D0948592

OVER ☆ THERE

OVER ☆ THERE

EDITED BY MARIA HÖHN AND SEUNGSOOK MOON

Living with the

U.S. Military Empire

from World War Two

to the Present

Duke University Press | Durham and London | 2010

© 2010 Duke University Press

All rights reserved

Printed in the United States of America on acid-free paper ∞

Designed by Heather Hensley

Typeset in Monotype Dante by Keystone Typesetting, Inc.

Library of Congress Cataloging-in-Publication Data appear on
the last printed page of this book.

Photograph on page ii courtesy *Der Stern*.

TO FARZIN AND CHARLES

CONTENTS

☆

ILLUSTRATIONS

☆

Maps

Figures

TABLES

☆

A NOTE ON FOREIGN LANGUAGE CONVENTIONS

☆

The romanization of Korean words and names in this book follows the McCune-Reischauer system except for names whose personal orthography is publicly known. The romanization of Japanese and Okinawan words and names follows the revised Hepburn system.

ACKNOWLEDGMENTS

☆

Over There: Living with the U.S. Military Empire from World War Two to the Present is a product of collaboration between a sociologist, whose research interest is South Korea, and a historian, whose work is concerned with West Germany. We benefited immensely from this scholarly collaboration, and are equal partners and contributors in this project. The order in which our names as co-editors are listed on the cover of this book and in the co-written introduction and conclusion reflects merely the convention of alphabetization in scholarly publishing, and is not indicative of any sort of hierarchy.

This volume would have not been produced without the crucial contributions from our collaborators, who were enthusiastic about the project from the beginning and professional and collegial throughout the process. We are deeply grateful to Mitchiko Takeuchi, Christopher Ames, and Christopher Nelson, whose expertise and thoughtful contributions made it possible to expand our focus and to include also Japan and Okinawa in our study. Donna Alvah and Robin Riley enrich this collection of essays by reminding us that the military empire has implications not only for women "Over There," but also for women at home in the United States. We are grateful that Christopher Nelson introduced us to Jeff Bennett, whose background in the U.S. Special Forces allowed him a unique angle for his perceptive and provocative essay on Abu Graibh. Thanks are also due to Meg Stuart, a GIS technician at Vassar College, for creating the maps for our volume. We are fortunate to have had a chance to work with her.

In the process of working on this book, we received various forms of financial support. We are grateful to the Freedman Foundation for making possible a study trip for Vassar faculty and students to South Korea in 2004 that generated the initial impetus for this volume. The Committee on Research at Vassar College generously funded our individual trips to South Korea (Jane Rosenthal Heimerdinger Fund) and Germany (Louise Boyd Dale Research Grants) to conduct research for our chapters in this book. We are also grateful to the Ford Foundation that provided us with opportunities to work with student researchers during the summers of 2005 and 2007. The Office of Dean of the Faculty partially funded our travels to participate in panels on the social costs of the global system of U.S. military bases at the Association for Asian Studies meeting in the spring of 2007. An NEH summer grant and funding from the American Philosophical Society made possible Maria Höhn's research in German archives. The Luce Asian Studies Program Fund supported Seungsook Moon's research in the National Archives in Washington in the winter of 2007; and the Leslie Koempel Fund in the Sociology Department partially helped finance her research for chapters in this book. Faculty travel funds from Vassar College also partially supported Moon's participation in panels that she organized on the global U.S. military empire at the Berkshire Conference on Women's History and the American Sociological Association meeting in the summer of 2005 and a panel on militarization of the everyday at the American Anthropological Association meeting in the fall of 2006.

Seungsook Moon would like to thank scholars and students who participated in her lectures and presentations based on her work for this volume delivered at Boston University; California State University, Dominguez Hill; Cornell University; DePaul University; Duke University; Ewha Womans University; University of California, Berkeley; University of California, Los Angeles; and University of Hawaii, Manoa. In particular, she thanks Shahla Haeri, Jung Sun Park, Naoki Sakai, Natalie Bennett, Haeyoung Kim, Eun Mee Kim, Elaine Kim, John Duncan, and Ned Shultz for providing forums for sharing her work and receiving thoughtful comments. These lectures and conversations that spanned a few years really helped her sharpen her work in progress. She is deeply thankful to Vladimir Tikhonov and Farzin Vahdat for their steady and enthusiastic support of her work and reading earlier versions of all of her chapters. She also extends thanks to Bruce Cumings and William Hoynes for reading parts of earlier versions of her work in this book. She is grateful to Hyeweol Choi, Cynthia Enloe, Katsuya Hirano, Annmaria Shimabuku, Setsu Shigematsu, and Theodore Jun Yoo for their warm encouragement and keen interest in her work. She would like to thank Richard Boylan, archivist at the National Archives and Records Administration, for his professional assistance in the sprawling archives and Shelby Jergens for her excellent work as Ford Scholar during the summer of 2007 and as research assistant for two years. She extends her thanks to wonderful colleagues and friends in the Asian Studies program: Martha Kaplan and Yu Zhou for creating and maintaining intellectual space; Pat Turner for providing excellent administrative assistance while she was working on this book; and Hiromi Dollase for assisting communication with Kuwabara Shisei, a photojournalist who permitted use of his wonderful photographs, for which she is grateful as well. Moon also thanks Young-im Yu, Dong-ryong Kim, Kyung-t'ae Park, Imha Yi, and Reverend Wu-sǒng Chǒn, for their generosity in sharing their valuable observations of camptowns in Korea and resources about them. Finally but not least, she would like to extend her thanks to Kang-sok Kim for allowing her to use his pictures of KATUSA service.

Maria Höhn benefited from the sharp eye of her friend and colleague Martin Klimke, who read drafts of all her chapters and the introduction and conclusions, offered his keen advice, and encouraged her in many ways. It has been an amazing scholarly collaboration working with Martin Klimke; everyone should have such a collaborator. She is also fortunate to be part of the study group *New York Women in German History*, whose members, over the years, have read her work in progress, vigorously picked chapters apart, raised hard questions, and then patted her on the back. Their thoughtful observations helped clarify many issues in the introduction. Thanks to Julie Sneeringer, Molly Nolan, Atina Grossmann, Rita Chin, Marion Kaplan, Belinda Davis, Nancy Reagin, Amy Hackett, Bonni Anderson, Dolores Augustin, Kathy Pence, Rebecca Boehling, Jane Caplan, Young Sun Hong, and Krista O'Donnell. Her former Vassar colleague Judith Weisenfeld, and current colleagues Peggy Piesche and Michael Hanagan, read early drafts of chapter 10, and provided keen insights, and she thanks them for taking time from their busy schedules.

Höhn has also benefited tremendously from working with her student research assistants Duane Bailey-Castro, Katie Paul, Katie Greenberg and Jessie Regunberg, who helped gather materials for this book over the years. Emma Woelk traveled with her to Germany as a Ford Scholar and worked through boxes and boxes of documents on student activists in Hamburg and Berlin archives. During the last stages, her research assistant Michael Ilardi saved the day with his sharp eye, attention to detail, and willingness to put in the extra time. She is grateful also to KD Wolff for all the insights on the

Black Panther Solidarity Campaign that he organized as a student activist. In Germany, Dieter Brünn, the curator of the Archiv für Soldatenrecht, e.V., has been wonderfully generous in granting access to his rich collection of materials from the GI movement. She thanks him, as well as Max Watts, who collected the materials, and the late Dave Harris, and his widow, Vicky Marx, who preserved them for all these years. For the use of photos in her essays she would like to thank Michael Geib from the Dokumentations- und Ausstellungszentrum zur Geschichte der Air Base Ramstein und der US-Amerikaner in Rheinland-Pfalz (docu center Ramstein), the late Heinrich Brucker from Birkenfeld, the late Karl Edinger from Baumholder, the late Walter Rödel, and Herbert Piel from Piel Media.

Our husbands, Farzin Vahdat and Charles Geiger, have lived with this project for many more years than we care to admit. Their patience and support, especially their good humor, sustained and comforted us at many difficult moments. For that and for all the other ways in which they bring joy to our lives, we thank them.

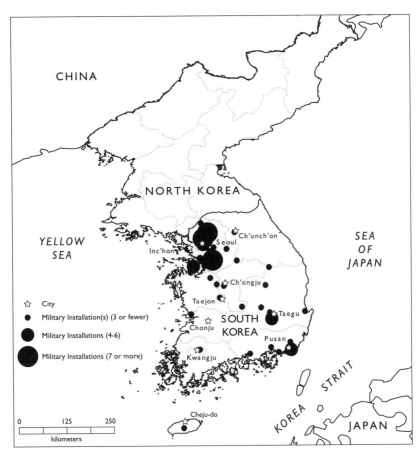

MAP 1. U.S. military bases in South Korea. BY MEG STEWART

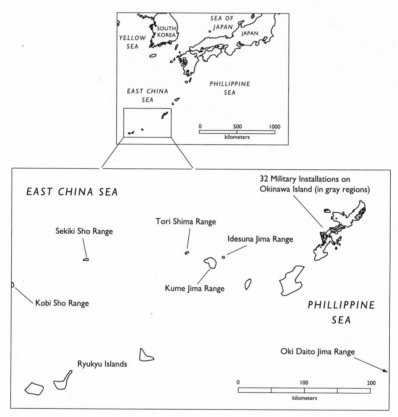

MAP 2. U.S. military bases in Japan and Okinawa. BY MEG STEWART

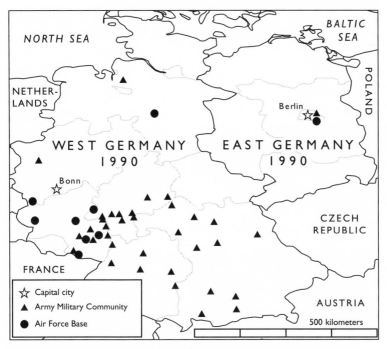

MAP 3-1. U.S. military bases in Germany, 1990. BY MEG STEWART

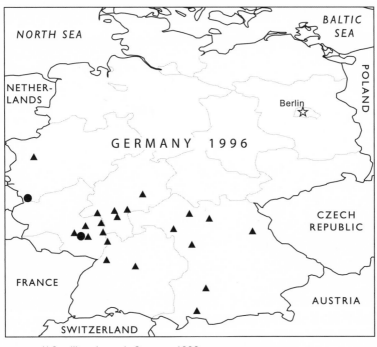

Map 3-2. U.S. military bases in Germany, 1996. BY MEG STEWART

THE POLITICS OF GENDER, SEXUALITY, RACE, AND CLASS IN THE U.S. MILITARY EMPIRE

☆

MARIA HÖHN AND SEUNGSOOK MOON

The idea for this book was born during a study trip with Vassar students to South Korea in the spring of 2004, when we visited Hooker Hill in It'aewŏn, the famous red-light district of Seoul that caters to American GIS. While It'aewŏn continues to draw American soldiers, as it has since the late 1940s, it has also become a bustling shopping district with fancy restaurants that offer international cuisine. During our visit to It'aewŏn, U.S. soldiers were milling about in the streets and enacting a ritual that was as old as the U.S. global military empire itself. The soldiers were hoping to escape the dreariness of military life by looking for drink, drugs, and women. Clubs catering to the soldiers in It'aewŏn, which are legally off-limits to most Koreans, all boomed with American music, and many sported names that evoked American sites. Business transactions were conducted in English, and most establishments replicated the social segregation of the races prevalent in American society. To keep order in this raucous atmosphere, uniformed Courtesy Patrols (CPS) instead of U.S. Military Police (MPS) walked the streets, routinely checking on the GIS inside the clubs. For the soldiers in search of a good time, and for the CP patrols making sure that things did not get out of hand, the clubs in It'aewŏn hardly differed from those around American military bases anywhere else in the world. Indeed, while some of the clubs predictably offered "girls, girls, girls" or "naughty nurses," others sported Bavarian décor, promising U.S. soldiers Wiener schnitzel and German beer, just like they used to get in "Good Old Germany." Indeed, the sergeants conducting the Courtesy Patrols told us laughingly that the last time they pulled this kind of duty was during a tour in Baumholder, one of America's largest military bases in Germany.[1]

What struck both of us during our visit to It'aewŏn was how familiar it seemed, although neither of us had ever visited these clubs in Seoul before. It seemed so familiar not only because both of us are scholars working on the impact of the U.S. military presence abroad, but also because both of us grew up in countries where the U.S. military presence has been part of everyday life since the end of the Second World War. What felt so "familiar" to us, of course, is a piece of the worldwide U.S. military-base system that is completely "foreign" to the majority of Americans. Since the introduction of an all-volunteer military in 1973, only about 0.3 percent of Americans serve in the military each year. Thus, most Americans have little understanding of the realities of military life, and they know even less about the unsavory side effects of large military deployments overseas. They know little about how their country imposes itself on "host" communities and how the daily lives of local women and men are affected by the presence of a militarized body composed mostly of young men and a few women. Furthermore, although the continental United States has its share of "camptowns" or "basetowns" surrounding military bases,[2] camptowns in Asia have existed under starkly different conditions. American soldiers stationed abroad are not only far away from home but are also operating in a foreign environment where they feel both a sense of racial and cultural superiority. The recent anointing of Second World War veterans as the "Greatest Generation," and the widely accepted commitment after the agony of the Vietnam War that the country must always "Support the Troops," leave little room for a more critical assessment of what effects the U.S. military has in the daily lives of the peoples who play host to the worldwide network of U.S. military bases. The attack on the United States on September 11, 2001, and the resulting "War on Terror" have only exacerbated this trend.

Over There: Living with the U.S. Military Empire from World War Two to the Present is a scholarly endeavor that brings closer to home just what the implications of such an expansive military empire are, both for the people "Over There" but also for Americans at home. Our collection of essays is the product of collaboration between scholars who were trained in very different disciplines (anthropology, history, religion, sociology, women and gender studies), and was edited by a sociologist (Moon) and a historian (Höhn). As we set out to imagine the shape of this volume as co-editors, it was easy enough to agree on the need for such a comparative and transnational volume, but we quickly found that we approached this project with very different assumptions. Trying to discover commonalities in the functioning of the U.S. military base system to help us develop a comprehensive theoretical model of empire, we also grappled to highlight the differences between the military deployments, how they have evolved since 1945, and the complexities of the encounters between American soldiers and local civilians. Our own "historical baggage" as participant-observers of the U.S. military in our respective home countries of South Korea and West Germany resulted in a number of spirited discussions on the implications of the U.S. military presence. In the end, though, it was our different national and personal experiences as well as our distinctive disciplinary approaches that made possible a much richer and more nuanced exploration of the global U.S. base system. We are equal partners and contributors in this project, and we both benefited immensely from this scholarly collaboration.

By bringing together some of the most current scholarship on how U.S. military bases affect social relations in foreign host countries, we intend to make visible this unprecedented empire of bases. Our comparative and multidisciplinary exploration is both theoretically and empirically compelling at a time when U.S. policymakers are debating the future shape of the global network of military bases. In the midst of an ongoing transformation of the worldwide U.S. base system after the collapse of the Soviet Union, the existing base structure is being replaced by new types of more mobile and flexible bases to reinforce America's new global posture as the only remaining superpower. While the huge European, mostly German, bases were cut back at the end of the Cold War, and bases were consolidated in South Korea and in Japan and Okinawa, new installations were created in the Middle East during the First Gulf War in 1990. After the terrorist attacks of 2001, U.S. policymakers identified a new "arc of instability" that reaches from Africa to the Middle East all the way through Central Asia and China, increasing the demand for more flexible "forward operating sites." Military bases have been constructed in Afghanistan, Pakistan, Kyrgyzstan, Uzbekistan, Tajikistan, Kuwait, Qatar, Turkey, Bulgaria, and, most recently and most controversially, Iraq.

In particular, the authors in this collection are interested in illuminating the various aspects of the politics of gender, sexuality, race, and class that are constitutive of the maintenance of America's global empire of bases. Exploring the American military as a global and transnational phenomenon, our contributors show that the U.S. military empire has bearing not only on the lives of soldiers and their families, but also on the lives of sex workers and residents of local host communities. By focusing on Korea, Japan and Okinawa, and West Germany, where more than two-thirds of American overseas military bases and troops have been concentrated for the past six decades, this collection illuminates recurring patterns and differentiations in the social costs of maintaining the empire, paying special attention to the hybrid spaces in and around U.S. military bases that blur the boundary between civilian society and the military. We also include two essays that examine the workings of the U.S. empire outside these three countries to account for the most recent shift in the expansion of the military basing system to the Middle East and to highlight the experience of female workers in the U.S. defense industry, which generates its own variant form of hybrid space.[3]

For our in-depth exploration of the U.S. military empire we have been inspired by the work of scholars who have examined European empires of the nineteenth century and early twentieth century (see McClintock 1995; Stoler 2002, 2006b; Young 1995). We have also benefited greatly from the work of scholars of American empire, who have rigorously exposed imperial expansion "as a dynamic engine of American history" (Go 2007, 2008; Go and Foster 2003; Kaplan, 2002; Kramer 2002, 2006a; Renda 2001). In particular, scholars such as Julian Go, Amy Kaplan, Paul Kramer, Melanie McAlister, and Mary Renda have placed American history firmly within the "overall history of colonial and post-colonial powers," and their important work has made visible what for too long has been disguised behind the assertion of "American exceptionalism" (Kaplan 2002, 2004, 6; Kramer 2006; McAlister 2001; Renda 2001). As Kaplan (2004, 3) argues in her research, the "denial and disavowal of empire has long served as the ideological cornerstone of American imperialism and a key component of American exceptionalism."

As crucial as the contributions of these scholars have been in exposing American empire, their work focuses foremost on the nineteenth century and early twentieth century and ignores American empire, buttressed by an extensive web of military bases, after 1945.[4] Against the backdrop of the unprecedented expansion of U.S. power after 1945, scholars who have been exploring American empire, both in the United States and abroad, have instead focused on what is generally called America's "soft power": the imposition of American-style consumer capitalism in the reconstruction of the post–Second World War world, the economic power of U.S. corporations, and the influence of American cultural productions worldwide (Nye 2002). These studies popularized such terms as "Coca-colonization," "Mc-

Donaldization," the "empire of consumption," and "irresistible empire" to underscore the dominance of American models of consumption and of the U.S.-dominated mass media in shaping the desires and dreams—or, as critics might see it, the nightmares—of millions of people in the world (Barber 2001; Bascara 2006; DeGrazia 2005; Gardner and Young 2005; Kroes 1996; Kuisel 1993; Ritzer 2000; Wagnleitner 1991, 1994). With their emphasis on cultural imperialism and the political economy of the United States, these studies are crucial in this era of globalization characterized by the increasing production and circulation of images, ideas, and information (see Appadurai 1996; Kroes 1996; Rosenberg 1982; Watson 2007), but they, too, ignore the "hard power" that buttresses American influence across the globe—namely, the worldwide web of American military bases.

Given the unprecedented size and reach of the American military empire since 1945, it is surprising that the military dimension of America's global power has garnered strikingly limited attention from scholars working outside the narrow circle of strategic studies and military history.[5] When the U.S. military does receive attention from scholars outside these disciplines, it usually comes from feminist scholars who explore the gendered working of the military and the conditions of women and sexual minorities in it.[6] While this wide range of scholarship illuminates how and to what extent gender and sexuality function as constitutive principles organizing the lives of individuals and institutional processes in the military during war and peace, it is largely confined to the institution of the military in a domestic context. Studies that do concern themselves with American military bases overseas tend to focus on the impact of those bases on just one country,[7] or else they explore the local political resistance that has emerged as a response to the bases.[8] As important and valuable as these studies are, they cannot fully capture the multiple interactions between the U.S. military and local populations over the course of the Cold War and how those relations changed in its aftermath.

While the focus of our collection of essays is on the post-1945 era when the U.S. global military empire reached its zenith, we argue that those bases are part of a much longer history of American expansion, and therefore future research on those bases should not be left to the disciplines of strategic studies or military history. For too long, claims of American exceptionalism have clouded the fact that military bases have been an integral part of American empire building, going back to America's westward expansion. During the nineteenth century, soldiers stationed in more than 250 military forts assured that expansion, and the establishment of military bases abroad, was central to the consolidation of America's fledging overseas empire, beginning with the Spanish-American War of 1898, and then in assuring American prerogatives in the newly acquired territories (Gillem 2007, 19; Weigley 1984, 267). Significantly, Arizona, New Mexico, and Oklahoma became states only *after* the United States had already "incorporated" or colonized Guam, Haiti, Hawaii, Panama, the Philippines, Puerto Rico, and the Virgin Islands (Renda 2001, 7). America's military and its intricate base structure, both in the nineteenth century and after the Second World War, should therefore be seen as crucial components in assuring this enduring expansion of American power.

Establishment of the Bases during the Second World War and in the Postwar Years

According to the 2009 Base Structure Report, nineteen years after the collapse of the Soviet Union and eight years after the terrorist attacks of September 11, 2001, the United States still commanded more than 1.8 million military personnel while also employing almost 500,000 civilians from the Department of Defense and 370,000 "other" personnel. These enormous numbers of individuals are scattered among military bases in the United States and abroad, with about 140,000 soldiers and an equal number of dependents, some 20,000 civilian employees and more than 72,000 "other" personnel serving on more than 700 military bases overseas. These substantial numbers of foreign-based military personnel are, of course, only a shadow of the Cold War deployments. For most of those years, some 500,000 soldiers, as well as tens of thousands of civilian employees and hundreds of thousands of family dependents, were stationed overseas.[9] The troop numbers from the 2009 report are also deceptive in that they do not include troops fighting in Iraq and Afghanistan, because the military does not consider those soldiers "stationed or based" but merely "deployed" abroad. Furthermore, those numbers do not include the tens of thousands of private defense contractors in Iraq and Afghanistan, such as Halliburton and Blackwater (renamed Xe in 2009), which provide construction, cooking and laundering, and an increasingly larger share of security and intelligence services (Kane 2006).[10]

To provide housing and training facilities for its personnel, the U.S. military controls almost 29 million acres of territory, with approximately 635,000 acres of that territory being made available to the U.S. by host governments. Such an expansive military reach has its price. The military installations in the continental United States are worth more than $600 billion, and it would cost American taxpayers $124 billion to replace the base structure the military controls overseas. The replacement cost for bases overseas does not include the massive and incredibly expensive bases currently being built in Iraq, Afghanistan, and Central Asia. Also not included in the 2009 report is the replacement value of the approximately 23,000 buildings, structures, and installations that the United States has been leasing in Europe and Asia. Not only is the United States the largest military power in the world; it is also the largest landlord and leaseholder in the world (Kane 2006).[11] How could the United States come to this point while insisting that it is not an empire?

The first U.S. military base outside the continental United States was established in Guantánamo, Cuba, in 1898 after the victory in the Spanish-American War; naval bases in the Philippines were a valuable booty of that same war. By 1938, the United States had established bases in Panama, Cuba, Puerto Rico, and the Virgin Islands in the Caribbean, while Hawaii and the Philippines served as major hubs of naval activity, supported by facilities on Guam, Midway, and Wake in the Pacific Ocean. Although small numbers of army personnel were stationed in Panama, Hawaii, and the Philippines, most pre–Second World War overseas basing involved the U.S. Navy and the Marines. Compared with the sprawling and extensive military empire of today, the 60,000 men serving in the U.S. Navy and staffing naval bases abroad was minimal. The real expansion of the American military base structure came during the Second World War with the beginning of Lend-Lease in 1941. Existing military bases were taken over from the British in the Caribbean to preempt possible German bases there and in Great Britain and Africa to prepare for the invasion of Germany. The attack on Pearl Harbor in December 1941 led not only to an accelerated expansion of base structures in the Pacific, but also to a growing sense that U.S. bases should be maintained as a "guarantor of an open, interdependent political-economic order" after the end of hostilities. By 1942, President Franklin D. Roosevelt had instructed his Joint Chiefs of Staff to prepare a proposal for an extended global network of U.S. bases to ensure that order (Calder 2007, 13).[12] One year after Pearl Harbor, the framework of the U.S. basing system with some 2,000 base sites in more than 100 countries was in place, and by 1945, the network of U.S. military fortifications stretched from the Arctic Circle to Antarctica (Blaker 1990; Calder 2007).

At the Potsdam Conference held from July 17 to August 2, 1945, President Harry S Truman reiterated his conviction that the U.S. "maintain the military bases necessary for the complete protection of our interests and of world peace" (Calder 2007, chap. 1; Sandars 2000, 3). Although the more than 2,000 overseas military installations of the war years had been reduced to 582 installations by 1949, military planners were determined to keep a Pacific arc of U.S. military bases, spanning from Okinawa to the Aleutian Islands, to ensure U.S. dominance of the seas. The United States was also eager to fill the vacuum left by the diminishing British empire, especially in the Middle East. The United States "inherited" its first base in the Middle East—Bahrain— from Great Britain in 1947 and transformed it into a vital U.S. Navy facility that would come to play an ever greater strategic role in ensuring unencumbered access to oil. By 1957, the United States had established 815 bases outside the United States, and by 1960, treaties had been signed with 43 nations to have U.S. troops stationed on their soil. By the end of the 1950s, a million troops, civilian employees, and family members resided overseas as part of the U.S. global network of military bases (Sandars 2000, 9).[13]

When thinking about the global web of U.S. military bases, the Cold War competition with the Soviet Union immediately comes to mind, given that the base system served three fundamental military strategies. A ring of air and missile bases around the Soviet Union, located mostly in Japan and Europe, would allow the United States to attack the Soviet Union by air, while naval forces in the Pacific could send aircraft carriers to any conflict zone in the world. Finally, combat forces of the U.S. Army stationed in West Germany and South Korea would avert any potential communist invasion.[14] At the same time, the bases served a broader goal. As military strategists like to put it: the bases kept the Americans in, the defeated Germans and Japanese down, and the Russians out (Calder 2007, 23).

It is not surprising, then, that the bulk of the U.S. military commitment was focused on two regions that were crucial to this larger goal: 52 percent of troops abroad were stationed in Western Europe; 41 percent, in northeastern Asia; and the rest, dispersed in Africa, the Americas, and the Middle East.[15] Of the 1,014 U.S. overseas bases that existed at the height of the Vietnam War, 673 were in Europe and the North Atlantic, and 271 were in the Pacific and Asia (see Blaker 1990, table 1.2). It was in South Korea, Japan and Okinawa, and West Germany that the bulk of the U.S. overseas military empire would be anchored and where the battle lines would be drawn between the so-called Free World and the Communist Bloc. Together, these three countries provided the basing locations that allowed the United States to span the globe during the Cold War, thereby ensuring the nation's strategic goals, as well as its political and economic ambitions (Walker 1991, 36).[16]

South Korea, Japan and Okinawa, and West Germany were intimately connected in the larger strategic military planning of the United States. Although the United States had already decided during the war to keep bases in Japan, military planners had not considered permanent military bases in

TABLE I.I *Number of U.S. troops in 1957 and 2005: Asia and Europe*

	1957	2005
Asia		
Japan	150,874	35,571
South Korea	71,043	30,983
Guam	15,869	3,018
Philippines	11,297	55
Taiwan	6,261	—
Hong Kong	4,539	—
Marshall Island	2,288	—
Midway	1,187	—
Vietnam	751	—
Thailand	410	114
Johnston Island	130	—
Pakistan	114	—
Cambodia	80	—
Singapore	—	169
China	—	67
India	52	—
Diego Garcia	—	683
Europe		
Germany	244,407	66,418
France	71,531	58
United Kingdom	63,008	10,752
Greece	15,360	428
Italy	11,289	11,841
Portugal	5,935	970
Iceland	5,246	1,270
Netherlands	4,415	583
Spain	4,299	1,660
Denmark	2,206	—
Norway	1,900	77
Gibraltar	1,377	—
Belgium	139	1,366
Yugoslavia	92	—
Serbia and Montenegro	—	1,801
Bosnia and Herzegovina	—	263
Soviet Union	48	—
Russia	—	44
Georgia	—	42

Note: All countries and territories with more than forty U.S. soldiers are listed.

TABLE I.2 *Number of U.S. troops in 1957 and 2005: North America and Latin America*

	1957	2005
North America		
Mainland United States	1,876,928	914,604
Hawaii	59,285	32,629
Alaska	44,439	18,169
Canada	18,297	150
Latin America		
Panama	9,516	—
Puerto Rico	9,387	219
Cuba	6,826	950
Bermuda	3,614	—
Bahamas	761	41
West Indies	702	—
Honduras	—	438
Brazil	189	—
Venezuela	98	—
Colombia	68	52
Peru	65	—
Ecuador	59	—
Argentina	51	—
Chile	51	—

Note: All countries and territories with more than forty U.S. soldiers are listed.

Germany after what they hoped would be a short and successful occupation. Neither had the United States made provisions to keep troops in South Korea after the country was liberated from Japan and once the United States concluded its occupation in 1948. The outbreak of the Korean War in June 1950, however, shifted U.S. military goals in Asia and Europe dramatically. To ensure that the Soviet Union could not use Korea as a "dagger" or a launching pad for an invasion of Japan, the United States together with North Atlantic Treaty Organization (NATO) troops defended South Korea against the North (Gerson and Birchard 1991, 174). This U.S. decision to take a stand against communism in the Korean Peninsula also shifted its strategy in Europe, as the United States feared Soviet expansionism there, as well. Truman's "Troops to Europe" decision in 1950 as a response to the conflict in Korea brought a reactivated Seventh Army and a significant Air Force presence to replace the small contingent of occupation troops in West Germany. Thus, the war in Korea brought about a radical revision of postwar strategic

	1957	2005
Middle East		
Morocco	12,141	—
Turkey	10,030	1,780
Libya	5,603	—
Saudi Arabia	1,340	258
Bahrain	766	1,641
Malta	620	—
Iran	479	—
Egypt	168	410
Iraq	48	150,000
Israel	45	42
Kuwait	—	42,600
Afghanistan	—	19,500
Qatar	—	463
United Arab Emirates	—	71
Cyprus	—	43
Africa		
Eritrea	1,239	—
South Africa	279	—
Ethiopia	46	—
Djibouti	—	522
Senegal	—	42

Note: All countries and territories with more than forty U.S. soldiers are listed.

planning and an extensive U.S. military buildup in both Korea and Germany. Some 70,000 combat and combat support troops were stationed in South Korea after hostilities ceased in 1953, and some 250,000 such troops were stationed in West Germany to deter a possible Soviet invasion.[17]

Aside from being "host countries" to almost 90 percent of U.S. troop deployment outside the U.S. during the Cold War, South Korea, Japan and Okinawa, and West Germany present paradigmatic case studies that allow us to compare how the human cost of establishing and maintaining the military empire has been handled from the perspectives of both the United States and the "host" nations. By highlighting the uneven social costs that are imposed on host communities, the unintended consequences of imperial expansions, and the eruptions of disorder and violence, this collection broadens existing theoretical discussion of empires by adding nuance and the human dimension.[18] The contributors also highlight the degree to which the U.S. empire is

TABLE I.4 *Number of U.S. troops in 1957 and 2005: Oceania*

OCEANIA	1957	2005
New Zealand	179	—
Australia	162	196

Sources: T. Kane, *Global U.S. Troop Deployment, 1950–2005*, The
Heritage Foundation, Center for Data Analysis Report #04-11, 2006,
www.heritage.org / Research / Reports / 2006 / 05 / Global-US-Troop-
Deployment-1950-2005 (accessed 12 April 2010).

forced to work with realities on the ground and how the experiences abroad
affect the United States at home. By shifting the focus of exploration from
the center to the peripheries of the empire, the contributors show, furthermore, that the contour of the U.S. military empire is not as monolithic as
might be expected. Interactions between the military and civilian populations are multilayered and hardly as static as existing studies, with their focus
on the metropole, suggest.

Mapping the U.S. Empire

When scholars debated the nature of American power during the Cold War,
they generally rejected the view of the United States as an empire, especially in its post-1945 incarnation (Aron 1974; Fulbright 1967; Kennedy 1989).[19]
These scholars highlight the distinct and often flexible characteristics of
American power, such as the absence of formal colonies and the reliance on
bilateral or multilateral security agreements and Status of Forces Agreements (SOFAS). They employ such terms as "informal empire" (Lord Beloff
1986), "empire by invitation" (Lundestad 1998), and "leasehold empire" (Sandars 2000), although most of the bases acquired after 1945 were part of the
spoils of war.[20] This conceptualization of the U.S. empire reflects these scholars' primary focus on the relationship between the United States and Western Europe and their disregard of the varying degrees of neocolonial arrangements that define relations between the United States and many of
the non-Western countries that host troops. In non-Western countries, the
power relations between the United States and the host nation as specified in
the SOFAS (or implied in security agreements without separate SOFAS) have
often been so asymmetrical as to completely remove the military and individual American soldiers from any local sovereignty and jurisdiction.[21] When
non-Western countries with deeply unequal agreements are included in the

conceptualization of the U.S. military empire, they are usually mentioned as unusual or unfortunate "aberrations" to the normative patterns that characterize America's interaction with Europe.[22]

The collapse of the Soviet Union triggered an interesting twist to the debate on American empire: as the sole superpower, the United States quickly asserted that the rest of the world was dependent on it for military security. Significantly, since September 11, 2001, the debate is focused not on whether the United States is an empire at all but on what kind of empire it is. Both neo-conservatives and liberals share a growing consensus that the United States is indeed an empire, albeit a "reluctant empire" or an "empire by necessity." With this important intellectual shift, their debate is mostly concerned with how the United States might appropriately deal with the challenges of empire and how to manage it more effectively. At the same time, critics of empire highlight its unsustainability, given its costs and the dangers it poses to democratic values at home.[23] Against the backdrop of this proliferation of debate about empire, we bring insights from critiques of "American exceptionalism" (see Kaplan 2002; Kaplan and Pease 1993; McAlister 2001; Stoler 2006b, 2006c) and from postcolonial studies (see Bhabha 1994, 1995; Mehta 1999; Memmi 2006; Williams and Chrisman 1994) and contend that "liberal imperialism" best characterizes U.S. power based on the global network of military bases in the post-1945 era.

By using the term "liberal imperialism," we underscore the fundamental significance of imperial expansion to the liberal self-conception and practice of U.S. global power since its emergence in the nineteenth century.[24] When the United States joined the European scramble for colonial expansion outside its borders, beginning with the Spanish-American War, the annexations of Hawaii, Guam, Cuba, Puerto Rico, and the Philippines were interpreted as "aberrations" to American exceptionalism, which was grounded in an ostensible rejection of European-style colonialism. After the bloody conquest and occupation of the Philippines, the United States realized that formal occupation of territory was not always necessary for its global ambitions and projected its power foremost through economic expansion and informal treaties rather than territorial conquest.[25] But as the nineteen-year occupation of Haiti (1915–34) and the numerous military interventions in Latin American countries in the first half of the twentieth century testify, the United States was more than willing to use its military might when treaties proved insufficient. Thus, while politicians, adopting the slogan "Dollar Diplomacy" during the 1920s, might have assured themselves and their country that the United States was not acting like European imperialists, the United States intervened militarily in Latin America more than a dozen times between 1910 and 1930 to ensure the region's compliance with the U.S. economic and political agenda (McAlister 2001, 30).

In the post–Second World War era characterized by decolonization and the founding of newly independent nation-states, American "exceptionalism" was infused with a liberal anticolonial rhetoric to counteract traditional European power in the Middle East and other regions of the world and to assure the dominant position of the United States as the leader of the "Free World."[26] In particular, the Truman Doctrine, initially declared in March 1947 to support the restored Greek monarchy against a communist insurgency, was used to justify U.S. intervention in the Third World to assist "free people to work out their destinies in their own ways." This self-perception of "benevolent supremacy" became the underlying logic of the postwar U.S. security policy outlined in the influential National Security Council document NSC-68 of 1950.[27] Significantly, this global security policy was fundamentally linked to the political-economic ambitions of the United States. The United States bound its major allies in Asia through the "San Francisco System" of asymmetrical economic relations, and in Germany (and Europe), the Marshall Plan achieved the same results. As Kent Calder argues persuasively, one of the key quid pro quos in this arrangement was acceptance of the U.S. bases in the "host countries," because the bases assured fickle investors in the United States that Japan and West Germany were worth the gamble and that they could expect bright economic futures under American tutelage. Although it was the Korean War that globalized America's policy of containing communism on every front, the bases in Korea were a mere footnote to the larger prize: Japan. Proponents of this Pax Americana praised the arrangement for ensuring the "dynamic capital flows that have been at the heart of post–World War II global economic recovery" (Calder 2007, 23). But this arrangement also assured that the United States would emerge from the Second World War as *the* hegemonic power to lead the so-called Free World.

Intricate SOFAS have been integral to the liberal self-perception of the United States after 1945. First signed between the United States and twelve NATO countries in 1951, SOFAS have regulated various issues, ranging from criminal jurisdiction over American military personnel and civilian employees and their dependents to custom duties for U.S. goods brought to the "host countries." During the 1950s, the United States signed SOFAS with forty-nine countries.[28] By 2008, the United States had publicly admitted to having SOFAS with more than one hundred nations, a number that did not include undisclosed SOFAS with Islamic countries. While SOFAS are professedly designed to ensure the smooth working of the military alliance between the United States and the "host" country, they are primarily concerned with guarding the "rights and privileges" of American soldiers stationed abroad (Mason 2008, 1–2). In principle, SOFAS protect GIS from foreign prosecution if a crime is committed "on duty" but allow for local jurisdiction if the crime is committed "off duty." In practice, however, the U.S. military has been known to "bend" the interpretation of these categories. Furthermore, the receiving state is expected to give "sympathetic consideration" to requests from the U.S. military authorities in handling criminal jurisdiction.[29] How equal or unequal the "concurrent jurisdiction" over GIS stationed abroad is depends entirely on the balance of power between the United States and receiving countries.[30] While the United States treads more carefully today so as not to undermine its alliances abroad, GIS (but not necessarily their families and civilian employees), for the most part, are subject to the judicial sovereignty of the U.S. military.[31] Despite the absence of formal colonies, these SOFAS have undermined national sovereignty in many ways and contain the contradiction of America's liberal imperialism.

In the aftermath of the Cold War, the liberal self-conception of the United States as the benevolent leader of the world, buttressed by a global network of military bases, has persisted. Although the "unilateralism" of the Bush administration (2001–9) after the terrorist attacks of September 2001 is commonly contrasted with the "multilateralism" of previous administrations, there has been far more continuity than rupture. For example, "A National Security Strategy for a New Century," issued by the Clinton administration in 1999, praised the "global interdependence" of the United States and insisted that Americans were "citizens of the world." Yet the report enunciated such uplifting rhetoric without an actual commitment to ensuring a more egalitarian membership in the global community for other countries (Muppidi 2004, 73). While the language of "globalization" has replaced that of the Cold War struggle with the Soviet Union in the liberal discourse of America's leadership in the world, the mainstays of liberal imperialism in relationship to other peoples in the world remain (Muppidi 2004, 64–65).[32]

As scholars of American empire in the late nineteenth century and early twentieth document vividly, the United States borrowed techniques of ruling from other imperial powers and flexibly modified them in accordance with local realities on the ground. The United States, for example, understood that the presence of an economically more prosperous and politically ambitious elite in the Philippines called for a different colonial regime from that which could be imposed on Guam or Samoa, two islands that lacked a developed economy and an educated elite that might have clamored for greater participation.³³ This collection makes equally clear that the face the U.S. empire presents via its expansive military base system is not as monolithic as many existing studies of the U.S. military presence abroad assume or imply. As we argue in more detail, it matters a great deal, for example, whether the stationing of troops takes place in a democratic country under the auspices of an increasingly egalitarian military and political alliance or whether the United States, for strategic purposes, is willing to collaborate with undemocratic regimes. Other factors contributing to the local variations in the working of the military empire include the branch of service and composition of troops stationed; the location of military bases vis-à-vis the civilian population; and the racial and cultural assumptions that informed encounters between the U.S. military and the host country.

As our contributors illustrate, within the context of our three countries, nowhere was the neocolonial character of the U.S. presence more evident than in South Korea. Despite its assertion of being the leader of the Free World, the United States was willing to tolerate Syngman Rhee's autocratic rule (1948–60) and then the military dictatorships of Park Chung Hee (1961–79) and Chun Doo Hwan (1980–87) because those regimes most consistently aligned with America's own anticommunism and supported the U.S. military strategy in the Asian Command. After the Korean War, the U.S. military continued its dominance by maintaining peacetime and wartime operational control of the entire Korean military until 1978 and of a majority of the country's military under the Combined Forces Command (CFC) after 1978.³⁴ While peacetime command of the South Korean military was finally returned in 1994, wartime command will not be returned until 2012.³⁵ The U.S.–South Korea military alliance has also involved KATUSAS, or young South Korean conscripts who have been attached to the U.S. Army. This institution, which resembles nineteenth-century European colonial military arrangements with native soldiers, was created during the Korean War to compensate for dire manpower shortages.³⁶ Although the Korean government formally agreed to transfer the control of its military to the United States, the broader geopolitical and economic context of the Korea–U.S. relation marked the relation neocolonial to a degree not found in either Japan or West Germany.³⁷ American support of the repressive Korean dictatorships contributed to popular antagonism toward the U.S. military presence that has grown since the 1980s. The continuing U.S. dominance over South Korea's foreign policy, the unwillingness of the United States to stop the South Korean military's brutal crackdown on democracy protesters in Kwangju in 1980, as well as the prevailing perception that South Korea was fortified only to secure Japan, Korea's former colonial master, fuels much of the popular anger toward the U.S. military.[38]

The U.S. deployment in Japan presents a more complicated picture. The United States was committed to democratizing Japan and spent considerable resources to achieve that goal. Yet the United States stationed the bulk of its forces on the island of Okinawa, a former colony of Japan, whose inhabitants were regarded as second-class members of the nation. Okinawa, some 860 miles away from Tokyo, makes up less than 0.6 percent of Japan's landmass but has housed 75 percent of all U.S. troops in Japan, shouldering a disproportionate burden of the U.S. military presence.[39] While Japan itself would regain its sovereignty by 1952, the island of Okinawa remained under U.S. military occupation until 1972. Because the United States occupied 25 percent of the land in Okinawa, and the local population was traditionally marginalized within Japanese society, a certain viceroy mentality defined many of the daily interactions between the military and the civilian population. The "doubly colonized" people of Okinawa also understood that their island served mostly as a deployment base to protect mainland Japan and to conduct U.S. military action elsewhere, such as during the Korean and Vietnam wars. Given these realities, the people of Okinawa developed a vocal and well-organized anti-base movement.

The situation was quite different in West Germany, America's "favored ally," where the United States invested unprecedented effort and resources to ensure democratization and integration into the American-sponsored political and military alliance. Because the U.S. military viewed West Germany not as a staging ground for warfare elsewhere but as *the* front line against possible Soviet aggression in Europe, the United States proceeded with much more care in its interactions with the local population. Because of that more egalitarian relationship, which, furthermore, was based on the assumption that this was an alliance between two white nations, the U.S. military enjoyed unquestioned support from West Germany's democratic government and the overwhelming number of West Germans.[40] While German peace activists protested vigorously against the deployment of Pershing missiles during the 1980s, their protests generally focused on nuclear and biological weapons, not the U.S. bases in general.

It also matters a great deal to host communities what kind of troops are sent for what duration of time. As the institution for waging war through the organized use of armed violence, the military developed a distinct culture to transform civilians into soldiers. Military culture glorifies the ideas of service and sacrifice, while camaraderie in this predominantly homosocial atmosphere is reinforced through an "ethos of male rivalry based on competitive claims to toughness and physical prowess" that are "enacted in the battlefield or the brothel" (Renda 2001, 71).[41] Hence, to the host nation it makes a significant difference whether the United States sends predominantly young single men for one-year deployments, as is still the case in Korea, or whether soldiers serve tours of duty that last two to three years, a policy that has been largely in effect in Japan and Okinawa and West Germany. The longer tour of duty by soldiers accompanied by families makes possible a much more "normalized" relationship between the military base and surrounding communities; it also allows soldiers to get acquainted with their host country. The difference between South Korea and the other two countries in their deployment patterns is crucial to understanding the divergence in how sexual and gender relations between the military and the host societies have been structured since 1945.

As the people in all three countries will attest, the branch of the military that is being deployed also has tremendous ramifications for civilian–military relations. The U.S. Air Force, with its generally better-educated personnel, stands in higher regard than the U.S. Army or the Marines, but it also brings a higher degree of noise pollution and environmental degradation to host communities. The U.S. Navy commands higher esteem than the U.S. Army, but the long deployments at sea confront communities surrounding U.S. Navy ports with cyclical upheavals when the sailors arrive for shore leaves that often culminate in search of drink and sex. The people of Okinawa stress that the presence of 17,000 Marines from the Third Expeditionary Force has always posed serious security problems for them, because these young soldiers are being trained and deployed for warfare elsewhere and generally rotate through the island at short intervals. Similarly, communities in West Germany that are home to command, intelligence, and combat support units report a more positive experience of the U.S. troop presence than communities that house primarily combat troops or are located in close vicinity to military training camps.

The spatial arrangements that govern how the U.S. garrison and surrounding civilian communities interact are also important for the civilian–military relationship. Korea again reveals the least favorable arrangement. While the three major cities—Seoul, Pusan, and Taegu—host about 20 percent of the U.S. military stationed in the country, a majority of the U.S. bases are heavily concentrated in rural and provincial areas, mostly in Kyŏnggi

Province. Those military bases are spartan and often dilapidated, consisting mainly of barracks to house soldiers and the military structures necessary for the mission along the demilitarized zone (DMZ). Soldiers on those bases relate to the South Korean civilian population mostly through the surrounding camptowns (*kijich'on*) rather than through Korean society at large. Populated by poor and marginalized Koreans, and stigmatized by the larger society, these camptowns bear the burden of the U.S. military presence and have allowed the autocratic regimes of South Korea to conceal the social cost of the U.S. presence. By having more than 75 percent of U.S. troops based in Okinawa, the Japanese government was similarly able to displace the burden from Japanese society as a whole and to conceal the worst aspects of the U.S. military presence, such as GI crime; the sex and entertainment industries that cater to the soldiers; and the environmental degradation that comes with such large bases. In West Germany, as well, much of the military buildup after the Korean War took place in the country's most marginalized area, a region along the French border that had already been heavily fortified during the Nazi regime. However, because U.S. bases in Germany are dispersed across German communities, the military had to take greater care to be "good neighbors." This greater concern for "neighborliness," which was fortified by cultural and racial affinities the United States did not share with South Korea and Japan / Okinawa, made possible a more egalitarian relationship between Germans and Americans.[42]

As all the essays in this volume convey to varying degrees, the U.S. military empire as a global and transnational phenomenon has also led to the formation of hybrid or ambiguous spaces that blur national boundaries and sovereignty. "Over There," these hybrid spaces exist in the form of "extraterritorial" military bases and in the "contact areas" or "transfer points of power," to use Ann Stoler's term, where American soldiers and local civilians interact. In the hybrid spaces where imperial power is exercised, different cultures intermingle, generating an amalgamation or creolization of languages and other cultural practices. At the same time, the hybrid spaces made possible by the establishment of military bases abroad have allowed local women and men to challenge their own countries' hierarchies based on gender, class, and race. Ironically, those same spaces have also allowed African American GIs to question and unsettle their country's color line. We found significant variations among the three countries in terms of the rigidity of the boundaries between U.S. military bases, the local communities bordering on them, and the larger civilian societies. How rigid or porous these boundaries were also shifted over time, depending on the changing power balance between the military and local communities that resulted from socioeconomic and political transformations in their own societies. Given the transnational character of the U.S. empire, we also identified hybrid spaces generated by the privately owned defense industry in the continental United States and the transnational migration of hundreds of thousands of military wives (American and foreign-born) who reside across military bases and civilian communities and between bases in the continental United States and those overseas.[43]

As our contributors convey explicitly and implicitly, hierarchical meanings of race, in conjunction with gender, sexuality, and class, have shaped the encounters and interactions that take place in these hybrid spaces, at home and abroad. In combination with strategic considerations, race informed how the U.S. military managed the social costs of the empire and how its soldiers were to relate to local women. We found, however, a significant difference between American empire in the postwar era and European colonial empires of the past and America's own empire of the late nineteenth century and early twentieth. Anxiety about transgressing racial boundaries was expressed not only by the United States but also by the host societies, which harbored their own assumptions about race. Adding fodder to this racial anxiety was the fact that, because of manpower needs, the United States was forced to rely on African American, Asian, Hispanic, and Native American soldiers.[44] Thus, a multiracial occupation (and, later, protective force) confronted racial others in Asia but encountered, for the most part, a homogenous white population in West Germany, which in turn was anxious about encountering soldiers of color.

In describing and analyzing the varied interactions between the United States (or what GIS usually call "the world") and the countries "Over There," the contributors to this volume bring innovative and new empirical research that illuminates the fascinating and complicated encounters between American soldiers and local civilians. To make sense of this history and its contemporary developments, to track change over time, and to underscore the complex inequalities and forms of resistance that shape these encounters and interactions, we have organized the essays into four parts: part I, "Monitored Liaisons: Local Women and GIS in the Making of the Empire"; part II, "Civilian Entanglements with the Empire: American and Foreign Women Abroad and Home"; part III, "Talking Back to the Empire: Local Men and Women"; and part IV, "The Empire under Siege: Racial Crisis, Abuse, and Violence."

In part I, Seungsook Moon, Michiko Takeuchi, and Maria Höhn focus on how the U.S. military regulated relations between GIS and local women in South Korea, Japan, and West Germany in the aftermath of the Second World War and the Korean War. The authors document that prostitution and cohabitation emerged as key sites in managing civilian–military relations during the founding years of the U.S. military empire in Asia and Europe. In their comprehensive analyses of each country, the authors illuminate the following commonalities and differences. First, the U.S. military displayed a colonial perception that women of occupied territories in Korea, Japan, and Germany should be sexually available for GIS, just as colonized women of color had been available to European colonialists, and just as women of color had been expected to be available to U.S. military personnel during America's empire building in the nineteenth century and early twentieth.[45] Second, although prostitution was prohibited in the United States and the U.S. military was legally bound to this prohibition, military commanders closely collaborated with local authorities to ensure a system of highly regulated prostitution to protect the health and welfare of soldiers and their combat readiness. Third, after the severe economic hardship of the postwar decades was overcome, a significant divergence occurred between Germany and the two Asian countries. As Germany recuperated economically and emerged as an almost equal political and military ally of the United States, widespread prostitution around U.S. military bases mostly disappeared. Change did not take place at a comparable pace in South Korea and Okinawa, despite similar trajectories of strategic partnership and economic transformation. Fourth, unlike European empires, which commonly established policies on the practice of "concubinage" in their colonies, the United States after 1945 did not establish an official policy on cohabitation; instead, it condoned it as a relationship preferable to interracial marriage or unregulated prostitution.[46] Hence, various forms of cohabitation became commonplace in all three countries. While practices of cohabitation had diminished in Germany by the mid-1960s, they continue to exist in South Korea and Okinawa to the present.

The three authors reveal that hierarchical meanings of race influenced various ways in which the military interacted with the host society. Was it the cultural and racial affinity with white Germans, for example, that convinced the U.S. military to keep defenseless American wives and children in

Berlin even during the Berlin Airlift in 1948–49, one of the hottest moments of the Cold War? On the other side of that spectrum of decision making is the case of South Korea. Although the U.S. military was fully cognizant of the deleterious implications that sending soldiers to South Korea on one-year rotations, without their families, would have on the neighboring communities, Korea was considered too dangerous a locale for American families. The. U.S. military announced a retreat from that policy only in late 2008.[47] Racial hierarchies, furthermore, informed how the United States dealt with prostitution and cohabitation. In particular, military commanders were acting on widely shared assumptions about the segregation of the races. Those assumptions about racial hierarchies found their legal expression in Jim Crow "anti-miscegenation" laws, which the U.S. Supreme Court did not rule unconstitutional until 1967.[48] Those laws made it very difficult if not impossible for black GIS to marry white German women and for white GIS to marry Asian women, since the military could not return such couples to states where such marriages were illegal. The racial assumptions undergirding those miscegenation laws also informed how the military regulated the sexual liaisons between local women and GIS. Given the demographics of Korea and Japan and Okinawa, the military was forced to manage interracial liaisons unless it was willing to "import" white women from the United States, as some European colonial powers had indeed done in the nineteenth century (Wildenthal 2001). Such a step was impossible. Due to the anti-miscegenation laws at home and pervasive racism within the military (on the individual and institutional levels), American efforts focused therefore foremost on protecting the internal U.S. color line by introducing and then condoning racially segregated entertainment establishments: women who served African American GIS should not serve white GIS.[49] In Korea, Japan, and Germany, local women who associated with American GIS internalized the American color line, as well, because no white soldier would date or be sexually involved with a woman who associated with soldiers of color.

It is noteworthy that elites in Korea, Japan, and Germany were equally concerned about protecting their own national boundaries and racial integrity. Eager to restore national sovereignty after the war, Japanese elites were more than willing to "sacrifice" lower-class women in collaborating with the U.S. military's regulation of its soldiers' sexuality. Drawing on the existing institution of comfort stations, Japanese authorities actively recruited destitute women so that the honor of "respectable" women and the purity of the Yamato race could be ensured. They also hoped, as Takeuchi argues, that such compliance would help them preserve their leadership in Asia by making them junior partners of the United States. During the Korean War, as Moon discusses, the institution of comfort women, established by the Japanese colonial authorities in Korea (1910–45), was revived to serve UN forces, and after the war, many of these women found their way to the camptowns bordering U.S. military bases.[50] In these camptowns, impoverished women were procured for prostitution to protect the purity of "respectable" Korean women and preserve the racial integrity of the nation. While German officials worked hard to convince the American military to establish brothels for its troops, there was no conscious and deliberate policy by government officials to provide "sacrificial" women for the Americans. However, there was a parallel anxiety about racial mixing. Thus, when periodic vice raids were conducted in garrison towns to appease the population, who were resentful about the thriving sex industry, it was mostly women who dated or catered to African American GIs who were harassed or prosecuted.

In part II, Donna Alvah, Christopher Ames, and Robin Riley examine various ways in which American and foreign women interact with the military in the hybrid spaces made possible by the transnational empire. In chapter 4, Alvah focuses on American military wives and children who dwell in and around military bases, both in the continental United States and overseas. By documenting the role of American military wives after the Second World War as "unofficial ambassadors" who disseminated American values and the American way of life, Alvah convincingly argues that they performed a central role in restoring discipline and morals and in "normalizing" gender relations with the Germans. For decades, the military thus considered the wives an integral part of the long-term deployment of troops. However, military planners in the post–Cold War era have re-envisioned the role of military spouses (who are still largely women) under the "New Global Posture," which emphasizes mobile forces sent on short-term deployments without families. As Alvah aptly points out, this shift to more mobile forces has far-reaching implications for gender and sexual relations with host societies. Alvah interprets the new strategy as an effort to re-masculinize the military in order to overcome the feminization that, in the eyes of many strategists, was rooted in the defeat in Vietnam and the introduction of women into the military.

In chapter 5, Christopher Ames focuses on Okinawan (and mainland Japanese) women who date or marry American soldiers in contemporary Okinawa and analyzes the complex processes of their marginalization and resistance in and around U.S. military bases. Given the construction of normative masculinity associated with power and control in many societies, local people in host societies have commonly perceived American soldiers as agents of the imperial power and have been both repulsed by and attracted to them. Local women who date or marry GIS frequently encounter derisive comments and ostracism from their own societies. Ames's discussion of the women's agency allows us to see the complex interplay of race, gender, sexuality, and class, often with unexpected twists and turns. He illuminates how Japanese women view American men, in both their actual physique and their idealized images projected through American movies, as desirable, romantic, and sexual objects. Japanese women who are attracted to American GIS perceive them to be less misogynistic and more chivalrous than Japanese men and assume that marriage to an American man will result in a more egalitarian partnership. Ames also shows that Japan's economic boom and the collapse of the U.S. dollar in the 1980s meant that newly prosperous young Japanese women from mainland Japan started traveling to Okinawa to find "exotic" American lovers, showering them with gifts of clothing, stereos, and even expensive cars. Fascinating are also Ames's findings that women from Okinawa who marry American GIS feel most at home not in the United States or in their own communities, but in the extraterritorial, hybrid spaces that the military housing areas provide.

In chapter 6, Robin Riley focuses on women working for the defense industry in the United States and helps us understand how civilian–military relations are mediated by it. Many American women are employed in the defense industry in various capacities, ranging from engineers and administrators to assembly-line workers and receptionists. What is revealing about the narratives of these "hidden soldiers," as Riley calls the women, is that regardless of their racial and class differences, they tend to subscribe to an ideology of national defense, commonly conflating the private companies they work for with the government. While these women justify their work in terms of their contribution to national defense, more mundane factors shape the normalization of their close involvement in the workings of the military empire: the economic incentive of secure employment, the code of secrecy about their work outside their workplace, and the ideological distinction between "innocuous defense work" and "other real" war stuff. As Riley suggests, while economic and ideological factors also color the perception of work among male workers in the defense industry, these women's gendered preoccupation with familial responsibilities seems to further contribute to ambiguity and conflation in their perception of what they do for a living. Their narratives expose the disjuncture between normative elements of militarized femininity because they do not embrace a militarized motherhood that glorifies sending their sons and daughters to the battlefield. This disjuncture is most visible in their ambivalence about their own children's potential military service.

In part III, Seungsook Moon, Maria Höhn, and Christopher Nelson highlight the (postcolonial) agency of local men and women that has become possible in contemporary South Korea, post-occupation West Germany, and contemporary Okinawa. Residing in the hybrid spaces created in and around U.S. military bases, local nationals are able to challenge existing hierarchical social relations of race, gender, sexuality, and class in their own societies through their interaction with the U.S. military. This type of resistance resembles the notion of postcolonial agency grounded in hybridity as a source of creativity and originality rather than that of impurity and bastardization. Such resistance is not necessarily organized and consciously politicized; nevertheless, it paradoxically subverts established power relations.[51] While simultaneous attraction and repulsion underlie the daily encounters between GIS and locals, racially marked cultural differences distinguish the ways in which local agencies are expressed. In chapter 7, Seungsook Moon explores contemporary change in the racial hierarchy tied to gender, sexuality, and class on U.S. military bases by focusing on the relationships between GIS and Korean male conscripts,[52] who have been serving as augmentation troops to the U.S. Army (KATUSAS) since 1950. In the 2000s, the nonfictional and fictional accounts spoken or written by KATUSAS about their experiences of serving in the U.S. military reveal criticism of arrogant male GIS and fantasies about sexual encounters with white female GIS. It is noteworthy that the power balance between KATUSAS and American GIS has shifted substantially over time because of economic and political developments in South Korea. As a result, since the 1980s, not only have a majority of KATUSAS been middle-class college students from elite universities in Korea; they have also found political space to articulate their criticism of the U.S. military. Against the backdrop of blatant racism against KATUSAS that has become subtle in recent decades and the continuing U.S. military and political dominance of Korea, these better-educated and affluent Korean conscripts often look down on American male GIS, whom they judge as ignorant and impulsive. Moon also points out that the sexual fantasy about white female GIS is a flip side of the KATUSAS' shared resentment of the history of camptown prostitution and the growing practice of dating between female Korean college students and GIS, preferably white officers.

In Chapter 8, Maria Höhn traces the interactions between local men and GIS in West Germany, which were much more positive than those that took place in South Korea. For young, male German teenagers after the Second World War, American GIS presented novel ideas of desirable masculinity. Their more relaxed styles and habitus proved seductive to a generation looking for a counter-model to the discredited and goose-stepping Nazi male of their fathers' generation. The image of a different sort of militarized masculinity—namely, that of the citizen soldier who also knew how to jitterbug and did not mind playing Santa Claus for German children—was endorsed by the American military as part of the democratization of German society. During the 1950s, this different meaning of masculinity was also enforced by such Hollywood stars as James Dean and popular-music figures such as Elvis Presley (who was stationed in Germany in 1958). The very qualities that made American GIS attractive to Germany's younger generation also convinced their elders that American GIS were "feminized" and were not manly enough to stand up to Soviet soldiers, and that it was foremost America's nuclear umbrella, rather than the prowess of its soldiers, that kept Germany safe. Höhn also shows the dramatic shift in perception of American GIS that took place after the all-volunteer force was introduced, especially since the American invasion of Iraq and the abuses at Abu Ghraib and Guantánamo.

In his evocative essay in chapter 9, Christopher Nelson adds a fascinating contribution to existing scholarship on grassroots resistance to military bases, which has developed in response to GI crime or as part of anti-base movements by peace and environmental activists. As Nelson illustrates in his discussion of *eisā*, a traditional Okinawan dance performed each summer in preparation for Obon (the festival of the dead), opposition or resistance to the U.S. military empire can take an apparently nonpolitical, asexual, and genderless form. This cultural affirmation is staged against the backdrop of a series of violent protests against the U.S. military, including the Koza Riots in Okinawa in 1970. In performing the dance to escort the spirits of the dead from their tombs to their homes, a young generation of working-class Okinawans endeavors to transcend the history of double colonization and contemporary lives dominated by the overwhelming U.S. military presence. Instead of criticizing male GIS' arrogance or the dating or marrying of GIS, or fantasizing about sexual liaisons with GIS, these young men and women dance together in the streets normally dominated by U.S. troops. For a few days during the local festival, the Okinawan youth take back the streets, which otherwise reverberate with the noise of U.S. military convoys and are illed with the "A-sign" establishments of bars, clubs, bathhouses, cafés, brothels, and restaurants that cater to the foreign soldiers.

As comparative historical studies of empires point out, empires—as complex political entities that develop over time in multiple relationships with other states—expand and maintain their dominance in the name of "order" and "civilization." Those same studies have shown that order and civilization, as enunciated by the metropole, often means disorder and violence for those outside the metropole. As the contributors to part IV analyze, various types of violence generated by the working of American empire can lead to racial crisis, abuse, and violence in and around U.S. military bases. The essays in part IV illuminate that the abuses at Guantánamo Bay, Abu Ghraib, and Haditha are not merely symptoms of the over-extension of the U.S. military in the ongoing war on terror. Even before the over-extension, the military was threatened by internal racial strife and a subculture shaped by sexism and homophobia. At the same time, U.S. military culture, imbued with notions and practices of hyper-masculinity, as well as of cultural and racial superiority, also contains a potential for violence against those who are outside its gender, sexual, and racial boundaries.[53]

One manifestation of the racial conflict within the military empire can be found in the racial crisis of 1970–71 that plagued U.S. military bases at home and abroad. In chapter 10, Maria Höhn argues that the racial crisis that played out on military bases across the United States and worldwide resulted from the vast contradiction between America's claim after 1945 to be the leader of the "Free World" and its unresolved racial question at home.[54] After the Second World War, it was the creation of the global network of U.S. military bases that brought the "American dilemma" to the world's scrutiny, making possible the desegregation of the military in 1948 and federal support of the civil-rights revolution that began in the 1950s (see chapter 3).[55] The problem of institutional racism in the U.S. military and in American society at large was, however, not overcome that easily. Thus, it was the widespread discrimination in the military, the strain of the Vietnam War, and the apparent failure of the liberal Civil Rights Movement that, had led to unprecedented levels of violence within the military by the late 1960s, but had also brought about a noticeable increase in violence against civilians living near U.S. bases. By comparing how events unfolded in South Korea and West Germany, Höhn reminds us just how severe the racial crisis in the military was. In fact, in Germany, the Seventh Army was close to collapse, and in South Korea, military–civilian relations were at a breaking point. However, her essay also illuminates how the democratization of Germany and the more egalitarian relationship between the Germans and the U.S. military allowed for a much

FIGURE I.1. Aerial view of Camp Page, which opened to the public to celebrate Citizens' Day (November 8, 2008) in Chunch'ŏn City, Kangwŏn Province.

more "democratic" solution than in South Korea, where the United States was aligned with a military dictatorship. Just as important, Höhn's discussion of the situation in West Germany reveals that the U.S. military was forced into drastic reform because a new generation of black activists was no longer willing to wait for promises that had been made as far back as the Second World War, and they enunciated their demands in the very country where the United States had pledged the defense of the "Free World."

In chapter 11, Seungsook Moon provides a cautionary tale of the abuse and violence inherent in the institution of camptown prostitution that has been based on racism, sexism, and uneven power relations between GIS and civilian society regulated by the imperial SOFA. The enduring practice of camptown prostitution in South Korea, which largely has been kept invisible to Americans at home, was exposed in the summer of 2002 when Fox News reported on the military's entanglement with camptown prostitution that relied heavily on trafficked women. In response to these embarrassing revelations, the U.S. Department of Defense implemented a zero-tolerance policy on prostitution and trafficking around U.S. military bases overseas, but this policy has not substantially reduced abuse of and violence against camptown women. Moon argues that, despite the military authorities' attempt to maintain control over camptown prostitution to ensure the smooth func-

FIGURE I.2. This partial view of the Baumholder military base shows how intimately the base and the surrounding German community are connected. COURTESY HERBERT PIEL.

tioning of the empire, the deeply unequal power relations between male GIS and camptown sex workers continue to precipitate abuse and violence. Opportunity for abuse has only increased since the end of the Cold War, as more and more women from the Philippines and the former Soviet Union have been replacing Korean sex workers. These transnational women are often trafficked and therefore are much more vulnerable to exploitation and abuse by both club owners and GIS than were earlier generations of Korean women.

In chapter 12, Jeff Bennett analyzes the highly sexualized and gendered forms of torture and violence perpetrated against prisoners in Abu Ghraib in occupied Iraq. He convincingly argues that this form of violence at Abu Ghraib prison is not merely a symptom of the current over-extension of the U.S. military in the ongoing war on terror, but also an outcome overdetermined by the elective affinity between interrogation techniques in prison and gendered and sexualized understanding of power in the subculture of the U.S. military. As he documents, this understanding of power extends beyond Abu Ghraib prison spatially and temporally; it informs social relations in the American penitentiary system and, before Abu Ghraib, had been normalized in Vietnam as a way to break down and convert prisoners of war. Bennett analyzes how, in the hybrid space of the military prison of Abu Ghraib, the established military chain of command based on official hierarchy of rank and regulation broke down and the relationships among prison guards were governed by informal "respect" for the alpha warrior, drawn from the "non-conventional warfare specialists" (Special Operations, Central Intelligence Agency operatives such as Delta Force, and private military contractors such as Blackwater/Xe). In the institutional context of celebrating male sexual potency as the marker of a collective imperial potential, female guards also internalize the prevailing attitudes of sexualized masculine domination or are pressured to act "tough" toward prisoners. Bennett thoughtfully concludes that the violence at Abu Ghraib prison was a predictable, though unintended, outcome of the profound contradiction inherent in a war that requires the loss of human life to win the "peace."

Notes

1. For a detailed study of Baumholder, a small community of 5,000 inhabitants with a U.S. military base that was home to some 30,000 personnel for most of the Cold War, see Höhn 2002.
2. See Lutz 2001 for a study of Fayetteville, North Carolina, outside Fort Bragg.
3. Ann Laura Stoler aptly observes that empires preceding the United States also relied on the creation and maintenance of hybrid or ambiguous spaces where boundaries between nations and between civilian society and the military are blurred: see Stoler 2006b, 54–58.
4. Melanie McAlister (2001) is an exception in that she focuses on the postwar period, but her concern is solely with cultural productions in the United States and not the impact of the military abroad.
5. For an exception to this tendency, see Carl Boggs (2003), who pointed out this lacuna.
6. For the studies of women's paid and unpaid labor in the military, see Freedman and Rhoads 1989; Howes and Stevenson 1993; Norman 1990; Zeiger 1999. On violence against women and homosexuals in the military, see Firestone and Harris 2003; Harris 1999; Miller 1998; Quester 2002; Scott and Stanley 1994; Shawver 1995; Wolinsky and Sherrill 1993; Zeeland 1996. On gendered workings of the military, see D'Amico and Weinstein 2000; DeGroot and Peniston-Bird 2000; Enloe 1983, 1989, 1993, 2000; Herbert 1998. On women's resistance to war and militarism, see Elshtain and Tobias 1990; Oldfield 1989; Tylee 1990.
7. For in-depth studies of individual countries, see Höhn 2002 (Germany); Leuerer 1997 (Germany); K. Moon 1997 (South Korea); Vine 2009 (Diego Garcia).
8. For comparative studies, see Cooley 2008; Lutz 2009; Gillem 2007; Baker 2004; Gerson and Birchard 1991; Johnson 2000, 2004; Sturdevant and Stoltzfus 1992.
9. On the development of the global network of U.S. military bases in the postwar era, see Blaker 1990; Calder 2007; Campbell and Ward 2003; Gerson and Birchard

1991; Grant 2002; Lindsay-Poland 1996, 1999; Sandars 2000; *Time*, December 29, 2003 / January 5, 2004.

10. See also Chalmers A. Johnson, "737 U.S. Military Bases Equals Global Empire," *Japan Focus*, vol. 22, February 2007, available online at http://japanfocus.org/products/topdf/2358. For the 2009 Base Structure Report, see Department of Defense: http://www.acq.osd.mil/ie/ie_library.shtml (accessed March 29, 2010).

11. See also Johnson, "737 U.S. Military Bases Equals Global Empire." The land on which overseas bases are constructed is usually not owned by the United States but is made available free of charge by the host country.

12. Kent Calder's book was published after we had conceptualized this volume and written our contributions. He sees the bases as a major stabilizing system in the postwar order while also acknowledging the high cost they exact on the local population. We find it telling that his focus is also on the three countries that we found most important to compare.

13. For a discussion of how many bases of the U.S. empire were inherited from the British empire beginning in the Second World War, see Calder 2007, 11–13. During 1950–2000, 535,540 troops on average were stationed abroad, reaching a high of 1,082,777 in 1968 and a low of 206,002 in 1999. For a detailed overview by country and region, see Kane 2006.

14. The U.S. military strategy was built on three premises: (1) nuclear-war fighting strategy and deterrence through mutually assured destruction; (2) deterrence of major conventional war in Europe and Asia; and (3) ability to engage or intervene in smaller wars throughout the world: see Walker 1991, 36.

15. As Tim Kane (2006, 4) concludes, until the terrorist attacks of 9/11, the commitment of American soldiers had been consistent in Europe, varied in Asia, and shallow in other parts of the globe, with Africa especially holding little interest to the United States.

16. According to the *2009 Base Structure Report* from the Department of Defense, accessible at the website of the Office of the Deputy Under Secretary of Defense at http://www.acq.osd.mil/ie/ie_library.shtml, these three countries continue to host more than two-thirds of overseas bases. We see our volume as an initial effort to globalize the study of the U.S. military empire. We do not want to suggest that other countries with U.S. troops merit less attention. Indeed, we hope that this volume will encourage future studies of military–civilian relationships in Africa and Central and South America; in countries such as Guam and the Philippines; and in Islamic countries such as Bahrain and Turkey.

17. During the Cold War, Germany accounted for 60 percent of all overseas bases: Duke 1989, 57; Sandars 2000, 206. Of the $9.6 billion that the United States spent on NATO in 1987, $6.4 billion went to military installations in West Germany: Kane 2006, 4.

18. Existing theories of empire and imperialism reveal a striking lack of concern with the human costs of empire and imperialism. While Marxist economic theories focus on the expansionist logic of capital, political theories highlight the pursuit of prestige by a

stronger state within the international system: see Doyle 1986; Harvey 2003; Mann 1984, 2003; Münkler 2007. Postmodern theories of empire tend to disregard specific political and economic conditions in their emphasis on the fluid nature of decentralized and amorphous imperial power: see Hardt and Negri 2000. Amy Kaplan (2002) and Melanie McAlister (2001) are mostly concerned with how American empire impacts cultural discourses within the United States.

19. See Eland 2004, chap. 2, for the discussion of how the United States conforms to various definitions of empire. See Williams 1972, 1980, for important exceptions.

20. The United States established basing rights by "virtue of conquest" not only in West Germany and Japan, but also in South Korea: see Sandars 2000, 13–14. Kent Calder (2007, chap. 1) makes an equally strong case that the United States "inherited" most of its bases from other empires or during the Second World War.

21. For an overview of the SOFAS, see Center for Strategic and International Studies 2002; Mason 2008. For country-specific discussions, see Gher 2002; Headquarters of the Movement to Root Out American Soldiers' Crime 2002; Johnson 2004b.

22. This Eurocentrism is so deep that a theoretical discussion critical of it ironically fails to discuss the historical and contemporary relationships between the U.S. empire and non-Western societies. For example, Herfried Münkler (2007, 27), after stressing that "theories of empire have to keep center and periphery equally in view, both in analysis of the formative period of empires and in relation to the era following their consolidation," limits his discussion of the U.S. empire primarily to its interactions with Western Europe.

23. For examples of the ambivalent discussion of America's empire, see Bender 2003; Ignatieff 2003; Maier 2006; Nye 2002; Waltzer 2003. For examples of supporters of American empire, see Cohen 2004; Ferguson 2002, 2005; Hodge 2005; Kissinger 2001; Mark Mazzetti, "Pax Americana," U.S. News and World Report, vol. 135, no. 11, 6 October 2003, 30–37. In addition to these two camps, there are critics of empire who question its impact on democratic traditions at home or attack it for the cost to the American taxpayer. For examples, see Bacevich 2003; Johnson 2000, 2004a; Michael T. Klare, "Imperial Reach: The Pentagon's New Basing Strategy," Nation, vol. 280, no. 16, 25 April 2005, 13–14, 16–18; Knauft 2007; Mann 2003; Misra 2003; Pilger 2004; Vidal 2002.

24. See Renda 2001, 115, on how Wilsonian paternalism based on liberal imperialism led to the nineteen-year military occupation of Haiti: Renda argues that the United States took Haiti not because of a failure of the liberal vision, but because of the logic of that vision, which is inscripted with racial, gender and class hierarchies. Julian Go (2008) uses the term "liberal imperialism" as well to trace the working of U.S. empire. See also Uday Singh Mehta (1999), who theorizes the link between liberalism and European colonialism. While liberal thought promoted a universal belief in liberty, autonomy, and self-rule, it justified colonial rule over conquered societies outside Europe with a paternalist outlook that equated the colonized with children who needed to be guided with a firm hand toward a progressive future.

25. In her study of the economic and cultural rise of the United States between 1890 and 1945, Emily Rosenberg (1982) calls this imperial ideology "liberal developmentalism."

A similar imperial ideology is observed by Andrew J. Bacevich (2002), a former military officer and self-identified conservative, in his examination of American diplomacy during the 1990s, whose origins he traces to the Second World War.

26. In practice, even today, the United States continues to have de facto colonies ambiguously named "territories" in the Pacific Ocean and the Caribbean Sea, where it has maintained several dozen military bases. According to the U.S. Department of Defense (2004a), there were 115 bases in U.S. territories, and the 2009 Base Structure Report (http://www.acq.osd.mil/ie/ie_library.shtml) identifies 121 bases in U.S. territories.

27. For a thoughtful discussion on this shift, see McAlister 2001, 47–55. The phrase "benevolent supremacy" was coined by Charles Hilliard in a right-wing tract in 1951. Although it was not widely used among policymakers in the 1950s, it captured common attitudes of a large segment of the American elite in the immediate postwar decades. The theme can be traced to Henry Luce, who published his influential editorial "The American Century" in 1941, glorifying the United States as "the powerhouse of the ideals of freedom and justice" and legitimizing not only its leadership in the world but also its supremacy: 17 February, 1941, *Life* magazine.

28. "Justice & Law in Status-of-Forces Agreements," *Time*, 17 June 1957, available online at http://www.time.com/time/printout/0,8816,867699,00.html (accessed on 4 March 2008).

29. The clause of sympathetic consideration and other unequal arrangements concerning concurrent jurisdiction have remained to this day. See U.S.–Republic of Korea SOFA, 1966, 1991, art. 22, 7(b), available online at http://www.shaps.hawaii.edu/security/us/sofa1966_1991.html (accessed on 24 April 2008). See the Status of U.S. Armed Forces in Japan signed on January 19, 1960, art. 17, 7(b), available online at http://www.niraikanai.wwma.net/pages/archive/sofa.html (accessed on 24 April 2008). See NATO SOFA, signed on June 19, 1951, art. 7, 3(c), available online at http://www.nato.int/docu/basictxt/b510619a.htm (accessed on 24 April 2008). In South Korea and Japan, as well as in West Germany, "sympathetic consideration" has been an established convention because the United States "automatically request[s] a waiver for U.S. personnel implicated in criminal activity": see Gher 2002, 234.

30. As activists in Korea and Okinawa have repeatedly pointed out, SOFAS with non–NATO countries have been so asymmetrical vis-à-vis the host nation that American soldiers have been virtually above the law: see Gillem 2007, 23; National Campaign to Eliminate Crimes Committed by U.S. Forces in Korea 1999, 2002; Sandars 2000, 326.

31. German authorities actually prefer to yield judicial authority over GIS to the United States because U.S. military law passes much harsher sentencing than German law. Germany, however, will insist on trying an American defendant when a case (such as a particularly gruesome rape or murder) provokes a major public outcry. Interestingly, given Germany's opposition to the death penalty, the SOFA negotiated with West Germany entails the provision that no GI prosecuted under U.S. military law can receive the death sentence for any crime committed on German soil.

32. Pierre Hassner (2002, 46), a critic of American empire, comments that the United States claims an absolute right "to make sovereign judgments on what is right or

wrong, particularly in the use of force, and to exempt itself with an absolute clear conscience from all the rules that it proclaims and applies to others."

33. Julian Go (2008) argues this in his comparison of American colonialism in the Philippines, Guam, and Samoa.

34. Reflecting the liberal imperialism discussed earlier, the security arrangement between South Korea and the United States has been convoluted, masking its unequal neocolonial nature with formalistic arrangements. From the Korean War to 1978, the commander of the U.S. forces in Korea was, at the same time, the commander of the UN forces in Korea, which exercised full operational control of the Korean military. Although the UN Forces Command Headquarters was in charge of defending South Korea during this period, it did not include a single Korean officer. The establishment of the CFC transferred the command of the Korean military formally from the commander of the UN forces to the commander of the U.S. forces: see Rhee 1986.

35. However, presidents Barack Obama and Lee Myung-bak agreed to postpone the return date to December 2015 at the G-20 Economic Summit meeting in Toronto, held in June 2010: see http://www.globalsecurity.org/military/agency/dod/usfk.htm (accessed on August 6, 2010).

36. This arrangement continues apparently to supplement the U.S. military's manpower commitment in Korea, the lesser ally. Korean conscripts have been used in place of more expensive (economically and politically) American soldiers since the Korean War and make up 12 percent to 24 percent of U.S. forces serving in South Korea: see chap. 7 in this book.

37. During the Korean War (which left 4 million people dead) and the postwar decades, marked by widespread poverty and a continuing threat from North Korea (which was economically and militarily superior to the South until the beginning of the 1970s), South Korea did not have a choice but to give up its control over the military. The Korean elites' willingness to cede control over the military again in 1978 was caused by a combination of the following factors: U.S. troop reductions in Korea in the 1970s, the vested political and economic interests of the ruling elite in maintaining the Cold War system that was used to justify dictatorship, the U.S. withdrawal from Vietnam and the subsequent takeover of Indochina, and the precipitation of oil crises during the 1970s.

38. According to nine opinion polls on U.S. Forces conducted between 1988 and 2002, a majority of Koreans supported a phased withdrawal or immediate withdrawal of U.S. Forces: J. Kim 2004, 272. In surveys conducted in the 1960s, a mere 13 percent of South Korean thought that Americans "liked them": K. Moon 1997, 119. That low number stands in sharp contrast to West Germany, where 70 percent of the population assumed that the Americans viewed them "as friends": Knauer 1987, 189–90.

39. Japan also repeated a strategy from the Second World War when Okinawa saw large-scale deployments of Japanese troops, and because of those deployments, was the only inhabited island of Japan that saw ground warfare. In these devastating battles, Okinawa lost a quarter of its population. The Third Marine Expeditionary Force is the only division-scale force stationed abroad. It has 17,000 officers and soldiers, account-

ing for 60 percent of all American servicemen stationed in Okinawa: see Baker 2004; Calder 2007. For more details, see "III Marine Expeditionary Force," n.d., available online at http://www.globalsecurity.org/military/agency/usmc/iii-mef.htm (accessed 1 April 2010).

40. Even at the low point of German–American relations during the 1980s missile crisis, 75 percent of Germans approved of the U.S. military presence: see Fleckenstein 1987, 5. For a detailed description of how intensely the United States fostered German-American relations, see Höhn 2002.

41. See also Enloe 1989, 1991, 1993, 2000; chap. 12 in this book.

42. The Berlin Brigade, for example, was made up of forty-two different installations. For a more detailed description of residential patterns in Germany, see Höhn 2002. Of the 37,000 Americans associated with the Ramstein/Landstuhl military communities during the 1980s, for example, 12,000 found housing in surrounding German towns and villages: "Wie in einem besetzen Land [As if in an occupied country]," Der Stern, 19 May 1982, 88. Since 9/11, this trend has been reversed. U.S. housing areas and military installations that used to be rather open and accessible, are now closed off with intimidating fences and barriers.

43. The defense industry has supplied a wide range of weapons for the military. During the 1980s, one in twenty jobs in the United States was directly or indirectly linked to the military, and 25 percent of scientists and engineers were involved in military work. During the 1990s, the contraction of military-procurement spending by more than 50 percent resulted in the heightened concentration of the defense industry. More than forty firms were merged to form the big four—Lockheed Martin, Boeing McDonnell Douglas, Raytheon Hughes, and Northrop Grumann: see Markusen 1999.

44. Until the introduction of the all-volunteer military, between 12 and 15 percent of troops were African American. Since the shift to a professional army, their proportion has grown to more than 30 percent.

45. On the pervasiveness of prostitution and concubinage in the British empire, see Levine 2003, 184–85. On the U.S. military and prostitution in the Philippines and Haiti, see Kramer 2006b; Renda 2001.

46. Concubinage in European colonies refers to cohabitation between a white man and a local woman outside marriage in which the woman could occupy various positions, ranging from that of live-in slave or coolie to that of lover with a good deal of power over a white partner.

47. This shift in policy will have to wait, however, until the bases have been completely relocated south of Seoul. The United States insisted that South Korea was still a war zone and that it was therefore too dangerous to bring families. We find this attitude to highlight a notable contrast to Germany: American families were kept in Berlin, even during the Berlin Airlift and subsequent crises, because the United States wanted to impress on the Soviets that America was willing to make the ultimate sacrifice.

48. In 1945 thirty states in the United States had such laws. During the 1950s and early 1960s, a number of western states discarded those laws, but it would take the Supreme Court ruling (Loving v. Virginia) in 1967 to get rid of those laws in southern states. For a

more comprehensive discussion, see Höhn 2002, 2005. For a discussion of how civil-rights activists in the United States used this contradiction to indict Jim Crow laws in the United States, see Höhn 2008c, 2011.

49. In doing so, the military followed a precedent set during the occupation of the Philippines at the beginning of the twentieth century and during the deployment of U.S. forces in Hawaii during the Second World War. For the Philippines see Kramer 2006a. For policies in Hawaii see Bailey and Farber 1994.

50. However, there were some significant differences between Japan and Korea in terms of their perceptions of the U.S. occupation. The Japanese elite, whose imperial military committed mass rapes against women in occupied territories, feared mass rapes of Japanese women by American soldiers. Korean elites were not so concerned, because Korea was not an enemy of the United States. As Moon documents in chap. 1 of this book, in the absence of a formal arrangement, widespread unregulated prostitution coexisted with prostitution regulated by the U.S. military. Koreans' concern about racial purity is revealed in the rejection of children of mixed race, who are usually the result of liaisons between camptown sex workers and GIs. Newspapers represented such biracial children as a serious social problem, and until very recently the Korean government maintained the policy of sending the children to the United States for adoption: see Kim et al. 2003.

51. Homi Bhabha grounds his theory of postcolonial agency in the positive affirmation of hybridity and mimicry. As the practice or art of imitating speech, behavior, and appearance, mimicry is not considered the absence of creativity and originality but, rather, a crucial strategy to turn the colonial power's ability to reform, regulate, and discipline the colonized into a subversive tool to disrupt such authority: see Bhabha 1995, 34.

52. See S. Moon 2001, 2002b, 2005b for a detailed discussion of the male-only conscription system and its significance for gendered nation building and the notion and practices of masculinity in contemporary Korea.

53. For an insider account of the widespread abuse at Guantánamo Bay, see Yee 2005.

54. This racial contradiction was derided by the Soviet Union in the Cold War rivalry, even though the Soviet Union had its own history of racism. For example, in 1937 Stalin ordered the deportation of approximately 180,000 Korean minorities from their homes in the Far Eastern part of the Soviet Union to barren areas in Kazakhstan. This forced displacement was motivated by security concerns due to Japan's imperial expansion in Asia throughout the 1930s. Stalin did not trust the Korean minority's loyalty to his regime in the event of a Japanese invasion, presumably because of the racial affinity between the Koreans and the Japanese: see Chung and Dibble 2007.

55. See also Höhn 2002, chap. 3, 2008b, 2008c; Höhn and Klimke 2010, as well as the website / digital archive they have created: aacvr-germany.org.

PART I

MONITORED LIAISONS

Local Women and GIs in the Making of Empire

ONE

REGULATING DESIRE, MANAGING THE EMPIRE
U.S. Military Prostitution in South Korea, 1945–1970

☆

SEUNGSOOK MOON

I am a comfort woman catering to foreign soldiers in the 7UP club in Yŏnp'ungni, Chunae Township, P'aju County, Kyŏnggi Province. Three years have passed since I came to [Yongjugol]. I've already been working as a comfort woman for over two years. I must get out of the bridle of this life. . . . I've been treated only with contempt because I am a comfort woman serving foreign soldiers, a woman with an inhumane job, but my writing can be of help to other people. Yet I'm not writing my repentance. Although my life may have been inhumane and vicious, I have never committed a crime or a sin. (Pak 1965, 6, 10; my translation)

Annie Pak (or Pak Ok-sun in Korean), whose words are quoted from her autobiography,[1] was conceived by a Korean woman and a white American soldier in January 1946. Her mother was a seventeen-year-old maiden employed in a men's suit factory in Seoul to alter American soldiers' uniforms, and her father was a young private who occasionally visited the factory. Her mother frequently worked until very late at night. On a very gusty winter night, when she came out of the factory to go home, an American military truck stopped in front of her. The soldier, whose face she knew, kindly offered her a ride home, and she thankfully got on the truck. But he took her to a remote place and raped her. Because he was in love with her mother,

Annie was told, he took her into his unit and lived with her for five days until she was found by his commanding officer and kicked out. She did not even know the soldier's name. Annie's mother revealed this secret of Annie's birth only after Annie herself had become a camptown sex worker in the mid-1960s (Pak 1965, 253–54).[2]

Left with a Eurasian daughter, Annie's mother began to work in military prostitution to raise her. Clever about multiplying her meager savings, her mother was able to buy a house and leave the work behind. Unfortunately, she then lost her money and houses to charlatans (all Korean men) who lived off her with the promise of marriage, which would have been a ticket to the respectable life for a woman. These vagaries of life evaporated her mother's plan to give Annie a secondary education. After struggling to make ends meet for a few years, her mother finally returned to Yongjugol, a thriving camptown, in the 1960s, where Annie started working in a convenience store patronized by American soldiers.[3] Annie's unusual Euro-American appearance attracted many American soldiers to the store, and at seventeen she fell in love with one of them—a white officer. They lived together like a newlywed couple for several months, and she became pregnant. Yet it turned out that the officer did not intend to marry her, as she had expected, and like numerous soldiers before and after him he left when his service in Korea ended. It is not clear whether Annie was able to leave the camptown for good and whether she is still alive. If she is, she would be living somewhere in Korea as a woman in her sixties.

This chapter traces the emergence and consolidation of U.S. military prostitution during the time span when these two generations of women came to sell sex for a living under conditions beyond their own choice and control. These conditions included the presence of imperial troops, the legacy of the comfort station that naturalized both military and civilian authorities' use of women's sexual labor to manage (male) soldiers, and the mass impoverishment generated by Japanese colonial exploitation and the Korean War. The confluence of these conditions generated the institution of camptown prostitution, which became a naturalized fixture of the American military presence in South Korea. The racialized cultural differences between Korea and the U.S. further amplified the making and spread of the institution. The estimated total of 180,000 camptown sex workers in the 1950s and roughly 10,000 camptown sex workers in the Tongduch'ŏn area alone in the mid-1960s were staggering in light of the annual number of American troops in South Korea, which fluctuated from 85,000 to 50,000 between 1955 and 1970 (Oh et al. 1990, 56).[4] In West Germany, by comparison (also a country divided by Cold War politics that steadily hosted more than a quarter-million American troops in the 1950s and 1960s), prostitution catering to American soldiers operated on a much smaller scale.

The history of the U.S. military presence in Korea began in September 1945, when the Twenty-Fourth Army Corps, consisting of some 72,000 soldiers and led by Lieutenant-General John R. Hodge, commanding general of the U.S. Armed Forces in Korea (USAFIK), arrived to transfer power from the crumbled Japanese colonial empire. As the agent of the American empire that commanded the global network of military bases, the military developed the unofficial but consistent system of regulated prostitution during its direct rule of Korea (1945–48). The U.S. Army Military Government (USAMG) suppressed unregulated prostitution to control the spread of venereal disease (VD) and, at the same time, regulated prostitution as an expedient means of entertaining and controlling male soldiers. The succeeding Korean government of President Syngman Rhee (1948–60) maintained a similarly contradictory position on prostitution that both criminalized it in law and supported it for American (and Korean) soldiers in practice. During the Korean War, the Korean government adopted the Japanese institution of "comfort stations" to serve Allied Forces and Korean soldiers in the name of protecting respectable women and rewarding soldiers for their sacrifice. During the 1950s, when the Korean War resulted in a semi-permanent U.S. military presence, the development of camptowns sped up to meet sex and other entertainment needs of the American soldiers, and regulated prostitution became an integral component of the camptown economy. During the 1960s, while continuing to criminalize prostitution in formal law, the military government of President Park Chung Hee further consolidated camptown prostitution through the creation of 104 "special districts" and the establishment of rules to support the camptown economy. This chapter contends that an unofficial yet consistent policy regarding prostitution existed despite the criminalization of prostitution in both countries from 1945 to 1970 (and even after). As Cynthia Enloe (1989) points out, political powers rely on certain notions of femininity and masculinity for their smooth working. Regulated military prostitution assumes soldiers as heterosexual men in need of constant sexual gratification and requires such construction of militarized masculinity. The emergence and consolidation of regulated military prostitution in Korea reveals that prostitution is an essential component of expanding and maintaining the American empire, as were the cases with European colonial empires, and it is sustained through the collaboration of local elites, at the expense of lower-class women, to serve their political and economic interests.

The intimate liaison between regulated prostitution and a foreign military in the Korean Peninsula preceded USAMG rule. Military prostitution catering to Japanese soldiers stationed in Korea began after Korea's "opening" by Japan in 1876, leading to the growing influx of Japanese merchants, soldiers, and laborers. In 1883, Japanese businesses opened concentrated brothels for Japanese soldiers in downtown Seoul. Their conspicuous existence incited a strong reaction from the local population. The Japanese authorities, however, condoned them and in 1904 finally began permitting public prostitution (*kongch'ang*) in Seoul (Son 1988, 286; Song 1989, 71). This legalization facilitated the spread of public prostitution districts in the midst of Japan's growing power over Korea, especially after its victory in the Russo-Japanese War of 1905. After Korea was colonized in 1910, the colonial state legalized the trafficking of women for prostitution under the Regulations Concerning the Acquisition of Prostitutes of 1916 (Kim 1989, 137; Yun 1987, 25–26). Under this system of public prostitution, the colonial state recognized prostitution as a legitimate form of business and collected taxes on it (Pak 1994, 65–68). The colonial authorities implemented their own VD control programs, including the periodic examination of licensed prostitutes (Yi 1997, 72).[5]

During the Japanese military expansion between 1930 and 1945, the Japanese colonial state actively consumed women's bodies in order to sexually feed and manage its imperial armies. Initially, private businesses recruited Japanese women from poor rural areas for "military comfort stations" in China and other conquered areas where large numbers of Japanese soldiers stayed. These women were called *karayuki san*, or "foreign-bound women." The sex workers were exploited in the name of "the last service for the nation" (Chai 1993; Chŏng 1997). After the Sino-Japanese War (1937), however, the Japanese military began to implement a policy to manage the comfort stations directly in order to check the rampant spread of venereal disease and drafted a large number of Korean women (Chŏng 1997, 105). Encountering the unwelcome partner of the colonial expansion, the military turned its attention to seventeen- to twenty-year-old Korean women as substitutes for Japanese sex workers. Aware that women in Korea's Confucian society were instilled with an education that valued rigid chastity, the military replaced Japanese sex workers with young Korean women who were chaste enough to be free of venereal disease and young enough to endure disease if it developed. "Military comfort women" were an integral part of Japan's military expansion, which spanned Korea, China, Southeast Asia, and Papua New Guinea. The women were sent to battlefields as "royal gifts" from the Japanese emperor (Kim 1997, 53).

The demise of colonial rule did not end the use of women's sexual labor for foreign soldiers in Korea. Projecting its image as a "benevolent liberator" to teach democracy to Koreans,[6] the U.S. military was deeply implicated in various forms of prostitution from the dawn of its occupation of Korea. Upon arriving in Korea, the U.S. military used dance halls that the Office of the (Japanese) Governor-General had opened to protect repatriating Japanese women from American soldiers (Yi 2004b, 272). The military also instituted separate clubs for officers and enlisted men because such a "service club program" provided "wholesome recreation for the troops" and proved to be valuable to the "improvement of morale of military personnel."[7] Hostesses in these clubs were locally procured. The so-called decolonizing process led by the U.S. military continued to provide fertile soil for the rapid growth of private and unregulated prostitution (*sach'ang*) in Seoul, Ascom, Taejŏn, Kwangju, and Pusan.[8] The boundary between hostesses and sex workers became blurred in impoverished Korea, where well-paid American soldiers aggressively sought out local women for sexual services.[9]

American GIS chased after Korean women in the context of racialized cultural difference, coupled with racism against the Koreans by GIS who were living and working in the racially segregated U.S. military. Military authorities had to deal with the pervasive problems of the deterioration of military courtesy, discipline, appearance, and training.[10] Under the category of courtesy, the authorities addressed widespread racism against the Koreans, ranging from the use of the racial slur "gooks," physical assaults, reckless driving, and undue arrests of Koreans to making aggressive passes at Korean women.[11] The courtesy drive launched by the Office of Commanding General Hodge in November 1946 summarized American racism in a surprisingly frank manner: "Americans are ignorant of Korean customs, show no appreciation of Korean art or culture, and openly ridicule the idea that there can be any good in anything Korean. . . . Americans act as though Koreans were a conquered nation rather than a liberated people."[12]

As the agents of the expanding American empire, "[GIS] in Korea think and act as though the world was made solely for them and their pleasure."[13] Within this imperialist mindset, GIS viewed sexual access to Korean women outside the respectability of marriage as their entitlement, as agents of European colonialism did toward colonized women of color. Seriously concerned about American racism as "one of the principle factors adverse to [the]

Korean–American relationship," the military authorities instructed GIS to learn about and respect Korean customs.[14] In a long, "restricted" message concerning how to change their bad behavior, Commanding General Hodge exhorted GIS to "keep [their] hands off Korean women."[15] Using a circular, the authorities attempted to teach GIS about the "vast cultural difference and social customs between Americans and Koreans" and urged them to "refrain from association with Korean women in public, except where such association is obviously of an impersonal or official nature." At the same time, the circular, to be read to "all male military and civilian personnel assigned or attached to the USAFIK," suggested that sexual relations with prostitutes be culturally acceptable but that all other forms of sexual relations with Korean women "[were] deemed by Koreans to be classed as an act[s] of rape."[16] The annual report of Medical Department activities for 1947 affirmed the condoning of prostitution on the grounds of cultural difference in its conclusion that, coupled with a dearth of adequate recreational facilities, Korean custom that segregated sexes in public tended to circumscribe encounters between GIS and Korean women to "brothels, dance halls, and street walkers."[17] Such tacit acceptance of GIS' sexual entitlement led to numerous liaisons between GIS and Korean women. Even married officers unaccompanied by their wives took "steady female partners,"[18] which resembled the practice of various forms of concubinage in European colonies.

Amid the rampant spread of private prostitution, the USAMG pursued duplicitous measures of condemning prostitution in law and inspecting sex workers and other categories of women who sexually served GIS. The USAMG issued the legal "prohibition of the trafficking in women or their sales contracts (*punyŏjaŭi maemae ttonŭn kŭ maemaegyeyagŭi kŭmji*)" in 1946. This law, however, did not prohibit prostitution that was presumably based on an agreement between a woman and her employer (Pak 1994, 85). Concerned about its image as a liberating force, the USAMG finally replaced the 1946 law with Public Act (PA) 7 of 1947. Proclaimed on November 14, 1947, and effective from February 1948 onward, PA 7 abolished the institution of public (or licensed) prostitution established by the Japanese colonial state.[19] The professed objectives of the law were to eliminate the "evil customs" of Japanese rule and to promote the democratic principle of "equality between men and women" (Pŏbjech'ŏ 1952, 179). Beneath the glib façade of emancipatory rhetoric lay convoluted political concerns. For the USAMG, prostitution was the object of effective regulation rather than of elimination. Alarmed by widespread VD and other communicable diseases, including tuberculosis, malaria, and leprosy, among the Koreans, the military authorities immediately established medical facilities and a public-health infrastructure (Smith 1950, 9–12).[20] Concluding that prostitution was a threat to American soldiers, the authorities initially placed "geisha houses" and "houses of prostitution" off-limits to American troops.[21] Yet the authorities did not attempt to criminalize prostitution, and it was argued that "a Korean prostitute was not disobeying the law unless she engaged in sexual intercourse with any member of the occupying forces while suffering from a VD in an infectious stage" (Meade 1951, 220–21). Following this logic, a medical officer "secured permission from [Sixth] Division Headquarters to keep the houses of prostitution on limits provid[ed] there would be weekly inspection of the working personnel" (Meade 1951, 220–21).

In May 1947, the USAMG established the VD Control Section under the Department of Public Health and Welfare and introduced periodic examination of, and treatment for, "entertaining girls." This category referred not only to licensed prostitutes (*kisaengs*), but also to dancers, bar girls, and waitresses. The practices of VD testing and treatment continued even after the abolition of public prostitution.[22] Failure to comply with the physical examination resulted in the loss of licenses. From May 1947 to July 1948, a total of 14,889 entertaining girls were examined, and almost 60 percent of them were infected with VD.[23] In addition, the first National Venereal Disease Center in Seoul officially opened in December 1947 to treat the infected (National Economic Board 1948, 191). During the first month, the military treated 191 formerly licensed prostitutes in outpatient services at Sunwha Hospital in Seoul and detained them at the Women's Jail until they were completely cleared of VD infection (National Economic Board 1947, 175).[24] Between 1946 and 1949, the U.S. military kept meticulous statistical records of various categories of women suspected of infecting American soldiers with VD. "Report on the Public Health Problems of South Korea" shows such statistics for "kisaengs," "waitresses," "servants," "dancers," and "prostitutes" who were subject to VD tests (Smith 1950, 69).

A majority of Korean women engaged in prostitution in the second half of the 1940s were impoverished expatriates who had been displaced during the colonial rule or were married women with families to support.[25] The first group of expatriates had previously worked as "dancers" in Shanghai and Manchuria during the colonial period. The second group consisted of women who worked in American military units as "coffee girls," "hair stylists," "house girls," "laundresses," and "typists." These women were escorted by American soldiers to dance parties at enlisted men's clubs. It is likely that many of the women who were engaged in prostitution in one way or another did not identify themselves as prostitutes and instead saw their involvement as an aberration or temporary sacrifice to be made in the face of dire poverty. It is important to recognize that the boundaries between professional prostitutes and various groups of women who had to work in the sex trade were blurred in the period of the USAMG rule. An implication of this fluidity is that there were discrepancies between the official labeling of prostitutes and the self-perceptions of women who sold sex. Many women catering to American soldiers, who were commonly called Western princesses (*yanggongju*) or "UN madams," may not have viewed themselves as prostitutes. Yet these women were subject to humiliating treatment in public that included stoning and cursing from children.[26] The U.S. military's expedient measures of criminalizing prostitution and, at the same time, regulating sex workers and the other categories of women who catered to GIs were part and parcel of its policy on controlling VD. While the military cracked down on prostitution when it caused VD to spread, it condoned and actively used prostitution when it took a form that allowed for the tight regulation of sex workers. This unofficial but consistent policy reflected the military's serious concern about the spread of VD as a major threat to soldiers' combat readiness during the period of USAMG rule and the subsequent decades. It also indicates the price that the military had to pay for normalizing heterosexual entitlement for male soldiers.

The U.S. Military Campaign against VD and the Regulation of Prostitution, 1945–1949

During the second half of the 1940s, the American military was involved in a campaign not only against communist forces in the Far East but also against an unexpected and formidable enemy: VD among its soldiers. The U.S. War Department, deeply concerned about the persistent problem of increasing VD rates in the USAFIK, issued the Army VD Control Program. The program aimed to reduce exposure to VD through the practice of "continence" (total abstinence from sexual activity) and by supplying the knowledge and materials necessary to prevent VD among soldiers who already had been exposed. Commanding General Hodge issued VD control measures to commanding generals and commanding officers through Circular 26 (February 21, 1947).[27] The campaign against VD was launched with the establishment of VD Control Councils that consisted of commanding officers, the Corps of Chaplains, the Special Service Division (which provided entertainment and recreation programs and facilities), the Provost Marshal, and the Medical Department. Toward the end of 1948, VD Control Councils were replaced by Character

Guidance Council to deal with all types of delinquency as well as VD. Essentially, the policy on VD control held commanding officers and noncommissioned officers responsible for the high incidence of VD in their units.[28] Their ineffectiveness in reducing VD rates was construed as a definite sign of inadequate leadership, thus discouraging accurate reporting of VD incidence in their units.

Various practices were implemented to combat VD. First, in compliance with the military's emphasis on continence, soldiers were indoctrinated with (Christian) sexual morality, citizenship, personal hygiene, and VD prevention. Those who had already contracted VD were treated and sent to the Rehabilitation Training Center in Chinhae.[29] Trainees were subjected to a forty-nine-hour-a-week training schedule to curb their "rampant promiscuity."[30] Second, various forms of wholesome recreation and entertainment were promoted that ranged from athletic activities, movies, and sightseeing tours to religious services.[31] Third, soldiers were required to obtain condoms and prophylactic kits before they obtained passes to leave their units. Those soldiers who returned intoxicated or late were subjected to mandatory treatment at prophylactic stations that were open for 24 hours.[32]

In practice on the ground, however, the VD control measures were not successful at all. A document sent out to "all commanders to include companies and separate detachments" indicated that too many unit commanders accepted an increase in VD as "inevitable" and did not carry out the ample directives in effect on the subject.[33] During USAMG rule, the USAFIK Provost Marshal revealed that a large percentage of the total military offenses were violations of "off-limits," "curfew," "uniform," and "pass" regulations, which were commonly linked to going out to drink and hire sex workers.[34] Three major sources of contradiction undermined VD control policy in South Korea. First, in September 1944, the War Department amended Section 2 of the Veterans Regulation Act, approved on May 17, 1926, to accommodate numerous veterans who had contracted VD during their service.[35] As a result, veterans could claim disability benefits for service hours lost due to the treatment of VD. This means that the military came to treat VD as an exception to a principle of Veterans Regulations that soldiers were prevented from receiving pensions "for any disability due to the claimant's own willful misconduct or vicious habits."[36] This legal change sent a green light to soldiers on the ground and contributed to the pervasive attitude among unit commanders at various levels of treating the VD indoctrination programs with laxity in the face of urgent needs for manpower.[37] Many soldiers with repeat cases of VD were sent back to the Rehabilitation Training Center without any serious consequences for their service, which rendered such training perfunctory.[38] These modifications reveal the military's normalization of soldier's heterosexual entitlement to reward and retain soldiers in the military. Second, "legitimate" recreational facilities such as service clubs and dance halls were commonly used as places of contact between soldiers and sex workers, generally via pimps. For example, the area around the service club in Inchŏn became a major point of contact between American soldiers and Korean pimps.[39] In a letter to Lieutenant-General Hodge, Major-General Orland Ward of the U.S. Army acknowledged that "our so-called city club, run by the hostesses, is the center of pimp activity."[40] The letter also revealed that in order to control the spread of VD, the military had conducted monthly physical examinations of the "Shanghai girls" who came to dance with American soldiers. The women were housed together, far away from military units, and transferred back and forth by their pimps. Third, other "wholesome" recreational facilities were insufficient in Korea. Although athletic activities were stressed as the "best" form of recreation,[41] facilities remained grossly inadequate in many areas due to "the normal delays in getting logistical support and the inability of the Army to obtain the necessary cooperation from the civilian police."[42] A similar problem existed for movie and other recreational facilities.[43]

Rank-based discrimination among soldiers who contracted VD also contributed to the ineffectiveness of the VD control policy. Commissioned officers infected with VD were not sent to the Rehabilitation Training Center in Chinhae but were kept in certain restricted areas. While noncommissioned officers were subjected to physical inspection to detect whether they had contracted VD, no commissioned officers were exposed to such intrusive examinations, which invited potential resistance among enlisted men and noncommissioned officers.[44] A possible reason for such an uneven practice was the apparent problem of a very high incidence of misconduct among noncommissioned officers. When reporting about "lowering discipline and more laxity in control," the Office of the Commanding General, in a letter to all commanders (including companies and separate detachments), indicated that "far too frequently noncommissioned officers are involved in such incidents" as robberies, assaults on persons, drunkenness, interference with the police, and "malicious and wanton molesting of Korean women."[45] Yet such an observation might itself have been colored by class and racial biases in the racially segregated U.S. military in Korea in favor of white commissioned officers, who mainly came from more affluent and better-connected families than the noncommissioned officers. It is noteworthy that the military kept separate statistics for "White" and "the Colored" in its weekly VD rates reports. Responding to higher rates of reported VD among "the Colored," military authorities even blamed black GIs for their inability to practice abstinence "on aesthetic grounds," as most white soldiers did.[46] This remark reveals racism not only against black GIs but also against Korean women, who were sexually unattractive to certain whites.

The VD control measures resulted, at best, in mixed effects. Successful declines in the reported VD rates in some units were commonly offset by alarming increases in other units. During the late 1940s, 1 in every 333 soldiers stationed in South Korea received VD treatment.[47] In most areas in South Korea, the reported VD rates were 100 cases per 1,000 soldiers per year.[48] Most important, the reported VD rates are not even an accurate indicator of the actual incidence of VD, given the military context of harsh discipline, punishment, and race- and rank-based discrimination.[49] Throughout the second half of the 1940s, despite periodic fluctuation in reported VD rates, the spread of VD remained a vexing problem for the USAFIK.[50]

In an effort to control the spread of VD, the Control Councils considered Public Act 7, which eliminated public prostitution, a problem rather than a solution. According to the documents generated by monthly VD Control Council meetings and related correspondence, the outlawing of public prostitution was repeatedly mentioned as one of the main causes of the rapid increase in VD rates among American soldiers. It was argued that the end of public prostitution resulted in the "scattering of prostitutes" who had once been clustered in restricted areas.[51] Yet this argument is not convincing for the following reasons. First, as mentioned above, the total number of licensed prostitutes was tiny compared with the rampant spread of private prostitution following the arrival of the USAFIK. Second, other VD Control Council documents indicated that women picked up by American soldiers were not licensed prostitutes who had in fact very little contact with American personnel.[52] On one rare occasion, the minutes of a VD Control Council meeting recognized that "the effects of prohibition of legalized prostitution on the VD rate among American soldiers cannot be determined at this time."[53] What is connoted in the presumed causality between the scattering of sex workers and increases in the VD rates is the military's loss of tight control over sex workers. The women were viewed as the raw material necessary to manage masculine soldiers and as carriers of VD posing a threat to those soldiers. Under the military rationale of VD control, prohibiting licensed prostitution was not necessarily desirable, implying the desirability of maintaining the physical examination of sex workers and therefore indicating an underlying acceptance of women's sexual service as a crucial means to manage young male soldiers. This preference for regulated prostitution rather than complete suppression of prostitution is a central undercurrent that shaped the relationship between prostitution and the U.S. military in South Korea.

Attempting to regain control over sex workers and pimps in the aftermath of the abolition of the institution of public prostitution, the Provost Marshal organized "vice squads" in the Seoul and Pusan areas. After arrests, sex workers and pimps were tried in the Army Provost Court and sentenced to imprisonment, but this practice came to an end with the inauguration of the Korean government in August 1948.[54] Because of overcrowding in prisons and jails, the government did not impose jail sentences for arrested sex workers and pimps.[55] Again, the military viewed the loss of control over prostitution as a primary factor contributing to the spread of VD among American soldiers.[56] However, on rare occasions minutes from VD Control Council meetings recognized the limits of vice squads; they succeeded "only in interruption of the activities for which they were organized and [were] maintained to discourage or eliminate."[57] In the Susaek area, one of the heaviest concentrations of prostitution, the Sixth Infantry Division was so "infested with prostitutes" that "vice squads [were] unable to keep up with the situation."[58]

What is obscured in the presumed causality between the decrease in the military's control over prostitution and the growth in VD rates as the naturalization of the male soldiers' sexual demands, which continued to generate the supply of private prostitution in the context of mass impoverishment after the end of public prostitution. As discussed above, even before public prostitution was abolished, private prostitution had grown rapidly in the Seoul area following the arrival of the U.S. military. After the end of USAMG rule in August 1948, the military's control over prostitution skidded further out of control. Unit commanders complained about prostitutes and solicitors who gathered outside their gates, which were located far away from Korean houses.[59] In September 1948, a sharp rise in the VD rates in the Pusan area (where prostitutes and pimps were particularly active) even drew the attention of the U.S. president.[60] As prostitution spread, it became common for American soldiers to use cartons of cigarettes (bought at Post Exchange [PX] shops) for payment.[61] As discussed below, this practice of using PX goods for payment continued into the 1960s.

The outbreak of war on June 25, 1950, poured some 300,000 Allied Forces into South Korea and amplified the persistent problems of (private) prostitution and the spread of venereal disease that had vexed the U.S. military since the dawn of its occupation of Korea. The confluence of at least two factors precipitated the adoption of the colonial institution of comfort stations by the newly born Korean government. Although this would be shocking to the public in South Korea and elsewhere who had been exposed to coverage condemning Japan's use of military "comfort women," civilian and military leaders of the new Republic of Korea borrowed the institution to protect respectable Korean women from foreign soldiers and to thank the soldiers for their sacrifice. In other words, regulated military prostitution serves not only the imperial interest in keeping soldiers entertained, but also local elites' interest in guarding the class boundary at the expense of lower-class women. Throughout the war, two separate types of comfort stations were maintained: UN comfort stations (*yuengun wianso*) for the Allied Forces and special comfort stations (*t'ŭsu wianso*) for Korean soldiers. During the war, the term "comfort women (*wianbu*)" referred to sex workers who catered to soldiers, as opposed to civilian customers. This meaning of "comfort women" survived well into the 1960s, and the term was commonly used, as noted by Annie Pak, whose writing is quoted in the beginning of this chapter, and who called herself a comfort woman. The organized use of women's sexual labor for foreign (and domestic) soldiers heralded the establishment of camptown prostitution around U.S. military bases in the postwar decade.

The earliest documented installation of UN comfort stations was in the city of Masan. On August 11 1950, the *Pusan Daily* reported:

> The municipal authorities have already issued the approval for establishing UN comfort stations in return for the Allied Forces' toil. In a few days, five stations will be set up in the downtown areas of new and old Masan. The authorities are asking citizens to give much cooperation in coming days. (Quoted in Yi 2004a, 122; my translation)

During the National Assembly Sessions of July 7 and October 19, 1951, lawmakers discussed the issue of providing entertainment for "foreign guests" and "soldiers" that would use women under the "Wartime Living Improvement Act" (Chŏnsisaenghwalgaesŏnbŏp). Because prostitution was made illegal by the PA 7 of 1947, lawmakers revived prostitution for foreigners and Korean soldiers as "special cases" (Chŏn, et al. 2005, 110, 111). The institution of UN comfort stations spread throughout South Korea, especially after the war came to a standstill between January and July 1951, when North Korea and the United States began to negotiate a truce. During this period, the Allied Forces grew rapidly from approximately 199,000 to 281,000, and maintaining control of the large numbers of new and old soldiers became urgent (Yi 2004a, 122). According to a secret memo dated May 1951 from the Office of the Presidential Secretary, with a personal signature by Prime Minister Myŏn Chang, UN comfort stations were to be administered collaboratively by provincial governors, mayors, and the police. On September 1 and 5, 1951, the *Cheju* newspaper documented the negotiation between the U.S. military and the Cheju Provincial Office over the installation of a comfort station (Yi 2004a, 123–24).

It is not entirely clear how many such comfort stations were set up throughout the war; nor is it known how many women worked in the comfort stations and how they were procured. Only fragmentary pieces of information on the comfort stations exist. In the southern city of Pusan, where Korean refugees were heavily concentrated, there were seventy-eight UN comfort stations in July 1952. In the city of Masan, adjacent to Pusan, there were seven such stations in July 1951 (Yi 2004a, 130). It appears that, while some women would have been trafficked through force and deception, the masses of impoverished Korean women, single and married, were mainly recruited by private businesses that secured approval from the authorities. The majority of women working in UN comfort stations were married, which suggests that sexual labor was a desperate attempt to feed children and families (Chŏn et al. 2005, 112). The force of abject poverty and the death, disability, and displacement of men during the Korean War further multiplied the number of women who had to prostitute themselves for survival.[62] In 1951, there were an estimated 64,934 sex workers of various types in Seoul alone, a number that indicates an increase of roughly 50,000 from 1948 (Sin 1989, 58–59).

What is clear about the institution of UN comfort stations is the persistence of the instrumental use of women's sexual labor by military and civilian authorities to entertain (and essentially control) soldiers, the agents of imperial and local political powers. The institution of UN comfort stations was not an isolated phenomenon but a component of a set of pervasive state-sanctioned practices exploiting women's sexual labor during wartime in the form of "special restaurants for foreigners," "dance halls," and social parties for high-ranking military and civilian officers (Chŏn et. al 2005, 111; Yi 2004a, 127). While prostitution remained ostensibly illegal during the Korean War, various categories of women working in state-approved facilities were subjected to physical examinations for VD. With the spread of UN comfort stations, the Ministry of Health (Bogŏnbu) required all sex workers to receive VD tests and carry "health certificates (kŏngangjŭngmyŏngsŏ)." The ministry also required doctors to withdraw health certificates from any sex workers who contracted VD—with the understanding that the certificates would be returned when VD tests were no longer positive. Still worse, sex workers without health certificates were sent to VD clinics and hospitals, when the police inspected them (Sin 1989, 59). Observing this pervasive practice, Joseph H. McNinch, a medical officer, remarked that the Korean government virtually revived licensed prostitution by reinstituting the periodic physical examination of sex workers for VD control and issuing them a "health card" (McNinch 1954, 147).

Meanwhile, despite its grave concern about venereal disease and (private) prostitution throughout the war,[63] the U.S. military entertained its combat-fatigued troops in South Korea with rest-and-recreation leaves, during which soldiers were flown to Japan for five-day stays. The military Special Services Division provided them with hotels and other recreational facilities, but many soldiers ventured out to seek female sex workers in postwar Japan (McNinch 1954, 146). In the face of the urgent need for loyal soldiers willing to fight and willing to be killed in a foreign country that they barely knew, the military found it more expedient to examine sex workers for VD infection than to suppress prostitution, the operation of which entailed little immediate cost for the military compared with other forms of recreation. This perception is reflected in the following comments articulated by the Office of the Commanding General: "Prostitution and attendant venereal disease are a real threat to the health and welfare of our troops. Due to the unusual amount of ready cash available through this operation, it is a widespread and well-organized activity, and most difficult to curb."[64] In the face of dire wartime poverty, the Korean government viewed prostitution as an inevitable means to feed its population. In the midst of the anticommunist war, the government also viewed it as a necessary means to entertain foreign soldiers who were fighting the war against North Korea.

The Spread of Regulated Prostitution in Camptowns and Rituals of Suppressing Private Prostitution, 1954–1960

During the postwar years, state-sanctioned prostitution, coupled with VD tests for sex workers who catered exclusively to American soldiers, spread in camptowns that sprang up around U.S. military bases. After the signing of the Korea-U.S. Mutual Defense Treaty in 1953, the growth of camptowns accelerated around semi-permanent U.S. military bases. During USAMG rule, camptowns had already developed around Yongsan in Seoul, Hialeah in the southern port city of Pusan, and in some areas in Chinhae, Taegu, Kwangju, and Chŏnju.[65] In the 1950s, eighteen camptowns grew throughout Korea in a symbiotic relationship with U.S. military bases (Munhwa Broadcasting Corporation 2003). Camptowns in South Korea became a virtually colonized space where Korean sovereignty was suspended and replaced by the U.S. military authorities, and GIs' buying power ruled Korean residents, whose livelihood largely depended on them. These Korean residents tended to be individuals and families of the lower classes, capitalizing on a last chance to eke out a living. Many of the camptown residents were refugees from North Korea, who faced discrimination in the south.[66] Camptowns were deeply stigmatized twilight zones fraught with prostitution, crime, and violence and were characterized by substandard community infrastructure where "respectable" or "ordinary" Koreans would not visit.[67] In *Camp Seneca's Camptown*, an autobiographical novel, Kŏ-il Pok discusses the growth of the camptowns in the late 1950s and portrays an ironic sense of separation between the camptowns and the rest of society: "A camptown is a sort of protective district. It is where people who cannot live outside gather and barely manage to survive. Those who make some money here and leave almost always come back because they cannot endure the outside world" (Pok 1994, 85; my translation). In the face of pervasive ostracism against camptown residents (which included not only sex workers and pimps but also others), camptowns became standing comfort zones. Stigma and ostracism stemmed from the nature of camptowns as places of abjection where the undesirable (such as sex workers for the foreign soldiers and their biracial children) were tucked away. Indeed, all camptown clubs and bars catering to GIs were legally off-limits to Korean nationals (except for registered sex workers).

The growth of camptown prostitution was explosive in the poverty-stricken postwar decade. According to statistics by the Ministry of Health and Social Affairs (MHSA), in 1956, there were approximately 400,000 "bar maids" (chŏbdaebu), and 65.5 percent of them were "UN madams" catering to American soldiers (Chŏn et al. 2005, 47). In 1958, similarly, there were an estimated 300,000 sex workers, and approximately 180,000 of them were camptown sex workers (Munhwa Broadcasting Corporation 2003). To gain tight control over sex workers who began to flock to camptowns, the U.S. military and the Korean government agreed to concentrate sex workers in several areas where American troops were stationed for the effective control of vd. In 1957, the usafik established ten designated clubs and dance halls in Seoul, twelve in Inchŏn, and two in Pusan, and for the first time permitted its soldiers to stay overnight outside their barracks (Ministry of Health and Social Affairs 1958, 13–14; Kim 1980, 274).[68] This arrangement accelerated the development of camptown prostitution. In the same year, the mhsa established eighty-nine vd clinics throughout Korea, with forty-three of them clustered on major U.S. military bases in Seoul, P'aju, Pusan, Py'ŏngt'aek, Taegu, and Yangju (Ministry of Health and Social Affairs 1958, 22). The official statistics on sex workers issued by the mhsa in the 1950s covered only those who were examined or treated for vd (Ministry of Health and Social Affairs 1958, 304–309). The statistics also included categories such as comfort woman (*wianbu*) and cohabitant with American soldiers (*migundonggŏ*), along with waitress, hostess, dancer, servant, and licensed prostitute (*kisaeng*). The duplicity between the prohibition of prostitution in principle and the presence of regulated camptown prostitution in practice would be a lasting feature of the U.S. military's presence in South Korea for decades to come.

As prostitution became an integral part of camptowns' local economies, camptown prostitution regulated by the U.S. military and the Korean government adjusted to coexist with periodic crackdowns on unregulated (private) prostitution. A major operation took place from December 15, 1955, to January 15, 1956, during which the Police Department launched a large campaign against pimps, procurers, and sex workers, including Western princesses, who were engaged in business outside the authorities' control.[69] Presumably, this type of periodic crackdown was intended to cleanse the social mores that had been contaminated by unchecked prostitution, but its real purpose was to eliminate sex workers infected with vd. Even during the 1955–56 campaign, the police were instructed not to interfere with women "cohabiting with a foreigner in single partnership."[70] Throughout the postwar years, the U.S. military police randomly inspected camptown sex workers in clubs and on the streets, and the U.S. military periodically demanded that the Korean government take over control of sex workers in order to check the spread of vd.[71] This type of ritualistic but functional cleansing and punishment of private prostitution persisted after the 1950s as a feature of the contradictory position on prostitution shared by U.S. military authorities and Korean authorities in postcolonial South Korea.

As camptown prostitution became a significant source of coveted U.S. dollars, camptown business owners and politicians began to entertain the idea of legalizing it in the name of national economic development. This unsettling notion was discussed during the fourth National Assembly session in 1960.[72] A National Assembly member, identified as "L," proposed instituting special districts for camptown prostitution and argued:

> As long as the United States remains our ally and its soldiers continue to stay, we need to recognize that a majority of those military men are single and they naturally desire certain entertainment. It would be better to come up with some sort of special measures to deal with this than to focus on problems caused by prostitutes, which would be ridiculous in my opinion. . . . For example, we can approve the development of special facilities catering to American soldiers on the outskirts of Seoul that are nice enough that the soldiers do not have to fly to Japan. (Quoted in Cho and Chang 1990, 92; my translation)

Since the days of the Korean War, American soldiers had frequently flown to Japan to spend their leaves seeking female companionship from Japanese sex workers (see chapter 2 in this book). Noticing this popular practice, Assemblyman "L" and others discussed ways to profitably redirect this flow of U.S. dollars. The National Assembly subsequently proposed instituting special measures to encourage American soldiers to frequent Korean sex workers instead of Japanese ones, including the legalization of camptown prostitution, the improvement of sex workers' etiquette, and the prevention of VD (Cho and Chang 1990, 92). In early 1960, the Ministry of Transportation announced a plan to build large-scale tourism facilities in Kyŏngju, Haeundae Beach, and Onyang "to earn foreign currency" and "to attract UN soldiers during their leaves."[73] As early as 1959, Kim Chu-ho, a police captain, had delivered an "enlightenment lecture" for some seven hundred "military hostesses (kunjŏbdaebu)" in Sinjang Village, Songt'an Township, P'yŏngt'aek County, Kyŏnggi Province.[74] As discussed below, the economic rationale for this debate became a reality in the 1960s when camptown prostitution became a full-blown enterprise sanctioned by Park Chung Hee's government.

The development of camptowns rapidly turned farming villages into commercial districts filled with GI clubs, makeshift rental dwellings for club women and GIs, international marriage agencies, convenience stores, pawn shops, barbershops, tailors' shops, photo and portrait shops, and drugstores catering to American soldiers (Kim 1980, 288).[75] For example, Tongduch'ŏn City, which eventually hosted one of the highest concentrations of GIs in South Korea, had originally been a village of rice paddies. But by 1955, it had become a thriving camptown with a bustling service economy and a population of 21,377 (Kim 1980, 277). The northern part of Kyŏnggi Province outside Seoul, including Tongduch'ŏn, P'aju, and P'och'ŏn, became a major camptown area, with a heavy concentration of clubs exclusively patronized by GIS who rested and enjoyed themselves during off-duty hours and on weekends. In southern Kyŏnggi Province, the P'yŏngt'aek area underwent a similar transformation.

Camptown prostitution in the 1950s had two noteworthy characteristics compared with the period of Park Chung Hee's rule in the 1960s. First, a large number of freelance sex workers operated outside the perimeter of official control. Although the military and civilian authorities made efforts to improve their ability to control sex workers catering to American GIS in the late 1950s, it took more time and better-organized political power to achieve this objective. It was not until 1962 that camptown prostitution became organized and developed into a distinct form of its own. As the category "cohabitation with an American soldier" used in Ministry of Health and Social Affairs statistics on prostitutes suggests, many women worked on their own, without pimps. Literary works of the 1950s portray such entrepreneurial women. In his novella Ssyori Kim (1957), Song Pyŏng-su portrayed the life of "elder sister darling (daling nuna)," a camptown sex worker who lived with the orphan boy Ssyori Kim in a trench constructed by Chinese soldiers during the Korean War. Ssyori casually frequented a U.S. military base and arranged rendezvous between the sex worker and American soldiers. He also kept his eye on the military police patrolling the area to prevent her and her clients from being caught. This monitoring reflected the fact that the U.S. military continued to crack down on private sex workers for VD control while it was discussing with the Korean government the establishment of regulated prostitution in camptowns. Similarly, in his A Stray Bullet (1959), Yi Pŏm-sŏn portrayed the life of Song Ch'ŏl-ho, an educated scribe, and his North Korean refugee family struggling to survive in the postwar decade. In the face of dismal poverty, Ch'ŏl-ho's younger sister, who lived with the family, worked as a "Western princess" apparently without being tied to a pimp.

Second, those women who worked for pimps in camptowns during the immediate postwar decade and the interregnum of the Second Republic enjoyed relatively more autonomy and more of a collective voice than their counterparts did in the later period. During the summer of 1960, some fifty Western princesses working in so-called Texas Village in Pusan protested against their exploitative employer, who, they said, treated them like slaves. The women spread thousands of fliers conveying their message about equality among human beings and agitated among other sex workers in private brothels in nearby Wanwŏl-dong and T'aepy'ŏng-dong.[76] The physical proximity between camptown prostitution and private brothels suggests that the boundary between the two was still ambiguous in the 1950s and early 1960s. In Pup'yŏng, some one hundred and fifty "comfort women dealing with American troops" protested strict restrictions on their access to enlisted men's clubs and demanded the improvement of their treatment by the U.S. military.[77] In It'aewŏn, some sixty Western princesses protested the death of a camptown sex worker after she jumped out of a military vehicle carrying sex workers arrested for alleged violations of regulations concerning health certificates. The military police commonly abused their discretionary power in arresting sex workers to punish those they did not like.[78] Moreover, military sex workers organized and ran autonomous support groups to protect their interests. Although this type of association was not a labor union and became co-opted by pimps and the local police,[79] it reflected military sex workers' initiative to empower themselves collectively. The White Lily Society (Paekhaphoe), formed during the Korean War, was one of the earliest examples of this type of association. Several other such organizations existed in the 1950s, including the Rose of Sharon Friendship Society (Mugunghwachi'nmokhoe), the Clover Society (K'ŭlobŏhoe), the Sprout Society (Saessakhoe), and the White Lotus Society (Paengnyŏnhoe).[80] These voluntary associations, and the existence of freelance sex workers, reveal the extent to which women who had to work in prostitution sustained their human agency under the extremely harsh conditions of dire poverty and the disciplinary power of domestic and foreign military and civilian authorities.

The Consolidation of Military Camptown Prostitution, 1961–1970

The ascendance of Park Chung Hee's junta through a military coup in May 1961 brought momentous change in the development of camptown prostitution during the 1960s. The military regime actively promoted the development of camptown prostitution through the following measures: (1) the establishment of "special districts (t'ŭkjŏngguyŏk or t'ŭkjŏngjiyŏk)"; (2) the enacting of the Tourism Promotion Law; and (3) the establishment of the Korean American Friendship Society (Hanmich'insŏnhoe). The military regime viewed camptown prostitution not only as necessary for American soldiers to continue protecting South Korea, but also as beneficial for economic development.[81] Throughout the 1960s, camptown prostitution was a significant source of the foreign currency that was zealously pursued by the

FIGURE 1.1. Busy street in camptown, north of Seoul, Kyŏnggi Province (1965). PHOTOGRAPH BY KUWABARA SHISEI: REPRINTED WITH PERMISSION.

FIGURE 1.2. Two couples in camptown, north of Seoul, Kyŏnggi Province (1965). PHOTOGRAPH BY KUWABARA SHISEI; REPRINTED WITH PERMISSION.

FIGURE 1.3. A black MP and two women in camptown, north of Seoul, Kyŏnggi Province (1965).
PHOTOGRAPH BY KUWABARA SHISEI; REPRINTED WITH PERMISSION.

FIGURE 1.4. Two black GIs and a woman, north of Seoul, Kyŏnggi Province (1965). PHOTOGRAPH BY
KUWABARA SHISEI; REPRINTED WITH PERMISSION.

FIGURE 1.5. A couple outside a GI club in P'aju, Kyŏnggi Province (1964). PHOTOGRAPH BY KUWABARA SHISEI; REPRINTED WITH PERMISSION.

Korean government, since it aggressively directed economic growth (Sin 1970; Sŏng and Chang 1970). As a result, camptown prostitution became consolidated as the crucial element of the camptown economy and enjoyed a heyday during the 1960s.

Immediately after the coup, the junta proclaimed the Prostitution Prevention Law (Yullakhaengwidŭng Pangjibŏp), which was drafted by the civilian regime it overthrew, to replace the Public Prostitution Elimination Law of 1947. This legal change was a rhetorical reassertion of the illegality of (private) prostitution and an ostentatious projection of the junta members' moral standing as patriotic soldiers eager to reconstruct the nation.[82] During its campaign against prostitution, the junta ironically required "barmaids and comfort women employed in approved entertainment business establishments to register in order to avoid confusion with private prostitution."[83] In

September 1961, the Seoul Police Department began registering "UN comfort women" through its "UN comfort women's VD control section."[84] In 1962, the junta established 104 special districts, including 32 U.S. military camptowns, where prostitution was not only allowed but was also closely monitored by the Ministry of Internal Affairs, the Ministry of Health and Social Affairs, and the Ministry of Law (Pak 1994, 111). The special districts outside camptowns were designated for foreigners who visited Korea for international events. The official rationale for the special districts was "to move away from the prosecution of prostitutes and guide them to rehabilitation in the 'benevolent areas,' where they could save up their earnings from prostitution to leave for other occupations."[85] This convoluted justification was overshadowed by the conventional view that prostitution is inevitable. As pointed out in the argument for special districts in the National Assembly session of 1960, male leaders tended to naturalize men's frequent heterosexual gratification. The societal perception of military prostitution as a necessary evil was hegemonic and shared by civilian-authoritarian, civilian-democratic, and military-authoritarian regimes. Although contesting arguments (which were deemed "ridiculous") surfaced during the parliamentary debate, the proposal for the special districts was finally adopted by the military regime.

In 1964, the number of special districts grew to 146, 60 percent of which were located in Kyŏnggi Province, where a majority of U.S. military camptowns were clustered (Chŏng 1988, 159). A survey conducted by the MHSA in 1964 revealed that Seoul alone had seventeen special districts, including Chong-no, Ch'angsin-dong, Hŭngin-dong, and Samgakji (Chŏng 1967, 66). According to 1969 health and social statistics, the total number of the special districts was seventy-five in 1967 and was reduced to seventy-one in late 1969, with a majority of them concentrated in Kyŏnggi Province (20), South Ch'ungch'ŏng Province (12), Kangwŏn Province (9), and Seoul (7), where U.S. military bases were located (Ministry of Health and Social Affairs 1969, n.p.).[86] The institution of the special districts meant the virtual revival of licensed prostitution both in camptowns for American soldiers and outside them for foreign visitors. These special districts were justified with the pretext of "protecting" sex workers from abusive pimps and bar owners and "guiding them into the right path" (Chŏng 1967, 84). The operation of the special districts was a blatant expression of the contradiction that has underlain the Korean government and the USAFIK's policy concerning prostitution: the institutionalized regulation of prostitution for American soldiers and the criminalization of unregulated prostitution.[87]

The second measure that promoted the development of camptown prostitution was the Tourism Promotion Law, enacted in August 1961, just three months before the promulgation of the Prostitution Prevention Law. Under the Tourism Promotion Law, camptown clubs that catered exclusively to American soldiers became "special tourism facility businesses (*t'ŭksu kwan-kwangsisŏl ŏpch'e*)" that were supplied with tax-free alcohol. Owners of the clubs organized the Special Tourism Association (T'ŭksu Kwankwang Hyŏphoe), whose major activities centered on the management of camp-town prostitution. In accordance with the Tourism Promotion Law, each camptown club was required to deposit $500 per month in its savings account as a way to contribute to the accumulation of capital necessary for the economic development of the nation. Noncompliance with this demand could lead to the withdrawal of business approval by the government (Sŏng and Chang 1970, 132).

The last element of the institution of camptown prostitution was the Korean American Friendship Society (KAFS). Established to alleviate the tension arising from violence against Korean civilians committed by American soldiers, KAFS became a formal channel for dealing with the relationship between Korean civilians and American soldiers in camptowns with the signing of the Status of Forces Agreement (SOFA) in 1966, which took effect on February 9, 1967 (Chŏn 1991, 170). Convening bimonthly, KAFS comprised a Korean chair, an American chair, and twelve members, commonly includ-ing the mayor of a host city, its police chief, Korean Central Intelligence Agency officers, the president of the Special Tourism Association, and the president of a local hospital, as well as the commanders and military police staff of the USAFIK. The Friendship Society's central office was located in Seoul, and local branches existed in almost all camptowns. From the time of its foundation, KAFS managed the tension between Korean civilians and American soldiers in a perfunctory way, with the veneer of friendship promo-tion and without addressing the root causes of the violence (Chŏn 1991, 170–72). In effect, KAFS worked to put pressure on bar owners to improve the quality of service given to American soldiers and functioned as a status symbol for its Korean members who could boast about their special connec-tion to American members (Chŏn 1991, 172).

These organizational and administrative arrangements worked to consoli-date camptown prostitution and its proliferation in the 1960s. Consolidated camptown prostitution came to include the following common features: (1) registered sex workers with health cards working in clubs owned by Korean businessmen; (2) a larger number of women working without regis-tered health cards as streetwalkers under more vulnerable conditions; (3) the rental of rooms, from club owners or other businesspeople, where women from both groups could rest and serve their GI customers; and (4) debt bondage, subjugating camptown sex workers to their club owners or land-lords. In April 1964, the Tongduch'ŏn area had approximately 10,000 camp-town sex workers, including some 3,000 comfort women registered with the county's Health Department and the U.S. Army Military Police Corps and a larger number of streetwalkers (hippari) who were not registered (Chŏng 1967, 66). Similarly, a study indicated that the number of camptown sex workers in Tongduch'ŏn was close to 7,000 during its heyday between 1962 and 1968 (Kim 1980, 284). Geographically, the Kyŏnggi Province had the larg-est concentration of camptown sex workers, accounting for 53.3 percent of the total number of registered military sex workers in South Korea due to the heavy concentration of U.S. military bases in the province. The next largest concentrations were in Seoul (2,231), Pusan (2,182), and North Kyŏngsang Province (1,113) (Chŏng 1967, 66, 67).

Camptown clubs were racially segregated, which reflected the segregated U.S. military in South Korea and elsewhere.[88] A camptown was often di-vided into a white entertainment area and a black entertainment area. Club women were also divided into those who served white GIs and those who served black GIs. Two distinct subcultures developed in terms of music and fashion among GIs and makeup and fashion of club women. While many club women found black GIs easier to relate to (because they were usually more expressive and warmer than white GIs), they had to make business decisions based on the fact that there were far more white GIs, and white GIs were often more affluent than black GIs. Crossing of the invisible boundary was rare, and such crossing commonly resulted in tension and violence. As Katharine Moon (1997) examines in her study of camptown prostitution in the 1970s, racial tension was simmering underneath this segregated racial order in camptowns (see chapter 10 of this book).

The consolidation of camptown prostitution proceeded hand in hand with the continued suppression of unregulated private prostitution during the 1960s. On the one hand, the Korean police continued to round up sex workers and send them to detention centers if they did not carry health cards. Kim Yŏn-ja, a former camptown sex worker who became a Christian missionary, observed in the fall of 1963 that the Municipal Women's Protec-tion Center (Siribbunyŏbohoso) in Seoul, which was established by Park Chung Hee's military junta immediately after the 1961 coup,[89] detained vari-ous types of private sex workers, ranging from streetwalkers to "high-class" hostesses, in the name of protection and rehabilitation (Kim 2005, 68, 71). On

the other hand, registered camptown sex workers were subjected to weekly
VD examinations and received "inspection cards," or state-issued health certificates. The U.S. military police screened camptown sex workers working in
clubs, and if a sex worker was not carrying the inspection card, she would be
arrested and sent to a local police station for a summary trial. The women
were fined for the violation and subject to imprisonment for five days if they
could not pay the fine. Those women who had contracted VD were sent to a
detention center for isolation and medical treatment by American military
doctors. One such facility, commonly known as the "monkey house" among
camptown sex workers, was located between Tongduch'ŏn and Ŭijŏngbu.[90]
If an American soldier was found with VD, the military authorities required
him to come up with a list of women with whom he had had sex. Those
women suspected of being VD carriers were taken to a detention center (Kim
2005, 105–6, 113).

Consolidated camptown prostitution accelerated the spread of cohabitation between American soldiers and sex workers, known as "cohabitating
prostitution." Another significant factor that contributed to the proliferation
of cohabitation was the U.S. military's policy on international marriage.
Although over a dozen marriages between Korean women and GIS took
place as early as in the summer of 1947,[91] the military had maintained multiple barriers against such marriages, reflecting the anti-miscegenation laws
in the United States, which had existed in the South until 1967. In 1951,
the military formally permitted such interracial marriage, and archival data
show hundreds of marriage applications throughout the 1950s.[92] Yet the
prospective groom was required to demonstrate his future financial ability
and plans to support his Korean wife. Military chaplains were also required
to speak to couples to ensure that they fully understood the possible consequences of the marriage and the potential challenges they might confront in
the future. Many of the marriage applications even included a statement
drafted by military chaplains and signed by prospective couples that they had
been informed of the improbability of the success of their unions. These
obstacles to interracial marriage revealed that the military was keenly concerned about the immigration of Korean brides to the United States when it
maintained extremely restrictive immigration laws against Asians. The military intended to guarantee that interracial marriage would not automatically
lead to the Korean bride's entry into the United States.

In arrangements of cohabitation, the woman generally stopped working
in clubs and maintained a monogamous relationship with her partner, who
gave her monthly living expenses, similar to the way a husband might (Ahn

2001, 165). Camptown sex workers usually preferred this to working in clubs because cohabitation could relieve them from the stress of daily dealings with customers and managers and opened the possibility of real marriages and immigration to the United States as military spouses (Kim 2005, 107).[93] American soldiers also favored cohabitation for economic and emotional reasons. It was generally cheaper to pay a monthly allowance for a live-in partner who ensured sexual service on demand and took care of housework than to pay sex workers by the hour or the night. Observing the widespread practices of drinking and prostitution in the form of cohabitation among American soldiers in South Korea, the Reverend Ernest W. Karsten, who served as a military chaplain in Korea, commented that "many men have their steadies. Some of them own their girls, complete with hooch and furniture. Before leaving Korea, they sell the package to a man who is just coming in."[94]

However, it would be a mistake to assume from Reverend Karsten's comments that those cohabitating camptown sex workers were merely passive pawns transferred between American soldiers who were leaving and arriving. As women had in the previous decade, these women organized themselves into self-help groups. In Tongduch'ŏn, camptown sex workers formed the Dandelion Society (Mindŭllehoe) in 1961 and subsequently expanded their local branches to promote their "human rights" and "protection" (Kim 1980, 284). This type of voluntary association was a rational and natural response to the extremely dangerous and exploitative conditions of their work, which commonly involved health hazards such as frequent pregnancies and miscarriages and exposure to VD and which made them vulnerable to violence committed by American soldiers who enjoyed extraterritoriality (Kim 2005, 110).[95] Unfortunately, such associations of camptown sex workers became less autonomous as the military regime escalated its surveillance over the general population and began to co-opt voluntary associations into its instruments of power. For example, on June 26, 1962, during the ruling period of Park Chung Hee's junta, 670 military sex workers gathered to organize a military sex workers' council and elected its first president, Ms. Ch'oi, who was a leading member of the Lily Society and the Rose of Sharon Friendship Society. Yet the event took place in the auditorium of a local police station, which suggests increasing military control over this type of organization.[96] Despite this change, the presence of such organizations enabled military sex workers to have some leverage vis-à-vis managers, pimps, and, occasionally, even the U.S. military.[97] In the 1970s, when Park's military regime intensified its repressive rule, such associations became anything but voluntary and autonomous.[98]

During the 1960s, camptown prostitution, as the central component of the camptown economy, served as an important means to earn U.S. dollars, which could help build the industrial economy in Korea. As discussed above, camptown prostitution was considered a "special tourism industry" that enabled the nation to "earn foreign currency without start-up capital" (Munhwa Broadcasting Corporation 2003), to quote T'ae-ha Paek, an ex-general who promoted the project to build the America Town in Kunsan (see chapter 11 in this book). Testifying at a National Assembly session, Kim Hang-yŏl, director of the powerful Economic Planning Board, which administered the Five-Year Economic Development Plans, reported that the annual amount of foreign currency earned from the U.S. military stationed in South Korea in 1969 was approximately $160 million, $43 million of which came from sales of goods and services to American soldiers (Sŏng and Chang 1970, 130, 138). This category of direct sales included revenue from camptown prostitution. He also added that the reduction of American troops by 30,000 would decrease the acquisition of foreign currency by $80 million per year (Sŏng and Chang 1970, 130). In 1969 alone, 46,000 Korean workers in camptowns earned $70 million (Sŏng and Chang 1970, 134). The economic benefits proved to be irresistible not only for a majority of the local populace dependent on the U.S. military for their living, but also for the government, which was pursuing its project of "militarized modernity" through industrialization and anticommunist military buildup.[99]

The economic significance of camptown prostitution in the 1960s was clearly reflected in a series of concerned responses to the impending withdrawal of American troops in 1970, in the aftermath of the Nixon Doctrine proclaimed in Guam in July 1969. As 20,000 soldiers were withdrawn, the general population in Korea became fearful of their impending abandonment by the United States and the possibility of a subsequent North Korean invasion, which resembled the situation prior to the Korean War (Kim 1970, 140). Because camptown prostitution was an important source of livelihood for a large number of Koreans in the war-stricken society, the fear was also economic. In 1970, the Department of Tourism and Transportation of Kyŏnggi Province estimated that Western princesses earned $8 million annually, and that each of these women supported an average of four family members. In the same year, there were approximately 40,000 (registered) sex workers in Kyŏnggi Province alone, including those in Tongduch'ŏn,

P'och'ŏn, and Ŭijŏngbu. The withdrawal of each American soldier would affect not only sex workers and their families but also local businesspeople who ran dry-cleaning and laundry shops, drugstores, hair salons, and convenience stores (Sŏng and Chang 1970, 131).

Conclusion

The history of prostitution regulated by the U.S. military and Korean authorities illuminates the underlying significance of this institution to the maintenance of soldiers who are constructed as heterosexual men in constant need of sexual gratification. Military prostitution is not simply an inevitable evil that "natural" men's sexual urge generates but an outcome of expedient calculation that imperial and local elites make to serve their political and economic interests. There is an underlying logic of economy in using marginalized lower-class women to keep soldiers happy and loyal to the military authorities; it is often cheaper than other alternative means, economically and politically. At the same time, there is a definite downside of maintaining such notions and practices of militarized masculinity, as indicated by the vexing problem of VD during the early decades of U.S. military presence in Korea. The military and civilian authorities are deeply circumscribed by unintended consequences.

By precipitating geopolitical and economic fear among the general population in Korea, the Nixon Doctrine paved the way for even more explicit government involvement in regulating camptown prostitution in the 1970s. To ensure "clean sex" as a necessary attraction to keep American soldiers in Korea, Park's regime set up a Blue House Committee and the Base Community Clean-up Committee to direct the so-called camptown-purification campaign that was launched in 1971. This shift in the regulation of camptown prostitution led to the enforcement of registration among sex workers, mandatory physical examination for VD checkups, and the detention of sex workers who had contracted VD (Moon 1997, 75–83). After this policy shift, the Tourism Promotion Law was revised in 1972, and the International Tourism Association was established in the same year. Business owners involved in camptown prostitution, who formed the Special Tourism Association a decade ago, opened local chapters in almost every camptown to protect their business interests. In particular, the Special Tourism Association ensured the supply of tax-exempt liquor to clubs that catered exclusively to American soldiers (Chŏn 1991, 171). In 1972, when the legal dictatorship under the

Yushin Constitution began, the special districts were temporarily eliminated in the name of social cleansing. Yet they were soon revived, with 119 special districts dealing mainly with local customers and 15 districts exclusively serving American soldiers in camptowns throughout the country.

As recently as 1989, the Korean government, which was formally democratized in the aftermath of the military-authoritarian rule, proclaimed that it would permit prostitution in the "areas in which prostitutes are guided." (Kim 1990, 90, 96). As a result, the police suspended the penalization of prostitution in special districts and in "special tourist hotels" that catered to foreign visitors (Pae 1989). This line of policy on camptown prostitution has dragged on without radical change amid otherwise swift socioeconomic and political transformation in South Korea. What has changed in the post–Cold War era is the face of camptown prostitution: in the process of accelerated globalization, Filipinas and Russian women have become the majority among military sex workers serving American soldiers stationed in South Korea (see chapter 11 in this book).

Notes

Research for this article was supported by the Jane Rosenthal Heimerdinger Fund from the Faculty Research Grants, Luce Asian Studies Program Fund, and Ford Scholars Program at Vassar College. I thank Richard Boylan, archivist at the National Archives and Records Administration, for his professional assistance. I also thank Shelby Jergens for her excellent research assistance. Earlier versions of this essay were presented at the American Anthropological Association meeting, San Jose, 2006, and at the Center for Korean Studies, University of California, Los Angeles, in 2006.

1. After its publication, this unusual book sold more than 10,000 copies and became a nonfiction bestseller of that year. An American reporter for *Time* and *Life* magazines went to Korea to meet with her and suggested that he could help her study in the United States if she wanted, but she refused the offer: "Tasinŭn pigŭgŏbge" (Tragedy, never again), *Kyŏnghyang*, December 2, 1965. In 2006, when I was looking for a copy of the book, it had been completely forgotten. Even activists working for camptown women had never heard of it.

2. I use the term "sex workers" to refer to prostitutes to destigmatize individual women and groups of women who had to work in prostitution. But I use the term "prostitution" to refer to the institution that sells women's sex, which was regulated by authorities.

3. A prostitution district emerged in Yongjugol immediately after the Korean War ended, and the village developed into a typical camptown around a U.S. military base during the 1950s. As American soldiers in the town were replaced by Korean soldiers throughout the 1970s, it catered to the domestic troops. By the 2000s, it had been transformed

into a new nightlife spot popular among Seoulites looking for affordable sexual services in a posh, clean setting: Chang 2000.

4. During the Korean War, the number of U.S. troops swelled to 325,000 but was rapidly reduced to 223,000 in 1954 and then to 85,000 in 1955: Oh et al. 1990, 56.

5. This information is corroborated by the U.S military record: see "VD Control Program in Korea," 27 July 1948, NARA, RG 554, box 147.

6. This positive self-image was juxtaposed with "tyrannical" Japanese rulers in U.S. military history: see "First Year in Korea," 3 February 1947, NARA, RG 554, box 70.

7. "Assignment of Army Hostesses," 9 October 1948, NARA, RG 554, box 50.

8. "History of Medical Activities from 1 October 1945 to 31 December 1945," 11 February 1946, NARA, RG 554, box 70. Ascom city was once the location of a Japanese military compound. During and after the Korean War, it became a central administrative and supply base in Korea for the U.S. military.

9. American soldiers enjoyed the abundant flow of cash because they were not only far better paid than most people in war-torn Korea but also were often engaged in black-market activities of selling American goods from PX shops for cash profit: "Circular 39: Prevention of Black Market Activities," 26 March 1947, NARA, RG 554, box 50. This relative wealth of GIS was common across many societies that were occupied by the U.S. military in the postwar decade: Baker 2004, 32.

10. "Report on Standards of Living Conditions, Military Courtesy Discipline, and Training" 29 April 1946; "Deterioration of Standards," 3 May 1946; "Courtesy Drive," 6 November 1946; "Message from the Commanding General, USAFIK," 17 January 1947; "Instructions to Courtesy Patrol Officers," 21 July 1948; "Personal Conduct," 27 August 1948, all in NARA, RG 554, box 50.

11. This problem of reckless driving was so common that the Office of the Commanding General announced, "Do not think of Korea as a conquered nation. It is not—it is a liberated nation. . . . We are here to help the Korean people—not run over them": "Message from the Commanding General, USAFIK," 3–4.

12. "Courtesy Drive."

13. "Message from the Commanding General, USAFIK," 1.

14. "Courtesy Drive."

15. "Message from the Commanding General, USAFIK."

16. "Association with Korean Women," 25 January 1947, NARA, RG 554, box 50.

17. Headquarters, Twenty-Fourth Corps, Office of the Surgeon, APO 235, "Annual Report of Medical Department Activities," 11 March 1947, NARA, RG 554, box 70.

18. "Deterioration of Standards"; "Personal Conduct."

19. In February 1948, there were some 2,000 licensed prostitutes in South Korea, including approximately 1,000 in Seoul, 200 at Inch'ŏn, and the remaining 800 scattered throughout the country. Some 1,400 of the 2,000 were to be placed in alternative employment arranged by welfare agencies: Headquarters, Twenty-Fourth Corps, APO 235, "Venereal Disease Council Meeting," 7 February 1948, NARA, RG 554, box 147. A Korean historian documents a similar record of this: in October 1947, there were an estimated 2,214 licensed prostitutes in Korea: Yi 1996, 168.

20. The problem of the VD epidemic was not limited to American soldiers. As reported by

Howard Smith (1950, 5), VD (along with tuberculosis) was a major public-health problem in Korea, especially in the city of Seoul and in Kyŏnggi Province, as a result of explosive population growth.

21. "History of Medical Activities from 1 October 1945 to 31 December 1945." This imposition of off-limits on "all houses of prostitution" remained a major component of the official VD policy of the military government; See Headquarters, Twenty-Fourth Corps, Office of the Surgeon, APO 235, "History of Surgeon's Section, Headquarters Twenty-Fourth Corps" [covering the period from 1 September 1945 to 30 June 1948], 24 August 1948, NARA, RG 554, box 70.

22. "Kongch'angp'yeji huŭi taech'aek" (Countermeasures after the abolition of public prostitution), Dong-a Daily, 20 February 1948.

23. See Headquarters, USAMGIK, APO 235, Unit 2, "Venereal Control Program in South Korea," 27 July 1948, NARA, RG 554, box 147.

24. Headquarters, Twenty-Fourth Corps, APO 235, "Venereal Disease Council Meeting," 7 January 1948, NARA, RG 554, box 147.

25. "Saenghwalgoro yullagŭi kil" (Economic hardship leading to the road of prostitution), Chosun Daily, 12 April 1947.

26. "Yanggalbo nolim p'inggye" (Western whores, objects of taunting), Dong-A Daily, 17 June 1949.

27. "Meeting of Venereal Disease Control (Report Control Symbol WDGPA-89), 10 February 1948," NARA, RG 554, box 147.

28. This responsibility was repeatedly mentioned in various documents: see "Summary of VD for the Week Ending January 9, 1948," 16 January 1948; Twenty-Fourth Corps, Office of the Commanding General, APO 235, "Venereal Rate and Discipline," 14 April 1948; WDAO-C 726.1, 31 January 1947, all in NARA, RG 554, box 147. The authorities sent out letters to individual commanders whose units had VD rates higher than the total average of the USAFIK: see USAFIK, APO 235, "Venereal Disease Control and Excessive Rate," 20 May 1948, NARA, RG 554, box 147.

29. The center opened on 4 November 1947 and closed on 15 September 1948, after the inauguration of the Korean government on 15 August 1948: USAFIK, APO 235, "Venereal Disease Rehabilitation Center," 14 August 1948, NARA, RG 554, box 147. Its rigorous program made trainees feel that they were being punished: Headquarters, Twenty-Fourth Corps, APO 235, "Visit to Venereal Disease Rehabilitation Training Center," 15 December 1947, NARA, RG 554, box 147.

30. "Venereal Disease Rates during the Last Six Months of 1948 and January 1949," 726.1, 2 February 1949, NARA, RG 554, box 147.

31. Along with organized sports activities, boxing matches were scheduled, football and baseball games were broadcast, and four different movies were shown each week to attract soldiers: Headquarters, Twenty-Fourth Corps, APO 235, "Venereal Disease Council Meeting," 27 September 1948; Headquarters, Eightieth Medical Group, APO 235, "Venereal Disease Control," 1 October 1948, both in NARA, RG 554, box 147.

32. These measures were instituted from the beginning of the occupation: see "History of Medical Activities from 1 October 1945 to 31 December 1945" and "History of Surgeon's Section, Headquarters Twenty-Fourth Corps" [covering from 1 September 1945

to 30 June 1948]. They were repeatedly discussed in many VD Control Council meetings and in Character Guidance Council meetings in 1949: see Headquarters, Eightieth Medical Group, APO 235, "Monthly Meeting of Venereal Disease Control Council," 20 April 1948; General Headquarters, Far East Command, APO 500, "Venereal Disease Responsibility," 8 April 1949; Headquarters, USAFIK, APO 235, "Venereal Disease Control Measures," 29 August 1946; Korea Base Command, APO 901, "Meeting of the Venereal Disease Council," 23 December 1947; idem, Headquarters, Korea Base Command, APO 901, "Venereal Disease Council Meeting," 1 June 1948; Office of the Chaplain Headquarters, Special Troops, Twenty-Fourth Corps, APO 235, "Command Employment of Chaplains of Venereal Disease Control," 25 October 1948; 790th Transportation Railway Operating Battalion, APO 6, Monthly Report of VD Council, 25 September 1948; USAFIK, APO 235, "Venereal Disease Rates in the Command," 7 June 1948; WDAO-C 726.1, all in NARA, RG 554, box 147.

33. Headquarters, Twenty-Fourth Corps, Office of the Commanding General, APO 235, "Venereal Rate and Discipline," 14 April 1948, RG 554, box 147. In his "message to commander of each and major and separate unit," Lieutenant-General Hodge deplored that "Too many of them [American soldiers] take the line why should I make any effort to keep myself clean and holy. My company and battalion officers don't do it and they don't give a damn. They sleepwalk through the day so they can get drunk again at night. They associate loosely with Korean women or any others they can get their hands on": see Headquarters United States Army Forces in Korea, APO 235, "Increase in Venereal Disease," 13 August 1947, NARA, RG 554, box 147.

34. "Deterioration of Standards"; "Reduction of Criminal and Military Offenses," 14 August 1948, NARA, RG 554, box 50.

35. John R. Hodge, commander-in-chief in Korea, believed that VD cases should be considered like any other injury or disease caused by personal misconduct, because "almost all cases result from violation of standing orders and instructions issued by all echelons of command." Yet this recommendation was not accepted by the Department of the Army under the rationale that the status of "not in the line of duty" would not be a major deterrent. Headquarters, USAFIK, APO 235, "Venereal Disease Cases Considered Not in Line of Duty," 18 February 1948, NARA, RG 554, box 147.

36. U.S. War Department, "Claims—Disability—Section 2, Act 17 May 1926, Repealed; Veterans Regulation Number 10 Amended," memorandum, 17 October 1944, NARA, RG 554, box 147.

37. Headquarters, USAFIK, APO 235, "Venereal Disease Council Meeting," 11 May 1948, NARA, RG 554, box 147.

38. "Repeated Cases of VD," 17 February 1948, NARA, RG 554, box 147.

39. Sixty-First Ordnance Group, APO 901, 28 September 1948, "Venereal Disease Control," NARA, RG 554, box 147.

40. Headquarters, Sixth Infantry Division, APO 6 [a letter sent to Lieutenant-General John R. Hodge by Major-General Orland Ward], 21 May 1948, NARA, RG 554, box 147.

41. Many documents on VD control emphasized that sports programs categorized as "special services" not only would reduce VD rates but would also raise the morale and "esprit de corps" of units: Headquarters, USAFIK, APO 235, "Venereal Disease Rates in

the Command," 7 June 1948; idem, "Venereal Disease Rates in the Command," 7 September 1948, NARA, RG 554, box 147; Eightieth Medical Group, APO 235, "Monthly Meeting of Venereal Disease Control Council," 22 September 1948, NARA, RG 554, box 147. One report attributed the low VD rate in a unit to its active and comprehensive special-service program: Eightieth Medical Group, APO 235, "Venereal Disease Control," 1 October 1948, NARA, RG 554, box 147.

42. "VD Rates during the Last Six Months of 1948 and January 1949."

43. Headquarters, Twenty-Fourth Corps, APO 235, 7 February 1948, NARA, RG 554, box 147; Korea Base Command, APO 901, "Venereal Disease Council Meeting," 1 June 1948.

44. See "Memo to Colonel Ward on Visit to the Training Center," 20 January 1948; "Procedures for Handling VD Cases," 20 January 1948, both in NARA, RG 554, box 147. Office of the Battalion Surgeon, Seventy-Sixth Signal Service Battalion, "Venereal Disease Control Survey," 17 March 1948, NARA, RG 554, box 147.

45. Twenty-Fourth Corps, Office of the Commanding General, APO 235, "Venereal Rate and Discipline," 14 April 1948.

46. "History of Medical Activities from 1 October 1945 to 31 December 1945."

47. See USAFIK, Office of the Surgeon, APO 235, "Casualty Report for Week Ending 29 October 1948," 4 November 1948, NARA, RG 554, box 147. In July 1948, the total number of USAFIK forces was 22,823: Minton 1948.

48. Headquarters, Special Troops, USAFIK, APO 235, Unit 1, "Minutes of Monthly Meeting, Character Guidance Council," 22 January 1949, NARA, RG 554, box 147. Curiously, after the end of the USAMG rule, the VD rate per 1,000 soldiers per annum more than doubled. During the 1949, the rates were 319 in January, 238 in February, 222 in March, 204 in April, and 207 in May: see "Supplement to History of Surgeon's Section, United States Army Forces in Korea, 15 January 1949 to 30 June 1949," p. 80, NARA, RG 554, box 70.

49. This discrepancy was occasionally admitted by members of various VD Control Councils: see Headquarters, USAFIK, APO 235, "Venereal Disease Control Measures," 29 August 1946; Headquarters, Twenty-Fourth Corps, APO 235, 11 January 1948, NARA, RG 554, box 147.

50. In the beginning of 1947, the U.S. War Department sent out a letter to the commanding general of USAFIK indicating that the "present annual rate of VD incidence in the army is higher than at any time in the past 30 years": WDAO-C, 726.1. On May 7, 1948, a special meeting was held at the Bando Hotel to discuss the reasons for increased VD rates and to formulate policies and coordinate plans for military-wide control activities: "Venereal Disease Council Meeting," TFYSG 726.1, 11 May 1948; USAFIK, Rehabilitation Center, Office of the Surgeon, APO 6, Unit 4, "Report of Essential Technical Medical Data," both in NARA, RG 554, box 147. During the winter of 1948 and 1949, the VD incidence reached the highest during the occupation of Korea: see USAFIK, Adjutant General, "Supplement to History of Surgeon's Section, USAFIK, 15 November 1948 to 15 January 1949," NARA, RG 554, box 70.

51. Headquarters, Twenty-Fourth Corps, APO 235, 5 April 1948; Sixth Infantry Division, APO 6, "Meeting of Venereal Disease Council (Report Control Symbol WDGPA-89)," 10 February 1948; idem, Headquarters, Sixth Infantry Division, APO 6, [a letter sent to

Lieutenant-General John R. Hodge by Major-General Orland Ward], 12 April 1948; "VD Council Meeting," all in NARA, RG 554, box 147

52. Headquarters, Twenty-Fourth Corps, APO 235, 7 January 1948.

53. Ibid.

54. "VD Rates during the Last Six Months of 1948 and January 1949."

55. Special Troops, Twenty-Fourth Corps, APO 235, "Venereal Disease Council," 20 November 1948, NARA, RG 554, box 147. The Women's Police was in charge of arresting sex workers. After arrests, they were sent to four dispensaries at the Women's Police stations in Seoul, Pusan, Taegu, and Inchŏn: Smith 1950, 33.

56. Headquarters, Sixth Infantry Division, APO 6, "Meeting of Venereal Disease Control Council (Report Control Symbol WDGPA 80)," 2 September 1948, NARA, RG 554, box 147; "VD Rates during the Last Six Months of 1948 and January 1949."

57. Sixth Infantry Division, APO 6, "Meeting of Venereal Disease Control Council (Report Control Symbol WDGPA 80)," 2 September 1948.

58. Headquarters, Twenty-Fourth Corps, APO 235, 27 September 1948.

59. Ibid.

60. Headquarters, Sixth Infantry Division, "Meeting of Venereal Disease Control Council (Report control Symbol WDGPA 80)," 5 October 1948, NARA, RG 554, box 147.

61. Headquarters, Korea Base Command, APO 901, "Report of Character Guidance Council Meeting," 28 October 1948, NARA, RG 554, box 147.

62. The sex ratio among the Korean population in 1944 (near the end of the Second World War), in 1949 (near the beginning of the Korean War), and in 1955 (two years after the end of the Korean War) indicates the extent to which adult men were killed during the wars. The number of men per 100 women age twenty to twenty-four was 90.75 in 1944, 101.14 in 1949, and 85.40 in 1955. Among the age twenty-five to twenty-nine cohort, the numbers were 94.67, 103.29, and 79.02, respectively. Among the thirty to thirty-four cohort, they were 96.13, 106.25, and 95.58, respectively: National Statistics Office, available online at http://kosis.nos.go.kr/cgi-bin/sws_999.cgi (accessed on April 6, 2008). According to the United Nations Population Division, the ratios are different: the sex ratios of males per 100 females were 102.1 in 1950 and 96.1 in 1955: see World Population Prospects: The 2004 Revision Population Database, available online at http://esa.un.org/unpp/p2kodata.asp (accessed on 18 September 2006).

63. Headquarters, Eighth United States Army Korea, APO 301, "Quarterly Venereal Disease Report QGA-92," 14 February 1953, NARA, RG 338, box 560).

64. Headquarters, Office of the Commanding General, "Prostitution and Venereal Disease," 3 October 1952, NARA, RG 338, box 844.

65. These were cities that hosted major units of the U.S. military from its arrival in Korea during the fall of 1945: see Headquarters, United States Army Service Command 24, Office of the Surgeon, "History of Medical Activities from 1 October 1945 to 31 December 1945," 11 February 1946, NARA, RG 554, box 70.

66. This information came up during my conversations with older Koreans of diverse backgrounds. This reality is also reflected in a few old films about camptown prostitution: see Cho 1964; Shin 1958.

67. These characteristics were vividly portrayed in *Chiokhwa* (Shin 1958), a film about

camptown sex workers and local residents. While it was not about a particular camptown, the film was set against the backdrop of Ascom City (Pup'yŏng in the present), one of the first U.S. military camptowns in South Korea.

68. In 1955, a similar idea of establishing "special districts" to cluster prostitutes together was broached in a public hearing organized by Seoul City's "committee for eradicating private prostitution." Participants of the hearing were lawmakers, professors, and leaders of women's organizations and religious organizations: see "Chigŭm tangjangŭn kollan" (Difficult to eliminate private prostitution right now), *Dong-A Daily*, 14 December 1955.

69. "250 yŏmyŏng kŏmgŏ" (Some 250 people arrested), *Dong-A Daily*, 8 December 1955; "Chigŭm tangjangŭn kollan" (Difficult to eliminate private prostitution right now), 14 December 1955; "Kŭdŭrŭi kalgosŭn magyŏn" (They do not know where to go), 16 December 1955.

70. Ibid., 16 December 1955.

71. "Yongsanildae maech'unbu tansok" (Control over prostitutes in the Yongsan area), *Don-A Daily*, 8 February 1959, "Ch'angnyŏ tansokkwŏn yoch'ŏngsŏl" (A rumor about a request for the authority to control prostitutes), *Dong-A Daily*, 30 October 1960. Chŏm-gyun Yun (1936–), a camptown sex worker in the 1950s and the 1970s, mentioned that the Korean police frequently raided clubs and brothels to collect fines. Such raid operations were called "*t'obŏl*": Yun 2005, 140.

72. It is noteworthy that this assembly convened during the short-lived Second Republic (April 1960–16 May 1961), which was established in the aftermath of the overthrow of the First Republic (1948–60) by student-led popular protests (19 April 1960). The democratic republic was soon overthrown in the military coup led by General Park Chung Hee.

73. "Kwankwangsisŏrŭl hwakch'ung" (Expanding tourism facilities), *Dong-A Daily*, 3 February 1960. In the 1959 Tourism Business Report, the Ministry of Transportation also estimated that American soldiers in Korea would annually spent $11.5 million for their regular leaves (three days and given frequently throughout a year), R & R leaves (one week and given twice a year), and annual leaves (thirty days a year): see Korea Travel Newspaper Special Report Team (1999), 91.

74. "Kyemonggangyŏnhoe, P'yŏngt'aekkun chŏbdaebudŭre" (Enlightenment lecture to barmaids in P'yŏngt'aek County), *Chosun Daily*, 13 March 1959.

75. Two novels on camptowns convey vivid portrayals of such transformations: see Cho 1974b, 253–54; Pok (1994), 12–33, 43–44.

76. "Ppira ppurigo siwi, Texas'ch'on ch'angnyŏdŭl" (Protesting and spreading leaflets, prostitutes of Texas Town), *Chosun Daily*, 19 July 1960.

77. Ibid., "Migun sangdaehanŭn yŏindŭri p'oktong" (Riot by women catering to American soldiers), 23 August 1960.

78. "Yanggongjuga temo" (Western princesses in protest), *Dong-A Daily*, 27 October 1960.

79. According to Yi Im-ha (2004a), these voluntary associations were controlled by the police and local government from the start, but the extent of this control is not clearly discussed. The 1950s allowed for relatively more autonomy for those associations than did the later decades, particularly when disciplinary authority was strengthened and

became more sophisticated under Park Chung Hee's military rule: see S. Moon (2005a), chapters 2 and 3.

80. "Migunwianbudŭri chach'ihoe chojik" (Comfort women for American soldiers organizing their association), *Chosun Daily*, 27 June 1962.

81. This use of sex workers to entertain American soldiers and to earn foreign currency was the flip side of the official nationalism promoted by Park's military regime, which promoted a "self-reliant" economy along with "self-reliant national defense": S. Moon 1998.

82. See S. Moon 2005a, chap. 1, for a more detailed discussion of the junta's nationalist orientation.

83. "Maech'unhaengwiro inhan ch'aekwŏnŭl muhyoro" (Writing off debt caused by prostitution), *Dong-A Daily*, 10 June 1961.

84. Ibid., "UNgun sangdae wianbu, 13ilbut'ŏ tŭngnok silsi" (Registration of comfort women for UN soldiers, effective from the 13th), 14 September 1961.

85. Ibid., "Ajigdo sarainnŭn pamŭi yohwa, sang" (Tempting flowers of night, still alive, part 1), 14 August 1962.

86. The page number is missing in the original document, which is an old government record. I contacted a librarian in the Korean National Assembly Library, but she could not identify it.

87. Faced with growing criticism of the blatantly contradictory policy, Park's regime temporarily abolished the special districts in 1970, but they were soon revived: Ministry of Health and Social Affairs 1987, 111.

88. Conversations with camptown activists, memoirs by sex workers, and novels about camptowns all confirm this deplorable situation. I talked to Young-im Yu, director of My Sister's Place in Ŭjŏngbu, on March 20–27, 2007, and to the Reverend Wu-sŏp Chŏn of Tabita Community in Tongduch'ŏn on June 30, 2007. For the memoirs, see Pak 1965; Kim 2005; Yun (2005). For the novels, see Cho 1974a, 1974b; Pok 1994.

89. See "Sirippohoso," *Dong-A Daily*, 3 October 1962.

90. During the 1970s, another monkey house was built near the America Town (see chapter 11 in this book) at Kusan Air Force Base. This information was given by a local activist when I visited the American Town in June 2007.

91. "Migunkwa kyŏronhanŭn chosŏnyŏja chŭngga" (Increase of Korean women marrying GIS), *Dong-A Daily*, 27 August 1947.

92. Eighth U.S. Army, Adjutant-General Section, General Correspondence, "Memorandum: Marriages between American Citizens and Korean Citizens (nationals)," 28 November 1951, NARA, RG 338, box 491; Eighth U.S. Army Korea, Office of the Adjutant General, APO 301, "Incoming Message" [concerning marriage between Americans and Koreans], 1 April 1951, NARA, RG 338, box 491. For examples of such marriage applications, see documents in Eighth U.S. Army Adjutant General Correspondence, 1956–1959, NARA, RG 338, box 645.

93. The arrangement of cohabitation is also extensively portrayed in two novels by Hae-il Cho 1974a, 1974b.

94. "South Korea: A Hooch is Not a Home," *Time*, 9 October 1964, 48.

95. It was not uncommon for this kind of violence perpetrated by American soldiers to

end in the killing of camptown sex workers. The highly unequal power relations between the soldier and the sex worker in terms of gender, nationality, race, and money allowed for the recurrence of deadly violence. According to official statistics released in response to grassroots movements against such violence, between 1968 and 1998, 45,183 American soldiers committed 39,452 crimes. This means that on average, two crimes were committed by GIs every day (Kim 2001, 8).

96. "Migunwianbudŭri chach'ihoe chojik" (Comfort women for American soldiers organizing their association), *Chosun Daily*, 27 June 1962.

97. This information is based on my conversation with Kim Yŏn-ja in the winter of 1995, when she visited Boston to give a public talk about American camptown prostitution in South Korea. I served as a simultaneous translator when Kim gave the talk in Boston. During that winter, she traveled to give similar talks in other major cities in the United States, including Chicago, Los Angeles, New York, San Francisco, and Washington, D.C.

98. Kim Yŏn-ja, the camptown woman who worked in Tongduch'ŏn in the 1960s and in Songt'an in the 1970s, observed this change in Songt'an in the first half of the 1970s. According to her, the Sisters Society (Cha'maehoe), a quasi-voluntary association of camptown sex workers, did not have any legal and administrative power to promote its members' rights. Instead, virtually functioning as an auxiliary to local authorities, the association organized a VD inspection schedule for its members, managed their inspection cards, and ensured that they attended "cultivating lectures" during which they were inculcated with patriotic values such as the utility of hard work to earn foreign currency and the importance of providing nice services to American soldiers. The Sisters Society frequently held such cultivating lectures, but "there was no single woman who attended voluntarily. They all came in order not to lose their inspection cards." These lectures were also attended by a county chief, a Security Department chief, a Welfare Department chief, and the president of the society: Kim 2005, 123, 136, 139.

99. See Moon 2005a for a detailed analysis of the project of militarized modernity.

TWO

"PAN-PAN GIRLS" PERFORMING
AND RESISTING NEOCOLONIALISM(S)
IN THE PACIFIC THEATER

U.S. Military Prostitution in Occupied Japan, 1945–1952

☆

MICHIKO TAKEUCHI

For Japan, the Second World War came to an end with the Japanese government's official acceptance of the Potsdam Declaration on August 15, 1945. Japan became an occupied country of the Allied nations and remained so until 1952.[1] In reality, it was the U.S. government that took command of all military and civilian aspects of the occupation through the Supreme Commander for the Allied Powers Headquarters (SCAP / GHQ) and its Supreme Commander, General Douglas MacArthur. In 1946, 465,000 former enemies found themselves in the midst of a country of 72 million exhausted and starving Japanese.[2]

The U.S. occupation of Japan is often referred to as the "workshop of democracy," with its implementation of the demilitarization and democratization policies of the first two years, exemplified in universal suffrage, land reform, and guaranteed equality between women and men in the new constitution. However, despite these lofty ideals, the U.S. occupation of Japan resulted in the emergence of the Japanese state-sponsored "special comfort women" system and the phenomenon of the "pan-pan girls" (private prostitutes and streetwalkers), who provided sexual services to GIs.[3] This chapter is concerned with Japanese women, many in their teens to mid-

twenties and impoverished by the war, who were subjected to and participated in this aspect of the occupation. I argue that controlling the sexuality of
these Japanese women was crucial to the establishment and maintenance of
U.S. hegemony over Japan and the reemergence of Japan in the postwar era.
By highlighting the experiences and voices of these Japanese women, I also
reexamine the nature of the U.S. occupation of Japan.

Methodology

The realization by scholars of the similarities and continuities between European colonial sexual politics toward indigenous women and U.S. politics
toward Japanese women has drawn critical attention to the nature of the U.S.
occupation. In fact, the similarities suggest that the U.S. occupation of Japan
was a form of neocolonialism. However, claiming U.S. neocolonialism remains a difficult task. Anne McClintock (1995, 13) argues that neocolonialism
is not simply a repeat performance of colonialism, but it brought Hegelian
merging of tradition and colonialism into some new, historic hybrid. She
continues:

> Since the 1940s, the U.S.' imperialism-without-colonies has taken a
> number of distinct forms (military, political, economic and cultural),
> some concealed, some half-concealed. The power of U.S. finance capi-
> tal, research, consumer goods, and media information around the
> world can exert a coercive power as great as any colonial gunboat. It is
> precisely the greater subtlety, innovation and variety of these forms of
> imperialism that make the historical rupture implied by the term post-
> colonial especially unwarranted. (McClintock 1995, 13)

McClintock points out the continuities with European colonialism, but
the unofficial nature of this U.S. imperialism-without-colonies in its variety of
distinct forms and concealed manner is what makes it difficult for scholars to
define U.S. neocolonialism after the Second World War. The study of European colonial sexual politics does not easily translate to the experience of
the U.S. occupation of Japan, either. Nonetheless, the investigation of European colonial continuities is essential because the U.S. formation of Euro-
American identity in the post–Second World War era has been palpable,
as manifested in the formation of the North Atlantic Treaty Organization
(NATO) (Lutz and Collins 1993, 2).[4]

Through an examination of the sexual politics of the United States and
Japan toward Japanese women and an exploration of these women's agency,

this chapter explores whether the U.S. occupation of Japan was a concealed U.S. neocolonial project.[5] To do this, I place my examination of sexual politics in the larger context of the Cold War. By focusing on sexual politics, I will show that the U.S. occupation was not merely a negotiation between two countries. It also involved the Soviet Union (Russia) and former colonies of Japan.

In addition, this chapter presents the pan-pan girls as main characters in U.S.-occupied Japan. Although they have been ignored and silenced, they were a vital presence in the bombed-out cities and devastated landscape of defeated Japan. An investigation of these women's everyday negotiations, struggles, and challenges reveals existing and new postwar Japanese social orders, as well as new sets of U.S. social orders. These are also critical in examining U.S. neocolonialism in Japan.

It is difficult to define prostitutes or pan-pan girls. The task is so difficult because most special comfort women (who can be defined as women involved in state-organized sexual slavery in Japan) became pan-pan girls, but also because almost every woman seen with a GI was considered a prostitute, even if she considered herself simply a girlfriend (a situation very similar to the one in postwar Germany). Therefore, rather than imposing categorical analyses that would generate a simplistic dichotomy of forced–voluntary and victim–agent evaluations, this chapter treats pan-pan girls as an overarching socioeconomic cultural phenomenon while respecting individual experiences and voices.[6]

To capture these women's experiences and voices, I conducted field research and worked at a GI bar in Yokosuka City, Kanagawa Prefecture, in 2007. Located at the entrance of Tokyo Bay, Yokosuka is approximately forty miles south of Tokyo. Due to its geographical convenience and deep-sea water, it was developed as a base town for the Japanese Imperial Navy in the late 1800s, and more than 40,000 people worked for the base by the end of the Second World War.[7] Since the U.S. Occupation Forces dropped anchor off Yokosuka on August 28, 1945, it has been the base host town for the U.S. Navy. I chose Yokosuka as the site of my field research because, in contrast to Tokyo and Yokohama (occupied by the Eighth Army), where communities were destroyed by U.S. air raids and postwar urban developments, communities in Yokosuka remained intact. Because Yokosuka did not experience significant U.S. air raids, people felt less antagonism toward Americans, and when the U.S. Navy arrived, people soon accepted it as a new employer.[8] Also, existing recreation centers there for Japanese Imperial Navy sailors, including prostitution quarters, were simply reorganized for use by U.S. Navy sailors and marines (Yokosuka Keisatsushoshi Hakkō Iinkai 1977, 124).

Although most people in Yokosuka today perceive the existence of the U.S. base as a way of life, some have been active in anti-base movements. They view the U.S. Navy and Marine personnel with a mixture of admiration and aversion. Many elderly men, who seem to avoid U.S. personnel, nevertheless wear U.S. Navy baseball caps purchased in front of the base, on Dobuita Street (known as "the Honch" to U.S. personnel). For some, associating with U.S. personnel is considered "cool." While many in Yokosuka consider Japanese who feel that way peculiar, the majority also wish to befriend the "Amerika-san (Americans)." When I was there, the people of Yokosuka talked about women who had associated with GIs as if they had evaporated into thin air. Yet the women were there, and though it took me a while, I did meet them. I collected voices of women in Yokosuka that were constructed in this specific power dynamic of memory and erasure.

Establishment of the Bilateral Prostitution System in the U.S. Occupation in Japan

As soon as the first postwar Higashikuni cabinet was established, on August 17, 1945, its members started to plan for special comfort women to provide sexual services to the U.S. Occupation Forces (Kobayashi and Murase 1992 [1961], 3).[9] Keeping in mind their own troops' brutal behavior toward other Asian women, they felt certain that such proactive steps were a matter of "national security" (Duus 1995 [1979], 21–24; Inoue 1962, 43; Kanzaki 1953b, 4). They acted on the assumption that *all* young men needed to be "fed" with female flesh; otherwise, a large population of women would be threatened (Duus 1995 [1979], 27; Kobayashi and Murase 1992 [1961], 146). Prior to the arrival of the Americans, there were widespread rumors that all Japanese women would be raped by Americans. Women were told to evacuate from cities, and some were given potassium cyanide to commit suicide should they become victims of rape (Sokāgakkai Fujin Heiwa Iinkai 1982, 149). The day after the cabinet was established, National Police Commissioner Shinya Saka of the Home Ministry was appointed to organize special comfort facilities (Duus 1995 [1979], 44; Inoue 1962, 43; Kanzaki 1953b, 4). Saka quickly contacted the Tokyo Restaurant Association about "the most important postwar diplomatic task" (Duus 1995 [1979], 31–33). The association became the backbone of the state-sponsored prostitution agency, the Recreation and Amusement Association (RAA). Financial support was guaranteed by Hayato

Ikeda of the Ministry of Finance (prime minister from 1960 to 1964), who stated that even 100 million yen was a cheap price to pay to protect the chastity of Japanese women and the purity of Yamato (Japanese) blood (Dower 1999, 126; Duus 1995 [1979], 44; Kobayashi and Murase 1992 [1961], 10). The Japanese officials hoped that special comfort women would provide an outlet for the occupiers' sexuality, help to prevent mixed blood, and serve as a buffer between "good" Japanese women and GIS.

A secret wireless order from the Home Ministry was sent directly to regional police officials on August 18, instructing them to prepare special comfort facilities. In Kanagawa Prefecture, local city police chiefs took direct responsibility for mobilizing brothel owners and "special comfort women." The Public Security Section of the Kanagawa Prefecture Police also established the Special Comfort Facility Measurement Headquarters, which cooperated with the Home Ministry in establishing city guidelines. As one brothel owner recalls, the chief of the Yokosuka City Police, Kunio Yamamoto, asked owners and women to cooperate:

> I feel as if my heart is breaking as I ask you this. Until yesterday, I encouraged fighting against America. I cannot bring myself to ask you to sell yourself to work for arriving GIS. But, to have sexual outlets for GIS and to prevent rapes and sexual crimes by GIS, we have to accommodate their needs [by providing special comfort women]. To help recover defeated Japan and to live for a great purpose, please help us [establish special comfort facilities]. (Yokosuka Keisatsushoshi Hakkō Iinkai 1977, 135, 138–39)

Finding women in Tokyo for this purpose was difficult due to the wartime ban "on pleasure" (1943) and the U.S. air raids, which had forced licensed prostitutes to evacuate and ultimately leave the city. Available prostitutes were scarce, but the Japanese officials had a certain target group: young women who had lost families, homes, or jobs as a result of total war. The strategic U.S. air raids had contributed significantly to class-based hardships, as they had targeted lower-class living quarters to preserve upper-class housing for the use of the Occupying Forces' officer corps (Dower 1999, 46–47). By one estimate, at least 60,000 young women had lost families or homes in the Tokyo-Yokohama area; nationally, the number was 400,000 (Kobayashi and Murase 1992 [1961], 28). A former U.S. Army Signal Corps enlistee (stationed in Yokohama in 1946–47) told me that the destruction was so severe that all of Yokohama was like a base for the Eighth Army, and the airfield literally existed in the middle of the city. Thus, when the RAA advertised for female clerks to participate in "the great task of comforting the Occupation Forces,"[10] many women were shocked, but impoverished and orphaned women had few other options and joined in order to survive.

The tactic of recruiting lower-class and impoverished women replicated the Japanese Imperial Military's "comfort women" system, which had treated such women as convenient, useful, and disposable.[11] If displaced women worked at the special comfort facilities, the Japanese government would not have to deal with issues of social welfare and possible future friction from their families. It could also evade social and moral pressures, because lower-class women had already been the major source of prostitutes for the licensed Japanese pleasure quarters. Women did not always volunteer, and some women were coerced. In some cases, the recruitment process involved rounding up and kidnapping orphaned women by Japanese police in cooperation with *yakuza* (mobsters). Sometimes women of the wartime Volunteer Corps were ordered to continue to serve the country and emperor in this new national duty.[12] This recruitment process illustrates the continuation of the colonial policy of Japanese officials toward lower-class women in Japan.

Many Japanese women raped by GIs ended up as special comfort women (Yoneda 1972, 123). Contrary to the image of a peaceful occupation propagated by the United States, incidents of rape occurred within hours of the U.S. Occupation Forces' landing and continued to take place throughout the occupation period. Reports of rape, as well as of fraternization between GIs and Japanese women, were suppressed by the SCAP / GHQ censorship codes of September 10, 1945 (Kobayashi and Murase 1992 [1961], 28–29, 69; Takemae 2002 [1983], 67; Yoneda 1972, 90, 124). Having come under the jurisdiction of the SCAP / GHQ, Japanese police were helpless to control American rapists (some of them U.S. Military Police [MP] personnel). Consequently, people in Yokosuka started to call their city police "Decker's Police," after Rear Admiral Benton W. Decker, commander of Fleet Activities in Yokosuka (1946–50) (Yokosuka Keisatsushoshi Hakkō Iinkai 1977, 315, 320).

Special comfort women were considered "*Onna no Tokkōtai* (female kamikaze)" and were supposed to serve the country by offering their bodies to foreign "attack" (Kanzaki 1953a, 198; Kawasaki 1988, 145). Condoms named "Be the First to Attack," which had been supplied to Japanese soldiers, were recycled for special comfort women and GIs (Duus 1995 [1979], 126). Whether these women felt patriotic or not, patriotism was used not only to eliminate individual shame for having sexual intercourse with GIs but also to legitimate the state's exploitation of women.

The first special comfort facility, with thirty-eight women, opened in

Tokyo on August 27, 1945. The next day, a group of U.S. Marines wasted no time visiting (Duus 1995 [1979], 70; Nishida 1953, 17). The U.S. policy on fraternization was incoherent; while fraternization with Japanese was originally forbidden, it was allowed after the first week in Yokosuka. Major Michael R. Yunck, commanding officer of Marine Fighter Squadron 311, explained that this shift was necessary because "the Japanese Geisha girls have taken a large share of the attention of the many curious sight-seers of the squadron" (quoted in Smith 1997, 15). In fact, the special comfort facilities were quite popular. The facility the war correspondent Clark Lee visited was jammed with American jeeps, and MPS were running around so excitedly that he thought an anti-American uprising had started (Lee 1947, 15). The price for a short visit was 15 yen (10 yen in Yokosuka)—almost equivalent to half a pack of cigarettes. The women received only 40 percent of this fee, with costs for board, food, clothing, and cosmetics taken out (Dower 1999, 130; Duus 1995 [1979], 72; Kobayashi and Murase 1992 [1961], 52; Yokosuka Keisatsushoshi Hakkō Iinkai 1977, 137, 433), and they served between fifteen and sixty GIs a day (Dower 1999, 129; Kobayashi and Murase 1992 [1961], 20; Nishida 1953, 20). The number of special comfort women eventually grew to 70,000 nationally (Oshima 1975, 94).[13]

In Yokosuka, an existing dormitory for Japanese Imperial Navy factory workers had been set up as the first special comfort facility, with 170 women, by September 3. The facility joined the 88 brothels in the Yasu'ura area and 45 brothels in the Minagasaku area. Observing that many U.S. Navy officers favored geishas (performing artists), the Yokosuka City Police designated 5 geisha houses, with 71 geishas, for the exclusive use of U.S. personnel. A total of 358 women worked in these special comfort facilities (Yokosuka Keisatsushoshi Hakkō Iinkai 1977, 136).

Within a few weeks of the operation, the Yokosuka City Police found that these facilities were inadequate to accommodate U.S. sailors and marines, as the U.S. Navy released thousands of men at once for shore leave. As many as 2,000 men (recorded on September 11) rushed to the facilities seeking brief sexual interactions before they were forced to return to their base or be confined on their ships (Yokosuka Keisatsushoshi Hakkō Iinkai 1977, 137). The Eighth Army soldiers in Tokyo and Yokohama resided in Quonset-hut housing villages within the cities; U.S. sailors and marines in Yokosuka were in a more restricted environment: a rigidly enclosed former Japanese military base and dormitories (that had remained untouched by U.S. air raids). Many U.S. Navy veterans to whom I spoke referred to this confinement and isolation at sea as factors that contributed to their eagerness to seek sexual interaction. To address these concerns, the Yokosuka City Police sought to find new buildings and collect more women by advertising—similarly to the RAA—in the *Kanagawa* newspaper. They enticed women by offering special distributions of rice, new identification papers, free public transportation, and by simplifying the process of changing their addresses (Yokosuka Keisatsushoshi Hakkō Iinkai 1977, 137–39).

Despite the existing military prohibition against encouraging or fostering prostitution, the U.S. military was involved in doing just that. In late August, Colonel Wilson, a Special Services officer of the Eighth Army, gave permission to the RAA to operate its facilities under the supervision of the Military Police (Gayn 1948, 233). The Yokosuka City Police received permission to proceed directly from the head of the Military Police (Yamamoto in Yokosuka Keisatsushoshi Hakkō Iinkai 1977, 431). On September 5, 1945, the Public Relations Office of the Eighth Army announced that "the Eight [*sic*] Army would take no notice of Japanese houses of prostitution unless they [became] centers of disease. Then they would be closed."[14]

The operation of the Japanese state-organized special comfort facilities was *officially* under the direction of the SCAP/GHQ. The U.S. Occupation Forces supervised the special comfort women (and, later, the pan-pan girls) via the Military Police, compulsory venereal disease (VD) examinations and American medical treatment under the SCAP/GHQ, the Public Health and Welfare Section (PHW), the VD Control Council sub-section, the Eighth Army Surgeon, and the Provost Marshal.[15] On September 28, VD Officer Lieutenant-Colonel James H. Gordon and Colonel A. G. Tuckerman, executive to the Provost Marshal-General, held their first VD control conference. Gordon presented the Japanese government's plan to reinstitute the licensed prostitution system to be adopted by the SCAP/GHQ to "insure successful operation of the system." Tuckerman voiced his "willingness to comply fully" with the desires of the consulting chief health officer and to request a complete survey of prostitutes from the chief of police in Tokyo, supplemented by Military Police observation. On the same day, Gordon held another meeting with the chief of PHW, Colonel Crawford Sams, and with Colonel Weaver to discuss VD measures to be adopted for and in the U.S. Occupation Forces. Sams then directed the Japanese government to reestablish its VD regulation system immediately.[16] According to Mitsuru Yosano, head of the municipal government's Hygiene Department, an Eighth Army surgeon, Colonel Bruce Webster, had already expressed the U.S. Occupation Forces' intentions to use all special comfort facilities in Tokyo, even before Yosano met Sams on the same day (Duus 1995 [1979], 119). Rather than prohibiting the Japanese state-licensed prostitution system, the U.S. occupation authorities used the system to ensure the health of U.S. soldiers.

Colonel Sams stated, "A lot of young and healthy men among the troops have no choice but to buy prostitutes [to satisfy their sexual desire]." Therefore, VD control was crucial (Sams 1986, 7). Significantly, the U.S. occupation authorities' attitude toward male sexuality was very similar to that of the Japanese patriarchal system. According to the journalist Masayo Duus (1995 [1979], 86), Sams stated with a bitter smile that "military discipline [anti-fraternization] and politics [anti-prostitution] do not always agree with [the] ecology [of men]." Thus, the Japanese state-organized special comfort women system was transformed into a U.S. military, police, medical, and sexual occupation of Japanese women's bodies.

On September 28, the SCAP / GHQ instructed the Japanese government to prepare a VD regulation law to locate the source of VD among women.[17] When the Kanagawa Prefecture police took this order to the Yokosuka City police, it stated that "there [were] GIS infected with VD, but SCAP / GHQ would not admit the fact that GIS spread it" (Yokosuka Keisatsushoshi Hakkō Iinkai 1977, 138). Instead, the special comfort women were ordered to undergo weekly VD examinations and carry a "VD check-up card" that verified their health to GIS (Kobayashi and Murase 1992 [1961], 65; Yokosuka Keisatsushoshi Hakkō Iinkai 1977, 138, 324). If a woman was found to be infected, she was forcibly hospitalized and treated with outdated penicillin from the U.S. military supply.[18] By the end of 1945, the new system of routine examination of prostitutes had been established by the PHW of the SCAP / GHQ, acting through the Japanese government's Ministry of Health and Welfare.[19] The modern Japanese licensed prostitution system was reinstituted to provide safe sex workers to GIS.[20]

The significance of the U.S. VD control system was that it applied to "all individuals whose occupations or activities involved a possible hazard of venereal disease transmission" to GIS.[21] It aimed to enforce VD regulations on previously unregulated groups of women, including dancers, waitresses, maids, and female Japanese employees of the U.S. Occupation Forces. The U.S. VD policy justified the systems of roundups and contact tracings—finding women who were suspected to be sources of VD and imposing examinations and medication on them—that eventually emerged. The U.S. occupation authorities also established prophylactic stations outside the special comfort facilities for GIS to use.[22] GIS were given two lectures on VD, or "Character Guidance Lectures," supplemented by a training film that emphasized the morality of objecting to prostitution.[23] A weekly VD checkup for GIS was also conducted.

In addition to gender and sexuality ideologies, the management of special comfort facilities by the U.S. Occupation Forces reflected its internal class and racial ideologies. The facilities were separated into those for officers, enlistees, blacks, and whites. In the conversation with Yosano referred to earlier, Webster had also expressed his concern over the integrated or shared use of special comfort facilities by Euro-Americans and African Americans (Duus 1995 [1979], 119).[24] To Euro-Americans, such an integrated establishment was impossible, given Jim Crow segregation in the United States and prevailing racist views about blacks' alleged inferiority.[25] Euro-American GIS did not want to share women who served African American GIS.

The U.S. military government was forced to change its position on special comfort facilities after only five months of operation. On January 21, 1946, MacArthur ordered the abolition of all public prostitution, declaring it a "contravention of the ideals of democracy" and a violation of women's rights.[26] At the same time, he released a statement to the Army chaplains, saying that "to protect the members of our occupying forces as far as possible from influences of evil, houses of prostitution and of ill repute have been placed off-limits."[27] Journalists and scholars agree that the main reason for this order was the increased rate of VD among GIS and the ineffectiveness of VD control in organized prostitution.[28] Consequently, special comfort facilities were placed off-limits in March 1946.[29] In response to the off-limits order, some units of the U.S. Occupation Forces enforced the use of prophylactic kits and treatment for those GIS who returned inebriated or late at their quarters.[30]

The 50,000–70,000 women who had been working as special comfort women were let go, without severance pay or offers of alternative employment from the Japanese government or the SCAP / GHQ. Without jobs and desperate to support themselves, they either joined privately owned brothels or sold their bodies on the street. These "freelance" prostitutes became known as pan-pan girls, and according to the Ministry of Health and Welfare's estimates, there were between 70,000 and 80,000 of them in 1951 (cited in Duus 1995 [1979], 303; Kobayashi and Murase 1992 [1961], 130). In Yokosuka City alone, there were some 4,000 pan-pan girls and about 1,200 women working in GI bars by 1948 (Yokosuka Keisatsushoshi Hakkō Iinkai 1977, 141, 143). The Japanese government viewed the pan-pan girls as a necessary social evil that was nonetheless required to maintain a buffer between "good" Japanese women and American GIS.

Although the U.S. military authorities were no longer officially sponsoring special comfort facilities, U.S.-administered VD control of Japanese women persisted throughout the occupation period. Indeed, the VD Control Section of the Provost Marshal's office in Tokyo instructed the Japanese Ministry of Health and Welfare and the Tokyo Metropolitan Police Bureau to enforce a system of roundups of women suspected of prostitution.[31] Significantly, according to an informal report made to the Government Section of the SCAP/GHQ, the Provost Marshal was acting on the authority of secret instructions from Washington, D.C.[32] The first roundup in Tokyo was conducted on January 28, 1946, and the first systematic nationwide roundups took place on August 28–30 of the same year.[33] The beginning of systematic roundups coincided with the order to end the forced issue of prophylactic kits and treatment of GIS by the Headquarters of the U.S. Army Forces, Pacific, on August 21, 1946.[34] On the recommendation of the Surgeon's Office of the Eighth Army, the U.S. occupation authorities had come to the conclusion that placing brothels off-limits and controlling Japanese women—both medically and physically—were "the only means to reduce venereal disease among troops and to prevent their further increase."[35]

The roundups of women were carried out by the Military Police in cooperation with the Japanese police and were carefully designed so as not to provoke any antagonism toward the U.S. Occupation Forces. The actual arrests were to be made by Japanese police, but in many instances women were actually arrested by American MPS. The roundups were indiscriminate; any Japanese woman who was outdoors after dark could be arrested and taken to a hospital for a VD inspection. Often enough, innocent women were arrested, and some of the women were found to be virgins. During the humiliating examinations, MPS and GIS were often present, making crude jokes and taunting the women.[36]

Contact tracing also had been established by late 1945 and was made legal practice in March 1946.[37] Infected GIS were required to report to medical officers and were then turned over to the Provost Marshal to identify the women with whom they had had contact. By 1950, the U.S. Navy in Sasebo was operating a school to train contact tracers for Navy and Army personnel (McNinch 1954). The contact tracing took extreme forms. The Military Police and Japanese police intruded into the homes of suspected women and imposed VD examinations.[38] They also accompanied infected GIS to bars and arrested any woman an infected GI identified. Many GIS did not remember the names or faces of women with whom they had had sexual intercourse. The information provided by GIS was often inaccurate, and many women were falsely accused.[39] The U.S. occupation authorities knew the ineffectiveness of this VD control measure. Their purpose was to implant a sense of fear of U.S. Military Police surveillance—or, in their own words, "To curb the more active individuals in a well organized traffic."[40]

On October 28, 1947, the vd Control Council of the General Headquarters, Far East Command, requested that the Provost Marshal prepare instructions for all commanders in Japan establishing the criminal liability of Japanese women who infected gis with vd. They were regarded as "committing an act of prejudice to the security of the Occupation Forces."[41] Women suspected of prostitution were prosecuted in the Military Occupation Courts (the Naval Provost Courts in Yokosuka). The Legal Section of the scap / ghq asserted that this "technique" had a "greater deterrent value in preventing acts of prostitution than trial[s] in the Japanese courts."[42]

In time, the pan-pan girl business grew to such proportions that it helped to stimulate Japan's postwar economy. According to unofficial estimates, occupation personnel spent between $90 million and $140 million on pan-pan girls (Sumitomo 1952, 70 cited in Dower 1999, 580; Nishida 1953, 236). In Yokosuka, the local business association even composed a theme song with these lyrics: "Japan, Yokosuka Wonderful; Beer and Girls Very Nice."[43] The journalist Setsuko Inoue called this phenomenon the "Japanese economy's Pan-Pan dependency era" (Inoue 1995, 129). The U.S. occupation authorities were not unaware of this situation and even discussed the possibility of taxing the pan-pan girls.[44] The system of bilateral exploitation of the sexuality of Japanese women thus was carefully crafted by both the Japanese government and the U.S. occupation government.

Pan-Pan Girls Performing in the U.S. Occupation in Japan

Well before the end of the Second World War, some Americans had expectations about Japanese women acting like "Madame Butterfly": passive, obedient, and self-sacrificing geisha who knew how to treat men. Young Japanese women in kimonos were called "Geisha Girls," which was synonymous with prostitutes in the minds of gis.[45] Similarly, the special comfort facilities and brothels were referred to as "Geisha Houses."[46] To avoid confusion, the *Guide to Japan*, distributed to gis, had to educate gis that geishas were not prostitutes.[47]

Young gis—arriving as conquerors, able to buy conquered women, and feeling that they were taking control of other human beings—experienced a tremendous sense of power. This was especially the case for inexperienced teenage gis who, even if they were not popular with women in the United States, learned that they could buy a sense of being in control, dominant, desired, and accepted by poor conquered women.[48] Being able to purchase women they considered racially inferior reconfirmed for many the myth of Madame Butterfly: the easy, readily available, forgiving, undemanding, and unthreatening Japanese woman. A former teenage GI stationed in Japan during the occupation period who is currently living in Japan approached me while I was having a conversation with other former GIS and addressed me this way: "So you're asking people about what we thought about Japanese people right after the war? I'll tell you this: I had a good impression of Japanese women." Then he burst into laughter and walked away.

Similar sentiments were expressed by American observers at the time. Noel F. Busch, a senior writer for *Life* magazine stationed in Japan, noted that a subordinate of the Eighth Army's Commanding General Robert Eichelberger had written that the sign on a rest camp, "YOU NEVER HAD IT SO GOOD," should have been placed on the porch of the Imperial Hotel in Tokyo. Busch continued, "Troops occupying Japan [were] suffering no hardship, and save that Frauleins [were] better looking than *neisans* (young Japanese women), their lot [was] clearly happier than that of their confreres in Germany" (Busch 1948, 26–27). A scene in a novel written by Don Richie, a member of the U.S. Occupation Forces, portrayed an older GI telling a younger one that "any (little) gook girl spread her legs if you ask[ed] her the right way" and that Japanese women were a "bunch of animals." The younger GI wondered, "The Army was full of men like him. . . . What happened to Americans abroad? They changed somehow. This fellow in the fields of Arkansas or the hills of Tennessee would have been a nice guy. But here he [became] a kind of monster" (Richie 1968 [1956], 64–65, 71–72). For young GIS, being able to control the sexuality of conquered Japanese women gave them a sense of empowerment; inexperienced country boys had become white masculine conquerors.

Colonel Sams believed that the sexual interaction between GIS and Japanese women gave young GIS not only physical comfort but also, for those separated from their families, psychological comfort (Duus 1995 [1979], 117). Combined with homesickness were the pressures and frustrations of being under strict military regimentation and hierarchy. For all GIS, there was also the fear of possible death, which became even greater after the outbreak of the Korean War. Sexual interactions were thus considered a recreational activity to release stress and tension (Parker 1952, 103). This understanding of "recreation" only increased once Japan (and especially Okinawa) became a rest-and-relaxation (R&R) center for American soldiers fighting in the Korean War. GIS tried to maintain their sense of confidence, power, and masculinity by taking control of the sexuality of obviously weaker conquered Japanese women. Their actions often led to taking out frustrations. From the perspective of the U.S. occupation authorities, Japanese women were convenient nurturers for inexperienced, young, lonesome, and frustrated men. Sexual liaisons between GIs and Japanese women also served the interests of the U.S. occupation authorities because they gave GIs a sense of attachment in a foreign land, which improved their efficiency on the job.

However, while talking with Japanese women who had associated with GIs (most of them had worked at GI bars), I have learned that they did not simply accept the inferior status imposed on them. They played and performed the myth of Japanese femininity to attract GIs for the sake of financial gain as well as social status. They took advantage of their inferior status, pretending to be inexperienced and ignorant to promote the GIs' sense of power in conversation and relationships so that the GIs would buy them drinks and food and possibly even pay their living expenses. One former bar woman told me that she often pretended not to speak English at all and to know nothing about the United States. Most bar women worked for profit on drinks that GIs brought, so acting inferior and demure was considered part of the job. The bar woman told me that most former bar women thought newly arrived young GIs were "suckers (ii kamo)" for them. The women I spoke to were also extremely knowledgeable about U.S. Navy structures and systems and the relationships among sailors. One former bar owner termed them the "Intelligence of the Night."

Japanese women who associated with GIs often took advantage of their local knowledge and performed the roles of mediator, interpreter, and tour guide for the GIs, for whom the connection with an indigenous woman was advantageous for getting around in a foreign country and interacting with local people. (At the Area Orientation Brief in Yokosuka in April 2007, one of the commanders told newly arrived sailors to go outside the base and explore Japan, saying, "If I were a young man, I would find a nice Japanese lady to show me around."[49]) In addition, Japanese women provided companionship for the men that did not revolve around the military competitions and rivalries involved in friendships with other GIs. The benefits that they provided allowed women to take some measure of control in their relationships with GIs, and sometimes Japanese women were treated well by GIs who appreciated the advantages of such a relationship.

The racial segregation that had defined the special comfort facilities of the immediate postwar era also infiltrated the management practices of later brothels, bars, and other entertainment facilities for GIs. As a consequence, pan-pan girls became a highly stratified group. This stratification was based on the racial and military hierarchies of the GIs with whom they associated, as well as on the women's own level of economic achievement and the specifics of their relationships with the GIs (e.g., exclusive girlfriend or concubine, called "Only," or streetwalker, called "Butterfly"). The pan-pan girls who associated with African American GIs ("Kuro-pan," or "Black pan-pan girls") were considered lower status than those who associated with Euro-American GIs ("Shiro-pan," or "White pan-pan girls"). Becoming the "Only" of a Euro-American GI, especially of the officer class, was regarded as having achieved a certain status in U.S. base–town communities. A former bar woman told me that some of her friends who had associated with officers started to act superior to bar women associated with enlisted men. Associating with a higher-rank Euro-American GI meant a rise in the status of a pan-pan girl. It also meant that a pan-pan girl would be well treated by her partner's subordinates and better perceived by other Japanese.

At the same time, one former bar woman told me that she intentionally had associated with enlistees. She called her sailor boyfriend, with whom she had cohabited, "Chopstick" (referring to the two lines on his uniform sleeves). She told me that it was better if a man was a little ignorant, because he would not be arrogant and would be kinder, and she could be in charge of the relationship that way. It seems that some Japanese women chose GIs of lower rank, someone they considered lower than themselves, to offset the fact that the GIs were white male dominating conquerors.

Many pan-pan girls did suffer from poverty, discrimination, VD, and violence from the GIs and other Japanese.[50] But for many pan-pan girls, prostitution also became the site to challenge sociocultural sets of ideas and conditions; it was a way to survive in the only way available, given their limited skills and opportunities in U.S.-occupied Japan. For many Japanese women who came from "undesirable" family backgrounds (e.g., outcasts, orphans, the illegitimate, and the physically challenged), prostitution was a site for life-affirming expression. Associating with the conquerors of Japan, the country where these women were classified as socially inferior, gave them a sense of power. For some Japanese women who did not fit into Japanese socioculturally constructed notions of beauty, walking on the street with conquerors and being desired by American men (even though they were exoticized and faced other forms of discrimination) were self-regarding expressions.[51] They may have considered associating with GIs to be an act of defiance against the sociocultural notion of how Japanese women should act and look in Japanese society. A former GI bar hostess whose father had divorced her mother and then married the hostess's own high-school friend, which made the girl run away from home when she was seventeen and become a *hiropon* (cocaine) addict, told me about her experiences going to the Enlisted Men's Club in Yokosuka with a GI. She mentioned that going to a place where other Japanese were forbidden to enter, escorted by a man (conqueror), listening to jazz, drinking alcohol not available to other Japanese, eating beefsteaks while others were starving, and receiving special treatment by a waiter made her feel above other Japanese, privileged, and like a princess. Thus, the sexual politics that regulated the relations between the United States and Japan were translated into the practice of everyday sexual interactions between the pan-pan girls and the GIs, but the pan-pan girls not only reinforced but sometimes also contested and even took advantage of the existing sexual politics to serve their individual interests through their performance.

Neocolonialism, Nationalism, and the Sexuality of Japanese Women

Masayo Duus has called the special comfort women system organized by the Japanese government a gift from the defeated nation to the victor, the United States. The conqueror, the U.S. Occupation Forces, accepted these women as a sign of victory and exercised its prerogative over the sexuality of the conquered women. Similarities to the sexual politics of European colonial countries and the United Sates are apparent. Yet the collaborative nature of sexual politics or the system of sexual exploitation in U.S.-"democratized" Japan also manifests the neocolonial character of the United States in Japan within the specific context of the Cold War.

This specificity can be seen in the sexual politics of the United States in ordering the closing of the so-called undemocratic special comfort facilities. This step came about to justify the continued maintenance of the sole domination of Japan by the United States, which was embedded in Cold War politics. As U.S. military authorities had quickly found, the existence of special comfort facilities was harmful to the construction of the post–Second World War American self-image: the "all-powerful, progressive, and paternalistic state called [to] the job of developing the world and protecting it from communism" (Lutz and Collins 1993, 139). The United States had to save face if it wanted to live up to its self-proclaimed mission of global leadership after the Second World War: to Japan, to itself, and to the Soviet Union (and, to some extent, to the world).

Similar to European colonial regimes, the projection of the respectability and moral superiority of the United States as a conqueror was an important element of establishing a salient distinction between civilized Americans and the uncivilized Japanese.[52] This was especially pressing, since the "civilizing" of Japan through American democracy was *the* rationale for America's continued presence. The use and supervision of Japanese state-organized brothels began to threaten the moral and cultural superiority the occupation asserted. The effort to maintain a clear distinction between civilized conquerors and the uncivilized conquered was also shown in censorship policies of Japanese movies during the U.S. occupation. The subject of fraternization, including portrayals of inter-ethnic marriage (which the United States perceived at the time as interracial marriage) between GIs, Japanese women, and children fathered by GIs, was forbidden. The presentation of any foreigner (presumably of European descent) was allowed only if he or she was depicted in a favorable light, as civilized (Hirano 1992, 58, 82, 85).[53]

The democratizing U.S. military government also had to save face with respect to its own people at home to bolster the emerging domestic ideology of the American way of life that was promoted as the benefit of capitalism, democracy, and ideological superiority over the Soviet Union. This ideology was constructed on the notion of the ideal American life—based on traditional gender roles (male breadwinners and female housewives) in the Puritan, white, middle-class nuclear families. It also conveniently cloaked internal conflicts of gender, race, class, and homophobia (May 1999 [1988], xviii, 65). With this rise of gender conservatism, the U.S. War Department quickly responded to complaints by female family members of GIs and chaplains stationed in Japan about the much publicized topic of the special comfort facilities.[54] Consequently, the War Department instructed MacArthur to deal with the situation.[55] The continued use of comfort stations also would have exposed the U.S. to charges of hypocrisy from the Soviet Union. The specific timing and suddenness of the abolition were, perhaps, a direct reaction to criticism from the Soviet Lieutenant-General Kuzma Derevyanko and Soviet journalists who pointed out that public prostitution and the trafficking of women were hardly conducive to a "democratic" Japan (Duus 1995 [1979], 172, 260).

The abolition of the special comfort facilities by the U.S. Occupation Forces was expressed in the cliché of the "liberation of Japanese women."[56] It was a part of the U.S. neocolonial project, specifically reflected in the Cold War context, used to justify U.S. domination of Japan and its *necessity*, because the special comfort women were thereby saved by the U.S. Occupation Forces from the Japanese feudal system. This abolition was also instrumental in establishing sole authority in Japan based on American cultural values over those of Soviet communism. The U.S. occupation of Japan did not become the kind of "workshop of democracy" for the people of Japan that many New Dealers had hoped for.[57] For the U.S. government, it became instead a construction site for the global image of the United States, used to campaign against the communist model of the Soviet Union. The "workshop of democracy" in Japan also served to publicize American democracy to other parts of the world. Turning "world-menacing Japan" into a "democratic Japan" under America's guidance had far-reaching implications in that it made American democracy and capitalism appear more attractive than communism, in order to gain and expand in overseas markets. Hence, the neocolonial domination of Japan by the United States, which was embodied in the regulation of Japanese women's sexuality, was carefully concealed by the rhetoric of democracy and the liberation of Japanese women. This was a particularly critical move in the context of the Cold War competition with the Soviet Union.

For the Japanese government, sending special comfort women as a gift was a calculated response to American neocolonial domination, serving the Japanese government's own interests in domestic reordering and foreign policies with the United States and former colonies.[58] The continued dominance of former Japanese colonial officials in postwar Japan was achieved not only because of the U.S. occupation's selective purge for the sake of indirect rule, but also through the sexual politics practiced toward Japanese women, using a sense of nationalism (both colonial nationalism and neo-nationalism) in reaction to the armed foreign occupation.[59] The institution of special comfort women was an attempt by male former Japanese colonial officials to reconstruct postwar social hierarchies at the expense of the sexuality of lower-class women.[60] It was used to reclaim the diminished sense of power and masculinity of male former colonial officials that had resulted from defeat in the Second World War and from foreign domination by reconfirming gender, class, and racial oppression. Lower-class women were to serve GIs for the sake of the nation, and at the same time, upper- and middle-class women were to preserve their chastity (e.g., by evacuating from major cities) so that they properly belonged to Japanese men. By allocating women based on class, and containing GIs in designated facilities, the male former colonial officials undertook to preserve the Yamato race, the cult of Japanese racial supremacy over other Asian people, that had been essential in the construction of the Greater East Asia Co-Prosperity Sphere. By sending this gift to the conquerors, the former Japanese colonial officials were looking for

FIGURE 2.1. "How do we survive under a foreign country's domination?" Remembering the U.S. occupation in Japan. ILLUSTRATION BY ORIKO, IN "SURVIVAL NOW," *BIG COMIC COMPACT: SAITO TAKAWO BEST 3*, VOL. 12, 2005; REPRINTED WITH PERMISSION FROM SHŌGAKUKAN.

reciprocity—namely, the affirmation by the United States of those former officials' maintenance of power within occupied Japanese society.[61]

By calling the special comfort women project "the most important diplomatic task," the Japanese government's intent in using special comfort women to achieve foreign-policy objectives is all too apparent. The Japanese government also hoped for reconciliation by accepting or intentionally submitting itself to the subordinated / neocolonial postwar relationship with the United States. Such a relationship was important to the Japanese government in the face of defeat and its new, uncertain position in Asia. Acknowledging Japan's neocolonized status, Minister of Finance Hayato Ikeda stated, "Japan is like a concubine of America."[62] Japan was a concubine, a symbol of American male power and privilege.[63] Ikeda's statement was not merely a representation of the gendered and sexualized relationship between the two nations embedded in European colonial practices. This unofficial male and female sexual bonding symbolized the neocolonial domination by the United States specific to Japan.[64]

Being a concubine of the United States brought tremendous benefits to Japan in the context of the Cold War. In the initial stages of the occupation, subordination to the United States meant having another military force to guard against a potential communist revolution by the starving masses of Japanese people. As Cold War tension rose in East Asia, Japan, as America's faithful ally, was the beneficiary of the U.S. push toward economic recovery and remilitarization. Japan's Cold War concubinage came to fruition during the Korean and Vietnam wars, which brought about Japan's economic miracle. Though unexpected by the United States, Japan's economic miracle provided more evidence to support the American claim of democratization in Japan, adding another historical layer of concealment to its neocolonial domination. Although this connection is often overlooked, Japan's economic miracle was achieved in part by supplying weapons and war supplies that victimized thousands of other Asian people (Onna Tachi no Ima wo Tou Kai 1986, 11).

Thus, the U.S.-Japanese alliance was also created at the expense of former Japanese colonies. The United States reinforced the Japanese sense of racial supremacy over other Asians via its political, economic, and military missions.[65] The maintenance and incorporation of Japanese colonial hierarchies in Asia was convenient for the United States and its Cold War strategy, as most former Japanese colonies, such as South Korea and Okinawa, became U.S. military bases and even battlefields. Within the specific context of this Cold War relationship, Japan's geopolitical importance to the United States enabled it to achieve economic neocolonial status—re-creating systems of economic and sexual exploitation of other Asian countries and maintaining an unchanged attitude toward other Asians. Hence, the U.S. occupation of Japan was also a construction site for Japan's postwar neocolonialism in Asia.

What Japan embraced on August 15, 1945, was not so much *Haisen* (defeat in war) as what the Japanese call *Shūsen* (the end of the war). What Japan also embraced was American domination, and ruling elites showed this by offering Japanese women as a gift to the victor. The control of the sexuality of Japanese women served to maintain former colonial officials' power within Japanese society and to define Japan's relationship with the United States and former colonies. It created grounds for the Japanese government to take a strategically subordinate position to the United States in order to serve its own political, economic, and military interests. U.S. neocolonialism over Japan was a bilateral process that simultaneously maintained colonial binaries between the United States and Japan and rebuilt former Japanese colonial hierarchies.

The form U.S. domination in Japan took was called "occupation"—seen as the proper consequence of the defeat and the desire to democratize Japan. The term served to obscure the nature of the domination and to differentiate the U.S. presence from European colonial domination. However, the U.S. "occupation" in Japan replicated some European colonial practices. U.S. sexual politics toward Japanese women were almost identical to the corresponding European practices. Yet an examination of the very similar sexual politics reveals the new and hybrid form of colonialism practiced by the United States. It was tactically concealed under the country's democratic and favorable economic policies, intended to remake Japan as a faithful Cold War ally in competition with the Soviet Union. U.S. neocolonialism was also concealed by Japan's willing self-subordination, to serve its own interests, to the American neocolonial structure, as was shown in the collaborative nature of sexual politics toward Japanese women. These were distinct forms of U.S. neocolonialism in Japan that were innovatively created *with* Japan.

U.S. Neocolonialism over Japanese Women

Despite the seemingly successful concealment of the neocolonial intentions of the United States toward Japan, the neocolonial relationship between the two nations was clearly reflected in the mentality and attitude of Euro-American GIS toward Japanese women—in their everyday sexual conquest and "occupation" of pan-pan girls.[66] The power imbalance between male conquerors and conquered women was irrefutable. Not only was it created by the lost war and the GIS' material and economic power, but it was also based on the notion of the "other." Japanese women, unlike German women, were the Other to Euro-American GIS in almost every possible way: gender, race, and class; non-Western and non–Judeo-Christian; and a former enemy. This Otherness promoted Euro-American GIS' prostitution activities and the Euro-American male heterosexual conquerors' exercise of power over Japanese conquered women.

The *New York Times* reported, "Only Fake Geishas Entertain GIS in Tokyo" and called Geisha Girls "[the GI's] little faker."[67] But GIS did not care whether the Geisha Girls were real geishas or not, because their enthusiasm for

FIGURE 2.2. Japanese women and American sailors in front of the U.S. Navy base in Yokosuka, Japan (ca. 1947). COURTESY WATASEI SHŌTEN.

"Maybe short, American—just right, Japanese!"

FIGURE 2.3. ''Babysan'': American sailors' image of Japanese women (1953). COURTESY WILLIAM S. HUME ESTATE.

Geisha Girls represented the American male masters' colonial fantasy of fetishized, exoticized little brown women. Japanese newspapers reported that women were referred to as *"Ki'iroi Benjo* [Yellow Public Restroom]" by some GIS. Their attitude toward Japanese women not only reflected the wartime racial antagonism; it also represented the characteristic colonial attitude because native Japanese women were regarded as "little more than available sexual objects."[68]

Although prohibition of prostitution was discussed, that step was never taken by the U.S. Occupation Forces. Unlike European colonial officials, who considered sex across the color line between white men and brown women as a threat to the European way of life, the U.S. occupation authorities in Japan encouraged consorting with local prostitutes and even informal living arrangements or concubinage (see Spickard 1989, 132). The use of the "Oriental tradition" of special comfort facilities was denounced as not reflecting the American way of life, but private prostitution between GIS and pan-pan girls was widely accepted as an individual choice. That model fit conveniently into the rhetoric of American capitalist democracy, even though U.S. occupation authorities fully understood that most of the women had no other options to make a living. Furthermore, the U.S. military forced a strict regime of VD control on the women.

The encouragement of prostitution also helped to discourage and prevent marriages between GIS and Japanese women, even "good" ones, because they were by definition (as defined by the still valid Exclusion Act of 1924) racially ineligible to immigrate to the United States (Spickard 1989, 132). The indiscriminate roundups of Japanese women represented a different colonial attitude, because the U.S. occupation authorities considered every Japanese morally weak and degenerate and thus a potential carrier of VD.[69] The indiscriminate roundups were also a powerful public display that enforced to the troops the sense that Japanese women were not considered proper wives for GIS. The U.S. neocolonial domination of Japan was also a domination of Japanese women's bodies and sexuality.

Sexual Politics and the Reexamination of the "Workshop of Democracy"

The matter of U.S. military prostitution policies in occupied Japan has prompted scholars to reevaluate prevailing interpretations of the U.S. occupation as a "workshop of democracy" by looking into the sexual regulations of other occupied spaces, including European and Japanese colonies. Their work has demonstrated that the regulation of indigenous people's sexuality was a crucial component of colonial rule and the core of defining and managing colonial privilege and its boundaries (Chaudhuri and Strobel 1992, 12; Stoler 1992, 339). Largely influenced by this approach, Mire Koikari (1999, 316, 329) argues that the striking similarities between the U.S. Occupation Forces' sexual politics toward Japanese women and that of European colonial countries toward indigenous women reveal that the U.S. occupation in Japan was a form of neocolonial process. Yuki Fujime (1999, 121, 2006) asserts that, as with other imperial troops, the invasion and occupation by U.S. military forces in foreign countries (in the past and present) destroys the indigenous economic foundation and forces occupied women into prostitution through its immense material power. In essence, she considers U.S. military prostitution as rape via power and money. Although examinations of the neocolonial / imperial nature of the U.S. occupation of Japan are not a new scholarly development (even though they have been marginalized as a left-wing approach), these scholars underscore the salience of sexual politics in their interpretations of the U.S. occupation of Japan.

By exploring similarities and continuities with European colonial practices when examining the sexual politics in U.S.-occupied Japan, an important difference emerges, since Japan was a former colonial power and, later, a neocolonial state. Koikari addresses the differences in an examination of the binary opposition between colonizer and colonized, arguing that in contrast to the situation in European colonies, the binary was fluid and contested at the site of U.S.-neocolonized Japan. She bases this claim on the fact that Japan was a former colonial power and fairly capable of negotiation and sometimes manipulation (e.g., in its preservation of the emperor system; Koikari 1999, 316, 329).

However, there appear to be dilemmas in the scholarship examining U.S. military prostitution in occupied Japan, particularly in the framework of European colonial sexual politics. First, many scholars seem to perceive the U.S. occupation in Japan as the operation of two countries, portraying Japan as neocolonized only in the nexus of power with the United States. Further complicating the analysis of U.S. military prostitution in "neocolonized Japan" is the fact that military prostitution was not imposed or unilaterally managed only by the SCAP / GHQ. The system of sexual exploitation of Japanese women was organized first and foremost by the Japanese government. It was the Japanese state-sponsored prostitution system specifically prepared for the U.S. Occupation Forces that laid the groundwork for systematic U.S. military prostitution in Japan. Hence, the Japanese government was not merely a secondary actor but one of the primary actors exploiting the

FIGURE 2.4. Popular Japanese comic strip by Tezuka Osamu (1975);
REPRINTED WITH PERMISSION © TEZUKA PRODUCTIONS.

sexuality of Japanese women. As I have explored, its sexual politics were deeply rooted in, and continuous with, its own colonial sexual politics.

Second, the existing scholarship on the history of U.S. military prostitution in occupied Japan is written largely based on documents, a legitimate methodology of history, which tends to focus on policies and attitudes *toward* Japanese women. Journalists and writers living around the U.S. bases were pioneers in shedding light on women's own experiences and voices. These writers represent women as mere victims, which, although also reductive and problematic, constituted a path-breaking shift from the representation of women as simply immoral and shameful. More important, women's own realization and claim of victimhood became a form of agency to challenge both their exploitation by the states and the people who condemned them.[70] In the case of pan-pan girls, a further complication is that their image as victims has served Japanese masculinity, because it conveniently denies the fact of their *own* women appearing to have been more attracted to the American conquerors than to Japanese men.

My chapter resolves the challenges faced by the current scholarship; I also have demonstrated that U.S. neocolonialism in Japan was embedded in a more complex nexus of power—namely, the Soviet Union and the former Japanese colonies. The establishment of U.S. neocolonialism was a bilateral process between the United States and Japan. I have also argued that the intricate existence of pan-pan girls and their agency were part of that nexus.

Conclusion

The consequence of the U.S. occupation of Japan, for the conqueror and the conquered, manifested itself in the control of the sexuality of Japanese women. These women were, in fact, central to the maintenance of the U.S. occupation from the perspectives of both the United States and Japan. For the United States, the control of Japanese women's commodified sexuality was instrumental in creating a post–Second World War hegemony in East Asia, establishing neocolonial domination of Japan while concealing it under the rhetoric of democracy in competition with Soviet communism. For Japanese neocolonized officials, controlling women's sexuality served to maintain their dominance in postwar Japanese society and to create new patterns of economic, political, and military development in the context of their subjugation to the United States. Japanese state regulation of women's sexuality was not only a nationalist construction of women under U.S. neocolonial domination; it was also a Japanese neocolonial project. The system of U.S. military prostitution in occupied Japan was a product of two countries and a process of U.S. neocolonialism and Japan's synchronous neocolonialism.

Pan-pan girls represented a condensed form of Euro-American neocolonial domination of Japan that involved the conquerors' sexual aggressions and Japanese gender, class, and racially oppressive systems. But the pan-pan girls did not simply submit to the given structures of power. Regardless of how they became involved in prostitution activities, many pan-pan girls exercised a form of agency in the best way that they could to achieve economic and personal prosperity and autonomy. It seems to me that pan-pan girls also attempted to contest and subvert their relationship with the male conquerors through physical, mental, intimate, and even loving sexual interactions.

Through my research, I have come to know many former GIS. I learned that, while former GIS overwhelmingly felt power over Japanese women, some also expressed compassion toward women. When an elderly former GI told me about meeting his girlfriend at a bar, for example, he seemed truly appreciative of having someone (not specifically an exotic Japanese woman) who was accepting, desiring, and loving toward a teenage country boy. Some GIS seemed to have learned to contest the boundaries of the conqueror through intimate relationships with Japanese women. As I have argued, the pan-pan girls were historical agents who shaped the history of the U.S. occupation of Japan in many ways.

Postscript: U.S. Military Prostitution in the Post-Occupation Japan

The end of the official U.S. occupation of Japan in 1952 did not bring an end to the U.S. Armed Forces "occupation" of Japan. To this day, Japan hosts the second-largest U.S. military installations and forces abroad and has become the biggest financial contributor to help defray the cost of the U.S. Common Defense.[71] The presence of the U.S. Armed Forces has continued, and so has the phenomenon of pan-pan girls. Although the Japanese government enacted the Prostitution Prevention Law in 1956, U.S. military prostitution continued to flourish in Japan until the mid-1970s, and it continues in Okinawa to this day.[72] In the 1970s, stimulated by the Vietnam War economic boom, Japanese living standards shifted dramatically. Many Japanese women who had engaged in prostitution for economic reasons started to disappear from prostitution. More important, Japanese women's new economic status made them more expensive as a sexual commodity for GIS; at the same time, Japanese women were also becoming available as dates, which meant that they were more time-consuming for GIS to consort with (time-consuming because courtship was involved).

The U.S. occupation of Japan, as the constructing site for the U.S. and Japanese neocolonial power(s), continues to manifest itself in the way U.S. military prostitution is conducted in Japan. Women from economically disadvantaged Asian countries have been forced to migrate to Japan to work in the U.S. military and Japanese sex industries. By the mid-1980s, Filipina, South Korean, Chinese, and Thai women (and, after the collapse of the Soviet Union, Russian women), called "massagy girls," had started to replace pan-pan girls. As one sailor on the USS *Kitty Hawk* recently said: " 'Doing a massagy' is almost a rite of passage for male sailors when they get to Yokosuka. . . . The younger guys get here, . . . [it's] like an experiment. It's not like the U.S."[73] Euro-American hegemony, the rite of passage for GIS, the continued dominance of the descendants of former colonial officials in the Japanese government, the sense of Yamato superiority, and the respectability of neocolonial Japanese women—all are sustained at the expense of the sexuality of new Other women in Japan within the U.S.-Japanese military prostitution system.

Notes

This article is based on my master's thesis (2001) and doctoral dissertation (2009). I owe thanks to Maria Höhn and Seungsook Moon for helping me to articulate my ideas in this chapter. I thank my former advisers at the University of California, Los Angeles (UCLA), Kathryn Norberg, F. G. Notehelfer, Mariko Tamanoi, and Sharon Traweek, and the late Miriam Silverberg. I also thank the following scholars for their valuable advice: Ann Marie Davis, James Fujii, Yuki Fujime, Erlend Gjelsvik, Sondra Hale, Hirofumi Hayashi, Helen Hopper, William Marotti, Marlene Mayo, Hideko Mitsui, Yukuo Sasamoto, Yoshimitsu Shimizu, Yasuhiro Suenami, Hirotaka Sugawara, Hiroki Sugita, Fumiko Suzuki, Kenji Takita, Lorella Tosone, and Akira Yamagiwa, and the members of Senryo / Sengoshi Kenkyūkai. I am indebted to my master's thesis advisers, Sharon Sievers and the late Xiaolan Bao of California State University, Long Beach. My opinions do not necessarily reflect those of the scholars listed, and all mistakes are mine. I am grateful to the Terasaki Center for Japanese Studies at UCLA and the War and Peace Research Group at the Graduate University of Advanced Studies (Sokendai) in Japan for their support of my field research.

1. This chapter is concerned with U.S. occupation policies in mainland Japan.
2. By 1948, the numbers had been reduced to 125,000. With the outbreak of the Korean War, the numbers increased again, to between 210,000 and 260,000 throughout the early 1950s: Johnson 1975, 62, cited in Hirano 1992, 265.
3. The term "pan-pan" (woman or prostitute) is believed to have originated in the South Seas.
4. For a discussion of the formation of "Euro-American" identity in relation to U.S. expansion in the "Far East," see Said 1978, 1–2, 18.
5. For a discussion of prostitutes' agency in connection to the dominant relations of power, see Kempadoo 1998, 8–9.
6. For discussions of the contextualization of prostitution as phenomenon, see Coomaraswamy 1995; Doezama 1998.
7. Yokosuka City Hall, available online at http://www.city.yokosuka.kanagawa.jp (accessed July 2008).
8. More than 16,000 Japanese were employed at the U.S. Navy base by 1950: Tompkins 1981, 83.
9. See also Duus 1995 (1979), 19.
10. The translation is in Dower 1999, 126–27.
11. For a discussion of the Japanese Imperial Military's tactics of "recruitment" or kidnapping of Korean women, see Song 1997.

12. For an example, see Yamada 1995, 5, 62–63, 273.

13. Yuki Tanaka (2002, 162) estimates the number to be about 150,000.

14. "Japanese Admit We Behave Well," *New York Times*, 5 September 1945, 2.

15. "HD: 726.1 Pacific Theater of Operation[s]," entry 31(z1), NARA, RG 112, box 1272; "Venereal Disease Control 1945–46," NARA, RG 331, box 9852.

16. "Venereal Disease Control 1945–46."

17. "720 to 829.1," NARA, RG 331, box 477.

18. Ibid.; "726–1 SCAP," NARA, RG 331, box 477; "HD: 726.1 Pacific Theater of Operation[s]."

19. "HD: 726.1 Pacific Theater of Operation[s]."

20. For the history of the Japanese licensed prostitution system, see Fujime 1998, 410.

21. "HD: 726.1 Pacific Theater of Operation[s]."

22. Ibid.

23. Ibid.; and "726–1 SCAP Reference Only," NARA, RG 331, box 477. See also Hayashi 2005.

24. It is not clear whether male-male sexual interaction facilities came under the management of the SCAP / GHQ. However, the SCAP / GHQ authorities acknowledged the existence of Japanese male prostitutes ("pan-pan boys") who provided sexual services to GIS and attempted to enforce regulations on them.

25. Segregated VD research was conducted; for an example, see Tobey 1948, 481.

26. "726–1 SCAP Reference Only"; *Asahi Shinbun*, 25 January 1946.

28. Public Relations Office, "Press Release," 2 April 1946, MMAL, RG 5: 376.

28. The VD rate in the Eighth Army was 238 per 1,000 per annum in January 1946 (the U.S. War Department had set the limit at 50 per 1,000 per annum): "HD: 726.1 Pacific Theater of Operation[s]." For a reference to controlled prostitution, see "HD: 726.1 (Discipline and Punitive Measures)," entry 31(z1), NARA, RG 112, box 1269. *Stars and Stripes*, 4 January 1946, reported that 75 percent of special comfort women were infected with VD: MMAL, no. 970–77.

29. "HD: 726.1 (Prostitution—Zone of Interior 1946)," entry 31(z1), NARA, RG 112, box 1272.

30. "726.1 (VD) January–March 1946," NARA, RG 338, box 312.

31. UMAA / SCAP, 82-A-1-1; Duus 1995 (1979), 238–40.

32. UMAA / SCAP, 82-A-1-1.

33. Ibid.; Duus 1995 (1979), 239; "726.1 (VD) August 1946," RG 338, box 312.

34. "726.1 (VD) January–March 1946."

35. UMAA / SCAP, 83-A-14-2; "762.1 (VD) April–May 1946," NARA, RG 338, box 312.

36. "726.1 (VD) August 1946"; UMAA / SCAP 82-A-9-1. SCAP / GHQ became concerned over the MPS' direct involvement in the roundups, seeing it as harming the image of the U.S. democratizing forces. The responsibility for roundups was turned over to the Japanese police in September 1949: see Duus 1995 (1979), 246.

37. "HD: 726.1 Pacific Theater of Operation[s]"; "726.1 (VD) April–May 1946."

38. "Venereal Disease Control Staff Visits," NARA, RG 331, box 9336; "Monthly Summary No. 11, May 1947," MMAL, no. 108–115.

39. "Venereal Disease Contact Tracing," NARA, RG 331, box 9370.

40. "HD: 726.1 Pacific Theater of Operation[s]."

41. "726–1 no. 1 1948 SCAP," NARA, RG 331, box 580.

42. Ibid.

43. "Tamaran bushi [Irresistibly wonderful song]," cited in Inoue 1962, 132.

44. UMAA/SCAP, 82-A-11-1; "726.1 Abolition of Licensed Prostitution," NARA, RG 331, box 9370.

45. The kimono is a traditional Japanese outfit: Schultz 2000.

46. "It's Legal Now," *Time*, 3 October 1949, 49; Duus 1995 (1979), 94.

47. *CINCPAC–CINCPOA Bulletin* 209–45, September 1945, LOC.

48. Many veterans I encountered mentioned that they had not been popular with girls in the United States and that they came from poor family backgrounds.

49. Another U.S. Navy commander had kindly arranged my participation.

50. Due to the limited space, the relationship between pan-pan girls and other Japanese is not discussed here.

51. For an examination of the prostitute's body as the site of life affirmation and self-regarding expression, see Bromberg 1999, 298, 302.

52. For an examination of the rise of European bourgeois respectability ideology and its application to colonies, see Mosse 1985, 5. For a discussion of the maintenance of the European colonizers' moral superiority, see Stoler 1991, 85.

53. The moral superiority toward Japan was expressed in several articles written in the United States: see Janeway 1945, 468–69.

54. "HD: 726.1 (Prostitution—Zone of Interior 1946)."

55. Ibid. See also Duus 1995 (1979), 140.

56. *Travel Magazine* reported the abolition of the special comfort facilities as follows: "The greatest significance attaches to General Douglas MacArthur. . . . Japanese girls no longer will have to submit to . . . human degradation. . . . This 'Emancipation Proclamation' for the Japanese woman gives her a new level of human dignity and decency": Hoyt McAfee, "The Passing of the Japanese Geisha," *Travel Magazine* 87 (1946): 28.

57. The progressive policies implemented in Japan were created by the more liberal members of SCAP/GHQ, who sympathized with Franklin D. Roosevelt's New Deal (1933–38).

58. For an explication of the practice of making women's sexual services available to GIS as a deliberate choice made by officials of host countries of U.S. bases to achieve their domestic and foreign policy objectives, see Enloe 1991, 101.

59. For discussions of colonized male elites' social reordering under anticolonial nationalism at the expense of the sexuality of women, see Chatterjee 1989, 632; Choi 1998, 5.

60. John W. Dower (1986, 308) has also observed that the establishment of the special comfort women system was a vivid example of how the Japanese virtue of self-sacrifice was used by Japan's male upper ruling class to maintain its domination in postwar Japan.

61. For the analysis of gift-giving practices and their social efficacy, see Bourdieu 1980, 99.

62. Ikeda made the comment on 22 May 1950: cited in Inoue 1962, 131.

63. For debates about the concubine system in modern Japan (1870s–1920s), see Sievers 1983, 31.

64. Dower's earlier work shows that Japan's military and political dependence on the United States was institutionalized by the Security Treaty of 1952, as in a marriage.

65. "When the issue of Japan's trustworthiness came up . . . in 1951 between the United States and the British, John Foster Dulles, a special ambassador for President Truman, suggested that the United States and England should make every effort to assure Japan's allegiance by exploiting the Japanese feeling of superiority toward other Asians. . . . [Dulles claimed that the] Japanese would be more attracted to the 'social prestige' of being associated with the Anglo-Saxons . . . rather than with the less developed masses of Asia": Dower 1986, 311.

66. Due to lack of sources, African American soldiers stationed in Japan are not discussed here.

67. "Only Fake Geishas Entertain GIs in Tokyo; Police Reveal Old Houses Are Still Closed," *New York Times*, 28 October, 1945, 2.

68. For a discussion of the characteristic colonial attitude, see K. Moon 1998, 167.

69. Katharine Moon (1998, 167) claims that the indiscriminate roundups of Korean women showed U.S. neocolonialism, because every Korean woman basically was considered a whore.

70. For a discussion of the exercise by "Comfort Women" of their agency as victims, see Mitsui 2006.

71. Japan is obliged to defray most expenses for the U.S Armed Forces in Japan under the Security Treaty of 1952. In 2002, Japan bore approximately $4.4 billion. Although its size has been reduced, the area occupied by the U.S. military runs to a total of 127,810 acres, and the number of U.S. military personnel (excluding civilians) stationed in Japan is 41,455 (ashore total 36,960) as of 2006: U.S. Department of Defense, "Base Structure Report (A Summary of DoD's Real Property Inventory): Fiscal Year 2006 Baseline" http://www.defenselink.mil/pubs/BSR_2006_Baseline.pdf (accessed October 2007); idem, "2004 Statistical Compendium on Allied Contributions to the Common Defense" http://www.defenselink.mil/pubs/allied_contrib2004/allied20 04.pdf (accessed October 2007); U.S. Forces, Japan, *Brochure*, October 2006, http://www.usfj.mil/ (accessed October 2007).

72. The Prostitution Prevention Law criminalized prostitution and made prostitutes more vulnerable to sexual exploitation: Fujime 1991, 21.

73. Allinson Batdorff and Hana Kusumoto. "Despite ban, Yokosuka sex trade flourishes," *Stars and Stripes*, Pacific edition, 22 October 2006, available online at http://www.stripesonline.com (accessed June 2007). The cost of a "massagy" (referring to sexual services, which vary from using a woman's hands or mouth to stimulate ejaculation to sexual intercourse) is $30–$150.

THREE

"YOU CAN'T PIN SERGEANT'S STRIPES ON AN ARCHANGEL"

Soldiering, Sexuality, and U.S. Army Policies in Germany

☆

MARIA HÖHN

After the Second World War, two powerful master narratives came to dominate popular memory of Germany's military defeat, and those memories of the country's "zero hour" reveal how sexualized, gendered, and racialized the end of the war and the humiliating years of occupation were experienced. Those narratives also emerged as powerful metaphors of the Cold War alliances of the two German states.[1] One narrative focuses on the mass rapes of German women by invading Soviet troops in retaliation for the horrific crimes Germans committed against Soviet civilians. For many Germans, the rapes of hundreds of thousands of German women confirmed the Nazis' racist diatribes of the "subhuman Slav" and Russia's "Asiatic hordes."[2] In contrast, the public memory of the American-controlled territories of Germany is dominated by the widespread fraternization between German women and U.S. soldiers, often in exchange for food, candy bars, or cigarettes. The celebratory coverage of the sixty-plus-year military and political alliance with the United States often portrays these women as the first fragile link of friendship with the Americans,[3] but during the years of military occupation they were decried as *Ami-Liebchen* or *Ami-Huren* (American lovers or American whores) who betrayed their fatherland and German soldiers. In both the narratives—of rape by Soviet soldiers and of seduction by American GIs (white and black)—German women were depicted as having "failed." A popular and particularly misogynist joke during the bitter occupation years lamented that German men fought six years, while German women fought for only five minutes (White 1947, 149).[4]

The widespread fraternization and the kind of sexual "free-for-all" that came to dominate the American zone is not what military planners in Washington had in mind when they prepared for the military occupation of Germany. Indeed, military planners had devised a policy of strict non-fraternization. Military commanders on the ground were, however, unable to enforce this ban; most of them were also not willing to stop the many kinds of sexual contact between their troops and German women. Despite a strict U.S. War Department policy not to condone or encourage prostitution, military commanders became deeply enmeshed in making sex partners available for their troops. A discussion of the military's effort to rein in venereal disease resulting from the widespread fraternization shows the degree to which postwar German gender norms were affected by these measures. The military's troubling racial divide and its policies toward the romantic and sexual relationships of African American GIs with German women also introduced American-style racial boundaries into German communities that bordered U.S. military bases.

The Failure of Non-Fraternization

During the war, U.S. military authorities debated how the relations between Germans and American occupiers were to be conducted once the war ended. In April 1944, Section G-2 (Military Intelligence Service) of the U.S. Army suggested a policy of strict non-fraternization. To achieve this goal, no troops were to be billeted with Germans, and to avoid the forming of attachment between occupiers and occupied, units were to be moved frequently throughout the American zone of occupation. There were to be no interactions with Germans; GIs were prohibited from having a conversation with, and even shaking the hand of, any German. This plan became official policy in late April 1944 and was integrated into Occupation Directive JCS 1067, which informed U.S. policy during the occupation.[5]

U.S. military officials also considered how to prevent GIs from seeking sexual relationships with German women, since such relationships could undermine the whole fraternization policy. Plans to set up bordellos in Germany under American military supervision, however, were rejected by the War Department, which ordered that all forms of prostitution "in all areas in

which troops . . . are quartered or through which they may pass" be suppressed. The War Department policy specifically forbade its commanders to
"directly or indirectly, condone prostitution" and to "aid in or condone the
establishment or maintenance of brothels, bordellos or similar establishments." Medical officers in the military shared the War Department's opposition to any sort of prostitution, because they believed that the "practice
of prostitution [was] contrary to the best principles of public health, and
harmful to the health, morale and efficiency of troops."[6] With that policy, the
military drew on the May Laws of 1941, which had made prostitution around
military bases in the United States a federal offense.

The War Department's policies regarding prostitution were established
for the whole European Theater of Operations; however, as became clear
already during the military advance in France after the invasion of Nor-
mandy on June 6, 1944 (D-Day), commanders on the ground did not always
share the convictions of their superiors in Washington. Whether or not
the War Department's *official* policy on the suppression of prostitution was
enforced thus depended largely on the attitudes of individual commanders. Since military commanders generally do not pass reports up the chain
of command on why or how they circumvented War Department policy,
sources other than military records prove instructive.[7] Those records suggest
that during the advance on Germany—and later, during the occupation of
Germany—commanders were not just turning a blind eye but were actively
involved in facilitating access to female companions, including prostitutes,
for their troops. Not only did the U.S. military actively participate in the
regulation of prostitution, it also insisted on an American-style color line.
Segregated bordellos for black and white troops were established in Cher-
bourg, France, for example, with the "military police stationed at the doors
to keep order when the queues formed." After the liberation of Paris, the
Provost Marshal of one section combed through local bordellos that had
catered to German Wehrmacht soldiers and selected groups of prostitutes to
service his officers, white enlisted soldiers, and black enlisted soldiers (Cosamas and Cowdrey 1992, 540–41).[8] Commanders subverted official War Department policy because they considered sex a "recreation needed and deserved by fighting men" and thus "attempted to provide it through regulated
prostitution" (Cosamas and Cowdrey 1992, 540–41).

Not surprisingly, once the American military reached Germany, the attitudes of commanders on the ground toward the sexual needs of their men
did not change substantially.[9] In Germany, however, commanders faced the
added challenge of the fraternization ban, which had not been an issue in the

allied countries Great Britain and France. Osmar White, an Australian war correspondent who accompanied the Third Army on its advance into Germany, had plenty of opportunities to observe how the attitudes of military commanders on the ground conflicted with those of policymakers in Washington. One high-ranking divisional officer let it be known that he considered the entire fraternization ban to be ludicrous, remarking, "This is surely the first time in history that a serious effort has been made to deny soldiers the use of women in a country they have conquered!" Another distinguished army commander expressed similar sentiments when he joked during a meeting that "copulation without conversation does not constitute fraternization" (quoted in White 1996, 98).[10] For these high-level commanders, "fraternization" foremost meant the GIS' right to have sexual relationships with the women of the conquered nation, which they understood as a prerogative of the victorious warrior.

The attitude of most military commanders toward the "sexual needs" of their soldiers was probably best conveyed by the expressions of the time that the military "is not a Boy Scout camp" and "You can't pin sergeant's stripes on an archangel."[11] While some commanders tried to enforce the War Department policy on non-fraternization, they "were not anxious," according to an observer of the American military occupation of Germany, "to enforce a policy which most of them believed ill-advised and unenforceable" (Bach 1946, 74). Most were pragmatic, telling their soldiers to keep their escapades with German women discreet and to carry condoms (Standifer 1997, 17). The "army standard," insisted a military report on venereal disease, is to "always use a rubber and always take a pro [prophylactic kit]."[12] Condoms the military did provide: some 50 million of them were handed out to American soldiers each month throughout the duration of the war, and in the closing months of the war, the military was not able to fill demands from the field (Brandt 1985, 164–65).

While romantic and sexual contacts between GIS and German women became a regularly noted occurrence during the military advance into Germany after September 1944, such contacts became a mass phenomenon after hostilities ceased on May 8, 1945. Given that the military had made no accommodations for the "sexual needs" of the 1.6 million U.S. soldiers amassed in Germany in May 1945, this development is hardly surprising. Numbers are hard to come by, but U.S. Army surveys show that in the fall of 1945, 54 percent of GIS reported that they had "talked to German girls" in that week, while 25 percent had spent at least ten hours "talking" to German "girls." Very few reported that they had talked to older Germans or German men their age (Ziemke 1975, 327). Given the limited foreign-language skills of most American GIS and most German women, it is probably safe to conclude that many of these contacts were of a romantic or sexual nature. While contacts between American soldiers and German women varied among army units (depending on whether they were located close to a town), a U.S. Army investigation in 1946 estimated that 50–90 percent of its troops had frater-nized with German women and that one in eight *married* GIS had a stable relationship with a German partner (Starr 1947, 98). The U.S. Army also reported that fraternization rates of officers did not differ from those of enlisted men. A survey conducted in 1949 confirmed that the U.S. Army's estimate from 1946 was not exaggerated: 87 percent of single GIS reported that they had had sex while stationed in Germany.[13] In the soldiers' parlance, informed by the attitudes of the commanding officers cited earlier, fraterni-zation or "going frattin'" solely came to mean having sexual relations with German women (Bach 1946, 76).

After hostilities ceased, sexual relations between GIS and German women took place for a number of reasons. The most important was the sheer suffering of the civilian population. While some stretches of German coun-tryside were barely touched by the war, German cities were destroyed be-yond recognition, and any area that had lain in the path of the conquering Allied armies was utterly devastated. Because the Nazi regime had ruthlessly exploited its occupied territories, Germans had not endured hunger during the war. The end of the war changed that radically, and for Germany the liberation from Nazism also meant the beginning of "the hunger years." The arrival of some 12 million refugees and expellees from the eastern parts of the former Reich only exacerbated an already grim situation. For the next four years, caloric rations in the American zone remained alarmingly low, and fuel to cook and heat often was not available at all. The black market thrived, and the only valid currency in this desperate situation was American ciga-rettes. One of the most sought-after food items was the high-calorie Hershey candy bar, which could easily be traded on the black market for other food supplies. It is easy to see how having an American "boyfriend" and access to American food rations could literally be a matter of life and death for a woman trying to feed herself and perhaps her children. Even as large num-bers of Germans scorned the *Ami-Liebchen* as loose women, at best, and as prostitutes, at worst, the women's families often tolerated or actively encour-aged these relationships to ensure survival.[14]

The pronounced gender imbalance in Germany after the war also contrib-uted to the fact that German women sought out American GIS. Some 3.5

million German soldiers had been killed in the war, and 9.2 million German men were prisoners of war (POWs) in 1945. For every 100 German men between twenty and thirty years old, there were 167 German women. Numbers did not look much better for women between thirty and forty years old, for whom the ratio was 151 women to 100 men. That gender ratio would improve as the POWs were released over the next four years,[15] but given the utter destruction and poverty in Germany, American GIs remained desirable romantic partners for many German women.[16] Just as important, German women, many of whom had fended for themselves since the beginning of war in 1939, were sexually attracted to the "exotic otherness" of the American GIs. Women commented on the soldiers' healthy looks, good teeth, and more relaxed habitus while also appreciating their carefree behavior, which differed markedly from that of the defeated and dejected German men (White 1947, 149).[17]

Rape, Romance, and Prostitution

While many German women fell in love with American GIs and hoped for marriage, during the hunger years of 1945–49, the boundary between love affairs, promiscuous behavior, prostitution, and rape were incredibly fluid because the power relations between occupier and occupied were so out of balance. While rape was not a major problem in the American-controlled areas, unlike in the Soviet zone, it was difficult to judge a woman's acquiescence to a sexual encounter. Especially during the military advance into Germany, American officials expressed concern about what they called the "spiral increase" of rapes.[18] While the Judge Advocate-General of the Seventh Army was reluctant to convict the GIs in many of the reported rape cases because of the severity of the punishment for the soldiers,[19] he had few illusions about the power relations involved: "A man who enters a strange house carrying a rifle in one hand is not justified in believing he has accomplished a seduction" (Ziemke 1975, 220).[20] But an official study on rape committed by American GIs was more lenient with the soldiers, arguing that the soldiers' assumption that all European women had loose morals "contributed to the prevalence of rape cases in Germany. The German women in such cases," the report continued, "were usually too terrified of the armed invader to offer much physical resistance. . . . Their apparent compliance toward the soldier's desire confirmed his contempt for the morality of Europe" (quoted in Kleinschmidt 1997, 104). Another observer of the occupation, a female journalist, even went as far as to portray the German women as the real villains in incidents of rape. She viewed the GIS as innocent "kids" who were "chased" into the bushes, concluding, "If there was rape, it certainly wasn't necessary" (Barden 1950, 165).

It was even more difficult to draw boundaries between "true" love affairs, promiscuity, and so-called hunger prostitution when German women were so desperately poor and the American GIS were well fed and rich. The destruction of German infrastructure and the utter collapse of the German economy only contributed to this morally hazy climate. Since the German currency was worthless, how does one assess the pound of coffee or bar of soap (instead of bouquet of flowers) that a GI brings to a first date? How is one to judge the woman who has accepted four buckets of coal from her American boyfriend, an offering worth a fortune in the bitter winter of 1946–47? Were these "gifts" romantic tokens of love, a sign of mercy toward a suffering people, or a business exchange for sexual favors? In the eyes of many Germans and Americans, the women who accepted such American goods were no better than the professional prostitutes who accepted cold, hard cash. The military's ban on all fraternization, which was not revoked until October 1945, and its refusal until December 1946 to allow marriages between GIS and German women only fed the widespread perception that these relationships were illicit and immoral.

Even though some German social workers pleaded for sympathy for women who were forced into "hunger" or "survival" prostitution, most Germans and Americans were appalled by the women's matter-of-fact approach to their sexuality. German officials suggested that in Berlin alone, 100,000 women (compared with 15,000 before the war) were engaged in "secret" or "occasional" prostitution in 1947.[21] Even as astute an observer of the occupation as Saul Padover, who was aware of the immense suffering in Germany, could not help himself from concluding that German women were "perhaps the easiest white women in the world" (Padover 1946, 263).

Many of the encounters between GIS and German women during the military advance into Germany and during the early, unsettled months of the occupation involved the one-time exchange of sexual favors for a handful of cigarettes or a bite to eat. Germany's bombed-out city landscape provided innumerable hiding places for these fleeting encounters. Once military units settled into more permanent locations, opportunities for such "pick-ups" became more formalized. In order to survive, hungry and desperate German women would gather outside military detachments and in front of the American Post Exchange (PX), where the soldiers did their shopping (Boyle 1963; Habe 1957).[22]

German women could also meet American GIs in the bars and clubs that catered to GIs in the vicinity of military detachments. Despite the fraternization ban, military commanders allowed enterprising individuals to open these venues to provide entertainment for the troops, who spent most of their free time in such places. Often, the clubs and bars were in dark and bombed-out buildings amid the rubble of Germany's cities, but they could also be fancy establishments that catered to officers. They usually offered American music, "exotic" dancers, floor shows, and plenty of American liquor, and they were generally off-limits to German men.[23] Not surprisingly, these establishments—like the military itself—were strictly segregated by race, with the soldiers and the military police enforcing racial boundaries (see Smith 1948; Standifer 1997).[24] The clubs were also a place for soldiers to make contacts with German women who worked there as taxi girls or waitresses, and as one soldier recalled, the "army wasn't strongly opposed to the prostitution or the sex shows" that were offered in these GI clubs (Standifer 1997, 176). In licensing these sorts of places, commanders provided sexual outlets for their troops without having to establish bordellos, but in doing so they clearly violated the official War Department policy that commanders must not condone or foster prostitution.

Another type of relationship that emerged during the occupation years was the so-called shack-up, an arrangement of convenience that replicated the institution of concubinage prevalent in nineteenth-century European empires. The relationship often evolved from a pick-up encounter and became a relationship of convenience for both partners. These sorts of arrangements were popular among both officers and enlisted men, and many married American soldiers preferred a stable partner to having to deal with pick-ups. The soldier would live with the woman until his unit was moved, supplying her with food and goods not available on the German market in exchange for sex and housekeeping. When the soldier was transferred back to the United States or was redeployed within Germany, the woman often would be passed to a buddy who had not been transferred (Habe 1957; White 1947, 147).[25] The "shack-up" proved one of the most popular ways to deal with what military commanders called the "boy-girl problem" and what soldiers called the "laundry problem." Such arrangements were widespread and would mark U.S. garrison towns in Germany until the mid-1960s, when Germany's economic miracle offered women much greater opportunities to make a living.[26]

Another phenomenon that came to define the occupation period and that lasted well into the 1950s was the so-called camp follower; German women who followed American military units as they were deployed across the American zone. Among them were many lost souls: young women who had lost their parents in the war, widows whose husbands had been killed in the war, women who had been bombed out of their homes, and refugees and expellees from the east who had no place to go in war-devastated Germany. These women attached themselves to military units, offering not only cleaning and laundry services but also sexual favors in exchange for food. Here too the boundaries between prostitution and romantic love were hard to discern. Many of the women who were considered camp followers had become attached to their American partners and hoped for more than an arrangement of convenience. They would follow the soldier when his unit was moved within the U.S. zone because the couple had fallen in love. Sometimes a woman would choose to stay with a unit because she was pregnant or because she already had a child by the soldier and they could not get married because of the military's ban on marriages (Starr 1947, 146–48).[27]

While the military command viewed the camp followers as pests, some commanders encouraged this development because they preferred their men to be in stable sexual relationships rather than establishing a "shack-up" at every new location. Stable sexual relationships improved morale and controlled venereal-disease (VD) rates.[28] Military commanders who allowed camp following would instruct the local German authorities that the women who arrived with their unit were not to be treated as prostitutes, even though they lived with the soldiers outside of marriage. German authorities were instructed to keep an eye on the women to ensure that they remained monogamous, and they were assisted in their efforts by American military police. German authorities, to their great chagrin, also had to provide the women with housing and food coupons drawn from the extremely limited resources available at the time (Starr 1947, 147; Willoughby 2001, 37–38).

Although U.S. observers tended to blame the sexual aggressiveness of German women and the naiveté of American GIS for the rampant fraternization and sexual disorder of the occupation, American GIS marveled in their power and aggressively pursued women in the street and at local dance halls. The call, "*Hallo, Fräulein!*" could be heard throughout garrison towns even in the 1950s and reflected how many American GIS related to any woman they encountered in the streets (Höhn 2002, chap. 8). GIS were at times so aggressive in their pursuits that military authorities had to post large "Off-Limits" signs on religious convents to inform their troops that the women there were to be left alone. Female employees of the U.S. military government and female visitors from the United States had to wear armbands that identified them as Americans to keep GIS from pursuing them as "just another German *Fräulein*" (Botting 1985, 169; Hutton and Rooney 1947, 38; Wilder 1949). While this precaution by the military government protected American women from the sexual advances of GIS, they also marked German women as "free for all" sexual objects for the GIS.

The Problem of VD

The military's inability to rein in the GIS' widespread fraternization with German woman angered many Americans at home; it also undermined the prestige of the occupation in the eyes of many Germans. But it was the explosion of venereal-disease rates that forced the military to become much more involved in the sexual lives of the troops. Aside from describing in the next section how the military responded, I will outline why U.S. policies to control the spiraling VD rates among its soldiers also had grave implications for German women.

Even before the advance into Germany, the same military planners who had concocted the non-fraternization policy also prepared for what they feared would be widespread contacts between U.S. soldiers, German women, and female displaced persons (DPS), who often were liberated slave laborers from Eastern Europe or survivors of the Holocaust. While VD rates had already increased in Great Britain and doubled in France, it was in Germany that they exploded.[29] In April 1945, 56 incidences of VD were reported for every 1,000 soldiers. By August, those rates had risen to 177 per 1,000; by January 1946, to 233 per 10,000; and by July 1946, to 305 per 1,000 men—that is, according to the numbers for July 1946, 30 percent of men would be infected with VD within the course of that year (Cosamas and Cowdrey 1992, 585; Starr 1947, 76).[30] To the great dismay of the military leadership, VD rates were barely lower for officers: from second lieutenants to colonels, all ranks were represented in the VD statistics. Infection rates for black GIS were up to three times higher, a fact that the military did not try to explain at the time other than to state that their "rate is, of course much higher than [that] among white soldiers."[31]

VD rates increased so dramatically because military hierarchy and discipline broke down after hostilities ceased. Troops shifted, zonal boundaries moved, and hundreds of thousands of soldiers were demobilized or redeployed to fight in the Pacific. More than a million men had been moved out of Germany by late 1945, and experienced combat troops often were replaced with new and less disciplined personnel from the United States. Rates initially also spiraled upward because the War Department withdrew the familiar V-Packette prophylactic kit. The plan was to replace the kit with a more effective product, but the War Department withdrew the V-Packette kits before it had adequate supplies of the new kits (Cosamas and Cowdrey 1992, 585). Furthermore, because of the strict fraternization ban, soldiers who were infected were reluctant to seek treatment because they could be fined $65 or perhaps even be court-martialed for fraternizing with German women (Starr 1947, 78–79). By 1946, military commanders were forced to admit that VD rates in Europe "were the highest in American military history" (Geis and Gray 1951, 35; Starr 1947, 77).

In light of these factors, the military had modified its regulations by June 1945 and ruled that a VD infection could not be used as evidence against a soldier for violating the fraternization ban (Starr 1947, 79).[32] "Pardoning" soldiers for fraternizing with German women was just the first step toward controlling the VD epidemic. Once the supply of prophylactic kits was ensured again, the military command started passing out condoms and VD kits at military barracks and railroad stations across German towns and cities.[33] It was much more difficult for African American GIS to get access to these kits, because white commanders of black troops were hesitant to encourage interracial sexuality. Furthermore, until the Negro Newspaper Publishers Association filed a complaint in January 1947, American Red Cross clubs in Germany —which also handed out kits—did not open their doors to black GIS.[34]

The military also started a comprehensive education campaign with posters in troop quarters and articles on VD in the military newspaper *Stars and Stripes*. Made popular in *Stars and Stripes* and on billboards across the American zone was the image of an attractive blond German woman in a trench coat that was stamped with the letters VD. Soldiers quickly named her "Veronika Danke-Schön (Thank You Very Much, Veronika)." Even more disturbing was the decision by some commanders to produce wanted-style posters of infected women. The women were displayed in the most unflattering way, with the poster warning the soldiers to stay away from them.[35]

In light of the exploding VD rates among their troops and in the German population, commanders wanted to ensure that soldiers spent more time with "decent" girls. Beginning in the summer of 1945, when all fraternization was still prohibited, some commanders experimented with "social passes" to allow young German women as companions into clubs and dances sponsored by the Americans. A woman who wanted to frequent an American Red Cross dance club had to answer a barrage of questions about her family background, morals, and politics. U.S. authorities then checked with the local German Health Office and Police Department to ascertain whether the woman had a record of VD or criminal convictions. Military officials considered codifying this ad hoc system throughout the zone in July 1946, but the plans were abandoned because too many of the German women the military hoped to attract viewed the social passes as similar to the registration cards issued to professional prostitutes (Geis and Gray 1951, 38; Starr 1947, 80, 136–38; Ziemke 1975, 327).

The military believed that the most effective way to bring down VD rates was to gain better control over the women who infected the soldiers. Thus, in August 1945 the military started its anti-venereal-disease program, which was overseen by the Americans but largely executed by German health officials. The emphasis of the program was to identify and cure the carriers of the disease in order to protect the American soldier first, and then society at large (Starr 1947, 80). Because both U.S. and German officials agreed that the main culprits were the women who infected the soldiers, efforts to control VD focused foremost on tracking down infected women. Since prostitution was legal in Germany, the first group to receive scrutiny was registered prostitutes—that is, women who self-identified as prostitutes and were registered with the Health Department. The professional prostitutes were rather easily controlled because they had always been obliged to undergo routine examinations for VD, with German officials conducting the exams at the Public Health Offices. The military also handed out condoms to registered prostitutes that catered to American GIS, since it was almost impossible to find condoms on the German market (Standifer 1997, 176).

The real problem in terms of spreading VD, however, was not the professional prostitutes but the women who had occasional sexual relationships with GIS. Scrupulous attention was thus paid to women who worked as waitresses, dancers, or taxi girls in American clubs.[36] Only after bringing evidence of a clean bill of health were the women allowed to work in such soldiers' clubs. The women then also had to submit to regular gynecological check-ups to keep their jobs. Other groups that were targeted were female food workers, hotel employees, and maids who worked in leisure and recreation establishments set up for U.S. soldiers (see Timm 1998).

In trying to protect its troops from infection, the U.S. military government significantly expanded the provisions for punishment, surveillance, and social control open to German officials. In May 1945, the Allies invalidated all laws that had been passed by the Nazi regime. To combat communicable diseases, German authorities were instructed to revert to the Law for the Prevention of Venereal Disease of 1927, passed by the democratic Weimar Republic. That law stressed welfare rather than punitive measures to control VD, and protected individuals from arbitrary police measures. The Allied Decree of September 1945 to battle venereal disease, however, severely weakened those provisions. Whereas the Weimar law required that the name of the infected individual be reported only if the person refused treatment, the new Allied Decree stipulated that all infected individuals had to be reported to German health authorities, who then passed the information on to the U.S. military government. In an even more drastic shift from the 1927 law, any person "suspected" of having VD, and all "promiscuous persons," could be forced to undergo gynecological examinations. Thus, any woman suspected of having infected an American soldier was given an exam and confined if she was sick. To stress the punitive measures of the new provisions, prison-like hospital wards and detention centers were set up across the American zone, where patients had to wear prison garb–like clothing. As Annette Timm has argued, the measures passed by the Allies (and applauded by many German officials eager to get the VD crisis under control) had more in common with the punitive Nazi VD control legislation of 1940 than with the more progressive Weimar law of 1927. The ethos of the 1927 law, with its emphasis on welfare and the rights of the individual, would not be restored until 1953 (Timm 1998, 185–86).

To trace all people suspected of carrying VD and all "promiscuous people," surveillance measures were drastically increased and VD controls and vice raids of all suspected establishments, homes, and neighborhoods were initiated. The most offensive and humiliating method to control VD—and one that was to remain at the core of the joint U.S. and German effort until the end of the 1950s—was the vice raid. Because the Americans were primarily interested in individuals who infected their soldiers, and because German officials have traditionally targeted women in the struggle against VD, the overwhelming majority of the individuals arrested in these VD raids were women (Heineman 1999, 102; Timm 1998, 188).[37] In Berlin, one enlightened U.S. military official finally included German men in his measures in spring 1947, when 300,000 returning German POWs were thought to present a new source of infection (Timm, 1998, 189). But these more progressive policies in the U.S. sector of Berlin did not reverberate in the rest of the U.S. zone of occupation, where 99 percent of the individuals arrested in vice raids in 1947 were women (Heineman 1999, 102).[38]

During the vice, or VD raids, U.S. military police, German police, and public-health workers raided bars and clubs frequented by American GIs and their German partners, arresting all of the women present, loading them onto U.S. Army trucks, and taking them to police stations. Often, young women without any record of VD who were simply out at a dance would be caught up in the dragnet. It was not unusual for the women to be kept overnight before being forced to endure gynecological exams and forcible treatment, if necessary, in one of the ninety-eight VD clinics that operated in the U.S. zone by 1948. These raids were incredibly humiliating; they also trampled on the civil liberties of German women, who were merely out for some fun and escape from the misery of postwar Germany. Allied officials estimated that, at most, 18.2 percent of the women apprehended in the U.S. vice raids were actually infected with VD (Heineman 1999, 102).[39] The reputations of the other 82 percent were tainted, and their dignity was affronted by the fact that they had to endure humiliating exams that often were conducted in front of the American military police and the German officials who had picked them up. Despite embarrassing mistakes (in one town, the mayor's daughter and the wives of several prominent local businessmen were arrested), American military officials did not give up on this method of source tracing (Heineman 1999, 102).[40]

The sharp increase in VD peaked in the summer of 1946, but by late 1947, the Americans, in close collaboration with the Germans, were able to lower the rate significantly. They were successful not because of their aggressive source tracing but, instead, because in October 1945 the military made penicillin available for the treatment of Germans infected with VD (Cosamas and Cowdrey 1992, 584).[41] The situation within the military also stabilized. Soldiers were moved into more permanent quarters, and the worst disciplinary problems associated with demobilization were resolved when a fearsome Constabulary Force was introduced and soldiers were subjected to more demanding drill regimes. The military also used fear tactics in order to get soldiers to be more careful by threatening dishonorable discharges for any soldier with repeat infections and by demoting officers who did not successfully address the issue in their units (Geis and Gray 1951, 38–39; Geis 1952, 76–83).[42] The military's education campaign also deserves mention: the GIS, according to German officials, became conscientious users of the condoms that their commanders placed with the sign-out book at every military barracks (Höhn 2002, 174; Standifer 1997, 17).[43]

Stabilizing the Occupation

The widespread fraternization of American GIS with German women and the spiraling VD rates presented the U.S. military authorities with a number of problems. In the United States, the public was appalled with developments in Germany. In an immensely popular movie on the topic, *A Foreign Affair*, a female U.S. senator traveling on a fact-finding tour of Berlin gives voice to the outrage by exclaiming that post-Nazi Germany was infected by a kind of "moral malaria" that needed to be "fumigated with all insecticides available" (Wilder 1948).[44] Reactions to the sexual disorder were just as grim in Germany itself. Returning German POWs and angry former Hitler Youth were resentful of the relationships between "their" women and GIs, and the few attacks perpetrated by German men on American GIs, as the Third Army reported, were usually incited by competition for German women (Bach 1946, 71–83; Starr 1947, 74).[45] But just as damning was the fact that the U.S. military leadership appeared weak and incapable of enforcing its own strict rules. Throughout 1945, efforts to remedy the situation had failed miserably. Soldiers laughed at the $65 fine that was imposed for fraternizing with German women, and they complained that the policy was on the books only "to give the brass a first crack at all the good-looking German women."[46] The wartime hopes that American female civilian employees and nurses might prevent soldiers from fraternizing proved delusional, since the small contingent of just 2,500 American women could never satisfy the needs of the hundreds of thousands of soldiers stationed in Germany. Furthermore, the nurses brought to Germany were all officers and were thus prohibited from associating with enlisted men.[47] When German officials broached the idea of establishing military brothels for the troops, American commanders responded that the American women's organizations would have "their head on a platter" if they permitted such houses of prostitution (Höhn 2002, 137).

Matters over the state of affairs in Germany came to a head in the spring of 1946, when the occupation army was plagued by widespread problems of morale and discipline. U.S. newspapers had a field day with stories about how American officers and soldiers who had been sent to democratize the Germans were instead getting rich on the black market and conducting illicit affairs with German women. The perception that service in the occupation army "was one big picnic"—with GIs swinging "in hammocks with blond *Fräuleins*," swapping "cigarettes for castles on the Rhine" and soaking their "feet in sparkling Moselle" (Wilder 1948)—dominated much of the coverage in the U.S media and in movies made during the occupation years.[48] To counter those perceptions and to rein in the widespread sexual relations with German women, military leaders decided to bring the families of officers and upper-rank soldiers to Germany. The "wives to Europe" decision, in Brigadier-General John S. Whitelaw's words, was made "to stop the adultery and loose living going on," and after the families arrived, Lieutenant-General

Lucius Clay, the Deputy Military Governor, breathed a sigh of relief, concluding that their presence "brought back a much higher moral standard" (Whitelaw, quoted in Kleinschmidt 1997, 135; Clay, quoted in Smith 1990, 325). While the importation of 30,000 wives and children may have significantly improved the morale and morality of the officers, it did little to provide "relief" for the enlisted men. For the hundreds of thousands of American troops who rotated through Germany in 1945–46, illicit and non-sanctioned relations with desperate and hungry German women remained the norm.

The romantic and sexual relationships between German women and American GIS were finally legitimized when "normalizing" relations with German men became a pressing issue. Once military authorities realized that they did not have the manpower to conduct an orderly occupation on their own, they recognized a need for German collaborators. Thus, as John Willoughby (2001, 29) has argued, the "routinization of intimacy was central" not only to making that collaboration with German men possible, but also for stabilizing the military's presence in Germany. Consequently, in December 1946, the military authorities allowed American soldiers to marry their German girlfriends. By the end of the occupation period in 1949, approximately 12,000 German women had married their American partners, and 8,000 more women had traveled to the United States to marry their partners there.[49]

Despite this shift in policy, the early occupation policies concerning romantic and sexual relationships with American GIS proved disastrous for German women. Until the ban on marriages was lifted in December 1946, the American policy basically deemed any relationship between a German woman and an American GI illicit, thus branding the women either as "indecent" or as prostitutes. The military's decision to protect American women (wives and civilian employees) from the sexual advances of GIS by making them wear armbands with an American flag was perhaps the most offensive expression of that mindset. In making that decision, the U.S. military implicitly drew boundaries of women's respectability. As Bud Hutton and Andy Rooney, who served in Germany and were severe critics of U.S. policy there, pointed out, GIS could do everything with German women except marry them, even when a woman expected a child (Hutton and Rooney 1947, 51). Some 90,000 illegitimate children were born from these relationships during the occupation years, tarnishing the women even further in the eyes of many Germans. The military finally shifted gears because of bitter complaints from GIS that the existing U.S. policy treaded on their democratic rights as Americans, but also because normalizing gender relations in Germany became crucial to ensuring an orderly occupation. Despite this shift in late 1946, the stigma of prostitution and promiscuity brought about by the earlier policy would linger for many years to come.[50]

From Occupation to Partnership

The end of the formal U.S. military occupation came with the division of Germany and the founding of the two German states in 1949. In that year, the Occupation Statute, which remained in effect until 1955, ended military rule in West Germany. With the end of military rule, the U.S. High Commissioner, based in the State Department, took the reins from the War Department. The accelerated rapprochement between the former enemies became possible because of the emerging Cold War with the Soviet Union. The Berlin Airlift in 1948–49, during which the Western Allies supplied the city for more than a year, sealed that shift. Just four years after the defeat of the Third Reich, West Germany could look forward to political rehabilitation and normalization when the United States started pushing for a rearmed Germany to help contain the Soviet threat. The outbreak of the Korean War in 1950 vastly accelerated the ongoing rehabilitation of the new West German state; it also convinced President Harry S. Truman that Europe could not be defended with the 80,000 occupation troops still stationed in Germany in 1949. Truman's "Troops to Europe" decision as a response to the far-away conflict in Asia would drastically change America's commitment in Europe and significantly expand the network of military bases that covered Western Europe, with the majority of military personnel stationed in Germany. In 1950, the Seventh Army was reactivated and redeployed to Germany, and within a year troop levels had been raised to almost 250,000 soldiers.[51]

The much desired "normalization" of Germany's political relationship with the United States, however, also meant that gender relations around U.S. military installations could not be "normalized" in the foreseeable future. While many a German woman fell in love with an American GI and marriages became more acceptable, "illicit" sexual relationships continued to dominate the debates in Germany on the implications of such a large foreign-troop presence. During the years of occupation, sexual relations between German women and American GIs and the thriving entertainment and sex industry that catered to the soldiers had been deeply upsetting to many Germans. The years after 1949 proved hardly less disconcerting.[52] Large German cities such as Berlin, Frankfurt, and Munich were able to absorb the troops and the social problems associated with their presence more easily than the provincial towns and rural communities where most of the soldiers were housed, but they, too, struggled when their traditional red-light districts and entertainment establishments started catering to large numbers of American GIs.

The absorption of so many young and single men, far away from home and removed from the bonds of family, was even more difficult for communities that had not previously hosted American troops and for the small, provincial towns of the Rhineland-Palatinate where much of the military buildup during the 1950s took place. For example, Baumholder, a small provincial town with just 3,000 inhabitants, saw an influx of almost 30,000 soldiers when the Americans reactivated a huge training camp that had been built by the Nazi regime. During the early 1950s, when much of the military buildup took place, the newly established American garrison towns did not have the law-enforcement capabilities to deal with the influx of so many single young men and all the social problems associated with a large foreign military presence. Exacerbating those problems was the fact that fewer than 30 percent of the soldiers sent to Germany were married, and an even lower percentage had brought their wives, a privilege that was available only to soldiers of the military rank of E-5 and above (Hough 1979, 46).[53] Even larger towns such as Kaiserslautern (80,000 inhabitants) struggled mightily to cope with the 40,000 troops that were stationed in the large military installations of Kaiserslautern, Ramstein, and Landstuhl. Neither Baumholder nor Kaiserslautern had an existing red-light district that could cater to the American troops. When these communities had hosted German Wehrmacht troops during the Third Reich, the German military had provided brothels for its soldiers.[54]

In all of these small and midsize garrison towns, the new troop deployments were accompanied by the emergence of boom towns (Höhn 2002, chaps. 2, 3).[55] Especially around the huge U.S. military training camps of Baumholder, Wildflecken, and Grafenwöhr, which saw regular and large-scale troop rotations, neighboring rural villages turned into seedy places with bars and clubs that offered American music, striptease, and all sorts of entertainment for the GIs.[56] The small town of Baumholder sported some eighty GI bars during the 1950s. Catering to the soldiers' needs created an unprecedented economic boom in all of the new garrison towns, but the boom came at a steep price. The dreaded "hunger prostitution" of the immediate postwar years gave way to what social workers called "occupation prostitution" as young women from all over Germany, and even from other European countries, flocked to the new U.S. military bases in search of their fortune. On the soldiers' payday, women arrived from the Netherlands,

FIGURE 3.1. Street with GI bars in the town of Baumholder, where 20,000 Americans lived side by side with 5,000 Germans. COURTESY HEINRICH BRUCKER.

Belgium, Italy, and Austria. Many came to make a fast dollar and left town only once the GIS' dollars were spent. But many other desperate women arrived hoping to find an American husband who would take them to the United States. Similar to the so-called shack-up relationships of the occupation years, these women entered into monogamous relationships with just one soldier, hoping for marriage, but just as often they were passed on to another GI once the soldier was transferred to the United States (Höhn 2002, chap. 4).

In the eyes of German officials, what distinguished the new phenomenon of "occupation prostitution" from the "hunger prostitution" of the immediate postwar years was the fact that the liaisons with the American GIS were no longer a matter of sheer physical survival. While the young women who flocked to American military bases often were still suffering from the effects of war (many were orphaned or widowed and few of them had prospects for decent jobs), they were also making a conscious choice. They believed that their liaisons with American soldiers offered them a better life than the low-paying jobs in factories or domestic service offered by German social-welfare agencies. It was these women's matter-of-fact "calculations" about their emotional and sexual lives that convinced German authorities that the relationships were not based on "real love" and that the women were indeed prostitutes.

German authorities in all of the garrison towns felt overwhelmed by the explosion of the entertainment industry and the introduction of cohabitation into their communities, and their state governments undertook decisive steps to get on top of the situation. While a loosening of sexual norms had been going on in German cities for decades, the provinces had no experience with striptease bars or with young couples living together outside of wedlock. Furthermore, the sexual disorder of the immediate postwar years was experienced as an unpleasant side effect of war. Now that those years were overcome, and Germany was on its path to regain full political sovereignty, there was much less tolerance of such sexual disorder. German authorities were convinced that only the establishment of bordellos would remedy the situation, but just as it had during the years of occupation, the American military refused all German pleas to establish bordellos for its troops. To rein in the situation, all German states that experienced large-scale American troop deployments outlawed prostitution in communities with fewer than 20,000 inhabitants. To enforce the new laws, huge vice raids were conducted in the places were soldiers congregated to expose and apprehend "secret prostitutes." Just as they had during the years of occupation, German police and American military police conducted the vice raids together. That collaboration was necessary because the Occupation Statute, which was in force until Germany gained full sovereignty in 1955, allowed American GIs to protect any female companion from the jurisdiction of the German police; the soldier merely had to claim that the woman in his company was his wife. Furthermore, without American material support in the form of trucks, vans, and busses, the large-scale raids would have been logistically impossible.

And just as they had been during the years of military occupation, plenty of "decent girls" were apprehended in the random raids. Local women in the company of American fiancés or steady boyfriends were often also picked up and brought to the Health Offices for gynecological exams. In light of such embarrassing mistakes, and because more liberal elements of the population thought that such indiscriminate raids trampled on the rights of young women, German and American officials developed a more differentiated strategy on how to conduct the vice raids. As the new garrison towns settled in with their new neighbors, and as Germans came to realize that the American military would be staying for the unforeseeable future, a "gentlemen's agreement" emerged about how best to protect "local women" from the sexual advances of the GIs. While prostitution was outlawed in all

FIGURE 3.2. Soldier's bride in Baumholder watching the troops marching through town. The young boys on bicycles are clearly taken with the soldiers. COURTESY *DER STERN*.

communities with fewer than 20,000 inhabitants that hosted American troops, "secret prostitution" and "shack-up" relationships were widely tolerated. Local communities subverted the newly passed laws of their state governments, because officials agreed that the so-called soldiers' brides (*Soldatenbräute*) willing to enter into cohabitation protected "decent local women" from the sexual advances of the soldiers. Furthermore, unlike the professional prostitutes who came from big cities only on the soldiers' paydays, the "soldiers' brides" who lived locally kept the GIs' dollars in town. As long as the women remained in monogamous, if serial, relationships, they would be left alone. The Americans agreed to this bargain, because protecting "decent local women" from the sexual advances of the GIS was crucial to maintaining civil relations with the German population.

As the prostitution-enforcement records in all garrison towns with American troops make all too clear, German and American officials and law-enforcement officers agreed that wherever there were soldiers, there would be prostitutes, and if prostitution could not be stopped, the worst excesses would have to be contained. Inherent in this unspoken understanding, as I show below, was the view that punishment would be reserved for the worst offenders: the women who associated with African American GIS. When German and American officials pursued this course of action during the

1950s, they followed precedents that had already been established during the years of occupation. By ritually cleansing the communities surrounding U.S. military bases of "vice and smut," German and American officials pacified conservative Christian Democrats who feared for Germany's soul but also appeased the leftist Social Democrats who had not yet reconciled themselves to Germany's remilitarization under American auspices. By focusing on black GIs and their white German girlfriends, officials assured furthermore that the precious German-American military and political alliance would not be threatened.

America's Troubling Racial Divide

No discussion of fraternization, prostitution, the fight against VD, and the sexual or romantic relations between GIs and German women would be complete without acknowledging the deep racial divide within the military. Having arrived in Germany to cure the Germans of the racial hatred that had culminated in the Holocaust, the U.S. military government, in one of its first acts, repealed the Nuremburg Race Laws. The Nazi regime had passed those laws in 1935 to criminalize sexual relations and marriage not only between so-called Aryan Germans and Jews but also between "Aryans" and "Gypsies" (Roma and Sinti) and people of color. That first step of de-Nazification was followed up with an extensive reeducation program to teach the Germans that "the whole concept of superiority . . . and intolerance of others is evil" and that America was the "living denial of Hitler's absurd theories of a superior race."[57] At the same time that the U.S. military government was implementing this noble agenda, Germany was being occupied and reeducated with a strictly segregated military that was disproportionately commanded by officers from Southern states. Despite Truman's Executive Order of 1948 to integrate the military, it would take until 1952 for military commanders, under much pressure from the State Department, finally to agree to integrate the European Command. That integration was accomplished in November 1953, largely to stop the relentless Soviet and East German propaganda that exposed as hypocrisy America's claim to be the leader of the so-called Free World (Höhn 2002, chap. 3; Höhn 2005; Höhn and Klimke, 2010, chaps. 3 and 4).[58]

Given the context of the Jim Crow U.S. Army and a German society freshly emerging from Nazism, it is hardly surprising that interracial couples faced widespread contempt from both Germans and Americans. German and American officials all too quickly assumed that any woman in the company of a black soldier was a prostitute.[59] The shared assumptions about these relationships and the close collaboration between Germans and American officials in reining in interracial couples convinced many Germans furthermore that their new democracy was fully compatible with opposition to interracial romances and marriages. Not surprisingly, the importation of an American-style color line into post–Nazi Germany had dire consequences for interracial couples. That color line would not be successfully challenged until the emergence of the American Civil Rights Movement and its reverberations in Germany (Höhn 2005, 2008b; Höhn and Klimke 2010, chaps. 4 and 8); see also chapter 10 in this book).

To understand how German racism was "Americanized" after 1945, it is necessary to explore in more detail how the creation of the American base system after 1945 also meant that the American color line was taken outside the United States. Given the makeup of the Army's officer corps, it is hardly surprising that commanders were less than thrilled to employ African American GIs for occupation duty in Germany, and officers made their opposition known to the War Department.[60] Initial efforts to have African American soldiers returned to the United States failed, however, because the War Department feared repercussions from African American civil-rights activists. Commanders, who disproportionately hailed from the U.S. South, nonetheless made every effort to limit African American GIs from experiencing a sense of empowerment in their role as occupiers and masters over a white population.[61] Time and again, black soldiers complained about how their commanders and the military police tried to discourage them from associating with the German population.[62] Commanders, for example, tried to limit the interaction between black GIs and German civilians by not granting passes to soldiers who wanted to visit German pubs. Since the military was racially segregated, it was also easy to isolate all-black units as far away as possible from the German civilian population.[63]

The fact that America's traditional color line was being undermined in post-Nazi Germany because of the widespread fraternization of black GIs with German women was even more disturbing to many commanders (Starr 1947, 88–89).[64] A military report from June 1945 reveals that, for many commanders, it was unfathomable that romantic or sexual relationships between black men and white women could be based on mutual attraction. In attempting to explain the widespread phenomenon of fraternization, the report concluded, the white soldier was "teased [by German women] until his physical make-up has been overtried." The report continued that, when it came to fraternizing, "Negro troops are perhaps the worst offenders. . . . When they see the opportunity they take it. Some 30 rape cases are now on

record of which the large majority is credited to Negro soldiers."[65] Given
how easily this observer slipped from commenting on the widespread "seduction" of white soldiers to rape by black soldiers, it is perhaps not surprising that black GIS, who constituted about 10 percent of U.S. Army personnel
in 1945, were found guilty of committing 48 percent of the 620 rapes brought
to trial between V-E Day and the end of June 1946 (Geis 1952a, 27, 1952b, 138).
Robert Lilly's examination of rape trials that ended in the death penalty
shows an even greater racial bias: 83 percent of soldiers executed for rape
were African American, and Lilly makes a forceful argument that the severity
of punishment was part of an effort by the military-justice system to reestablish the American color line that had been undermined starting with the
American troop deployment in Great Britain in 1943.[66]

The condemnation of interracial romantic relationships within the overall
military command structure also found expression in how the American military police treated such couples. Military police, as African American civil-
rights leaders complained, employed "strong-arm methods" at the "mere
sight of a Negro soldier and a white girl." They regularly tried to separate such
couples, arresting the women for prostitution and brutalizing the soldiers.[67]
While some German parents were willing to overcome their own racial prejudices and embraced the black boyfriends their daughters brought home, they
were in the minority. Plenty of Germans appreciated the generosity of the
black GIS and mocked the widespread racism of their American mentors, but
they also did not approve of the black soldiers' romantic and sexual relationships with German women (Höhn 2002, chaps. 3, 5, 8).

I have shown how pragmatic the military could be when it allowed the
German "girlfriends" or "fiancées" of their troops to follow units to different
deployments in Germany. This camp following was tolerated because having
stable partners was seen as crucial to maintaining morale among the soldiers.
No such tolerance could be found when it came to camp followers of African
American GIS, whose units were generally under the command of white officers.[68] White, Southern military commanders of black units would not be
likely to "sponsor" their soldiers' white girlfriends when a unit was moved,
and in light of the material shortages, German officials were less than eager
to support newcomers to town, especially if the women were living in
intimate relationships with black men. Thus, many of the women who
associated with black GIS led lives of marginality and illegality, often following redeployed troops without the necessary papers and permits. That
pattern of marginality continued even after the end of military government in 1949, when it became much easier for Germans to move outside the

zonal boundaries. Many of the women who followed their soldier boyfriends ended up in sordid squatter camps outside of the towns and villages where black units were deployed, or they lived in traditionally marginal neighborhoods where landlords were less concerned about observing bourgeois notions of propriety (Höhn 2002, 202).[69]

Because of their socially marginalized circumstance and their choice of boyfriends, such women were also much more prone to be included in the dragnet of a vice or VD raid during the 1950s, since these raids usually were aimed at places where the "worst offenders" could be found. Thus, when American military police and German officials made decisions on where to conduct raids, they usually agreed that the marginal neighborhoods where the girlfriends of black soldiers lived, were to be policed most stringently. The same officials also agreed that bars and clubs frequented by black GIS would net the highest numbers of suspected prostitutes or carriers of VD. While all places that catered to GIS could be possible targets for vice raids, during the height of the struggle against VD in the immediate postwar years authorities were sensitive to strike only what they considered to be the "worst offenders" and the "seediest establishments." Given the prevalent racism among American and German police officers, all too often, this meant places that were popular among African American GIS and their German women friends. This strategy of targeting black-only bars came to define the collaborative German–American struggle against prostitution in all garrison towns (Höhn 2002, chaps. 7–8).[70]

The records in all garrison towns show clearly that the combined efforts of German and American police officers to contain *all* prostitution turned instead into a containment of interracial sexuality. The prostitution records in the town of Baumholder are especially instructive. Although only about 12 percent of the troops stationed in Germany were African American, 70–80 percent of the women indicted for prostitution appeared before the local court because they had been arrested in a bar or club frequented by black GIS. Interestingly enough, the strategy of singling out women who had relationships with black GIS can also be observed in larger towns and cities where prostitution was legal. Although both white and black soldiers frequented prostitutes and had shack-up relationships with German women, the great majority of vice raids—often under the pretense of discovering tax-free American goods—were conducted in those neighborhoods where African American GIS and their female friends resided. Many raids to uncover "secret prostitutes" were also initiated under the cover of exposing landlords or hotel owners who rented rooms or apartments to unmarried couples,

FIGURE 3.3. German–American vice raid in the late 1950s outside Ramstein Air Base. COURTESY DOKUMENTATIONS- UND AUSSTELLUNGSZENTRUM ZUR GESCHICHTE DER AIR BASE RAMSTEIN UND DER US-AMERIKANER IN RHEINLAND-PFALZ.

which, unlike prostitution, was illegal in Germany at the time. Here too, the record shows that hotels and landlords who rented rooms or apartments to black GIs and their women partners faced much closer scrutiny (Höhn 2002, chaps. 7–8).

For all these reasons, women who associated with African American GIs were much more vulnerable to police measures than women who associated with white GIs. But they were easy targets also because of still existing racial legislation in the United States. We have seen how crucial the shift in late 1946 to let GIs marry their German partners was in at least partly "legitimizing" the relationships between German women and white GIs. This legitimization did not happen for black GIs and their white partners. Due to the anti-miscegenation laws that still existed in many of the U.S. states until 1967, commanders remained reluctant, if not outright opposed, to grant wedding permits for black GIs and German women.[71] Not surprisingly, commanders' approval rates for black GIs to marry German women stood in sharp contrast to the approval rates for white GIS. In 1948, 64.3 percent of the marriage applications of white GIS were approved, while the other 35.7 percent were merely "temporarily suspended due to administrative difficulties." In 1949, only 22 out of 280 applications of black GIS had received a positive reply; 91 were denied; 57 never received a response; and 110 were allegedly still "in process."[72] Black GIS argued that these long delays were used to prevent marriages, and they complained bitterly to the National Association for the Advancement of Colored People (NAACP) that they were not allowed to make honest women out of their girlfriends, let alone legitimize their children.[73]

Since the military by the early 1950s had committed itself to equality before the law regardless of race, commanders reluctant to allow black GIS to bring home "white brides" used all sorts of strategies to prevent such marriages. They were obviously very successful. Out of 110 applications for interracial marriage in 1952, only 4 received their commanders' approval, even though all of the men already had children with their German partners (Frankenstein 1954, 26).[74] Applications were routinely lost; soldiers who applied for permits would be reassigned to other commands in Germany or even worse, were shipped back to the United States.[75] This strategy was even used when a woman was pregnant, earning black GIS a reputation for abandoning their babies, even though the record shows that they provided much more regularly for their offspring than did white GIS (Geis 1952b, 160–62). Other soldiers were granted permission to marry but were then informed that they would ship out to the United States within a few days, thus preventing the marriage from taking place. Another hurdle that the military imposed was the provision that the soldier had to prove his financial ability to "keep" a wife so that she would not become a public charge. Although that rule applied equally to white and black soldiers, it left plenty of room for discriminatory practices. Since the military regulations did not specify the financial resources that this mandate entailed, it was up to individual commanders to assess soldiers' future ability to be good providers. As late as 1957, some commanders granted wedding permits to interracial couples only if the soldier had enough financial resources to return his wife to Germany should the marriage fail. In light of the expense of transatlantic travel at the time, the provision created an almost impossible barrier. This was a particularly harsh burden for lower-rank personnel, because the military also did not pay for the wives' travel to the United States.[76]

Attitudes within the military toward interracial marriages shifted slowly, and it would take the advances of the Civil Rights Movement and the U.S. Supreme Court's decision in *Loving v. Virginia* (1967), which finally made anti-miscegenation laws unconstitutional, to make it easier for black GIS to marry their German partners. By the early 1970s, 10–15 percent of all marriages between American soldiers and German women involved a black partner, a ratio that was much more representative of the number of African American GIS stationed in Germany (Hough 1979, 198). Despite this shift, the damage to black-white romantic relationships had been done, since the military used all measures available to discourage such marriages for so many years (Höhn 2010b; Höhn 2011).

Epilogue

The boomtowns around American military bases, unlike the boomtowns in Japan and Korea, started to go downhill with the coming of West Germany's economic miracle. That economic boom, fueled to a large degree by the war in Korea, came later for German women than for society at large, and as a consequence West Germany's economic miracle of the late 1950s led to a decrease in, but not an end to, the boomtown industry. However, as better jobs became available in the early 1960s, fewer women were willing to find their fortunes in garrison towns hosting American troops. The death knell of the boomtowns, however, came only when the administration of President Richard M. Nixon uncoupled the dollar from the gold standard in the early 1970s and the dollar started its precipitous slide downward. As German society was prospering, the American GIS were no longer an economic force to be reckoned with. Further, with the emergence of the drug culture in the military in the 1960s and 1970s, more GIS started venturing to Amsterdam or to large German cities on weekend trips, where both sex *and* drugs were readily available. By the early 1970s, many of the bars and clubs that had caused outrage in German provincial towns that hosted American troops during the 1950s and 1960s had been forced to close their doors. Former boomtowns such as Baumholder, which had been home to some eighty GI bars in the 1950s, sported fewer than a handful of clubs in the 1980s, and none in the 1990s. As a consequence of the boomtown collapse, most of the entertainment industry relocated to large urban centers. There, GIS frequent houses of prostitution that cater to German clients, tourists, and Germany's immigrant workers. During the 1980s, one of the most popular establishments catering to U.S. soldiers, the Crazy Sexy Bordello in Frankfurt, was packed with GIS on every payday, with the U.S. military's Courtesy Patrols walking the halls to keep order (Seiler 1985, 139).

In Germany, unlike in Japan and Okinawa or Korea, the boomtowns were also doomed because of the shift to an all-volunteer U.S. Army, with a much more developed professional ethos and esprit de corps than had prevailed during the draft. Soldiers who were going to make their lives in the military were also much more likely to be settled in their personal lives. Unlike in the 1950s, when only about 30 percent of soldiers were married, 40 percent of enlisted men were married in 1973. After the introduction of the all-volunteer military, that percentage rose to 57 percent in 1994 and had stabilized at about 55 percent by 2007.[77] In contradistinction to Korea, where soldiers serve without families and for only one year, a large percentage of soldiers serving in Germany bring their families. The members of the U.S. military, just like American society as a whole, have also become more religious in the past few decades, with a larger proportion belonging to fundamentalist churches that frown on drinking and vice. In Baumholder, as in many other former boomtowns, many of the onetime bars and striptease joints have been converted into evangelical or fundamentalist churches that cater to the GIS and their families.

The military's decision in the early 1980s to integrate women into its all-male units also brought about a much more inward-looking military. Not only are more enlisted men married in today's military and have their wives and families with them in Germany, but single soldiers also have more opportunity to find sexual partners in the military. As the ratio of women in the military rose from 8 percent in the late 1970s to 17 percent in 2002, the need to find female companionship in neighboring German communities diminished substantially. Whereas 129 marriages took place between American GIS and German women in the town of Kaiserslautern in 1960, twenty years later, a mere 37 GIS took German wives.[78] In the 1980s, German inns and hotels that once catered to American GIS and German *Fräuleins* started to rent to intra-military lovers who rented rooms over weekends to escape the dreariness of barracks life. But just as often, these couples would marry, because marriage made them eligible for family housing on the base.[79]

Even after the drawdown of American troops in the wake of communism's collapse, some 70,000 American military personnel and their families are still stationed in Germany today. Despite this substantial presence, many of the American garrison towns are shadows of their former selves. The attacks on military installations by Red Army terrorists during the 1970s and 1980, the German peace movement of the 1980s, and, finally, the rise of Islamic terrorism in the past few years have forced Americans behind ever higher barricades and thicker coils of barbed wire. The swagger of the postwar years—the grinning "max nix" (not to worry) attitude of the American soldiers in the 1950s as well as the widespread fraternization of American GIS with German women—belong to a distant past that no longer reverberates for Germany's younger generation or for American troops stationed there now. An anthropological study of U.S. military bases in Germany during the 1990s reveals just how dramatic a shift has taken place: there is not one mention of the entertainment industry or of sexual relations between American GIS and German women (Hawkins 2001).

America's latest wars in Iraq and Afghanistan, however, have brought about a reversal. Baumholder, for example, which is home to the First Armored Division, has watched "its" soldiers being sent to Iraq five times, with the division's last deployment taking place in November 2009. Just as they did during the Korean War and the Vietnam War, city officials and the local community are struggling to integrate returning troops who not only have been brutalized by war but are also ready to have a good time. As a result of the war in Iraq, all garrison towns in Germany have been experiencing increased levels of crime, drug use, brawling soldiers, and vandalism. The war in Iraq also has brought a whole new chapter of the sex industry. Baumholder again has a number of clubs that offer hot music, striptease, lap dancing, and prostitutes. To rein in the worst excesses of young soldiers out about town, and to quell the complaints of local residents about an increasingly intolerable situation, Baumholder's military commander imposed a 2 A.M. curfew on his soldiers in September 2007, demanding that all downtown establishments close by that time. With that drastic step, the commander hopes to eliminate some of the worst excesses by having soldiers off the street and back in the barracks by 2 A.M. Such a drastic step, as well as the commanders' threat of an off-limits order if local bar owners do not comply, was last taken during the Vietnam War, and before that during the Korean War, thus revealing once more the global connections of America's military empire.[80]

Notes

1. Relationships between French soldiers and German women were limited by the fact that the French brought the soldiers' families and provided bordellos (segregated for its white and colonial soldiers) for single soldiers. The British military did not provide bordellos for its soldiers, but romantic relationships with German women occurred on a much more limited basis for a variety of reasons. Stricter military discipline, the memory of the London Blitz, and the relative poverty of British soldiers (compared with that of American GIS) did much to limit interactions.

2. As historians of the Russian zone have shown, approximately one million German

women were raped when the Red Army advanced into Germany and during the weeks following the fall of Berlin. By mid-1947, Soviet military authorities had moved their enlisted men to tightly controlled compounds, and by 1948, they effectively had been cut off from East German society. This rigid separation of troops from the civilian population would remain the norm until the drawdown of Soviet troops after the collapse of communism. For the rapes after the Second World War, see Grossmann 1995, 43–63; Naimark 1995, 116–21; Timm, 1998, 174–215. For women's descriptions of the rapes, see Anonymous 1959.

3. The exhibit in the Museum of the History of the Federal Republic in Bonn (built when Bonn was still the capital of Germany, before unification in 1990) features images of GIS and German women arm in arm etched into a steel wall that greets visitors at they enter. For an excellent discussion of Germany's zero hour and gender relations, see Heinemann 1996.

4. The women who had been raped received some sympathy from Germans, but many other Germans also wondered whether they had fought off their attackers hard enough or whether perhaps only "morally weak" women fell victim to Soviet soldiers: see Heinemann 1996. See also *Worüber kaum gesprochen wurde: Frauen und alliierte Soldaten* [Something hardly ever talked about; women and allied soldiers], exhibition catalogue, Heimatmuseum Berlin-Charlottenburg, 20, 27.

5. *Handbook for Unit Commanders (Germany)*, 1944, AMHI, 57–62. For a detailed discussion of the development of the ban on fraternization and its demise, see Kleinschmidt 1997, 35–39, 67.

6. The G-2 memo that suggests the creation of bordellos is cited in Kleinschmidt 1997, 36. The two quotes are from Circular no. 49, HQ ETO (European Theater of Operations), 2 May 1944, and "Preventive Medicine Division OofdCSurg, HQ ETOUSA (European Theater of Operations USA), Annual Report, 1944," and are cited in Cosamas and Cowdrey 1992, 173. See also Geis and Gray 1951, 35 for specific instructions for Germany.

7. Aside from drawing on military reports and histories written by the Army's Historical Division, I consulted memoirs, participant observer reports, newspaper coverage of the occupation, and popular movies produced at the time.

8. It is noteworthy that the U.S. military was much more willing to circumvent official War Department policy outside the physical boundaries of the United States. In a thoughtful essay, Paul Kramer (2006) made that case for the Philippines during the Spanish-American War, and Beth Bailey and David Farber (Bailey and Farber 1994) have argued thus regarding U.S. policies in Hawaii during the Second World War.

9. Despite the strict orders from Washington, D.C., to avoid all contacts with the defeated Germans, fraternization was widespread from the moment U.S. forces entered German territory. Unable to enforce their own discipline, military leaders relented partially, and in June 1945, children younger than ten were excluded from the non-fraternization policy. By 1 October 1945, the fraternization ban was further relaxed, because the military commanders' inability to control their troops seriously undermined the prestige of the occupation authority in the eyes of the Germans.

Despite this relaxation, two important exclusions remained: GIS still could not be billeted with German families and they were not allowed to marry Germany women: see Kleinschmidt 1997, 133, 166.

10. Unfortunately, White does not provide the names of these commanders.

11. This view was put forth in the popular film *A Foreign Affair* (Wilder 1948), which depicted the sexual exploits of U.S. occupation troops in Germany. Wilder, a Jewish refugee from Austria, was part of the American military occupation in Germany and thus had an insider's view of the situation. For a similar view of the military that "angels rightfully belong in heaven," see Brandt 1985, 164.

12. "VD Survey, Armed Forces Europe no. 96," 25 April 1949, NARA, RG 549, box 2193, 12.

13. Ibid. Interestingly, the same survey showed that 34 percent of single GIS believed that it was wrong to have sex outside marriage: ibid., 10.

14. See the iconic German movie of such a relationship, *The Marriage of Maria Braun* (Fassbinder 1979), and the postwar novel *Off Limits* (Habe 1957). Habe was a European émigré who had fled Nazism and returned as an officer as part of the American military occupation.

15. By the end of the war, about 9.2 million German soldiers were POWs. By the end of 1945, about 4.4 million POWs had returned to Germany; 1.8 million more had been released by the end of 1946; 1.6 million had been released by the end of 1947; about 811,000 had been released by the end of 1948; about 443,000 had been released by the end of 1949; and about 23,000 had been released by the end of 1950: Meyer and Schulz 1985, 223, 253.

16. Even after troop rotations to Japan and demobilization to the United States, approximately 614,000 GIS remained in Germany at the end of 1945. The smooth occupation of Germany meant that troop reductions continued in 1946, when 400,000 more GIS were returned to the United States. By 1948, a mere 90,374 soldiers were deemed necessary to ensure the goals of the occupation: see Kleinschmidt 1997, 133.

17. For women's comments on why they found GIS attractive, see Domentat 1998; Scibetta and Shukert 1988; Goedde 2003; and chapter 8 in this book.

18. Joseph Starr (1947, 80–82) describes how surprised authorities were at the "large number of rapes." American military records indicate that about 1,000 German women brought charges of rape against advancing American troops in the spring of 1945. See Graham Cosamas and Albert Cowdrey (1992, 584) for their conclusion that "rape by American soldiers was common, often requiring neither violence [n]or threats." Osmar White was an Australian war correspondent with the Third Army in Germany and he writes, "There was a good deal of rape by combat troops and those immediately following them. The incidence varied between unit and unit according to the attitude of the commanding officer." He also reports that African Americans were executed if the crime was considered "brutal or perverted" but that plenty of white soldiers brutally raped German women without being thus punished: White 1996, 97.

19. If convicted, the offender could face the death penalty or life in prison. By July 1945, 169 soldiers had been tried for rape, with 29 soldiers executed for rape and 14 executed for rape that resulted in the death of the victim. In all, 70 soldiers were executed in the European Theater of Operation between 1941 and 1946, and 5 more had been executed by 1950: see Kleinschmidt 1997, 104.

20. Starr (1947, 83) cites 402 cases in March; 501 in April; and 241 in May. After that, reported rape cases stabilized at 45 a month.

21. The numbers are from Heineman 1999, 283, n. 95.

22. Walter Slatoff, "GI Morals in Germany," *The Nation*, 13 May 1946.

23. Wonderful depictions of such places can be seen in the movies *A Foreign Affair* and *The Marriage of Maria Braun*. For a colorful description of one of these clubs and the sorts of shows that were put on, see Standifer 1997, 171–73.

24. Höhn and Klimke 2010, chaps. 3, 4. For the 1950s, see Höhn 2002, chap. 3.

25. High-ranking officers could easily requisition apartments for themselves from German families and set up house with their German mistresses. For the 1950s, see Höhn 2002, chap. 4.

26. Saul Padover, "Why Americans Like German Women," *American Mercury*, vol. 63, no. 273, September 1946, 354–57. "The Conquerors," *Christian Century*, April 1946, describes in detail how widespread these arrangements were among enlisted men and officers.

27. For this phenomenon in the 1950s see Höhn 2002, chap. 4.

28. "VD Survey, Armed Forces Europe no. 96," 16, endorsed the view that steady girlfriends significantly lowered the number of infections.

29. Many U.S. soldiers were already infected in France, and German women had often been infected by German partners on leave from the front. The mass rapes in the Soviet zone also contributed to these incredible high rates of infection in postwar Germany.

30. For VD rates see, NARA, RG 549, box 2207.

31. On VD rates among officers, see Geis and Gray 1951, 36. On attitudes of the military toward VD rates among blacks, see "McNarney Ignores Report, Isolates GIS," *Pittsburgh Courier*, 26 October 1946. Ulysses Grant Lee (1966, 276–81) has argued that rates for African Americans were higher because many black GIS arrived in Europe already infected because they had been unable to receive treatment due to the inadequate health care in the states of the American South.

32. During the First World War, the military established a policy that soldiers would not receive pay while being treated for VD. In 1926, Congress made that policy into a law, but by September 1944, the law was repealed.

33. An interview with James Boyd, an African American officer, describing how commanders tried to rein in VD is in NARA, RG 107, box 265.

34. See "Memorandum, Sec[retary] of War Robert Patterson for Deputy Chief of Staff, 7 January 1947," written by Marcus Ray, reprinted in Nalty and McGregor 1981, 217.

35. See, e.g., the photograph of such a poster in *Life*, 10 February 1947. I am grateful to Jan Lambertz for sharing this information with me. On the poster campaign, see Starr 1947, 26.

36. In *The Marriage of Maria Braun* (Fassbinder 1979), the main character has to get a gynecological exam from her doctor before she can work as a taxi girl in an American club.

37. Jennifer Evans (2001, 164–69) shows that young male adolescents were not included in the vice raids. The U.S. military never acknowledged homosexuality and thus never included male prostitutes as a possible source of infection for its troops. When male

prostitutes were observed and apprehended by German authorities, it was because homosexuality was criminalized.

38. Such vice raids were conducted in the 1950s largely to uncover "secret" heterosexual prostitution and thus also targeted only women: see Höhn 2002, 184, 202.

39. In the German state of Hesse, which was part of the American zone of occupation, 6,719 people were picked up in this manner between February and July 1947. Vivid depictions of such all-encompassing vice raids can be seen in the films *A Foreign Affair* (Wilder 1948) and *Fräulein* (Koster 1958). See also Evans 2001, 163–64.

40. The same sorts of mistakes were made during the 1950s when the vice raids were largely conducted to stamp out prostitution in U.S. garrison towns in Germany: see Höhn 2002, 184–85.

41. Doctors were not allowed to use the issued penicillin for other illnesses. The military instituted strict controls to prevent German physicians from giving it to patients who did not have VD.

42. The "elimination of undesirables" among soldiers who showed repeated infection was part of the program. They were forced to leave the service without an honorable discharge.

43. For the military's education efforts, see NARA, RG 549, box 2193.

44. *A Foreign Affair* brought the sexual excesses of the U.S. occupation to a wide American audience. See also "The Conqueror"; "Occupation: The GI Legacy in Germany," *Newsweek*, 16 June 1947; "Fraternization: The Word Takes on a Brand New Meaning in Germany," *Life*, 2 July 1945; "German Girls: U.S. Army Boycott Fails to Stop GIs from Fraternizing with Them," *Life*, 23 July 1945.

45. "Fraternizing Irks Reich's Ex-Soldiers," *New York Times*, 23 August 1945. See also Biddiscombe 2001, 611–47.

46. For a critical overview of the U.S. policy and how it had hurt U.S. prestige, see "Occupation: The GI Legacy in Germany." The article claims that the ban on fraternization had led to "mass disobedience that destroyed the Army's prestige and morale, a blow from which it is only now recovering": *Newsweek*, 16 June 1947. See also Ziemke 1975, 324.

47. Lieutenant General Frederick E. Morgan, deputy commander of the Supreme Headquarters Allied Expeditionary Force, suggested in a memo to G-1 (Deputy Chief of Staff-Personnel) dated August 1944 that female employees of the military and the Red Cross could provide appropriate companionship to the troops and thus would prevent them from seeking out German women: cited in Kleinschmidt 1997, 40, 120.

48. See, e.g., "Black Market Crackdown," *Newsweek*, 9 December 1946; "Curbing a Conqueror's Complex," *Newsweek*, 6 May 1946. See also Koster 1958; Habe 1949, 1957; Padover, "Why Americans Like German Women"; Smith 1948.

49. On the military's policies toward marriage, see Geis 1951, 20–29. To protect "innocent" soldiers from "crafty" German women, cumbersome procedures were installed. Any soldier younger than twenty-one had to get permission from his parents. The soldier also had to get permission from his commanding officer, and the application for any such marriage could be filed only in a narrow time frame (no earlier than six months and no later than three months before the wedding). The wedding itself

could only be performed one month before the soldier's return to the United States to ensure that the wife would not live in Germany as a military dependent spouse and thus benefit from the American standard of living. Furthermore, the prospective wife had to undergo a barrage of tests and examinations that assured her mental, physical, moral, and political integrity. For numbers of marriages, see Kleinschmidt 1997, 166–70.

50. In the mid-1970s, Patricia Hough interviewed numerous German women who had married GIS, and they all felt compelled to inform her "that they were not the typical kind" associating with American GIS: see Hough 1979, 128.

51. See Höhn 2002 for an extensive discussion of the impact of the deployments in the 1950s.

52. While the United States made every effort to convince the Germans that the Americans were no longer an occupying power but, instead, allies and a protective force, Germans, in private conversations, official documents, and news coverage, continued to refer to the Americans as "the occupation" for years to come. The deep gulf between the standard of living of Americans and Germans continued well into the 1950s, exacerbating the sense of German subjection to American might. At a time when a married German worker with two children earned, on average, about 280 deutsche marks, the lowest-grade private was paid $100, or the equivalent of 420 deutsche marks, and had his room and board paid for: see Höhn 2002, 43, 87.

53. On the special case of Baumholder, one of the U.S. military's largest trainings camps outside the United States, see Höhn 2002.

54. The discussion of developments during the 1950s is based on Höhn 2002.

55. For a description of an American boomtown, see Lutz 2001.

56. For a detailed description of the entertainment industry in Baumholder and Kaiserslautern, see Höhn 2002 chaps 3, 4, 8.

57. "Orientation Program for Dependents," AMHI, Occupation of Germany, 1944–48, miscellaneous files, 7, 17.

58. See also Fehrenbach 2005.

59. Arthur Harris to Secretary of War, letter regarding interracial marriage, NARA, RG 407, box 719. See also Starr 1947, 146–53.

60. On efforts to remove black soldiers from Germany, see Geis 1952b, 16, 142–44.

61. Secretary of War, "Civil Aide to the Secretary, Attitudes of Negro Soldiers, July 1945," NARA, RG 107, Box 265, lists numerous exit interviews with white and black soldiers that give a sense of just how liberating the war experience was for black GIS and how threatened many white Americans were because black GIS had experienced power over a white population in Europe. For a detailed description of that experience see Höhn 2002, chaps. 3, 4; Höhn and Klimke 2010, chapters 2 and 3.

62. "Report of the Negro Newspaper Publishers Association to the Honorable Secretary of War, Judge Robert P. Patterson, on Troop Conditions in Europe," 18 July 1946, NARA, RG 407, box 719, 6.

63. "McNarney Ignores Report, Isolates GIS"; Smith 1948. "Report of the Negro Newspaper Publishers Association to the Honorable Secretary of War, Judge Robert P. Patterson, on Troop Conditions in Europe," 8.

64. German women were attracted to the "otherness" of the African American GIs, but just as prevalent in recollections of these encounters is the fact that black soldiers treated the Germans very kindly. Since the vast majority of black GIs were deployed not in combat units but in labor, supply, and service units, they had unlimited access to treasured American goods, and their generosity in sharing those goods with the desperate and hungry German people remains a powerful metaphor of the occupation to this day. For contemporary depictions of these relationships, see Boyle 1963; Habe 1957; Smith 1948; Standifer 1997, 142. See coverage in the African American press: "Tan Yanks Still Popular with Germans although Chocolate Bars no Longer Buy Friends as in Early Occupation," *Ebony*, January 1952; "Tan Yanks Shared Their Food and Won Hearts of German Girls," *Pittsburgh Courier*, 8 December 1945. See also Höhn 2005, 2009 and Höhn and Klimke 2010, chap. 3.

65. "Report of the XXIII Corps," 22 June 1945, reprinted in Wünschel 1985, 341. See also, "First U.S. Army G5 Historical Report," May 1945, NARA, RG 407, which alleges that 55 percent of all sexual crime was committed by African American GIs, although they only made up 3.3 percent of the First Army's troop strength. When I viewed these documents they were not yet archived by NARA, but were part of a large collection of military records stored at NARA in moving cartons.

66. Lilly 1995 and Lilly and Thomson 1997 show the bias in U.S. military justice in detail.

67. "Report of the Negro Newspaper Publishers Association to the Honorable Secretary of War, Judge Robert P. Patterson, on Troop Conditions in Europe," 6; Starr 1947, 152–53. See also Davis 2000, 79–91; Smith 1948; Standifer 1997, 171. For the 1950s, see Höhn 2002, chapter 3.

68. Starr (1947, 148) states that "the problem of camp followers was particularly serious in American Negro units." Efforts by American and German authorities to disband the camps by arresting the women often led to violent confrontations between the African American GIs and the German police: see Schroer 2007.

69. Such squatter camps still existed in the 1950s, especially in the first few years of the military buildup: see Höhn 2002, 120.

70. The practice of conducting vice raids primarily in black-only bars had already been established in Great Britain during the war: see Rose 1997, 146–60.

71. In 1948, thirty states had such laws. In 1948, California became the first state to abandon the law. Seven western states quietly invalidated the laws during the 1950s, with four more states following suit before 1965. The remaining holdouts in the U.S. South were forced to invalidate their laws after the Supreme Court decision in *Loving v. Virginia* (1967) declared such laws unconstitutional. For a more detailed discussion, see Höhn 2005, Höhn 2011).

72. For rates among white GIs, see Geis and Gray 1951, 26. For rates among black soldiers for 1949, see Stone 1949, 583.

73. "Soldiers' Marriage Files," Discrimination in the Armed Forces, part 9, reel 15, NAACP. See also Habe 1949 for a depiction of the struggle of a black GI to marry the mother of his child.

74. In 1952, when Luise Frankenstein interviewed 552 women who had had children with

black soldiers, she found that 20 percent planned to marry their partner. Yet of all of these couples, only four had been granted wedding permits: Frankenstein 1954, 26.

75. ES / 56, 18 November 1957, LK, 602.06. In this case, a black soldier was transferred to the United States for expressing outrage when his commanding officer rudely questioned his German fiancée's decision to marry a black man.

76. "When Negro Servicemen Bring Home White Brides," *U.S. News and World Report*, 11 October 1957.

77. Office of the Undersecretary of Defense, Personnel, and Readiness, "Population Representation in the Military Services," available online at http://www.dod.mil/pr home/poprep2002/summary/summary.htm (accessed 18 November 2009).

78. "Wie in einem besetzen Land [As if in an occupied country]," *Der Stern*, 19 May 1982, 94. Until the late 1960s, approximately 5,000 such marriages took place in Germany every year.

79. For the 1980s, see Seiler 1985. Signe Seiler describes intra-military sexual relations and points out that gays in the U.S. military frequent bars in Frankfurt according to racial preference.

80. "Army Enacting 2 A.M. Curfew in Baumholder," *Stars and Stripes*, 20 September 2007.

PART II

CIVILIAN ENTANGLEMENTS WITH THE EMPIRE

American and Foreign Women Abroad and at Home

FOUR

U.S. MILITARY FAMILIES ABROAD
IN THE POST–COLD WAR ERA AND
THE "NEW GLOBAL POSTURE"

☆

DONNA ALVAH

In September 2004, a little more than 202,000 children and other relatives of servicemen and servicewomen resided abroad, well over a decade after the Cold War ended and numerous overseas bases subsequently closed.[1] The previous month, President George W. Bush had announced in a speech to the Veterans of Foreign Wars preliminary plans for what his administration called "a new global posture" that would reduce the number of military personnel stationed abroad by up to 70,000 and the number of "family members and civilian employees" by approximately 100,000. Besides creating a "more agile and flexible force," Bush said, the realignment would result in savings to taxpayers, as well as "greater stability" for military families because service personnel would spend more time in the United States, and family members would move and change jobs less frequently.[2] In promoting the new policy as beneficial to military families, the Bush administration assumed that maintaining them in the United States was preferable to their living abroad. That contrasts with early Cold War–era military wives' arguments that living overseas not only allowed families to be together and to aid the Armed Forces' mission through the support of military husbands, but also enhanced their children's upbringing and offered opportunities for family members to strengthen relations between the United States and the peoples of other nations. Between the late 1940s and the 1980s, when the Soviet Union was the chief rival of the United States, military spouses and policymakers made compelling cases for families to join military personnel posted overseas in stationary, defensive positions to counter perceived threats of invasion from communist nation-states. But those making policy in the aftermath of the September 11, 2001, terrorist attacks believed that having fewer families abroad would allow the United States to deploy its Armed Forces abroad much more quickly and effectively than in earlier decades.

This chapter considers the implications of the new global posture for American military families and for U.S. global militarism. The George W. Bush administration's plan to maintain fewer military families abroad, even as the United States established its military presence in new locations, was just one part of the Department of Defense's effort to shift the emphasis of the Armed Forces "from crisis response—to shaping the future"; "from static defense garrison forces—to mobile, expeditionary operations"; and from "a battle-ready force (peace)—to battle-hardened forces (war)" (U.S. Department of Defense 2006, vi). This renovation can be understood in gendered terms as a re-masculinization of the U.S. military presence abroad, which became more feminized and family-friendly in the aftermath of the Second World War. The concept and implementation of the new global posture, in drastically cutting back the number of American families abroad, revealed a perception of the world as ideally divided between the safe home front demarcated by the geographical boundaries of the United States and the rest of the globe, a domain where U.S. Armed Forces (consisting of women as well as men, although still far more of the latter) venture, fight, and serve in support roles. Yet although the U.S. Armed Forces and, it seems, many military spouses and children themselves have been less inclined than their predecessors six decades ago to see civilian military families living abroad as valuable for sustaining personnel at foreign posts and even for contributing to U.S. diplomatic aims, the U.S. military continues to rely heavily on feminine work "at home" to bolster the overseas activities of its personnel.

In her recent examination of gendered qualities in U.S. military personnel, Regina F. Titunik correctly points out that "the military is a complex environment embodying sometimes contradictory traditions and tendencies." She argues that it is "overly simplistic" to view the U.S. military "as a bastion of aggressive masculinity where dominance and assertiveness are promoted," and that the military inculcates in its personnel many qualities considered feminine, such as "teamwork, submission, obedience, and self-sacrifice" (Titunik 2008, 147). Nevertheless, I argue that the concept of a new global posture *envisions* (even if it does not wholly rely on) a military outside of the United States that is less encumbered by the presence of family members and will respond with a masculinity predominantly imagined as swifter, more assertive, and more "lethal." That is constructed against the idea of an inadequate masculinity attributed to the Cold War and pre–9/11 eras, which is outmoded and too vulnerable for the types of conflicts—for example, terrorist attacks—that pose a great threat in today's world.

Military Families Abroad as Occupation and Cold War Assets

In the late 1980s and early 1990s, as the Cold War that had dominated U.S. foreign relations for more than four decades wound down, defense planners tried to envision the future composition and role of the U.S. Armed Forces. Now that the Soviet Union no longer loomed as the chief adversary of the United States (and ceased to exist as of December 1991), U.S. government representatives searched for ways to shrink military expenses, which had skyrocketed in the early 1980s (Sherry 1995, 401–3). Responding to a request by the Senate Appropriations Committee that the U.S. Department of Defense (DOD) "report on practicable ways to reduce the costs of maintaining dependents of military personnel and DOD civilian employees overseas," the Defense Department adamantly urged that the policy of allowing families to join personnel wherever possible be continued and that the facilities and services for supporting families abroad also remain intact, since they were crucial to maintaining the morale of family members and, by extension, military personnel (U.S. Department of Defense 1990, iii). In a report to Congress in 1988, the Defense Department had declared that

> the fact that the Department of Defense considers families to be a force multiplier, in recognition of their contribution to overall readiness and the fact that family separation is a major determinant in Service members' decisions to leave the military make highly undesirable any option for reducing dependents overseas that cause[s] increases in the amount of family separation. Although both the Department and Congress have tried to reduce dependents overseas in the past, neither has been able to find any sustainable alternatives to present practices.[3]

The idea of military families overseas as a "force multiplier"—that is, as enhancements to military missions abroad—was not new. It had emerged in the aftermath of the Second World War, when military planners sought ways to reconcile demands for an end to the family separation endured during the war with the plan to maintain military personnel abroad, especially in occupied Germany and Japan. General Dwight Eisenhower, supreme commander of the Allied Forces in Europe, was among the first to articulate ideas for sending spouses to join military personnel in foreign countries after the war.[4] Armed Forces officials who supported sending families abroad did so primarily because they considered the opportunity to live with one's family essential to the morale of servicemen (the vast majority of military personnel with families were men, more so than in the early twenty-first century) and a determinant in the men's decisions to join and reenlist in the military. Military officials, however, also came to view family members, especially wives, as potential assets in the occupations of Germany and Japan and during the Cold War.

The extent of the post–Second World War and early–Cold War recognition and encouragement of family members, especially wives, as valuable contributors to international military goals was unprecedented. Families had long accompanied soldiers and officers on their travels and campaigns, with military wives sustaining their husbands, and sometimes other men, as well by doing essential tasks such as foraging, cooking, laundering, and nursing (Albano 1994, 287; Shinseki 2003, 1–3). Family members also joined military personnel in overseas U.S. territories such as the Philippines, even during the insurgency there against U.S. rule in the early 1900s. But as Cynthia Enloe (2000, 37) has noted, historically the U.S. Armed Forces tended to characterize wives and children as "camp followers," denoting a parasitic relationship that obscured the military's heavy reliance on women's unpaid labor and preserved a masculine image of the Armed Forces by discounting women's indispensable contributions to their maintenance.

Despite the continuation of the draft after the Second World War (Congress allowed it to lapse in 1947 but reinstated it in 1948), military leaders found that maintaining a large standing army for the post–Second World War occupations and the Cold War military buildup required them to accept that personnel were more likely to be married and have children than in previous eras when the nation was not in a hot war. The marriage and baby booms that had commenced during the war, and the postwar glorification of the nuclear family, would have made it difficult for the military to recruit and retain men who did not have wives or children. Although the military remained a masculine institution, it became more willing to concede that families were a part of it and even provided crucial social influence and support (Alvah 2007, 62–65). As Enloe points out, "Military commanders and their civilian political superiors . . . try to make use of those women who have married soldiers. If those women can be socialised to become 'military wives,' they can perhaps further some of the military's own goals" (Enloe 1983, 48). In making plans to send families to Europe, officials hoped that "normal family ties" would reduce fraternization between American soldiers and German women (*Domestic Economy* 1947, 2; U.S. Air Forces in Europe 1953, xvi–xvii). In addition, it was expected that men whose families were present would be more likely to stay out of trouble and that American families would help to create a more stable environment for all soldiers, which in turn would allow bases to operate more smoothly and would reduce problems for military and political leaders. Servicemen's disruptive and sometimes criminal behavior included relationships with local women, drunkenness, fighting, robbery, buying and selling goods on the black market, sexual assault, and murder. Assessments of the occupation in Germany correlated the decline in servicemen's criminal behavior with the arrival of families (Davis 1967, 191; Frederiksen 1953, 111).

Military officials viewed sending families abroad primarily as a means to bolster servicemen's morale and to help keep the men in line so that they would not engage in crime and other activities that disrupted occupied and host communities and offend local people. Yet they wanted family members, especially wives, to aid the foreign-relations goals of occupation and of the Cold War in other ways as well. Official military guidebooks and orientations for dependents, as well as many wives, some servicemen husbands and fathers, and occasionally teenagers, urged American family members abroad to consider themselves "unofficial ambassadors" who represented the United States in aiding in the "re-education" of peoples of occupied Japan and Germany by modeling and teaching them about democracy, projecting American interest in and respect for local cultures and customs and the desire for international cooperation, and demonstrating the alleged superiority of the American way of life in the ideological Cold War battle against communism. Military wives and children abroad encountered local peoples in a variety of activities, on and off U.S. bases, in homes, shops, churches, schools, and clubs and on recreational excursions (Alvah 2007, 102–16, chaps. 4–6).

The notion of American military family members as unofficial ambassadors enjoyed its heyday between the 1950s and mid-1960s, before the escalation of the Vietnam War and the widespread international and domestic disillusionment with the United States as a shining champion of democracy

Her world is wider and more demanding than most women's—more challenging and far more rewarding. It is:

The World Itself

Any time she may be living in lands as far flung as Formosa or Turkey, wherever the American Armed Forces serve and she is permitted to follow.

A U. S. LADY'S WORLD

By Jean D. Andrew

All of America

She lives the length and breadth of her homeland at posts, stations and bases. Wherever she lives in the world itself, she represents America and its women.

The Armed Forces

Wherever she lives as a service dependent, her welfare, safety, economic security and happiness are a reflection of the esteem her country feels for her service husband and his contribution to America.

Her Service

Be she an Army, Navy, Marine or Air Force wife, she is a part of a team that has its special rules, joys and problems. Her part on that team she plays with pride—as part of a bigger defense team.

Her Unit

She lives with a group of other wives and families as part of a squadron, regiment or division or wing. She must think of helping others in this unit, as they think of helping her.

Her Post, Station or Base

She lives in a small service community that needs her help in post activities to make the post a better community—in Red Cross, youth activities or recreation groups.

Her Local Community

She often lives near or in a city and has her part there to help in Church, P.T.A. or civic clubs.

Her Own Home

Wherever she may be living, she has home ties with her family, and her civic duties of voting absentee, thereby exercising her rights and duties of citizenship.

Her Family

No matter how wide the world of a U.S. Lady, it centers in the spot where her husband and children are—and where her children are when her husband cannot be there—all too often. Because her world is so much wider than most women's, her heart makes a home for her loved ones any place.

She is a U.S. LADY

FIGURE 4.1.
Illustration from
U.S. Lady magazine
(1956) conveying
a view of military
wives as supporting
their families,
neighborhoods, and
the Armed Forces
and as playing an
international role.

and morality in the fight against global communism. Still, as the Cold War came to an end and the Defense Department issued its report to Congress in 1990 on the costs of maintaining family members abroad, the population of military dependents overseas was 40 percent larger than it would be in the early 2000s. The highest census count stood at 462,504 in 1960, many times more than an estimated 90,000 abroad in 1950, and certainly far more than had resided abroad before the Second World War. Following the escalation of the Vietnam War in the mid-1960s, the number of military family members abroad dropped to approximately 318,000 in 1970, but by 1980 the number had increased to 353,641. A census analysis gave the number of Armed Forces dependents abroad in 1990 as 344,936 (U.S. Bureau of the Census 1964, VIII, table B, 1973, VII, table 1; U.S. Department of Defense 1981, 263; Mills 1993, 65).[5]

Despite the Defense Department's advocacy of maintaining families abroad after the Cold War's demise, the overseas presence of American military families, like the number of service personnel abroad, diminished over the next decade. From 1990 to September 1996, the number of family members in foreign countries fell by nearly 38 percent, to 214,327. Their number dropped further, to approximately 202,000, over the next five years.[6] Nevertheless, because deployments unaccompanied by family members are considered "hardship, arduous, or separation tours," Armed Forces policy generally continued to allow family members to join personnel abroad where they could be accommodated.[7]

The rationale and logistics of the new global posture can be understood in gendered terms, even if those articulating the plan do not consciously see this. Although ideas for redesigning the Armed Forces stretch back to the end of the Cold War, the terrorist attacks of 9/11 gave impetus to plans that in effect would re-masculinize the U.S. military, which critics worried was too weak to prevent attacks and too slow to respond to crises. The re-masculinization of the military does not, to most planners, entail the elimination or reduction of women in the Armed Forces; concerns about the ability to recruit enough personnel discourage such thinking, as does the evidence that female military personnel have performed their jobs adeptly. Rather, the goal is to improve the U.S. military's ability to move swiftly and aggressively against enemies—that is, to engage more effectively in martial activities gendered masculine.

The language used to explain and promote the global military transformation reveals underlying gendered assumptions about the new vision of the military and the place of families in relation to it. Although it is not surprising that the terms used to describe the transformation in various articles from the Defense Department's DefenseLink news service and in its policy documents underscore the masculinity of the military's activities, it is noteworthy that the various descriptions contrast the image of an reinvigorated, newly powerful Armed Forces with a military portrayed as outdated, weakly positioned, and perhaps even emasculated. A DefenseLink article quotes Donald Rumsfeld as saying, "It's as if, for example, Germany is still bracing for a Soviet tank invasion across the north German plain." Elsewhere, the article depicts the new "U.S. global posture" as "a more agile and efficient force," with more effective "joint capabilities" and greater "lethality," that employs improved technology such as "precision bombs [that] allow one aircraft to

TABLE 4.1 *Family members of U.S. Armed Forces abroad in 1960 and 1970*

	1960	1970
Europe and Soviet Union	327,446	204,049
Asia	81,540	98,129
Africa	15,581	4,359
Canada and Mexico	12,718	2,903
Americas (except Canada and Mexico)	5,284	6,022
Other	19,935	2,537
Total	462,504	317,999

Sources: U.S. Bureau of the Census, 1964, 52–57, table 9; 1973, 1–2, table 1.

kill a number of targets, rather than the old paradigm of a number of planes dropping bombs to take out one target" and that uses "beefed up special operations forces." Such an Armed Forces will be "better positioned to prevail in combat where war cannot be prevented." Although the report *Strengthening U.S. Global Defense Posture* (U.S. Department of Defense 2004b) states repeatedly that the cultivation of diplomatic and military relationships with "allies and partners" that will host U.S. military sites is integral to implementing the plan, indicating an awareness of the necessity of cooperating with other nations (an activity gendered feminine), there is no doubt that the United States is the dominant partner in such relationships and that the fundamental purpose of the global military renovation is to make the U.S. Armed Forces mightier than ever.[8]

Also strikingly juxtaposed to these portrayals of a revitalized military is the repeated rationalization of how the transformation will affect families. The flip side of the attempted re-masculinization of the military is the greater domestication of family members, whose overseas presence will decline as official personnel assume the new global posture. Under the new plan, a larger proportion of family members, who represent a feminine dimension of (and a feminizing influence on) the U.S. military, will reside in the United States—the "home front," also gendered feminine—rather than abroad. The domestication of family members also pertains to the continued fading of their participation in international roles—residing abroad in support of military personnel and, by extension, the larger U.S. military presence, and sometimes even serving to help further U.S. foreign-relations aims.

Explanations for the new global posture's proposed drastic reduction in the number of family members with personnel overseas to approximately 100,000 do not state that the central goal is to reduce the financial costs of

TABLE 4.2 *Family members of U.S. Armed Forces abroad in September 2005*

	COMMAND-SPONSORED MILITARY DEPENDENTS	NON-COMMAND-SPONSORED MILITARY DEPENDENTS
United States and Territories (including Guam and Puerto Rico)	1,757,082	8,306
Europe	112,949	9,965
Former Soviet Union	87	36
East Asia and Pacific	49,534	22,801
North Africa, Near East, South Asia	301	467
Sub-Saharan Africa	179	127
Western Hemisphere (including Canada and Mexico)	682	959
Undistributed	1,982	1,099
Total in Foreign Countries	165,714	35,454

Source: U.S. Department of Defense 2005a, 1–5.

maintaining them in foreign countries (although this may well be a factor, especially considering the weakness of the U.S. dollar abroad in recent years). As the Overseas Basing Commission has noted, under the new plan the United States will still have to pay for facilities and programs to help support the larger number of military families who will live on or near bases in the United States.[9]

Nor does the most prominent rationale for drawing down the number of military-family members abroad—that it will contribute to creating a leaner, "lighter, more agile" force better able to respond rapidly to threats anywhere in the world—disclose a fear that terrorists might target spouses and children of military personnel, although policymakers must have considered the possibility.[10] During the Cold War, U.S. government officials, as well as authors of articles in the popular media, worried about the possibility of military families' getting caught in the crossfire between communist and anticommunist forces and even occasionally expressed concern that communist enemies in Europe or Asia might deliberately harm these civilian Americans. Such concerns suggested a view of American family members as vulnerable and potential victims of global affairs more than as vital contributors to military personnel's morale and readiness and to good relations between the United

States and the nations housing its military bases. The idea of families as valuable supporters of military missions and as representatives of the steadfast U.S. commitment to anticommunism manifested itself during the Soviet blockade of Berlin between June 1948 and May 1949 and again during the Berlin Wall crisis of 1961, when U.S. officials decided to maintain rather than evacuate American military families in the city considered the bastion of freedom and democracy within communist Europe. Military officials and wives viewed the decisions to keep American women and children in West Berlin as a proclamation to the Soviet Union that the United States would stand its ground there under any circumstances (Alvah 2007, 139–40, 161; Leuerer 1997, 166–67). By contrast, evacuations of military-family members occurred at historic times of Cold War animosities that either did precede or nearly led to hot wars: the North Korean invasion of South Korea in June 1950; the Cuban Missile Crisis in October 1962; and the Johnson administration's decision to escalate the U.S. war in Vietnam in early 1965 (Alvah 2007, 226, 228–29).

While public statements and unclassified reports explaining the new global-posture rationale for reducing the number of American military family members on foreign posts do not divulge a fear of terrorism, they do reveal an incapacity for conceiving of families as positive contributors to military missions abroad, either in terms of shoring up service members' morale and readiness at foreign bases or, especially, in terms of seeing families as potential actors in forming and maintaining positive relations between the United States and host nations. In advocating the policy toward families in the proposed transformation of the military (which is already under way), President Bush and other civilian, as well as high-ranking military officials, depicted the changes as ultimately beneficial to military families. "This is really about the well-being of our soldiers and their families," said General Richard Cody, the Army's vice-chief of staff, "to provide them stabilization and predictability." According to Cody, the Army envisions stationing a soldier at one "installation" for four to five years; presumably, the families will live on or near this site and will have the opportunity to remain there when the service member is deployed.[11] The plan's backers, often using the same talking points to explain its benefits for families, emphasize the greater stability that families will allegedly enjoy due to the global military restructuring: spouses will not have to give up jobs when husbands (or wives, although approximately 94 percent of military spouses are women) are deployed from a base where the family is settled (a problem experienced by thousands of spouses), and children will not have to transfer from one school to another (although many military children have enjoyed and benefited from living abroad; see Ender 1996, 131–33; Houppert 2005, xix; Goodwin and Musil 2006). In President Bush's words, "Our military spouses will have fewer job changes, greater stability, more time for their kids and to spend time with their families at home."[12]

Bush's characterization of how life for military families will improve under the new global posture disclosed a view of them as longing to become homebodies who are not forced to uproot themselves and venture out into the world as frequently as they now do. (Usually the "tour of duty" for personnel stationed abroad with their families is three years.) Implicit in this view is that the role of military spouses (besides paid employment, if they have this, to help support their families) whose husbands or wives are deployed is to hold down the household on the home front and provide emotional support to the partner from afar. Bush did not mention the immense amount of volunteer work that wives provide at bases in the United States (Houppert 2005, 166–67, 198–99, 213, 226). Nor was there mention of ways that wives and children have contributed, and could continue to contribute, to U.S. military and foreign-relations goals in host nations. The predominant official view of military families, who cumulatively have lived abroad in the millions following the Second World War, has separated them from international military missions. In Bush's mind, their role in supporting service members and the larger Armed Forces was exclusively a domestic one, albeit one that relied heavily on the work of spouses and other family members.

Writing about the First Gulf War, Lynda E. Boose states, "By being positioned as the virtuously beribboned feminine [referring to the ubiquitous yellow ribbons that signified support for the military personnel fighting in the war], the civilian home front not only invoked the binary that reemphasized the exclusively masculine position of the military but effectively delegitimated resistance to the war from either men or women" (Boose 1993, 76–77). Boose interprets the backing of the war by a vast majority of women (73 percent, according to Harris polls), and women's prominent role in urging all Americans to support the troops (and thereby espouse a military intervention that many Americans had doubted shortly before), as reinforcing, even stridently imposing, positions gendered in traditional terms—the feminine, devoted, sustaining home front and the masculine, aggressive military front. These positions complemented each other in justifying and encouraging U.S. military action. Boose also sees this reaction to the war as "help[ing] to undo two alternative versions of gender that had first been imagined on a broad scale in the 1960s and 1970s: the masculinity that had been oppositionally constituted around resistance and militant pacifism, and the alternative femininity that had imagined divorcing itself from playing dutiful spouse / maternal producer for the needs of the masculine, military state" (Boose 1993, 76–77). Many Americans, even some who doubted the U.S. war in Vietnam, had responded angrily and resentfully to these alternative constructions of gender, especially to male antiwar activists.

In the early 2000s, the distinction between "front" and "home front" became starker, as did the gendered roles of military personnel and military families. While soldiers, men as well as women, were to be deployed to war zones and other sites far from the comforts of family, books and websites for military wives (sometimes addressing husbands of women soldiers) urged them to maintain stability in the household and sustain connections between children and faraway fathers (or mothers) and to prepare to aid the service member, as well as the rest of the family, in readjusting upon return. Thus, the military spouse performs a public service in helping her or his partner to recover from the traumas of overseas service (presumably so that the service member will be able to carry on with life in the United States and not become a problem for the military or the community). Yet this is also a private, domestic labor that places a great deal of responsibility on military spouses.[13]

Although thousands of military families still reside abroad with personnel, the predominant images of them, in television news stories, newspaper photographs and articles, and on websites, depict them as struggling on the home front to deal with the deployment of spouses (usually husbands)—tearfully saying goodbye to soldier partners and soldier parents, joyfully reuniting with them when they return, and straining financially to make ends meet. Since the 1970s, the government, social workers, and the media have given greater attention to problems suffered by military families—including domestic violence, separation, post-traumatic stress disorder, and poverty—but the families are seen less as agents in national and international political affairs than as martyrs. To advocates of U.S. militarism, showing support for military families (often, it seems, simply by acknowledging that they endure the hardships of military life, such as low pay, frequent moves, and deployments of loved ones) is a patriotic act, similar to exhorting all Americans, even those critical of U.S. militarism, to declare that they "support the troops." In this view, the trials of military families, as well as expressions of moral support for the families, are useful for demanding public acquiescence to the U.S. government's deployment of the nation's military.[14] But critics of U.S. foreign and military policies also uphold military families as symbols of the human costs of U.S. empire.

FIGURE 4.2.
Advertisement from
U.S. Lady (July 1958),
published primarily for
American military wives,
promulgating an image
of Air Force men as
civilianized and family-
oriented.

As the role of families becomes even more domesticated, the role of military personnel abroad becomes re-masculinized. The militarization of masculinity, however, is specific to historical and cultural contexts (Enloe 1993, 72–76). During the first two decades of the Cold War, images of military men as husbands and fathers became more prevalent in American culture than in previous eras. For example, in *U.S. Lady*, a magazine mainly for military wives, the Air Force promoted an image of itself in the 1950s as family-friendly in numerous full-page advertisements addressing wives that depicted men as civilianized, affectionate, family-oriented husbands and fathers. The militarized masculinity of this period allowed male soldiers to be both family men and fighting men, even as military policies, reinforced by the civilian federal government, discouraged marriage and motherhood for its female soldiers and even allowed for the discharge of women who were mothers (Segal and Segal 2004, 30).

Although the new global posture envisions a re-masculinized, gung-ho Armed Forces abroad, the many scenes of military personnel parting from and rejoining their families in the United States offer an alternative image. In these scenes, personnel, often wearing military garb, engage in emotional, intimate (although observed by the public) interactions with family members. Usually these scenes involve male personnel, although occasionally one sees female personnel.[15] Thus, the men and women of the Armed Forces are not represented simply as fighters; they are also depicted, especially in the context of the United States (and for domestic consumption), as fundamentally gentle and loving people attached to families.

Military Families in (and Apart from) the Post–Cold War and Post–9/11 U.S. Military Empire

During and after the Vietnam War, large percentages of military personnel were married (some wives had supported the war; others had opposed it) and had children, though the role of military families abroad was not as prominent and their total numbers abroad were not as large as in the late 1950s and early 1960s. More military spouses held paying jobs and found less time for the kind of volunteer work they had performed in Germany, Japan, and other locations after the Second World War, such as aiding "war orphans" and "GI babies" and their mothers and teaching English to host-nation students. Moreover, influenced by the feminist movement, the new generation of military wives proved less inclined than their predecessors to provide unpaid labor to the Armed Forces (Alvah 2007, 103–6, 144–46, 178, 180; Brown 2005, 233–45).

The attitude in the first two decades of the Cold War that military families should interact with people whose countries hosted U.S. bases, learn about their cultures and customs, engage in charitable activities on behalf of poor local peoples, and demonstrate the superiority of the American way of life (including gender relations) receded after the 1960s. By the early 2000s, it was no longer a prominent sentiment. Working at paid jobs (often while also working a "second shift" of caring for households and children) took up more of military wives' time. The weak dollar, combined with admonitions to families to spend money on the base rather than in host communities, as well as increased anti–American sentiment, made family members more reluctant to venture off bases (Alvah 2007, 230; Hawkins 2001, 167–80). In addition, families seem to have received less encouragement from the Armed Forces and from military spouses in leadership roles to "make friends" for their country, in contrast to the advice widely dispensed in the 1950s, when many Americans in military families considered it their duty to participate in the ideological fight against communism by projecting their nation's freedom and prosperity to host-nation peoples and cultivating their alliances. Books and websites for military wives from the early 2000s express less interest in interacting with local peoples than did the writings by and for military wives in the 1950s and 1960s. One book for military wives that does include a chapter on "Living Overseas" (among other chapters on such topics as benefits for family members, protocol for social events in military communities, wives' careers, and money management) advises them to learn the local language and get out into the host community but emphasizes this more as a means to personal enrichment than as an effort at personal diplomacy (Cline 2003, 210–28).

The apparent self-seclusion of many Americans affiliated with the military from host-nation communities suggests that the post–Vietnam War imperialism of the United States differs from the imperialism and colonialism of other countries and of the United States in previous eras. Unlike European colonists who enacted ways to delineate differences between themselves and Asians and Africans (Stoler 2002, 201–4), and unlike U.S. military wives from the mid-1940s to the nmid-1960s who considered their contacts with occupied and host-nation peoples influential in securing their support for U.S. Cold War goals, it seems that military families abroad in the late twentieth century and early twenty-first marked the boundaries between themselves and local peoples generally by having little to do with them—whether out of a fear of venturing into an unfamiliar community, lack of money or time, or sheer lack of interest. (An anthropologist who studied Americans with the military in West Germany in the 1980s observed that many also were wary of socializing and becoming too friendly with fellow Americans [Hawkins 2001].) American reclusiveness might convey the impression that Americans consider themselves superior to host nationals and that the Americans just want to use the host-nation sites to conduct military operations, with little or no concern for or interest in the host country. Still, one must bear in mind that military bases, especially those with the infrastructure to support families in countries considered friendly enough to Americans, are not necessarily off-limits to host nationals, who may work at the bases in American homes and in military facilities such as Post Exchanges and schools. Some American families do make excursions into, and live in, host-nation communities. Moreover, a number of military families comprise American service members who marry and have children with host nationals, thereby blurring boundaries between Americans and local peoples.

The restructuring of the global U.S. military presence in the first decade of the twenty-first century will make it more difficult, although not impossible, for families to join personnel abroad. The new global defense plan "envisions three tiers of bases." The Armed Forces will downsize or eliminate many Main Operating Bases (MOBS), which the Defense Department describes as "permanent bases with resident forces and robust infrastructure." This is the type of base considered best suited to accommodate family members and where families will still be allowed to join service personnel. An example of an MOB is Ramstein Air Force Base in Germany, which has "all the comforts of the U.S.—family housing, schools, supermarkets, convenience stores, theaters, and populations in the tens of thousands." U.S. Armed Forces will increasingly be deployed to "more austere facilities," or Forward Operating Sites (FOSS), that are "intended for rotational use by operational forces," and to Cooperative Security Locations (CSLS) in host nations that U.S. forces will use on a "contingency" basis. In August 2004, former Secretary of Defense Donald Rumsfeld stated that Forward Operating Locations are not "permanent bases: they're not large places where you have families; they are not places where you have large numbers of U.S. military on a permanent basis . . . [but places] where you'd locate people in and out or where you use it for refueling—these types of things" (Klare 2005, 14; see also Critchlow 2005).[16] Defense Department officials who advocate the restructuring describe it in terms of the U.S. military leaving a "lighter footprint" in host nations—that is, keeping a low profile and being a less intrusive presence among host populations.[17]

The goal is to transform the global U.S. military presence from the more stationary positioning of the Cold War era and the 1990s—"primarily in Western Europe and Northeast Asia," where the vast majority of military families lived and where U.S. forces were situated "to fight where they were stationed," or in the region where they were stationed—into a more "expeditionary" kind of army that responds with "flexibility" and is better able to "surge . . . from a global posture to respond to crises" (U.S. Department of Defense 2005ab, 5, 17–19).[18] Maintaining hundreds of thousands of military-family members abroad is not a part of this plan; their presence would necessitate extensive support facilities that, in the view of defense policymakers, would burden military missions and impede the readiness and mobility of soldiers.

Although the Bush administration announced the new global posture in

2004, the assumptions about transforming the U.S. military and using it preemptively to achieve foreign-relations objectives date back to 1993, during President Bill Clinton's first administration (Mann 2005, 7). A contingent termed "RMA [Revolution in Military Affairs] enthusiasts" pushed for a focus on research and development to create new military technology. "RMA enthusiasts," states Frederick Kagan of the American Enterprise Institute—President Bush among them—generally favor using long-range airpower instead of ground forces as a solution to military problems. Kagan reports that the expenses generated by creating, maintaining, fueling, and upgrading the new technology, combined with the costs of improving quality-of-life initiatives that help to retain and recruit military personnel, are leading to decisions to maintain lower personnel levels than are needed to successfully wage war, conduct occupations, and engage in other kinds of crucial activities that do not directly entail combat (Kagan 2006, 106–8).[19]

In the Bush administration's conception of what it termed the "war on terror," the most effective way to deal with threats from rogue states and non-state actors and maintain U.S. global pre-eminence demanded a tough-talking, individualistic approach that relied heavily on technology and the threat of force. It disdained "feminine" diplomatic, multilateral engagements that it viewed as ineffective and as creating an impression of the United States as weak and vulnerable. "Threats, bombings, and invasions," writes Michael Mann, "now dominate its foreign policy." But in its dependence on force at the expense of other forms of power (economic, political, and ideological), the "new militarism" of the Bush administration, as Mann sees it, will not bolster U.S. power but ultimately undermine it (Mann 2005, 1–3, 252). By the final year of the administration, it had received much international as well as domestic censure for what its critics viewed as a heavy-handed approach to foreign relations that did more harm than good to U.S. national security and other interests, as well as to the people of nations affected by its military actions.

In the meantime, even as the U.S. global military empire closes some of its large, "traditional" bases (the ones best equipped to support military families), it will expand its potential reach through "Forward Operating Sites" (FOSS) and "Cooperative Security Locations" (CSLs). Family members will continue to be allowed to accompany military personnel to certain overseas stations, where the facilities, political climate, and posture of forces can accommodate them, but they will dwindle elsewhere, such as in Western Europe, and will not be accommodated at established and new FOSS and CSLs. The heavy reliance on high-tech weapons and personnel removed from the comfort and social influences of families to augment U.S. international power indicates a mindset that values the potential for force ("hard power," gendered masculine) over "soft power," or the potential to influence others through persuasion and attraction rather than coercion and gendered feminine (Nye 2004, 5–9). The reduction or absence of families at Armed Forces sites abroad could create a more militarized atmosphere at these locations, separating military families from military missions even more than they are now and allowing the U.S. government to use the Armed Forces more readily—and perhaps with greater impunity—around the globe. It is important, however, to acknowledge that military personnel, including those in Afghanistan and Iraq, where the United States is at war, engage in interpersonal interactions with local people, informally and in official capacities, in ways that can moderate the impression of U.S. forces as harsh invaders. In American culture, such behavior is associated with a feminine approach to human relations (which, of course, is not to say that only girls and women engage in this behavior or that it is generally considered undesirable for men to behave in this manner). Nevertheless, the Bush administration did not emphasize such an approach in its statements and policies.

Those who fear the feminizing, softening influences of families and of female soldiers on the Armed Forces probably will view the reduction of families abroad as long overdue, though not going far enough to re-masculinize the military. American concerns and complaints about large numbers of U.S. families at overseas bases appeared as their numbers grew in the 1950s and 1960s, expressing dismay that maintaining them abroad wasted taxpayers' dollars, distracted soldiers from their missions, and sapped the fighting spirit of military personnel (Alvah 2007, 125–26, 161). Criticism of the family-friendliness and feminization of the military (including the growing number of women in the Armed Forces and women serving in combat-related roles) continued after the end of the Cold War. Allan Carlson, president of the conservative Rockford Institute in 1993, argued for "a return to a bachelor military force" in the aftermath of the Cold War on the grounds that families impede military readiness, cause soldiers to divide their loyalties between their military duties and their families, and cost too much for the government to support. He believed that the United States should maintain a "bachelor regular army, to be used for small conflicts and as an expeditionary force," but also be able to turn to a "vastly larger" number of men (who did not need to be unmarried and childless) as a "citizen force" organized for larger wars (Carlson 1993, 45–46, 52; see also Gutmann 2001; Mitchell 1989, 1998). While such arguments decry the alleged emasculation of the warrior culture by families, female soldiers, and feminists, a "return" to a mythical all-male or bachelor Armed Forces (a longing evidently not shared by the 15 percent of military personnel who are women or the approximately 51 percent of personnel who were married as of 2002) seems unlikely anytime soon. In an all-volunteer Armed Forces, the recruitment and retention of capable personnel simply would not be possible if they were not allowed to have families.[20] Still, one way to return some of the masculinity to U.S. forces abroad is to keep families at a distance from the "battlefields" where the fighting and killing take place—which, in the minds of the new militarists, are found all over the world outside the United States (Mann 2005, 5).

Effects of the New Global Posture on Host Nations and on U.S. Military Families

The attempted re-masculinization of the military will affect not only U.S. military families but also the nations that host U.S. forces. Some sectors of host-nation populations will undoubtedly react positively to the overall reduction of U.S. forces in their countries. The increasingly masculine—and, at sites without American families, purely military—profile of the U.S. presence, however, may trouble citizens of host countries concerned about the dangers and disruptions posed by single men in their communities, such as the creation or expansion of "camptowns" that cater to American military men's expectations that the emotional hardship of being stationed in a foreign country entitles them to find relief in bars, sex clubs, and brothels (Moon 1997, 36; Takagi and Park 1995). Furthermore, the transformation will reinforce an image of the international U.S. presence as oriented toward military domination.

What might be other negative—and, perhaps, positive—consequences of drastically reducing the number of U.S. military families abroad? It depends on the perspective. From the point of view of some military-family members, the prospect of fewer moves and shorter deployments for service members may indeed be attractive. For its study of the plans for a new global posture, the Overseas Basing Commission received input from a representative of the National Military Family Association (NMFA), which originated in 1969 and promotes the economic and social well-being of military families. The NMFA, which describes itself as "The Voice *for* Military Families," and whose theme for its thirty-fifth anniversary in 2004 was "Strong Families—Strong Force," has issued a position paper on the global military transformation indicating that the association's prime demands are for the U.S. government to ensure that military families scheduled to return to the United States will receive all necessary support (health care, child care, access to commissaries) until the moment of their departure from foreign stations, and that communities in the United States will be well prepared to accommodate them immediately when they arrive. The NMFA position paper does not question the plan to dramatically reduce the number of military families overseas (National Military Family Association 2005, 2006, 1–3).

The results for military families, however, may not be as rosy as proponents of the new global posture have portrayed them. The Overseas Basing Commission expressed concern in its report in August 2005 that under the new plan, even though its advocates say otherwise, military families will quite possibly experience numerous periods of separation:

> Even should peace prevail everywhere, active force units could find themselves away from home for an extended period (6–12 months) once in every three or four years; reserve forces once in every five or six years. When operational deployments in response to crises and combat operations are added to the rotational base, the number and duration of time away from home are likely to become even more severe.[21]

The commissioners noted that "in a married force, which is the predominant nature of our current structure, we would do well to remember that separation from family and loved ones itself is likely to extract a severe hardship on those involved."[22] Not only might numerous separations from families harm the morale of service personnel and undermine their ability to do their jobs well; it could also diminish retention and recruitment. Furthermore, considering the current U.S. military missions in Afghanistan and Iraq; the fact that numerous service personnel have already experienced multiple, back-to-back, or extended deployments since 2001; and that conflicts now under way are unlikely to end anytime soon, the likelihood of frequent deployments for personnel in the future is quite high. It is not realistic for the Department of Defense to lead military families to think that the new global posture will bring more family togetherness, at least not in the near future. In the meantime, the NMFA concludes from a survey of military families that "service members and military families are experiencing increased levels of anxiety, fatigue, and stress" due to heightened demands on and deployments of Armed Forces personnel.[23]

In describing the plan to station fewer military families abroad, its advocates seem to ignore that family members might actually prefer opportunities to live overseas. A report to Congress points out that the "DOD . . . appears to assume the overseas stationing in permanent European bases (such as Germany, Italy) is undesirable to military families, which is . . . often not the case. In fact, the opportunity to periodically live overseas is, for some, an advantage of a military career" (Critchlow 2005). Moreover, military family members have displayed determination to join service personnel not just in Western European locations such as Germany and Italy, where tens of thousands of "command-sponsored" spots—that is, "where an accompanied tour is authorized" by the U.S. government—have been available (more than 90,000 as of September 2005). Unlike command-sponsored military family members, non-command-sponsored (NCS) spouses, children, and other "dependents" are not entitled to government-funded transportation to and from the overseas station. Also, personnel living abroad with NCS family members do not receive the " 'with dependents' rate station allowance." Despite the greater economic onus, thousands of NCS family members live overseas with personnel, including in Turkey (911 as of September 2005), Japan (9,079), and the Republic of Korea (13,201), according to the U.S. Department of Defense (2005a, 1–2, 5, 44–45). In fact, of the 201,168 "dependents" in foreign countries in 2005, 35,454 (17.6 percent) were non-command-sponsored. Under the new global posture, it is likely that many family members not sponsored by a military command will continue to seek ways to join personnel abroad at their own expense.

From the perspectives of host-nation citizens, would the reduction of U.S. military families be a positive or negative development? Of course, the reactions of host nationals could be diverse and would be influenced by local, regional, and international politics; economic conditions; and personal attitudes toward the U.S. military, Americans in general, and the simple fact of one's nation housing a foreign military presence. Businesses that benefit economically from the U.S. military presence might miss having large numbers of family members as well as military personnel. Since U.S. bases have agreements with host nations guaranteeing the employment of certain numbers of host nationals, it is likely that shrinking or eliminating overseas bases will result in a regretted loss of such jobs.[24] Conversely, local citizens opposed to U.S. bases in their countries are likely to be happy to see a reduction in, if not the elimination of, the U.S. military presence, including its supporting personnel and the families that help to sustain them.

According to the Overseas Basing Commission, "Reductions in Germany and Korea account for the preponderance of the 60,000 to 70,000 military and 100,000 family members the [Defense] Department plans to return to the U.S. and accommodate at stateside military installations."[25] Since the end of the Second World War, Germany has hosted the largest portion of U.S.

military family members abroad. As of September 2005, 81,370 American military family members (approximately 40 percent of the total number in all foreign countries) resided in Germany (U.S. Department of Defense 2005a, 1).[26] Although the United States established its post–Second World War military presence in Germany through occupation, the emergence of the Cold War and the cultivation of cultural connections and friendships (influenced by a shared anticommunism and a shared sense of whiteness) helped to forge a bond between Americans and West Germans. the likes of which did not exist in other nations housing a large U.S. military presence, such as South Korea (Alvah 2007, 91, 95–103, 222). Although frictions did (and do) exist between Germans and the Americans affiliated with the U.S. military, and although increasing numbers of Germans have opposed the foreign military presence since the 1970s, Germany has proved the country most tolerant of U.S. bases and American military families.

Citizens in Asian host nations might respond with mixed feelings to reductions of American military families there. Opposition to the presence of U.S. bases is strong in Japan, especially in Okinawa Prefecture, but its government permits the bases because it views them as providing protection against aggression from North Korea and generally as a means to sustain a favorable relationship with the United States.[27] Yet what will it mean to continue to maintain U.S. military personnel in Japan (even at reduced levels) but also fewer family members? Opponents of the U.S. military presence may welcome any diminution of it, including families, who ultimately help to sustain the U.S. Armed Forces in those countries, and U.S. global dominance. In Okinawa Prefecture, where the majority of U.S. military personnel in Japan are located, American families, along with the rest of the U.S. military infrastructure, take up large areas of the small main island's precious space.[28] Thousands of U.S. Marines leaving Okinawa are moving to Guam, a U.S. territory. Although the people of Guam are U.S. citizens, they are apprehensive about what the Defense Department describes as "the biggest military move in Guam since the Second World War." While some expect that the influx of 8,000 U.S. Marines and their 9,000 family members will benefit the economy, other residents of Guam also worry about an increase in crime, appropriation of land from indigenous people, and the effects of the increased military presence on Guam's infrastructure and resources.[29]

The government of South Korea has seen the reduction of the U.S. military presence and the move of U.S. bases away from the demilitarized zone as steps toward a friendlier relationship with North Korea. While the U.S.

military planned to reduce the number of personnel, it planned to increase its accommodation of military family members by about 4,000. An American missionary in Tongduch'ŏn, South Korea, where Camp Casey is located, argued that the United States should make it possible for more military families to join servicemen there. The missionary stated, "If more families were allowed here, there would be less problems. When you have more families around you have less drinking, less prostitution, less pornography and less gambling. It would be a more wholesome community." The article reporting the missionary's statement noted, however, that "even if the command were to make it easier for soldiers to have their families with them . . . 57 percent have no families to bring because they are single."[30]

Moreover, despite the presence of thousands of command-sponsored American family members in Okinawa, numerous bars and sex clubs cater to U.S. personnel. In addition, the presence of relatively large numbers of American family members there has not prevented U.S. servicemen from continuing to sexually assault Okinawan girls and women and commit numerous other crimes.[31] According to an editorial by Kuniichi Tanida in the Japanese newspaper *Asahi Shimbun*, what did make a difference in reducing the number of crimes committed by U.S. military personnel in Okinawa between 2003 and 2004 was the shipment of approximately 5,000 Marine combat forces out of the prefecture to Iraq. Tanida urged the Japanese government in its negotiations with the United States regarding "the realignment of U.S. troops in Japan" to push for the removal of U.S. combat units in particular, despite the insistence of U.S. officials that "the units need to stay in Okinawa as a regional deterrent force."[32]

Although American military families abroad fundamentally function to uphold the U.S. global military through the support of personnel, the planners of the new global posture consider reducing their numbers overseas as integral to creating "a more assertive, usable combat force." While the numbers of military personnel will be much smaller than during the Cold War, and the overall U.S. military presence will perhaps be more detached from host nations' populations, the reach of the U.S. Armed Forces will be far more extensive in the post–Cold War, post–9/11 world. Even as the Pentagon scales down U.S. forces abroad and closes bases constructed during the Cold War, it is in the process of establishing new military sites (Rumsfeld tried to avoid the term "bases," which, Michael Klare says, connotes "a permanent, colonial-like presence") in other regions, such as Eastern Europe and Central Asia, to the dismay of many who reside there (Klare 2005, 13, 16).

Conclusion

Although it agreed with the Department of Defense's proclaimed need to extensively transform the U.S. military to render it more effective in protecting U.S. interests, the Overseas Basing Commission also described several reservations about the plan, among them that the renovation would cost billions more than the Defense Department has anticipated, that the reduction of U.S. forces in countries (such as Germany) with which the United States has enjoyed "longstanding relationships" would jeopardize diplomatic relations with those allies and U.S. influence in those nations, that the "quality of life" of military families could be diminished, and that the Defense Department was needlessly rushing to implement changes without thinking them through. Although Defense Department officials disagreed with the Overseas Basing Commission's concerns and criticisms, implementing the new global posture at this point is still a work in progress.[33] In fact, since the publication of the commission's report in 2005, Secretary of Defense Robert Gates (who replaced Rumsfeld in December 2006) has amended plans approved by Rumsfeld and President Bush in 2004 to reduce the number of U.S. Army personnel in Germany and Italy from 62,000 to 24,000.[34] In addition, after removing 9,000 U.S. military personnel from South Korea between 2004 and 2006, U.S. Armed Forces in Korea will maintain approximately 28,000 rather than the initially envisioned 25,000.[35] As the U.S. government transforms its military's global presence (although with alterations to the original plans), people in host nations and potential host nations are expressing concern about, and actively protesting, the prospect of a new or continued U.S. military presence in or near their countries.[36]

The Overseas Basing Commission concluded that, before the Defense Department hurries to further its strategy, "The nation would benefit from a more inclusive discussion on how to best secure the greater security of the United States." It recommended that the Defense Department communicate more extensively with other federal departments, and that Congress exercise its oversight role, to determine the best way to transform the military.[37] This "more inclusive discussion" and congressional scrutiny of the plan also should pay heed to the voices of military family members; the peoples of other nations, especially those where the U.S. Armed Forces will be located and those who will be affected by a new global posture; and those, Americans included, who envision alternatives to global U.S. militarism.

Notes

I greatly appreciate the editors' and anonymous reviewers' helpful suggestions for this chapter.

1. "Total Military, Civilian, and Dependent Strengths by Regional Area and by Country (309)," in U.S. Department of Defense 2005a, 5.

2. John D. Banusiewicz, "Bush Announces Global Posture Changes over Next Decade," 16 August 2004, available online at http://www.defenselink.mil (accessed 23 November 2005). The new global posture is also known as the "Global Posture Review," the "Integrated Global Presence and Basing Strategy, and the "Global Defense Posture Realignment." U.S. Department of Defense 2004b, 9. See also Critchlow 2005, 2.

3. "Appendix F: "Executive Summary of the Department of Defense's Report to Congress on Dependents Overseas, June 1988," in U.S. Department of Defense 1990, 41.

4. Dwight Eisenhower to Mamie Eisenhower, 12 May 1945, in Eisenhower 1978, 253.

5. According to Karen Mills, the number of family members given in the 1990 census is probably lower than the actual number.

6. Commission on Review of Overseas Military Facility Structure of the United States (Overseas Basing Commission), *Report to the President and Congress*, 15 August 2005, 5, available online at http://fido.gov/obc/reports.asp (accessed 31 March 2009); U.S. Department of Defense, "Table 4–1: Non Command Sponsored and Command Sponsored Dependent Strengths of Active Duty Military by Regional Area and by Country," September 30, 1996, available online at http://siadapp.dior.whs.mil/personnel/MOIFY96SMS4IBR.htm (accessed 28 August 2006). These numbers do not include members of military families in U.S. territories (Guam, Puerto Rico, Johnston Atoll, Marshall Islands).

7. On "hardship tours," see Cline 2003, 231.

8. Jim Garamone, "Rumsfeld, Myers Discuss Military Global Posture," DefenseLink News, 23 September 2004, available online at www.defenselink.mil (accessed 16 September 2006); U.S. Department of Defense 2004b, 4, 7, 9, 11–15.

9. Overseas Basing Commission, *Report to the President and Congress*, iv, xi, 25–26.

10. Sergeant First Class Doug Sample, "Changing [the Department of Defense's] Global Posture an 'Enormous Undertaking,'" 17 March 2005, American Forces Press Service News Articles, available online at www.defenselink.mil (accessed 21 May 2007). Michael Mann (2005, 259) states that the increased militarism of the United States provokes more terrorism against American targets abroad, including civilians.

11. Sergeant Sara Wood, "Army Announces Repositioning Plans," 27 July 2005, American Forces Press Service News Articles, available online at http://www.defense.gov/news/ (accessed 31 March 2010).

12. Banusiewicz, "Bush Announces Global Posture Changes over Next Decade."

13. Daniel Zwerdling, "Military Wives Fight Army to Help Husbands," broadcast, National Public Radio, 17 May 2008, available online at http://www.npr.org (accessed 17 May 2008).

14. On the imperative to "support the troops" (or "love our boys") as a means to gain support of U.S. military actions, see Boose 1993, 76–77.

15. See, e.g., the scenes of Ensign Susan Clapp, an air-traffic-control supervisor, and her children in the PBS documentary *Carrier* (Chermayeff 2008). The riveting ten-hour program follows a six-month deployment of the USS *Nimitz* in 2005.

16. Rumsfeld's statement seems to combine the terms "Forward Operating Sites" and "Cooperative Security Locations."

17. Kathleen T. Rhem, "Policymakers 'Plan to Be Surprised' in New Global Posture," American Forces Press Service News Articles, 30 June 2004, available online at www .defenselink.mil (accessed 21 May 2007).

18. Overseas Basing Commission, *Report to President and the Congress*, app. O, 3.

19. Furthermore, Kagan states that this "military manpower crisis" results in large part from the Bush administration's assumption that "war is fundamentally about killing people and destroying things." The core problem, argues Kagan, is that successful warfare is much more than this: not just combat, but also ensuing occupations, require large numbers of service personnel on the ground to succeed, and it is a mistake to rely so disproportionately on long-range technology—the kind advocated by "RMA enthusiasts"—to do the necessary work. Kagan sees the difficulties in quelling insurgencies in Iraq and Afghanistan and establishing stable, democratic governments as resulting in large part from the United States not providing enough military personnel on the ground.

20. Statistics on marriage and children of military personnel, as well as a concise discussion of military families, are in Segal and Segal 2004, 30–37.

21. Overseas Basing Commission, *Report to President and the Congress*, C4, E1, N6, n. 7.

22. Ibid., iii, 24.

23. "Study Shows Multiple Deployments Taking Toll on Military Families," U.S. Newswire, 28 March 2006. See also Representative John P. Murtha [and Representative David Obey], "United States Army Military Readiness," U.S. Fed News, 13 September 2006.

24. For example, in England, where peace activists have protested at U.S. bases, Armed Forces Minister Adam Ingram lamented the U.S. Army's withdrawal from the Hythe Royal Air Force base because of the loss of jobs to be suffered by the "more than 200 civilians [who] service and repair American military boats": "Loyalty Can Not Save US Base," U.K. Newsquest Regional Press—This Is Hampshire, 11 May 2006; Pete Lazenby, "We'll Stop US Base, Says Helen," *Yorkshire Evening Post*, 5 November 2004; "Former UN Inspector Joins Protest at Base," U.K. Newsquest Regional Press—This Is the Northeast, 6 July 2005. Regarding economic fears of a U.S. Army base closing in Schweinfurt, Germany, see "German Town's Future Is Uncertain if U.S. Base Closures Are Carried Out," *Watertown Daily Times*, 22 August 2004, A8.

25. Overseas Basing Commission, *Report to President and the Congress*, app. O, 1.

26. The Defense Department reports 77,326 command-sponsored dependents in Germany and 4,044 non-command-sponsored dependents.

27. Yoshio Okubo, "Political Pulse: Moving U.S. Bases Splits Nation," *Daily Yomiuri*, 2 December 2004.

28. The following articles discuss the U.S. military presence in Okinawa and in Japan in general, not American military families specifically: "Thousands Protest to Close U.S.

Base in Japan's Okinawa," Agence France-Presse–English, 15 May 2005; "Japan, U.S. Endorse U.S. Military Realignment in Japan," Jiji Press Ticker Service, 29 October 2005; "U.S. Military Realignment," *Asahi Shimbun*, 21 January 2006.

29. Michele Catahay, "Activists Demand Back Story on Marine Migration," KUAM News, 12 July 2007, available online at http://www.kuam.com (accessed 29 July 2007); Gaynor Dumat-ol Daleno, "Twenty Years of Growth in Five: Guam Population Will Add 42,000 by 2013," *Pacific Sunday News*, 14 September 2008, http://www.guampdn.com (accessed 21 September 2008); Ronna Sweeney, "With Population Boom, DEPCOR [Department of Corrections] Will Have to Expand," 14 September 2008, available online at http://www.kuam.com (accessed 21 September 2008).

30. Seth Robson, "Missionary: More Families Would Curb Bad Behavior in Area 1," *Stars and Stripes*, 23 November 2005. See also Moon 1997, 36.

31. Just two recent examples of such crimes are described in "U.S. Troops in Japan's Okinawa under Curfew after Pedophile Case Stirs Anger," Agence France-Presse–English, 8 July 2005; "Japan Police Arrest U.S. Sailor in Woman's Murder Case: Report," Agence France-Press, 7 January 2006.

32. Kuniichi Tanida, "Analysis," *Asahi Shimbun*, 31 October 2005.

33. Critchlow 2005; Overseas Basing Commission, *Report to President and the Congress*, vii–xiii.

34. Thom Shanker, "U.S. to Halt Troop Cuts in Europe; Military Wants 40,000-Soldier Force, Double Rumsfeld's Plan," *International Herald Tribune*, 22 November 2007.

35. Jung Sung-ki, "U.S. to Pause in Troop Reductions in S[outh] Korea," *Korea Times*, 4 February 2008.

36. "Czechs Protest against Possible US Base," *BBC Monitoring Europe–Political*, 12 September 2006; "Hundreds Protest in Okinawa over US Bases," Agence France-Presse–English, 25 May 2006; "Police and Villagers Clash near Seoul; 1,000 Protesters Fight U.S. Base's Expansion," *International Herald Tribune*, 5 May 2006; "Turkish Leftists Protest against Port Becoming US Naval Base," *BBC Monitoring International Reports*, 13 April 2006; "US Bases in Bulgaria Will Not Harm Environment—Defence Minister," *BBC Monitoring Europe–Political*, 27 March 2006; "Poll Shows Most Bulgarians Want Restrictions on Use of Possible US Bases," *BBC Monitoring International Reports*, 30 November 2005; "Hundreds Protest at US Base on Italian Island," Agence France-Presse–English, 29 October 2005; "Afghan Paper Lists Arguments against Permanent US Bases in Country," *BBC Monitoring International Reports*, 30 May 2005; "Most Poles against US Bases in Poland," *BBC Monitoring International Reports*, 5 January 2005.

37. Overseas Basing Commission, *Report to President and the Congress*, xii–xiii.

FIVE

CROSSFIRE COUPLES
*Marginality and Agency among Okinawan Women
in Relationships with U.S. Military Men*

☆

CHRIS AMES

Okinawan women who date or marry U.S. military men face challenges on both sides of the base fences that cordon off 20 percent of
Japan's Okinawa Island. Through six decades of American basing,
these women's choice of partners has made them targets of criticism from multiple directions: from parents who worry that their
daughter will live in a distant foreign country; from relatives and
counselors who fear that Okinawan-American marriages are likely
to end in unhappiness or divorce; from early-occupation U.S. military authorities forbidding "fraternization"; from Okinawan anti-
base activists who view such women as collaborators; and from
racists on both sides of the Pacific who oppose miscegenation. Okinawan women in relationships with military men have resisted marginalization by refusing or reappropriating pejorative labels such
as *"Amejo* (American woman)" while working with other women
who face the same challenges to garner support for themselves and
their families.

During my two years of ethnographic fieldwork in Okinawa, I
worked with roughly three dozen women in relationships with U.S.
military men.[1] I learned about their dreams and struggles through
participant observation, joining in their activities and interviewing
them about how they and their families negotiate membership in

both Okinawan and military-base communities. Attempting to grasp the challenges these women face also required understanding the perspectives of their American partners and Okinawan peers. Among contemporary Okinawans, disdain for such international romantic relationships is as widespread as frustration with the seemingly permanent U.S. military bases. Amid significant social change during the postwar era, a relative constant has been Okinawan society's negation of these women and their children as detracting from, rather than contributing to, imagined ethnic futures. Amerasian children are usually called "*haafu* (half)," derogatorily implying their incompleteness both as persons and as Okinawans. In anti-base discourse and postwar literature, relationships between American GIS and Okinawan women suggest a hijacking of Okinawa's future fecundity in the same way that military bases have rendered land taken from Okinawan farmers fallow (Molasky 1999).

Locating Okinawa Historically and Geographically

Romantic relationships between Okinawan women and U.S. military men in Okinawa are situated in complex social and historical milieus that also involve mainland Japan. Okinawa's dual colonial experience under mainland Japan from the late nineteenth century and the U.S. military occupation from 1945 through 1972 contextualize inter-ethnic love within a web of larger historical power relations. Couples consisting of Okinawan women and U.S. military men are conspicuous, taking on a historically symbolic meaning that shifts in accordance with events and public perceptions of the military bases with which these relationships are viewed as inevitably entwined.

Okinawa Island is located in the Ryūkyū Archipelago between the four main islands of Japan to the north and the island of Taiwan to the south. The Ryūkyūs were ruled by an independent kingdom until the seventeenth century, when samurai from the Satsuma Domain on mainland Japan's Kyūshū island invaded and began taxing Ryūkyūans. When the Japanese state modernized in the late nineteenth century, it annexed the Ryūkyūs and attempted to assimilate residents of the archipelago while treating them as second-class Japanese. Japan's aggressive expansion eventually led to the Pacific War, which was a collision between it and imperialist Western powers, primarily the United States. Although many Okinawans gave patriotic support to the war efforts—in part to prove themselves as first-rate Japanese—the Pacific War is widely perceived in Okinawa today as Japan's war, a conflict that brought only suffering for Okinawans. Okinawa Island was the location of the only ground battle on Japanese soil during the war. More than one-quarter of the island's civilian population died in what historians have called the "Typhoon of Steel."

The American military came ashore near the present location of the American Village shopping mall on April 1, 1945, and stayed. The United States occupied the island for twenty-seven years with absolute authority over island residents for two decades longer than mainland Japan's occupation. A massive social movement in Okinawa and mainland Japan realized reversion to Japanese sovereignty in 1972. After reversion, the American bases remained under the U.S.-Japan Security Treaty. For more than sixty years, Okinawa Island has hosted one of the world's highest concentrations of U.S. military bases, as well as one of the most organized movements against the U.S. presence abroad. In 2008, almost 50,000 Americans connected with the military resided on Okinawa Island, where all four branches of the U.S. military have bases.

Decreasing Postwar Power Asymmetries

Since 1945, relationships between American military men and Okinawan women have been marked by a decreasing power asymmetry. During and immediately after the Second World War, Okinawans were so impoverished by the battle's destruction that involvement between military men and local women was a means of material support for not only women, but also for their kin. From the earliest days of the occupation, intimacy across base fences had myriad forms that were distinguished mainly by the length of relationship and level of mutual emotional investment. Commercial sex transactions involving cash or goods were conducted until the end of the occupation at military-approved "A-Sign" establishments, which ranged from restaurants and cafés to bathhouses and quasi-brothel bars and clubs. Throughout the occupation in 1945–72, some GIS also kept local women as "*onrii* (only)" or "*hanii* (honey)" mistresses, paying their rent and giving them gifts and financial assistance. This blurry relationship continuum culminated in steady dating relationships and marriage, which have been the most common relationship forms between American military men and Okinawan women since the 1970s, when rising Okinawan prosperity decreased the need for local women to prostitute themselves to GIS. Military prostitution in Okinawa today involves largely Filipinas and other foreign women, a fact that is easily confirmed during a walk past the seedy strip shows that line Kadena Air Base's Gate 2 in Okinawa City (Sturdevant and Stoltzfus 1993).

Reversion to Japanese sovereignty in 1972 brought rising incomes and massive investment in infrastructure to Okinawa Island, reducing the economic gap between Okinawans and U.S. military personnel. Reversion also realized protection for Okinawans under the Japanese constitution and subjected the U.S. military to greater restrictions. Contemporary Okinawa Prefecture continues to have the lowest per capita income of any prefecture in Japan.[2] However, if Okinawa Prefecture were considered separately from Japan, its residents would have the ninth-highest average per capita income in the world—higher than that in many European Union nations and just slightly lower than the national average in the United States (Allen 2002).[3] Rising incomes in Okinawa during the past few decades have all but eliminated the extreme poverty that plagued the islands historically. Yet power differentials between Okinawan women and American GIs cannot be reduced simply to economic terms. Race and gender are also deeply entwined with economic class.

Occupation-Era Institutionalized Racism

Throughout the early U.S. occupation of Okinawa the military officially disapproved of relationships between military men and Okinawan women, a policy enforced most stringently during the initial four years of American administration. Occupation headquarters in Tokyo forbade intermarriage during the period from September 15, 1945, to May 31, 1946, based on racist American immigration policies and various state anti-miscegenation laws that discriminated against people of Asian ancestry. Military policies making marriage between military men and Okinawan women difficult existed alongside official acknowledgment of a massive sex industry in Okinawa involving GIs and local women. Despite these institutional barriers to stable, loving relationships, love and marriage between American military men and Okinawan women flourished. In late June 1947, the Soldier Brides Act relaxed immigration quotas for Japanese women who married military men during a month-long period in the summer of 1947. Nearly 1,000 couples in occupied mainland Japan took advantage of the law, while 53 American-Okinawan couples in Okinawa did so. Three years to the day after the U.S. forces invaded Okinawa, on April 1, 1948, the occupation again banned marriages between GIs and Okinawan women, a draconian measure that proved to be both ineffective and short-lived, as it was withdrawn four months after being issued. Thus, from late 1948 on, American GIs and Okinawan women could marry, but if the new couple wished to keep their household intact, their only option was to reside outside the United States because U.S. immigration policies continued to discriminate against Asians. In 1952, the U.S. Congress passed the McCarran-Walter Act, which allowed up to 185 Japanese military brides to immigrate to the United States (Forgash 2004). Okinawan brides of U.S. military men find it easier today to get visas for residence in the United States, although women from some countries married to servicemen still reportedly face hurdles.

Global American Military Basing and the Politicization of International Romance

Gender, militarism, and empire interact in unpredictable and complex ways. Marginalization and resistance among non-American women married to U.S. servicemen stationed abroad is a transnational phenomenon with a long history, as Maria Höhn's study of German women in the 1950s attests (Höhn 2002). Höhn discusses how early postwar nationalists on both the left and the right attempted to stem what they feared was the morally degenerative influence of American culture, and analyzes how German women who dated American GIs contested this political agenda. The Okinawan case illustrates that political attempts to regulate the love lives of women by condemning their relationships with American military men have been pursued by nationalists in a society that is different historically and culturally from Germany. At a broader level, my research aims to contribute to an emerging body of work on how the postwar American military empire has produced similar social effects across societies that host American garrisons, from European nations with which Americans have more equitable racial and economic relations to developing countries such as the Philippines, where racial and economic power asymmetries between members of the U.S. military and their hosts have been extreme (Sturdevant and Stoltzfus 1993). During the postwar period, Okinawan society has moved from impoverishment to become a province of one of world's wealthiest nations; for Okinawan women in relationships with U.S. military men, this shift has influenced, but not eliminated, the challenges they face on both sides of the base fences.

As Höhn has shown, political discourses ostensibly aimed at liberation from American military imperialism sometimes rely on oppressive means. In Okinawa, anti-base anger erupted in 1995 following the rape of a schoolgirl by three U.S. servicemen. Subsequently, women in relationships with military men reemerged as targets of local scorn after two decades of increased tolerance that corresponded to the relative dormancy of the base problem from the late 1970s through 1995. One Okinawan informant, who returned to the island with her military husband in 1996 after being transferred from a base in California, found the social climate in Okinawa far less hospitable for mixed couples after the rape in 1995. Ultimately, she and her husband avoided going off-base together for most of 1996, "until things cooled off." Although few Okinawan women today work as military prostitutes, repetition of activists' claims that "nothing has changed" since the occupation help to dredge up the specter of love between local women and GIs as organically linked to the sex industry, projecting the image of hapless prostitutes or bar girls onto these women via comments, stares, snickers, and pointed fingers.[4] In the decade following the peak in anti-base sentiment shortly after the rape in 1995, women in relationships with military men have continued to face public scrutiny, although my informants report that it has lessened substantially in recent years.

In situations permeated by imperial power, it is often unclear who is an insider or outsider. Among the challenges faced by the women in this study, negotiating liminal status in the Okinawan and base communities presented the most salient day-to-day difficulties. Flow between these two communities threatens nationalist resistance binaries of "us" and "them"; Okinawan women with American military husbands or boyfriends personify this permeability. Empires are not easily held together by military force. Their strongest glue resides in the structures of ambivalence—co-optation—that bind local and imperial power. Political, economic, and social ties, such as kinship, blur local interests with those of the imperial state. Such ties are deeply rooted in Okinawa due to the scale and length of its history of U.S. bases, the first of which was established there in 1853.[5]

Protest and Compensation, Compensation and Protest

In recent years, Okinawan voters have consistently elected base-accepting conservative candidates over their anti-base progressive peers in gubernatorial as well as key mayoral races. The gubernatorial election of 1998, in which the activist Ōta Masahide was defeated by an oil tycoon, served as a watershed in this transition. In the gubernatorial race of late 2006, a conservative who downplayed the base issue again defeated a staunchly anti-base opponent to realize a decade of conservative governors, parallel to that of the 1980s. The Okinawan author and activist Medoruma Shun has decried the proliferation of Japanese media stories simplistically explaining the recent string of conservative victories in Okinawa as indicating that Okinawans do not mind guns as long as they get enough butter; anti-base activists often criticize the Japanese government for attempting to purchase acquiescence by fostering economic dependence via a quid pro quo of subsidies for bases.[6] Contemporary Okinawan prosperity, in Medoruma's view, has become a trap that forces the bases on an unwilling population. This perspective fits in with the general history of the American military empire's development after the Second World War, as vanquished and victorious nation-states with devastated economies from Europe to Asia accepted U.S. bases along with— and perhaps in exchange for—economic benefits from the United States. The Cold War turbocharged this dynamic. Kent Calder's recent work suggests that such compensation politics in Okinawa and mainland Japan has yielded the most stable structure for basing among all nation-states hosting overseas U.S. garrisons worldwide (Calder 2007). These political-economic practices maintain the status quo on basing while responding to local voices of opposition with payoffs that quiet antipathy among the general population, even if they aggravate more radical critiques such as Medoruma's.

Gendered Byproducts of Nationalist Discourse

In locations such as Okinawa, nationalist movements seeking to dislodge U.S. bases at times have perceived that they have no choice but to dehumanize members of the U.S. military and marginalize compatriots who have ties to the military.[7] Among Okinawans with such ties, women in relationships with military men are the easiest to criticize. Unlike Okinawan base workers, who labor in the prefecture with Japan's highest unemployment rate, and Amerasian individuals, who were unable to select their own parents, these women freely choose to date or marry GIs and thus are seen as suitable targets for criticism. Considering the influence of gender in this dynamic, questions arise concerning the forms of power that finance nationalist resistance. Michael Molasky suggests that Okinawan literary works written by men, such as the prizewinning *Cocktail Party*, published in 1967, "condemn the sexual appropriation of local women by their foreign occupiers while these same texts appropriate the abstract figure of 'woman' to construct the male protagonist's sense of victimhood" (Molasky 1999, 28). Postwar Okinawan literature and journalism are saturated with stories of barbaric U.S. military men preying on female Okinawan victims, a trope that Molasky argues collapses violated innocent women's lives with the nation as represented by the Okinawan landscape. These narratives leave little symbolic space for consensual relationships. Ultimately, activists promise to free Okinawan women from violence by American GIS, only to re-subordinate these women to Okinawan masculine domination.

Cynthia Enloe is critical of such gendered nationalist movements. She writes: "Rape and prostitution have been central to many men's constructions of the nationalist cause. They have permitted men to hear the feminized nation beckoning them to act as 'her' protectors. The external enemy is imagined to be other men, men who would defile and denigrate the nation" (Enloe 1993, 239). Enloe makes an important, albeit insufficient, point for understanding the anathemization of Okinawan women in relationships with military men. Gendering Okinawa as a victimized woman is a trope deployed by female Okinawan anti-base activists, as well. In her public statements, the politician and feminist activist Takazato Suzuyo frequently likens Okinawa to Japan's "prostituted stepdaughter" to emphasize the prefecture's subordination in multiple senses; "prostitute" in these statements appears to be both a literal reference to the humiliating history of Okinawan women being forced by poverty to work in the sex industry and to Okinawa's being exploited for Japanese and American imperial interests, the ultimate example of which is the Battle of Okinawa (Takazato 1996).

A Concatenation of Racisms

As Ann Stoler's work on colonialism in Indonesia so compellingly illustrates, gender cannot be viewed in isolation because it is always already entwined with social class and "race" or ethnicity (Stoler 2002). Racism has long been rife in Okinawa, although its ubiquity does not imply homogenous practices. Japanese militarists during and before the Pacific War expected Okinawans to make the sacrifices they required of imperial subjects while simultaneously treating them as rustic second-class citizens; Okinawans' efforts to prove themselves as Japanese subjects while the Battle of Okinawa raged resulted in great loss of life without ameliorating discrimination, leaving only bitterness toward mainland Japan and profound distaste for war (Christy 1995). Wartime propaganda led many Okinawans to believe that American invaders were goblin-like monsters hell bent on torturing them in the cruelest imaginable ways; fearing beastly Americans, hundreds of Okinawans committed "compulsory group suicide (*shudan jiketsu*)" rather than face anticipated rape and torture at American hands.[8]

During the Battle of Okinawa and the occupation, the U.S. military and its members exported American racism—which was officially institutionalized within the Armed Forces at the time—by extending prejudice and discrimination reserved for people of color at home to America's new Okinawan charges. Over time, some Okinawans picked up on Americans' white–black racial antipathy and fashioned it into their own version, most often looking down on African American soldiers as the nadir of the island's social hierarchy. In contrast, some Okinawan nationalists, such as Arakawa Akira, expressed a sense of commonality with African Americans as fellow people of color, a category held together by anger against white members of the American military (Molasky 1999). Amid such conflict and anger spanning more than half a century, tens of thousands of Okinawan women and American military men have fallen in love, only to find that few people on either side of the base fences approve of their relationships. Probably the harshest example of denigration of these relationships in postwar literature is Arakawa's 1956 poem "The Yellow Race":

THE YELLOW RACE (PART II)
Within the Yellow Race
Are various types of people.

There are those
Who guard the purity of our blood
Who believe in the purity of our blood,
Who stand by one another, unfailing,
and march forth in unison

And there are those who
Betray our blood,
Who sell our blood,
Who hide their ugly simian face
behind a clever mask
Opportunists, shameless sycophants.

We will be watching,
To tear away their masks
and lay them beneath the bright sunlight.
We will be watching,
to expose the traps set by those
Who pollute our blood.
Our eyes wide open, always,
We will be watching.

We, the Yellow Race,
Take pride in being the Yellow Race.
Our eyes wide open,
We will march,
Watching for those apes within the Yellow Race,
Watching, ready to slit open the fat bellies
of those white wolves who
threaten our blood.
Our eyes wide open,
We will march. (Molasky 1999, 99–100)

In the popular imagination, the fallen Okinawan woman and her male military partner are conjoined by two forms of illegitimate blood work, the "selling" of Okinawan blood for the love of men who are in the business of bloodshed. Twin stereotypes of prostitute and GI emerge to police and homogenize perceptions of co-mingling foreign minds, lives, and bodies as necessarily exploitative, politically counterproductive acts brought together as literal embodiments of false consciousness. Yet, as I have noted, extremely few Okinawan women work as military prostitutes today, although some are employed as bartenders and hostesses at businesses that cater to predominately military clienteles. As Arakawa's poem states, there is palpable fear among some nationalist men that local women will "Betray our blood."[9] The notion of protecting Okinawan blood and putting this onus on Okinawan women is not limited to Arakawa. One informant, whose late father, a fellow journalist and contemporary of Arakawa's, recalled her father telling her: "You must protect your beautiful Ryūkyūan blood; you are forbidden to marry an American, a mainland Japanese or someone from Miyako Island [the disparaged penal colony during the Ryūkyū Kingdom]." She eventually married a mainland Japanese, divorced, and had a second marriage with an American that also ended in divorce. She and other women whose marriages with Americans did not last must endure eternal "I told you so" comments from relatives and peers.

Legendary Deceptions

The tragic plot of Okinawan women being victimized by foreign military men—not only raped but also deceived in consensual relationships—recalls a legend regarding the inception of Okinawa's troubled relationship with mainland Japan. In the story, a typhoon shipwrecked the mainland Japanese warrior Minamoto no Tametomo (1138–77?) on Okinawa Island, where he eventually married the daughter of a local chieftain. The couple had a son, who later founded the first dynasty of Ryūkyūan kings. Tametomo and his family attempted to sail to mainland Japan together, but a storm struck, and they were forced to return to the port, where the ship's captain argued that the sea god was angry because a woman was in the boat. Tametomo decided that he had no choice but to abandon his new family to return to mainland Japan, which he did when the skies cleared.[10] His wife and child waited faithfully for his return while residing in a cave near what henceforth has been known as "Waiting Port."[11] Tametomo never returned, however, because he supposedly committed suicide during a futile battle with a rival clan in 1177. Today, the harbor's shoreline is dominated by a U.S. Marine Corps base bearing its name, Makiminato.[12] Tametomo's masculine prowess as one of Japan's greatest warriors and his abandonment of his Okinawan family presage the attraction and tragic consequences many in Okinawa believe define relationships between foreign military men and Okinawan women. The tale also hints at the uneven power relationship between mainland Japan and Okinawa.

"The Bases Themselves Are Pollution"

Contemporary Okinawans continue to chafe at the concentration of U.S. bases, which is seen as disproportionately benefiting mainland Japanese and American interests while Okinawans shoulder the costs of military accidents, aircraft noise, crime, and, most important, a painful awareness that a foreign military controls much of their crowded island. For many, military male and Okinawan female couples are an interpersonal-level manifestation of foreign domination and deception, legitimating disapproval of these relationships and marginalization of the Okinawan women involved. Some Okinawans continue to discriminate against these couples' so-called *haafu* children, as well, treating Amerasians as living embodiments of "unnatural" relationships and embarrassing symbols of Okinawa's tragic history of subjugation.[13]

Okinawan activists' derision for the bases and everything connected with them contributes to the marginalization of Amerasians and women with American partners. Takazato's oft-quoted remark, "The bases themselves are pollution," is representative of totalizing strategies deployed to dislodge the bases by propagating "good" and "evil" binarist discourses that intentionally or unintentionally sweep some Okinawans into the latter camp due to their employment and kinship ties with the bases. Takazato has repeatedly stated publicly that she believes military training yields service members who are inherently violent people, one of many activists' comments that sting Okinawans with a U.S. military husband, father, or friend.[14] In my interview with her, Takazato expressed concern about discrimination against Amerasian children and against women who are in relationships with military men, although she did not recognize her own remarks as contributing to the anti-base backlash against these people or their American military kin. A recent volume edited by Arasaki Moriteru, an activist and professor at Okinawa University, takes up this issue squarely, however, noting:

> Anti-American sentiment is deeply ingrained in the heart of Okinawans due to the island's long history of hosting large-scale American military bases. As a result, it sometimes takes the form of discrimination and prejudice against Amerasians, who symbolize to them the military bases. It is no exaggeration to say that this is a violation of human rights committed by Okinawans, who were themselves discriminated against by both Japan and America. And it is a blind spot often overlooked by Okinawans. (Arasaki 2000, 161)

Mediated Sentiments and the Contradictions of Resistance

Anti-base discourse produced by activists and politicians such as Takazato are disseminated through the simplifying mechanism of Okinawa's two widely circulated nationalist newspapers, contributing to negative sentiment against everyone connected with the bases. In my view, such attempts to clarify ethnic boundaries police the binary of "Okinawan" versus "not Okinawan" through social praxis founded on fear of spiritual and physical pollution, a classical anthropological approach pioneered by Mary Douglas (1984 [1966]). Accordingly, when an Okinawan woman openly maintains a relationship with a military man, Okinawans often use linguistic slurs such as "*Amejo* (American woman)" or "*Kokujo* (black woman)" to attempt to classify her as an American "other." Such categorical relegation approaches binary discreteness due to hegemonic conceptions of Japan as a mono-ethnic nation and a corresponding unacceptability of hybrid identities (Hein and Selden 2003, 23). Ironically, activists' criticism of mainland Japanese mono-ethnic ideology as marginalizing or forcibly assimilating Okinawans does not prevent anti-base leaders from replicating mono-ethnic marginalizing strategies against internal others. Okinawan elites such as the former Prefectural Governor Ōta Masahide have long attempted to posit a homogenous *Uchinaanchu* (Okinawan) identity that masks internal heterogeneity in service of specific political agendas.[15] Ota has used what Gayatri Spivak termed "strategic essentialism" to position the Okinawan people as a historically pacifist group subjected to age after age of indignities by militaristic outsiders.[16] Identity politics ultimately reproduces the structures of domination activists ostensibly oppose as U.S. military bases become enemy strongholds populated by polluted others.

Talking with informants made me aware of how Okinawan women married to or dating military men experience implied, but seldom directly stated, suggestions that they are traitors. An Okinawan woman who works on a military base and is in a long-term relationship with a military man, awoke one morning shortly after the rape in 1995 to find the word "traitor (hiko-kumin)" scrawled in black spray paint on the hood of her white Nissan sedan. This incident crystallizes how a movement aimed at peace can be used by some individuals as an opportunity to pursue reactionary courses of action. The choice of words in this case is ironic, since the slur "hikokumin" had currency before and during the Pacific War as a means of badgering critics of Japan's militarist aggression as well as people such as Okinawans whose ethnic purity or patriotism was questionable. My informant interpreted the crime as criticism of her relationship with a member of the American military. She never found out who had vandalized her car. Anticipating criticism of her relationship with an American military man and violation of her privacy, she decided not to call the police.

This incident and other cases of harassment reported by my informants presaged the appropriation of anti-base rhetoric by Japanese neo-fascists in the early years of the twenty-first century. The right-wing cartoonist Kobayashi Yoshinori, whose earlier works questioned the existence of an official system of forced prostitution during the Pacific War while portraying Japanese aggression in Asia as libratory, created a series of cartoons on Okinawan history that ran in the reactionary magazine *Sapio* during 2004. In the summer of 2005, the series was published as the *manga* (cartoon book) *Okinawa-ron* (Treatise on Okinawa [Kobayashi 2005]). Mainlander Kobayashi's nationalistic manga idealizes ancient Ryūkyū and contemporary Okinawa as being more Japanese than mainland Japan itself; he attempted to flatter Okinawans by composing an afterword that advocates the cultural Okina-wanization of Japan, inverting the historical power relationship. Most of the volume's 407 pages is a venomously critical history of the postwar U.S. military in Okinawa. In one chapter, Kobayashi questions widely shared Okinawan perceptions that the U.S. military was comparatively kind to Okinawans during and immediately after the Battle of Okinawa. Conveniently, although he covers ancient history, Kobayashi leaves the Battle of Okinawa and Japanese wartime atrocities committed against Okinawans "for another time," preferring to fan Okinawan anger against the U.S. military to risking alienating Okinawan readers by repeating his earlier claims elsewhere that Okinawan compulsory group suicides enforced by the Japanese military were voluntary (Kobayashi 2005, 11).

In *Okinawa-ron*, Kobayashi expresses dismay that he shares the anti-American and anti-base sentiments of leftist Okinawan activists, if not for the same reasons. Such affinity led Diet Representative Itokazu Keiko, a leftist anti-base activist who was defeated in the 2006 gubernatorial race, to appear on stage at a local convention center with Kobayashi in 2005 during his visit to Okinawa, an act that shocked Takazato and other leftist activists. There are structural similarities between Japanese wartime fascism / neo-fascism and the Okinawan anti-base movement: both marshal nationalistic concepts of ethnic homogeneity and unity to oppose American empire while battling the U.S. military with similar levels of self-righteousness. There are also important differences, however, since most contemporary Okinawan anti-base activists, unlike their wartime fascist and neo-facist counterparts, *are* anti-war, usually eschew violence, and maintain anti-base positions within a constellation of other political opinions that are clearly progressive. With public support for the anti-base movement on the wane after 1996, some activists, such as Medoruma, have become critical of the movement's reliance on peaceful protest, suggesting that violence, including killing Americans in Okinawa, may be needed to further the cause (Molasky 2003, 161–91). This turn in the anti-base movement, the structural similarities between it and Japanese fascism, and the fact that Kobayashi's manga was a bestseller in Okinawa all suggest that Okinawan anti-base nationalism is amenable to valence switching from left to right. Harassment of Amerasians and Okinawan women with American military partners is thus more than an unfortunate byproduct of ethnic unity required to rid the island of bases. It is also a demonstration of the contradictions at the heart of ostensibly leftist nationalism operating through identity politics.

The Incomplete Project of Liberation

With a few exceptions, such as Linda Angst, scholars have rarely examined how an anti-base movement ostensibly directed at liberation has resulted in the marginalization of other disempowered persons (Angst 2003, 135–60). Angst critiques how Okinawan activists, including former Prefectural Governor Ōta Masahide, have used cases of violence against women by members of the military to bolster and illustrate symbolic claims of violence perpetuated against Okinawa by the U.S. military and mainland Japan. She notes that Okinawan activists—even some feminist activists—positing "pure" Okinawan women as innocent victims obscures and even denigrates the suffering of other women, such as sex workers, who have also paid an enormous price due to militarism. Angst concludes:

> Protest leaders, who define an idea of collective cultural self through reference to a pristine, precolonial past, draw upon images of purity and chastity, such as the Himeyuri and the raped schoolgirl (the Himeyuri or Princess Lily Student Corps was a group of elite girls from an Okinawan school who served as field nurses during the Battle of Okinawa in 1945. Most perished with their teachers in the battle, some committing suicide out of fear that they would be raped and tortured by American troops, as Japanese wartime propaganda suggested.); in the process, the real prostituted daughters of Okinawa are excluded. Indeed, in many ways, bar and brothel women are lingering and unwanted images of prewar era Okinawa as low ethnic other, while Filipina women, the new sex workers, are largely absent from the discussion. Despite their many sacrifices, these women are coded as less deserving of public concern by many groups because they are not "pure." (Angst 2003, 152)

Her work is highly critical of activists' insistence on a unified front against the bases as a strategic error that displays "an inherently patriarchal political outlook, . . . subordinating issues of women's human rights to the cause of Okinawan nationalism" (Angst 2003, 152–53).[17]

Accounts of sexual crimes by American GIS against Okinawan women receive differential treatment, creating and reflecting public opinion that certain women are innocent victims while others are less so.[18] If the victim is suspected of being a so-called Amejo or, to an even greater degree, a Kokujo, the incident receives comparatively little media attention and is accompanied by relatively low levels of social outrage. "She had it coming. Anyone associating with military people gets what they deserve is the logic behind this. Amejo are already on the other side, like military people themselves," explained a male reporter I interviewed who worked at a local newspaper. If the woman works in a bar or visits a club frequented by American GIS, the crime lacks the requisite "innocent victim" profile. Coverage of, and public response to, the rape committed by an Air Force enlisted man in 2001 in the parking lot of the American Village shopping mall demonstrated this bias, since his victim was deemed culpable for going to a club frequented by servicemen and voluntarily leaving with the assailant. Takazato noted, "There has been a lot of victim-bashing in this case, especially in the press."[19] In contrast to the rape of a schoolgirl by three servicemen in 1995, which led to protests that drew as many as 80,000 Okinawans, attempts to organize an anti-base rally after the rape in 2001 fizzled due to lack of interest among activists based on the demographic profile of the victim. Women who date military men garner little sympathy because of the logic of "approach to danger," which faults them for choosing to associate with GIs. Curiously, some of the same individuals who express this logic with respect to victims of sexual crimes also tend to object to the Japanese courts' refusal, on grounds of "approach to danger," to grant damages to people living near air bases who claim that aircraft noise interferes with their lives. In these cases, the courts have stated on multiple occasions that people who move in next to the bases knew there would be aircraft noise.

If, as the activist Uezato Kazumi (2000) suggests, many Okinawan men oppose international relationships because they fear the sexual competition presented by the hyper-masculine GI stereotype, Okinawan women tend to oppose Okinawan–GI relationships from pragmatic perspectives. My female informants who were critical of Okinawan military relationships claimed their opposition was rooted in the high divorce rate such couples experience, the lack of social acceptance their marriage or children are likely to receive in Okinawan society, and anecdotal evidence from friends and relatives about the interpersonal challenges of international marriage. One ordinarily reserved mother of a woman marrying an American GI made an impassioned speech at her daughter's wedding, saying, "I opposed this marriage because I love my daughter and I feared you would go far away and never come back, like so many Okinawan women before you have done, but it is your life and I support you now." Although family opposition to daughters' dating or marrying a GI is common, several of my informants had parents—or at least one parent—who approved of their relationships. One woman even began dating Americans after her mother, who was disgruntled in her own marriage to an Okinawan man, suggested American men as an alternative based on her perception of American men's "ladies first" chivalric tradition, an image, her daughter later noted, that was acquired from Hollywood love stories. Some informants had very unsympathetic parents. "My parents refused to acknowledge my husband because he is an American GI, but after our first child was born, my mother warmed up a little bit. My father still sometimes calls our son a 'kuronbo [literally, 'black baby,' a slur],' " noted an Okinawan woman married for six years to a U.S. Marine.

Performing Ethnicity under the Romantic Gaze

Ironically, there seems to be a pattern in some relationships wherein American GIS find themselves attracted to their ideal of an "Oriental lady" as someone submissive and undemanding, while their Okinawan partners report being attracted to their ideal of American men as "feminists (*feminisuto*)," which in Japanese can simply mean "men who are considerate to women." A counselor who works with Okinawan–American couples noted, "When they are dating they tend to see the ideal rather than the person, but once they marry they must come to terms with the person and discard stereotypical ideals." Curiously, military men's Orientalism has its counterpart in the essentialist ways some women in Okinawa view their boyfriends and husbands. The objectification of military men by Japanese and Okinawan women is a gaze reversal of the stereotypical "Oriental lady" fetish said to be common among military men stationed in Asia. Karen Kelsky researched Japanese mainland women's "romantic longing (*akogare*)" for Western men, drawing on Michel Foucault's notion that "where there is desire, the power relation is always present" (Foucault 1990, 81, cited in Kelsky 2001, 10). Hollywood has played a huge role in Japan supporting akogare among women for the sensitive but strong Western men of their imaginations. It is not unusual to hear Okinawan women debate which famous actor or musician their foreign boyfriends or husbands most resemble. The mainland Japanese author Yamada Eimi's perennially popular novels touting African American men as lovers also fuel the development of akogare. An Okinawan dentist dating an African American soldier proudly showed me her collection of Yamada's works, which filled a large bookcase. Films such as *Top Gun* and *An Officer and a Gentleman* depict American military men in modes that appeal to young Okinawan women as fantastic, gentlemanly alternatives to the barbaric stereotypes of these men propagated by anti-base activists.

I conducted fieldwork for this essay at a soul-music bar in my neighborhood called 24–7, after the title of a novel by Yamada. Okinawan and Japanese women who prefer African American men frequent this bar. A regular customer in her mid-twenties explained her distaste for some of her younger peers at the bar, saying, "They have no respect for their men. These young girls treat them like accessories, trying to show off their black man to impress their friends and piss off their parents. I think they are racists in some twisted sense." An African American friend in the Air Force had come to a similar conclusion after being stationed in Okinawa for only six months:

> At first I thought, "Wow, I have never been so attractive to women before." Back home I was just plain old Mike, but here I was like a hip-hop superstar. After a while it began to bother me, though, when women came up to me and called me "brutha." I have never talked Ebonics. My folks are English teachers in suburban New Jersey. I just could not perform for those girls anymore. It wasn't always clear to me whether my girlfriend liked Mike or just wanted an African American boyfriend.

Tiring of performing ethnicity for one's lover is not limited to heterosexual relationships. A female American English teacher in Okinawa said she had stopped dating Okinawan women because she began to have doubts similar to those Mike experienced. Despite her misgivings about the military as an institution, she developed a happy relationship with an active-duty woman.[20]

Kelsky (2001) notes that in the hierarchy of desirable Western male partners for Japanese women, military men rank near the bottom. My findings suggest precisely the opposite in Okinawa, where military men seem to be desirable as hyper-masculine men with stable jobs. I found that some young women in Okinawa who enjoy serial relationships with GIS reveal perspectives on their relationships that defy the victimized image of these women as deceived by military men. A nurse in her twenties explained:

> I don't accept the victim label many in Okinawa would like to stick on me for dating GIS. My girlfriends and I are not stupid, you know. We all went to the University of the Ryūkyūs [Okinawa's top university], and if these men are using us, well, then we are using them, too. To tell the truth, unlike Okinawan women during the occupation who cried when their GI left them, we don't mind saying goodbye because it's exciting to see who we will meet next.

In a reversal of GIS' paying the rent or buying food and luxuries for a girl-friend and her family during the occupation, some contemporary Okinawan women give lavish gifts to American GI boyfriends who claim to be poor even though tax-free housing and subsistence allowances leaves them with sufficient disposable income to lodge them clearly in the U.S. middle class. My informants had bought boyfriends new cars, expensive stereos, and luxury vacations. One well-heeled woman reported buying her boyfriend a late-model Mercedes-Benz when he asked for one. Nevertheless, although the vast majority of Okinawan women do not struggle with the degree of poverty that their grandmothers faced, most must work hard for relatively low wages in the service sector that dominates the prefectural economy. Many young women in my study had disposable income because they lived rent-free with family members. In this respect, their economic situations were similar to those of their partners in the military, whose seemingly low salaries were mostly discretionary funds thanks to a variety of tax-free allowances for housing, education, health care, and food. Although Okinawan women living at home and dating military men reported having difficulties maintaining privacy in their love lives, my informants also said that doing so provided significant emotional support. Those living on their own often visited their natal home or socialized with female friends, many of whom were also dating or married to military men.

Foreign Selves Refashioned

Kelsky discusses scholarly debates over the place of women in Japanese society in her study of Japanese women's romantic longing for Western men, noting that some scholars assert that "women are imagined in Japan as already 'partially foreign'" (Kelsky 2001, 10). For Okinawan women in relationships with military men, women's marginality becomes alloyed with seemingly subversive love justifying otherization as the natural result of a personal choice of partners. My Okinawan informants identified the stereotypical Amejo or Kokujo as a woman who is ruled by her desire for difference; she is imagined as dressing and acting flamboyantly, the near-opposite of valorized images of Okinawan women as paragons of reserve and strength. Considering the challenges that they face, my informants in relationships with military men were uniformly strong women. Their putative "lack of reserve" was something several of these informants equated with being liberated from what they perceived as the weight of Okinawan traditions through their expanded cultural affiliation with America, a finding consistent with Kelsky's interpretation of mainland Japanese women seeking American partners as a way of refashioning themselves.

Not all women in relationships with military men viewed lack of reserve as a positive or agentic expression of self, however. In her study of transnational military marriage in Okinawa, Rebecca Forgash (2004) notes that her informants attempted to distance themselves from the "low-class" stereotypes of bar girls by dressing conservatively, insisting that Amejo and Kokujo are predominately mainland Japanese or Filipina women or emphasizing their own educational and career achievements. Among my informants who had contemporary or past relationships with military men were a custodian, a surgeon, college students, schoolteachers, housewives, base workers, municipal office employees, nurses, retail saleswomen, and women in other occupations. The group included only one stereotypical bar hostess.[21] Most of my informants volunteered their perspectives of the association between "international marriage" in Okinawa and the stereotype of bar hostesses. Although some resorted to the tactic of projecting negative images onto mainland women or Filipinas, others reappropriated pejorative the "Amejo" and "Kokujo" labels as a source of pride, resistance, and social distinction, embracing elements of the stereotype to demonstrate courage to be different. Three informants used the contemporary catchphrase of Japanese youthful individualism—"*Jibun rashii* (To be myself)"—to explain apparent lack of concern at being called "Amejo" or "Kokujo." Indeed, a standing joke among friends in this group of women was to call one another "Amejo" or "Kokujo" in playful rivalry over who demonstrated stereotypical characteristics to the greatest degree. As Christopher Nelson (2009) has shown, Okinawans have used humor to establish a sense of commonality and make the unbearable bearable during the islands' painful modern history. Similarly, attention to the role of community building among Okinawan women in relationships with U.S. military men reveals engagement among them that works to counter marginalization.

Resisting Marginalization through Mutual Support

The Japanese Wives Club in Okinawa is an independently organized group that tries to provide support for Japanese and Okinawan women engaged or married to American military men. Members hold regular meetings, manage a listserv, and have parties. Women who joined the group reported hoping that it would relieve feelings of isolation, despite the fact that they were all still residing in their own country. Group members meet to make new friends, learn about military and American lifestyles, and exchange experiences and information while providing support for each other. Courses on international marriage introduced the women to the rhythms of military life while offering information on visa applications, permanent residence, and citizenship in the United States. Women also met to cook together, exchanging recipes for American food as well as for Japanese and Okinawan cuisine. Those with husbands deployed to other bases, or to war fronts in Iraq or Afghanistan, met to release stress in the Kirin Group.[22] Leaders encouraged members to get involved in community service by conducting volunteer activities on- and off-base and raising money for charity.

The Japanese Wives Club struggles with unity and fragmentation mainly as byproducts of the criticism its members seek to challenge both on and off the base. Like Japanese society, Okinawan society has a pronounced hierarchy determined partially by gender, age, local origin, and class. Although members reported joining the club to escape from the oppressive gaze of Okinawans judging their choice of partners, many found that the same hierarchical forces permeated the activities of the organization. Knowledge of American culture and the constantly changing, arcane aspects of military life were clearly markers of status and power among the most active members. The division between officers' wives and enlisted men's wives conditioned interaction between women even when their husbands were not present. Experience living abroad, degree of fluency in English, race or ethnic origin of the husband, and so forth all militated against members' forming the unity they optimistically had hoped the Japanese Wives Club would offer. Further tension was demonstrated between Okinawan and mainland Japanese members, with each perceiving the other has having preconceived, essentialist notions. Okinawan women reported feeling as if some mainland Japanese members "look down on us." Conversely, mainland Japanese members said they felt as if "certain Okinawan members seem to think we are uppity." The geographic division between Okinawa and mainland Japan was frequently played out in interpersonal proxemics at parties; Okinawan and mainland women tended to self-segregate.

Another challenge members faced was suspicion among husbands about the time their wives were spending with club members. Women invited their husbands and children to participate in club parties and other activities to demonstrate a spirit of openness. The level of spousal participation also became a marker of status within the group, offering higher-status members the opportunity to make explicit their family's place in the hierarchy by introducing the principal source of that status.

It is through their husbands that these women usually interact with the military as an institution. American spouses and foreign spouses of military personnel are placed in a dependent relationship on the "sponsor," and the military institution itself, as "dependents." Familial hierarchy is thus continually reified by institutional structure, circumscribing the agentic potential of dependents such as Okinawan women married to military men. In one reading, the resistance of loving military men promises to free Okinawan women from the oppressive structure of Okinawan male domination off-base, only to re-submit them to the domination of the social rules of the military community as mediated by their spouses as "sponsors" on-base.

The appeal of the Japanese Wives Club is in its potential, however incomplete, for serving as a third space ideally free of the gendered subordination these women face off and on military bases. Ultimately, masculine foreclosure of agentic space is incomplete, because as long as the couple resides in Okinawa, the wives play an important mediating role between their husbands and Okinawan society. Indicative of residual power asymmetries, however, are widespread social practices requiring Okinawan wives of military men to become proficient in English and knowledgeable about military and American culture. Military men rarely face expectations or demands that they learn the Japanese language, even though they reside physically in Japanese territory. Some men do learn Japanese, but many more—even those who choose to live in Okinawa for decades—opt to lead lives centered on the military base, with limited contact outside the fences. As interviews with both partners in numerous couples made clear, lack of linguistic ability among military men married to Okinawan women makes these husbands dependent on their wives for even the simplest tasks attempted off-base.

If the military social structure limits Okinawan wives' agency, it also provides openings for its expression. As couples, Okinawan women and their military partners in Okinawa have succeeded in negotiating spaces for themselves and their families amid challenges and criticism from numerous directions. A surprising number of Okinawan women married to military men have sought to reside in the garrisons rather than in Okinawan communities. Women who had lived in the United States with their husbands tended to prefer living on-base in Okinawa to living in America or off-base in Okinawa. Several informants explained that residing on-base in Okinawa provided a comfortable mix or cultural compromise between Okinawa, the military, and America, allowing them to regulate interaction and social obligations between themselves and their Okinawan families while providing a refuge away from Okinawan "cold stares" questioning their partner preferences. As the Japanese Wives Club's goals suggest, meeting with other women who are negotiating the same sets of challenges is also an advantage of living on-base.

Okinawan women in relationships with U.S. military men who are stationed in Okinawa face marginalization from multiple angles. As I have attempted to show, these women challenge marginalization by agentically expressing confidence in themselves and their choices amid widespread nationalist criticism by fellow Okinawans. Sustained contact between the U.S. military and the societies that host its overseas installations show the contradictions inherent in empire, yielding nationalist resistance movements that grapple with, and sometimes reproduce, further inequities and contradictions. This essay has attempted to demonstrate the uneven aspects of the Okinawan anti-base movement and its impact on Okinawans whose daily lives are intimately entwined with base-community members. I have also emphasized that American empire and the resistance it breeds must be considered at the micro-level of interpersonal interaction, as well as at the macro-level of institutions and social movements. Organizations such as the Japanese Wives Club play a key role in fostering these women's individual and collective agency by bringing women together to share information and experiences germane to their common situations. Through this organization, members created a community of Okinawan and Japanese women married to American military men that could be passed along to incoming military families, forging connections that would provide support no matter where their family resides. Although the club's goals were hampered to some degree by internal tension, most participants found it comforting to interact with other women like themselves.

Decades of public disapproval clearly have not prevented Okinawan women and U.S. military men from pursuing relationships. Repellence structures that play on fear of marginalization as "fallen women" associated with low-status sex work exist in dynamic tension with attraction to American men as exotic alternatives to their Okinawan counterparts. These women's agency is often truncated, co-opted, and twisted by critics of such relationships into support for structures policing sexuality. For Okinawan women in relationships with American military men, anti-base sentiment founded on treating all aspects of the bases as pollution has presented a bumpy road over the past sixty years. However, the activities of the Japanese Wives Club and of individual women suggest that resistance to marginalization among these women has emerged in myriad forms to match the multiple directions from which they face scrutiny.

Notes

1. My study had more than one hundred participants, including Okinawans, members of the American military community, mainland Japanese residents of Okinawa, Fili-

pinas, and several people from other countries. Their ages ranged from twenty years old, the legal age of adulthood in Japan, to eighty-five. I acquired most my data through participant observation. My seven-year marriage with an Okinawan woman provided opportunities to attempt to understand her contemporaries, many of whom had also dated or married Americans. I attended parties hosted by the Japanese Wives Club, an organization for Okinawan and Japanese women married to military men; visited clubs and bars where Okinawan women and U.S. military men interacted; and participated in international exchange events sponsored by local nonprofit organizations. I was fortunate to work with Okinawan, mainland Japanese, and American military colleagues for seven years in the field of local-level international relations at an Okinawan municipal office and on Kadena Air Base, the largest U.S. base on Okinawa Island. My informants also included limited numbers of people in same-sex relationships between Okinawans and members of the military, as well as relationships between Okinawan men and U.S. military women, although this essay focuses only on the more common couple configuration of an Okinawan woman partnered with a U.S. military man.

2. Differences in average annual income between rural prefectures in Japan are slight in comparison with the gap between urban and rural areas. Okinawa Prefecture's average annual figures are a few hundred dollars (40,000 yen in 2005) lower than those in neighboring Kagoshima Prefecture, which was home to the Satsuma domain in early modern Japan that became Okinawa's first in a succession of exploitative outside rulers after an invasion in 1609. For comparative data on Japanese prefectures, see *Deeta de Miru Kensei* [Japanese on the Prefectures of Japan], published annually by the firm Kokusei-sha.

3. See also James and Tamamori 1996, 17. This book includes a chart comparing average per capita incomes in various Japanese prefectures with those in developed nations' economies. Okinawa's figures were roughly equal to those of France using 1993 statistics.

4. See "Makeru no wa Nihon Seifu da [The loser will be the Japanese government]," *Sekai*, April 2006, for a roundtable discussion of contemporary base issues among three of Okinawa's representatives to the Japanese National Diet: Teruya Kantoku, Itokazu Keiko, and Shimoji Mikio. "Nothing has changed" is a major theme emphasized by all three. The theme has had widespread usage at least since testimony by former Prefectural Governor Ōta Masahide's before the Japanese Supreme Court deployed it to protest the central government's forcing him to coerce military land owners to lease land shortly after the rape incident in 1995.

5. The first U.S. base in Okinawa was established in July 1853, when Commodore Matthew Perry visited Okinawa Island shortly before pressuring Japan to open its doors to trade and diplomacy. Backed by two hundred U.S. Marines, Perry marched up the hill to Shuri Castle and demanded to see the Ryūkyūan king. The base remained for one year while Perry forced unequal treaties on both Japan and the Kingdom of Ryūkyū. American military personnel accompanying Perry caused social upheaval in the local community, particularly after a drunken seaman named William Board raped an

elderly Okinawan woman and was subsequently chased off a cliff to his death by local residents. Board's grave remains in Naha's Cemetery for Foreigners near Tomari Port.

6. Medoruma's column "Kichi ka Keizai ka' de Kataruna [Don't chalk it up to 'Either bases or the economy')" appeared in the mainland's *Asahi Shimbun*, 25 November 2006, 17.

7. Some Okinawan activists have eschewed the temptation to dehumanize their opponents. Among them, the late Ahagon Shoko who is sometimes called "Okinawa's Gandhi," is the most notable. Ahagon was a devout Christian and admirer of American democratic values who also stood up with his fellow Ie Island community members against appropriations of land for the U.S. military during the occupation. He insisted that movement members avoid talking with GIs in abusive language, stick to the principles of nonviolence, and attempt to make their points through reason. Even Ahagon sometimes resorted to referring to members of the U.S. military as "devils," a fact that is understandable to some degree when one considers that the U.S. military took his and other Ie Islanders' homes at gunpoint and destroyed them with bulldozers: see Ahagon 1989.

8. Norma Field (1993) discusses the activist Chibana Shoichi's efforts to research and preserve the tragedy of compulsory group suicide in Okinawa. Chibana, who was one of my informants, is noteworthy for avoiding vilification of people associated with the bases, opting instead to focus his resistance against the military institution and the political machinery that keeps it in place.

9. Arakawa is the foremost advocate of Okinawan independence from Japan. It is noteworthy that he is what some Okinawans call a "Shima-haafu [literally, half-islander]," with an Okinawan father and a mainland Japanese mother. His work makes it clear that he identifies with his father's ethnic group more strongly.

10. There are several variants of this legend. The version I draw on for this essay was taken from Kawahira 1970.

11. The area is called Makiminato in contemporary Okinawa, a "Japanized" word that draws on the pronunciation of the older Ryūkyūan place name Machinatuu.

12. The base is also called Camp Kinser.

13. One middle-age female informant expressed dismay that Okinawans and Americans can have children together due to what she perceived as their radical differences, both physical and cultural. Amerasians in Okinawa continue to suffer severe discrimination, especially at schools. The fact that some people of Okinawan and American ancestry are now older than sixty has not eliminated their exclusion.

14. Most people in America's current all-volunteer Armed Forces tend to join the military because capitalism and globalization have acted violently against them as poor or minority Americans, leaving many with limited economic choices and access to health care outside the military. Joining up provides a middle-class income, free college tuition, stock-based and non-stock-based retirement annuities, free rent, free health care, preferential hiring in the civil service, and numerous other benefits that are increasingly rare in America's private and public sectors.

15. In an editorial published in the mainland's progressive newspaper *Asahi Shimbun* on

19 October 1996, the historian Takara Kurayoshi criticized Okinawans for marginalizing minority voices within the prefecture that were at odds with the anti-base sentiment that had been sparked by three servicemen's rape of a schoolgirl. Takara pled for consideration of the opinions of people such as Okinawan women married to U.S. military men, stating, "The sight of Uchinaanchu [Okinawans] who themselves continue to make claims of suffering as a minority within Japanese society giving insufficient attention to minority voices within Okinawa saddens me. This is a topic that must be considered today and in the future by everyone living in Okinawa": Takara 1997, 111.

16. Ōta's testimony in 1996 before the Japanese Supreme Court, translated into English in Ōta 2000, is a classic example of strategic essentialist discourse. See also Teruya 2001 for a discussion of how the myth of innate Ryūkyūan pacifism developed before Ōta and anti-base activists re-appropriated it to serve the contemporary anti-base movement.

17. Although she does not specifically discuss discrimination against Okinawan women in relationships with military men, her critique can be applied compellingly to the subject of this essay.

18. Both major Okinawan newspapers, the *Okinawa Times* and *Ryūkyū Shimpo*, give tremendous attention to military crimes, ranging from theft of a plastic lighter at a bar to rapes and murders; at the same time, they pay comparatively little attention to such crimes when committed by Okinawans. Prefectural police statistics indicate that since the 1980s, at least, the military-base community's per capita crime rates across all categories of crime are only a fraction of the rates for Okinawans themselves. Takazato criticized comparing crime statistics from these two communities, saying, "Such comparisons themselves are wrongheaded." For a detailed discussion of comparative crime statistics between U.S. military stationed in Japan, crime committed by other foreigners, and crimes committed by Japanese nationals, see Michael Hassett, "U.S. Military Crime: SOFA So Good?" *Japan Times*, 26 February 2008, available online at http://search.japantimes.co.jp/cgi-bin/f120080226zg.html (accessed 30 March 2010).

19. "Japanese Media Try Character of Alleged Rape Victim in Okinawa," *Pacific Stars and Stripes*, 26 August 2001, 1. The racial politics of this case received worldwide media attention through *Time*, *Newsweek*, and other publications arguing that Japanese and Okinawan racism motivated criticism of the Okinawan victim for associating with African American men.

20. Although this essay is hetero-centric due to space constraints, exploring Okinawa–GI same-sex relationships is an important topic for research. The U.S. military's homophobic institutional policies, however, present even greater challenges for researchers.

21. The only person in my study who claimed to have exchanged compensation (in the form of "presents") for sexual services was a former male member of the military who had arranged meetings with mainland tourists looking for African American men during their vacations. In Japanese, this is called "*gyaku-enko* (reverse compensated dating)." Although legions of women in Japan work as bar hostesses nurturing the

egos of male customers, there are also significant numbers of "host bars" where men serve women. Such bars are popular among hostesses, who often drop by the host clubs after their own bars shut down for the evening to reverse the direction of gender service.

22. The *kirin* is a chimerical dragon-like creature said to bring serenity. The word also means "giraffe" in modern Japanese.

SIX

HIDDEN SOLDIERS

Working for the "National Defense"

☆

ROBIN RILEY

The war against Afghanistan and Iraq and the occupation of Iraq are being carried out by a military that relies on women's explicit participation. The ideas about gender—masculinity and femininity—on which militarism has traditionally relied, however, have meant that the preparation for and carrying out of war has been the sole purview of men. Idealized militarized femininity has dictated that women should not be interested in war, either as participants, preparers, or decision makers. These notions about the role of men and women have been extremely powerful in allowing war to be waged for the protection or salvation of "weak" women.

In this study of women who worked in the U.S. defense industry in the late 1990s through the early 2000s, the actual practice of militarized femininity has meant that the construct of the peace-loving woman, the weak and dependent woman, or the militaristic cheerleader all fail to describe adequately the reality of these women's lives. Here women make weapons for a living while claiming that what they do does not contribute to war. Here women are extraordinarily strong in bearing the burden of home lives that include mostly absent male partners, and some raise children to resist military enlistment. Here these women practice a militarized femininity, far from the ideal, that allows them to make weapon-delivery systems while thinking of the end result as defensive products. In this way, both in the home and in the workplace, militarized femininity now means that they can contribute to the waging of war while not believing that they do so and give tacit agreement to global imperialism—after all, it is for "our own protection."

Over the past fifty years, the primary beneficiaries of one aspect of militarism—the U.S. obsession with continual preparation for war—have been private defense contractors who rely mostly on U.S. government contracts for their business.[1] U.S. defense contractors often hire retired military officials as upper-level executives.[2] This practice not only enables the company or corporation to have the inside track on getting new contracts through the former military officers' contacts, but it also transfers militarized ways of organization and management into the companies.[3] So the hiring of mostly male retired military officers, along with the male dominance of professions such as aerospace engineering, means that these corporations become sites where militarized paradigms prevail, hierarchical methods of management are emphasized, and militarized masculinity is privileged (Heinrichs 2007).[4] The number of non-military women who work in these corporations is small, and the minority status of women within these highly masculinized sites frequently means difficult working conditions. Their work is often devalued by their employers and by the women themselves, and they have difficulty naming and conceptualizing their contributions to the corporation, to the nation, to militarism, to imperialism, to war.

Of course, gender is at work in how the women are seen and see themselves in society in general and within these sites of militarized masculinity. As Martin Shaw (1991, 12) suggests, militarism refers to a combination of war preparation and social relations. The perpetuation and spread of militarism in the United States relies on the belief in particularly rigid constructions of masculinity and femininity, and the participation and endorsement of both men and women is necessary for the process of militarization (Enloe 1993, 2000). That is, traditional constructions of masculinity and femininity must be ideologically adhered to for militarism to thrive. While such gender constructs operate in and around all of us, I wondered whether women who work in or are partners to people working in the U.S. defense industry are particularly prone to the imposition of a specific construction of gender heavily influenced by the privileging of a militarized masculinity. I was interested in what it meant for women to work there in terms of their sense of themselves as women and as citizens, both of the United States and of the world. Ideas about the proper practice of femininity in a militarized society suggested that the women were likely to see themselves as producers of children rather than of weapons, as helpers to husbands who are the head of the family / nation rather than as the ones who are in charge, and as upholders of the peace rather than contributors to war.[5]

Historically, some women have been acknowledged contributors to war. Among the most studied U.S. women who served to bolster the intense militarization of U.S. society during the Second World War years of 1941–45 were those women, both African American and white, who were deliberately recruited into weapons-making factories to replace male factory workers the government drafted into its military. Popularly nicknamed "Rosie the Riveter," these women have been the objects of numerous studies of their own perceptions of what this experience meant for their self-confidence and their economic security and of how employers and government policymakers strategized to enlist women in formerly masculinized jobs. These women were lauded for their patriotism and service to their country and subsequently urged to further demonstrate their propensity for self-sacrifice to the greater good by going back into the home after the war so that defense jobs would be made available to the men who were returning from war.

Yet the Cold War meant that business boomed for defense corporations long after the Second World War, and following the women's liberation movement of the 1960s and 1970s in the United States, women seeking stable, well-compensated employment quietly began to be employed by defense corporations. They have continued to work there in small numbers in spite of militarized ideas about femininity that suggest that women, rather than participating in such work, are the ones who require defending.

This ideology of militarism relies on ideas about men's supremacy and women's weakness and does not allow acknowledgment of the ways that the actual practice of femininity differs from the ideological ideal. Women and men both inside and outside the military take part in the perpetuation of militarism and the preparation for war. Still, these gender roles—that is, the particular meanings and practices of masculinity and femininity that make militarism possible and allow it to continue—are quite rigid and oppressive to both men and women as they rely on old understandings of the abilities, interests, and intellects of women. In reality, women play an important role in terms of preparing the nation for war and contemporarily in the actual fighting of the war. Yet if women were to be recognized for having a key role in war readiness, it might threaten the belief in women's need for protection that legitimates men's decision making about questions of conflict and war.

As a consequence, little gender-focused research has been conducted on those U.S. women who worked in companies producing military goods under government and defense contracts in the later eras of the Cold War and recent post–Cold War period.[6] So little attention has been paid to these women, these hidden soldiers, that it is as if women did not exist inside defense corporations after the Second World War. It is these women's experiences, consciousness, and daily strategies that interested me. Did they associate their daily work with war and with imperialism? Did they see themselves as part of the war effort? What can we learn from their stories about how militarism is perpetuated and thus contributes to the new imperialism?

In an effort to answer these questions and thereby to contribute to the transnational exploration of the nature and causes of gendered militarization, I conducted an in-depth study of a small but diverse group of women in two small cities in upstate New York who work for private defense corporations.[7] In this study, I conducted in-depth interviews, analyzed industrial products, and visited one of the work areas. The women who participated in the study were self-selected in that I had met several of them in various venues, and they volunteered when they heard about the study. I then asked them to refer others they thought might be interested in participating. The women worked in various positions within the corporations: in human-resource departments, on assembly lines, as contract administrators, and as engineers. Within these corporations, engineers occupy a position at the top of the hierarchy and are overwhelmingly male. The women and sometimes their male partners were employed at three different corporations,[8] all of which are named in the top-ten profit makers among defense corporations. The women in the study were employed at four different corporate sites. I visited one of the sites on two occasions by tagging along when a colleague taught a class that visited the company. While U.S. defense contractors have sites in most states in the United States and some sites abroad, these small cities in upstate New York have been quite dependent on the presence and profitability of these corporations for their economic well-being.

The women in this study use language to obscure their actions in ways that are similar to the men studied by Carol Cohn (1993, 1994) and Hugh Gusterson (1996). What is different about these women, however, is that they are not recognized by the government for being patriots or even good citizens as Rosie the Riveter was. Their communities do not laud them or regard them with the respect and awe accorded to scientists, and they cannot acknowledge what they do in their own minds without endangering their sense of themselves as feminine, as women, as mothers. The obscurity of the language at work, however, allows them to contribute to war and imperialism while at the same time thinking of themselves as removed from war and acting not as aggressors but, rather, as "protectors" of the nation.

Accidental Warriors

SUE: There's some people who work on this stuff who really get into it, some of them because it's defense, others just because they're really into engineering. I sort of fell into it, and it works for me, so I stick with it, but it's not something that I get really, really excited about. It's a job, and so with that, I'm doing my job. I'm not out there trying to make the next atom bomb or something [laughs].
RR: Do you remember how you thought about that when you got hired?
SUE: Defense, well, make[s] things that could kill people. Yeah, but it's a job, a nice paycheck. I think it was more a matter of thinking I should feel bad about it [laughing].

Sue is a twenty-seven-year-old European American, lesbian mechanical engineer who works for a company I call Universal Exports. She says that she chose Universal Exports over the other companies that recruited her out of college because the company offered to pay for courses toward her master's degree. Her comment about how she initially gained employment by "falling into" a job at Universal Exports is similar to the stories of other women's initial employment in defense. Her current thinking—"I'm not out there trying to make the next atom bomb or something"—and economic rationalization for doing defense work is representative of many of the other women's narratives on this topic: "It's a job, a nice paycheck."[9]

A heavily militarized discourse permeates these industries and, by extension, the homes of the families included in this study. Within this discourse, concepts of family and nation are interwoven with ideas about war, safety, defense, good citizenship, and "national security." Because talk in the workplace and at home is circumscribed by an ethic of secrecy, the questions I asked seemed to present a rare occasion for them to think about the work as connected to war. The talk that does occur at the workplace is made up of what Carol Cohn (1993, 290) refers to as "techno-strategic language." This language is deliberately abstruse and exchanges words that would convey the seriousness and lethality of the products being made for commonplace terms and phrases. The everyday discourse of the industry and of their homes then connects work with economic stability and parental and patriotic duty, not to a contribution to global militarism.

In talking about the meaning of doing defense work to themselves, their families, and the nation, the women refer to "national defense," "national safety," "protection," and the prevention of war. Several of the women also compare working at defense companies to various other occupations such as medicine, the manufacture of household appliances, domestic police work, and the production of foodstuffs. They insist that no conversations take place about their work contributing to war, death, militarism, or U.S. military aggression or imperialism. In this project, they talk about the meaning of what they call "national defense," how they think about war, how they make distinctions between "us" and "them"—at the time of the study, an amorphous, unknown enemy threat—and their sense of what it means to be patriotic.

> RR: Do you think about the building of weapons?
> ANGEL: No [long pause]. I can't say that I do. No, nothing like that has ever crossed my mind.

Angel, an African American woman in her mid thirties, gives a response that is startling in that she has long been employed in work that directly contributes to war. Some of the women are willing to acknowledge the purpose of the products they help make but are careful to make distinctions that distance them from the intended use of the product by diminishing their role in production. When I asked Teresa, a European American women in her early forties, what it was like to work at Universal Exports, she interpreted the question as a suggestion that the work she does there is different from other kinds of work. She was, however, resistant to that possibility even though it was apparent that she had some discomfort in talking about her work:

> Working for a national contractor, I gotta tell you, it's like working for a big corporation. They weren't making, you know, nuclear subs or anything like that. Because basically, we worked in a . . . we were a corporation. Because you were building weapons or . . . mostly we were building radar and sensor systems on ships. You know, for land mines and all that, depending what program you were on. They hired people from the military because . . . those people would know how . . . well, they could deal with the people, like military personnel. But it never affected me. Universal Exports was Universal Exports.

In this very defensive, confusing passage, Teresa contradicts herself several times about how she thinks about her work. First, she refers to Universal Exports, a private defense corporation, as a "national contractor." This blurring of the conceptual lines between government, nation, and private industry was frequently repeated by the women in the study. They often spoke of their work in private defense corporations as "working for the government." The conceptual ground, the way into interpreting, explaining, and theorizing, is set for this confusion by the emphasis on capitalism in popular culture, nationalist discourses, and the commingling of notions of democracy and capitalism.

Teresa began to acknowledge that she was contributing to the production of weapons but immediately stopped herself and referred to building radar and sonar systems. Focusing on her part in the production of what she defined as defensive rather than offensive weapons prevented Teresa from acknowledging her part in war and the preparation for war. Her reference to how her work at Universal Exports did not "affect her life" reflects the invisibility of relations of ruling that order her life. Her narrative's many twists and turns, her insistence that Universal Exports is like any other corporation, and the mention of weapons production immediately conflated or obscured with talk of radar and sonar points to Teresa's reluctance to be associated with war production. She was looking for work, she seems to be saying, not for an ethical dilemma or to make a contribution to global militarism.

Several of the women interviewed for this project made a conceptual distinction between offensive and defensive military products. This is reminiscent of the scientists in Gusterson's (1986, 56) study who somehow had convinced themselves that working on nuclear weapons was more moral than working on conventional weapons.

The women who worked at Universal Exports seemed particularly intent on elaborating the contrast between offensive and defensive weapons. The distinction is a false one, however, as radar in particular is used as part of the guidance system for antiballistic and Titan missiles.

Many times the women referred to not making guns or bombs as an important differentiation between this kind of seemingly innocuous defense work and the other, "real" war stuff. In talking about how she thinks about her work, Nancy, a European American woman close to retirement age, insisted on making the distinction between offensive and defensive products:

RR: Do you think about what it is that you're doing?

NANCY: You mean as to whether they're war? Actually, I don't, and that may sound peculiar. I mean, I think about it as a defense mechanism because we make radar. It's not like we're making machine guns, which obviously some plants do. We don't, so I guess I've never thought about it as a war product other than as a defense product. Oh no, certainly I knew that they were used for military purposes, but they're not, like, aiming a cannon at you or shooting you. They're for our own protection. I felt they're for our own protection.

Nancy seems to be suggesting that unless one is directly participating in the production of guns, then one can be excused from any culpability in war production. She reveals here that she really does not like to think of herself as contributing to war. Nancy's allusion to guns or weapons as being "aim[ed] at you" is interesting, as it seems to impart how she makes a division in her thinking about defensive weapons being about protecting "us" in the United States rather than weapons that can be used by "others" against "us."

While Teresa, who held various clerical and assembly jobs at Aeroco, denied that what she did there had any special significance for her, her co-workers, the nation, or the world, she hinted that there was some talk at work about the wider implications of what they were doing:

To me it was an inventory system. It was like working anywhere else. But, you know, we weren't really doing anything. It wasn't a big intricate part of the . . . where we were gonna drop bombs on somebody. . . . It was mostly computerized, and our engineering—you know, our engineering, um, division—was mostly, you know . . . we mostly talked to them. I never understood what they were talking about, [until], at one point, [thought], "Oh, big deal, you know? All I know is, I need the paperwork for this, and I gotta know." No, not really because it was basically just office work. You know—something that I was just always used to doing. It was the same thing to me tracking those parts as it was tracking Maxwell House Coffee and Jello and Cool Whip. So that was, we never really got into that—no. You know, they were very . . . a lot of the people that worked there, were very into . . . a lot of them were ex-military people, so their views on it were, we got to keep up the military, we got to do this, so basically that was their ideals, you know their—the way that they thought.

Even though the work she was doing was precisely directed at the ability to "drop bombs on people," Teresa still created a distinction between the production of radar and sonar, on the one hand, and the production of bombs or participation in the delivery of them, on the other. Her part in defense work seems innocuous when she asserts that she and her co-workers "weren't really doing anything" to prepare for or facilitate war. Perhaps preparation for war is a goal she does not want to think of herself as working toward. Maybe she really did not know what the parts she was counting would do. In an attempt to remove ideas about war from her work, she compared tracking parts for submarines with counting food products. She further distanced herself from the lethal potential of what she was helping to produce by claiming ignorance in her interactions with engineers who—she seems to be saying—are the real villains of the story. While she claimed that, to her, "it was an inventory system," she acknowledged that others she worked with were more interested in the intent of the production. Carol Cohn (1988, 296) talks about the power of this techno-strategic discourse to facilitate, in this case, the women's denial: "The imagery that domesticates, that humanizes insentient weapons, may also serve, paradoxically, to make it all right to ignore sentient human bodies, human lives."

Teresa and the other women interviewed for this study simply borrow from this strategy of naming and the use of metaphor (Gusterson 1996) employed by scientists at the highest levels of defense work to make their work ordinary.

Safety and Security?

Lorraine, a middle-age African American woman, differentiated between her role in the production of weapons and the role of the company for which she worked. Like the female British defense workers during the Falklands War in the study by Hillary Wainwright (1983), Lorraine explained that it was only during the First Gulf War that ideas about what she was helping produce became concrete for her:

> I didn't, because it was a job. Um, I wasn't doing anything to, you know . . . I knew . . . I mean, like in terms of what I'm doing could kill somebody's life. No, I didn't think that. The only time I did was when the war was in Saudi Arabia. And you realize that the equipment that you made, or that your company made—because I didn't physically

put any of the parts together—that would [either] fail or work. I did a lot of administrative stuff. But you don't think of the systems killing people; you think of the systems working to help your country. So then you take on responsibility and you want everything to work right. I think it put more pride. You don't think in terms . . . and like it could be another block that you put up if you're not that type of person that thinks of killing people, weapons systems.

Lorraine makes personally tenable her participation in the production of weapons that may result in someone's death by differentiating between her individual part versus the company's part in the production of the implements of war. She suggests that the meaning of her participation in this war machine did not occur to her because she is not "that type of person." Does she mean to suggest that there are people working in these plants who are that type of person, for whom the building of weapons is satisfying? Given her troubled history of racism and frustrated aspirations toward promotion within that workplace, it is not so surprising that she would characterize her co-workers as intent on hurting others or as evil. Elsewhere, Lorraine made a strong point of asserting her intelligence within the workplace, and yet here she characterizes herself as an innocent bystander of sorts.

Other respondents concentrated less on creating distance between themselves and knowledge of the intended use of the products or absolving themselves of responsibility for preparing for war and, instead, used strategies of rationalization to justify their continued participation in this kind of work. Jane, a middle-age European American woman, used a combination of Cold War rhetoric and nationalist-protectionist discourse to explain her part in defense work:

I had to think about whether I wanted to work for a defense . . . Gattling guns I couldn't have done. But I looked at radar and sonar as maybe being able to avoid death or avoid war. Some people could look at radar as trying to build things to kill people, but I didn't look at it that way, because I know when they were setting them up, it was for the defense of our country, the perimeters. And what they knew was amazing to me—what Russia was thinking and doing at the time. So I think we didn't want communism here, so that's how I rationalized that.

Jane acknowledges in this quote that her work is in fact different from other kinds of manufacturing work. Yet she, too, works to enforce the distinction between the creation of "gattling" guns (i.e., offensive weapons) and radars and sonars (defensive weapons) when she refers to "avoid[ing] death or avoid[ing] war." Unlike some of the other women employed at Aeroco and Universal Exports, she called participation in defense work "a problem" and admitted to having an internal struggle over the appropriateness of doing the work.

In addition to expressing a distaste for communism, Jane uses images from the 1960s and the Cold War to justify her participation in defense work. She says she did not understand what the company produced when she was first hired, but once she realized what was happening, she used her personal knowledge of history to support her continued employment:

> My first job was in employee relations, and that's how I found out about radar. And at one time I went over to the electronics laboratory. They do a lot of research and development. But I don't know—national defense to me being at that time, with the Vietnam War . . . I like history. I know what communism could do to you, and we were brought up with the idea that we could be taken over one day. Khrushchev had made remarks. . . . My dad went to Korea, and, you know, you hear some stories about the war. You hear about and you see things like someone being killed, and all that to you is very offensive. You have to protect your family. So to me, it is very important to have national defense. Now we're getting into global invasion and we aren't being so cloistered, I guess might be the word. We're allowing more and more countries and companies to buy more of our buildings and our land and everything. And we're buying over there and we're sharing more. It wasn't like that back then. Back then, it was all for us, so it was very important.

By referring to U.S. participation in the Korean and Vietnam wars in this passage, Jane moves from ideas of "avoid[ing] death or avoid[ing] war" as justifications for her participation in defense work to more concrete images of war. As she continues, Jane makes it sound, on the one hand, as if participating in defense work in the late 1990s no longer makes sense; on the other hand, she believes that, at the end of the twentieth century, the threat of "global invasion" of some sort seemed much more imminent. Her use of this phrase contradicts her description of the United States as being less "cloistered" and "sharing more." Her comment about global invasion in the present context seems prescient, although surely she did not foresee such an overt U.S. turn toward global imperialism. Jane also made the move seamlessly from talking about a desire to protect her family to "national defense."

Karen, a forty-something-year-old European American woman, gave a thoughtful but similarly nationalistic rationale for continued participation in defense work:

> How do you make friends with it? It's like, well, there again I guess it has to deal with the political party and stuff you're in. But it just . . . it's like I still think this is the best country in the world to live in, and if you can do something to help. And you have to wonder sometimes, are we, you know, instigating? Or are we really looking out for the good of the world? We're all humans. Everyone has a different agenda, you know? I mean, you just figure I'd rather be on the defense side of things and try to keep the country strong, you know, to . . . In my mind it was, like, OK if we can come up with something like the Stealth Bomber, which is enough of a threat, you know? Just knowing that we have it is enough so that somebody wouldn't want to do something, whether we use it or not. I'd hate to think that we build it and then we'd have to use it. But in my mind, that's kind of how it's justified.

Karen makes a number of interesting conflations here. While the idea of national defense clearly runs throughout this passage, she also suggests that perhaps defense is not all that U.S. foreign policy is about. She mixes ideas about the United States as global protector, or global instigator, with a frequently articulated justification for defense buildup from the time of the Cold War—that is, that American possession of large numbers of very scary weapons will inhibit aggression by others. While this nationalistic rhetoric is pervasive in U.S. culture, Karen conflates it with political-party affiliation.

Karen also alluded to her work as "help[ing]" the United States and expressed naiveté regarding the use of the products by the United States and others by suggesting that they exist simply as a threat that she would "hate" to see used. In response to a question about her husband's work, Karen employed the common strategy among these women of referring to other kinds of business the company is supposedly seeking:

> KAREN: Yes, I mean, . . . [my husband is] also trying to find new business and stuff for the company, and there's a lot of good ways to take this. I have no idea, really. He doesn't really talk about what he does and the conferences he goes off to and stuff, but, I mean, there's a lot going on. I feel comfortable with him doing it. I don't feel comfortable necessarily with me doing it [laughs]. And you know, it's just, I can only do what's right for me. You know, everyone has their own opin-

ion, and for the most part if you take the mindset that you're building a defense product, uh, to give a show of force and not necessarily to be used it's, um . . . I suppose you can even think of vaccines and things. I mean, it's deadly in its own right because it's killing something else, but yet it protects you, you know? I mean, there's certain levels where you kind of go to this point and just hope you don't have to go beyond, you know, so, but yet if you don't put up the fences. . . .

RR: You don't want to put up the fences?

KAREN: I don't want to [laughs]. I'll maybe paint the fence, um, but I don't know. It's because I have . . . there again, it's the beauty of being a female, where I have some options. But if I was a single female, and it was something I didn't really want to do but it was gonna provide for my family, I would be doing it.

Secrecy allows vague ideas about other uses for defense products to seem real. Karen uses ideas about gender to explain the contradiction apparent in her discomfort with her participation in defense work and the lack of it when it comes to her husband's work. Patriarchal ideas about gender allow her to think of herself as removed from the dirty business of defense that appropriately occupies her husband. Karen refers to these gendered expectations as a luxury—the "beauty of being a female."

Like several of the other women, Karen removed lethality from defense work by comparing it to the development of vaccines. Yet to make this comparison, Karen, like Jane, had to make a conceptual move that constructs people outside U.S. society as less than human. She continued:

You get yourself to a point where you're on this treadmill and you gotta keep going or you're just gonna fall right off. There again, you don't just go in and say, "Today we're gonna make a B1 bomber," you know? It's all so incremental. You might be just sitting at a computer and writing all these lines of code that is gonna make this switch move that thing, you know? So it's like: How do we get the fuel from this wing to . . . where it's needed? It's all so minute and intense, so to deal with it . . . the levels, you know, no one person can go from here to there. So it's not like you really feel . . . And that's part of the frustration . . . Engineering at this level is . . . your job is never finished, and you never have a final product to show. All you've got is code. It's not like going to work at a manufacturing plant and at the end of the day, I've made ten dozen shoes. There's no end product. And then when your end product is available to be used, you want it to be used.

It's kind of an "OK, we've done it, but what do we have?" I don't know, it's, um . . . it's a strange industry, at least from my point of view. Technology can be good or it can be bad, and there are these thrusts to get you to these different levels. And once you're there, you're standing on the brink, and you think, "Oh, gee, we've been able to get ourselves to the edge." And it's, like, OK—we've been able to push the limit, but where has that gotten us now? For my part, it was like, I say, if I had to categorize things—money. The security factor of being there.

One might assume from this passage that a bifurcated consciousness about doing defense work is assisted by the actual process of doing the work. The scientists at the Los Alamos and Sandia national laboratories who work on nuclear weapons also remove themselves conceptually from their work by concentrating on "a single small thing, a tiny technically interesting part of a larger project" (Rosenthal 1990, 44). Individual components may not have real meaning when they exist only in the form of computer codes. Wainwright (1983, 138) also refers to "ignorance reinforced by the extreme fragmentation of the production process in the arms industry." Karen also reveals, however, that there is full consciousness of what one is contributing to in defense work—and, indeed, frustration about the inability to view the entire product or see it working. Unlike the comparison she made in an earlier quote between doing defense work and policing, here, like Jane, she acknowledges that defense work is unlike other kinds of manufacturing work. Karen also uses the term "technology" to refer to weapons production. While she carefully suggests that technology's impact can be bad, she also seems to be removing any responsibility for its destructive use from her own hands by asserting that one cannot know in advance the end result of the development of such technology. Finally, she, too, makes the frightening suggestion that once the product is completed, there is a desire on the part of the people who contributed to its creation to see it used. Yet that desire, she implies, is based on technical interest rather than on imperialist aggression.

Another, more frequently repeated rationalization for continuing to do defense work has to do with various definitions of "national security." Some women make excuses for themselves such as immaturity, financial necessity, ignorance, or lack of intention. Others, as Karen and Jane show, draw on conflicting discourses, many of which have fear of an unknown "other" at their foundation, to attempt to articulate, or not articulate, the mixed feelings they have about doing defense work. Audrey was unclear about exactly what threat she was guarding against, yet she was much more explicit about how to do it:

RR: What do you think about this thing you're calling national safety?
AUDREY: I think about it from the standpoint that, um, if they were making a bomber of some kind, it's for the nation, for protecting our country, our nation. And that's how I see it from that standpoint—a bomber, the Stealth, the whatever—any kind of, uh, aircraft that's war-oriented, it's for the safety of the country.

How does one come to believe that a bomber, an obviously offensive weapon, is necessary for the "safety of our country"? Audrey, who identifies as Caribbean American and who is in her early forties, is participating in a discourse of fear that can be historically traced to the 1960s and the manufactured "arms race" with the Soviet Union. This discourse continues to be propagated by the media, mostly through news programs on television and newspaper stories intent on focusing on the threat of "terrorism" by a distinctly untrustworthy and irrational "other," who are usually people of color. Carol Cohn (1988, 305) discusses the use of techno-strategic discourse and its effects on users: "This discourse has become virtually the only response to the question of how to achieve security that is recognized as legitimate." Despite the fact that Stealth Bombers and the like are of little use in defending against people who are intent on carrying out terrorist activities, in a world that can appear increasingly dangerous, military might is presented as the only answer. Audrey never actually explained what she meant by national safety; instead, she used her response to further justify her own participation in defense work. Maybe, though, she was revealing the effectiveness of militarized thinking when she indicated that she thought the Stealth Bomber had been developed to protect U.S. citizens. Maybe that kind of thinking, coupled with fear of an unknown (often person of color), adds up in the minds of these women, even those of color, to a justification of imperialism (to protect) rather than as an offensive war move to which they might (albeit quietly) object.

For these women, and for other defense workers, the silences of the industry make talking directly about the work outside the workplace impossible. Accustomed to not talking about what they do, defense workers become removed from the reality of their work. It loses conceptual significance. "Secrecy also inhibits members from developing an overall picture of or sense of responsibility for an organization's work" (Gusterson 1996, 90). The diminishing of the meaning of what they do is assisted by a discourse that works hard not to name war production as war production (Cohn 1988). Carol Cohn (1993, 227) tells a story about a physicist who, in an unguarded moment, spoke with horror about how the other men in the room were dispassionately discussing the annihilation of 30 million people. The reaction of his colleagues was to ignore him, and he related that he "felt like a woman" for stepping outside the appropriate gendered behavior that is pro-scribed within highly militarized sites. Not talking about something also makes thinking about it unfamiliar and unclear. When asked directly how they think about their work, then, it is difficult—if not impossible—for these women to find words to name what they do or how they think about it.

"I'm Not Ever for War"

The possibility of war and what that means to the women, their partners, their children, the nation, and the victims of war often seems far removed from the women's narratives about their work, either because they work hard to omit it or because the notions of femininity under which they are operating make it impossible for them to see themselves as connected to such an event. Although current events sometimes force them to acknowl-edge their roles within militarized international relations, they still often eschew their part in war by focusing on ideological opposition to war.

> RR: So you think if you were making something else—like if you were making bombs or something like that?
> TERESA: I think that would be different. I don't think I would have; I don't know. That's a course that . . . why make them if you're not gonna use them? I mean, my husband goes in the woods and shoots; doesn't kill any animals, though, just targets. . . . I told him I didn't want [our son] into this—but that's beside the point. You know, every time I see a little brown-eyed deer, I don't care how big they are—just don't run into my car—but I'm not gonna shoot one.

Teresa again deflects talk about making deadly weapons onto something else. A question that alludes to war immediately brings to her mind her role as a mother. Protecting her children, she begins to say before stopping herself, is the only acceptable role for women to play in relation to war. If it is unacceptable for her to consider killing a deer, how can she possibly come to terms with the idea that what she does for a living could contribute to the killing of human beings? Staving off such thinking requires constant intellec-tual energy and discursive ingenuity.

When the question of actual armed combat arose, the women's responses to my questions were much more pointedly antiwar. Most of the women interviewed for this study were employed in the defense industry during the Persian Gulf War of 1990–91. They almost all related an increased sense of pride around their work as the occasion of the war provided an opportunity to see the products to which they had contributed in action. Of course, this pride in the work belied all of their protests that what they do at work does not contribute to war. Their reactions to that war were varied, but most expressed some ambivalence about American participation:

> RR: So what did you think during the war with Iraq?
> LORRAINE: Oh, I thought it was just terrible. And I was worried about our people. When our military went out on Desert Storm and they held up those white shirts, they were just giving in, you know? So the lives that were lost were just ridiculous. Um, I'm not ever for war, because the innocent people . . . even the men that go to fight, they don't want to fight. So it was, like, you just hate to see anybody's life gone, but it's just one of those things. You have to do it to protect some things, but I don't know. . . . I certainly wouldn't have liked my sons to have gone, you know? Or when you have someone involved in it, then that's when life and death really hit you.

Lorraine articulates a position mostly in opposition to war that is in direct contradiction to what her paid work contributed to for fifteen years. She also reluctantly acknowledges that war may at times be necessary, "to protect," but is unable to define who or under what conditions such protection may be necessary.

Several of the other women articulated more pacifist positions on war than the one at which Lorraine hints. Despite her adherence to, and reliance on, Cold War rhetoric to justify her participation in a defense buildup, Kate voiced distaste for war:

> RR: Are you a person that is opposed to war in general?
> KATE: If it can be avoided, yes. If there's a way to talk things out sincerely and compromise, I think that's where we should go, but on the other hand, do I want to be taken over by another country like we do to other people for their own good? I think we're spoiled here; we're not used to that. I wouldn't like that. I don't know if I could kill another human being, but if you put me to the test—if someone were to hurt my child—I don't know what I would do. I don't like it, and I think it's terrible; it's horrible and should be avoided at all costs. It's not . . . one of those things you want to get into and wave the flag. It's only if we

get into it for a reason that can't be avoided. During the Gulf War, I prayed to God it [would be] over quickly and that not too many people [would get] hurt. I don't . . . we don't need another world war.

While Kate indicates that war should be avoided "at all costs," she does not seem to object to U.S. military participation in the Persian Gulf War, a situation many analysts now believe was unnecessary (see Hiro 1992; Peters 1992). She also indicates that she would hate for the United States to be treated internationally in the same fashion that "we do to other people for their own good." Her earlier reference to "global invasion" seems to have morphed into a much more benign form of imperialism.

When our second interview took place, the United States was once again threatening war with Iraq. Audrey's response to my question about war reflects the views of the time and her general attitude toward war:

RR: Do you think about war at all in a general sense?
AUDREY: No. Yeah, you hear it on the news, but it doesn't really get to me [laughs]. There is so much out of our hands that if we were to worry about all of these things, we would absolutely go crazy. And I realize that, um, if we were to go, if we were in a war situation, we would just have to make the best of the situation. There's nothing that we could do. There's no way that we could change anything, so why worry about it?

Audrey's rather cavalier response to the question was contradicted by later statements she made about how she would feel about her son's participation in a war and in her discussion of the Persian Gulf War with her husband:

We did not have the same point of view on that at all. He felt something had to be done. And I saw it from the other side: . . . if we go to war, what is the consequence? And what are we as a nation? If we go to war, how will we be harmed? And maybe that's the mother instinct in me. That's how I saw it. I was more concerned about us and what could happen to us as a nation.

Audrey's description of her conversation with her husband shows the contradictions inherent in militarized versions of femininity. While militarized femininity dictates that as a woman she should be more peaceful than her husband, it also requires her unconditional support of militarized men in times of war. Her contributions to war readiness through paid work, however, are in opposition to her role as mother and protector of sons. Of course, militarized femininity requires that Audrey be willing to sacrifice her sons for the good of the nation, but she does not want to do that. As she moves discursively back and forth between ideas of nation and motherhood, she conflates notions of patriotism and family.

Some Other Mother's Son

One of the greatest contradictions apparent in these women's narratives is their ongoing contribution to readiness for war or the defense of the nation and their open articulation of resistance to having their children participate in war. Within the militarized paradigm of gender operating in their lives, these women are supposed to be willing, if not eager, to sacrifice their children for the protection of the nation or for the patriotic ideals of democracy. Yet in addition to Audrey, all of the other women with children interviewed for this study expressed similar reluctance to have their children sacrificed in war. None of these women referred to daughters' being required to fight; rather, they thought of daughters as needing protection from militaries and war in a fashion similar to their own imagined needs for protection by male partners. The women were mostly concerned about how war would affect their sons. As Angel noted, "Yeah I . . . have a feeling that something is gonna happen soon. Um, and you know, I've worked with all of this for a while, and I just pray that my son won't have to go."

In that statement, Angel is making a connection between her work for the U.S. Department of Defense and her son's potential military service. She seems to be suggesting that proximity to war preparation in her work makes her more reluctant to see her son go to war. Yet as she went on to tell the story of her son's reluctance to participate in peacekeeping missions in Eastern Europe, she did her discursive duty as a militarized mother of sons: "Oh, yes, my oldest son is in the Army Reserves. They were gonna send him to Hungary. And he was like, 'I'm not going,' and this and that. And I said, 'You gotta go.' But half of his unit went to Bosnia, and he said, 'I'm not going, mom.'"

For Angel, the important aspect of this story seems to be her son's expressed refusal to go rather than her own adherence to the rules. Ultimately, he did not have to make the decision because he was not assigned to Eastern Europe. Perhaps being an African American single mother supplies part of Angel's motivation. In late-twentieth-century U.S. society, few avenues were open to African American for achieving full citizenship. One was through her own military participation. The other was to offer her sons for the nation.

Not all militarized mothers, however, obediently follow the rules and willingly provide sons for cannon fodder. Lorraine rejected the idea of military participation for her sons. While she, like Angel, is African American, the economic status of her family—her husband is an engineer at Aeroco—may have allowed her this option without jeopardizing her status as a good citizen:

> Um [sighs], I have mixed feelings because, um, I'm an American. I would like my country to be protected. And I wouldn't like for people to be able to come here and invade it and kill me. But when it comes to my children, I wouldn't want them to go into someone else's country and kill them—whether it's for their own country that we live in or not. It's just something—as a mother—protective instincts. So I wouldn't ever want them to have to go and fight in a war. If they had to give their information or their thinking ability in what they can do, I would always want that to be first. If you can work it out rationally, or help somebody discussing war in the administration, if they had to do it that way, but to literally go with guns and fight? My kids—I wouldn't want them to ever have to do that [laughs]. That's a mother's instinct.

Thus for her sons, Lorraine would choose the much less dangerous roles of intellectual or negotiator for her sons than soldier. She objects rather explicitly to U.S. imperialism here. Yet she and her husband both had worked for years in the defense industry. Although Lorraine no longer did so, it was her husband's generous defense-industry salary that had allowed her to take time off to recover from what she described as the trauma inflicted by her experiences in the industry. Her husband's "thinking ability" was what kept him employed and working for the security of the nation. Yet Lorraine did show some tension around this assertion, as she seemed to understand that being a proper patriotic American required different kinds of activity in times of war.

Jane was the only interviewee without sons. Financial necessity, however, had prompted her daughter to consider entering the U.S. Navy to cover college costs. Jane had been downsized several times at Universal Exports; her husband worked as a contractor and was not employed in the defense industry. One of their two daughters has had significant health problems, and during Jane's layoffs, the family had no health insurance. She talked about how her children have learned to think about war:

> They haven't had to live through a lot of it. They've seen the Croatians. And we've tried to explain to them historically how we grew up with it—the war in our living room and how that wasn't a norm. We tried to

explain to them the emotions and [about] the families that were torn apart because of it. I pray that my children never know war. And I pray that their children don't, but I have feeling that any war there is is gonna be bad, if there is one. Um, I came close to having my oldest daughter go into the Navy. She unfortunately . . . I think [the recruiters] get these kids early, and they promote the college education. That's why we sat right here several times, and I questioned them very carefully. I gave [my daughter] some of the cons. [The recruiters] were giving her all the pros. I said, "What happens if a war comes? What happens if you have to go to Saudi Arabia?"

Jane sees her daughter as needing protection not only from the imagined foreign other, but also from the U.S. military, which will take advantage of her innocence. Jane never really said that she tells her children that war is wrong, only that it is difficult for families. There does not seem to be an issue of military service as a means of achieving patriotism here. Perhaps Jane is secure in her status as a patriot because her father and husband both served in the military.

Audrey fell back on traditional ideas that construct women as more peace loving to justify her reticence to engage in war. Her expressed willingness to hide her son in Jamaica if he was drafted, however, contradicted her proper role as a mother within militarized paradigms:

RR: Do you think about war as a necessary thing?
AUDREY: I think maybe it's the feminist side of me—the feminine side of me that says, you know, we really shouldn't have to get to that point. I don't know if war is the answer for some of the problems that I hear about. Sometimes I absolutely tune out what I am hearing because . . . maybe it's a way of not handling, you know, what's possible, that possibility. And I also, you know, hope that my children would never have to encounter any of that. At one point when [my son] was . . . well it was before he started college, I always used to threaten him. I'd say, "Well, I guess I could send you to your grandmother in Jamaica." But he never wanted to. His biggest statement to me was, "Mom, I did that, and if there was a war, I would have to go. I don't want to go." You know, he loves aircraft [and] that's what he wants to do—aerospace. But he says, "I will not do anything for any of the forces. I don't want to do that situation." So I respected that and went along with what he had in mind for himself. I was just concerned when he was eighteen or so in case something would happen and he would get drafted or something like that.

Audrey's son's refusal to participate within the military itself was also contradicted by his intention to follow in his father's "footsteps" by becoming an aerospace engineer. Perhaps he was simply mirroring the bifurcation that his mother is articulating when she suggests that she works every day at a defense corporation and yet "tunes out" the possibility that war will occur. Her son also exercises the middle-class privilege of refusing military participation, as both of his parents are well compensated for their work in defense.

> RR: Do you think that it's being in the military that your son's objecting to?
> AUDREY: I think it's war. I think it's war.
> RR: So did he ever question what you all do?
> AUDREY: No, because I think he basically wants to follow in the footsteps of his dad. He wants to do engineering similar to what his dad does, you know? So, um, he's always been intrigued with aircraft. I think it's the war that makes him . . . I think it frightens him more than anything else, you know, and he just knew that that's not what he wanted to do.

In telling her son's story, Audrey may have been giving a hint of how not only she and her husband, but all the families involved in this study, think about doing defense work. Perhaps one of the main motivating forces, individually and collectively, is the fear of the "them" and of war. Maybe working at defense companies provides just enough sense of patriotic duty and devotion to nation to keep the fear of others at bay.

Conclusion

Perhaps because the participants in this study have so successfully conceptually removed themselves from thinking about how what they do contributes to war, they can no longer think about their work as beneficial to the nation—or patriotic. Nor can they focus on the ways they help make global imperialism possible. Maybe the difficulty is that for these women, steeped in the language of offensive versus defensive, the idea of imperialism as something that is connected to them, to what they do, does not allow them to feel good about the nation they are dedicated to "protecting." Part of distancing themselves from the processes of militarization and imperialism includes distancing from war in general. Monette, an African American woman in her early fifties, told a story that personifies the conundrum women face trying to live within the confines of such a restrictive version of femininity:

> You know what was interesting? We . . . hired a female. Great—oh, man, she was so smart. She was a physicist and she just had great credentials. She came to work one week and quit. She had a change of heart. She said, "I cannot. I cannot do this." She had worked on systems and bombs and all kinds of stuff to kill people before, but what we didn't know at the time was that she was pregnant. It changed the way she thought about it. . . . I didn't know she was pregnant, and I just couldn't figure out why she changed her mind like that all of a sudden. It was just the talk of that area for months because nobody could believe that she could do that. And yet and still, I guess I understand her. But on the other hand, for the defense of this country, we need to do these things. And people say, "Well, why do these people want to make bombs?" Except . . . if Saddam Hussein knew that we were not able to defend ourselves, guess what? We'd be dead. So it's just that simple [laughs].

Torn between a sense of duty to child and to country, the physicist opted out of the business. For the women left behind, the mystery of her exit was solved when her pregnancy was revealed. Even though the seemingly brilliant woman had a history of working on "systems and bombs and all kinds of stuff to kill people," in the end anatomy ruled, and duty to child prevailed over duty to company or nation. Of course, the woman's behavior provides a good example to corporate administrators of why women cannot be taken seriously within the defense industry, and yet the women in this study face a similar predicament every day and do not opt out in the same fashion.

They do put family and children first, but they also continue to work for "national security." It is impossible to determine whether these women are thinking about working in defense as patriotic or as a means to achieve full citizenship status; whether they are attempting to stave off fear of the dangerous unknown "other" or simply are seeking stable, well-compensated employment. When Monette represents all of the people outside the defense industry who ask, "Why do these people want to make bombs?" it reminds me of my thinking when I first began this study. The response I would now give is best represented by a story Sue told me. When asked whether there was talk about the meaning of the work at her work site, she described a colleague's thought processes: "My cube mate was taking an engineering ethics course. She kept going on and on and on about how could she be doing this. Finally, she finished the course and went on to other things."

Women who are responsible not only for contributing to the "national defense," for keeping dangerous "others" away, but also for keeping the secret of women's active participation in militarism are also busy bearing and nurturing children, mostly on their own. They are buying and maintaining homes; doing unacknowledged emotional and social work both in the workplace and at home; washing, cleaning, driving, caring. They stop thinking about how what they are doing contributes to war, and go on to other things. Going on to other things is facilitated by gender ideology, economic necessity, fear of "others," and the techno-strategic discourse that sets the parameters of the conversation about war and weapons production in a way that not only keeps the women focused on other things, but also impedes any thoughts of alternative ways of living and allows militarism and imperialism to flourish.

Notes

Cynthia Enloe has provided ideas, inspiration, and encouragement from the inception of this project. I am indebted to her for her generosity and her spirit. Thanks also to Sari Biklen and Marjorie Devault for encouragement and assistance and for asking thorny questions. Margaret Himley always has my deepest gratitude.

1. In talking about private U.S. defense contractors, I am not referring to companies like the subsidiaries of Halliburton that provide services to the military. Rather, I am referring to corporations based inside the United States that manufacture the implements of war.

2. Ken Silverstein, "Heavy Metal: Revolving Door between Pentagon and Defense Industry Jobs," *Mother Jones*, vol. 23, no. 6, November–December 1998, 58–61. The U.S. federal budget proposal for 2007 contains a defense expenditure of $513 billion (Lincoln 2006, 4). In 2005, Lockheed Martin, the largest defense contractor in the world, reported sales of $37.2 billion. Raytheon, also in the top ten among defense industries, claimed revenue of $21.9 billion that same year: Kathleen Yanity, "Raytheon Posts Rise in Profits but Still Lags behind Rivals," *Providence Journal*, 1 June 2006, F1 (accessed at http://www.highbeam.com/doc/1G1-146558314.html).

3. The records on the number of military officers who are hired by defense contractors are difficult to access. Ken Silverstein accessed records from 1992–95 and discovered that in those three years, 3,288 former members of the military were subsequently employed by defense contractors: Silverstein, "Heavy Metal," 60.

4. Statistics on the gender breakdown of employees within these corporations are difficult to obtain, but the women interviewed for this project certainly perceived them-

selves to be in the minority within these workplaces. Recently, a female engineer at a particular company speculated that over the past few years, the percentage of women in her workplace had gone from none to 30 percent: Heinrichs 2007.

5. The role of women in war has changed enormously over the past ten to fifteen years. The large number of American women who served in the military during the First Gulf War and the high visibility of the women currently serving in Afghanistan and Iraq will necessitate a reexamination of the ideological construction of femininity that justifies male supremacy and legitimates men as protectors and that, consequently, upholds militarism. Some feminist scholars have speculated on how ideas about femininity have shifted and what that will mean for the perpetuation of militarism: see, e.g., Eisenstein 2007; Riley 2006; Young 2003a.

6. The interviews were conducted between 1996 and 1999. All were completed before 11 September 2001. Although several of the women talked about the First Gulf War in their responses, their narratives may be very different in the post-9/11 period.

7. The U.S. defense industry of the 1990s and 2000s consists of private businesses that rely mostly on government contracts to create, build, and test military hardware and products.

8. The actual corporations must remain unnamed to protect the anonymity of the participants in the study. All participants and companies have been given pseudonyms.

9. I did not ask the participants to identify their socioeconomic class, but because I visited their homes, I can speculate on the socioeconomic status. While most seemed to live in middle-class or upper-middle-class neighborhoods, the homes and neighborhoods of several others indicated lower-middle-class or working-class status.

PART III

TALKING BACK TO THE EMPIRE

Local Men and Women

SEVEN

IN THE U.S. ARMY BUT NOT QUITE OF IT

Contesting the Imperial Power in a Discourse of KATUSAs

☆

SEUNGSOOK MOON

In its March 5, 2003, issue, *Sisajŏnŏl*, a popular Korean current-affairs weekly, characterized the Korean Augmentation Troops to the U.S. Army (KATUSAS) as "a deformed baby born out of the Korean War." To most Koreans, KATUSAS have been known as conscripts who serve in the U.S. Army in American uniform and can learn English from native speakers, coveted cultural capital in the era of globalization. Despite their familiarity with the term, though, most Koreans are oblivious about why Korean conscripts serve in the U.S. Army instead of in the Korean military, and most people are also unaware of when this curious arrangement began. What triggered the media coverage of this familiar but obscure subject was an incident of sexual violence against a new KATUSA committed by a group of three GIs at Camp Jackson in Ŭijŏngbu on March 3, 2002.[1] It was allegedly the first publicized incident of sexual violence against a KATUSA since the creation of the institution in 1950.[2] In this chapter, approaching the institution of KATUSA as a liminal entity generated by Cold War politics, I explore the complicated working of the global U.S. military empire that expanded ostensibly in the era of decolonization.

I will use two novels written by former KATUSAS, a guidebook written by a former KATUSA, and ten interviews with former KATUSAS that I conducted during May 2006. The novels and the guidebook were published in the early 2000s, when the conventional view among Koreans of the United States as a "friendly nation (*ubang*)" was questioned to the point of generating a sustained public debate about the withdrawal of the U.S. military. This debate commonly has been associated with a radical student movement on the left. Politically, the public debate arose after the momentous South–North summit meeting between Kim Dae Jung and Kim Jŏng Il held in June 2000. Economically, it was also during the period that followed the Asian financial crisis of 1997, which had pressed Koreans to rethink their dominant model of economic growth. Such shifting sociopolitical and economic contexts allowed for the public articulation of KATUSAS' experiences, shaped by the complex alliance between South Korea and the United States that has survived beyond the end of the Cold War. Ten interviews were conducted with former KATUSAS in May 2006. All of them were college students in Seoul at the time of interviews and completed their service in the 2000s. This group reflects a majority of contemporary KATUSAS who come from prestigious universities in Seoul. This homogeneous composition is due to a competitive recruitment test (among conscripts) that was implemented in the early 1980s.[3]

Despite their difference in genre, the novels, guidebook, and interviews convey a thematically coherent discourse that shows KATUSAS' common experience of imperial power during their mandatory service on U.S. military bases. This discourse reveals how the imperial power is exercised and resisted at its margins, which are inhabited by KATUSAS and GIS, in the specific context of post-military-rule Korea. In particular, the KATUSA discourse shows how the hierarchical boundary between the U.S. as the empire and South Korea as its client is expressed and contested in actual and fictional discussions of nation, race, gender, sexuality, and class. My interpretive reading intends to highlight the duplicitous nature of the imperial use of the military bases in South Korea (and, by implication, elsewhere). In this ambiguous space, KATUSAS live with the imperial power that GIS embody in their pervasive sense of superiority toward KATUSAS. This sense of superiority as the agent and citizen of the empire is not always racialized along the dichotomy of white and non-white, because racial minorities are heavily represented in the U.S. military. Yet in the interviews and the fictional and nonfictional texts, KATUSAS continue to use racial distinctions to differentiate brotherly GIS, who can sympathize with Korean sentiments, from arrogant ones. KATUSAS question GIS' superiority based on American citizenship from their vantage point as college students from affluent middle-class families. In the fictional universe, main characters disrupt the hierarchy between the empire and its client through casual and romantic relationships with white female GIS. In this universe, some KATUSAS develop sympathy toward GIS as pawns of imperial power who come from disadvantaged families in the United States, and others pursue individual guerrilla tactics and collective movement to challenge GIS' extraterritoriality in South Korea and their sexual access to camptown women.

Contextualizing the Global U.S. Military Empire and the KATUSA Discourse

Emerging victoriously from the Second World War, the United States firmly established itself as a superpower in the Cold War global order. The politics of the Cold War provided the United States with the ideological impetus to expand and maintain its sprawling global network of military bases. During the Cold War, the overseas bases were intended to project conventional military power into the areas of U.S. concerns and thereby served as symbols of its imperial power. The bases also functioned as "tripwires" that ensured prompt American responses to military attacks and served as preparation for a nuclear war (Johnson 2004a, 151). As the essential tool of imperial politics, these bases have become hybrid spaces that were neither foreign nor domestic and therefore presumably "deterritorialized." Defining itself ideologically against the territorially based colonialism of the old European empires, the United States has maintained these hybrid spaces to exercise military, economic, and cultural power (Kaplan 2002, 96). In the ostentatious absence of formal colonies, these military bases, which are unevenly scattered throughout the world, territorialize the U.S. empire. From the perspectives of people living in areas that host U.S. military bases, the U.S. empire has never been deterritorialized. Unlike colonial empires that ruled occupied territories, the United States has developed and maintained a wide range of flexible relationships with host countries in the form of defense treaties and security arrangements. Specific contents of these treaties and arrangements have depended on the particular nature of the relationship between the United States and a host country in a given period of time. Although the nature of this relationship has ranged from virtually colonial to temporarily contractual, it is noteworthy that the United States established its basing rights as an occupying force in South Korea, Germany, and Japan (mostly Okinawa), the three hubs of its global military deployment during the entire span of the postwar era.[4]

In the aftermath of the Cold War, the U.S. empire has undergone significant changes and has become the uncontested military superpower ready for pre-emptive military action. This drift toward military aggression can be traced to the early years of President Bill Clinton's administration. In 1993, during his speech at the Citadel military academy, President Clinton voiced his willingness to use military force not as the "last resort" but as a preferred option "if other options seemed 'less practicable' " (Mann 2003, 7). Yet throughout the 1990s, the U.S. imperial exercises remained within the Cold War framework of viewing military power primarily as a pragmatic and defensive tool. This framework shifted after September 11, 2001, and this shift has been materially supported by the availability of "smart" weapons that conjure up the image of a "clean and quick" war. A year later, in September 2002, the "National Security Strategy of the United States of America" unequivocally stated the intention to use the U.S. military offensively.[5] This grand strategy of pre-emption turned the vision of omnipotent military empire into a reality.

In 2004, between 92 and 101 U.S. military bases were scattered across South Korea, depending on how military bases were being defined and counted. Occupying the vast tract of land freely granted by the Korean government, two-thirds of these bases have been concentrated in the capital city, Seoul, and in Kyŏnggi Province (Green United and the Coalition of Movements to Reclaim U.S. Military Bases 2004, 13, 221). Several major U.S. military bases located in major cities were initially constructed by Japanese colonial authorities and transferred to the United States during its military-government rule and during the Korean War.[6] As in other locations, U.S. military bases in Korea are highly visible but off-limits to the public. They take up immense space in the midst of densely populated cities and depopulated, poor rural areas but are not marked on maps. Army Post Office addresses in Korea are considered American addresses (Green United and the Coalition of Movements to Reclaim U.S. Military Bases 2004, 37). These bases have enjoyed extraterritoriality, marking them virtually as U.S. territories where Korean sovereignty ends. The U.S. military bases (and camptowns) in Korea resemble Puerto Rico, a U.S. colony, which was legally constructed as an "unincorporated territory" of the United States. In *Downes v. Bidwell* (1901), the U.S. Supreme Court ruled that Puerto Rico "was not a foreign country, since it was subject to the sovereignty of and was owned by the United States"; instead, it "was foreign to the United States in a domestic sense, because the island had not been incorporated into the United States" (Kaplan 2002, 2). This ruling was issued to settle the disputed import tax charged to Downes and Company, a business firm importing oranges from Puerto Rico to the

Port of New York. The company disputed the tax because Puerto Rico was part of the United States, but its claim was denied because Puerto Rico was deemed an "unincorporated territory" of the United States. Deployed on more than eighty U.S. military bases across Korea (Dakyuinp'o 2004, 88), KATUSAS inhabit a similar type of ambiguous space as an entity between the U.S. Army and the Korean military.

Recent scholarship on imperialism and empires has shifted the analytical focus from the political economy of imperial expansion to the construction of hierarchical differences between the colonizers and the colonized (Kaplan 2002; Levine 2003; McClintock 1995; Stoler 2002; Young 1995). The production and reproduction of such differences rely on existing social relations of race, gender, sexuality, and class. They also involve not only the use of instrumental knowledge, but also the generation of group fantasy and desires characterized by simultaneous attraction to and repulsion from the colonized. In his discussion of British colonialism, Robert Young focuses on the racial theories of the nineteenth century as being constitutive of the colonialism that generated the white desire for the non-white and children of such unions that disrupted racialized boundaries between the colonizer and the colonized. In Dutch colonies in Indonesia and India, Ann Stoler argues, sexual control constituted the colonial policies on race, as well as their symbolic iconography. "Sex in the colonies had to do with sexual access and reproduction, class distinction and racial distinctions, nationalism and European identity," she writes. "Sexual control was both an instrumental image for the body politic and itself fundamental to how racial policies were secured and how colonial projects were carried out" (Stoler 2002, 78).

The KATUSA discourse, which reflects daily interactions between KATUSAS and GIS in the context of post-military-rule Korea, demonstrates the comparable dynamic of gender, sexuality, nation, race, and class. It allows us to see the intimate working of the contemporary U.S. empire in its periphery, which is so obscured in the United States proper. The KATUSA discourse illuminates how KATUSAS, agents of the client state who are literally attached to the imperial troops, experience imperial power and how they try to challenge the hierarchical boundary between themselves and GIS in daily life and the realm of fiction. The spoken and written words of KATUSAS allow us to see the "material geopolitics of [imperial encounters] as an agonistic narrative of desire" (Young 1995, 174). Other KATUSA discourses would be articulated by older generations of KATUSAS who served during civilian authoritarian rule or military rule in Korea, when the official view of the United States as a "friendly nation" was rarely questioned. Those discourses may convey themes and sensibilities different from the contemporary KATUSA discourse I interpret in this chapter. With this caveat in mind, the following section will discuss how the KATUSA was created and has been maintained.

A History of KATUSAs (1950 to the Present)

The institution of Korean Augmentation Troops to the U.S. Army was haphazardly born in August 1950, during the Korean War, when the Allied Forces under U.S. Army command faced a dire shortage of troops. The immediate cause of this shortage was enormous casualties in the Allied Forces during the initial phase of the war.[7] Two elements of U.S. strategic policy in the aftermath of the Second World War contributed to the problem. First, the United States had steadily and drastically reduced its overstretched troops.[8] Second, by prioritizing its military commitment in Western Europe, the United States had allocated sparse and inferior military resources in the Far East.[9] Although South Korea stayed outside the Far East Defense Parameter (Korean Military Support Corps for the U.S. Eighth Army 1993, 5), the unexpected outbreak of the Korean War was alarming enough for the United States to reverse its earlier strategic policy. The problem of troop shortage was so severe that new American recruits were sent to the battlefield even before they had practiced shooting, let alone received proper basic military training (Schnabel 1972, 130). Under these pressing circumstances, 133 Korean policemen worked in the Seventh Division, prior to the formal institution of the KATUSA, to identify North Korean guerrilla forces disguised among civilians. After a series of informal discussions, President Syngman Rhee transferred the operational command of the Korean military to General Douglas MacArthur, supreme commander of the Allied Forces, and the two agreed to attach Korean soldiers to the U.S. Army as a temporary measure to cope with the shortage of troops.[10]

During the Korean War, an estimated 70,000–80,000 Korean men were drafted to serve as KATUSAS (Korean Military Support Corps for the U.S. Eighth Army 1993, 91). These men were sent to Japan to receive basic military training and equipment and were attached to the U.S. Army when they returned. Although they served as riflemen, artillerymen, and ammunition handlers during the early stage of the war, they were most commonly used in supporting tasks to relieve GIS who were in combat (Korean Military Support Corps for the U.S. Eighth Army 1993, 71).[11] Between 1954 and 1959, approximately 15,000 Korean soldiers were attached annually to the U.S. Army.[12] During the 1960s, roughly 11,000 Korean soldiers were attached annually to

FIGURE 7.1. KATUSAS carrying meals: Members of the Korean Service Corps carry New Year's Day dinner to the Twenty-First Infantry, Company L, near Kunsong, Korea, during the Korean War.
REPRINTED WITH PERMISSION OF U.S. ARMY TRANSPORTATION MUSEUM.

the U.S. Army, which made up approximately one-fifth of the U.S. troops stationed in Korea in a given period of time (Korean Military Support Corps for the U.S. Eighth Army 1993, preface). With the reduction in the number of U.S. troops in Korea, the total number of KATUSAS also contracted, to approximately 7,200 in 1971 and further to some 4,000 in 1987, which size has been maintained to the present. The quantitative changes were also accompanied by policy changes.[13]

The continuous existence of KATUSAS after the Korean War can be attributed to the relative insignificance of South Korea to the global U.S. military strategy. Viewing Korea as marginal to its military strategy, the United States has maintained its fundamental reservation about extensive military commitment and has relied on KATUSAS to fill the manpower shortage in its army. That is, conscripted KATUSAS are a cheap and reliable human resource that has stood in the place of American GIS, who are expensive in both the economic and the political sense.[14] Since the 1970s, KATUSAS have accounted for approximately 15 percent of U.S. troops stationed in Korea (Dakyuinp'o

2004, 88). Consequently, the KATUSA has been a semi-permanent fixture in U.S.–South Korean relations for the past six decades without any legal grounds.

The only formal basis of the institution of KATUSA was a letter sent by President Rhee to General MacArthur to transfer the operational command of the Korean military to the U.S. Army at the beginning of the Korean War (Korean Military Support Corps for the U.S. Eighth Army 1993, 20).[15] The only written documentation regulating the KATUSA consists of U.S. Eighth Army Regulation 600–2 and the Status of Forces Agreements (SOFA), signed in 1966 (Korean Military Support Corps for the U.S. Eighth Army 1993, 95, 146). However, these official documents are ambiguous about the status of KATUSAS. According to regulation 600–2, KATUSAS belong to the U.S. Army, but they are not subject to U.S. Army law. In contrast, the SOFA (art. 23, item 12) states that they are considered members of the U.S. Army with regard to claims (Korean Military Support Corps for the U.S. Eighth Army 1993, 194). In practice, KATUSAS have served in the U.S. Army, but personnel matters concerning promotions, awards and punishments, and leaves have been governed by the Korean military (Korean Military Support Corps for the U.S. Eighth Army 1993, 36, 145).[16] The term "KATUSA" formally appeared for the first time in the SOFA (app. clause B) when the agreement restricted the maximum number of troops in the Korean Army to 600,000 troops, including KATUSAS (Korean Military Support Corps for the U.S. Eighth Army 1993, 95). On July 23, 1958, the U.S. Department of the Army ordered the U.S. commanders to place a cap on the total number of KATUSAS at 11,000. The Army Department also allowed KATUSAS to use U.S. Army movie theaters for free and granted KATUSAS access to snack bars and clubs on U.S. military bases. These guidelines implied that, despite the ambiguities, the institution of KATUSA was recognized and approved of by both civilian and military authorities in the United States beyond the Eighth Army in South Korea (Korean Military Support Corps for the U.S. Eighth Army 1993, 95).

However, the KATUSA has remained invisible to outsiders (in Korea and in the American military), and even a scholar writing about U.S. militarism is oblivious about it. In his attempt to characterize America's "incoherent empire" in this postcolonial era, Michael Mann (2003, 27) asserts that "the U.S. army contains no 'natives' at all and not even any foreign mercenaries (like the French Foreign Legion or the British Gurkhas)." From a comparative historical perspective, the KATUSA closely resembles the type of imperial strategy that uses a native population to maintain the military security of a local territory deemed relatively insignificant but that cannot be ignored

FIGURE 7.2. Pie fund raising (winter 2006). Annual fund-raising event in a U.S. military unit in which the photographer served. PHOTOGRAPH BY KANG-SEOK KIM; REPRINTED WITH PERMISSION.

completely. The British colonial empire relied even more on its local allies in "the less valuable African colonies," and essentially ruled them through "the authority of loyal chiefs and tribal and village councils" that it propped up (Mann 2003, 26). In the history of the contemporary U.S. empire, KATUSAS are comparable to soldiers from Latin American countries trained at the School of the Americas, which in 2001 was renamed the Western Hemisphere Institute of Security Cooperation (Gill 2004); all of these soldiers are incorporated into global imperial relationships that instruct not only military knowledge and skills, but also, to varying degrees, superiority of American values and institutions. But there is a significant difference between KATUSAS and those Latin American soldiers: the former serve in the U.S. Army stationed in Korea, whereas the latter serve in their national militaries in their own countries.

It is noteworthy, however, that the United States was divided between civilian authority and military authority on the use of Koreans in its army. While the U.S. State Department favored the Korean attachment to the army, the U.S. Army opposed it. John J. Muccio, U.S. Ambassador to South Korea (1949–52), supported the Korean attachment to the U.S. Army as "the biggest human resources to destroy communists and save American lives" (U.S. Department of State 1976, 511). On the other hand, General Walker and his staff were opposed to the attachment for fear of deflating American soldiers' morale rather than increasing their combat capability (Korean Military Support Corps for the U.S. Eighth Army 1993, 26). According to correspondence by Everett F. Drumright, adviser to the ambassador, such resistance waned in the face of the exigency of fighting guerrilla forces often disguised among civilians (Noble 1975, 152). Although such military resistance to the incorporation of Korean soldiers was tied to the racialized imperial distinction between the United States as "the protector" and Korea as "the protected," as the contemporary KATUSA discourse shows, such explicit racialization of the hierarchical difference has been replaced by a more complex and apparently de-racialized construction of the difference. The next section will examine how the hierarchical difference between South Korea and the United States is experienced and how such a boundary is contested by KATUSAS in contemporary Korea.

Reading the KATUSA Discourse

Experience of Imperial Power at the Margin of U.S. Military Bases in South Korea

In the KATUSA discourse, one of the most frequently recurring themes is a pervasive sense of superiority among GIS over KATUSAS. This superiority is an expression of the hierarchical difference between the empire and its client, rooted in the peculiar military arrangement between the United States and South Korea. Although South Korea formally became an independent country, the U.S Army has exercised operational command of the Korean military since the Korean War.[17] As Dipesh Chakrabarty (2000, 8) suggests, independence from colonial rule was eclipsed by the presumed need for tutelage and pre-maturity for self-rule and, by implication, an inability for self-defense. During the Korean War, the Korean government wanted to be the main force fighting the war as long as necessary military assistance was provided. In contrast, the U.S. Army viewed Korea merely as a backward country that was unable to defend itself (Korean Military Support Corps for the U.S. Eighth Army 1993, 18–20, 27–29). This incapacity for self-defense has been coupled with Korea's supposed inability to administer justice; American soldiers in Korea as agents of the empire have embodied the privilege of extraterritoriality inside and outside U.S. military bases. Since U.S. Army Military Government rule ended in 1948, Korean jurisdiction over GIS who commit serious crimes against Koreans, both on the bases and outside, has been severely truncated. Even after two revisions of the SOFA in 1991 and 2001, the U.S. military is still entitled to request that the Korean government give up its jurisdiction over such GIS, and the Korean government is supposed to oblige except in "very important cases" (C. Yi 2004, 448, 450).[18] During the Cold War and in its aftermath, the postcolonial condition of ambiguous national sovereignty has continued to fuel the pervasive sense of superiority among GIS over Korea and KATUSAS.

Contrary to the explicitly racialized differences between colonizers and the colonized that European colonialism constructed, this sense of superiority is not explicitly racialized around the dichotomy of white and non-white. Rather, it is expressed in terms of space and material abundance. The military bases on which KATUSAS serve display the affluence as well as the military power of the United States. Showered with the blessing of American capital, the bases look like well-maintained resort towns equipped with spacious, modern facilities such as gymnasiums, swimming pools, libraries, theaters, clubs, and playgrounds (Gillem 2007; Pak 2002; C. Yi 2001). In the midst of affluent yet cramped urban space and underdeveloped rural space, these military bases boast impeccably manicured lawns and trees laced with neatly paved roads. During field-training periods, the overwhelming abundance of goods available to GIS and KATUSAS, including food and beverages, as well as ammunition and firearms, speaks volumes to American economic power and its imperial excess. This spatial display of conspicuous consumption is the visible source of a sense of superiority that American soldiers display.[19] Yet this sense of superiority is not readily racialized along the dichotomy of white and non-white because about a third of the active-duty U.S. Armed Forces consists of racial minorities, including Hispanics, blacks, Asians, Native Americans, and various mixed groups.[20] The proportion of racial minorities among GIS stationed in South Korea is likely to be higher than the total average, because a majority of the GIS in Korea serve in combat positions in which racial minorities are heavily represented.[21] Their citizenship in the wealthy and powerful empire, rather than their membership in their race, apparently bolsters the American GIS' pervasive sense of superiority.

The hierarchical difference between multiracial GIS and KATUSAS has manifested itself in discriminatory treatment of KATUSAS in their own country in mundane practices. For example, in the past GIS received feather sleeping bags whereas KATUSAS received blanket sleeping bags during field training. Post Exchange (PX) shops were not open to KATUSAS in rear areas, and KATUSAS were allowed to enter Army theaters only when seats were left after GIS had been admitted (Korean Military Support Corps for the U.S. Eighth Army 1993, 87). Although this type of outright segregation and discrimination has largely disappeared, the practice of discriminatory theater admission persists.[22] The practice of escorted entrance exists, as well, and a KATUSA may enter a theater without queuing behind GIS if he is escorted by a GI.[23] Similarly, KATUSAS can enter camptown clubs, which are categorized "foreigners-only entertainment business" and therefore legally off-limits to Koreans (except registered sex workers), if they are accompanied by GIS. The disappearance of explicit discrimination to a significant degree stems from individual and collective struggle by KATUSAS in the context of Korean economic development and democratization.[24] But such residual practices remind us of the not-so-distant past when white GIS called KATUSAS "yellow niggers," "gooks," or "Orientals" in their own country (Korean Military Support Corps for the U.S. Eighth Army 1993, 86, 88).[25] In the U.S. Army, where rank has been the primary source of authority, GIS did not recognize KATUSA ranks, and GI privates rarely saluted Korean officers (Korean Military Support Corps for the U.S. Eighth Army 1993, 113). KATUSAS initially internalized this racism and protested when they were paired with black soldiers in the buddy system.[26]

In response to racial conflict and protest, and to appease the KATUSAS, the U.S. Army abolished the practice of returning KATUSAS to the Korean military after eighteen months in the U.S. Army (wŏnbokjedo) in 1967. KATUSAS generally dreaded this return because they were often subjected to severe treatment and abuse by compatriot soldiers resentful of their comfortable and easy life on U.S. military bases. Korean commanders did not want them because KATUSAS were perceived as lacking strict discipline due to their exposure to material abundance and "loose" regulations in the U.S. Army (Korean Military Support Corps for the U.S. Eighth Army 1993, 67, 68, 89). In 1969, a research team led by John W. McCrary of George Washington University published the "Commander's KATUSA Program Checklist," and in 1973 the Office of the Adjutant-General of the Eighth Army Headquarters issued "Report of the Eighth Army KATUSA Program Special Study Group." Both were intended to improve the KATUSA system. Alluding to the negative effects of discrimination, the checklist concluded that KATUSAS tended to replace their initially favorable views of American soldiers with negative ones as they interacted with them over time in the U.S. Army. In 1978, to protect the rights of KATUSAS, education for human-rights-advocacy counseling staff was implemented for the first time. The report focused on how to achieve short-term, concrete results in improving the administration of the KATUSA system without examining the fundamental problem, which was the absence of any legal grounds for the system itself (Korean Military Support Corps for the U.S. Eighth Army 1993, 114–18). During the mid-1980s, the Korean military and the U.S army collaborated to improve service conditions for KATUSAS. As a result, U.S. Army Regulation 600–2 stated that "a KATUSA is entitled to equal rights with an American soldier of the same rank."[27]

Against the backdrop of racialized hierarchical differences of the recent past, KATUSAS in contemporary Korea experience the boundary between the empire and its client in terms of bodily strength and size in the multiracial U.S. Army. The KATUSA discourse contains numerous references, jocular and serious, to the body size and physical strength of GIS. It is noteworthy that this discourse does not racialize the physical difference. The popular guide-book for KATUSAS attributes the lack of physical stamina among Korean men in general, and among KATUSAS in particular, to a lack of physical exercise among Korean students, whose education has been geared toward the college entrance exam. Also, the guidebook partially attributes this difference in stamina to the ubiquitous practice of excessive drinking among Korean college students and working adults (Pak and Oh 2003, 140). Finally, half of the interviewees attributed the physical difference to diet: GIS eat more meat than Koreans.

The hierarchical difference between GIS and KATUSAS is also experienced in terms of assigned tasks. Even in the 2000s, a majority of KATUSAS have continued to perform simple manual or clerical tasks, despite their high levels of education. Even when they are assigned to "technical positions," they often serve as drivers (C. Yi 2004, 94–95).[28] This distinction is not only a matter of difference between Korean conscripts and professional American soldiers. It indicates little interest in making effective use of highly educated soldiers on the part of both the U.S. Army and the Korean Army. It also suggests the imperial nature of the KATUSA system that has existed underneath the economic account of their continued presence. Although KATUSA service remains the most popular form of military service among Korean conscripts, this reality of KATUSA service is "demoralizing" (according to my interviewees). Some of them called KATUSA service a "high-quality labor corps (kohangnyŏk nogada budae)." Such job assignments convey an unspoken message that Korean conscripts from elite universities are worth less than American GIS, who often have high-school diplomas or even less education. Ultimately, it echoes a colonial view that the colonized are not only the source of cheap labor but also inferior to colonizers, regardless of their educational qualifications and potential.

According to the KATUSA discourse, GIS' sense of superiority is reflected in their attitudes toward Korean culture, which are characterized by indifference, disrespect, and ignorance. Few GIS try to understand or learn about cultural differences between Korea and the United States.[29] Instead, American GIS opt to perceive such differences as indicators of Korean backwardness or inferiority. A KATUSA's unfamiliarity with certain American cultural practices (as trivial as eating hamburgers with utensils instead of with their hands) and their lack of proficiency in English are also construed to be the evidence of Korean inferiority.

The sense of superiority is manifested in the GIS' predatory attitude toward Korean women, including college students as well as camptown sex workers. A majority of my interviewees made numerous references to GI friends' or acquaintances' joking about sleeping with "pretty college students." A younger generation of GIS seems to be more interested in female college students than in stigmatized camptown sex workers, whom they have to pay. My interviewees and the guidebook complained that a large number of female college students visited military bases with white GIS. The sources came to know about the college students because the visitors had to leave their picture identification cards at U.S. Military Police checkpoints. While this practice has become popular rather recently, such a desire for "pretty" college students among GIS has existed for many years. For example, Pu-yŏng Hwang, a former KATUSA who served from 1985 to 1988, recalled a GI singing a song at a barbecue whose lyrics referred to sleeping with pretty Korean (female) college students.[30] The guidebook narrates a common anecdote about a group of rude GIS on the back of a military truck shouting at young women as they passed by.[31]

Certainly, the deeper issue concerning the pervasive sense of sexual entitlement among GIS is the institution of camptown prostitution, which has existed for more than half a century (see chapter 1). A majority of GIS continue to buy sexual service from camptown club women and often practice cohabitation (outside marriage) that is very similar to the institution of "concubinage" in European colonies (Stoler 2002).[32] While specific details of cohabitation may vary from one couple to another, the structural inequality between a GI and a camptown woman based on gender, race, and nationality is very conducive to abuse and violence against the woman. As a result of socioeconomic and political change in Korea and accelerated globalization in the past decade, Korean sex workers rapidly have been replaced by migrant foreign women from the Philippines and the former Soviet Union (Sŏl et al. 2003b). Yet the underlying structure of inequality that regulates the relationship between GIS and camptown women persists (see chapter 11). While regulated military prostitution continues to safeguard GIS' (hetero)sexual access to women in Korea, the Korean public has begun to question their sexual privilege and other privileges in post-military-rule Korea. The next section will discuss the ways in which KATUSAS challenge the pervasive sense of GI superiority and negotiate the hierarchical difference between Korea and the United States in their daily lives.

Contesting the Hierarchy through Class Advantage and Racial Solidarity with GIs of Color

The KATUSA discourse questions the sense of imperial superiority so pervasive among GIS from the Korean soldiers' own vantage point as middle-class students at elite universities in Korea. Although the discourse mentions certain positive qualities of GIS,[33] the recurring theme is that, although GIS happen to be members of a stronger and wealthier nation, they tend to be impulsive, stupid, and shallow, and the KATUSAS, as individuals and as a group, are smarter and more capable.[34] According to the discourse, KATUSAS learn quickly and perform different types of tasks competently; many GIS, by contrast, live for the moment and are not interested in planning their lives for the future. They spend their leisure time partying, drinking at clubs, and sleeping with women. The GIS' absence of intellectual ability and curiosity is reflected in their indifference to and ignorance of Korean culture, as well as in their unwillingness to learn about cultural and historical differences between Korea and the United States. By and large, the KATUSA discourse conveys, GIS judge KATUSAS and Korean culture using a narrow ethnocentric yardstick because they do not have the knowledge or experience to see things comparatively.

The class difference between KATUSAS and GIS accentuates inferior qualities of GIS, especially the privates and non-commissioned officers with whom KATUSAS, as conscripts, deal every day. This class difference has been widened as a result of socioeconomic and political change in both South Korea and the United States over the past three decades. During the 1950s and 1960s, KATUSAS were drafted from the general pool of conscripts who had completed grade school and passed basic physical tests. In 1961, 51 percent of KATUSAS had received elementary-level education only and did not receive any English education. In the face of problems caused by the language barrier, the U.S. Army asked to raise the educational criteria to the completion of high school. Yet although 30 percent of KATUSAS were college graduates in 1968 (Korean Military Support Corps for the U.S. Eighth Army 1993, 109), the overall educational qualification among KATUSAS was somewhat lower than that of GIS in the 1960s. While 70 percent of GIS were high-school graduates in 1968, only 60 percent of KATUSAS had attained this level (Korean Military Support Corps for the U.S. Eighth Army 1993, 108). The educational difference was reversed after the U.S. military became an all-volunteer force in 1973 and educational levels steadily increased among Koreans throughout the 1970s. In the process of industrialization and urbanization, more young Koreans pursued higher education for better employment opportunities. The Korean government doubled the enrollment of college students in the beginning of the 1980s. In January 1982, a competitive test was introduced to select KATUSAS, and many college students have taken it because the U.S. Army offers certain advantages unavailable in the Korean military, such as off-duty hours with privacy and not being subjected to harassment and beatings by, and providing personal services for, their immediate superiors. They also enjoy comfortable facilities, receive weekly leaves to visit their families, and can learn English. These benefits have made the KATUSA service highly popular.[35] The importance of English proficiency to this test contributed to the over-representation of students of elite universities among KATUSAS. Consequently, in contemporary Korea a majority of KATUSAS are from affluent, urban middle-class families, whereas a majority of GIS (especially privates) come from rural and impoverished families and lack high-school diplomas.

While my interviewees question the pervasive sense of superiority among GIS without explicit reference to social class, the fictional texts explore the class difference between KATUSAS and GIS more imaginatively. In *Yellow Submarine* (C. Yi 2001), an autobiographical novel, some of the main characters build solidarity with GIS as powerless pawns of the imperial power, a position that KATUSAS share. Set at Camp Humphreys, which actually exists in Pyŏngt'aek City, where the largest concentration of the U.S. troops in South Korea is located (Green United and the Coalition of Movements to Reclaim U.S. Military Bases 2004, 19),[36] the novel highlights the lack of choice among, and peril for, GIS of various races, all of whom come from poor families. It focuses on a friendship between Courtney, a white GI from rural Texas, and Chae-hyŏk, an English major from an elite university in Seoul, and on a friendship between Chin-uk, a college student from Pusan, and Jenny, a white female captain who commands a company, along with interactions among other KATUSAS and GIS. During weekend leaves, Chae-hyŏk invites Courtney to his family house in an affluent area of Seoul,[37] and his mother treats them to freshly fried squid, a popular Korean dish that many GIS do not like (according to the KATUSAS I interviewed). Courtney, who joined the U.S. Army to escape the "black hole–like poverty" and violence of his neighborhood, is impressed by

FIGURE 7.3. The recent transformation of Camp Humphreys in P'yŏngt'aek, South Korea. In 2005, there were fewer than ten family housing units. Large-scale housing complexes, equipped with tennis and basketball courts, have now been constructed to accommodate hundreds of military families. PHOTOGRAPH BY EDWARD JOHNSON, IMCOM-K PUBLIC AFFAIRS.

Chae-hyŏk's house and loving family. He says to Chae-hyŏk, "You yuppies have a lot of things. The only thing I could decide before [joining the army] was a TV channel" (C. Yi 2001, 2:247–48, my translation).

Nash, one of GI characters in *Yellow Submarine*, is a fashionable African American family man who joined the army because it was one of the fastest ways to make money. He endures hardship of military labor in Korea and sends most of his salary to his wife and daughter. To his devastation, he is notified that his wife has been shot to death. Through this type of humanizing interpersonal experience with GIs of various races, Chae-hyŏk develops a sense of sympathy for them. When he gets into a heated argument with Chŏng-t'ae, a college classmate and fellow KATUSA who supports the withdrawal of the U.S. military from Korea, Chae-hyŏk retorts: "Frankly, these guys [GIS] are not thrilled about coming all the way here and staying in this foreign country. They are not responsible. The real issue is the reality of our country. In a way, these American privates are victims, as well" (C. Yi 2001, 2:204–5; my translation).

This sense of victimhood among KATUSAS is poignantly articulated by Chŏng-t'ae, the anti-U.S. military KATUSA. He asserts poignantly that

KATUSAS are like a "male version of comfort women" because they are unfree labor drafted to serve the foreign army (C. Yi 2001, 1:41). To make the matter even more complicated, KATUSAS have long been subjected to envy from Korean men who consider KATUSA service a better form of mandatory military service. Their ambiguous position has invited suspicion and distrust since the beginning. On September 15, 1950, when the U.S. navy landed in Inch'ŏn to recapture Seoul, the Seventh Division included a large number of KATUSAS (1,873), and Korean civilians were very surprised at the sight of Koreans marching in the formerly occupying U.S. forces. These KATUSAS played a crucial role in communicating with civilians who might otherwise have viewed the foreign forces negatively (Korean Military Support Corps for the U.S. Eighth Army 1993, 51, 53). During the Korean War, they were doubly hated by North Koreans as "American Imperialists' dogs." North Korean and Chinese soldiers treated American soldiers less abusively than KATUSAS when they were captured. While American prisoners of war (POWS) were sometimes released as political propaganda, all KATUSA POWS were executed (Korean Military Support Corps for the U.S. Eighth Army 1993, 89–90). When they were returned to the Korean Army after the Korean War ended, other Korean soldiers treated them very harshly because "they deserved some suffering after a period of luxurious lives in the U.S. army" (Korean Military Support Corps for the U.S. Eighth Army 1993, 94). Korean commanders were often suspicious of KATUSAS' loyalty when they returned to the Korean Army. Against this checkered history marked by ambivalence, Chŏng-t'ae conveys his nationalist view on the U.S. military to Jenny, the white female officer, who is willing to learn about Korea and therefore represents a positive model of GIS:

> Is it indeed for peace and out of the overflowing sense of justice that GIS came to Korea? The Allied Forces joined the Korean War to fight the ideological force of communism. Unfortunately, our country became the battle ground. Isn't it the same with the Vietnam War? . . . Can you say that "because we [Americans] have shed a lot of blood for a democratic world order, we can exercise privilege in the place where we shed our blood even if such privilege entails some trouble?" Such a claim would be possible only between sentimental individuals. Moreover, it'd be senseless to talk about sacrifice and all that when blood was shed strictly because of self-interest. (C. Yi 2001, 2:95; my translation)

Unlike Chae-hyŏk's individual humanist position, this remark does not lead to a sense of sympathy among KATUSAS with GIS as pawns of imperial power.

Another way in which the KATUSA discourse contests the hierarchy between the empire and its client is by differentiating brotherly (*hyŏngjegat'ŭn*) GIs from arrogant (*kŏnbangjin*) ones. Some of my interviewees indicated that black GIs were better than white GIs in relating to Korean sentiments formed by the historical experiences of oppression and suffering. The guidebook even categorizes black GIs according to the degree of their biological mix with white people. Those who are dark, with small builds, are almost like brothers to KATUSAS. Those who look like athletes and show significant mixing with whites are usually playful and optimistic; this group tends to be neutral toward KATUSAS. Those who look almost white often show a sense of superiority toward KATUSAS (Pak and Oh 2003, 42). The novels also depict Native American GIs who genuinely love camptown sex workers. These GIs are contrasted to white GIs who consider Korean women, particularly sex workers, consumable playthings. An official history of the KATUSA documents a similar sense of solidarity with black GIs, who were subjected to blatant racism in the segregated U.S. Army (Korean Military Support Corps for the U.S. Eighth Army 1993, 88).

Contesting the Hierarchy through Sexual Unions

As recent studies of imperialism and empires argue, social relations of gender and sexuality figure into the working of an imperial power not as a peripheral issue but as a constitutive aspect of producing and maintaining the boundary between the colonizer and the colonized. This dynamic of gender and sexuality is never unidirectional, and the KATUSA discourse reveals resistance articulated around sexual relations between KATUSAS and female GIs. While my interviewees shied away from articulating their sexual relationships with female GIs and their sexual fantasies, the novels narrate sexual and romantic relationships between white female GIs and KATUSAS. It is noteworthy that the object of desire in these relationships is not the female GI of color. In *Yellow Submarine*, during the first training session immediately after his arrival at Camp Humphreys, Chae-hyŏk jokes about "riding a white horse" as good luck that may happen to him (C. Yi 2001, 1:15). This slang expression gained currency among Korean men in the context of the growing migration of white women from the former Soviet Union as "entertainers" who have worked in the sex industry since the mid-1990s. In *Do You Think You're GIs?* (Pak 2002), Sang-hun, one of the protagonists who serves in a Military Police company at Camp Hialeah in Pusan, becomes acquainted with Jennifer, a white GI with a chubby body and a simple smile. While he is not strongly attracted to her sexually, he accepts her interest in him, and they spend a carefree night together. He finds the experience "pleasant" and mulls over why in a chapter titled, "I Rode a White Horse That Night":

> Wasn't it just curiosity about a white woman who had a different hair color and a different eye color? Perhaps I became rather proud of a chance to *enjoy* such "rare stock." People like being with their pets and shower them with care and affection. They also feel proud of having a special stock that other people don't have.
>
> To me she was like a cute poodle with cottony hair that wags its tail when I touch it. If she felt like me, she would have considered me an indigenous Jindo dog. When this idea came to my mind, I could not help laughing at myself. (Pak 2002, 2:172; my translation; emphasis added).

This casual sexual encounter with a white woman based on mutual consent unsettles the hierarchical boundary between the empire and its client because it assumes equality between the two individuals. Entangled with white racism that sets hierarchy among women as the object of desire and places white women on its pedestal, this encounter goes against the grain of (colonial) white racism that constructs a white woman as an inaccessible object of desire for men of color. It also goes against the grain of masculinist nationalism that calls for revenge against white men (and a white nation) who have violated Korean women for more than half a century. Sang-hun "enjoys" Jennifer as an exotic rarity but understands the possibility of his own exotic appeal as a rare pet. He narrates, "I not only rode a white horse but also was ridden by the horse" (Pak 2002, 2:171).

In contrast to this casual encounter, *Yellow Submarine* portrays a troubled romantic relationship between Minwoo, Chae-hyŏk's classmate, a model student and the only son and heir (*changson*) in a middle-class family, and Irene, a white GI and former drug addict from an impoverished broken family in Florida. They are mutually attracted to each other, but Minwoo initially resists her approach because he is recovering from a first love. She asks him to show her Seoul; one weekend, he takes her there and to a dinner at his home. Although his mother cooks for them, she is appalled because Irene has not gone to college and has tattoos on her shoulders. (Irene also has a tongue piercing, which Minwoo's mother fails to notice.) Believing that Irene is as worthless as trash, the mother throws away plates she used during dinner. After dinner, Minwoo takes Irene to a café in a fashionable district south of the Han River. Like Courtney, Chae-hyŏk's white GI friend, Irene is impressed by Minwoo's family, house, and area where he hangs out. While

Irene is excited about their meeting, Minwoo worries about trouble in their fledgling relationship, including his unresolved first love, his mother's hostility, and Irene's pending return to the United States after her duty is completed. They stop seeing each other and agonize over their relationship for a while. During ten days of open combat training, however, they run into each other as night guards. Irene asks Minwoo what is really holding him back, and he finally tells her about his unresolved love for her. That night, they are sexually united. From then on, until they complete their military service, they spend their weekends together, learning about each other and traveling to different areas in Korea without worrying about the future. When they part ways, Minwoo asks Irene whether she will continue to learn Korean, and she promises to write to him in Korean. Minwoo promises her to send his favorite book of poetry. After the separation, Minwoo suffers from Irene's absence. The novel ends with Minwoo in an airplane, flying to the United States to meet Irene, and leaving behind a letter to his parents.

The love between Minwoo and Irene transgresses multiple barriers of class, nation, and race and disrupts the hierarchy between the empire and its client. It unsettles the deeply racialized class difference between white affluence and poverty and misery of people of color that commonly stems from colonial rule of the past. It is Irene, the poor young white woman, who is deemed dirty and worthless by the middle-class Korean mother. Like Sang-hun's sexual union with Jennifer, Minwoo and Irene's sexual union is postnationalist and challenges the colonial sexual order that prohibited access to white women for men of color, and vice versa. At the same time, this union reproduces racism that places white women at the top of the sexual hierarchy of desirability. Unlike the casual and fleeting union between Sang-hun and Jennifer, this union between Minwoo and Irene is represented as a lasting commitment nurtured by efforts to learn about each other. Irene's interest in learning Korean and eagerness to see different areas in Korea is diagonally opposed to the ignorance and indifference that classically reflect the imperial superiority among GIS. This hope for mutual understanding and love that can undermine the hierarchical difference between Korea and the United States is captured by the novel's title. "Yellow Submarine," adopted from the popular Beatles song, refers to a utopian space where all people can live together and become lovers and friends. It is "a land of love and peace filled with music instead of the noise of gun shots" (C. Yi 2001, 2:226).

What remains largely unexplored in these sexual relationships between KATUSAS and white female GIS is the colonial construction of men's entitlement (as agents of imperial power) to non-white women's sexual service.

While such men were usually white in European colonialism, they are multi-racial in the contemporary U.S. military empire. Confined by their structural position at the margins of that military empire, KATUSAS are left with few options for challenging such entitlement. In *Yellow Submarine*, Chŏng-t'ae, the anti-U.S. military, nationalist KATUSA, attempts to challenge such imperial privilege with a guerrilla tactic during his military service and through activism against crimes committed by GIS against Koreans after his duty is over. He falls in love with Hye-ju, a camptown woman whose English name is also Irene, and tries to help her leave prostitution. Initially suspicious of him and cynical about his motives, she gradually opens up to him, and he continues to care for her and shows her kindness. But she is involved with Marquez, a Hispanic GI who has a bad reputation in his company.[38] Embodying the predatory GI who is violent toward sex workers, Marquez plans to kill Hye-ju because he believes that camptown women "are like dirty toilet paper that [the Korean] government provides" (C. Yi 2001, 1:197). He boasts that he will kill a sex worker and leave Korea without being caught and carries the horrible thought into action. At the scene of his attempted murder of Hye-ju, Chŏng-t'ae, who has followed Marquez because he is behaving suspiciously, kills him. While Chŏng-t'ae manages to complete his service without being caught, Hye-ju is killed by a group of GIS who want to avenge Marquez's death. The military authorities simply close the case to avoid any escalation of revenge killings by Koreans and GIS.

Conclusion

The KATUSA discourse, which consists of nonfictional and fictional accounts of Korean conscripts' military service on U.S. bases in Korea, illuminates the complex workings of the U.S. military empire. In the apparent absence of colonies, U.S. military bases in South Korea (and elsewhere, especially in non-Western countries) have become virtual colonies where national sovereignty is suspended. American soldiers as the agents of imperial power embody extraterritoriality wherever they are in South Korea, as indicated by the U.S. military's and Korean justice system's treatment of GI crimes for decades. Even after the revisions in 1991 and 2001, the SOFA continues to restrict the legitimate exercise of Korean jurisdiction over GIS who have committed crimes against Koreans on Korean soil. KATUSAS' close encounters with imperial power gives them a vantage point from which to articulate how the boundary of the U.S. empire is maintained in the peculiar context of Korea as a divided country in a state of a ceasefire. The KATUSA discourse reveals that the hierarchical distinction between the empire and its client relies on a pervasive sense of superiority among GIS over KATUSAS.

The KATUSA discourse also contests the complex imperial hierarchy through KATUSAS' use of their class privilege vis-à-vis rank-and-file GIS and sexual unions with white female GIS. Although this discourse reflects a voice of middle-class college students, this voice is not an isolated one in the context of contemporary South Korea. Instead, the KATUSA voice is a component of a grassroots movement to question the normalized presence of U.S. military bases in Korea. As South Korea is democratized, grassroots non-governmental organizations (NGOS) have publicized the taboo issues of serious crimes committed by GIS against Korean civilians and the problems generated by U.S. military bases that residents of host communities have been forced to tolerate (Ko 2007).[39] For example, the National Campaign to Eliminate Crimes Committed by U.S. Forces in Korea has worked for the realization of an equal Korean-U.S. relationship. The Coalition of Movements to Reclaim U.S. Military Bases has worked to protect the livelihood and health of residents of host communities. These forces are small in the face of the imperial power and Korean authorities that have collaborated with it, but the outcome of these collective efforts may be substantial.

Notes

Research for this chapter was supported by the Jane Rosenthal Heimerdinger Fund for Faculty Research at Vassar College. Earlier versions were presented at the Association for Asian Studies Meeting, Boston, 2007, and Nordic Association for Japanese and Korean Studies, Copenhagen, 2007. I thank my interviewees for sharing their experiences of KATUSA service with me. I also thank Barbara Durniak for her professional assistance in finding crucial information and Seunghee Moon for sending me a rare material on KATUSA history.

1. Camp Jackson contains the KATUSA Training Academy, where new KATUSAS receive basic training before they are sent out to individual companies.

2. Che-gyu Ko, "Hŏnbŏbwie 'katusa' innŭnga [Is KATUSA above the constitution]?" *Sisajŏnŏl*, 5 March 2003, 48–49. *Pacific Stars and Stripes*, 15 February 2003, "Sergeant gets 30 years in sexual assault on S. Korean soldier" reported on the incident: "According to the victim's testimony, and an August confession by Sok [one of the three soldiers] to military investigators, the three U.S. soldiers approached the victim while he was alone in an outdoor latrine. Sok grabbed the victim by the throat and brandished a knife. The three soldiers forced the victim to perform various sexual acts, then left him, unconscious, in a toilet stall." A general court-martial panel found U.S. Sergeant Leng Sok guilty of "sodomy, aiding and abetting sodomy, conspiracy to commit sodomy, assault, indecent acts and making a false official statement." Sok was sen-

tenced to thirty years in prison; the other two U.S. Army sergeants (whose names were not disclosed, despite formal charges against them) "were discharged administratively from the service" without other punitive measures: "Charges dropped in KATUSA assault," *Pacific Stars and Stripes*, 26 September 2003.

3. While there are no formal statistics for this, all of my interviewees mentioned that more than 80 percent of KATUSAS would have been students at renowned universities in Seoul, because KATUSA service requires proficiency in the English language. I met my interviewees through personal contacts, and each interview lasted approximately an hour. Although these interviews were open-ended, I focused on the following questions: (1) How did you come to serve as a KATUSA? (2) What aspects of the service did you like or dislike and why? (3) What struck you most during your service and why? (4) What did you learn about the U.S. military, GIs, and American culture and society during your service? and (5) What do you think of the U.S. military in Korea and the relationship between Korea and the United States?

4. For extensive examples of varied military-base arrangements between the United States and host countries, see Cooley (2008), Lutz (2009), Johnson 2004a, chap. 6; Sandars 2000.

5. It reads: "We will not hesitate to act alone, if necessary, to exercise our right of self-defense by acting preemptively. . . . Our best defense is a good offense."

6. Such major bases include Yongsan Garrison in Seoul, Camp Walker in Taegu, Camp Hialeah in Pusan, Camp Humphreys in P'yŏngt'aek, and Kunsan Air Base (Wolf Pack) in Kunsan: Green United and the Coalition of Movements to Reclaim U.S. Military Bases 2004. According to the *Base Structure Report*, there were eighty-seven U.S. military bases in South Korea in 2008: U.S. Department of Defense 2009.

7. When the Korean War began, the South Korean Army had roughly 105,000 troops, and the North Korean Army had roughly 198,000 troops. But in some forty days, South Korean casualties mounted to approximately 70,000. Similarly, U.S. casualties reached 19,000 during the first two months of the war: Korean Military Support Corps for the U.S. Eighth Army 1993, 16–18.

8. During the Second World War, the number of U.S. Army peaked at more than 8 million, but this number had contracted dramatically, to 591,000 (active forces), by June 1950: Schnabel 1972, 43.

9. The Far East Command under General MacArthur was reduced to 120,000 troops, and the U.S. Eighth Army, the major combat force under this command, had only 26,494 soldiers in 1949: Korean Military Support Corps for the U.S. Eighth Army 1993, 13. However, because the Eighth Army was primarily responsible for the postwar occupation of Japan, these combat soldiers were neither continuously trained nor provided with adequate weapons and equipment. In addition, new recruits to the Eighth Army showed much lower abilities than new recruits elsewhere, as measured by the Army General Classification Test: ibid., 14–15.

10. During the Korean War, President Syngman Rhee believed that Koreans should protect their own nation and would be much more eager to do so than American soldiers, and he demanded an active role for Koreans in the war. In contrast, distrusting Korea's ability to perform in combat, American commanders did not take his

demand seriously and declined to increase the number of Korean troops. Instead, the proposal to allow Korean soldiers to serve in the U.S. Army was chosen as a compromise: ibid., 20.

11. They served as medics, guards, welders, and electricians.

12. This number was far larger than the one the Korean legislature had approved (10,472). The disparity reflects the U.S. military's imperial dominance over South Korea after the transfer of operational command of the Korean military to the U.S. Army at the start of the Korean War: Korean Military Support Corps for the U.S. Eighth Army 1993, 100.

13. Until 1967, KATUSAS were to be returned to the Korean Army after eighteen months of service in the U.S. Army. Since 1982, a competitive test has been used to select KATUSAS among new conscripts: ibid, app., 3–5. Since 2004, a lottery system has been combined with the test because KATUSA service is the favored form of military service among conscripts: Dakyuinp'o 2004, 90.

14. Colin L. Powell, secretary of state during the Bush administration (2001–8), served at Camp Casey (constructed in 1952) in Tongduch'ŏn in 1973–74. He observed, "We had troops called Katusas . . . who could run forever. Our units were always understrength. My battalion rated seven hundred men and I never had more than five hundred. We filled out the ranks with Koreans": Powell with Persico 1995, 186.

15. Kim So-hŭi, "Pulbŏpp'agyŏn, katusa, cŏmhom! [Illegal dispatch, KATUSA, come home!]," Hangyŏre 21, vol. 561, 31 May 2005, 40–49.

16. These ambiguous practices were frequently pointed out by my interviewees and were also mentioned in the novels and the guidebook analyzed in this essay.

17. United Nations Forces Headquarters (controlled by the U.S. military) remained in Korea until December 1974, when operational command was officially transferred to the U.S. Army. Although operational command of the Korean military during peacetime was returned to Korea in 1994, such control during wartime still remains in the hands of the U.S. Army: Kim, "Pulbŏpp'agyŏn, katusa, cŏmhom!" 43; Korean Military Support Corps for the U.S. Eighth Army 1993, 231.

18. Between 1948 and 1952, South Korea and the United States signed a series of unequal agreements to guarantee the extraterritoriality of U.S. military personnel in South Korea and to exempt the United States from liability for damage inflicted on Koreans by on-duty military personnel. The SOFA signed in 1966 allowed for very limited exercise of criminal jurisdiction and compensation claims by the Koreans, but it has continued to protect GIS who commit crimes against Koreans at the expense of victims: C. Yi 2004, 448–49.

19. Mark Gillem (2007, chap. 4) discusses material and spatial affluence as a common feature of overseas U.S. military bases.

20. These figures are based on "F[iscal] Y[ear] 2004 Active Component Enlisted Members by Race / Ethnicity," available online at http://www.dod.mil/prhome/poprep2004/appendixb/b_24.html (accessed on 25 March 2009); "FY 2004 Active Component Officer Accessions and Officer Corps by Race / Ethnicity, available online at http://www.dod.mil/prhome/poprep2004/appendixb/b_33.html (accessed on 25 March 2009).

21. In 1991, 73.3 percent of GIS stationed in South Korea served in combat units: Korean Military Support Corps for the U.S. Eighth Army 1993, 156.

22. Kim, "Pulbŏpp'agyŏn, katusa, cŏmhom!" 45. Oddly enough, GIS pay entrance fees; KATUSAS are admitted free, but only when there are seats left. My interviewees were puzzled about why this difference has existed when they were more than willing to pay the fees.

23. This anachronistic practice was mentioned by and in all of my sources.

24. Severe racism against KATUSAS precipitated the murder of a GI by a KATUSA in 1965. The KATUSA committed suicide, leaving behind a detailed description of the unequal treatment to which he had been subjected. In 1966, a group of thirty-four KATUSAS attempted to escape a military base to protest their unequal treatment: Korean Military Support Corps for the U.S. Eighth Army 1993, 114. From the postwar decade to the 1970s, the economic difference between the United States and South Korea was immense. In 1961, an American private was paid more than a Korean general. There was acute conflict around incidents of theft on U.S. military bases, and KATUSAS were often suspected of committing such crimes: ibid., 111; Kim, "Pulbŏpp'agyŏn, katusa, cŏmhom!" 48.

25. Despite their crucial role in fighting the Korean War, KATUSAS were frequently subjected to racism in the segregated U.S. Army. American officers thought that KATUSAS were dirty and unhygienic. One officer in the Seventh Division recalled, "Koreans have lived differently from us. Our loose rules are not suitable to them. Discipline in the Korean Army is very strict and arbitrarily violent. They grew up under this rule and therefore do not understand other types of rules. Korean attachments are not satisfactory. While they eat our food, ride our trucks, and use our supplies, they have little use other than for simple tasks": Stanton 1989, 53. The lack of education, language barrier, and lack of integration because of racism confined the KATUSAS to simple manual tasks: Korean Military Support Corps for the U.S. Eighth Army 1993, 110.

26. To facilitate the integration of KATUSAS, the Far East Command recommended a buddy system that paired a KATUSA with a GI during service. This failed because of the language barrier and because American soldiers did not accept Koreans as buddies. After the war, a different version of the buddy system was introduced as the "sponsor system," which also coupled a KATUSA with a GI mentor: ibid. 48, 50.

27. Kim, "Pulbŏpp'agyŏn, katusa, cŏmhom!" 45.

28. My interviewees confirmed these prevalent practices.

29. Such cultural indifference and ignorance stemming from a pervasive sense of superiority was noticed as a major problem by the U.S. military authorities that ruled South Korea from 1945 to 1948: see the first essay in this volume.

30. Kim, "Pulbŏpp'agyŏn, katusa, cŏmhom!" 48. The Korean military has not treated women that much better. See S. Moon (2002a) for an analysis of persistent sexism in the military against professional female soldiers, who were integrated in the name of gender equality.

31. This practice goes back to the period of U.S. military occupation and the Korean War. GIS then called young (and not so young) Korean women they saw as sexual objects

"*saekssi* (bride)." Wan-sŏ Pak (1998), a renowned female writer, vividly portrays this type of predatory sex between GIS and Korean women during the war.

32. Powell observed such sexual arrangements at Camp Casey, one of the most populous U.S. military bases in South Korea, in mid-1970s. He writes, "I was struck by the number of short-term AWOLS, men usually gone only a few hours. 'Yobos [a colloquial Korean word for spouses],' my executive officer explained. Yobos? Any eighteen-year-old who had had trouble getting a date in high school could have an apartment and a girl, a yobo of his own, in Tong Du Chon, the town next to Camp Casey, and for only $180 a month": Powell with Persico 1995, 183.

33. For instance, according to my interviewees, GIS generally have jolly attitudes and are disciplined about their responsibilities and safety. They are also rational about their self-interest and deal with others on the basis of mutual interests, which makes them act fairly without expecting personal services. These KATUSAS envy that GIS, as Americans, appear not to care about what other people think about them.

34. This image of smart KATUSAS is not merely a self-aggrandizing one. Powell corroborates it and writes positively about the KATUSAS he worked with at Camp Casey. "The Katusas were among the finest troops I have ever commanded. They never showed up drunk or failed to show up at all. They were indefatigable, disciplined, and quick to learn. And they earned $3 a month, less than [what] one of our men would blow on beer in a night in Tong Du Chon": Powell with Persico 1995, 187.

35. Before the KATUSA test was implemented, several dozen conscripts would apply for a single KATUSA position. After the change, the application rate plummeted and has remained steady at two or three for each position: Dakyuinp'o 2004, 90.

36. The city will host the Yongsan Garrison in Seoul to be relocated by 2014 and the Second Infantry Division units deployed in the north of Seoul by 2015: "S. Korea, US Near Base Relocation Agreement," 29 April 2009, *Korea Times*. Although relocating this huge military base in the center of the capital city had been under discussion since 1990, its execution was delayed by a disagreement between South Korea and the United States over the specific terms of the move. In 2004, the two countries uneasily agreed to move Yongsan Garrison to P'yŏngt'aek and agreed that the Korean government would provide the land: Green United and the Coalition of Movements to Reclaim U.S. Military Bases 2004, 27.

37. A program called "volunteer invitation (*chagach'och'ŏng*)" on U.S. military bases is designed to promote friendships between KATUSAS and GIS. Under the program, a KATUSA invites a GI to his family home and often gives a guided tour of some part of Korea. The host has to pay for the expenses.

38. I wonder whether there is an issue of internalized white racism in this portrayal, because white GIS most frequently have been involved in highly publicized cases of murdering camptown sex workers in Korea: see From Nogŭnri to Maehyangri Publication Committee 2001.

39. See Gillem 2007, chap. 3, for the general discussion of negative socio-spatial effects of U.S. military bases overseas.

EIGHT

"THE AMERICAN SOLDIER DANCES, THE GERMAN SOLDIER MARCHES"

*The Transformation of German Views on
GIs, Masculinity, and Militarism*

☆

MARIA HÖHN

In the popular imagination of the U.S. occupation of Germany, certain stereotypes of the American GI have taken hold. No historical exhibit or popular history book on the postwar years is complete without a picture of a smiling GI, preferably a black GI, handing candy to a German child. That same exhibit will also feature pictorial evidence of the enthusiasm with which many German women welcomed the American GIs, both white and black. The Berlin Airlift of 1948–49 was another important turning point that cemented the image of GIs as protectors of West Germany and as the guarantors of the country's emerging democracy. The same airplanes that just a few years prior had obliterated the city had been turned into "raisin bombers" that brought food to the starving city and dropped candy for Berlin's children. The GIs might have come as conquerors, but within just a few years they had become protectors and then allies of the German people in the Cold War conflict with the Soviet Union.

After the creation of the Federal Republic of Germany in 1949, many Germans continued to refer to the Americans as "the occupation," but most Germans, in light of the growing tension with the Soviet Union, also acknowledged how important the Americans' presence was for the security of West Germany and Europe. By 1953, an astounding 67 percent of West Germans wanted the Americans to stay, and that high level of support would hover around 75 percent over the next five decades. The numbers dropped only slightly during the most difficult years of the early 1970s, when the military switched to an all-volunteer army after the convulsions of Vietnam. Even during the contentious Pershing missile crisis during the early 1980s, which presented an absolute low point in German–American relations, only one-quarter of the population called for the Americans to withdraw their troops (Fleckenstein 1987, 15; Merritt and Merritt 1980, 208).

The consistently high numbers of Germans who saw the U.S. military as their country's best hope in the East–West conflict, however, do not reflect the more nuanced views that Germans held of their protectors from across the Atlantic. Just as consistently as they have expressed approval of the American mission in West Germany over the years, Germans have expressed deep skepticism concerning the overall fighting quality of American GIs. Interestingly, even as the American military as an institution was seen as West Germany's most reliable and forceful protector, the individual soldiers themselves were exposed to deep scrutiny.

To show the complexity of the German–American encounter, I will explore how Germans after 1945 viewed the GIs and how that perception changed after the all-volunteer army was introduced and, especially, after the invasion of Iraq in 2003. Significantly, German stereotypes of "emasculating" American women and "feminized" and weak American men, which go back to the 1920s, informed much of the encounter in the postwar decade. The attraction of German youth, both male and female, to the GIs' different physical styles and American popular culture only increased the sense among many older Germans that American GIs were not "real men" and definitely not the kind of "tough soldiers" that were needed to stand up to the Soviet threat. By juxtaposing the views of these two different generations, I will show that the U.S. military presence created the sort of "ambiguous space" that Amy Kaplan refers to in her work on American empire. In that space, the U.S. soldiers, fortified by American popular culture, introduced new models of masculinity into West Germany that were eagerly adopted by young German men. I will conclude with a short overview of how the German relationship to all things military and to soldierly virtues has evolved since 1945 and how that transformation has brought about a whole new perception of American GIs.

First Impressions and Years of Occupation

Germans first encountered American GIs in the First World War, and during the short-lived occupation of the Rhineland, but those encounters were few and far between, given the small U.S. military presence in Europe after 1918. The real encounter with "America" came during the "golden years" (1924–28) of the Weimar Republic (1918–1933) when the injection of American private loans brought not only American companies but also American popular culture and consumer goods. The Ford Motor Company, Charley Chaplin, jazz music, and Coca-Cola all heralded that a new age had dawned, and many young Germans in urban centers embraced the foreign influx with enthusiasm. But not all Germans shared this exuberance. After having lost the war and their monarchy, Germany's educated and conservative upper classes (*Kulturbürger*) felt besieged. Therefore, debates on the meaning of the American juggernaut and what it meant to be "German" in light of this cultural onslaught were not only extensive but heated.

When Germany's conservative elites looked to America, they saw nothing but trouble. In their eyes, the American model of consumer capitalism posed immense challenges not only to German *Kultur* (high culture), but also to traditional class, gender, and generational hierarchies. German elites were especially haunted by images of the "new woman" who seemed to epitomize all that was wrong with the American model. Significantly, German observers formulated their anxiety foremost about white American women from the middle and upper classes, who not only enjoyed greater legal equality than their German counterparts but were also much more visible in the workplace and in the philanthropic sector. Because of this narrow focus on privileged white women, German bourgeois observers concluded that American women had not only taken control over mass consumption in the home, but that they also allegedly had taken charge of Kultur, a sphere traditionally controlled by upper-class men in Germany. In doing so, women had "feminized" Kultur and thus emasculated American men. Germany's conservative upper classes were convinced that husbands not only showed "verbal deference" to their wives, but also allegedly washed the dishes and cared for the children. One German man, speaking for many, declared that the American woman was the "queen of the home," whereas in Europe the man was "lord of his castle." American-style consumer capitalism, West Germany's conservative bourgeoisie was convinced, produced hyper-aggressive women and emasculated men.[1]

Those long-established stereotypes of feminized American men and emasculating women were only further enforced by Nazi war propaganda. Beginning with the U.S. entry into the war, Goebbels's propaganda machine belittled American GIs as feminized "Tango dancers" or "Jitterbugs" who lacked the discipline of the German Wehrmacht soldier (Henke 1995, 167). German schoolchildren were told that the Americans could never win the war because the "American soldier dances, whereas the German soldier marches."[2] The regime reversed the image of the feminized American soldier drastically, however, during the closing days of the war. American GIs were depicted as "Anglo-American war criminals" or as "Anglo-American Soldateska" who aimed at the "complete destruction of the German *Volk*" (Ruhl 1980, 14, 1985, 88–91). The civilian population's resistance to the American invaders, however, was hardly fortified by this fear-mongering. There was no mass flight from the Americans on the Western front, and angry Nazi officials reported that people assured themselves that they were not being invaded by the Russians but by a "civilized people" (Ruhl 1980, 83). Even the efforts of the Nazi regime to depict African American GIs as brutal, "syphilis-infected rapists" intent on the complete humiliation of German women, could not convince the civilian population to resist the American onslaught (Henke 1995, 962). Instead of fearing the invaders, most Germans awaited the American soldiers with nervous anticipation or a sense of relief.[3]

The image that the defeated Germans were able to form of American GIs was, of course, not monolithic. For Germans, who had strongly identified with National Socialism, the invasion of the American victors was often coupled with a sense of helpless anger and sometimes even hatred. For many such Germans, it was incomprehensible that these "childlike" and "overweight chaps who constantly chewed gum" could have prevailed over German soldiers (quoted in Kleinschmidt 1997, 101). For many other Germans, however, the arrival of the GIs meant the end of the bombings of German cities and a chance to get a better look at these "strange creatures." In the contemporary depictions of these first encounters, but also in the recollections many decades later, certain themes emerge again and again.[4] Germans marveled at the unbelievable technical superiority of the American equipment; they commented on how big and well fed the soldiers were and how cool and relaxed they appeared to be. Another prominent theme that emerged was the GIs' generosity, especially toward children. A clergyman in Neckarsgemünd spoke for many Germans when he described the arrival of the victorious Americans and their "avalanche of steel" in this manner:

How unbelievably well equipped this American army was! . . . The soldiers looked stunning, healthy and well fed, dressed in uniforms of the finest cloth and their boots were made of the best leather. On top of that their fantastic vehicles. We were able to convince ourselves in every aspect of the technical superiority of the Americans . . . They ate lily-white bread, . . . and had chocolates in abundance and smoked constantly. (Quoted in Henke 1995, 962)

The soldiers were not only better fed and better equipped; they were also described as "big, friendly, relaxed boys" who appeared to many Germans like "apparitions from another star" (quoted in Kleinschmidt 1997, 100). Those first encounters for many Germans, but especially for children, also often were connected with oral satisfaction. To this day, the memories of that first piece of Hershey's chocolate or pack of Wrigley's gum tossed from a passing tank hold a prominent place in Germans' recollection.[5]

The contrast between the well-fed, sovereign American GIs and the "the malnourished, badly equipped, fleeing, and desperate" German soldiers, however, did not necessarily convince German observers that the American GI had been the better warrior (Henke 1995, 961). Quite the contrary: many Germans were convinced that the American victory over Germany "was not that honorable" and that the Americans had "defeated the Germans because they were better equipped and not because their soldiers were better fighters" (Ruhl 1985, 154). As we will see, this widely held conviction of the postwar years—that the American GIs were not such great soldiers and that the Americans could win wars only because of their technical superiority and overwhelming air power—would have a long afterlife in West Germany.

Because Germans were not allowed to criticize the occupation, it is difficult to get a sense of how Germans viewed the American soldiers during those years (1945–49). Surveys and reports by the U.S. military government, however, show that the prestige of the American GI deteriorated substantially because of widespread discipline problems, with German opinion reaching a low point by mid-1947. The occupation army lost much esteem and respect when the military proved unable to enforce its fraternization ban, especially in regard to fraternization with German women (see chapter 3). The decision to demobilize highly disciplined combat units as quickly as possible and to replace them with poorly trained recruits and volunteers only led to even greater discipline problems.[6] The military government reported with much distress that Germans have come to believe that "American soldiers are men who drink to excess; have no respect for the uniform they wear; are prone to rowdyism and beat civilians with no regard for human rights; and benefit themselves through the black market"(quoted in Ziemke 1975, 421). An appalled army leadership agreed that the situation had gotten out of hand, and General Joseph T. McNarney, the U.S. military governor in Germany, declared in May 1946 that the undisciplined behavior of the GIs had dishonored the American military.[7]

Given the larger American goal of democratizing German society, the U.S. Army was deeply worried about the soldiers' discipline and morale problems. The soldiers' lack of discipline also tarnished the image of the "GI as democratic citizen in uniform," which the Americans envisioned as a crucial element in their reeducation efforts in West Germany.[8] Effective response to the widespread problems came only in the late spring of 1947, when increasing fears of the Soviets led to a comprehensive effort to improve troop readiness, morale, and discipline (Willoughby 2001, chap. 5). The army brought a fearsome Constabulary Force to Germany to rein in the soldiers, and more permanent quarters helped improve discipline and morale. These efforts soon paid off, and by 1950 two-thirds of Germans were declaring that the behavior of the American soldiers was good or very good (Merritt and Merritt 1980, 58).[9]

Years of Rapproachment (1949–1955) and the Golden Years (1955–1965)

The 1950s are often referred to as the golden years in the relationship between Germans and Americans (Nelson 1987, 51–61; Schwarz 1981, 375–428).[10] Beginning with the Berlin Airlift, the former occupiers turned into protectors, and the granting of semi-sovereignty to West Germany in 1949 confirmed that the country was to be readmitted into the family of nations. Dean Acheson called those years a "period of not only settling differences but of growth and understanding" between the U.S. and West Germany (quoted in Schwartz 1991, 248). Surveys conducted at the beginning and end of the decade suggest just how much progress was made. By 1961, 70 percent of West Germans believed that the United States saw them as friends, and only 10 percent thought that Americans still viewed them as enemies. This is a dramatic turnaround from just ten years earlier, when a full 60 percent of Germans were convinced that the United States considered Germans their enemy, and only 20 percent believed that the United States was West Germany's friend (Knauer 1987, 189–90).

The military, however, had a much harder time convincing the Germans that its soldiers were up to the task of defending Europe. While 58 percent of

FIGURE 8.1. Military parade in Kaiserslautern (1950s). Such parades were meant to impress the Germans that the United States could stand up to the Soviet threat while assuring the French that the Germans were under control. COURTESY WALTER RÖDEL.

West Germans insisted by late 1952 that the U.S. Armed Forces should remain in West Germany to ensure the country's security, a significant number of Germans also believed that the American soldiers were not up to the challenge.[11] Just a few years after its triumphant victory over Germany, the U.S. military found itself in the awkward position of having to assure the Germans of its soldiers' military prowess.

Given Germany's long history of equating "manliness" and "Germanness" with military service, toughness, and self-sacrifice, the relaxed and indulged GIS who strolled through German communities with their seesaw walk, hands in pocket, all the while chewing gum, elicited many a smirk rather than awe. The American military was appalled with survey results in 1952 indicating that only 27 percent of Germans believed that the Americans could stand up to the Soviet threat. Even though West Germany would not reestablish its own military until 1956, 77 percent of West Germans declared in that same survey that German soldiers were the best soldiers in the world, while Soviet soldiers received that praise from 31 percent of Germans. Americans were stunned to hear that only 12 percent of Germans thought that American soldiers were deserving of that category (Merritt and Merritt 1980,

151–52). In a survey taken a year later, 38 percent of Germans described the American soldiers as "not brave," "soft," "undisciplined," or "badly trained," while another 47 percent of Germans still believed that the American military had only been able to prevail over the Germans in 1945 because its soldiers had been much better equipped than the German soldiers (Merritt and Merritt 1980, 207–8).

How does one explain the less than enthusiastic endorsement of the fighting qualities of American GIS? German assessments of the American victory in the war, which stressed the material advantage and technological superiority of the U.S. military, were still circulating widely. The widespread discipline and morale problems of American soldiers during the early occupation years also did much to undermine German confidence in the GIS' prowess. That Germans assessed the manliness and "soldierliness" of American GIS so negatively might also have been brought about by the many humanitarian activities of the U.S. military during the occupation years, such as the Christmas parties that soldiers organized for German war orphans. While these activities were much appreciated during the harsh postwar years, they did little to convince anxious Germans that the American soldier was as tough a fighter as his Soviet counterpart. In light of the abysmal numbers in the survey from 1952, the Public Information Office of the U.S. Army in Europe (USAREUR) instructed military commanders in West Germany that, "in the previous period, the problem was to convince West Germans that the American soldier was a friendly, tolerant person who wished them well. . . . The time has now arrived for stressing the fighting qualities of the troops, their desire and ability to hold back an invasion."[12]

Convincing the Germans of the soldierliness and toughness of the American GI was one of the largest challenges the U.S. Army faced in West Germany. To be accepted, first as an occupation army and then as a protective force, the U.S. military did everything in its power to present its GIS as democratic citizen soldiers, to shower Germans with American largesse, and to present GIS also as friendly ambassadors of the American way of life. Furthermore, the U.S. State Department made it very clear that the Cold War battle was to be fought not just militarily but also with American consumer goods and American popular culture (Höhn 2002, chap. 2; Poiger 1999). In this effort, the military took on an active role also by bringing the promises of the American way of life into German communities. The American military, unlike its Soviet counterpart in East Germany—and unlike in South Korea—actively encouraged its soldiers to go out and make friends with the Germans, to join clubs, and to become philanthropists in German

FIGURE 8.2. German–American Friendship Week (early 1960s). In rural communities, this event was the highlight of the year, with the Americans handing out ice cream, cupcakes, and hamburgers. COURTESY HEINRICH BRUCKER.

communities. These extensive community-relations efforts made it possible for the American military to insert such a large troop presence and to convince Germans to accept that presence over the past sixty years (Höhn 2002, esp. chaps. 1–2).

Unbeknownst to the military, however, there was a real downside to all these efforts at building community relations. The military's effort to highlight the "human" aspects of the soldiers created a situation in which the image of the American GI was defined not so much by his "soldierly qualities" as by his cool and relaxed American style. As we will later see, it was precisely these qualities that attracted young teenagers to the American soldiers, but older Germans could not hide a sense of unease that the American soldiers were not as "soldierly" as many Germans hoped for. The American GI was well dressed, well groomed, and possessed a marvelous set of wheels, and it was his consumer wealth, rather than his soldierly qualities that made him "the man" he was.[13] The *Ami-Soldat* (American soldier) was friendly and kind, West Germans declared in 1954, but lacked "aggressiveness and hardness," the very qualities Germans still deemed essential to good soldiering (Merritt and Merritt 1980, 238).

Just as important, for much of the 1950s, the stereotypes from the 1920s of the emasculated American man and the aggressive American woman were reproduced by widespread media coverage of the "new neighbors" in West Germany's garrison towns. At a time when West Germany's conservative Christian Democratic government was eager to restore "traditional" gender roles to distance the country from both its Nazi past and the communist present in East Germany, the coverage of the new neighbors revealed a sense not only of marvel but also of dread. American military wives allegedly ruled supreme in the American home on base, spending much of their time shopping or in philanthropic endeavors (instead of cooking for their husbands). German women may have been in awe that even officers occasionally took out the garbage for their wives or helped with the children, but such gender relations only confirmed for German men that "the natural order" had been turned on its head in the American family. The perception of the emasculated and henpecked American man was still widespread in the 1950s, and Germans often teased that the American "generals in the Seventh Army were only afraid of McCarthy and the American women's organization."[14]

Although the bloody toll of the Second World War and the almost complete destruction of Germany's cities had convinced many Germans that their country should not rearm, the German understanding of "soldierly qualities" and "manliness" had not yet been transformed. Throughout the 1950s and into the mid-1960s, that understanding remained directly tied to Germany's long tradition of militarism. A "real soldier" was able to endure harsh discipline, deprivation, and sacrifice; he did not live the spoiled and indulged life of the American GI. If rearmament and the reinstitution of conscription could not be avoided in light of America's efforts to integrate West Germany into the Western military alliance, then young men should be taught "order and discipline." Until the social transformation of the 1960s, the ideal of the military as *the* identity-creating institution of "manliness" and as the "school of the nation," was still alive in the minds of many Germans despite the Nazi catastrophe (Frevert 2004, 274).[15]

The Dollar's Collapse and Vietnam War

The overwhelmingly positive assessment regarding the friendliness and kindness of the American GIs, and the somewhat less enthusiastic assessment of their soldierly qualities, lasted until the late 1960s. Beginning with America's growing involvement in the war in Vietnam, American prestige and that of U.S. soldiers would take an unprecedented downturn. The war and the way in which the U.S. government dealt with the damage inflicted on the Seventh

Army in West Germany because of Vietnam also created a gulf between Americans and Germans that would become ever wider.

For German politicians and the people living around U.S. bases, the Vietnam War brought an unprecedented crisis in German–American relations— a crisis that, at the same time, reveals the transnational quality of the U.S. military empire. The Seventh Army in West Germany was bled dry to feed the war machine in Vietnam, resulting in a crippling collapse of morale and discipline among the troops. As I describe in chapter 10, the Seventh Army in West Germany was close to collapse and confronted with widespread desertion, alcohol and drug abuse, and racial tension. At military roll calls, commanders sometimes were greeted with the soldiers' cry of "FTA" (for "fuck the Army"). In some instances, grenades were lobbed into commanders' offices, and unit-wide incidents of insubordination were reported (see Höhn 2008, 133–54; Höhn and Klimke 2010, chap. 8; Vazansky 2008).

Desertion and AWOL (absent without leave) rates skyrocketed, and out-of-control drug and alcohol abuse led to an ever-rising number of attacks on German civilians. The situation around U.S. military bases was so violent by the late 1960s and early 1970s that the American political scientist Daniel Nelson (1987, 108) called it a "reign of terror." In 1971, GIs committed 2,319 violent crimes against Germans, a 75 percent increase over 1969.[16] The *Frankfurter Allgemeine Zeitung*, one of West Germany's most distinguished and pro–American newspapers, came to a similar conclusion when it reported in the late summer of 1972 that certain military barracks and their surroundings had become dangerous areas for U.S. soldiers as well as German civilians: "Gangsters in uniform blackmail or rob their comrades on base [and] gangs made up of [American] soldiers terrorize the local population outside the bases."[17] Commentaries in German newspapers regularly asked whether such a demoralized military was capable of mobilizing an effective attack against the armies of the Warsaw Pact (Nelson 1987, 192–93).

What gave further fuel to the Vietnam-induced crisis of the 1970s was the unprecedented collapse of the dollar as a result of the Nixon administration's decision to uncouple the currency from the gold standard. The dollar, which brought 3.90 deutsche marks in 1967, was worth only 3.63 deutsche marks by 1970 and had dropped to 2.50 deutsche marks by 1975. The dollar reached its lowest point in October 1978, when it was worth a mere 1.72 deutsche marks (Nelson 1987, 174). Mayors in garrison towns pleaded with German landlords to reach out to the Americans and to lower their rent. Many landlords complied, but the economic descent of the formerly wealthy American GIs could not be stopped. By the 1970s, fewer and fewer Americans could be seen about town, and their German neighbors were appalled to hear that lower-rank soldiers often were able to manage only with the help of food stamps. In 1979, 16,000 American military families in West Germany lived below the poverty line. Even the care packages that German families donated in 1978 for poverty-stricken GIs and their families were a mere drop in the bucket (Leuerer 1997, 185). The *Frankfurter Allgemeine Zeitung* reported with dismay that the "rich uncles from times past [had become] the poor devils from overseas."[18]

The American government's decision in 1973 to replace the draft with an all-volunteer military was envisioned as a resolute answer to the problems of discipline and morale that had crippled military bases across the globe, but the professional military brought a new set of challenges with it. Because of the low military pay and the weakness of the dollar, the military could not compete with the free market in the United States. Consequently, it was often individuals with limited professional options, who joined the military during those difficult years of transition.[19] During the 1970s furthermore, plenty of young GIs found themselves in West Germany because a juvenile court had offered them military service as an alternative to serving a prison sentence. Matters were not helped by the low-level of educational attainment that many of the early volunteers suffered from. During the years of the draft, soldiers were recruited from all strata of society, and more than 14 percent had college degrees. In this more representative sample of American society, only 18 percent of troops could be found in the lowest category of the Armed Forces Qualification Test (AFQT). After the all-volunteer army was introduced, that ratio rose to 41 percent in 1977; in 1980, 50 percent of new recruits scored in the lowest category of the AFQT (Nelson 1987, 116). In the same year, the *Frankfurter Allgemeine Zeitung* reported, with much dismay, that 4 percent of American GIs were illiterate and that one-third of them had problems reading even simple texts.[20]

Because the United States occupied Germany after the war with a segregated military, but also because only a tiny percentage of African Americans served in the officer corps and in leadership positions, Germans had always understood their alliance with America to be foremost an alliance between two white nations (Höhn 2002, chaps. 3 and 4). The introduction of the all-volunteer army changed that perception because it brought a much higher percentage of people of color to the Armed Forces. While only about 13 percent of the soldiers stationed in West Germany before 1974 were African American, the ratio had increased to 31.4 percent by 1983. Considering, furthermore, that 4.2 percent of soldiers were Hispanic and 3.4 percent came from other minority groups, Americans with a white European background constituted only 60 percent of the U.S. military (Nelson 1987, 146; Seiler 1985, 186). The introduction of women into the military hurt its prestige even more than the increasing number of minorities (Nelson 1987, 20).[21] Even though female soldiers on the whole were better educated and trained than male soldiers, and accumulated fewer sick days than their male comrades, conservative German observers could not overcome their sense of unease that something was wrong with the picture.[22]

All of the demographic changes within the military, as concerned observers of U.S.–German relations repeatedly pointed out, weakened the bond between Germans and Americans that was based on a "shared West European culture."[23] But German commentators also wondered whether the American superpower fully understood the implications of this new military. An extensive and probing essay in the pro-American *Frankfurter Allgemeine Zeitung* raised the questions, "[Is it] politically smart that American society has placed the responsibility and burden of national defense foremost on its socially marginal classes? . . . Is this an appropriate response given the importance of such an existential calling? Will these minorities perhaps see themselves some day as mercenaries for 'the others'?" The author of the essay, Günter Gillessen, also asked whether the loyalties of America's "people of color" might "be uncertain in a future conflict in the Third World."[24] The First Gulf War in 1991 and the American invasion and occupation of Afghanistan and Iraq have proved his concerns unfounded, but even in America, more and more voices are being raised asking whether it is democratic and whether it is just to leave such a large degree of the burden and sacrifice of national defense to Americans recruited from minority or economically disadvantaged backgrounds.

Germans, the Military, and Gender Assumptions

When French pollsters asked West Germans in 1983 who the Federal Republic of Germany's "two best friends" were, 77 percent named the Americans, about half chose the French, 25 percent named the British, and only 2 percent mentioned the Soviets. This incredibly high rating for the Americans at the low point in German–American relations, during the Pershing missiles crisis that led to emergence of a vibrant and outspoken German peace movement, speaks volumes about the complicated relationship between Germans and Americans. The Americans were well liked, and, as I have shown, a substantial majority of Germans wanted the U.S. military to remain in West Germany. Thus, even though many Germans never quite came around to appreciating the individual American soldier as a "manly" or "soldierly" fighter, Germans were the first to point out that the Americans had provided security for them for decades. The reliance on the American strategy of nuclear weapons, I suggest, made it possible for Germans to question the fighting qualities of the American soldier while simultaneously insisting that the American military, because of its nuclear superiority, ensured security for West Germany.[25]

Yet despite the consistently high approval rating for a continued U.S. troop presence, the gulf between West Germans and American GIs has widened considerably since the 1980s.[26] How does one explain the dramatic transformation between the 1950s and the 1980s? The changing demographics of the military caused by the all-volunteer army certainly played a role. Another contributing factor was the more insular ethos of the professional army, which defined itself by widely using the advertising slogan "Army of One." The attacks on U.S. military installations by members of the terrorist Red Army Faction in the 1970s and 1980s also did much to create a "bunker" mentality in the military and to foster more self-reliant and inward-looking troop cohesion (Nelson 1987, 174). The demonstrations by the German peace movement in the 1980s contributed to this development, despite the demonstrators' efforts not to conflate the individual soldiers with the politics of Ronald Reagan. The calls to remove nuclear missiles and to take "Poison Gas Out" of West Germany all too often were perceived by American soldiers as "Ami go home."[27] This siege mentality within the U.S. military has only increased since the terrorist attacks of September 11, 2001. In stark contrast to the situation in earlier decades, military bases and housing areas for American families in West Germany are now not only heavily guarded; they are almost completely cut off from the rest of German society.

The most important cause of the deep gulf between Germans and American soldiers, however, is not the American military and the soldiers it sends to Germany. We need, instead, to look at how German society has been transformed since the 1950s. Although only a small section of German society was active in the peace movement in the 1980s, the movement's convictions and goals reflected a much broader societal consensus. Since the end of the Second World War, West German society has been undergoing a process of transformation in which the military and "soldierly virtues" no longer hold identity-creating values in what it means to be a German. Many Germans who came of age in the 1920s and 1930s still waxed nostalgic in the 1950s and early 1960s about the unmatched discipline and toughness of German soldiers. By the 1970s, however, most Germans were proud of the peaceful mission of West Germany's "citizens in uniform," whose main job was to guarantee that there would "never again be another war." The traditionally militarist Germans had been transformed into pacifists who put their faith in multilateral action, multinational institutions, and political solutions to deal with conflicts. In light of the death and destruction brought about by German militarism, this transformation is all too understandable.

The trauma of the Second World War, Germany's genocide of the Jews, and the slaughter of millions of other innocents are not sufficient to explain this important shift. Since the late 1950s, German society has also been undergoing a significant modernization of social and cultural norms that has produced new models of masculinity. Unlike in the past, these models of masculinity no longer rely on the military and such qualities as hardness and violence. Instead, they refer to role models in youth and popular culture, sports, and technology. As scholars of postwar German history have shown, the U.S. military occupation, and the predominance of American consumption patterns and popular culture, certainly contributed to this transformation in cultural norms. In this important shift, the profession of the soldier is no longer understood as *the* defining symbol of masculinity, and the military is no longer understood as the "school of the nation" (Frevert 2004, 280). By the early 1970s, 80 percent of Germans from age sixteen years to twenty-nine were insisting that draftees should have a free choice between serving in the military or paying their dues to the nation through alternative service (*Zivildienst*)—that is, by working in hospitals, nursing homes, or day-care programs for children. West Germany Chancellor Willy Brandt affirmed that view in the early 1970s when he insisted that in a democratic society, *schools* are the "school of the nation," and not the military. With this important transformation of society, the military's century-old monopoly as the fount of a specifically German masculinity and of national sovereignty had been broken (Frevert 2004, 282).

Just how much the German understanding of "masculinity" and the population's attitude toward all things military have changed since 1945 can best be seen when one looks at how young Germans have viewed American GIS over the decades. During the 1940s and 1950s, the GIS' relaxed style and privileged way of life prompted older Germans to question their masculinity and their soldierliness. However, it was precisely the qualities that their elders abhorred that made the American GIS so attractive to young West Germans after the Second World War. Especially during the so-called golden age of German–American relations in the 1950s and '60s, young Germans saw in the

GIS ambassadors of the American way of life, of a better and easier life, and this understanding has deeply penetrated German recollections of these years.[28] American blue jeans and the mighty American limousines (*Strassenkreuzer*) driven through town by young GIS made a terrific impression on German teenagers. Young West Germans, male and female, were equally impressed by the relaxed American style. One man spoke for many in his generation when he recalled that, in the 1950s, "we saw in the GIS a symbol of a country with a way of life that we did not even know but longed for so desperately."[29] Another man remembered fondly, "The American GIS opened a whole new world to us."[30]

West Germany's young people were crazy for American consumer goods, but they also admired the much more relaxed American approach to life. Germans who were teenagers during the golden years recall that "the [soldiers'] whole way of carrying themselves, their clothing, their mode of behavior had a tremendous impact."[31] After the hard discipline of Nazi Germany, West Germany's teenagers were especially taken with the casual American manner. As one early fan recalled:

> What impressed me personally . . . to an incredible degree was when you saw . . . these young GIS, who were so relaxed when they put their hand to their cap in their casual manner, while I still had all this . . . heel clicking in the back of my head. That's how they were. . . . . Such comradely relations that the subordinates had with their bosses. . . . I was incredibly impressed by that. (Quoted in Maase 1992, 215)

After 1945, West Germany was flooded with that different American style of "being in the world" through new role models such as the movie actors Marlon Brando and James Dean and through rock-and-roll icons such as Elvis Presley. Most Germans had plenty of opportunity to observe and mimic American film and popular-culture idols, but teenagers around U.S. military bases experienced the much admired American "cool casualness (*Lässigkeit*)" daily and on a much more intimate basis. Much as male teenagers throughout West Germany copied the American role models of the big screen, teenagers in U.S. garrison towns observed the confident seesaw walk of the smartly dressed GIS around them. They marveled at the American GIS' laidback manner as they walked the streets "with their hands in their pockets." Walking with hands in pockets, sitting backward on a chair, putting feet up on a table—all of these gestures became a new way to express an informal habitus that set the young generation apart from the more inflexible and formal world of their elders.[32] It was this American way of "being in the

FIGURE 8.3. The military took full advantage of Elvis Presley, who was serving a tour of duty in Friedberg, to convince reluctant Germans not to oppose the American-sponsored remilitarization of the country. Here Elvis is helping restore a First World War memorial. PHOTOGRAPH BY HORST SCHÜLER, COURTESY STADTARCHIV FRIEDBERG (HESSEN).

world" that attracted young women and that gave male teenagers in postwar West Germany a different role model of masculinity—one that was based not on military discipline, but on a relaxed style, expertise in the latest dance steps, and a well-groomed hairdo.

That fascination with and admiration of all things American could not be undermined by the older generation, who warned their teenager children in the 1950s that they were acting and looking like Americans when they chewed gum or put their feet on the coffee table. As Reinhold Wagnleitner, an early fan of the relaxed American style, recalls, "That is how we wanted to look like" (Wagnleiter 1994, ix). Thus, many young German men saw the American GIs as a cool alternative to the goose-stepping and discredited German Wehrmacht soldier. The GIs were adored precisely because they were not tough fighters. Instead, they carried the promise of a better life literally on their bodies.

That infatuation with all things American began to shift in the mid-1960s.

As German youth became much more critical toward the domestic- and foreign-policy objectives of the U.S. government, and as the war in Vietnam escalated, a much different attitude toward the GIs emerged. The journalist Niklas Frank, who was a child when he saw with much excitement his first American soldier, probably spoke for many a disenchanted German of his generation when he wrote, "And then we discovered a war, way beyond Turkey, in Vietnam—and suddenly the smooth dancers and blues swingers, the rock-and-roll acrobats and relaxed gum chewers, were transformed into the ugly Americans who devastated the forests with Agent Orange and bludgeoned innocents in thousands of My Lais."[33]

For many in the postwar generation, the Vietnam War destroyed the image of the friendly GI who smoothly tucked a pack of Lucky Strikes into the sleeve of his T-shirt and brought the newest dance steps from the United States. But that same war also caused a different strata of German youth to take note of the GIs in their midst—namely, university students from West Germany's educated upper classes. During the 1950s young men and women from that social strata had mostly stayed away from American GIs, looking to French culture as a role model instead. In the 1960s, they shifted their outlook; many had spent time at American high schools or as exchange students at American universities, where they learned about American grassroots democracy, the Civil Rights Movement, and the emerging student unrest against the war in Vietnam (Klimke 2010, chap. 2). Beginning in the mid-1960s, an extensive collaboration emerged between German students, who were mostly from the educated upper classes, and American GIs stationed in West Germany to end the war in Vietnam.

All German garrison towns with American troops, just like garrison towns in the United States, saw the emergence of GI cafés, and legal and logistical networks were established to help willing deserters get to Sweden and France, two countries that were not obligated by North Atlantic Treaty Organization statutes to return those soldiers to U.S. authorities. Thus, when German students protested against the war in Vietnam in cities across Germany, they wore discarded U.S. military parkas and sang "We Shall Overcome," the anthem of the American Civil Rights Movement (Wagnleitner 1994, x). Significantly, the students' protest was a protest "together with America against America," and German students went out of their way to win American GIs to the antiwar cause (Gassert 2002, 757; Höhn 2008, 2010; Höhn and Klimke 2010, chap. 8; Klimke 2010; Brünn 1986). Furthermore, these young student radicals challenged the understanding that the bond between Germany and the United States was built on an alliance between

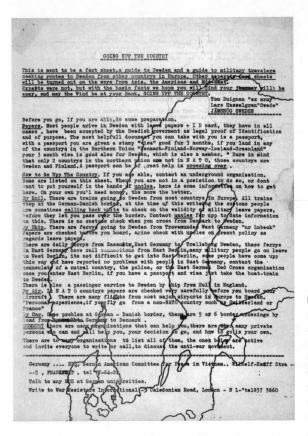

FIGURE 8.4. Flyer produced by the German sds (Sozialistischer Deutscher Studentenbund) advising American GIs on how to desert and find refuge in Sweden. COURTESY ARCHIV FÜR SOLDATENRECHT.

two white nations. Indeed, they reached out specifically to radicalized Black Panther GIS, because they represented a masculinity and authentic revolutionary subjectivity of which white and privileged middle-class German students could only dream (Höhn 2008; Klimke 2010, chap. 4; Höhn and Klimke 2010, chap. 8; see also chapter 10 in this volume).

This kind of collaboration between young Germans and similarly young GIS has become almost impossible since the introduction of the all-volunteer U.S. Army. The difference not only in education, but also in cultural background, between German students and GIS, for whom military service is often the only chance for upward mobility, is just too big. Furthermore, in today's military, more than 50 percent of soldiers are married and bring their families, and many spend most of their time in the self-reliant "Little Americas" on the military bases. Because so many Americans who serve in the military are politically and culturally more conservative than most German youths their own age, interactions are also less likely (Nelson 1987,

149). In a dramatic shift from the earlier postwar decades, most German youth began looking down on the American GIS, seeing them as the losers of their own society.[34]

The most dramatic reversal in how Germans view the American GIS, however, came with Al Quaeda's attack on the United States in September 2001, which led to the war in Afghanistan, the invasion of Iraq in 2003, and America's neo-conservative vision of the "global war on terror." Because of those wars and the escalating growth of unconventional fighting forces, including the Special Forces, the Central Intelligence Agency's Delta Force, and privatized mercenaries from companies such as Blackwater (renamed Xe), a radically new perception of the American military and the GIS has emerged. That perception is only strengthened by American popular culture's celebration of the individual "warrior and hero" in movies and thousands of war and commando videos (see chapter 12). George Bush's decision to discard the Geneva Convention in his global War on Terror, and the resulting brutalities committed by American soldiers in Abu Ghraib, Afghanistan, und Guatánamo, have only enforced the perception that the U.S. military is tough as nails and that GIS are ruthless executioners of American foreign policy. The friendly, cool, and generous GIS of years past—those "marvelous creatures" from another world, as young Germans called them after the Second World War—have in the view of many Germans turned into efficient and deadly mercenaries. Their voluminous body armor and mirrored aviator glasses, which are standard equipment on the streets of Baghdad, also dominate the images that filter into German homes via television and newspaper coverage. That coverage is almost unanimously antiwar. Significantly, the perception of the GIS as ruthless enforcers of American foreign policy is more nuanced in communities where soldiers are actually based. But even there, the self-imposed isolation of the U.S. empire under siege makes it almost impossible to counter the prevailing media images from the war in Iraq with the sort of images of GIS that so enchanted a different generation of Germans after the Second World War and convinced so many of them to give democracy a chance.[35]

Notes

1. For a thoughtful description of bourgeois gender anxieties in the 1920, see Nolan 1994, 125; Peukert 1992.
2. Gabrielle Simon Edgcomb, conversation with the author, Washington, D.C., summer 1995.

3. The Oral History Collection, IANAS, contains a wonderful collection of how Germans remember these first encounters.

4. Ibid.

5. Video Archive, IANAS, videos 5, 8, 11, 14, 57, 63.

6. For a detailed description of these problems, see esp. Kleinschmidt 1997, chap. 6; Schraut 1993, 153; Willoughby 1993, chaps. 1, 3.

7. "Overseas: Curbing a Conqueror's Complex," *Newsweek*, 6 May 1946.

8. On GIS as "ambassadors of democracy," see Kleinschmidt 1997, 198–204. Renwick C. Kennedy, "The Conqueror," *Christian Century*, April 1946, describes in detail how many chances for democratization and for winning the Germans over to the American way of life were lost because of the bad behavior of the GIS. For similar sentiments, see Hutton and Rooney 1947.

9. Fleckenstein 1987, 5, contains public-opinion surveys since 1956.

10. See also Video Archive, IANAS, videos 37, 47, for a description of the 1950s as the "Golden '50s."

11. USAREUR Public Information Division, Classified Decimal File 1952, and HICOG survey 152, 15 September 1952, NARA, RG 338, box 1, folder 014.13.

12. "A Note on Anti-Americanism in Germany," n.d. [ca. 1952], Classified Decimal File 1952, NARA, RG 338, box 1, folder 014.13.

13. "Dicke Luft in Kaiserslautern. Man sieht kaum einen französischen Soldaten auf der Strasse [Trouble brewing in Kaiserlautern: One sees hardly a French soldier on the streets]," *Saarbrücker Zeitung*, 9 December 1952.

14. "Laufende Razzien beunruhigen Geschäftemacher [Constant raids are upsetting shady businesses]," *Die Freiheit*, 18 December 1954. On how German women perceived the Americans and gender relations in the U.S., see Höhn 2002, chap. 2.

15. See also Bald 1994, chap. 3; Geyer 2001, 376–408. Michael Geyer shows that Germans were hardly pacifists in the 1950s but that the romance with the state, which also was closely tied to the military, was broken. It was this break that allowed Germans to build a democratic civil society.

16. "Wir mussten die Siebte Armee ruinieren [We had to wreck the Seventh Army]," *Der Spiegel*, 17 April 1972; Adalbert Weinstein, "Die Siebte Armee erholt sich von Vietnam [The Seventh Army is recuperating from Vietnam]," *Frankfurter Allgemeine Zeitung*, 25 August 1972.

17. Weinstein, "Die Siebte Armee erholt sich von Vietnam."

18. Margrit Gerste, "Die armen Teufel aus Übersee. Der Dollarverfall fesselt die GIS noch stärker an ihre Kasernen [The poor devils from across the Atlantic. The collapse of the dollar forces them to stay put in their bases]," *Die Zeit*, June 1979.

19. Ibid.

20. Günter Gillessen, "Jeder Dritte Soldat ist ein Schwarzer [Every third soldier is black]," *Frankfurter Allgemeine Zeitung*, 22 August 1980.

21. For German views on U.S. female soldiers, see also Bald 1994, 109–13.

22. Gillessen, "Jeder Dritte Soldat ist ein Schwarzer"; idem, "Es kostet Mut über die Hemmungen hinwegzukommen [It takes courage to overcome these inhibitions]," *Frankfurter Allgemeine Zeitung*, 6 August 1980. See also, Video Archive, IANAS, video 11.

23. Gillessen, "Jeder Dritte Soldat ist ein Schwarzer."

24. Ibid.

25. On the role nuclear deterrence played in shifting German views of militarism, see Bald 1994, chap. 3.

26. A headline in *Neckarzeitung* (23 February 1988) declared ominously, "The GI—the Unknown Creature Isolated in the Military Barracks," giving voice to how alienated Germans and Americans had become.

27. "Wie in einem besetzten Land [As if in an occupied country]," *Der Stern*, 19 May 1982. On the German peace movement, see Müller 1986. Significantly, even substantial segments of the peace movement were opposed mostly to the stationing of nuclear weapons, not to the U.S. military presence in general.

28. The presence of such large numbers of young and mostly single men also brought problems. Too much German beer and competition for German women often led to brawls and vandalism. German observers, however, usually stressed that the new German draftees would be acting up in the same way if they had the financial resources of the American GIs: Höhn 2002, chap. 3; Leuerer 1997, 196.

29. See "Zweibrücken Zusammenstellung, 2c," IANAS. Reinhold Wagnleitner's introduction in Wagnleitner 1994 (the American translation of Wagnleitner 1991) contains marvelous reflections on how seductive the GIs, their consumer goods, and their cool style were to young Germans (and Austrians).

30. Video Archive, IANAS, video 34.

31. Ibid., video 1.

32. Heide Fehrenbach (1995, 165–68) suggests that "consumption, personal style, and leisure activity took on a symbolic significance as German youth employed American culture to mark their difference from received notions of German identity." On this fascination of German teenagers with the American style, see also Höhn 2002; Maase 1992; Poiger 1999.

33. Niklas Frank, "Ami Good Bye," *Der Stern*, 7 January 1993.

34. On how radically the attitudes of German youth toward American soldiers have changed, see *Neckarzeitung*, 23 February 1988, 4; Nelson 1987, 174.

35. During a recent book tour in Germany in 2008, I was struck by the deep gulf in the audience between those Germans who knew Americans in the 1950s and 1960s and a younger generation whose understanding of the American military is foremost informed by U.S. policies in the Middle East since the early 1990s.

NINE

IN THE MIDDLE OF THE ROAD I STAND TRANSFIXED

☆

CHRISTOPHER NELSON

In Okinawa, like perhaps anywhere else, the past exists uneasily alongside the present. It can pass unnoticed, occasionally rising for a moment of recognition, slipping away again under the weight of the routine tasks of daily life. And like the unexploded bombs that still lie close to the surface of the Okinawan landscape, it can erupt into the present, casting its shadow over a future not yet experienced. Memories, wrenching and traumatic, can tear the fabric of the everyday, plunging those who experience them into despair and even madness. They haunt the present with their melancholy demands for repression, making their presence known in the prohibitions that they have engendered.[1]

For decades, Okinawans have tried to come to grips with a past that reaches so insistently into the present—memories of the battlefield, repressive colonial policies, and the disinterested neglect of the American-led reconstruction.[2] At the same time, they must also confront troubling memories of moments of intimacy, what Ann Stoler (2002, 7) has called "the affective grid of colonial politics," a colonial history that has been grounded at every point in the quotidian activities of everyday life. It is, of course, a history that took shape on cane plantations and military parade grounds; in police barracks and classrooms; and amid throngs of demonstrators. However, the relationships that emerged out of this experience were also enmeshed in metaphors and practices of closeness, sexual and familial. They have been enacted, criticized, and challenged at kitchen tables and household altars; in farmhouse bedrooms, neighborhood bars, and backstreet brothels. These intimate moments of daily life are subject to appropriation by soldiers and bureaucrats, entrepreneurs and ethnographers. The ideal of a respectful and affectionate subordination to parental authority was cultivated through myriad institutions and discourses during the Japanese colonial era; filial affect was then bound to a fascist imperial ideology and its demands for loyalty to the emperor and absolute sacrifice (see Tomiyama 1995). The Japanese army laid claim to the valorized bonds of maternal love as soldiers encouraged mothers to murder their children and commit suicide rather than surrender to invading American soldiers (Field 1993). Under the American Occupation, the division of domestic labor within farming families was reified and commodified, providing servants, gardeners, and cooks for military households, as well as sex workers for the bars and brothels of newly constructed base towns (Molasky 1999, 53–59; Sturdevant and Stolzfus 1993, 240–99).

The collective struggle of Okinawan survivors, secondary witnesses, and activists to critically reexamine the past unearths complex and overdetermined traces inscribed in memory and in graphic representation. Those traces are not simply—if such a thing could ever be simple—of deprivation and exploitation, of terror and loss. The Okinawan past—the history that extends beyond the Japanese colonial era to the Kingdom of Ryūkyū—is also a reservoir of possibility. Once stigmatized as backward and oppressive, it has become a powerful archive of romantic imagery and practices for Japanese nativist artists, scholars, and politicians, as well as for Okinawans themselves. Traditional Okinawan villages are represented as sites where the Japanese people (for these discourses often appropriate Okinawans as something like living traces of the ancestral Japanese) could truly dwell, places of organic totality lost to life in the modern world. Work was meaningful; relationships were close and continuing. Life could be lived from birth to death in the same site; men and women, spirits and deities living and laboring in harmony. Agrarian rituals, songs of thanksgiving, the ruses of traders, the sexual autonomy of the *moashibi* (a gathering of young men and women in prewar agrarian communities and an important object of academic and popular remembrance in contemporary Okinawa), invocations of ancestral spirits and local deities await nothing more than recovery in the practices of the present.

Beautiful women and handsome men in homespun kimonos; villages of small wooden houses with thatch or tile roofs and walled courtyards; songs of romantic obsession, the promise of sexual intimacy, separation and melancholy. The production and circulation of these images of the rural Okinawan past as signs are characterized by the powerful and unsettling ambiguity of trauma and possibility. Recollections conjure intertwined and contradictory feelings of hope and loss, pleasure and horror, origin and apocalypse. It seems that however carefully the narrative is crafted to emphasize one aspect, its counterpart remains just at the edge of perception. I do not mean to suggest that this is a natural property of the sign; rather, it is the outcome of the interwoven practices of progressive historiography, native ethnology, popular folksongs, imperial apologia, storytelling, conversations with the dead, political debate, and more.

As the American military occupation continues, young artists and performers turn to these images, working to reappropriate the affect with which they were once charged. For dancers such as members of the Sonda Seinenkai—the youth group that I discuss in the pages to follow—they are saturated with possibilities that may be realized in the present. While their performances do not deal explicitly with images of tragedy and oppression, they are shadowed by this past in the most intimate ways. Every day the dancers feel it in the ache of their tired limbs, their joints bent and twisted by labor long before the ravages of age take them, their skin burned and dried by long hours in the sun. They feel the shame of occupation in the long detours that American bases impose on their travel to work, in the way a word like "houseboy" rolls off their grandfather's tongue, in the money from base leases that fills their pockets after trickling down through grandparents, uncles, and parents. They know it in the longing for a lover who is away searching for work in Osaka or Kawasaki or spending the evening pouring drinks for a businessman in a neighborhood bar. They feel it in the desire for a new car, a comfortable house, a private room that they will never own. They see it in the faces of their mixed-blood siblings, in the tears that streak their grandmother's cheeks as she kneels in prayer at the family tomb. They hear it in the laughter of drunken Marines and affluent Japanese tourists. They taste it in the *awamori*, the Okinawan rice liquor, that they drink through long afternoons and evenings of boredom, frustrated by the lack of work. Feeling this, they turn to other images of the past as they search for ways to make and remake themselves. Working in the most intimate spaces of everyday life—their homes, their neighborhood streets—they struggle to transform the world.

Two Films, Two Dances

During the summer of 2003, I returned to an Okinawa once again caught up in intense reflection on its exploitation by Japan and the United States. Discussions continued about the brutal rape of an Okinawan schoolgirl by American servicemen in 1995, the repression of yet another attempt to challenge compulsory leases of Okinawan land for military bases in 1997, and conservative attempts to censor images of the Battle of Okinawa in the new Prefectural Peace Museum in 1999. At the same time, Okinawans were deeply divided over the proposed construction of a new Marine base in Henoko. The past again erupted into the present (see Angst 2003; Yonetani 2003).

And so it was with great interest that I took my seat in a crowded theater in Naha for a screening of Nakae Yūji's film *Hoteru Haibisukasu* (Hotel Hibiscus; Nakae Yuji, dir. 2002). Nakae is a well-known mainland Japanese filmmaker who studied at the University of the Ryūkyūs and often speaks of his deep affection for the islands. All of his films have been about Okinawa; they have gained considerable popularity among mainland devotees of Okinawan culture and performing arts, as well as with Okinawans themselves. *Hotel Hibiscus* follows the picaresque adventures of Mieko, a young girl growing up in Okinawa.[3] Like Nakae's earlier *Nabī no Koi* (Nabbie's love; Nakae Yuji, dir. 1999), it is saturated with a sentimental focus on the natural wholeness of the Okinawan life world.

Mieko's life is bound up in the rhythms of rural life—schoolyard games and lazy summer holidays, vibrant seasonal festivals and deeply meaningful household rituals. Woven into this narrative are encounters with the ghostly inhabitants of lost villages, shy forest sprites, and kindly ancestral spirits. Nakae's film, with its languid, episodic pacing, presents each moment as commonplace while still highlighting the exceptionality of the exotic and the uncanny for metropolitan viewers. However, the setting is not the tiny isolated island of pristine white beaches and quaint villages of *Nabbie's Love*—or of a host of other recent films and television specials that celebrate Okinawan authenticity. Mieko lives in a base town, desolate and impoverished, clinging to the perimeter of an American military garrison. The temporality of the film is ambiguous—somewhere in a hazy moment that stretches from the reversion of American-occupied Okinawa to Japanese sovereignty in 1972 to the present.

The jarring representation of crumbling concrete buildings, asphalt streets, and barbed-wire fences is a surprising departure for a film such as this. Still, Nakae retains something of an ethnographic focus, particularly in his emphasis on the organization of the Okinawan household. This long-standing obsession of Japanese nativist ethnologists also powerfully underlies representations of Okinawa in Japanese popular culture. No stereotype of Okinawan domestic life escapes Nakae's camera: Mieko's father, Masao, is an amiable idler; her mother, Chiyoko, capable and energetic; her siblings, happy and supportive. Her paternal grandmother—played by the iconic Taira Tomi—aging and wise, provides a linkage to the spirit world as well as virtually every other recent film and television drama about Okinawa.

However, there is something about Mieko's family that exceeds the conventional representation of the Okinawan household. Her father whiles away his days in a deserted billiard hall on the first floor of a nearly derelict family-run hotel that probably had been built to accommodate transient Americans and assignations between GIs and Okinawan prostitiutes during the booming days of the American occupation. Her mother presides over the household by day, leaving at night to work at a local nightclub that caters to U.S. soldiers. Her older brother, an aspiring boxer, is half black; her older sister, with vivid blond hair, is half white. Only Mieko seems to be Masao's child. And yet, like her encounters with the spirit world, Mieko's family situation is presented as both unremarkable and unusual.[4]

Although she is absent for a significant part of the film, her activities are central to the narrative. Clever and resourceful, she engages in a kind of practical polyandry: her family and their hotel are supported by the relationships that she maintains with her Okinawan and American lovers. While Chiyoko's practical activities are so important to the film, Nakae's camera avoids the bar where she works. There are no representations of the workplace, no intimations of how her relationships with her lovers were initiated or organized. However, the director's apparent reticence is belied by the signs that mark Chiyoko's social skin—her garish makeup, her red lingerie, the red dress that she wears as she leaves the hotel in the evening (see Turner 2007).

The juxtaposition of Mieko's dreamlike adventures against representation of postwar Okinawa has the effect of draining the everyday world of its actuality, of distancing the film from the historical experiences of Okinawan men and women. I felt this most strongly when Mieko, her sister, and her mother were shown doing the laundry on the roof of the hotel. Their aging washing machine broke, and the women moved the laundry to an inflatable pool. Churning the soapy water with their feet, they begin to dance, then burst into an impromptu song about their lives:

At our Hotel Hibiscus—
We're an international family!

I cringed at the double appropriation of Okinawan history: the first, as it effaced a past charged with Okinawan exploitation; the second, for what it represented in its place.

What does it mean to speak of an Okinawan family as "international?" Has it been internationalized in its destruction by both the United States and Japan? Is it an international family if it has had its conventions transformed, its practical existence reconfigured by the new demands that it is subjected to at the nexus of the Japanese and American states? It is here that the Okinawan past calls out for attention. In the aftermath of the Battle of Okinawa, nearly 140,000 Okinawans were dead, their homes ruined, their families scattered. In abandoned fields and confiscated farms, the American military began to build the bases and airfields that remain to this day. They also helped Okinawans to rebuild their shattered villages, relocating those whose land had been appropriated for base construction. In the newly established base towns, they worked together to create an orderly grid of streets and alleys: not the lone Hotel Hibiscus but hundreds of similar bars and hotels, tiny houses, and cramped apartment buildings close to the bases, linked with wide, paved highways. The postwar conversion of these Okinawan communities was so thorough, the spatialized division of labor so intensive, that they were not simply sites of the residences where Okinawan base laborers— houseboys, maids, gardeners, cooks, and janitors—retired to eat and sleep. Even domestic space itself became a site of productive wage labor. The streets and highways that brought Okinawan workers to the bases also carried American soldiers in the opposite direction—to the shops, bars, brothels, and hotels that existed among and within Okinawan houses. The home was not only the site of domestic labor. For thousands of Okinawan women, it became a workshop for commodified sexual labor, as well.[5] Higashi Mineo's award-winning novel *Child of Okinawa* describes this transformation in its crushing banality—in a building like the Hotel Hibiscus, a child grudgingly gives up his bed to a prostitute working at his family's bar and the GI who has paid to accompany her (Higashi 1992, 83).

Why did Okinawans accept these conditions? Desperation and a lack of alternatives. Experience of trauma so intense that the problems of the moment seemed inconsequential. A fierce determination to do whatever was necessary to save their families. Fantasies of an American way of life. The lure of a world beyond the drudgery of an agricultural village and the duties of an

Okinawan household. Faith that the Japanese or the American states would deliver them from these conditions (see Molasky 1999). These are only a few of the motivations that could have been explored; however, there is little intimation of any of this in Nakae's film.

Nakae's sunny images of Okinawan life were released to theaters at a time when issues surrounding the American military presence, its impact on Okinawan life, and the responsibilities of the Japanese state to its citizens remained hotly contested. For me, the film resonated with remarks that I heard Hashimoto Ryūtarō, then the prime minister of Japan, make in 1997 in a speech in Naha.[6] Despite the severity of the base crisis that threatened his administration, Hashimoto took time to praise the depth of Okinawan culture and traditional practices and the gentleness and optimism of the people of the islands. "These are things that did not simply endure the American occupation," he said, "They have prospered." This is certainly good news for those who fear for the erosion of tradition by the relentless march of capitalist modernity. And yet is there any impetus to alleviate social problems when we know that Okinawan culture, strong and enduring, lies beyond their reach? Hashimoto's words were kind, but the aspirations of the people can be policed through compliments and flattery as well as through discipline and repression. And the policing of Okinawa was surely one of the objectives of Hashimoto's visit: to once again fix in place the spatial division of labor that constitutes the Japanese nation-state. An order in which, unfortunately, it falls to Okinawa to provide a home for 75 percent of the American military forces in Japan, as well as for the Japanese security forces that support their operations. How close to the vision articulated in Nakae's film: you've satisfied the sexual desires of American GIs, you've shouldered the burden of their children, you've sacrificed your share in Japanese prosperity, and you're still happy and energetic! You really do know what's important in life—what more could you need?

For Hashimoto, everyday life and traditional practices are the compensation for oppression; for Nakae, they are also the sites of the most intimate kind of exploitation. And for both, the power that these intimate relationships contain can be appropriated as representations for the benefit and the pleasure of the rest of Japan. In the end, Nakae's film seems to offer precisely the same reward as Hashimoto's address: warm words of praise and assurances that the rent will keep coming.

Throughout the screening, I watched faces of the people who sat around me—excited, laughing, actively listening. I saw them talking and joking as they left for home, an old man happily bouncing his grandson in his arms, enjoying the final moments of a relaxing interlude in their busy lives. I expected to hear complaints or catcalls, but there was nothing of the sort. I wondered at their thoughts as they made their way out of the theater, as they reflected on their own experiences, as they discussed the film with their friends and relatives.

Something about the moment also made me think of a film by Moriguchi Katsu that I had seen several years earlier in the theatre at the Okinawan Prefectural Archives. A film that explored the same terrain, and yet represented the eruption of the political in the intimate, the revolutionary in the everyday. This was Breaking Through Hard Ground: Okinawa '71, a documentary that included images of the Koza Riot—a violent uprising against the Americans who had occupied Okinawa for twenty-five years. Scenes began on the evening of December 20, 1970. The streets of the base town Koza—now Okinawa City—crowded up against the massive American Air Force base at Kadena. Moriguchi's camera pans along rows of concrete buildings, sweeping over the seemingly numberless shops, bars, and brothels that cater to American soldiers, a street much like the one that runs in front of the Hotel Hibiscus. The incident that sparked the riot—an American GI striking an Okinawan pedestrian with his car—has already taken place off camera. Okinawan men and women crowd the streets, pulling American servicemen from their cars, hurling rocks, debris, bottles of burning gasoline. Okinawan police and American soldiers struggle ineffectively to restore order. The wreckage of dozens of cars smolders in the streets. Lit from behind by the flames, a woman dances. She is dressed in a dark Okinawan kimono, her hair worn in the traditional *kanpu*, or chignon. After decades of lifestyle reforms, this attire is only seen in dance studios, at neighborhood festivals, and on local stages. Perhaps she is a musician or a hostess from one of the *minyō*—popular traditional music—pubs in the neighborhood. She steps and turns, her hands describing wavelike patterns in the air as she dances the *kachāshī*, an exuberant expression of celebration.

I am fascinated by the irreducibility of the references to the past evoked by the image of the dancer—of life in an idealized rural village, of the stigmatized and abandoned fashions of Ryūkyū, of women's labor in the bars of the base towns, of rebellion dressed in the costume of subservience (see Tomiyama 1998). And what of her dance? Time after time, people have told me that a celebration is inconceivable without kachāshī. It is an invitation: to dance kachāshī is to call to others to join in, to participate in the creation of a celebration. It is a physical expression of pleasure and happiness. It also signals the completion of a performance. Concerts, festivals, plays—even

FIGURE 9.1. American cars burning during the Koza Riot (December 20, 1970). COURTESY *OKINAWA TIMES*.

lectures, films, and demonstrations—end with the kachāshī. To see a dancer begin its sweeping gestures is to know that a moment is coming to a close.

I feel a kind of awe as I recall the dancer in Moriguchi's film. I wonder at the conflicted invitation that I saw in her dance. *Come join in—it is about to end!* How could someone who stood in these streets at a moment of such crisis weigh all of her possibilities and find the courage to dance? Dancing among the burning cars, dancing as rioters stream around her in the street, dancing as soldiers advance toward her in riot formation.

Performing, Remembering, Becoming

I spent every evening during the summer of 1998 at the Sonda Community Center in Okinawa City, about a mile or so south of the point where the Koza Riot began. As I had done the summer before, I joined dozens of men and women in the pounded clay courtyard as they prepared to dance *eisā*. I joined them as a visitor, a student, and a friend, struggling to learn something of the way that Okinawans came to grips with a past that weighed so heavily on the present. In fields and parking lots across central Okinawa, thousands of young Okinawan men and women practice eisā throughout the summer, preparing for three nights of dancing during Obon, the festival of the dead.

In recent years, many scholars have worked to understand the politics of remembrance in Okinawa (see Field 1993; Figal 2001; Molasky 1999). However, little attention has been paid to eisā, the most widespread modality of public memorative practice in the islands. As my friends often told me, eisā was necessary so that they could respond to the demands and desires of their ancestral spirits, to the hundreds of thousands who were killed during the war. Eisā is danced to escort the spirits of the dead from their tombs back to their homes and to entertain them during Obon; to narrate and embody the history of impoverished Okinawan courtiers sent down from the capital; to express and sustain the pride and honor of these neighborhoods, the power and the artistry of the dancers; to create and share *karī*, the gift of happiness and belonging produced in performance, necessary for life.

Okinawa City was still a base town, its crowded neighborhoods of concrete buildings clustered along the fence of Kadena Air Base like a coral reef. And yet the long struggle of local activists has worn at the American presence; the number of Marines and airmen in the streets has also been reduced by new regulations imposed by their commands. In recent years, the once thriving base economy has collapsed as a result of the long slide of the dollar against the yen, as well as the construction of on-base communities that claim the GI dollars once spent in Okinawa City. Row after row of buildings thrown up in the frenzy of a Vietnam-era boom are now falling to ruin; the bar district is quiet; prostitution has virtually disappeared. Filipina and Russian women work in the bars that remain. Most Japanese tourists avoid Okinawa City, preferring the resort hotels of Onna and the southern islands, the shopping malls and nightclubs in Mihama. The bases remain, dominating the Okinawan landscape, a staging area for wars in Afghanistan and Iraq, a beachhead held against dreams of developing central Okinawa in other ways.[7]

After the Pacific War, this area of uninhabited wooded hillocks and swampy lowlands was settled by impoverished former Ryūkyūan courtiers who had lived in Nishizato, a farming village several miles to the west. Their homes had been destroyed in the Battle of Okinawa; their land confiscated in the construction of Kadena Air Base.[8] They were joined by displaced or unemployed farmers from all over central and northern Okinawa, workers from Kyūshū and Amami Ōshima, and laborers from other outlying islands. While they worked on the American bases that now dominate the island or in the cities that were quickly constructed around them, they built this crowded neighborhood of narrow streets and small wooden or concrete houses. At its center stood the community center, surrounded by a group of massive family tombs.

In many ways, the community center echoes the space of the tomb. Before the war, dancers and musicians from Nishizato gathered on summer evenings in the courtyards of the crypts that lay on the edge of their hamlet. Night after night, they danced and sang before the spirits of their ancestors, practicing for the day that would bring eisā again to the streets of their villages and the courtyards of their homes. Pleasurable and demanding, away from the fields where they labored each day, from the discipline of the home, from the regulation of the state, resisting the pressure and the lure of labor migration to the mainland or the South Pacific. In the company of their friends and the spirits of their ancestors, farmers and laborers became dancers and musicians.

Those tombs and villages are gone. The material presence of the ancestors, so painstakingly ordered and attended by their families, was fragmented and dispersed—destroyed along with many of the lives of those who commemorated them. For those who survived, relationships with ancestral spirits were too precious to lose; obligations to the dead were too great to ignore. Rebuilding the tombs and recollecting the ancestors was one of the first priorities of Okinawan households in the postwar reconstruction. However, tombs and household altars are not the only places in which the spatial fields of the ancestors were reinstalled. The community center itself has been a site of repeated daily labor to situate and recall the dead. It is a space that is filled with the creative activity of dancers who struggle to express their desire to understand—and to change—the world around them.

Virtually every inch of available wall space is covered with the graphic traces of Sonda's past. Banners commemorating their victories in competitions. Row after row of framed photographs showing generations of dancers. Certificates noting the youth group's performances in decades of annual eisā competition in Okinawa City and their appearances throughout Japan. Letters of appreciation from prominent Japanese politicians, performers, and admiring fans. Images that organize powerful constellations of gender, work, and creativity.

The oldest picture, a framed black-and-white group photograph above the door, shows a group of men, lean and sunburned, staring gravely at the camera. They are dressed in short, working kimonos and wearing farmers' woven conical hats. One or two men hold *sanshin*—the Okinawan shamisen —and several drums are lined up in the foreground. These are the first dancers to come together to dance eisā after the war. In the early 1950s, Kohama Shuei, a well-known musician as well as a member of one of the leading families in the area, gathered the young men of the neighborhood together in the Quonset hut that served as their community center. Together they worked to master not only the steps and the songs of the eisā, but also the style that marked the performances during the festival of the dead in the streets of Nishizato, their lost village. In central Okinawa, only young men of noble ancestry had been allowed to participate in eisā, and then only with the groups from their natal communities. Until Shuei decided to resume the dance after the war, it was inconceivable that outsiders would be allowed to join. Over the objections of many of his neighbors, Shuei broke with tradition. He not only allowed but encouraged all the young men to dance. If the disparate group that had come together in his neighborhood were to survive the aftermath of the war, he was sure that they would need eisā.

Faded color photographs show that women had joined the group by the late 1950s or early 1960s. The decision to eliminate gender as well as class restrictions seems to have been both principled and pragmatic. Kohama said that he and his friends were grateful for the contribution of women to the life of the community, their work and their sacrifice. At the same time, they thought that the addition of women would add to the complexity of the dance and certainly appeal to the audiences at public performances.

The clothing of the dancers also changed. When they were all déclassé nobles, they proudly wore the modest kimonos of the farming village where their families were born. When participation in the seinenkai was opened to everyone, noble or commoner, native or outsider, men began to wear the garb of a stylized Okinawan samurai; women wore the equally stylized kimonos of rural farmers. Kohama Shuei told me that he and his friends were inspired to select costumes that would help the young men and women of the neighborhood create a dramatic impression on the audience and judges at performances. One cannot help but notice the powerful representations of gender and class in these images, in contrast to the conditions of Okinawan daily life. Imagine the attraction that representations of strong, handsome Ryūkyūan warriors had for a cook at a base club or a servant in an American household; to think of the possibilities that a graceful, laughing rural dancer presented to a maid at a cheap hotel or a prostitute in a crowded club. What seems to be a gendered assignment of class also speaks to the history of the community: men's martial attire evokes the remembered world of the Ryūkyūan Court; women's simple yet elegant kimonos reference the rural villages where déclassé nobles labored to build new lives.

At the same time, these costumes were not simple representations of the Okinawan past. Rather, they were selected from the most popular plays and dances of the Okinawan theater—the Uchinā Shibai. It was in Okinawan popular theater—a genre also suppressed by the Japanese colonial authorities—that performers could move effortlessly from a tragedy depicting court intrigues and martial prowess to a romanticized peasant dance. Thus, costumes not only referred to favorite images and idealized qualities of the past;

they also suggested the protean expressiveness of theatrical performance. However, in transforming themselves, dancers also opened themselves to the judgment of the audience gathered for performances: an appropriated image could be maintained only if the dancers demonstrated that they were deserving of it.

The images displayed in the community center are important elements in mediating the transmission of the varying versions of the seinenkai's past. They provide visual linkages between the interior space of the building and other people, places, and events distributed over space and time—traces of other moments, graphic reminders that figure practices of recollection, for the storytelling that is as much a part of eisā as the dance.

Outside, the members of the seinenkai prepared for rehearsal, just as they did every evening during the three months preceding Obon. Most of the dancers came to practice directly from work. From the dress of the members of the youth group, it was clear that Sonda was a working-class neighborhood. A majority of the young men were in *sagyōfuku* (work clothes)—baggy, calf-length trousers in vivid pastel colors, white T-shirts, towels knotted around their heads. High-school boys were still in school uniforms of black trousers and white shirts. The remaining young men were dressed in current hip-hop fashion: shiny sweats or baggy denim shorts or pants; large, blocky sneakers; oversize jerseys emblazoned with Fubu, Mecca, or the Japanese national soccer team. Young women wore fashionably tight blouses with wide collars and flared pants; a few matching knee-length skirts and vests, the uniform of local banks and offices. None of the high-school girls still wore their school uniforms; younger girls dressed in wide-leg jeans; clunky, thick-soled sneakers or sandals; undersize military T-shirts. Fashion means attention to detail: the right jewelry, a cool G-Shock wristwatch, good haircut—bleached or dyed. Color contacts—green or variegated blue best of all.

The *jikata* (sanshin musicians) sat at the front, tuning their instruments and warming up their voices. Dancers removed their cellular phones, pagers, watches, lighters, cigarette packs, and wallets, leaving them on windowsills and along the steps. Everyone filed down onto the watered clay surface of the courtyard. The lead jikata laughed, shouting to the new dancers, "Unless you decide that you're going to try to do this better than everyone else, your dancing won't ever amount to anything!"

Dancers came to the community center to play, but it is a form of play that has costs. The dancers have shrugged off many of the more conventional chances for recreation that contemporary Japanese society offers, even in Okinawa. They have—if only for the moment—refused the distractions of mass culture, of television, bars, games, parks, and films. Although they may dance side by side with the young men or women—neighbors, co-workers, or classmates—whom they might otherwise date, they have deferred the opportunity to do so.[9] At the same time, they have refused certain kinds of work, such as more profitable employment in the dense urban areas of Naha or Urasoe, in mainland Japan, or in America, and labor in the remaining bars and brothels, nightclubs, and snack bars of nearby Nakanomachi. They cannot meet the demands of employers for overtime, for different hours, for selfless devotion to their jobs. For the most part, they have turned their backs on university labor and intellectual labor. The dancers have also sacrificed one of the most treasured goals of a worker: sleep. The toll taken on laboring bodies is inescapable, but sleep offers a daily refuge from work, a chance to recover one's strength, to heal—perhaps even the opportunity to dream. Instead, they commit themselves to hours of arduous and demanding activity that, until the recent popularization of Okinawan performing arts, marked them as hooligans and lowlifes.

Standing in the courtyard, the drummers—all men—adjusted the carriage of their instruments, and dancers shifted their bodily hexis to that of the dance. The male dancers lowered their hips, turned their knees out, and sank into a wide stance: head up, shoulders back, hands on hips, a look of quiet confidence on the face. Women stood with feet together, legs and backs straight, hands at their hips, faintly smiling. The men's position is hard; the women's is more relaxed.[10] Older members moved through the formation physically correcting the dancers.

To the front, the jikata counted out the beat and drove into "Nandaki Bushi (The Ballad of the Southern Grove)," the first song of the eleven pieces that make up their eisā. With the simultaneous sound of fifty drums being struck, the dance began. The song is sung in unison, the lyrics in Okinawan. For twenty minutes or more, the songs continue and the dancers dance. Women work to make the stately grace of the dance seem effortless. Along with the male dancers, their performance draws heavily on Okinawan folk and classical genres, creating the figure that organizes the eisā, elegant and controlled. The drummers dance a counterpoint to this. Leaping and turning, beating out a rhythm that is sometimes straight, sometimes syncopated, they struggle to maintain Sonda's reputation for speed and physicality—dancers whose bodies are already exhausted and injured from long hours of harsh, physical labor, and for whom this evening's exertions are a respite before another day of work. Sweat from the dancers splashes the ground. Some people say that if you scratch away the clay, it's salt all the way down to the roofs of the tombs at the bottom of the hill. Their performance conjures the account of a journey, assembléd and sung from narratives of the past. A complex secondary genre, eisā is a cycle of narratives that recount the diaspora of the Ryūkyūan nobility that began in the nineteenth century, their impoverishment and exile to the mountainous northern forests, their struggle to return to the capital once more. Each of the songs narrates the experiences of a particular time and place where the former nobles lived along their journey. Some are songs that were composed during the period that they represent; others are later representations of that time and place. With their own particular chronotopes, their own narrative organization of space and time, the songs are bound together by the formal structure and the performative production of the dance. All are woven together, harmonized in performance by the powerful rhythm of the drums that opens the dance—eisā's heartbeat, say the dancers. These songs also fit together by the similar stylistics of the dance: stepping and spinning, first clockwise, then counterclockwise. The understated, graceful movement of the women demonstrates the influence of Okinawan traditional dance, as does the way the *shimedaiko* (small, hand-held drums) are extended at arms length by the men, then swung in dramatic underhand arcs.

The initial songs are elegiac narratives of the past, narrating what could be called Ryūkyūan mythic time—a powerful fusion of time and space. Even the titles of the songs—"Nandaki Bushi," "Chunjun Nagari," and "Kudaka"—are redolent of the Ryūkyūan past. The past to be sure, but a past that differs significantly from conventional historical representations. There is no more than a glimpse of the everyday world that gives shape to festival and ritual. There is no definite sense of the conditions of agricultural labor, trade, courtly governance, or war. There are no suggestions of hardship or loss; only mastery, pleasure, and plenty. The moment recounted in the song eschews any reference to the expected subjects of Okinawan history: diplomatic relations with China, military expansion into the Amami islands, Satsuma's invasion of Shuri, Japanese colonialism.

Instead, there is a strange compressed immediacy to the performance. The singers' voices are filled with the reported speech of nobles, their gender unspecified, the time indeterminate. Singing of eisā today in the words, the voices of eisā from the past. In this transposition, the performers sensuously experience the narratives of the past as they create them again in the moment.

Midway through the cycle of songs, the performance changed. Before the Pacific War, the songs that followed continued to advance the sequence of spatial representations of the courtiers' diaspora. In the aftermath of the war, musicians such as Kohama Shuei felt that there was something incomplete about the old cycle of songs. Why should the manifest form of the dance express sentiments—the bitterness of exile, longing for a return to the capital—that the performers no longer shared? They decided to shift the emphasis of this part of the performance to songs that more closely expressed the desires and experiences of neighborhood youths. In the postwar world, the courtiers were no longer dependent on the backward glance to Shuri or their lost villages. Instead, they created their place, producing it in their confident, expressive actions.

The movements of the performers also became more dynamic and complex. The pattern of earlier dances was taken and transformed by changes in rhythm and tempo, pauses, dramatic shifts in the level of the dancers. The new songs were exuberant compositions characterized by syncopated rhythms and intricate sanshin finger work—a departure from the stately pace and pastoral lyrics of the first section. The anonymous narrators of earlier songs were replaced with the clear voices of young men and women. They recounted their intimate experiences of anticipation and hope, of desire that is intensely and explicitly sexual: the feverish need for the return of affection, yearning for the evening's revelries and a passionate embrace.

I'm in love with a seafaring rogue and I can't even eat. In the middle of the road I stand, transfixed. My parents are heartbroken.

Here, in the words of a young Okinawan woman, the singers describe the intensity of their emotions—they are entranced, immobilized by longing. The moment that the narrator describes, that they have created, leaves no room for anything else. They also sing of defiance and transgression—refusing to accept an arranged marriage demanded by Japanese convention (see Okuno 1978, 93–134), rejecting dutiful labor and submission to authority in favor of creative performances, drinking, and romantic celebrations. Dancers create narratives of uncommodified sexuality and personal choice in the time that they might otherwise spend in bars and clubs. Who is to say which is more real or more fulfilling? At the same time, the moments recreated in the performance suggest that their determination has a cost. Autonomy has its bounds, and desire cannot always be fulfilled. A powerful tension emerges in the performance: the tension between hope and loss.

Like the voices heard in these songs, the dancers face the consequences of their dance: fatigue, disappointment, sacrifice of opportunities for material advancement. Still, they throw themselves into the moment, determined to master the most forceful strikes, the most furious arcs of the drums, the most

FIGURE 9.2. Okinawans dancing eisā at Kadena Air Base in a field that once belonged to their ancestral village. COURTESY *OKINAWA TIMES*.

spectacular spins and dreaming that they will equal the forms of the past, adding something new, something of their own creation. Hence, the lead jikata's comment, "Unless you decide that you're going to try to do this better than everyone else, your dancing will never amount to anything!" Close to exhaustion, their voices horse, uniforms dripping with sweat, they conclude the dance with an exultant burst of energy.

Eisā speaks in many voices. Of course, it calls out to the audience present: friends and family, ancestral spirits, tourists. It speaks to others, as well: absent parents, companions, and lovers, drawing on the captured speech of singers represented by jikata of long ago. It would also be possible to think of another level of address: the singer speaks to herself in her words and her actions, repeating again and again these narratives of what she can do, of who she is. Through this repetition, the singers bring the world of eisā, the world of the work, into themselves, into their everyday lives.

Writing of the existential problem of ethics, Paul Ricoeur (2004) has said that to recall the objects of memory opens the possibility of astonishment for the remembering subject. The recognition of the relationship between action and agent can be profoundly disturbing. One is no longer able to dissociate the general idea of a personal history that led to this moment from the memory of a particular act that was performed in the past. How is it that the

"I" that I am now was capable of the specific act of the remembered "I"? Can I feel that feeling again in this moment? Eisā compounds this by transposing the words and gestures of others into direct speech and action, into performance. The experience of each moment represented in the work is embodied by the dancers. The past is mobilized in a manifold of experiences in the present. The singers feel the authority of these voices in their own song, the power of the dances in their own bodies. They are challenged by the familiarity and the strangeness of the performance. Can I feel the experience of others in the performance that I am now creating? Am I also the narrator to whom I give voice?

These questions are important to the members, a sign of their determination to transform themselves from the young men and women who began learning the eisā together into those who are fully capable of the dance, to become those who are able to produce karî. Describing it as a gift of happiness and belonging, my friends have told me that karî is essential to life. As performers, it is their responsibility to create karī and "attach" it to their relatives, friends, and neighbors. Karī strengthens and renews the bond between the living, the ancestral spirits, and those yet to be born. In eisā, the dancers draw on their aesthetic, productive powers to recollect and re-create the very relationships that make life worth living, in which the living and the dead can join each other in happiness. *Chura nashun*, people say—to make beautiful. In the moment of the dance, filled with the complex patterns described by their bodies in movement, their voices raised in song, the rhythm measured out by their drums, they create a place and a time of beauty.

Can this beauty obscure as it creates? As Ricoeur (2004, 456) has written, there are consequences to representations of the past if they put history at the risk of forgetting. Is this true of the time and space filled by eisā? Certainly, the cycle of songs eschews any direct reference to the abjection, the horror of the eras that they depict—although songs that take up these themes certainly exist. Nonetheless, as I have suggested, any reference to the past always carries the charged ambiguity of a beauty underwritten by the memory of pain and loss, a joy tempered by sadness and despair. The beauty of the performances begun by Kohama and his friends was driven by the need to renew life in a shattered world. The dancers who still gather to learn and to perform the eisā know this well. How can it be completely forgotten in the dance?

Instead, they have the courage to put aside memories of horror and abjection, to allow these inescapable fears and anxieties to slip into a kind of oblivion during the performance. In the courtyard of the community center, in the space soaked with the sweat of generations of dancers, they create something of beauty in the shadow of the horrors of the past. This is why today's dancers no longer need to be of noble ancestry. They have learned to do the things in practice that were once the exclusive provenance of those of noble birth. Hour after hour, night after night, they have developed the skill and artistry to dance the eisā, to create karī, to rebuild what has been broken, to make a place for the living and the dead in the world that they have been given.

Dancing in the Street

It was the night of September 4, 1998—*ūkui*, the third and final night of Obon. We had already been dancing through the narrow streets and alleys of Sonda for several hours. Women in indigo kimonos, men in the attire of Ryūkyūan warriors—dressed like the images of generations of dancers lining the walls of the community center. For the previous three nights, we had covered what seemed to be every road, every path in the neighborhood. We had entertained the spirits of the dead who had returned to their homes and accepted the hospitality and the gifts of the households and businesses that we visited. I was exhausted. My left hand was stiff from carrying my drum, and the heavy calluses lining my fingers had begun to tear away. My right shoulder ached from an old injury. Too much drinking, too little sleep. It was much the same with everyone else. Around me, dancers and drummers—particularly the veteran performers—favored damaged knees and shoulders, struggled with increasingly painful back injuries. The everyday world of labor exacts a price from those who struggle to escape its regulation—or perhaps I should say that those who do so are painfully reminded of the price already paid by all who labor.

Although everyone was clearly exhausted, enthusiasm crackled through the formation. It was nearly time for *ōrāsē*, a fight between neighboring seinenkai. Older members often spoke of the violent clashes with other groups that marked the eisā of earlier years. Rocks and bottles were thrown from the audience; groups might even attack one another with heavy bamboo staffs or lash out with fists. Now the battle was waged with sanshin and drums, with dancing bodies and raised voices.

Soon, the long column of our dancers emerged into the brightly lit arc of a dingy bar district just south of Sonda. Passing the open doors of a tiny club, I felt a sour blast of dank air from the air-conditioned interior. I was breathing hard, my chest pounding with fatigue, feeling what I feared was my last surge of adrenaline. Far back in the formation, I could hear a muted call and response from the dancers. One of the men was shouting out something, lost in the pounding of the drums; the women, their voices keen in response. "Give us some *sake!*" Ahead of us, our banner bobbed up and down as the standard bearer danced to the rhythm of the drums.

Thousands of spectators of all ages thronged the streets. They parted before us as we advanced, pressing up against the walls and storefronts. The spectators laughed and waved, children darting through our formation as we advanced. People come together in these streets—people who would be unlikely to associate under other circumstances. They are not just locals, but Okinawans and mainland Japanese from across a broad spectrum of classes, as well as American soldiers from the bases. Tourists, scholars, performers, broadcasters. Older members gently remind spectators to keep back and moved aside those who ignored their warnings.

The sanshin continued to repeat the same droning figure, and we followed the standard bearer deeper and deeper into the bar district. Then, on a signal from the jikata, the standard was lifted high, and everything stopped. People rushed at us from all sides. Elderly bar owners hurried their hostesses into the street, carrying trays full of glasses of iced oolong tea or *awamori* to us. Reporters from local radio stations moved in to question cooperative-looking dancers. Cameramen moved up and down the ranks. Tourists asked to join the dancers in photos. Local merchants signaled to older members, formally handing them envelopes bearing offerings or asking for dancers to enter their clubs for brief performances. The offerings were accepted; the requests were politely declined. Now was not the time for distractions— ōrāsē was only moments away.

The crowd before us literally seethed. For the past decade or so, eisā has been growing in popularity, and tourists throng to performances throughout Okinawa. This is also true of performances on the mainland; however, an eisā festival in the Okinawan community in Osaka has been riven by controversy. Local activists encouraged young men and women to dance to develop their pride in being Okinawan. They also hoped that the dance would be a source of pride to older members of the community who have suffered from Japanese prejudice throughout their lives: stigmatized as dirty, primitive, menial laborers. In many ways, their eisā was an enormous success. Thousands of people come each year to watch the performances. However, the presence of so many aggressive spectators discourages the older members of the community from attending. After enduring years of discrimination, they were unwilling to publicly participate in performances that identified them as

Okinawans before a Japanese audience, regardless of any putatively positive valuation. At the same time, the insistent clamoring of tourists to join the dance has created other problems. For activists such as Kinjo Kaoru, the festival has become yet another occasion for Japanese tourists to demonstrate the colonizer's thoughtless appropriation of the most intimate practices of the colonized, the insolent consumer's unconstrained desire. As he reflected bitterly, any Japanese who honestly respected Okinawan culture should simply stay away (Kinjō Kaoru, cited in Nomura 2005, 175–77, n. 128).

Sonda has been subjected to the same flood of visitors. Mainland tourists come to Sonda throughout the summer, but their numbers swell during the days of Obon and the festival that follows. The members of the seinenkai anticipate these visits and are prepared to deal with their nearly overwhelming numbers. During performances, volunteers direct traffic and control the tourists, keeping them out of the way of the dancers and insisting that they not interfere with local residents. While never quite extended the warm embrace of belonging that they might hope for, tourists are treated as guests, with kindness and respect. The dancers allow them to beat on the drums after practice, seat them at tables in the community center, offer them food and drink, entertain their questions, include them in conversations, even teach them to dance. Moments such as this are opportunities for the dancers to demonstrate their confidence and their pride in their dance.

Iha Masakazu, the charismatic young leader of the seinenkai, told me that members of the youth group dance for many reasons: to be with their friends, to carry on a family tradition, to show respect for their ancestors. Still, he said that the most important reason is to be seen.[11] Most of the members spend their working hours in garages, buses, grocery stores, hotel lobbies, restaurant kitchens, at shop counters, technical schools. They long to be seen as something else, and in the images of the past and present, members of the seinenkai that line the kōminkan, they have an object for their longing. Jacques Ranciere has written: "All my work on workers' emancipation has shown me that the most prominent of the claims put forward by the workers and the poor was precisely the claim to visibility, a will to enter the political realm of appearance, the affirmation of a capacity for appearance" (Ranciere and Hallward 2003, 202). When the young men and women perform in the streets of Sonda, on the field surrounded by thousands of spectators at the Zentō Eisā Matsuri, before a busload of mainland high-school students, they know not only that they will be seen, but that they will be seen as powerful, dynamic dancers of the Sonda Eisā. Time and time again members have told me about the pride, the pleasure, and the sense of duty that they feel when they are seen in this way by friends and family, ancestral spirits, Japanese tourists, and American spectators.

This confidence is reflected in the equal treatment that they accord to their visitors. Young tourists and aging schoolteachers, native ethnologists and professional performing artists, well-known athletes and television personalities all seem to be given the same consideration. However, this does not seem to be an attempt to flatten social distinction. The courtesies extended to guests in Sonda acknowledge the importance of these visitors. As Iha himself wrote in a collection of essays about eisā: "We dance the eisā holding in our hearts the idea that each one of our viewers is our judge. What's more, we are committed to show them a performance that will live up to the expectations that they have for the Sonda eisā" (Iha 1998, 306). Without diminishing themselves, dancers acknowledge that their guests possess the skill and knowledge to make valid aesthetic judgments. This is an important element in the construction of the work. It enables the dancers to appropriate their audience in the same way Kinjō feared that spectators in Taishō-ku would appropriate the performance.

The youth group from neighboring Kubota approached us from the end of the street, pushing through the crowd like an icebreaker. As they moved closer, the sounds of their performance filled the silence that we had created. Finally, they halted when they were no more than ten yards to our front. A space opened between us, and the standard bearers of both groups stepped into the opening, lifting and shaking the huge flags as the crowd roared. Without waiting for Kubota to be completely prepared, our jikata played the opening notes of "Chunjun Nagari." Ōrāsē had begun. We all struck our drums in unison—the sound was tremendous. Kubota had also begun, its version of the song echoing seconds behind our own. For a moment, I worried about the distraction of their competing melody, feared being drawn away from our rhythm. But there was no time for that kind of concern—the dance demanded my whole attention. Every moment had to demonstrate pride, poise, perfection.

The crowd was joining us, too—long wailing whistles, shouted responses. I glimpsed an elderly man dancing in a doorway, the eisā of decades ago. I heard the responses of the women behind me, sharp and strong, and saw the dancers next to me, behind and in front of me, matching me in every move, perfectly synchronized. How can I describe their expressions—rapturous? I could no longer hear Kubota at all. I could not see anything beyond the front of our formation. There was no time, no space, for anything but the dance. The repetitions of the figures of the dance came effortlessly. I felt as if I was hitting the drum harder than I ever had before, stepping higher, swinging the drum in powerful arcs. We danced through the cycle of songs, then repeated it.

We all began to push forward. Our columns collapsed until we were all standing shoulder to shoulder, beating the drums furiously. Behind us, the dancers moved forward, as well, adding their voices and their clapping to the dance. I had lost all track of Kubota. Their standard bearer and ours circled each other, bobbing and leaping in the space between groups. The tempo increased, the sanshin booming and percussive. We pressed forward, hammering away as if we could physically drive them back with the intensity of our drumming. I was blinded with sweat; my arms ached with the effort. I was beginning to worry that I could not go on when I noticed Iha whistling and waving us forward as he danced with the standard. Dancers from both groups set their drums on the ground and leaped into the space between the formations. More and more dancers joined. Two first-year members rushed past me, one on the other's shoulders.

The jikata shifted to a different version of the standard "Tōshindoi (The Chinese Treasure Ship Has Come)," moving from the driving, percussive rhythms of eisā to a folk style that showcased their speed and agility. And as quickly as the tempo and the style of the performance changed, the feeling of conflict slipped away. Everyone from Kubota and Sonda came together, men and women, laughing and dancing. Everyone was shouting "Kachāshī,! Kachāshī!" Tourists were being pulled from the crowd into the street. The dancers offered them their drums, demonstrated gestures, drew them into the dance. Many of the tourists hesitated, laughing nervously; others rushed to join in, waving their arms in imitation of kachāshī, the ecstatic dance that ends every performance. Taking up the drumsticks and the drums that dancers handed to them, they tried to strike up a rhythm of their own.

One of the former leaders of the seinenkai told me that he loved ōrāsē, the chance to put Sonda's skill and artistry on the line in front of an audience, to confront a rival group and show it exactly what Sonda could do. However, he said that the violence that once went along with ōrāsē ruined the moment. Everyone in Sonda was proud of being tough, he said, but a lot of other people in Okinawa were tough, too. However, no one else could dance like Sonda. Violence detracted from the performance, diminished the group's accomplishments. What is more, it made enemies in the neighboring communities who should have been brought together by the dance. In the current performance of eisā, dancers like Iha have found a way to bring neighbors together while still demonstrating the beauty of their dance.

Once, after a long and demanding practice, I asked several of the older dancers why they still performed. Zukeran Masahide—one of the most active older members and a colorful jikata—answered without hesitation: "We still have to put the world back together." This is what the dancers work together to create. In the streets where Okinawans have labored for decades, running bars and shops that cater to American GIs and Japanese tourists. In the streets lined with faltering businesses, with Naha-based banks and mainland convenience stores, where young men and women from the neighborhood are waitresses and clerks, parking lot attendants and idlers. In the streets that are the lines of communication for the American bases, where Japanese and American strategic decisions are executed, along which troops and supplies are moved. In the streets where Okinawans once rioted against American oppression, burning vehicles, beating their occupants, storming the gates of the base.

In these streets, the spectators and performers come together, linked in the production of karī. As I have suggested, this is not simply the distribution of good fortune but the creation of a network of relationships that includes the performers, the diverse group of Okinawans and mainland Japanese, the spirits of the dead. In this place, once built by the labor of their ancestors, a moment is created for them once again. Through the beauty of the performance, the stylish self-presentation of the dancers, the pain and sacrifice, the artistry and expressiveness of the dance, ancestral spirits are gathered from their homes and entertained once more. They are given the gift of the eisā before leaving to return to their tombs, to the other world, to the places where they are believed to dwell until they return again. Memories of every other performance, every other Obon are drawn into the constellation; the ancestral spirits are shown that the dance that they worked so hard to create is still vibrant. Eisā is not just repeated without change from year to year. It is transformed to honor the legacy of the past and to meet the demands of the present. This is why the peaceful resolution of the ōrāsē is so important: in the place where there has been war, suffering, and death, a struggle can be resolved peacefully, a victory can be won without loss, a conflict can end in friendship.

This is why the presence of outsiders is so critical to the creation of the work. It cannot be that the painful burden of the past is easier to bear in Okinawa City than it is in Osaka. Eisā is danced in fields where battles once raged and where other ways of life were destroyed, in streets that bear the material signs of colonial subjugation, poverty and military occupation, prostitution and menial labor, before spectators whose class and ethnicity has long dominated the lives of the dancers. And yet they have found a tremendous resource in other memories, in other formulations of the past. They are able to draw on all of their performances of eisā, year after year, mile after mile, danced in the courtyard of the community center and the streets of Okinawa City; at festivals in Naha and throughout Okinawa; at Expo '70 in Osaka; in schoolyards, stadiums, and television studios across Japan.

All of these memories are brought into a manifold relationship in the present, conjoined to the work that is created by the musicians and dancers. For the duration of the dance, in the moment marked out by the rhythm and artistry of eisā, a hierarchy of relationships is performed as other memories, other histories fade into a moment of oblivion. Building on Ranciere's observations, the performers make themselves visible: they appear before their audience as dancers beautiful and strong, confident and kind. The audience is also constituted in the performance, given an opportunity to be a part of the festival. They are able to join in the dance before them; to be treated as discerning and capable guests; to receive the gift of good fortune. Finally, the spirits of the dead are brought together with them, honored for what they have done, assured that their legacy remains important, and given the promise of performances yet to come.

Inevitably, the moment ends. As the duration of the dance comes to a close, the memories that had been kept at bay fill the space and the time that had been cleared for the performance. The uneasy accommodation that performers maintain between the worker, the samurai, and the dancer cannot be maintained; the same can be said for the tension between the enthralled spectator, the uneasy visitor to the rundown streets of Koza, the tourist returned from the battlefield, the metropolitan traveler who suddenly realizes that Tokyo is very far away.

As the crowd begins to disperse, we fall into formation once again, laughing and exhausted. Dancing through the darkened streets, we make our way back to the community center. Families return to their homes; tourists, to their hotels; the spirits of the dead, to wherever it is that they dwell—their tombs, the other world, the island paradise known as *nirai kanai*.

What extends beyond the moment? New images have been produced; old images have been reinvigorated; old practices have been reappropriated. Representations of the performance circulate in tourist campaigns and commercial advertising, in banal television series and experimental film. A massive banner depicting a powerful dancer in Sonda's attire was hung as a backdrop at an anti-base rally in Naha. Both the dancers and their audience carry the memories of the performance into their everyday lives; the dancers also bear the physical transformation of their experiences. After years of dancing with the seinenkai, two older men have become members of a popular Okinawan musical group that works to fuse traditional and contemporary forms. A young woman has formed a well-known vocal duo. Several members told me that they quit their jobs at local clubs or distanced themselves from local gangs. Others have built on their experiences to become local politicians—both progressive and conservative—and some have been selected to become municipal bureaucrats. In every case, they have told me, their experience of eisā played a critical role in their decision. I have also heard of stories of dancers who quit jobs on the mainland and moved back to Okinawa so that they—or their children—could dance. Others refused promotions or transfers so they could remain active in the group. More common, however, are stories of the traces left in memory: the sense that one is more than who she appears to be in the working world; that alternatives exist to a daily life that is relentlessly commodified and stripped of meaning. The memories of eisā are often brought up against daily experience, informing the way that the world is perceived and understood. It is in this space, open to contradiction and question, that other possibilities exist, that new choices are made legible, that the possibilities of transformative action are explored.

At the same time, I do not want to take away from the importance of the moment itself. It seems that practices are too often considered only to expose their reference to other situations, their relationship to other times and places. Eisā is more than a resistance to social pressure, a rejection of stigmatized categories of class and gender, a displacement of concerns that cannot be addressed in any other way. Eisā should also be understood as subject itself, created and re-created in the coordinated activity of the dancers, their audiences, and the ancestral spirits. It is steeped in the forms of the past, yet driven by creative action in the present. It is an expression of individual and collective artistry, an archive of historical representations, and a source of strength and renewal. It marks a determination to define themselves—as men and women, as artists, as Okinawans—on their own terms. When I recall the image of the dancer in Moriguchi's film, I know that I will never understand the meaning of her dance or what gave her the courage to raise her hands so gracefully in that burning street. Yet I do understand the courage to ignore the judgment and expectations of others—to put aside the repressiveness of everyday life, the restrictions of gender and class, the constant pressures of labor, fatigue, and boredom. I understand the courage to act and to create. I have seen it in those very same streets.

Notes

This essay was drawn from fieldwork funded by a Fellowship from the Fulbright Foundation (1996–98), a grant from he Gakujutsu Furontiā project at Rikkyo University (1999), and Research and Travel Grants from the Carolina Asia Center and the Freeman Fund (2005). I wrote the first draft during a semester at the Institute for Arts and Humanities at the University of North Carolina, Chapel Hill, in 2006.

1. Here I am thinking of Judith Butler's recent work on melancholy and the constitutive role that the internalization of loss has in the construction of the self. While I find Butler's argument about the repression of the originary experience of homosexual desire compelling, I would like to broaden this category of melancholy objects to include other forms of internalized historical experience (Butler 1997).

2. Dominick LaCapra (1991) has argued that therapeutic strategies to de-cathect oneself from a lost object and to articulate conceptual and affective bonds once again with the world at hand are both necessary and inadequate. Loss must be addressed collectively, not simply at the level of individual experience. Moreover, actual historical loss must be acknowledged and attended. The failure to do so can lead to the conversion of the historical experience of loss into a structuring sense of absence, an a-historical originary account that authorizes repetitions of violence and ideologies of subjugation. In this failure, subjects may find themselves at an impasse of endless melancholy and impossible mourning, trapped in naturalized, repetitive cycles that seem to be beyond their understanding and control.

3. The film is based on a popular series of semi-autobiographical *manga* (comic books) by the Okinawan author Nakasone Mīko.

4. The hotel also accommodates a lone lodger, a Japanese tourist who perhaps represents the perspective of the Japanese audience. Virtually silent, he shows no interest in Chiyoko's sexual availability. He seems content to pay for his room and to have access to the intimate domestic space of the family.

5. Saundra Sturdevant and Brenda Stolzfus (1992, 251) quote the estimate (cited in Takazato 1996) by the government of the Ryūkyūs of 7,362 full-time sex workers in base towns during the Vietnam era.

6. From a speech to the Okinawa Regional Conference of the Japanese Junior Chamber of Commerce (Jaycees) in Naha, Okinawa, 23 August 1997.

7. The Okinawan bases do continue to generate revenue in the form of payments made to landowners who either voluntarily lease their land to the Japanese government or are compelled to do so. This land is then provided for use by American military forces.

8. Like the *hansen jinushi* who testified at the prefectural hearing, many of the residents of Sonda continue to own land within the U.S. bases. However, like most Okinawan landowners, very few are active in oppositional organizations such as the hansen jinushi.

9. Young men and women spend a great deal of time together, but rehearsals are controlled, and there is little free time. Occasionally relationships emerge, and a number of couples I know have married. Many others date people from work or school

with no connection to the seinenkai. Surprisingly, there seem to be few relationships with the admiring mainland visitors who attend rehearsals and performances.

10. Although women have danced in the seinenkai for decades, they have never become drummers or sanshin musicians. While local women professed to be content with this, several complained that it was difficult for women to socialize at the community center once they stop performing.

11. For an interesting discussion of the desire to be seen among Japanese youth, see Sato 1991.

PART IV

THE EMPIRE UNDER SIEGE

Racial Crisis, Abuse, and Violence

TEN

THE RACIAL CRISIS OF 1971 IN THE U.S. MILITARY
Finding Solutions in West Germany and South Korea

☆

MARIA HÖHN

The documentary *Sir! No Sir!* (Zeiger 2005) about GI dissent in the Unites States during the late 1960s and early 1970s was a bitter reminder for many Americans of just how tumultuous those years had been and in what dire straits one of the world's mightiest military powers found itself because of widespread dissent in the ranks.[1] As a consequence of the Vietnam War and the societal upheaval of the 1960s, military commanders reported the collapse of morale and military discipline, widespread desertion, and mounting racial tensions. Not surprisingly, West Germany, Japan, and South Korea, the three countries with which this collection is concerned, all experienced turmoil similar to that taking place in and around military bases in Vietnam and the United States. By comparing the unfolding of the crisis and how, in particular, the unprecedented racial crisis in the military was approached in West Germany and South Korea, it becomes clear that the U.S. military empire is not as monolithic as is often assumed. Indeed, it matters a great deal whether the U.S. military's interaction with civilian society takes place within the context of a democratic society, as in West Germany, or whether the United States, for reasons of national security, was willing to collaborate with a repressive military dictatorship, as it did in South Korea. Furthermore, such a comparison will illustrate that the U.S. decision not to allow soldiers to bring their families to Korea led to a significantly different approach to how the racial crisis was solved.

To illuminate how the very different military–civilian relationships in West Germany and South Korea created the cultural framework for dealing with the racial crisis of 1970–71, I will first describe events in West Germany. This chapter will be weighted heavily toward West Germany, because the source base for that country, for a number of reasons, is much more diverse and broad. Most important, and unlike in South Korea, scholars have access to a wealth of sources to give voice to the complaints of African American GIs because leftist German students reached out to them as possible revolutionary allies. Because of this highly unlikely alliance between students and soldiers, sources outside U.S. military records were produced that made public a much more nuanced view of the grievances and demands of black soldiers.[2] For the South Korean perspective, I will rely on Katharine Moon's important analysis of how the crisis played out in South Korea and how the Eighth Army and South Korean officials responded to quell the crisis not only within the military, but also between the military and local communities.

I will juxtapose the gender-focused South Korean solution of ensuring African American soldiers equal access to local sex workers to how the racial crisis was resolved in West Germany. In doing so, I will argue that the kind of troop deployment in West Germany—namely, a mix of single soldiers and married GIs with families—as well as the by now well-established structures of German democracy prompted German and American officials to search for a much more comprehensive solution to address the grievances of African American soldiers. My discussion of the German case will also show that the racial crisis in 1970–71 was a much more complex problem than access to local women. Intense political grievances related to the slow pace of civil rights, and entrenched racism within the military justice system were at the heart of discontent among black GIs in 1970–71.[3] In West Germany, as in South Korea, the competition between white and black GIs over access to local women was merely the most visible and, for observers, most recognizable expression of African American discontent and the widespread racial strife within the U.S. military.

The U.S. Army, German Society, and the Solution to the Racial Crisis

The Seventh Army in West Germany was among the victorious U.S. armies that had crushed the Nazi menace in 1945, but little of that glory was left in the late 1960s, as American journalists visiting military bases in West Germany pointed out with great concern. The backbone of the European defense strategy in the Cold War struggle with the Soviet Union was close to collapse. Because the Pentagon used the Seventh Army in West Germany as a materiel and personnel reserve for the war in Vietnam, military units in West Germany lacked 50 percent of their majors and 37 percent of their captains and lieutenants. Furthermore, officers serving in West Germany often rotated every four months, undermining any sort of continuity in leadership and unit cohesion. Deteriorating living conditions in crumbling military barracks, mostly built during the late nineteenth century or the Third Reich, and the gaps in the command structure led to unprecedented discipline and morale problems (Hauser 1973; Wilson and Johnson 1971; Nelson 1987, 102–8).[4] Because the military had lowered recruitment standards, and because judges offered juvenile offenders the chance to consider enlisting in the military to avoid serving a prison sentence, the quality of manpower suffered, aggravating an already difficult situation (Wilson and Johnson 1971, 29, 36). Morale was hurt by the fact that West Germany served not only as a deployment base to Vietnam but also as a way station for returning GIS to cool off before they were sent back to the United States. The deterioration of morale in the Seventh Army did not remain hidden behind the gates of the military bases, and with clandestine support from American antiwar activists, German students, and German unions, ever larger numbers of American soldiers went AWOL (absent without leave) or deserted their units in West Germany.[5]

Brutalized by war and alienated by mind-numbing military drills and the boredom of army life in West Germany, soldiers increasingly turned to alcohol or drugs. Military studies show that drug use among GIS stationed in West Germany was even higher than that of soldiers in the United States, and only GIS in Vietnam had higher consumption levels. The same studies show that 46 percent of GIS stationed in West Germany smoked hashish regularly, and the military estimated that 10–15 percent of its personnel used heroin daily. Drinking alcohol to excess was an even bigger problem than drugs, and by 1972 the military was operating some eighty-four detoxification centers in West Germany.[6] Not surprisingly, crime rates among American GIS also exploded. At the height of the crisis in 1971, American GIS committed 2,319 violent crimes against German civilians living in communities around military bases. Those numbers represented an increase of 40 percent over the crime rates in 1970 and an increase of 75 percent over the rates from 1969.[7] American observers and German commentators agreed that U.S. soldiers were exposing surrounding communities to a "reign of terror" (Nelson 1987, 108).[8]

By the late 1960s, as a much more vocal and radical generation of African American soldiers was sent abroad, it had also become clear that the U.S. military had not kept pace with the dramatic changes taking place in U.S. racial politics. Many of the white soldiers resented the Black Power Movement and expressions of black pride by soldiers of color—the elaborate and time-consuming handshakes known as "dabbing," Afro hairstyles, and the insistence that soul music be played at servicemen's clubs. In some spectacular instances, white GIS organized Ku Klux Klan formations and burned crosses in front of barracks where black GIS lived.[9] Black soldiers, inspired by the Black Panther Party for Self-Defense, responded by organizing self-defense groups. By 1970–71 and at the height of black discontent in the military, dozens of militant black organizations had been founded on U.S. military bases across West Germany.[10] Racial tensions among enlisted men were intense, and effective military leadership needed to deal with the crisis was sorely missing. Not only was the military command structure depleted because of the war in Vietnam, but the military had also failed to keep up with developments in American society at large and had not educated its commanders on how to deal with the more assertive and outspoken African American soldiers being drafted.[11]

German officials watched with dismay as the U.S. military faced this unprecedented crisis, but they also expressed concern because the violent racial strife between white and black GIS increasingly spilled into German communities bordering on American military bases.[12] Interior spaces of German bars and discothèques were routinely demolished when black soldiers tried to enter places that white soldiers had traditionally claimed as their own. Often enough, white GIS threatened the German owners of these establishments with an economic boycott if they allowed black soldiers on their premises, but plenty of German club owners did not need encouragement from white GIS to keep black GIS out. Existing tensions were only stoked further because many white GIS resented the fact that African American GIS dated white German women, or because German women preferred dancing with black GIS at local discothèques. The combination of too much alcohol and the competition over access to local women and off-base entertainment facilities often proved explosive, and just as often led to violence.

Interracial romantic relationships had been offensive and unacceptable to white GIS and military commanders going back to 1945 (see chapter 3). The context in which such relationships took place in the late 1960s and early 1970s had dramatically changed, however. By the late 1960s, African American soldiers—enlisted men as well as officers—no longer tolerated harassment by white GIS or their superiors for dating white German women or threats that such relationships might imperil their chances for promotion. They also no longer accepted that certain establishments in German garrison communities "belonged" to white GIS and were thus off-limits to African American soldiers.[13]

For the casual observer of events taking place in German communities bordering U.S. military bases in 1970–71, it would be easy enough to conclude that most of the racial strife taking place between white and black GIS was the result of too many drugs, too much alcohol, and competition for German women. A glance at German or American newspapers at the time would easily lead to that conclusion.[14] Because the grievances of African American GIS received a hearing outside the often sensationalist media coverage of the garrison towns, a much more differentiated picture than that of white and black GIS fighting over German women is available.

As mentioned, so much more is known about the mood of African American GIS in West Germany because support from German students gave them a voice far beyond the military gates, making possible a varied historical record of their grievances. Leftist German students, many of them the product of American efforts to reeducate and democratize German society after 1945, faced their former mentor with nothing but cynicism by the mid–1960s: students who in years past had embraced American ideals and culture as an alternative to the discredited German Nazi past now viewed America as just another racist and genocidal regime. The war in Vietnam, U.S. policies in the non-Western world, the murder of Dr. Martin Luther King Jr., the failure of the liberal Civil Rights Movement, and the brutal crackdown on the Black Panthers in the United States convinced many student activists that more radical measures were called for. Enamored with the militant posture of the Black Panther Party for Self-Defense, and inspired by the writings of Huey Newton, Eldridge Cleaver, and Frantz Fanon, German students discovered in militant Black Panther GIS stationed in Germany new forms of masculinity and a revolutionary authenticity of which white and privileged middle-class German students could only dream (Höhn, 2008a, Klimke 2010, chap. 4).

To forge an alliance with the Black Panthers in the United States, and especially with the Black Panther GIS in Germany, radical German students organized Black Panther Solidarity Committees in German university towns that also hosted U.S. military bases. In collaboration with activist black GIS, students produced (and fully funded) underground newspapers, such as the *Voice of the Lumpen* to inform others about the connection between American

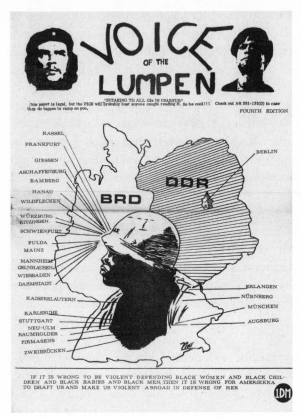

FIGURE 10.1. *Voice of the Lumpen* (1970). The cover of this underground newspaper indicates to African American GIs the degree to which they are part of the military-base structure in West Germany. COURTESY ARCHIV FÜR SOLDATENRECHT.

racism and American imperialist ambitions in the Third World. African American GI activists and students organized rallies and teach-ins all over German universities in 1969 to bring their message to a broader audience.[15] The students and their collaborators in the military also brought the demands of African Americans into the middle of German cities and thus gave black soldiers a political voice outside the narrow circle of leftist activists. During numerous demonstrations in the spring of 1970, for example, black GIS marched with German students through downtown Frankfurt, and numerous other German cities, protesting the war in Vietnam and calling, "Freedom for Bobby Seale," the imprisoned Black Panther leader.[16]

Even more attention was drawn to the grievances and demands of black GIS when students and African American soldiers organized the first "Call for Justice Meeting" at Heidelberg University on the Fourth of July in 1970. More than 1,000 Black Panther GIS and hundreds of their German student supporters met to indict America for the war in Vietnam and for its unfulfilled civil-

FIGURE 10.2. Black Panther Solidarity demonstration in downtown Frankfurt (1969), organized by German students, African American GIs, and black veterans who had taken their military discharge in Germany. PHOTOGRAPH BY HANS REMPFER, INSTITUT FUR STADTGESCHICHTE FRANKFURT AM MAIN. COURTESY STADTARCHIV FRANKFURT.

rights agenda. In a clear reference to the discrimination that black GIs and their families experienced off-base in German communities, the protesters also demanded equal access to housing.[17] The students and African American activists garnered even more exposure in October 1970, when the popular German TV show *Panorama* dedicated large segments of its weekly news coverage to another huge Black Panther Solidarity rally in Kaiserslautern.[18]

The ever more radical struggle of America's black minority had been brought to West Germany through the American military-base system. In this "globalization" of the American race question, the disenchantment and anger that African Americans expressed toward their own society became more widely and intimately known to German society because the students were savvy in attracting the attention of the national media. While the German media had been consistently covering the civil-rights struggle in the United States, the alliance between students and black GIs brought that struggle and its increasing radicalization much closer to home. By arranging interviews with some of West Germany's most important media outlets, students helped black GIs get a platform that they otherwise would not have had. The students, for example, arranged an interview with *Der Spiegel*, West Germany's most prestigious news magazine, for two black Vietnam War veterans who had left their unit in Berlin after a series of racist attacks by white soldiers. The black soldiers told *Der Spiegel* that they had deserted because they finally understood their own role in maintaining the worldwide U.S. empire: "The same thing that is happening to our people at home, well, that is what the black man in the army is doing to other people around the world."[19] In another story on black dissent in West Germany, *Der Spiegel* informed its readers that African American GIs declared that "because of the dirty stinking ghettos in Atlanta, Detroit, or Jacksonville [Florida], they were no longer willing to fight a war for the whites and instead demanded weapons to liberate their brothers and sisters at home."[20] The *Süddeutsche Zeitung*, another national newspaper also commented on the radicalization of African American GIs by quoting a young black soldier who said, "I bled for my country in Vietnam; now I will bleed for myself and, if necessary, for my people."[21]

The German students' collaboration with militant black GIs and their many public demonstrations on university campuses, in the streets of German university towns, and even in the deepest provinces educated Germans about the situation of African Americans in the United States and about racism in the U.S. military. Their militant posture also rang alarm bells in both the American and German governments. While German and American officials had been concerned for some time about the radicalization of African American GIs, it was the "Call for Justice" meeting on the Fourth of July, 1970, at Heidelberg University that prompted German and American officials to act.[22] Not only had that meeting been held in of one of West Germany's most distinguished universities—with the explicit support of the university's president—but Heidelberg was also home to the headquarters of the U.S. Army in Europe (USAREUR). In response to the Fourth of July protest, government agencies at the highest levels in both the United States and West Germany came to believe that the radicalization of black GIs and their deteriorating morale not only undermined military discipline but also threatened the security of West Germany in the Cold War struggle.[23] Furthermore, action was called for because officials in West Germany and the United States feared that the alliance between radical black GIs and German students, and their "political philosophy," could prove attractive to "millions of [disenchanted black] Americans" and might lead to a closer collaboration with the communist regime in East Germany.[24]

Looking back from the perch of the post–Cold War world, one might be

FIGURE 10.3. Solidarity demonstration for the Ramstein 2 in Zweibrücken (March 1970).
COURTESY ARCHIV FÜR SOLDATENRECHT.

tempted to write off these assessments as overly anxious and exaggerated, but for German and American officials at the time, the fears were very real. Consequently, intervention at the highest level was called for. The political radicalization of black GIS, made visible and audible through the extensive support they received from German students, brought about a comprehensive Pentagon program to deal with the deeply embedded racism within the military. In September 1970, as a direct response to the Fourth of July protest, a commission sponsored by the White House and the Pentagon, known as the Render Commission, traveled to West Germany to take a hard look at the increasingly unmanageable situation on military bases there. In the spring of 1971, the Render Commission investigation was followed by a visit from the National Association for the Advancement of Colored People (NAACP), which interviewed more than 500 African American GIS. The Congressional Black Caucus also sent an investigative team led by Thaddeus Garrett Jr., assistant to Representative Shirley Chisholm (D-NY), for a six-week tour of military bases in Europe, with a special focus on West Germany. In their conclusions, the Render Commission (Render 1970) and the NAACP investigation made starkly clear that the racial crisis in West Germany went far beyond territorial struggles over discothèques and access to local women. Both reports exposed and indicted the discrimination that black GIS faced in

German communities, mostly from landlords and pub owners, but they also stressed that it was the widespread and institutionalized racism *within* the military that was the root cause of the deteriorating racial situation in the Seventh Army (Render 1970 and National Association for the Advancement of Colored People 1971).

The Render Commission's and NAACP's findings showed that, although about 13 percent of the U.S. soldiers in West Germany were African American, only 2.6 percent of officers were African American, and at the junior-officer level black leadership was almost completely missing. Their investigation of the military justice system revealed even more shocking revelations about widespread discrimination against soldiers of color. Black GIS were disciplined and imprisoned not only more often, but also for infractions that brought no punishment for white GIS. African American GIS complained that officers interpreted any questioning of authority and any sign of nonconformity or expression of black pride as a sign of militancy. Thus, while discipline and morale had deteriorated for both white and black soldiers, it was black GIS who suffered the brunt of disciplinary action: in 1970, at a time when a mere 13 percent of soldiers were African American, two-thirds of sentences for insubordination were handed out to black GIS, and more than 50 percent of inmates in U.S. military stockades in West Germany were African American. The NAACP also found that commanders disproportionately used pretrial confinement for black GIS to remove so-called black militants from their units. The pretrial confinement rule allowed commanders to keep alleged offenders imprisoned for up to thirty days without filing charges, and in 1970, three out of five black prisoners in the stockades were held under this prerogative. In that same year, the NAACP found, 28 percent of African American prisoners (912 individuals) had been released without charges ever having been pressed. These GIS had basically been imprisoned to intimidate them and to silence "troublemakers" or "militants" (National Association for the Advancement of Colored People 1971; Render 1970).[25]

The Render Commission's report and the NAACP's investigation were a stinging indictment of the pervasive and widespread institutional racism in the Seventh Army and brought about a series of congressional hearings and an extensive program to eliminate those injustices (U.S. Department of Defense 1972). General Michael Davison, who in the spring of 1971 replaced General James Polk as the commander of USAREUR, acknowledged much more forthrightly just how deep-seated the problems were, especially in the administration of military justice, and he insisted that the situation could not improve unless officers became more sensitive to the needs of black GIS and

FIGURE 10.4. Cover of *Voice of the Lumpen* (June 1970). Two activists were on trial for allegedly wounding a German guard who had refused to let them onto the base to hang posters to advertise Kathleen Cleaver's talk in Frankfurt. The paper used the incident to depict Germany as a puppet of U.S. militarism. COURTESY ARCHIV FÜR SOLDATENRECHT, BERLIN.

stopped interpreting every expression of racial pride as a challenge to their authority. The NAACP and Render Commission reports as well as the hearings initiated by the Congressional Black Caucus also brought about an unprecedented affirmative-action program by the military. To "truly integrate the Army," Davison insisted that his command needed to be much more racially diversified. To make African Americans and their families feel that the military was also *their* military, the Seventh Army needed "more black teachers, more black lawyers, more black counselors, more black chaplains, and more black officers and non-commissioned officers." Davison also called for more "black content" in the overseas school system run by the Department of Defense for the children of service personnel, "not only in faculty but also in curricula, [the] civilian work force, and in our management echelon."[26] A comprehensive affirmative action program to attract more minority officers was also complemented with mandatory race-sensitivity workshops for all officers and noncommissioned officers.[27] Finally, the NAACP's report also resulted in the establishment of a branch office of the association in West Germany to represent the interests of the 28,000–30,000 black GIS stationed there.[28]

A change in attitude and practices was also necessary for the host nation because the racial crisis in Germany had erupted at the very moment when congressmen such as Mike Mansfield (D-Mont.), who was also the Senate Majority Leader, were questioning the rationale of continuing the extensive U.S. military presence in Germany. These critics emerged in light of West Germany's ongoing détente with Eastern Europe (*Ostpolitik*) and the resulting reduction in tension with the Soviet Union. Mansfield and his allies quickly gained ground when representatives of the NAACP and the Congressional Black Caucus in the United States, upset over reports from Germany, joined them. Thus, every report of German discrimination against African American GIS gave fodder to those who agitated for withdrawal of the troops.[29] The U.S. military's rapid and comprehensive response to the racial crisis thus has to be viewed in this larger Cold War context, because Mansfield's demand for a drawdown of U.S. troops in Germany posed a serious threat to the Pentagon's European defense strategy, which was based on maintaining military forces in Germany at their current level. Not surprisingly, given Germany's precarious location in the Cold War struggle, the West German government was as eager as the Pentagon to preserve U.S. troop strength.[30]

To assure their American alliance partner as well as the African American community in the United States that West Germany was not hostile toward black soldiers, both Chancellor Willy Brandt and Secretary of Defense Helmut Schmidt made public statements. They repudiated any sort of discrimination that black soldiers might encounter in West Germany when searching for apartments or trying to enter a club or a discotheque. President Gustav Heinemann met personally with General Davison to express his concern over reported instances of discrimination from German landlords and pub owners.[31] The West German government also initiated an extensive and expensive construction program (some $600 million) to modernize deteriorated military barracks that housed single soldiers and soldiers serving in West Germany without their families. To alleviate the situation in West Germany's notoriously tight housing market, the German government furthermore built new family housing for U.S. military personnel.[32] While this program benefited both white and black soldiers and their families, its impetus was to address black GIs' complaints about housing shortages and discrimination.

Meetings about how to ensure nondiscriminatory policies were held at the federal, state, and local levels and in collaboration with civic and business associations to educate landlords and owners of bars, discothèques, and restaurants. Strict new rules were set in place that imposed economic sanctions on individuals who continued the practice of not renting to black soldiers and their families or of keeping black GIs out of their clubs or discothèques. German government officials instructed media outlets to stop identifying alleged offenders by race when covering crimes committed by U.S. soldiers. Newspaper editors were also urged to make a greater effort to educate Germans about the accomplishments and contributions of African Americans to American history.[33] These steps were necessary, as Helmut Schmidt made clear in his instructions to state governors, because the problems and "concerns of [black] American soldiers in the Federal Republic must also be our concerns."[34]

The elevation of the race question to the highest level of the U.S. and West German governments was a dramatic shift from the 1950s, when charges of racism by black GIs were largely denied, or the early 1960s, when such charges at most brought about ad hoc and often reluctant responses by individual U.S. military commanders and German mayors in garrison communities.[35] After the crisis in the military in 1970–71, the situation of African American GIs in the military became a foreign policy priority of the German and American governments. The moderate demands of the Civil Rights Movement going back to the Second World War finally became reality, because protests by more radical groups forced the German and American governments to act.[36]

South Korea and the Sexualization of the Racial Crisis in the U.S. Military

The way the Seventh Army and German officials dealt with the anger of African American soldiers differed sharply from how the situation was handled in South Korea, where soldiers of color experienced and expressed similar anger, but where the solution to the problem would be vastly different. As Katharine Moon (1997) has shown, just like their counterparts in West Germany, U.S. military and South Korean government officials came to believe that the deterioration of morale, the rising use of drugs and alcohol, and the escalating racial tension within the military undermined South

Korea's security in the Cold War struggle. Officials were furthermore concerned that relationships with neighboring civilian communities had become ever more antagonistic as a result of the crisis within the military—and needed to be mended. The solution agreed upon by the Eighth Army and the South Korean government on how to solve the crisis in the military and how to improve military–civilian relations, however, focused solely on regulating the relationships between South Korean sex workers and African American GIS.

Black GIS in South Korea, especially those who might have already served a tour of duty in Vietnam, were expressing similar grievances and discontent over the disproportionate cost of the war for African Americans, the slow advance of civil rights, the murder of Martin Luther King Jr. in 1968, and the continuing and widespread racial discrimination in the military. While military observers at the time concluded that the racial strife in West Germany was the most severe in all of the military commands overseas, I would argue that this was experienced as such only because black GIS in West Germany—due to their collaboration with German students—were able to speak more loudly and be heard. In addition, the U.S. military has traditionally emphasized the strategic importance of the West German command and thus was more concerned about developments there. In fact, African American soldiers serving in South Korea had more cause for complaint. Not only were the overwhelming number of them deployed without their families (only 10 percent of all soldiers were accompanied by families, and a disproportionate number of those who brought families were officers), but the military's infrastructure in South Korea was in even worse shape than that in West Germany. Military bases, hastily erected during the Korean War, were often built as temporary structures and consequently were often in a state of utter dilapidation by the late 1960s.

Compared with those in West Germany, American soldiers stationed in South Korea were much more isolated from society at large because so many of the military bases were in desolate areas close to the demilitarized zone. Not only were most soldiers removed from interacting with the broader South Korean society; in the overwhelmingly small base structure that prevailed in South Korea, there was also less variety in the leisure activities offered on the bases. While the centralized bases in and around Seoul, Dagan, and Pusan had all of the luxuries that life in America offered, the smaller bases often lacked adequate leisure facilities, and soldiers had to rely to a much larger degree on what the surrounding camptowns had to offer. Because of the deep cultural distance between Americans and the larger South Korean society, fewer soldiers than in West Germany were willing to explore Korean society beyond the narrow confines of the camptowns. South Korea's relative poverty at the time, as well as the harsh rule of Park Chung Hee's military dictatorship, did little to induce American GIs to venture beyond the safe gates of the base or the relative familiarity of the surrounding camptown.

The alliance between America and West Germany was built on the understanding that the two sides shared the same Western culture, especially in light of America's extensive reeducation program after the Second World War, but this assumption was largely lacking in the case of South Korea. Not only was the country culturally alien to most Americans, but the United States also had never insisted that it be democratic. Indeed, the United States was willing to tolerate Syngman Rhee's autocratic rule (1948–60) and then the military dictatorships of Park Chung Hee (1961–80) and Chun Doo Hwan (1980–87) because those regimes most consistently shared American anti-communism and thus supported eagerly the U.S. military strategy in the Asian Command. This willingness not only to tolerate but also to support the repressive regimes of Rhee, Park, and Hwan bred a much more antagonistic attitude toward the United States among broad sections of South Korean society. The fact that the South Korean regimes had confiscated land from local farmers to construct U.S. bases through eminent domain rather than compensation only contributed to the bitter relationship between the American military and the civilian population.[37]

Just as important, the interactions between American military personnel and South Koreans were also defined by the fact that the U.S. military viewed South Koreans as racially inferior, and the prevailing attitude of commanders and personnel toward military service in South Korea as a hardship tour only exacerbated this sense. The military newspaper *Stars and Stripes* reflected this attitude shamelessly when it highlighted the advantages of a tour of duty in South Korea by focusing on the easy sexual availability and docility of South Korean women: "Picture having three or four of the loveliest creatures God ever created hovering around you, singing, dancing, feeding you, washing what they feed you down with rice wine or beer, all saying at once: 'you are the greatest.' This is the Orient you heard about and came to find." The Seventh Army had a very different pitch; advertising travel to the Bavarian Alps and the castles of the Rhine as fringe benefits of a tour of duty in West Germany.[38] Opinion polls conducted in the 1960s show that these haughty attitudes toward the Koreans did not go unnoticed. A mere 13 percent of

South Koreans thought that the Americans "liked them"; by contrast, 70 percent of West Germans assumed that the Americans viewed them "as friends" (Moon 1997, 119; Knauer 1987, 189–90).

Given the absence of military families, the spatial arrangements of the bases, persisting South Korean poverty, and the unequal cultural and racial context of the American–South Korean interaction, it is not surprising that, for most of the American troops in South Korea, the surrounding camptowns and the sex workers employed in the many GI clubs were almost their only contact with South Korean society. It was the sex workers, as Moon (1997, 53) argues, who provided the "daily glue" between the military base and the civilian community.

While contact with sex workers may have constituted the sole encounter with German society for *some* of the GIS serving in West Germany, this was generally not the norm. Interactions between the military and German civilians were more multifaceted because a much larger percentage of U.S. troops came with families and lived in German communities. Because some 30 percent of soldiers in 1970 had brought their wives, and because so many couples lived in German communities, the public face of the GI was not only that of the single, carousing soldier. Because of the presence of military wives, and their involvement in the life of the military community, an article such as the one cited earlier would have never been printed in the USAREUR edition of *Stars and Stripes*. Gender relations in West Germany also differed from those in South Korea because soldiers stationed in Germany tended to serve tours of duty that lasted two to three years. These longer tours of duty allowed for a much larger degree of cultural comfort and acculturation, as well as the chance to establish and nurture serious relationships with German partners.

Thus, the much narrower scope of interaction that was the norm between American soldiers and South Korean civilians, the lack of partnership built on equality between the two countries, and the reality of the South Korean military dictatorship defined in profound ways how the racial crisis of 1970–71 would be resolved. By drawing on Moon's important work on the violence that occurred in the camptown of Anjŏngni, I will show how vastly different the solution to the racial crisis in South Korea was from that in West Germany and the crucial role that equal access to sex workers played in solving the crisis.

The camptown of Anjŏngni was home to some 4,795 South Koreans and abutted Camp Humphreys, a military base with some 1,700 GIS, of whom about 500 were African American. At a time when African Americans made up only about 13 percent of GIS serving in the U.S. military, almost 30 percent of the soldiers at Camp Humphreys were black (Nelson 1987, 146).[39] Also, an astounding 970 women in Anjŏngni made their living as sex workers, and most of those who had registered as sex workers were employed in one of twelve clubs that catered to GIS. To avoid tensions between soldiers and South Korean men, all of the clubs were off-limits to South Korean men. Similar to West Germany, the clubs were segregated along the American color line. The town also had its share of unregistered sex workers, who mostly made contact with GIS by walking the streets. The ratio of sex worker to GIS in Anjŏngni and at Camp Humphreys (and in South Korea as a whole) is truly mind-boggling (Moon 1997, 30).[40] Not surprisingly, 84 percent of soldiers who had served in South Korea reported having used the services of sex workers (Moon 1997, 37).[41]

The racial crisis in South Korea, just like the one playing out in West Germany, had been brewing for some time. Beginning in the late 1960s, racial strife had increased between the soldiers on-base and off-base; attacks on South Korean nationals were also on the rise. Similar to the situation in West Germany, the racial strife among the soldiers often played out in the clubs that catered to GIS. Arguments most often ensued, after too much alcohol, over access to women, over the kind of music to be played (country and western or soul), and over who "owned" a particular club. As in West Germany and all other overseas military bases, white GIS in South Korea had drawn a strict color line to keep black GIS out of their clubs; that color line ensured that the sex workers employed by those clubs did not provide their services to black soldiers. In the past, that color line had been grudgingly accepted by black soldiers, and in response they had created their own, all-black spaces where white GIS would not be tolerated. Military commanders implicitly and often explicitly endorsed this Jim Crow color line because too many racial confrontations might hurt their military record. In many commands the military police ensured that the racial boundaries were not violated (President's Committee on Equal Opportunity in the Armed Forces 1963, 1964).[42] As it did in West Germany, the growing politicization and radicalization brought about by changes in American society led many black GIS in South Korea to question those territorial boundaries based on color.

The racial crisis in South Korea came to a head in the camptown of Anjŏngni in July 1971, when fifty African American GIS simultaneously entered five different clubs that refused service to black GIS. The violent protest stands out mostly because it had clearly been planned ahead and was well orchestrated. The soldiers ordered people to leave the premises and then proceeded to demolish the interior of the establishments. They declared that they had resorted to this violence to punish the owners of the clubs and the sex workers employed by them for refusing service to African American GIs. Similar destruction of the interior of bars or clubs also occurred in West Germany during this period, but the reaction of the South Koreans suggests how much more antagonistic military–civilian relations were in South Korea. Having endured the growing racial tension between U.S. troops for some time, and lacking any other recourse, locals decided to take the law into their own hands. About 1,000 individuals pursued the black soldiers with sickles and rocks, leading to an escalation of the violence. It would take 170 U.S. Military Police, 80 South Korean police officers, and the use of tear gas and warning shots to get the volatile situation under control. To calm the situation, and to punish the locals for taking the law into their own hands, the military commander of Camp Humphreys declared Anjŏngni off-limits to his soldiers for an indeterminate time.

The violent protest by the black soldiers, as well as the vigilante response by the local population, reveals important differences between the military–civilian relationships in South Korea and West Germany. Prior to the Anjŏngni incident, no established or effective channels of communication and crisis management existed between the military and the civilian community that could have addressed the brewing crisis (Moon 1997, 80). It speaks volumes about U.S. military attitudes toward the neighboring South Korean communities that Community Relations Committees were established only in 1971; in West Germany such committees had been established as early as 1950, because cordial relations with the Germans were seen as essential to the American mission. Second, although black GIs at times acted out violently in West Germany, they also found allies among German students, American students of color, and African students studying at German universities. These alliances were possible largely because West Germany had matured into a democratic country. Consequently, the demands of African American soldiers were not only amplified by the students; they were also debated extensively by the public and taken seriously by those in power. Because of the deep gulf that separated the U.S. military bases from South Korean society at large, and because South Korea's military dictatorship had crippled the development of a democratic civil society, black GIs in South Korea were much more isolated and thus lacked the structural support to voice their dissent constructively. Third, the violent reaction of the local population indicates not only an overwhelming sense of helplessness but also a long-brewing frustration over the uneven power balance vis-à-vis the U.S. troops. The decision by the American commander of Camp Humphreys to issue an off-limits order for the whole town only confirmed for the locals how utterly dependent they were on the goodwill of the U.S. military. A lasting off-limits would have meant the economic ruin of the town and its 4,795 inhabitants.[43]

As Moon has shown, the Anjŏngni incident provided an important catalyst to devise measures that would calm the anger of African American GIS, settle the racial tension among the troops, and improve the severe deterioration in South Korean–American relations that had been caused by the drawdown of U.S. troops as a result of the Nixon Doctrine. In South Korea, as in West Germany, the concerted response to the racial crisis largely came about because American and local officials feared that disenchanted and radicalized black GIS might become easy targets for communist appeals. In one such assessment of that danger, the U.S. military's Psychological Operations Division (PsyOp) concluded that, "for some time, the North Korean Communists have been directing some of their propaganda attacks toward the American Negro Soldier in an effort to encourage him to rebel against his military leaders, desert the army, abandon the defense of the [Republic of Korea]" (quoted in Moon 1997, 88–89). Moon, however, also shows that the U.S. military foremost looked outward in trying to quell the crisis. Instead of scrutinizing the institutionalized racism within the military, or the military's complicity in creating the racial boundaries that were being contested by black soldiers, it looked to the South Korean civilian population.

The racial crisis in West Germany brought about a comprehensive evaluation of racism in the military and in German communities, but events unfolded very differently in South Korea. Because black soldiers "acted out," as they did in the Anjŏngni incident, the U.S. military and its South Korean partners in the newly established Community Relations Committees identified South Korean sex workers as *the* source of the widespread racial unrest. Even though the racial tension came about because black GIS were fed up with the racism they encountered in the military and in the civilian host community—similar to events in West Germany—American and South Korean officials identified South Korean sex workers' refusal to "serve" black GIS as the chief cause of the crisis. If South Korean sex workers were at the root of the racial conflict, it was all too obvious to the officials charged with alleviating the crisis that the sex workers could also be the solution (Moon 1997, 85). Thus, both the town's government officials and U.S. military representatives assigned the town's sex workers the main burden of mending the tensions between white and black military personnel. It would also be up to the sex workers to mend the relationships that had reached a crisis level between the U.S. military and the Korean civilian population (Moon 1997, 84).[44]

To deal with the racial crisis, South Korean and American officials agreed that African American GIs in South Korea had to be assured equal access to bars and clubs and equal and courteous service by South Korean hostesses and sex workers. To ensure that club owners and sex workers understood the severity of the crisis and their own crucial role in solving it, PsyOp devised flyers that were handed out to sex workers and posted in the clubs for their information. One such flyer instructed the women not to discriminate against black soldiers by appealing to their nationalism. When they refused service to black customers, club owners and sex workers were told that they were "unconsciously helping [the] enemy, while weakening the internal security of [the] nation." To "keep your business and help the security of your country," the flyer continued, "you are urged to treat all U.S. customers equally." To efface the authorship of the flyer, PsyOp presented it as an appeal from South Korean officials (Moon 1997, 89), but the reference to the economic implications of failure to comply probably revealed its true origin to both the club owners and the women working for them. Thus, the United States exploited the South Koreans' fear of communism and the military's economic weapon of issuing off-limits orders to ensure compliance with its most unusual "affirmative-action" program in the GI clubs.[45]

Another aspect of the effort to improve troop morale culminated in an effort to rein in the abysmal venereal-disease (VD) rates among South Korean sex workers. To accomplish that goal, the South Koreans, with logistical support from the U.S. military, set up an extensive regime of VD control. Women working in the clubs were examined weekly; they had to carry picture identification and had to sport a registration number on their clothing so infected GIs could identify the source of infection. To achieve the goal of assuring safe and equally accessible sex for its soldiers while keeping VD rates in check, the U.S. military had to be intimately and directly involved in the regulation and supervision of prostitution. For the so-called Camptown Campaign, the South Korean authorities drew on support from the U.S. Military Police, Equal Opportunity Treatment Office, Public Affairs Office, Provost Marshal, Criminal Investigation Division, Office of Preventive Medicine, and Inspector-General (Moon 1987, 133). Thus, despite the U.S. military's official policy of not condoning prostitution, it was collaboration between the U.S. military and South Korean officials that ensured equal and safe access to sex workers for American soldiers. This policy became a central aspect of maintaining racial peace in the Eighth Army and of ensuring better relations between the U.S. military and the South Korean civilian population.

It is important to point out that the far-reaching reforms brought about in the U.S. military because of the crisis in West Germany did benefit African American soldiers in military commands elsewhere. The military's decision to attract more minority officers, improve the record of the military justice system, appoint affirmative-action officers, and establish race relation workshops was a policy shift that improved the situation for African American soldiers in general. In fact, the response to this crisis transformed the military into the most inclusive institution in the United States, setting in motion the "New American Revolution," as the Congressional Black Caucus called the government's response to the crisis.[46] But we have also seen that the crisis in West Germany resulted in extensive German investments to improve the crumbling base infrastructure. Furthermore, Germans and Americans worked attentively to assure African American soldiers that West Germany was a country worth fighting—and, perhaps, dying—for. In South Korea, the solution was much more misogynistic and one-dimensional, but it was also much cheaper. While American soldiers in South Korea benefited from the extensive programs to combat racism in the military brought about by the Render Report, the NAACP's investigation, and the Congressional Black Caucus's hearings, resolving the racial tensions within the military and the improvement of community-military relations in South Korea were largely shouldered by Korean sex workers.

The sexualization of the racial crisis of 1970–71 in South Korea reveals how "local" we need to keep the focus when exploring the U.S. military empire and its implications for gender, sexuality, and race. The solution to the crisis was so different from that in West Germany because, in the eyes of U.S. military planners, South Korea had always been the "lesser ally." A deep cultural gap separated Americans and South Koreans, and that gulf was made worse by the prevailing sense of racial superiority that Americans expressed toward the South Koreans. America's support of the successive South Korean dictatorships meant that no democratic institutions had been able to prosper, and the absence of such democratic institutions had deep implications for how the military–civilian relationship was handled and how the racial crisis of 1970–71 was solved. Perhaps most significantly, because South Korea was considered a hardship post, fewer than 10 percent of the troops stationed there were able to bring their families, with the privilege being mostly granted to high-ranking personnel. Given this context, the easy and convenient access to sex workers was a fact of life to manage the thousands of single young soldiers far away from home. Military planners may do well to keep the deleterious implications of this policy in mind as they consider one-year deployments without the emotional support and the social stability of soldiers' families.

Notes

1. On GI dissent on military bases in West Germany, see Brünn 1986; Cortright 1975.
2. For a much more detailed depiction of how the crisis developed and was addressed, see Höhn 2008a, 2010, and Höhn and Klimke 2010, chap. 8, all of which focus on different aspects of this crisis. See also Vazansky 2008, which explores the collapse of the Seventh Army in West Germany.
3. While Katharine Moon (1997) acknowledges that the increasing militancy of black soldiers upset the strictly drawn color line in South Korean camptowns, and thus brought about racial strife among soldiers (and with South Korean civilians), the focus of her analysis stays on the competition over local women.
4. For a German depiction of events, see Adalbert Weinstein, "Die Siebte Armee erholt sich von Vietnam (The Seventh Army is recuperating from Vietnam)," *Frankfurter Allgemeine Zeitung*, 25 August 1972; "Wir mussten die Siebte Armee ruinieren (We had to wreck the Seventh Army)," *Der Spiegel*, 17 April 1972; "Die Armee schafft sich immer neue Neger (The Army is constantly creating new Negroes)," *Der Spiegel*, 21 June 1971.
5. Most of these deserters eventually returned to their units, but the prestige of the military suffered substantially due to the lack of discipline. On dissent in the ranks, see Brünn 1986; Cortright 1975.
6. "Wir mussten die Siebte Armee ruinieren"; 65; Wilson and Johnson 1971, 26. On the drug problems in the military, see "Orientierungsbericht Deutsche Botschaft [Informational overview German embassy], 10 August 10, 1971, Drogenmissbrauch in der US Armee [Drug abuse in the U.S. Army]," AAA, B 31/346.
7. Weinstein, "Die Siebte Armee erholt sich von Vietnam"; "Wir mussten die Siebte Armee ruinieren"; "Die Armee schafft sich immer neue Neger."
8. See also Weinstein, "Die Siebte Armee erholt sich von Vietnam."
9. For German newspaper coverage, see "Nicht zuständig für das Seelenheil von U.S.-Soldaten [Not responsible for the spiritual and psychological well-being of U.S. soldiers]," *Abendzeitung*, 21 January 1966; "Die letzte Warnung: Holzkreuze verbrannt [Final Warning: Wooden crosses were burned]," *Abendzeitung*, 16 September 1968; "Ku-Klux-Klan in Deutschland [Ku Klux Klan in Germany]," *Der Stern*, 11 October 1970; "Brennendes Kreuz vor der Kaserne—Militärpolizei ermittelt [Burning Cross in front of the barracks—Military police are investigating]," *Mannheimer Morgen*, 15 September 1970. See also "Wir mussten die Siebte Armee ruinieren"; "Die Armee schafft sich immer neue Neger." For detailed depictions of the racial strife in the U.S. press, see Hauser 1973; Wilson and Johnson 1971. For contemporary coverage in the U.S. media, see Paul Delaney, "U.S. to Study Race Issues Among Troops in Europe," *New*

York Times, 31 August, 1970; Thomas Johnson, " 'I'll Bleed for Myself,' Says Black U.S. Soldier in Europe," *New York Times*, 11 October, 1970.

10. For the growth of militant groups see, Brünn 1986, 90; Weinstein, "Die Siebte Armee erholt sich von Vietnam."

11. See also, "Race Relations: A New Military Mission for the New American Revolution," 92nd Cong., 1st sess., *Congressional Record* 117 (March 9, 1971): H 5650–52; "The United States and NATO: Troop Reductions–VIII," Congressional Record, 92nd Congress, 1st Session, July 16, 1971, 25540–43; "Racism in the Military," 92nd Cong., 2nd sess., *Congressional Record* 118 (13–14 October 1972), 36582–36596. The October 1972 record was actually the transcript from the ad-hoc hearings that the Congressional Black Caucus (CBC) held 16–18 November 1971 because the House Armed Service Committee refused to hold hearings. In May 1972, the CBC prepared a report that was then entered into the Congressional record in October 1972.

12. "Wir mussten die Siebte Armee ruinieren."

13. William Hauser (1973, 78) cites comments from a speech Frank W. Render gave about how central the resentment of white soldiers over interracial dating was in stoking the crisis in West Germany. Harold Sims of the National Urban League stressed the same point: Ibid., 81. See also Wilson and Johnson 1971, 47.

14. "GI Crime, Violence Climb Overseas: Race, Drugs, Idleness Mix Together in Explosive Combination," *Washington Post*, 13 September 1971; " 'Modern und exclusiv.' Zum Tanzen bitte weisse Haut ["Modern and exclusive." Only white skin at the dance, please]," *Frankfurter Rundschau*, 3 May 1971.

15. BK, RG B 106/39985, contains numerous reports by the Bundesministerium für Verfassungsschutz and the Innenministerium on the pro–Black Panther meetings that took place all over West Germany in December 1969 and January 1970. Up to 1,000 individuals took part in each of these teach-ins.

16. Sz-Sammlung A 9986, SF, contains an extensive collection of newspaper articles dealing with such protests in Frankfurt: see, e.g., "Black Panther Freunde demonstrieren am Samstag [Friends of the Black Panthers to demonstrate on Saturday]," *Neue Presse*, 24 November 1970; "Solidarisch mit Black Panther [Solidarity with the Black Panthers]," *Frankfurter Rundschau*, 24 November 1970; "Demonstration in der Innenstadt [Demonstration downtown]," *Frankfurter Allgemeine Zeitung*, 30 November 1970. See also Höhn 2008a, 2010; Klimke 2010, chap. 4; and Höhn and Klimke, chap. 8 for a detailed depiction of the breadth of the collaboration).

17. "Ku-Klux-Klan in Deutschland"; "Treten farbige GIS in Aktion? [Are black GIS taking action?]," *Rhein-Neckar Zeitung*, 27 June 1970; "Einmischung [Meddling]," *Die Welt*, 7 July 1970; Bernd Armbruster, "Schwarze GIS: 'Wir wollen Freiheit jetzt' " [Black GIS: "We want freedom now"], *Heidelberger Tageblatt*, 6 July 1970; "700 farbige US-Soldaten in der neuen Aula" [700 colored US-soldiers in the new lecture hall], *Rhein-Neckar-Zeitung*, 6 July 1970.

18. Kulturamt, Akte Fruchthalle Vermietung, SK; also *Black Panther Info* (Kaiserslautern: Black Panther Solidarity Committee, 1971), 16, Wolff Papers, HIS; "Black Panther,"

report from the Ministry of Justice to the Foreign Office, 15 February 1971, AAA, RG B 31/346.

19. "Die Armee schafft sich immer neue Neger"; "Höherer Grad [Higher Degree]," *Der Spiegel*, 21 June 1971. The transcript of the interview with the two deserters, Robert Bolden and Samuel Robertson, is at ASR, Berlin.

20. The quote is from "Wir mussten die Siebte Armee ruinieren," 72. See also "Schwarze Frustration [Frustration among blacks]," *Der Spiegel*, 25 January 1971; "Wie Coca Cola [Like Coca-Cola]," *Der Spiegel*, 23 August 1971; "Die Armee schafft sich immer neue Neger."

21. "Panther-Sprung nach Europa. Auch die U.S. Truppen in Deutschland sind in wachsendem Maße Rassenspannungen ausgesetzt [Panther's leap to Europe. U.S. troops in Germany are also increasingly affected by racial tensions]," *Süddeutsche Zeitung*, 18 December 1970. For a depiction of how radical black soldiers had become, see Wallace 1970.

22. "Rassenstreit der Amerikaner in Europe [American Racial Strife in Europe]," *Frankfurter Allgemeine Zeitung*, 7 September 1970, credits the Fourth of July meeting of Black Panthers at Heidelberg University in 1970 for having set in motion the U.S. government's investigation into discrimination in the armed forces.

23. AAA, RG B 86/1425 and RG B86/1392 show how concerned German government officials were that the increasing anger of black GIS over German racism would undermine their morale and thus threaten German security. For responses to the crisis at the state level, see HH, Staatskanzlei 502–7425/26 and LK RG 860/6490. For newspaper coverage of initiatives set in motion by the protests, see "Farbige fühlen sich ausgeschlossen. Gespräche mit amerikanischen Soldaten in Deutschland [Blacks feel shut out: Conversations with American soldiers in Germany]," *Frankfurter Rundschau*, 13 February 1971; "US Neger in Deutschland beklagen Diskriminierung [U.S. Negroes in Germany complain about discrimination]," *General Anzeiger*, 6 June 1971. On American debates, see note 11.

24. Deutsche Botschaft, Militärattachéstab, Orientierungsbericht, 15 June 1971, AAA, RG B 86/1425.

25. See Höhn and Klimke 2010, chapter 8 for a more comprehensive discussion of the investigations and the congressional hearings that came in their wake. For German coverage of the widespread racism in the U.S. military, see " 'Schwierigkeiten' im Militärgefängnis eine Folge von Rassenhass und Schikanen? ['Trouble' in the military stockades. Result of racial hatred and harassment?]," *Mannheimer Morgen*, 15 August 1970; "Ku-Klux-Klan in Deutschland."

26. General Michael Davison, speech delivered at the Equal Opportunity Conference, Berchtesgaden, Germany, 10 November 1971. All quotes are from that speech; a German translation of that speech is in HH, Staatskanzlei 502–7426, 105–9. As part of the improvement for black soldiers and their families, the military began to stock black beauty products and books by African American authors and began training German barbers and hairdressers how to cut and style hair for their African American clientele.

27. "The United States and NATO: Troop Reductions–VIII," 25542. Racial tensions were also escalating in the United States, and of course in Vietnam. Thus, it was a combina-

tion of riots and uprisings at military prisons in the United States, Vietnam, and West Germany that brought about this dramatic change in policy. How crucial developments in West Germany were to bringing about these reforms has thus far been ignored: see, e.g., Alan M. Osur, "Black–White Relations in the U.S. Military, 1940–1972," *Air University Review*, November-December 1981, available online at http://www.airpower.maxwell.af.mil/ (accessed 28 March 2010). Osur's focus is solely on the racial crisis in the United States.

28. HH, Staatskanzlei 502–7426, 112; "NAACP to Open German Branch: Cries of Negro Americans Spur Action by Group," *New York Times*, 22 July 1971. For a more detailed discussion, see Höhn and Klimke 2010, chap. 8.

29. Headquarters, U.S. Army in Europe, "Equal Opportunity and Human Relations," 2 December 1971, AAA, RG B 86/1425.

30. Bundesminister der Verteidigung, letter to Deutsche Botschaft, Miltärattachéstab, 15 June 1971, AAA, RG B 86/1425; HH, Staatskanzlei 502/7425–26.

31. HH, Staatskanzlei 502–7426, 112, 114.

32. That initiative helped soldiers who were not eligible for command-sponsored tours because of their low military rank. The extra family housing built for command-sponsored GIS furthermore alleviated the pressure on Germany's notoriously tight housing market.

33. See AAA, RG B 86/1425 and RG B86/1392 for the extensive programs that were initiated. These are also discussed in greater detail in Höhn and Klimke 2010, chap. 8.

34. Ministry of Defense to prime minister of Baden-Württemberg, letter, 16 November 1971, AAA, RG B86/1425.

35. The Gesell report of 1963–64 was intended to do away with widespread racism in the military, but as the former Secretary of Defense Robert McNamara acknowledged in hindsight, after issuing directives to alleviate racism in housing and at off-base stores, diners, and clubs, the Pentagon turned its attention elsewhere. For McNamara's self-criticism, see Osur, 1981. On the military's reluctance to intervene on behalf of African American GIS in Germany during the 1950s and 1960s, see Höhn 2002, chap. 3 and Höhn and Klimke 2010, chap. 4.

36. For a detailed discussion of how civil-rights concerns were carried by the U.S. military to Germany beginning with the Second World War, see Höhn 2002, chap. 3, 2008b; Höhn and Klimke 2010, chap. 3 and 4. See also the award-winning website and digital archive that Höhn and Kimke have created (and are continuing to expand) that explores the connection between the U.S. military base system and the advance of civil rights in the United States: aacvr-germany.org. A much more comprehensive exploration of how the deployment of African American GIS impacted that struggle in countries other than Germany is still needed.

37. For a thoughtful discussion of why military–civilian relations in South Korea are so much more fraught because of these land issues, see Calder 2007.

38. The *Stars and Stripes* article is quoted in Moon 1997, 33. On how very differently Germany was advertised to the troops, see for example USAREUR, "Special Issue: Germany," 1971, AAA, RG B 86/1426.

39. Of the 250,000 GIS stationed in West Germany, about 28,000 were African American.

The disproportionate percentage of minority soldiers at Camp Humphreys reflects the fact that mostly combat troops were stationed there. Any military base in West Germany that had similar deployment of combat troops would have reflected the same racial makeup.

40. The numbers for Anjŏngni reflect larger trends in South Korea. In 1965, for example, some 20,000 prostitutes catered to the 62,000 American GIS stationed there. As Moon (1997, 28) points out, these numbers are similar to those of the Philippines at the time, where 55,000 prostitutes worked at some 2,182 rest-and-recreation establishments catering to American soldiers stationed at Subic Bay and Clark Air Force Base.

41. These numbers stand in stark contrast to West Germany. Not only did no such off-limits clubs exist, but the number of sex workers was decidedly smaller. In fact, at the height of the American boom during the 1950s in Kaiserslautern, approximately 200 sex workers catered to a military community of some 40,000 GIS. One of the reasons for the much smaller numbers is the fact that many GIS arrived with families or were able to initiate long-term relationships with German women due to the three-year deployment schedule that was the norm in Germany: see Höhn 2002.

42. For a more detailed depiction of how Jim Crow laws were introduced in West Germany, see Höhn 2002, chap. 3; Höhn and Klimke 2010, chaps. 3 and 4.

43. In South Korean camptowns, 60–80 percent of income was generated by the military: Moon 1997, 29. On the more balanced economic interaction in West Germany, see Höhn 2002, chap. 2. An off-limits was declared in 1957 against a German town that did not "play ball," but such a step would have been inconceivable in West Germany in the 1970s. For a discussion of the incident in 1957, see Höhn 2002, chap. 8.

44. Moon (1997, 110–20) also makes a convincing argument that the sex workers were expected to alleviate the tensions between the United States and South Korea over the planned drawdown of troops in South Korea as part of the Nixon Doctrine.

45. When the U.S. military imposed the off-limits order on Anjŏngni, the town's economy was severely hurt. When locals and sex workers protested the order in front of the military base, the military used tear gas to disperse them: Moon 1987, 81, 145. Such a drastic response to protests of civilians would have been utterly inconceivable in West Germany.

46. "Race Relations."

ELEVEN

CAMPTOWN PROSTITUTION AND THE IMPERIAL SOFA

*Abuse and Violence against Transnational
Camptown Women in South Korea*

☆

SEUNGSOOK MOON

"America Town" in Kunsan, North Chŏlla Province, was a hallmark
of camptown prostitution regulated by Korean and U.S. military
authorities and run by private business in South Korea. Resembling
the French model of enclosed prostitution that Alain Cobin (1990)
documents, America Town (A-Town) was a bordered space filled
with clubs, restaurants, and other small businesses that catered to
GIS. Built in 1969 by a Korean businessman with the government's
approval for "special tourism facilities," it was located 2.5 miles
away from local residential areas around the sprawling Kunsan Air
Base (home to the Eighth Fighter Wing, known as the Wolfpack),
which has occupied the rural area since 1951. The core of A-Town
was a cluster of several hundred row houses built on hilly land.
During A-Town's heyday in the 1970s, each of these tiny houses,
made up of a room, a kitchenette, and a toilet, was rented out to
"camptown women (*kijich'on yŏsŏng*)" selling sex to GIS in a brief
encounter or long-term cohabitation.[1]

When I visited A-Town one Friday in June 2007,[2] the row houses
had been abandoned for more than a decade, and the walls that separated it from neighboring rice paddies and towns were gone. The
houses were boarded up, with wooden panels nailed to doors and
windows and some windows broken. Relatively new houses had

FIGURE 11.1. Abandoned houses in America Town. PHOTOGRAPH BY DONG-RYUNG KIM; REPRINTED WITH PERMISSION.

sprouted in A-Town and were being rented to Filipinas and their GI partners. Since the implementation of the zero-tolerance policy on prostitution and trafficking of women (discussed below), cohabitation and marriage between Filipinas and GIS have increased. While the walls were demolished to improve the town's image, a rectangular signpost remained to mark the street leading to the entrance to A-Town. This sign is paired with a red plastic palm tree standing oddly in the middle of green rice paddies that extend along a four-lane, concrete rural road. Unlike in the prosperous days of camptown prostitution in South Korea during the 1960s and 1970s, weekend evenings no longer bustled with GIS enjoying liquor and women. Although a team of two young U.S. Military Police (MPS) patrolled alleys of A-Town, many clubs were not open yet when our group visited, and the few clubs that were open were almost empty. Loud rock music and a few Filipina club women seemed to chase away the emptiness.

Against the backdrop of the apparent decline of camptown prostitution in South Korea, this chapter examines how and why foreign migrant workers (who become transnational camptown women) continue to be subjected to abuse and violence and what this situation illuminates about the workings of the U.S. military empire. Direct perpetrators of such abuse and violence are Korean owners and managers of camptown clubs, recruiting agencies that

FIGURE 11.2. Entrance to A-Town. PHOTOGRAPH BY DONG-RYUNG KIM; REPRINTED WITH PERMISSION.

often collaborate with their Filipino and Russian counterparts to deal with local recruiting, and GIS who date, cohabitate with, or marry these transnational women. I argue, however, that such acts of abuse and violence are not merely individual but also structurally precipitated by the hierarchical status distinction between GIS and transnational camptown women. This distinction was created, and has been maintained, by the institution of camptown prostitution and the Status of Forces Agreement (SOFA) between Korea and the United States.

The first section of this chapter discusses how and why camptown prostitution became transnational and how this was accompanied by the trafficking of migrant women mostly from the Philippines and the former Soviet Union. The second section examines the extent to which the Korean authorities and U.S. military authorities continue to be implicated in the workings of camptown prostitution. The growing influx of foreign migrant workers as "entertainers" into camptown clubs since the mid-1990s has not only aggravated abuse and violence against these women. It has also heightened the visibility of camptown prostitution, which has become entangled with transnational trafficking. As a result, the U.S. military was forced to investigate the situation and implement the zero-tolerance policy in January 2004. Grassroots activism in a few major camptowns also pressed the Korean government to deal with the problem of trafficking. While the recent turnaround in policy may protect the U.S. military's own image and have some positive effects on camptown women's ability to fight their employers and managers, its implementation has not dismantled the institution of camptown prostitution. Ironically, the policy has coexisted with the inveterate practices of VD testing for camptown club women and the regulation of camptown clubs by the Korean and U.S. military authorities. As a result, although transnational entertainers are no longer blatantly forced into prostitution by club owners and managers, these women, under highly exploitative labor conditions in camptown clubs, are pressured to engage in prostitution to support themselves and their families back home.

The third section discusses various forms of abuse and violence committed by GIs against the transnational camptown women, ranging from deceptive marriage and abandonment to beating, rape, and murder. Since the zero-tolerance policy was implemented, and as cohabitation and marriage became preferable to prostitution, the problems of deceptive marriage and abandonment, leading to the burdens of pregnancy, childbirth, and child care, have grown. These abuses and violence need to be understood in the larger legal and geopolitical context that establishes and maintains the hierarchical relationship between GIs and transnational camptown women. While both groups generally come from impoverished families and reside in Korea as temporary employees, the asymmetry of power between a GI and a camptown woman is striking. While GIs enjoy the privilege of extraterritoriality as agents of imperial power under the SOFA, transnational camptown women carry the vulnerable status of migrant laborers. The women become illegal aliens the moment they step out of their exploitative and abusive workplace to live with their boyfriends or husbands. This legal structure makes them not only vulnerable but also dependent on their men.

Examining the labor exploitation, abuse, and violence that have affected transnational camptown women reveals that what is at stake are more than the human rights of trafficked camptown women that ostensibly have been championed by the zero-tolerance policy. What lies at the heart of these problems is an anarchic tendency that undermines the smooth working of the military empire, which has relied on the reproduction of militarized masculinity that naturalizes a need for constant heterosexual gratification. The limits of the zero-tolerance policy point to the underlying problems of camptown prostitution as the mechanism to bolster militarized masculinity and extraterritorial privileges soldiers enjoy as agents of the empire.

Transnationalization of the Camptown Prostitution:
Labor Exploitation and Trafficking

While the institution of camptown prostitution has outlived the Cold War in South Korea,[3] the demise of the Cold War contributed to its transnationalization. A handful of Filipina "entertainers (*yŏnyein*)" were already present in Korean camptowns in the late 1980s. The number of foreign entertainers began to grow in the mid-1990s, however, replacing Korean women in camptown clubs and other entertainment businesses catering to GIS. In the late 1990s, a majority of Filipinas in South Korea was clustered in Tongduch'ŏn City and P'yŏngt'aek City, two major areas of concentration for U.S. troops, where some fifty camptown clubs were patronized by GIS (Enriquez 1999, 96). In the first decade of the twenty-first century, 70–90 percent of camptown club women serving GIS are Filipinas and Russians (My Sister's Place 2003, 24).[4] These foreign women can be better described as transnational migrants because they live across national boundaries in their search for better employment opportunities and life chances. Many of them straddle Korea, their own countries, and the United States as they move from one club to another and cohabit with GIS or marry them. In the face of dire economic prospects in their own countries, a majority of these migrant women are forced to continue their migration after their initial contracts in Korea have ended. Many Filipinas who migrate to Korea have already worked in other Asian countries, including Japan, Malaysia, and Thailand.[5] That is, foreign women become transnational once they enter the labyrinth of global labor migration, which is very likely to continue.

The growing influx of these transnational women into U.S. military camptowns in South Korea needs to be understood in the context of globalization accompanied by the explosion of the sex industry not only in Korea, but also in many other countries in the world. The free movement of capital and the not-so-free but massive transnational movement of labor in this era of globalization generated the rise of the business elite and the increase of vulnerable migrant workers, both of whom rely on commercialized personal services to secure food, lodging, cleaning, rest, and entertainment. The sex industry is part and parcel of the explosion of businesses selling these services (Ling 1999). In the process of globalization, women from poor countries have increasingly migrated to relatively rich countries as service workers selling domestic labor and sexual labor in search of better economic opportunities (Sassen 1998).

Camptown business owners in Korea discovered that foreign migrant women were amply available as they faced a mounting shortage of labor in the 1980s. These businessmen had experienced a decline in the camptown economy during the 1970s, when the number of U.S. troops in Korea was reduced by 20,000 and the value of the U.S. dollar depreciated significantly. Yet the supply of young and undereducated Korean women desperate enough to work in camptown clubs remained steady. In the process of rapid industrialization and urbanization, however, native Korean women found better employment opportunities elsewhere,[6] and the business owners asked the Korean government to allow them to import foreign workers. In 1996, the Korean Ministry of Culture and Sports granted the Korea Special Tourism Association (KSTA), an organization of camptown club owners,[7] the privilege to invite foreign entertainers to work in the clubs (Ko et al. 2006, 40–41). Initially, the business owners imported foreign entertainers from several countries, from Nepal to Peru,[8] but found Filipinas and Russian women most suitable for their businesses.

The key component of this mechanism of supplying transnational entertainers has been the E-6 visa, which was created in 1993 (Sŏl et al. 2003b, 44).[9] While the visa has admitted both male and female entertainers, women have represented a majority of such entertainers since 1996. In 2001, when the entry of foreign entertainers peaked, women accounted for 81.2 percent of the total number of 8,586 foreign entertainers who entered Korea (Ko et al. 2006, 65). Generally, owners of camptown entertainment businesses collaborated with some sort of recruiting agencies in Korea and foreign countries. It is important to recognize that not all of the foreign entertainers were taken to camptown clubs, but most of them were: more than 90 percent of foreign women with E-6 visas were employed in the sex industry, both inside and outside camptowns (Sŏl et al. 2003b, 47). While a majority of Filipinas worked in camptown clubs catering to GIs, a majority of Russian women worked in nightclubs patronized by Korean men, who tended to prefer exotic white women (Sŏl et al. 2003b, ix). The process, from recruitment to employment, involved ample cases of deception, bribery, and debt bondage, which made the boundary between voluntary employment and trafficking rather ambiguous.[10]

According to a study conducted in 2003 of 106 Filipina women and 89 Russian women who had worked in camptown clubs, a majority of migrant women who came to Korea with the E-6 visa did not know the details of the sexual nature of their work. They vaguely knew that they would be entertainers who would dance on stage and serve customers with conversation in clubs. Although they had signed employment contracts, most of them were not given copies of the contracts, and most of them experienced discrepancies between their contracts and actual working conditions (Sŏl et al. 2003b, 65). In a nutshell, while not all migrant women workers recruited for the entertainment industry were trafficked, the "entertainer" category has been the façade for a main channel of trafficking women into prostitution. In August 1999, Kyŏng-su Kim, owner of the Palace Club in Tongduch'ŏn and president of the KSTA, was arrested for receiving about $160,000 in kickbacks from 234 owners of camptown clubs. From July 1996, Kim, who was also a member of the Provincial Assembly in Kyŏnggi Province, had conspired with recruiting agencies to procure entertainers from Vladivostok and Manila and introduced 1,093 foreign women to camptown clubs. Six brokers of recruiting agencies were also arrested for forcing these transnational entertainers into prostitution and extracting some $130,000 from them.[11]

Once employed at camptown clubs, a majority of foreign entertainers were exposed to various forms of labor exploitation.[12] The most common included delayed or unpaid wages, arbitrary imposition of fines, extended working hours, lack of day off and health insurance, and inadequate food and housing. It is noteworthy that all of these problems stem from the violation of employment contracts that the transnational women had signed in their own languages and in their own countries, alluding to the deceptive nature of the transnational employment entangled with trafficking. Working conditions in camptown clubs deteriorated as a result of the redeployment of U.S. military bases, which began in 2001, through the merging and closing of old bases in northern Kyŏnggi Province. Not only were these women subjected to increasing pressure to sell more drinks and even engage in prostitution to compensate for falling profits, but they also had to serve (illegally) Korean customers and foreign migrant male workers after midnight when GIS returned to their bases (Ko et al. 2006, 46).

The Apparent Decline of the Camptown Prostitution and Complicity of the Authorities

The criminal incidents and labor exploitation discussed earlier show that the E-6 visa is abused by unscrupulous business owners. A close examination of the system further reveals that this visa is a new component of the camptown prostitution system in the age of globalization. The Korean authorities not only condone abuses of the E-6 visa; they also actively regulate the working conditions of transnational entertainers. The following statement by the president of a recruiting agency poignantly reveals the Korean authorities' continuous and deep involvement in camptown prostitution:

> In fact, [these women] are called entertainers but they came as hostesses. The government cannot issue visas for hostesses, can it? Anyhow, because our business has been in serious decline, the government felt responsible and came up with this idea of issuing visas for entertainers. To induce American soldiers to spend money outside their bases and *earn the foreign currency*, we need to give them what they don't have inside the bases. The only thing they don't have inside is women. That's why we procured women. (Ko et al. 2006, 40–41; my translation and emphasis)

What is startling about his remarks is the rhetoric of earning foreign currency, which echoes the patriotic rationale the Korean military government popularized during the 1960s when, in close collaboration with the U.S. military authorities, it consolidated camptown prostitution by instituting "foreigners-only entertainment restaurants (*oeguginjŏnyong yuhŭng'ŭmsigjŏm*)" as special tourism facilities around U.S. military bases to entertain American soldiers (see chapter 1). His remarks reveal the continuity of the covert official sanction of regulated prostitution in camptowns. Under these conditions, it is not accidental that some club owners in the Tongduch'ŏn area maintain personal ties to the local police, develop new personal ties to immigration officers, and are employed by the U.S. military. Although they are not as emboldened in the 2000s as they were at the peak of camptown prostitution during the 1960s and 1970s, they act as community leaders in organizing protests against the relocation of U.S. military bases (My Sister's Place 2007, 43).

The criminal case involving President Kim of the KSTA took place in the late 1990s, when the Ministry of Culture and Tourism loosened its regulations on importing foreign entertainers. It is noteworthy that Kim claimed that he had followed legal procedure and that he was released on the grounds of insufficient evidence. His case was closed.[13] Agencies that recruit and import foreign entertainers into Korea have existed since the early 1960s to bring music bands to perform at enlisted men's clubs inside U.S. military bases. Their number remained small until the 1980s. From 1962 to 1999, foreign entertainers came to Korea only through recruiting agencies that had been formally approved by a government ministry. Since 1999, however, such entertainers have been able to enter Korea with recommendations only. With this change, the total number of recruiting agencies multiplied to 54 in

1999 and then to 157 in 2002 (Ko et al. 2006, 64–65). Between 2001 and 2003, foreigners-only entertainment businesses also mushroomed. One hundred four establishments out of the total 292 such businesses opened during this two-year period (Ko et al. 2006, 42).

The origin of the practice of importing foreign entertainers also points to the significant degree to which the U.S. military is implicated in the current practice of E-6 visa abuse. Since 1962, the U.S. military authorities have actually regulated matters concerning the recruitment, importation, and performance of foreign entertainers for camptown clubs in South Korea. Recruiting agencies are required to register with the Military Purveyance Section of the Ministry of Commerce and Industry and to obtain the military purveyor's approval; they must also obtain identity references and security checks from the U.S. Eighth Army (stationed in South Korea). Recognizing this autonomy, the Korean Ministry of Culture and Tourism excluded "performance for commercial promotion" from the definition of the kinds of performance it regulates when it revised the Performance Act in 1999 (Ko et al. 2006, 64, 70). This suggests that the Ministry of Culture and Tourism tried to reduce its involvement in regulating foreign entertainers who cater to GIs. Indeed, specific details of the policy concerning the importation of foreign entertainers are not open to the public and are governed by internal guidelines (Ko et al. 2006, 71).

In the midst of the secrecy and discretion surrounding the U.S. military authorities' involvement, a written agreement between the U.S. military and the city of Songt'an,[14] "Standards and Guides for Off-Base Establishments," was exposed.[15] The agreement was signed in April 1992 by Mayor O-jang Kwŏn of Songt'an and John M. Spiegel, commander of the Pacific Air Force Fifty-First Combat Support Group. Under the agreement, the municipal government transferred its jurisdiction to inspect and punish camptown clubs and businesses to the U.S. military authorities. It allowed the U.S. military commander to impose off-limits orders on camptown clubs that violated military standards on public hygiene, fire safety, and equal treatment of nonwhite GIs. The off-limits punishment lasted at least three months and hurt business. The military authorities conducted inspections so that only registered hostesses were working in camptown clubs and all club employees used their name tags properly. In the cases of drug dealing and outbreaks of VD, off-limits punishment was immediately imposed without a warning or grace period. Although this privilege has been justified in the rhetoric of benefiting local businesses and mutual understanding, respect, and cooperation between the Osan Air Base and the city, it has placed camptowns squarely under U.S. military control, rendering them virtually colonial space. While the written agreement in Songt'an is exceptional, the de facto exercise of U.S. military jurisdiction over camptowns—particularly the privilege to impose off-limits punishment on clubs—has been fairly well established in many camptowns, including Tongduch'ŏn, without a written agreement or other formal arrangement.[16]

After decades of complicity in maintaining regulated prostitution, the U.S. military has been forced by media coverage to shift its position drastically. In the summer of 2002, a television station in Ohio broadcast a hidden-camera recording of Courtesy Patrols that were overseeing GIS' interaction with women trafficked into camptown clubs around Camp Casey in Tongduch'ŏn City.[17] Camp Casey has accommodated a majority of the 13,000 soldiers of the Second Infantry Division, which constitutes almost a third of 37,000 U.S. troops stationed in South Korea.[18] In the same year, *Time* magazine published an article about Filipinas and Russian women trafficked into camptown clubs that catered to GIS in South Korea.[19] This type of exposure made a mockery of the Victims of Trafficking and Violence Protection Act that the U.S. Congress had legislated in 2000. Under the law, the U.S. State Department released its annual "trafficking in persons" report, which evaluated eighty-nine countries for their efforts in combating human trafficking.[20]

In response, Lieutenant-General Daniel Zanini, commander of the Eighth U.S. Army—the main U.S. force stationed in South Korea—issued a statement saying that the command "does not condone or support the illegal activities of human trafficking and prostitution," which was widely circulated among U.S. units in Korea.[21] In September 2003, the U.S. Department of Defense introduced the zero-tolerance policy with regard to the trafficking of humans. Under the policy, the Office of the Inspector-General in the Defense Department launched an investigation into the trafficking of women into camptown prostitution around major U.S. military bases in Korea. The Inspector-General also reviewed policies and programs of the U.S. military authorities concerning prostitution and human trafficking. In 2004, more than 400 GIS stationed in South Korea were punished for prostitution-related offenses, including violations of off-limits regulations.[22] In 2005, the U.S. military authorities in Korea placed twenty-nine camptown clubs suspected of hiring trafficked women off-limits to GIS (Ko et al. 2006, 95). The authorities also have stressed educating GIS about the illegality of prostitution and have tried to expand on-base recreational facilities to offset the popularity of off-base prostitution.[23] In October 2005, President George W. Bush signed Presidential Decree 13387 to punish "those who encourage prostitution" as a violation of Article 134 of the Uniform Code of Military Justice (Kirk 2007, 140).

Meanwhile, Korean nongovernmental organizations (NGOS) that have provided advocacy services for transnational camptown women in Kyŏnggi Province put pressure on the Korean government to deal with the problem of trafficking women. Korea Church Women United conducted seminal field studies of transnational camptown women and published investigative reports in 1999 and 2002. Local women's organizations such as Turebang (My Sister's Place) and Saewumt'ŏ (Sprouting Place) also published reports (Kang et al. 2001; My Sister's Place 2003, 2005a, 2005b, 2005c, 2007). In October 2002, the Philippine government filed a lawsuit against the owner of the Double Deuce club for coercing eleven Filipinas, who had escaped from the club, into prostitution. The case was reported to the International Organization for Migration in Geneva, generating much publicity.[24] The aggregation of these types of public exposure led to some change in policy. The Korean government began to collaborate with the NGOs to establish two shelters for transnational camptown women and to fund fact-finding research, outreach programs, and counseling services (My Sister's Place 2003, 9). The Korean police launched a campaign against camptown clubs' violations of their workers' human rights, including forced prostitution and restriction on the freedom of movement.[25] The Korean government also began to punish business owners and managers who deprived women of their passports or identification cards, and it stopped issuing E-6 visas for Russian "dancers" on June 1, 2003 (My Sister's Place 2003, 9).

The combination of NGO activism and policy changes in the U.S. military and in the Korean government has brought some positive changes. For example, blatant forms of sexual services on clubs' premises, which had been quite common, have disappeared, as have the practices of depriving foreign women of their passports (Ko et al. 2006, 7, 93; My Sister's Place 2005b, 12). While the various forms of labor exploitation discussed above have persisted, the problem of forced prostitution has been subdued (with variations in terms of its frequency and the level of pressure exerted by employers and managers on women from one camptown area to another and, at times, from one club to another).[26] Yet the difference is rather tricky, because transnational camptown women are still pressured to engage in prostitution by the exploitative working conditions that threaten their livelihoods and the exigency of sending money to their impoverished families back home (My Sister's Place 2005d, 16).

The recent policy changes in the U.S. military and the Korean government are duplicitous because the institution of camptown prostitution regulated by these authorities persists. The backbone of camptown prostitution in South Korea, including VD tests imposed on camptown women and the subsequent issuing of health cards to women who do not have sexually transmitted diseases, remains intact (My Sister's Place 2005d, 41). In particular, the E-6 is the only category of visa that requires applicants to submit HIV test certificates. In Kyŏnggi Province, which has hosted more than two-thirds of the U.S. military bases in Korea, foreign female entertainers working in camptown clubs are still required to have monthly VD tests under the Contagious Disease Management Act (Ko et al. 2006, 39; My Sister's Place 2003, 20). Transnational entertainers on major U.S. military bases in Kunsan, Pusan, Songt'an, Tongduch'ŏn, and Ŭijŏngbu are required to undergo VD tests and HIV tests every three months (Korea Church Women United 1999, 37; My Sister's Place 2003, 25, 28). Although the specific logistics of the VD test have varied, the practice itself, which involves intrusive vaginal examination, has remained.

The Korean authorities and U.S. military authorities have played direct and indirect roles in establishing and maintaining this practice. Until the 1980s, VD clinics around major U.S. military bases had been separate from local health clinics (pogŏnso), where poor camptown residents received minimum medical services. Women infected with VD were immediately sent to hospitals—constructed in the style of internment camps—and treated for a few days, until they were free of VD.[27] In the 1990s, this coercive practice disappeared, and club women could get a monthly VD test in any hospital they chose. Yet, as a physician who worked at a health clinic in Ŭijŏngbu observed, for almost six decades there has been no serious attempt to integrate other health examinations into the VD test (Moon 2005, 328, 334).

Other established components of camptown prostitution remain anachronistically intact against the backdrop of rapidly evolving socioeconomic contexts in camptowns. In 1993, the Ministry of Culture and Tourism introduced the "tourism special district (kwankwangt ŭkgu)" to promote tourism with tax-free shopping and entertainment. This notion of tourism tied to camptowns was recycled from the 1960s, when camptowns were isolated from the larger society as a buffer zone between Korean society and U.S. military bases. The later tourism special districts blurred the boundary between camptowns and that larger society. As some camptowns were turned into special tourism districts,[28] more and more Korean civilians and other foreign (civilian) visitors frequented camptown entertainment businesses. In the midst of this significant change, Article 2 of the Tourism Promotion Law Ordinance continues to allow camptown clubs patronized by GIS to hire "hostesses" who can provide GI guests with drink, song, and dance. Article 115 of the Taxation Special Cases Restriction Law continues to grant these clubs tax exemptions for liquor sold on their premises. Article 19 of the Special Consumption Tax Law continues to guarantee the supply of tax-free Korean liquor to be sold to GIS and foreign sailors, who are categorized as "foreign troops stationed in Korea" (*chuhan oegukkun*) (Ko et al. 2006, 85–87).

Specific initiatives under the zero-tolerance policy also reveal the continuing complicity of the U.S. military authorities in maintaining regulated prostitution on the ground. On October 1, 2004, the Second Infantry Division, a major U.S. military unit in Korea, and the KSTA introduced the "Guidelines for Model Business Practices" to communicate the military's firm stance against prostitution and human trafficking. Professedly intended to promote mutual benefits for the military and the KSTA, but resembling the Songt'an agreement discussed earlier, the document grants the military discretionary power to impose off-limits orders on clubs that violate the guidelines. These guidelines include the regulation of hygiene in clubs, as well as the protection of troops, prevention of terrorism, fire safety, courteous behavior, and the maintenance of order.[29] The VD test appears to fall under "regulation of hygiene." On March 14, 2005, a similar document, the "Memorandum of Understanding between the U.S. Army Support Activity Area III and the KSTA regarding the Prohibition of Prostitution and Human Trafficking," was introduced.[30] In theory, MPs are given power to impose off-limits orders on camptown clubs to enforce the anti-prostitution and anti-trafficking policy. Simultaneously, they enforce the VD testing of club women discreetly through the use of off-limit measures against clubs with VD cases. The duplicitous nature of the zero-tolerance policy has generated unintended (but predictable) consequences. Club owners complain that MPs have abused their off-limits orders to receive bribes from them and sexual favors from their female workers. At Osan Air Base, a U.S. Air Force first lieutenant, who led the military police team that patrolled the bar district outside the base, abused the authority to impose off-limits orders and was charged with "bribery, extortion, rape" and other misconduct, including assault, larceny, and making false official statements.[31]

The military authorities may want to claim that this type of corruption is an exception committed by a few egregious MPs. Yet the long history of camptown prostitution suggests otherwise. It has not been the lack of law, policy, or official rhetoric that has caused camptown prostitution to proliferate, but its expediency as a means to maintain militarized masculinity (hinged on constant heterosexual gratification). It is noteworthy that the zero-tolerance policy, through the imposition of off-limits orders on clubs, is primarily concerned with distancing the military and its soldiers from camptown prostitution tainted with trafficking. The policy is nebulous about the use of (poor) women's sexual labor presumably without force or trafficking to keep male soldiers docile and useful. It continues to normalize male soldiers' heterosexual entitlement at the expense of marginalized women. Some military leaders, such as Major General John R. Wood of the U.S. Second Infantry Division at Camp Red Cloud, Ŭijŏngbu City, support the transformation of camptown prostitution: "I think the entertainment districts [in camptowns] are a bit of an anachronism. I would like our troops to have the opportunity to benefit from the new modern entertainment establishments that you find in Seoul that no doubt the business climate up here would support."[32] But it is not entirely clear what Wood means by "new modern entertainment establishments." Given that the entertainment districts in Seoul are saturated with the sex industry, however, they may well include various forms of women's sexual labor, presumably without force and trafficking, in more upscale environments. The conventional acceptance of the inevitability of prostitution is also implied in a remark by Major General James Soligan, deputy chief of staff for U.S. Armed Forces in South Korea, who has said that he is "unsure what to do beyond keeping soldiers confined to their bases or barring them from clubs with Russian or Philippine hostesses."[33] The comment suggests that the zero-tolerance policy (or any similar policy) is not sustainable, especially as the U.S. military has been thinly stretched and recruiting has become difficult during the wars in Iraq and Afghanistan. As was the case during the Korean War and the Vietnam War, the military authorities may have to give up their enforcement against prostitution as long as they view prostitution, which relies on marginalized women's sexual labor and therefore has minimal economic and political costs to the military, as the expedient means to manage soldiers who are also recruited predominantly from poor sectors of American society. This entrenched idea about prostitution is deeply at odds with the zero-tolerance policy, which requires the moral cost of maintaining a positive image of a military that is separate from forced prostitution and the trafficking of women.

Janus-Faced GIs: Helpers and Violators of the Transnational Camptown Women

As customers, boyfriends, and husbands, GIS perpetrate abuse and violence against transnational camptown women. They play much more convoluted roles than business owners and managers. On the one hand, abusive and exploitative working conditions in camptown clubs make GIS not only the crucial source of club women's income but also their potential husbands. As customers, they buy drinks ("juice") and thereby help the club women meet the sales quotas that are common in many camptown clubs. While working, many of these women meet "good" customers who sympathize with their situations and buy drinks regularly. The women often develop intimate relationships with this type of customer, who became boyfriends or fiancés. As boyfriends, some GIS give camptown women money to buy food or, at times, to support their families in their home countries. As husbands, GIS can secure the women's vulnerable status as temporary migrants in Korea and sponsor their immigration to the United States. For the transnational camptown women, heterosexual relationships with GIS are almost the only avenue to get some relief, or even escape, from the exploitative, strenuous, and degrading work in camptown clubs. On the other hand, GIS in these diverse roles can and do perpetrate abuse and violence against the women, ranging from deceptive marriage and monetary deprivation to such serious crimes as battery, rape, and murder (My Sister's Place 2005b, 2005d; Yea 2004).

Although no separate official statistics are available on crimes against camptown women, a journalist's compilation of Korean newspapers during the period 1945–90, covered incidents of violent crime committed by GIS against these women for the first time in 1957 (Oh 1990), when camptown prostitution began to concentrate around major U.S. military bases in South Korea. The first reported incident of rape and murder of a "camptown prostitute"—thirty-year-old Hyŏn-suk Song—took place in P'aju, one of the major camptowns near the demilitarized zone, on May 6, 1957. Since then, numerous camptown women have been victimized by violent crimes. According to a survey of 243 camptown women in Kyŏnggi Province, 67.5 percent had experienced crimes committed by their customers (mostly GIS and some Korean men) that involved beating, sexual violence, theft, and robbery, in declining order of frequency. The older a respondent was, the more likely she was to have been victimized this way; 89.5 percent of the respondents older than fifty reported having been exposed to GIS crimes (Kang et al. 2001). This may mean that age increases camptown women's vulnerability to crimes by GIS or that older women have been exposed to violent situations longer than younger women. It may also mean that GI crimes have been in relative decline. The possible increase of vulnerability with old age suggests that crimes in general, and GI crimes in particular, are not entirely random; instead, perpetrators calculate their chances of being caught and punished by assessing their relative power vis-à-vis their potential victims. As discussed later, the unequal power relationship between transnational camptown women and GIS was established, and has been maintained, by the SOFA and Korean immigration laws.

In the aftermath of the implementation of the zero-tolerance policy, one of the most common abuses perpetrated by GIS against camptown women has been deceptive marriage and abandonment.[34] Although problems of deceptive marriage and abandonment have a long history and were endured by Korean women before Filipinas and Russians arrived in the camptowns, the conspicuous suppression of prostitution under the zero-tolerance policy has contributed to their spread by making cohabitation and marriage more attractive than prostitution. Indeed, the practice of cohabitation is as old as the presence of U.S. military bases in South Korea. This arrangement of convenience, which resembles the institution of concubinage in European colonies, has blurred the boundaries of prostitution and marriage. Hence, cohabitation in the context of a camptown is also known as "cohabitating prostitution (*tonggŏmaech'un*)." In cohabitation, a GI pays for food and housing in exchange for the sex, housework, and emotional labor provided by his partner. It also is not uncommon now to encounter GIS who also marry camptown women to take advantage of their family allowances, which can range from $231.90 to $277.50 a month,[35] depending on their rank (My Sister's Place 2007, 33). As their predecessors did for decades to Korean camptown women, contemporary GI fathers commonly leave these relationships of convenience when their tours of duty in Korea end and abandon their women and children.[36]

While deceptive marriage and abandonment are not defined as crime, this type of abuse leads to complicated problems of pregnancy, childbirth and child rearing, and illegal immigration status (My Sister's Place 2005d, 13, 2007, 37). In the Tongduch'ŏn area, where Filipinas make up the majority of camptown women, a growing number of them are raising children alone because their GI boyfriends or husbands have returned to the United States (My Sister's Place 2003, 84). A sizable community of Russian women married to GIS who have abandoned them also live in the area as illegal aliens (My

Sister's Place 2005d, 21). Thus, widespread abandonment after deceptive marriages has encumbered transnational camptown women with financial difficulties and with bearing and raising children alone (Ko et al. 2006, 48).[37] These mothers commonly become illegal residents in Korea after their husbands leave, because their husbands have to sponsor their applications for SOFA visas after their E-6 visas expire. These women are also suspended in legal limbo because they are not formally divorced. With assistance from local NGOs, some camptown women file civil lawsuits against GI husbands to receive financial support for their children and divorces. The U.S. military authorities provide some counseling services for these women through the Family Assistance Center and the Office of the Inspector General. But these efforts are grossly inadequate to deal with the problems (My Sister's Place 2007, 35).

Because the covert acceptance of camptown prostitution has allowed owners and managers of camptown businesses and recruiting agencies outside camptowns to exploit transnational women, deceptive marriage and abandonment are not merely domestic troubles between two individuals but also symptoms of the profoundly unequal status between the women and their GI partners. Transnational camptown women often see cohabitation or marriage as providing relief, or even escape, from exploitative and abusive working conditions; low-ranking GIS view the women as relief from lonely and tedious daily routines away from their own families. As a GI takes advantage of the family allowance, his wife manipulates emotional ties and trust to get resources from the husband. At the same time, while both the women and their GI partners often come from impoverished families in their own societies, there is a big gulf between the GIS' status as agents of the American empire and the women as vulnerable migrant workers. The GIS' privileged status of extraterritoriality in Korea has a long history that goes back to the arrival of U.S. troops as an occupying force in 1945 and the three-year direct rule of Korea by the U.S. Army Military Government. Under the Taejŏn Agreement, signed on July 12, 1950, and the Myer Agreement, signed on May 24, 1952—during the Korean War—the U.S. military in Korea exercised exclusive criminal and civil jurisdiction over GIS. Although the Korean government demanded a SOFA after the Mutual Defense Treaty was signed in October 1953, the United States resisted the demand until it faced mounting popular protests and recognized that it needed Korea's cooperation during the Vietnam War and in the rapprochement with Japan.[38] Before the SOFA was finally signed in 1966, GIS enjoyed almost absolute freedom from Korean jurisdiction even when they committed serious crimes of rape, robbery, and murder against Koreans (Headquarters of the Movement to Root Out American Soldiers' Crime 2002, 19).

The SOFA did not transform the virtually colonial relationship between the two countries. On the first day the SOFA became effective in 1967, the Korean government, to comply with the "favorable consideration" clause in the agreement, gave up jurisdiction over three crimes committed by GIS (S. Yi 2001, 275). In practice, the courtesy clause automatically transferred Korean criminal jurisdiction over GIS to the U.S. military, leaving the SOFA toothless. Throughout the 1980s, the Korean government exercised criminal jurisdiction over fewer than 1 percent of the total reported GI crimes that it was entitled to handle (National Campaign to Eliminate Crimes Committed by U.S. Forces in Korea 1999, 476). After such jurisdiction is transferred to the U.S. military, a majority of criminal offenders have received warnings or administrative discipline rather than criminal prosecution and appropriate sentencing.[39] In the absence of substantial accountability and punishment, GIS committed numerous crimes. Between 1967 and 1991, when the SOFA was first revised, 1,100–2,300 crimes committed by GIS, their families, and other civilian employees of the U.S. military were reported annually (National Campaign to Eliminate Crimes Committed by U.S. Forces in Korea 1999, 19). GIS were responsible for 85 to 90 percent of these crimes and violent crimes accounted for roughly 30 percent of the total incidences of crime in the early 1980s (National Campaign to Eliminate Crimes Committed by U.S. Forces in Korea 1999, 147–48).

Although political and socioeconomic transformations in South Korea have somewhat mitigated the deeply colonial nature of the SOFA, Korea's criminal jurisdiction over GIS remains grossly truncated, even after two revisions of the agreement in 1991 and 2001.[40] While the overall rate of reported crimes has declined to an annual average of 700–800 since 1992, throughout the 1990s, an average of 24.2 percent of GIS who committed crimes were perpetrators of violent crime (National Campaign to Eliminate Crimes Committed by U.S. Forces in Korea 1999, 148). In 1999, the Korean government exercised its jurisdiction over merely 3.6 percent of GIS crimes and transferred all other cases to the U.S. military (S. Yi 2001, 273). Although the revision in 2001 strengthened Korean jurisdiction for twelve serious crimes, including robbery, rape, and murder, Korea's exclusive jurisdiction in Korean territory is still expected to be given up in practice when the U.S. military requests. Moreover, Korea cannot exercise jurisdiction over crimes committed by GIS during "official duty," and U.S. military officials have sole discretion in defining what "official duty" means (Headquarters of the Movement to Root Out American Soldiers' Crime 2002, 35, 38, 40). Based on Article 22, clause 9, of the SOFA, GIS' extraterritoriality encompasses a set of privileges that exempt them from appearing in their own criminal trials. They have the right not to attend court when circumstances are considered physically and mentally inadequate. They are also entitled not to be hand-cuffed and not to be prosecuted if trial conditions are not adequate to the prestige (*wisin*) of the U.S. Army (National Campaign to Eliminate Crimes Committed by U.S. Forces in Korea 1999, 131). These conditions are subject to widely varying interpretations that are entirely at the discretion of the U.S. military. In stark contrast, the U.S. military has arrested Korean civilians and put them in handcuffs on the sole basis of a GI's report. In a nutshell, the U.S.-Korean SOFA has remained far more unequal than comparable agree-ments in Japan, Germany, and most North Atlantic Treaty Organization countries.[41]

Under the SOFA, Korean citizens are virtually colonial subjects in their own territory. Although the public perception of the U.S. military as Korea's protector increasingly has been questioned since the 1980s,[42] the Korean and U.S. military authorities have long sanctioned GIS' extraterritorial status. For Korean camptown women, a highly stigmatized and marginalized group, this colonial relationship has intensified. When the victim of a violent crime by a GI is a camptown woman, even Korean government officials showed callous indifference. In 1992, the highly publicized and grotesque brutal mur-der of Kŭm-i Yun in Tongduch'ŏn City shocked the Korean public, trigger-ing the emergence of a grassroots movement to deal with GI crimes for the first time. In October 1993, the movement developed into the National Cam-paign to Eradicate Crimes against Civilians committed by American Soldiers. In response to the growing popular movement, a city official commented, "We should not make a crack in the Korea-U.S. alliance just because a lowly woman died." And when the National Campaign requested approval to publicly protest a murder case in 1996, a police officer replied, "[North Korea] is now sending down a submarine, and . . . we are in semi-war situation. It does not help national security for you to make a fuss about a GI crime in front of the military base. We need to help American soldiers" (National Campaign to Eliminate Crimes Committed by U.S. Forces in Korea 1999, 377). This old Cold War ideology in the post–Cold War era that prioritizes militarized national security over security of camptown women and other civilians in daily lives has also colored GIS' hegemonic perception of their place in South Korea. The National Campaign had been staging protests on

Fridays to eliminate GI crimes and revise the SOFA. In May 1998, a GI passed a note to protesters that contained the following message: "If you don't like American soldiers, you can go to North Korea. Over there you have no GIS and no freedom" (National Campaign to Eliminate Crimes Committed by U.S. Forces in Korea 1999, 377).

The transnational camptown women, who are not even Korean citizens, confront an enormous hierarchy in their relationships with GIS. In contrast to GIS' extraterritorial privileges, the transnational camptown women are subjected to multiple legal constraints. They are temporary employees whose legal residence in Korea depends exclusively on their employment in the highly exploitative entertainment industry. In the absence of other sources of support, sexual relations with boyfriends become materially and emotionally necessary for club women, even when they are aware that the relationships may not last. Like other migrant laborers, they are merely carriers of expendable cheap labor. Marriage to a GI is alluring, because it presents the possibility of immigration to the United States, but it does not guarantee a camptown woman automatic legalization of her status in Korea. If she leaves a camptown club to live with a boyfriend or husband before her E-6 visa expires, the club's owner or the manager of the agency that recruited her can report her to the immigration office. She immediately becomes an illegal resident and can be penalized with heavy fines and deportation. Many women marry their GI boyfriends to reduce the heavy fine; after paying the penalty, she can apply for a SOFA visa as a GI's spouse (Bautista 2005, 104). It is imperative that her GI husband sponsor her application to obtain a SOFA identification card, which is necessary to obtain the A-3 visa for U.S. military personnel and diplomatic personnel (Ko et al. 2006, 50). This legal structure, coupled with the GI's extraterritorial privileges, thus renders transnational camptown women very vulnerable to abuse and violence.

The long history of extraterritorial privilege that the U.S. military has enjoyed in Korea sends an implicit but powerful message that emboldens GIS in their relationships with camptown women as sex workers, girlfriends, or wives. If GIS are rarely held accountable for serious crimes they commit against Korean civilians on Korean soil, why should they care about vulnerable transnational women? After all, these women are supposed to entertain them; they work at camptown clubs set up under the aegis of the military authorities and the Korean government and are regulated by these authorities to protect GIS from VD.

As a young woman from Uzbekistan who worked at a camptown club in Tongduch'ŏn City told an NGO staff member in January 2005:

Young GIs just want to have a good time. Some GIs marry because they want to live outside their units and have a good time. In fact, many young GIs marry in Korea because they want to have a good time here in Korea. There are some GIs serious about making a good family. That kind of GI tends to think that women in their own countries are bad. They are too money-oriented and selfish. (Kim 2007, 73; my translation)

In other words, individual GIs believe they are entitled to have a good time (which camptown prostitution is supposed to deliver) and enjoy extraterritorial privileges because they do the strenuous and traumatizing work of maintaining and expanding the U.S. military empire. This rationale reproduces the militarized masculinity that naturalizes the need for constant heterosexual gratification. The young woman's comments also expose an insidious Orientalist view among these GIs of Asian women as submissive and family-oriented.

Conclusion

The various forms of abuse and violence against transnational camptown women that are perpetrated by GIs and by camptown business owners and managers speak volumes to the limitations and duplicity of the zero-tolerance policy. The trouble with this policy, and with related measures, points to the serious problem with which the U.S. military has to deal, in Korea and elsewhere, as it transforms itself into a more mobile force rapidly swaggering around the globe. How can the military efficiently manage its soldiers and maintain their respectability (the ostensible goal of the zero-tolerance policy) when it is asking those same soldiers to endure long separations from their families and perform tedious and arduous labor in foreign countries with which they have little cultural affinity? Given that a hyper-sexualized version of masculinity has been integral to the smooth operation of the U.S. military, how long can the military sustain the zero-tolerance policy in Korea and elsewhere—or, for that matter, any similar prohibitive measures—and still solve its serious recruiting problem? These questions reveal that the problem with camptown prostitution is not merely the violation of the human rights of some trafficked women; it is also tied into the fundamental assumptions about militarized masculinity on which the military has relied. The global visibility of the U.S. military presses it hard to look for a viable alternative to regulated prostitution that relies on sexual labor of poor and marginalized women beyond duplicitously prohibiting it.

A critical reassessment of militarized masculinity coupled with camptown prostitution is not only a moral issue. It is also a practical issue that affects the reproduction of the military as an institution. In this era of globalization, elite men and women go into finance to make immense fortunes, and the educated population in the United States is generally less inclined to serve in the military, especially as rank-and-file soldiers, as long as other decent employment is available. As was the case in the past, high unemployment among young people is the single most significant factor that enables the U.S. Army to meet its recruitment quotas.[43] The military needs new recruits most desperately during wartime; at the same time, potential recruits are much less likely to enlist during wars because of the heightened risk. It is not surprising that approximately 21,100 legal immigrants who are not U.S. citizens are currently serving in the U.S. Armed Forces to take advantage of expedited naturalization.[44] It is not unfathomable that the U.S. Army has granted "moral waivers" to recruit people convicted of minor and serious crimes, including armed robbery, sexual abuse, and vehicular homicide. Since the United States invaded Iraq in March 2003, GIs in South Korea have been transferred to meet the dire shortage of troops there. In the midst of this global circulation of troops, 8,129 moral waivers have been issued, accounting for more than 10 percent of new U.S. Army recruits.[45]

In the presence of the underlying issue of recruitment, the zero-tolerance policy fails to address the deeper problems of extraterritorial privilege and militarized masculinity. That the U.S. military is aware of this problem is suggested by Defense Secretary Robert M. Gates's recent decision to replace unaccompanied twelve-month tours to South Korea with family-sponsored three-year tours.[46] At the same time, the U.S. military continues to transform itself into a "lean" and "mobile" global fighting machine through the deployment of single soldiers on strategic forward bases (lily pads). Until it dismantles the hypersexual construction of militarized masculinity sanctioned by extraterritorial privilege, prostitution around U.S. military bases is likely to increase.

Notes

I thank Young-im Yu, director of My Sister's Place; Dong-ryong Kim; Kyung-t'ae Park, both independent filmmakers; and Reverend Wu-sŏng Chŏn, director of the Tabitha Community, for their generosity in sharing valuable resources and observations on camptowns.

1. Korean NGOs working with sex workers who catered to American soldiers coined the term "camptown women" to replace the deeply stigmatized categories of Western

princess (*yanggongju*) and whore (*ch'angnyŏ*). These NGOS also avoid using the notion of sex workers because they believe that selling one's body is not conducive to a positive meaning of work. Mainstream feminists in Korea argue that prostitution cannot be considered a form of work that women can freely choose, given that most women who enter prostitution, particularly camptown prostitution, are indigent, and their economic marginality is almost always coupled with the lack of viable job opportunities. While I do not agree completely with this position, I choose to adopt the notion of camptown women because its broad connotation can encompass various categories of women who cater to GIS, including registered club women employed at "class 1" businesses selling liquor, which have been controlled by the KSTA, who are de facto professional sex workers; and unregistered women employed in restaurants approved as "class 2" and "class 3" businesses that sell prepared food but no liquor. In the mid-1970s, several hundred women catered to GIS within the enclosed space of A-Town, but only several dozen of them were officially registered: Kim 2005, 171, 173.

Resistance to categorizing camptown women uniformly as prostitutes has been observed among transnational camptown women themselves. According to in-depth interviews with forty-nine women who have worked in camptown clubs, some Filipinas insist that they are "entertainers" different from "those Korean women engaging in prostitution." Some Russian women convey that it is unbearable that Koreans tend to perceive Russian women as prostitutes: Sŏl et al. 2003a, 2003b, 199.

2. This field trip would not have been possible without Tong-nyŏng Kim and Kyŏng-t'ae Park, who have made documentary films about camptown prostitution in South Korea.

3. In the late 1980s, a noticeable change in the form of camptown prostitution took place. Traditional brothels were replaced by a sex industry that combined prostitution with other types of legitimate service businesses, such as massage parlors, hair salons, coffee shops, and restaurants. While this type of sex industry had been exploding in Korea since the 1970s, it did not affect camptown enclaves, which were closely monitored by Korean and U.S. authorities. After the shift, women from outside periodically gathered in the camptowns on paydays and weekends to make quick money by selling sex to GIS. Registered club women looked down on these transitory women.

4. As of December 2004, approximately 87 percent of women working in GI clubs in major camptowns were foreign migrant workers: "Migungiji ingŭn kijich'on oegugin-yŏsŏng inkwŏnch'imhae simgak" (Camptown foreign women, serious violation of human rights), *Naeil Newspaper*, 21 February 2005.

5. Barbara Demick, "Off-Base Behavior in Korea: By Allowing GIS to Patronize Certain Clubs, the U.S. Military is Seen as Condoning the Trafficking of Foreign Women for Prostitution," *Los Angeles Times*, 26 September 2002.

6. Korean women were marginalized in the process of industrialization: S. Moon 2005a, chap. 3. In the 1980s, ironically, they encountered opportunities to get jobs in the entertainment industry that paid relatively well. The explosion of entertainment businesses selling food and drink along with women's sexual service can be attributed to

small and medium-sized businesses' seeking quick profits from relatively limited capital investments. The Korean state severely discriminated against such businesses as it fostered economic conglomerates as an engine of economic growth based on exports; the two oil crises in the 1970s aggravated the adversity small and medium-sized businesses faced. In response, they invested their capital in domestic entertainment: Chŏng 1988, 160. In 1988, more than 350,000 registered entertainment businesses sold food and drink in Korea, and a majority of them also sold women's sexual services. An estimated 400,000 unregistered entertainment businesses that sold women's sexual services also existed, employing some 120,000–150,000 women. This suggested that a fifth of young Korean women age fifteen to twenty-nine were working in the domestic sex industry: Kang 1989, 123.

7. In 2002, this association was composed of 189 owners of camptown clubs: Gustavo Capdevila, "South Korea: UN Says Sex Industry Employs 5,000 Women for GI's," Global Informational Network, 3 September 2002, 1. In 2002, there were 222 camptown clubs serving 37,000 U.S. troops stationed in South Korea: "Prosecution Combats Brothels near US Bases," *Korea Times*, 11 October 2002.

8. Gustavo Capdevila, "Korea's New 'Comfort Women,' " *Asia Times*, 5 September 2002.

9. The number of female foreign entertainers admitted through the E-6 visa system grew from 235 in 1994 to 3,392 in 1999. The number peaked in 2001, at 6,971, and then declined to 2,498 in 2004, after the entry of Russian "dancers" was suspended in June 2003. The number increased again in 2005, to 3,111: Ko et al. 2006, 64–65. Between 1999 and 2003, women from Russia accounted for the largest number, followed by Filipinas, but after the dancer category was eliminated in 2003, the number of Russian women plummeted and Filipinas became the largest group of foreign entertainers: ibid., 69.

10. The official definition of sex trafficking is limited to "the transport, sale and purchase of women and girls for prostitution, bonded labor and sexual enslavement within the country and abroad": quoted in Korea Church Women United 1999, 51. According to Hyun Ung Goh, head of the Seoul office of the International Organization for Migration, "virtually all Filipina women trafficked for the sex and entertainment industry in South Korea cater to the military camptown: see Vivion Vinson, "Base Intentions: The US Military Whitewashes the Exploitation and Trafficking of Women in S. Korea," available at http://www.afsc.org/pwork/0405/040506.htm (accessed on 23 January 2006).

11. Il-lan Kim, "Chigŭm kijich'onŭn ŏdiro kago inna, 3" (Where is the camptown headed now? Part 3), *Ilda*, 13 September 2004: available (in Korean) online at http://webcache .googleusercontent.com/search?q=cache:Eq38zpUrYqkJ:hcy.jinbo.net/zbx (accessed on 11 April 2010).

12. A large-scale research project sponsored by the Korean Ministry of Gender Equality investigated situations of transnational camptown women in Seoul, Ŭijŏngbu, Tongduch'ŏn, Anyang, Pusan, Ch'angwŏn, and Kunsan in 2003. These camptown women were virtually rented out by their managers to clubs for a few days, several weeks, or several months. For each woman, a manager received several hundred dollars in rental fees from a club owner. A majority of these camptown women

worked every day, without a holiday, usually from 5 or 6 P.M. until midnight, when GIS returned to their bases (to comply with the curfew imposed after 9/11). During weekends and soldiers' paydays, these women's work began as early as 1 or 2 P.M. The women often continued to work as long as clubs had customers, sometimes until 3 or even 5 A.M. In these late-night hours, customers were often Korean men and migrant foreign workers from Bangladesh, Pakistan, the Philippines, and Turkey. There were also some young white men who had come to Korea to work as English teachers. The camptown women often were paid less than their employment contracts had stated, because they were frequently forced to pay arbitrarily imposed fines, fees, and debts. Monthly wages were not usually given directly to the women, because their employers were concerned that they would try to escape the harsh working conditions. Monthly wages were withheld by employers or deposited to the women's bank accounts, which were controlled by the employers: Sŏl et al. 2003b, 89, 98–99. The following studies also show the commonalities among transnational camptown women in different locations in South Korea: Kang et al. 2001; Ko et al. 2006; My Sister's Place 2003, 2005a, 2005b; Sŏl et al. 2003a, 2003b; Yea 2004.

13. Donald Macintyre, "Base Instinct," *Time*, 5 August 2002.

14. Songt'an City has hosted the Osan Air Base, the largest U.S. Air Force base in the Pacific region, since the Clark Air Base in the Philippines closed. In 1996, this city was incorporated into the city of P'yŏngta'ek. which has become the host for the majority of U.S. military bases relocated from northern Kyŏnggi Province and Seoul.

15. This discovery generated a simmering controversy in the local community and among anti-base activists nationwide, because the agreement was perceived as an unequal, colonial-style document that was anachronistic and therefore to be abolished. Ironically, however, some club owners criticized the agreement because it interfered with their business. In light of the recent transformation of the Songt'an and P'yŏngt'aek areas into special tourism districts in 1997, such business owners have argued that GIS should not delude themselves into believing that they own the clubs because there are many other foreign (civilian) visitors, such as engineers: In-jin Ch'oi, "SOFAboda tŏ nappŭn akpŏp"(A law worse than the SOFA), *Kyŏnghyang*, 1 April 2005.

16. In-jin Ch'oi, Sang-ho Yi, and T'ae-wu Pak, "P'yŏngt'aek yuhŭngŏpso tansokkwŏn yangdo p'amun" (Stir from surrendering the power to regulate entertainment establishments in P'yŏngt'aek), *Kyŏnghyang* 31 March 2005.

17. Mary Jacoby, "Does U.S. abet Korean Sex Trade?," *St. Petersburg Times*, 9 December 2002. This reportage, filmed by Fox television's affiliate in Cleveland, was triggered by local coverage of Korean women working in prostitution at massage parlors in Cleveland. The women had come to the United States with their GI husbands, but their marital relationships had deteriorated. Abandoned or sold by their husbands, they were forced to become sex workers to support themselves.

18. Don Kirk, "From Russia without 'love': GI Bars in South Korea," *International Herald Tribune*, 20 September 2002.

19. Donald Macintyre, "Base Instincts," *Time*, 5 August 2002.

20. Christopher H. Smith, "Modern Slavery: U.S. Must Battle Countries Participating in Human Trafficking," *Washington Times*, 18 June 2002.

21. Don Kirk, "From Russia without 'love': GI Bars in South Korea," *International Herald Tribune*, 20 September 2002.

22. Hyung-jin Kim, "US Military's Anti-Prostitution Campaign Makes Headway in South Korea," *Yonhap News*, 31 January 2005.

23. In 2006, the U.S. military authorities continued to try to educate GIS arriving in South Korea about the anti-prostitution and anti-trafficking policies and programs: Ko et al. 2006, 95. The authorities banned GIS from paying bar fines or buying out employment contracts for foreign club women they had met or dated. They also established a twenty-four-hour telephone hot line to receive reports on human trafficking and other illegal activities and have provided some counseling services. The military authorities proposed collaborative patrols between Korean police and the MPS in camptowns across the country. The military authorities also have engaged in dialogue with camptown businesses to promote guidelines for model business practices and cooperation in prohibiting prostitution and the trafficking of women: ibid., 96.

24. "Shameless Exploitation," *Korea Herald*, 21 October 2002; Mary Jacoby, "Does U.S. abet Korean Sex Trade?," *St. Petersburg Times*, 9 December 2002.

25. "Prosecution Combats Brothels near US Bases," *Korea Times*, 11 October 2002.

26. In camptown slang, prostitution is commonly called "the second round (*ich'a*)," connoting that it is an activity in which club women engage after doing their primary job of selling alcoholic drinks and interacting with the customers who buy them. The second round is usually done outside clubs, but at some clubs, women sold quick sexual services to GI customers in "VIP rooms." According to the study sponsored by the Ministry of Gender Equality in 2003, customers paid $20–$50 for sex in a VIP room, depending on the type of service, and a club woman received roughly 20 percent of each sale. To go out with a club woman, a customer had to pay "bar fines" (this going out is called the second round). Customers paid $50 for a "short time" (thirty to forty minutes) and $200–$400 for a "long time" (overnight). The average club woman performed intercourse at least once per day. The customer paid an average $230 for intercourse; the sex worker herself received 20–30 percent of the fee: Sŏl et al. 2003b, 98–99.

27. In the 1960s, this type of VD clinic was directly run by the U.S. military authorities in South Korea. The authorities also demanded that pictures of women who had passed the VD test be posted at the entrance to clubs so GIS could avoid the women whose pictures were not on display. Camptown club women also had to undergo semi-monthly VD tests, and clubs with infected women were placed off-limits. In the 1970s, the Korean government took over the administration of the VD tests, after the Camptown Clean-Up Campaign demanded by the U.S. military, and maintained regular VD tests and forced treatment in isolation: Moon 2005, 327.

28. Mayors and governors can apply to the Ministry of Culture and Tourism for this favorable status. To take advantage of the change and deal with the problem of declining camptown prostitution, many owners of camptown entertainment businesses try to turn their businesses into tourism businesses. In 1994, Kyŏnggi Province, where the largest number of U.S. troops and military bases have been concentrated,

applied for the status of tourism special district. The city of P'yŏngt'aek became a tourism special district in 1997.

29. My Sister's Place provided me with a copy of the Korean translation of the document sent to camptown club owners.

30. A copy of this document, in English and Korean, was also provided by My Sister's Place.

31. Chuhan mi hŏnbyŏng chungwi 'pŏmjoi paekhwajŏm' ch'unggyŏk ("A US Military Police Lieutenant, shocking 'crime department store),' " *Yonhap News*, 13 May 2005; Franklin Fisher, "Osan Officer Facing Multiple Charges in Shakedown Scandal," *Stars and Stripes Pacific Edtion*, 15 May 2005.

32. "US General Feels Enduring Link to Korea," *Korea Times*, 31 October 2002.

33. Barbara Demick, "Off-Base Behavior in Korea: By Allowing GIS to Patronize Certain Clubs, the U.S. Military is Seen as Condoning the Trafficking of Foreign Women for Prostitution," *Los Angeles Times*, 26 September 2002.

34. According to the informal meeting between U.S. military personnel and the director and staff of My Sister's Place that took place in Yongsan Garrison in Seoul on 4 December 2004, the military authorities were aware of this growing problem. The minutes of the meeting were provided to me by My Sister's Place.

35. This numbers are based on FY 2006 BAH Type II Payment Rates. This document was provided by My Sister's Place, but its detailed publication information is missing.

36. According to a study of GIS and their Korean wives conducted in the mid-1990s, the most common reasons for abandonment after marriage were physical separation after the termination of the GIS service in Korea and the absence of the intention to marry from the beginning: Okazawa-Rey 2005, 197.

37. During 2004, My Sister's Place provided counseling services for 333 camptown women in northern Kyŏnggi Province. Among these women, 16 percent reported the following problems: pregnancy, childbirth, child care, and divorce and immigration status. The two most common problems they reported were an urgent lack of income for living expenses (25.5 percent) and illness (19 percent). These problems are often closely related to deceptive marriage and abandonment by GI fiancés or husbands: My Sister's Place 2005d, 19.

38. A series of violent crimes against Koreans in the early 1960s galvanized public pressure to draft a SOFA. On 2 June 1962, several GIS lynched a local Korean man who collected scrap metal (for a living) in an off-limits area of P'aju. They beat him with shotguns, bats, and military boots; dragged him onto their base; and hanged him. Then they tied his ankles and dragged him off the base to a hill, where they stripped him and beat him. They spit in his face and put dirt in his eyes, nose, and mouth. Finally, they hung him upside down from an electric post. In February 1964, four brutal shooting incidents took place that left three civilians dead and one seriously injured: S. Yi 2001, 274. In response to these crimes, the U.S. military authorities commented that, in the face of the communist threat, "U.N. Forces" needed to maintain maximum security for military supplies and that such shootings were inevitable to avoid theft of the supplies. This cold indifference intensified public protests to institute a SOFA: ibid.,

277. To avoid the growing anti-Americanism, the South Korean government and the U.S military struck a deal and agreed to institute a SOFA in exchange for sending Korean soldiers to Vietnam and signing a Korea–Japan Diplomatic Treaty that would normalize relations between the two countries: ibid., 275.

39. According to the Korean Parliamentary Inspection of the Administration in 2000, among the total 246 criminal cases transferred to the U.S. military in 1997 and the total 292 criminal cases transferred to it in 1999, no case against a GI had resulted in a prison sentence. In 1998, only three prison sentences were handed down in the total 212 criminal cases transferred to the U.S. military: ibid., 273.

40. The first revision was provoked by growing anti-Americanism in South Korea during the 1980s, when radicalized movements for democratization were developing against Chun Doo Hwan's regime. This military regime took state power through a military coup in late 1979 and the massacre of citizens in Kwangju in 1980, in which the U.S. military was implicated. The general public, which was not necessarily radicalized, also developed a critical attitude toward the United States because of the overbearing arrogance and ignorance the U.S. mass media displayed during the Seoul Olympics in 1988. The negotiations to revise the SOFA began in 1988 and took three years to complete. The Korean public pressed for the second revision in the 1990s as the result of a series of brutal crimes against civilians and arrogant responses by U.S. officials to them. The crimes included the brutal murder in 1992 of the Korean camptown woman Kŭm-i Yun; the detention and brutal beating of three Korean women (a sixty-eight-year-old mother and her two adult daughters) by four MPS at the Yongsan Garrison in 1994; and the brutal beating of a Korean man by thirteen GIS and their families at the Ch'ungmuro subway station in Seoul: Headquarters of the Movement to Root Out American Soldiers' Crime 2002, 20, 21; National Campaign to Eliminate Crimes Committed by U.S. Forces in Korea 1999, 62, 66.

41. As late as 1993, and for the first time in Korean history, a group of Korean legal scholars and attorneys formed a research committee to examine the Korean SOFA and compared it with other SOFAS: Headquarters of the Movement to Root Out American Soldiers' Crime 2002, preface. This severe inequality contributes to the far higher incidence of GI crimes in Korea than even in Okinawa. From 1999 to 2001, the rate in South Korea was 11.2 crimes per 1,000 GIS; the rate was 2.4 crimes per 1,000 GIS in Okinawa: Gillem 2007, 48–49.

42. This altered public sentiment is well reflected in the following comments by Yo-wang Yun (2001, 169), an NGO activist in Wŏnju, Kangwŏn Province, a very conservative garrison city: "Because [Americans] helped us fifty years ago, Koreans have been subjected to humiliation as members of a weaker nation. We need to reclaim our sovereignty and gain the second independence. GIS have been able to leave Korea without remorse and any punishment after they kill people for no reason, rape our daughters, and steal our possessions. We need to teach the strongest country in the world the plain truth that people must be punished when they do wrong."

43. Lizette Alvarez, "More Americans Joining Military as Jobs Dwindle," *New York Times*, 19 January 2009.

44. Clyde Haberman, "Becoming an American Citizen, the Hardest Way,," *New York Times*, 18 September 2007.

45. Lizette Alvarez, "Army Giving More Waivers in Recruiting," *New York Times*, 14 February; "Moral Waivers and the Military," *New York Times*, 20 February 2007.

46. Eric Schmitt, "Gates Approves of 3-year Tours for U.S. Troops in South Korea," *New York Times*, 4 June 2008.

TWELVE

ABU GHRAIB
A Predictable Tragedy?

☆

JEFF BENNETT

Perfect masculinity is sociopathic.
Stan Goff

Torturously exacted confession and conversion are no longer things we fight against: these are now part of our own arsenal, weapons of our own struggle.
Marshall Sahlins

The report "AR 15–6 Investigation of the Abu Ghraib Detention Facility and the 205th Military Intelligence Brigade" (Fay and Jones 2004), describing the abuses perpetrated by Americans at the Abu Ghraib prison facility, states clearly that the incidents cannot be explained with reference to a single cause. It also concludes that confusion regarding the roles of military police (MPS) and intelligence, along with a general lack of control over the multiple agencies and organizations involved in interrogation, were important factors in the abuse equation. Finally, it claims that the abuses at Abu Ghraib were of two types—"intentional violent or sexual abuses" and "incidents that resulted from misinterpretations of law or policy"—while admitting that "some abuses may in fact fall in between these two categories or have elements of both" (Fay and Jones 2004, 4).

Although I think these findings are both accurate and informative, the Fay and Jones report, like the Schlesinger and Taguba reports (Schlesinger et al. 2004; Taguba 2004), was designed to review the formal conduct of operations at the Abu Ghraib prison facility to confirm that the abuses of detainees resulted (primarily) from individual criminal misconduct rather than higher-order perversions of established military procedures and regulations. As a result, the report leaves much unsaid, and it never adequately accounts for the explicitly sexual nature of the abuses at Abu Ghraib. Nor does it discuss the role the Bush administration's new torture protocol might have played in manufacturing the abuses. Further, although the Fay and Jones report makes it clear that the crimes at Abu Ghraib took place in a highly dysfunctional environment where lower enlisted soldiers were forced perpetually to juggle contradictions and cope with confusions generated by the Bush administration's "gloves off" approach to combating terrorism, it refuses to establish any *causal* links between this environment and the incidents of "violent and sexual abuse" that took place at the prison (Fay and Jones 2004, 4). Instead, the official U.S. Army reports all suggest that the chaotic situation at the prison presented a few morally corrupt soldiers with an opportunity to act out their idiosyncratic, sadistic fantasies and subsequently (and, in part, successfully) defend their misconduct as a case of policy confusion.[1]

Alternatively, Amnesty International, the American Civil Liberties Union (ACLU), and a host of investigative journalists and lawyers have acquired evidence that suggests that the abuses at Abu Ghraib were the *direct* results of new laws and policies established by the Bush administration rather than misinterpretations of those policies or the work of a few perverse soldiers (Mayer 2008; Sands 2008).[2] In fact, evidence amassed since 2003 makes it clear that the new torture protocol Secretary of Defense Donald Rumsfeld approved for use at Guantánamo Bay in November 2002 was signed by General Ricardo Sanchez in September 2003, authorizing the use of many of the aggressive interrogation techniques depicted in the infamous Abu Ghraib photos. Thus, there seems to be good reason to view the Abu Ghraib incidents as the byproducts of a secret, top-down plan to extract intelligence from detainees through the use of torture. However, if the goal is to understand how the abuses occurred and why they took the specific forms that they did, this information cannot serve as more than a point of departure. I say this because there are simply too many human links in the chain connecting Washington, D.C., to the hinterlands of Iraq that still need to be examined— links that played active roles in manufacturing the outcomes depicted in the Abu Ghraib photos. Dave Brant, a former Bush administration official, suggested as much when he admitted, before the Abu Ghraib story broke, that we'd sit around and say, you know what's going to happen. You've got guys who have been pumping gas in Nebraska or a cop on a beat in New York City suddenly thrown together in the war in Iraq, face to face with a terrorist, and you know it's a ticket for problems. It's just going to happen. It [the Abu Ghraib tragedy] was inevitable. (Quoted in Mayer 2008, 237)

Indeed. In fact, the ACLU's paper "Allegations of Detainee Abuse in Iraq and Afghanistan" claims that even before the Abu Ghraib photos were presented to the American public, at least sixty-two cases of abuse of detainees by Americans had already been investigated. These involved a wide range of criminal offenses, including:

> Assaults, punching, kicking and beatings, mock executions, sexual assault of a female detainee, threatening to kill an Iraqi child to "send a message to other Iraqis," stripping detainees, beating them and shocking them with a blasting device, throwing rocks at handcuffed Iraqi children, choking detainees with knots of their scarves and interrogations at gunpoint.[3]

I do not believe that Pentagon officials authorized or were even aware of most of these cases. However, I do believe that these abuses were informed by the same sense of impunity and desire for vengeance that underwrote the invasion in 2003. In other words, I think it is clear that the "ticket for problems" that Brant foresaw existed long before the abuses at Abu Ghraib actually occurred, and it may still exist today—even after so many stories of U.S.-sponsored torture have come to light. Thus, in my opinion, the "torture protocol" explanation for the abuses at Abu Ghraib is no less partial than the explanation offered by the Fay and Jones report.

To reiterate, I believe the official U.S. Army reports regarding the happenings at Abu Ghraib are mostly correct. I also think the various attempts that have been made to link the abuses to the Bush administration's new torture protocol are crucial to understanding the problem. However, if the goal is to *understand* the abuses, we need not discard one explanation in favor of the other. Rather, we need to understand better how these competing explanations may be linked and what they both may be overlooking. With this in mind, in this essay I suggest that neither explanation addresses the range of social-psychological factors that may have contributed to the abuses, or the ways military sociology and culture may have shaped the dispositions and behaviors of the soldiers who perpetrated the abuses. More specifically, I argue that an elective affinity existed between the Bush administration's newly authorized interrogation protocol and certain understandings of sex and power fostered within the ranks of the U.S. Army. The behaviors of those convicted of abuse at the prison are thus better viewed as the overdetermined byproducts of a situation that allowed sexual and sadistic themes already present in the U.S. military subculture to be both literalized and officially operationalized—that is, acted out by a group of American soldiers artificially freed from customary social and legal constraints. I also maintain that this situation was symptomatic of contradictions inherent in the war itself, and for this reason the illicit use of violence by American soldiers in Iraq will almost certainly occur in alternative contexts until or unless sweeping policy changes are effected. Finally, I suggest that the U.S. military subculture is transforming in unexpected ways as a consequence of the ongoing war in Iraq and conflicts elsewhere, and much more work needs to be done to chart and monitor these transformations.

The Insurgency, the Prison, and the Program

The *Final Report of the Independent Panel to Review Department of Defense Detention Operations* (Schlesinger et al. 2004) is a summary account of investigations mounted in the wake of the Abu Ghraib prison scandal. At the most basic level, the report argues that the abuses at Abu Ghraib were committed by a few "morally corrupt" soldiers who were neither adequately trained nor supervised. It also notes that the abuses might not have occurred if prison overcrowding and personnel shortages had not become chronic problems during the summer and fall of 2003.

However, in the course of offering this explanation the report also makes several other important claims. To begin, it states unequivocally that the war in Iraq is "not at all like Desert Storm or even analogous to Vietnam" (Schlesinger et al. 2004, 28). At least from the American perspective, the operational environment in Iraq is more complex than it was in these earlier conflicts, and both the mission and the enemy in Iraq have become highly unconventional (Schlesinger et al. 2004, 28). As a result, America has been forced to conduct the war in a way that "inevitably generates detainees— enemy combatants, opportunists, trouble-makers, saboteurs, common criminals, former regime officials, and some innocents as well" (Schlesinger et al. 2004, 27). In short, in the minds of U.S. planners, winning the war in Iraq mandates capturing, sorting, processing, and interrogating sometimes large portions of the Iraqi civilian population in the service of bringing the nation as a whole under control.[4] Further, in spite of the fact that the U.S. Supreme Court ruled on June 28, 2004, that "the purpose of detention is to prevent captured personnel from returning to the field of battle and taking up arms again," (*Hamdan v. Rumsfeld*, 548 U.S. 557, 2006) the panel insisted that detention was also a legitimate means to the end of *intelligence gathering*. Therefore, it noted that detention operations in the "new war" mandated that MPS and intelligence personnel work together in new, mutually reinforcing ways.

While I clearly disagree with the notion that the report represents the final word on the Abu Ghraib scandal, I do think the panel's explanation for the abuses at the Abu Ghraib prison deserve serious consideration. A spike in American casualties in the late summer and fall of 2003 due to the mounting insurgency in Iraq resulted in thousands of people being detained around the country, including many women and children. For a variety of reasons, it also left detention facilities hopelessly understaffed. At the Abu Ghraib facility, many detainees waited for as long as ninety days before they were processed and interrogated, and the U.S. Army's Inspector-General later estimated that up to 80 percent of these detainees might have been eligible for immediate release (Schlesinger et al. 2004, 61). However, it is clear that many Iraqi detainees were processed in the fall of 2003, when population within the Abu Ghraib prison grew to more than 7,000, and it is also apparent that a new working relationship was established between prison guards and intelligence personnel at the prison during this period. In fact, the linked issues of detention and interrogation of prisoners had been on the minds of U.S. officials since the September 11, 2001, attacks, and an entirely new plan for dealing with enemy captives in Iraq had been developed prior to the invasion.

According to Seymour Hersh,

> The notion that Arabs are particularly vulnerable to sexual humiliation became a talking point among pro-war Washington conservatives in the months before the March, 2003, invasion of Iraq. One book that was frequently cited was "The Arab Mind," a study of Arab culture and psychology, first published in 1973, by Raphael Patai, a cultural anthropologist who taught at, among other universities, Columbia and Princeton, and who died in 1996. The book includes a twenty-five-page chapter on Arabs and sex, depicting sex as a taboo vested with shame and repression. "The segregation of the sexes, the veiling of the women . . . and all the other minute rules that govern and restrict contact between men and women, have the effect of making sex a prime mental preoccupation in the Arab world," Patai wrote. Homo-

sexual activity, "or any indication of homosexual leanings, as with all other expressions of sexuality, is never given any publicity. These are private affairs and remain in private." The Patai book, an academic told me, was "the bible of the neocons on Arab behavior." In their discussions, he said, two themes emerged—"one, that Arabs only understand force and, two, that the biggest weakness of Arabs is shame and humiliation."[5]

Speaking of the notorious photos that quickly became symbols of the Abu Ghraib prison scandal, Hersh went on to report:

The government consultant said that there may have been a serious goal, in the beginning, behind the sexual humiliation and the posed photographs. It was thought that some prisoners would do anything— including spying on their associates—to avoid dissemination of the shameful photos to family and friends. The government consultant said, "I was told that the purpose of the photographs was to create an army of informants, people you could insert back in the population." The idea was that they would be motivated by fear of exposure, and gather information about pending insurgency action, the consultant said.[6]

In light of Hersh's exposé and a still flowing stream of new information regarding the treatment of prisoners at Guantánamo Bay, it is now clear that, in spite of first appearances, there was nothing arbitrary or bizarre about photographing innocent—or, perhaps, softly committed—Iraqi partisans in sexually compromising positions at Abu Ghraib. As Hersh noted, this particular form of abuse was practiced by members of a secret counterterrorism task force formed well in advance of the invasion of Iraq, and it had "across-the-board approval" from the Bush administration.[7] What is truly important to understand, then, is *how* this tactic was implemented as part of a larger strategy aimed at putting down the burgeoning insurgency in Iraq in the fall of 2003—an insurgency that had created a real sense of political desperation in both Baghdad and Washington due to the American military's inability to contain it as the myriad costs of the occupation soared.

Here, I want to assume that a certain degree of consensus exists regarding the fact that the Bush administration was under considerable political pressure to stabilize Iraq from the outset of the conflict and that this pressure was translated into military action focused on ending the insurgency.[8] In terms of the military situation, then, the following seems clear: unable to penetrate what in classical military terms is referred to as the underground, and unable to locate and destroy a guerrilla force capable of attacking American targets and then melting back into a vast urban population, American planners in Iraq were forced to turn their attention to the third branch of any organized insurgency—the "auxiliary." That is, they were forced to focus on civilians who had the potential to lend assistance to active insurgents by safeguarding or transporting weapons, supplies, and people in support of actions opposed to U.S. interests. Recruiting members of this vast, mainstream population (the same population that might be convinced to give up "terrorist" leaders for ransom or simply to trade information for favors of various kinds) would be crucial in disrupting the work of the underground and denying the active guerrilla forces both sanctuary and mobility.

With these ends in mind, tested methods of winning the hearts and minds of the ordinary civilian inhabitants of key Iraqi neighborhoods and cities (through civil affairs and humanitarian assistance work) began and in some places enjoyed provisional success. However, political exigency, troop shortages, and an utter lack of moral and legal constraints also seem to have permitted another, less orthodox set of methods to emerge and flourish. Large numbers of innocent Iraqis were rounded up via home searches, roadblocks, and sweeps performed in areas where roadside bombings were taking American lives, and they were herded into detention facilities where they were duly interrogated by members of the Central Intelligence Agency (CIA), privately contracted defense workers, and military-intelligence personnel.

Mass detention was also used widely by the French in Algeria as a counterinsurgency measure, and here I am reminded of a statement made by the notorious French General (and accused war criminal) Paul Aussaresses, who was responsible for eradicating the National Liberation Front threat in Algiers between 1957 and 1959 before he left to train American Special Forces personnel bound for Vietnam:

> I don't think I ever tortured or executed people who were innocent. . . . It must be remembered that for every bomb, whether or not it had exploded, there was a chemist, a bomb maker, a driver, a lookout, and a terrorist who set the detonator. Up to twenty people each time. In my view the responsibility of each one of the accomplices was overwhelming, even though the perpetrators may have thought they were merely the links in a long chain. (Aussaresses 2006, 129)

In other words, as was the case in the Casbah in Algiers, in a variety of neighborhoods in major Iraqi cities anyone who appeared to condone insurgent violence was presumed guilty and treated as a link in a long chain that had to be broken in the name of "Iraqi Freedom." And in the minds of American commanders, breaking that chain apparently would require transforming selected Iraqi prisoners into intelligence assets that might be used to locate "higher-value" targets.

The "Night Shift"

An article in the January 11, 2005, edition of the *Baltimore Sun* claimed that Ivan "Chip" Frederick and Charles Graner, the alleged "ringleaders" in the Abu Ghraib prison abuse case, were viewed as senior leaders in their unit due to their experience as civilian corrections officers. If true, this fact highlights the shift in attitude and authority that took place when the Maryland National Guard unit entered a real-world combat zone. Charles Graner was a mere Army specialist with no formal authority to command troops whatsoever. However, he happened to be a former Marine, a Gulf War veteran, and a civilian corrections officer accustomed to dealing with prison violence at the Fayette County Prison near his home in Pennsylvania. Under circumstances that included a blossoming insurgency, mass detention of prisoners, chronic shortages of personnel, and political pressure to elicit "actionable" intelligence from selected detainees at Abu Ghraib, Graner's background and special talents suddenly provided him new respect from peers and superiors. But this is only half the story.

In his court-martial testimony, Graner stated that shortly after he had arrived in Iraq, he came under the influence of a civilian contractor nicknamed "Big Steve" (Steven Stefanowicz), whose orders he had followed *simply because he knew he was working with intelligence.*[9] Graner also testified that a CIA operative referred to as "Agent Romero" had given him orders, which he followed without consulting his supervisor. I suspect that Graner found these early contacts (with people he probably viewed as covert operatives) exhilarating, and they likely enabled him to render his experience as an ordinary prison guard more meaningful at a variety of levels. Similarly, Chip Frederick, Graner's supervisor, testified at his court-martial that various interrogators repeatedly had instructed him to harass and abuse detainees and to pass the word down to Graner and the rest of his soldiers that they were doing a fine job—even though these interrogators were not in Frederick's chain of command. It thus seems that Frederick, like Graner, was seduced by the mystery and power he associated with interrogators and civilian contractors affiliated with the so-called other government agencies (OGAS), and like

Graner he developed a love–hate relationship with these authority figures and everything they came to stand for.

Here it is important to recognize that the authority granted to commissioned and noncommissioned officers in the U.S. military is guaranteed by the Uniform Code of Military Justice. In other words, subordinates are legally obliged to follow orders communicated to them by their superiors, regardless of how they may feel about the person or people giving the orders. I mention this to highlight the fact that there is a significant difference between following a directive simply because someone of superior rank has ordered it and following a directive because the person who ordered it genuinely commands what, for lack of a better term, I will call "respect." When commands are contradictory or authority is imperfectly aligned, "respect" frequently trumps rank, which is to say that troops are often more loyal to experienced leaders of small units than they are to high-ranking officers or to the codified rules and regulations that otherwise govern military life.

Going further, a complex system of classification exists in the U.S. Army that organizes individuals and whole units into hierarchies that are only loosely connected to rank. Regular army troops stand above reserve and National Guard troops. Combat veterans stand above troops who have not seen combat. Combat arms troops stand above support troops. Airborne troops stand above "legs." Special Operations troops stand above conventional troops, and so on. And members of "secret" organizations such as Delta Force or the CIA's paramilitary branch sit at the top of the pyramid, where they tend to attract all the awe and ire of minor gods. Such is the calculus of symbolic power in the U.S. Army.

Finally, it is worth noting that in the army, all of these differences are routinely encoded and displayed on the uniform itself, which functions as a text of sorts that soldiers "read" to establish practical understandings of where they "stand" in relation to one another. It is often the absence of these conventional signs that signifies that one is dealing with a member of a government agency or some secret task force. After all, not knowing—or, better, being prohibited from knowing—exactly who these individuals are and what they do (and have done) is precisely what makes them imaginatively and symbolically powerful.

This is important because I believe that, at the Abu Ghraib prison facility, lower enlisted troops regressively identified with individuals who, in a very Freudian sense, symbolically replaced individual ego ideals. Rank and regulations were thus trumped by "respect" at the prison, and a heavy dose of fantasy and idealization was introduced into the working relationships that developed among and between the various actors working in what came to be known as the "hard site." As Freud (1959, 57) once noted, "Conscience has no application to anything that is done for the sake of the object [that has taken the place of the ego ideal]; in the blindness of love remorselessness is carried to the pitch of a crime."[10]

So what, exactly, did Graner and the men and women who participated in the activities he organized during the night shift (4 P.M.–4 A.M.) do at the bequest of the various interrogators with whom they interacted? At the most general level, they stripped detainees naked, photographed them in sexually compromising positions, "hooded" them with sandbags and placed them in "stress positions" for long periods of time, intimidated them with dogs, and humiliated them by having female guards and interrogators come into physically close and culturally inappropriate contact with them. However, all of these measures had been pre-approved by the Bush administration and tested at various locations since the invasion of Afghanistan almost two years earlier. In a strict sense, none of these activities actually constituted "offenses." This was further confirmed in Frederick's court-martial testimony; he eventually claimed that, although interrogators had directed him to begin using a set of new techniques for "softening up" the prisoners in tier 1A,[11] they had not directly ordered him or soldiers operating under his supervision to commit the specific abuses for which they were eventually tried, which involved inflicting forms of physical violence and sexual humiliation on Iraqi prisoners that went beyond what the Pentagon had authorized.

Most of the *unauthorized* abuses committed by the "night shift" have been described in newsprint, and many were documented in the now famous Abu Ghraib photographs.[12] Here I will simply add that the depositions of the victims make it clear that they were routinely beaten, especially by Graner, and at least one detainee was raped while another prisoner was allegedly sodomized with a nightstick. Detainees were also forced to masturbate in front of female guards and to simulate homosexual and oral sex. In addition, several Iraqis had pictures of women drawn on their backs before being forced to bend over and spread their buttocks as if to submit to rape. They were also forced to eat pork, and at least one detainee had liquor poured into his mouth. Finally, the guards seemed to have taken special pleasure in nicknaming detainees ("Shit Boy," "Gilligan," "The Claw," "Mr. Clean") and openly joking about the humiliation and anguish they suffered.

The two questions I want to address in the remainder of this chapter, then, are (1) Why did the abuses perpetrated by Graner and the others take the particular forms they did? What are we to make of the human pyramids, the dog leash, episodes of forced masturbation, and real and threatened rape? And, more important, (2) What compelled Graner and the dozen or so others who have been implicated in the Abu Ghraib scandal to take matters into their own hands and push beyond the prescribed forms of what has since been defined as torture?

A Provisional Explanation

In regard to the first question, I suggest that once the lower enlisted MPs at Abu Ghraib were authorized and instructed to use sexual humiliation and other forms of taboo violation, along with sensory deprivation and extreme physical stress, to break down the Iraqi detainees in their charge, they began to project their own (sub)cultural assumptions regarding sex, gender, and domination onto the prisoners—and they began acting on and out those assumptions. This is also to say that an *elective affinity existed between the prescribed forms of humiliation outlined by Hersh's informant and attitudes toward sex, gender, and domination that already existed within the military subculture.* In other words, simulating sex with detainees and even sodomizing them were relatively "natural" extensions of the language of masculine power and domination that already existed within the ranks, and the literal enactment of these metaphorical relationships in a *prison* environment was already experientially familiar to Frederick and Graner, who imported scripts from their work as civilian corrections officers into a war zone to dominate, emasculate, and "break" the alleged criminals or enemies in their charge. Let me explain.

The language of masculine domination permeates everyday life in the U.S. Army.[13] By this I mean that, within the ranks, virility, strength, and power are openly equated with the phallus, and homophobic and misogynistic references are routinely used to connote weakness, subservience, and "otherness." Put differently, the U.S. Army is a place where being called an "animal," a "stud," or a "monster" is a recognizable compliment and where derogatory labels such as "pussy," "whiner," and "fag" are commonly attached to personnel who display inadequate levels of masculinity, aggression, or competence.

This language and the attitudes it reflects are, to a certain extent, representative of the cultural prejudices of the mostly male, eighteen- to twenty-five-year-old enlisted majority that makes up the U.S. military. The language is deployed with great effect during basic training, when new recruits are radically re-socialized and encouraged to display high levels of discipline, aggression, and "intestinal fortitude" as they confront various obstacles, including instructors' ongoing attempts to "break" them and compel them to quit (like "little girls"), a process often referred to as being "dogged out." Accordingly, the reward for succeeding in this environment—that is, for "sucking it up" and effectively demonstrating a high degree of commitment and competence—is the social conferring of "manhood," or the gift of phallic power. This repeatable rite of initiation has been instituted in such a way that those who go further and volunteer to attend the U.S. Army's various "whip me, beat me" schools eventually emerge as "alpha males" of sorts who are accorded inordinate degrees of "respect" for their demonstrated ability to suffer proudly and to do harm to others, pointing to the close tie that exists between sadomasochism and hyper-masculinity within the ranks (Goff 2006).[14]

As an extension of this, pornography is a pervasive component of barracks life in the U.S. Army, as is daily banter concerning both the real and fabricated sexual exploits of soldiers of all ranks. Moreover, in several units I belonged to, small-unit leaders worked hard to promote local mythologies concerning the extraordinary sexual powers of the soldiers in the unit, which were variously celebrated on duty and during the long bouts of drinking and storytelling that rounded out day-to-day life between deployments. It is not an overstatement to say that within the unit, it was implicitly understood that one's sexual appetite and virility were directly related to one's thirst for combat and potential for heroic self-sacrifice—and vice versa. As Stan Goff (2006) has made clear, "sex and war" interpenetrate and congeal to form a social-psychological complex within the American military, which may account, in part, for the pervasiveness of rape as a metaphor for military invasion and conquest; it translates the institutionalized celebration of male sexual potency into an affirmation of collective imperial potential.[15] Here, let me simply add that I once worked for a platoon sergeant who insisted that his troops parachute with a pair of "soiled" panties stuffed in their helmet liners to magically preserve their sexual powers on the battlefield.

Of course, things have changed a great deal in the past decade or so, and concerted efforts have been made to cultivate greater sensitivity regarding gender inequality and discrimination, sexual harassment and abuse, and domestic violence on U.S. Army installations in both the United States and abroad. I clearly remember the time in the late 1980s when units began briefing soldiers on the topic of sexual harassment. It coincided with the evolution of co-educational basic training and the formal prohibition of formerly traditional PT (physical training) songs with lyrics such as:

If I die on the Russian front,
Bury me with a Russian cunt,
If I die on the Cuban shore,
Bury me with a Cuban whore.

However, what I have referred to as the language of "masculine domination" has continued to survive and even flourish as a *"joking"* register of speech used by both men and women in the course of everyday military life. Thus, while both male and female enlisted soldiers exercise greater discretion with their use of language than ever before, it is not altogether uncommon to hear comments such as "She (the First Sergeant) is fucking us again" or " "we're always taking it up the ass," among enlisted personnel in co-ed military units today. In fact, one female noncommissioned officer who was serving in Iraq when the Abu Ghraib prison scandal broke told me that when female soldiers in her unit attempted to make their living spaces "prettier," other women responded by saying, "That's so gay!" and by calling the women "fags," thereby ventriloquizing the masculine voice to which I have been referring.

Interestingly, a similar language saturates everyday life inside the walls of the American penitentiary system. However, there the metaphors of male virility and rape are routinely made literal, and real sexual violence is used as a tool to establish and maintain a complex masculine hierarchy. As Ian O'Donnell (2004, 242) has noted, "Prison rape is an acting out of power roles within an all-male, authoritarian environment where strength and dominance are emphasized. This is why men who anally penetrate young and vulnerable men against their will are first, not considered rapists and second, do not incur the stigma that such an offence would attract if perpetrated outside the prison walls." Emasculation is also, therefore, a dominant theme within the American prison system, where "weaker" men are forced into submissive, "female" roles and labeled "punks," "fags," and "fairies," effectively reinforcing heterosexual norms (O'Donnell 2004, 243). Finally, it is important to note that the guards whose job it is to maintain order in this hyper-masculine environment necessarily participate in this system, and they do so by deploying whatever resources are available to them to communicate and maintain their dominance over the "criminal" population.

Thus, it seems that in the military, where a vast array of formal rules, regulations, ranks, and ready-made mechanisms for sublimating sexual and aggressive energies exists, latent cultural assumptions regarding masculine domination generally manifest themselves in informal figures of speech and tolerated (if not authorized) attitudes and expressions of various sorts. In prison, however, where the scope of the social universe has been radically constricted and rendered (at least temporarily) inescapable, a similar set of attitudes and assumptions are actualized to separate the population into masculine predators, feminized victims, and guards charged with regulating violence and preserving a highly gendered social order.

Considering this, it is telling that Special Agent Paul Arthur, who headed the first investigation of the Abu Ghraib abuses, initially claimed, "They [the MPS] were just joking around, having some fun, on the night shift."[16] Similarly, at one point in Graner's court-martial hearing, his lawyer suggested that piling naked Iraqi detainees into a pyramid was simply an innocent parody of American cheerleading. Further, in response to the question of why she and her fellow guards chose to photograph detainees being sexually humiliated on tier IA, Lynndie England replied, "We thought it looked funny so pictures were taken."[17] In each of these cases, then, military personnel defended the abusers' actions by casting them as a kind of "hazing" or game that bored American soldiers played with detainees who, in their minds, apparently deserved far worse. In short, it was all a joke.

However, if the testimony of the defendants in the abuse trials means anything, then we are confronted with a disconnect; there is almost universal agreement that the abuses at Abu Ghraib violated both the U.S. Uniform Code of Military Justice and international humanitarian law. Yet the perpetrators of the abuses seem to have understood them as pranks—not serious crimes. Insofar as it is possible to explain this slippage, I refer back to the fuzzy boundary separating military and prison life that I mentioned earlier. It seems clear that Abu Ghraib, a military prison staffed in part by the former civilian corrections officers Charles Graner and Chip Frederick in the midst of a conflict marked by the Bush administration's *criminalization* of the "enemy," became a hybrid space of sorts where latent (sub)cultural understandings of masculinity and domination were acutely freed to manifest themselves in extremely cruel and brutal ways and still be viewed as "jokes" or pranks by the military personnel externalizing those understandings.

It is also worth noting that a number of the incriminating pictures that were taken, including the famous photo of England controlling a detainee with a dog leash, involved female guards demonstrating their dominance over male Iraqi prisoners—dominance that was typically expressed in the form of female guards laughing and gesturing at the genitalia of naked Iraqi prisoners or standing behind them and actually simulating anal intercourse. Thus, if the photos are reliable representations of what went on on tier IA, female soldiers tended to victimize Iraqi men via acts of symbolic castration and sodomy, reinscribing the schemes to which I have already referred. In fact, in this respect the cycle of sexual domination seems to have taken the form of a generalized exchange where the alleged Arab "terrorists" were dominated by American women, who were dominated by American men, who, at some level, viewed insurgent violence as an expression of Arab dominance and control.[18]

Alternatively, the pictures of Graner and Frederick typically show the men either perpetrating acts of *physical violence* against the Iraqi prisoners or posing in positions that signify their absolute control over both the Iraqi detainees and the American women. Further, the depositions provided by the Iraqi victims of abuse make it clear that Graner routinely beat and physically intimidated the Iraqi prisoners in his charge—acts not associated with the female soldiers accused of abuse. Graner's proclivity for physical violence was further supported by the testimony of Joseph Darby (the soldier who eventually blew the whistle on the abuses), who claimed that at one point Graner had explained, "The Christian in me says [abusing detainees is] wrong, but the corrections officer in me says, 'I love to make a grown man piss himself.'"[19] Frederick also made it clear at his court-martial that once he and his fellow MPs began playing an active role in "breaking" Iraqi detainees, Graner began improvising and orchestrating scenes of abuse to demonstrate his control of the cellblock to fellow soldiers, especially to the female, lower-enlisted soldiers with whom he was romantically involved—namely, Private First Class Sabrina Harmann and Private First Class Lynndie England.

This is interesting because when I questioned a group of former (female) soldiers about the roles England and Harmann played in the Abu Ghraib scandal, they responded by saying that in the U.S. Army most women either "want to be men" or they "want to have men." To them it was obvious that the two women "wanted something" from Graner and were willing to make him happy to get it.[20] In short, they completely rejected the notion that the co-ed organization of the MP unit might have had a hyper-masculinizing effect on the female soldiers or that they had taken it upon themselves to torment Iraqi prisoners. In fact, one soldier complained that the women in her unit were really only "tough" and "aggressive" when men were *absent*; she claimed that once a male soldier showed up, the women normally deferred to him and became passive. When asked why, she claimed that it made it possible for women to "get over"—that is, to do less (or, at least, less arduous) work. Another former soldier claimed that the majority of enlisted women in her unit had been "girlie girls" who had adopted an explicitly feminine (and usually subordinate) position vis-à-vis the men in the co-ed unit at least partly for this reason. In the course of our discussion, it became clear that this had placed pressure on other women in the unit (like herself) to follow suit or risk ridicule. Meanwhile, she claimed that the men (like many women) responded to the "girlie-girl" phenomenon with a certain degree of ambivalence; they resented that the women were not "pulling their weight," but they also enjoyed their sense of dominance. Finally, she claimed that "almost everyone" in her unit was having sex, so it was not surprising to her that Graner had been involved with both women.[21] This last claim was echoed by a female noncommissioned officer who complained that she had had to manage numerous relationship dramas linked to sex between soldiers while she was stationed in Iraq and that she was even forced to prohibit male and female soldiers from pulling guard duty together be- cause the potential for sexual fraternization was so great.[22] She added that she had been more afraid of being raped on her military base in Iraq than she had ever been "at home."[23]

If these particular claims have any general relevance—and the Abu Ghraib case seems to suggest that they might—then sexual tensions and gender relations are affecting conduct in co-ed military units in Iraq in ways and to degrees that they normally do not during peacetime. Or better, perhaps, tensions that are normally latent during peacetime seem to be openly mani- festing themselves in Iraq, where wartime fears and anxieties, coupled with various forms of deprivation, frustration, and the constriction of social net- works, appear to be altering the ways soldiers normally relate to one an- other. In the Abu Ghraib case, Graner is alleged to have forced hooded Iraqi detainees to masturbate in front of England as a birthday present, and it seems that a good deal of the abuse that took place was related to relation- ship pressures and issues of gender and authority among and between Amer- ican soldiers working in the prison.

To sum things up, the male MPs convicted of abusing detainees at Abu Ghraib behaved in *physically violent* ways toward the detainees in their charge. They were also responsible for assigning the female MPs specific roles in the scenes of abuse they staged and photographed, and those roles almost always involved *sexually humiliating* detainees by forcing them to submit to simu- lated acts of sodomy (perpetrated by female MPs), oral sex (prisoner to prisoner), or other forms of behavior that were culturally offensive to the prisoners and expressive of the fact that they had been "broken" or were "owned" by American women as well as American men. In keeping with the rhetoric of the global war on terror, then, the guards treated their Arab victims like imprisoned *criminals*. However, for them this meant both viewing them as and forcing them to act like *animals* (specifically dogs). It also meant *emasculating* (or de-virilizing) them in an effort to strip them of their "manhood" and honor. And it meant branding the prisoners with demeaning nicknames, effectively reducing them to *property* or playthings of the guards. Above all, however, it meant *tormenting* the detainees in their charge, first to produce a sign that might confirm the prisoner's guilt, and second to *punish* the prisoner for his or her anti-Americanism. In short, it meant placing the Arab detainees in an inescapable double bind: if the prisoners passively accepted being abused, they were treated with disgust, nicknamed, and perpetually tormented; if they resisted, they were treated as dangerous "enemies" that needed to be broken and taught a very physical lesson about domination and resistance.

Having come this far, however, it is also crucial to understand that Graner and his co-abusers were also trapped in a latticework of contradictions and double binds that distorted their judgments and behavior in significant ways. In fact, as I have alluded, I believe that, in large part, this was what motivated the abuses. To clarify this, however, a very short history lesson is in order.

Indochina, Algeria, Iraq, and the "Destruction of Conscience"

In 1964, Peter Paret published a short monograph entitled *French Revolutionary Warfare from Indochina to Algeria*. The book provided a detailed analysis of French counterinsurgency doctrine that quickly became required reading at the U.S. Army War College, heavily influencing the development of U.S. unconventional and psychological warfare doctrine for the duration of the Cold War. Part of what is remarkable about the book is that, rather than beginning with a series of technical notes about the conduct of counterinsurgency warfare, Paret begins by noting that when the French began to prosecute the wars in Indochina and then Algeria to preserve their colonial dominion, they suffered from a dangerous lack of popular support for the war at home. At the time, France was a multiparty liberal democracy riddled with social, economic, and political divisions. Therefore, it was virtually impossible for the French government to manufacture a counter-ideology to legitimate war that could compete with the manifestos of national liberation promoted by their insurgent enemies in the colonies. The solution to this

dilemma, however, turned out to be frighteningly simple: the French government vociferously claimed that the colonial insurgents had forced France to
participate in a *global war against terror* whose new frontlines had become
Indochina and Algeria:

> The Army, it declared, was engaged in a permanent world-wide revo-
> lutionary conflict in which the differences between anticolonialism,
> non-Western nationalism, and Communism were insignificant, and in
> which the traditional distinctions between war and peace had disap-
> peared. . . . Not military power alone, but all means at the disposal of a
> highly developed society had to be committed. The war, furthermore,
> could end only with the effective—if not total—defeat of the enemy;
> negotiations, compromise, the acceptance of limited goals could only
> damage one's own cause. (Paret 1964, 29–30)

Privately, however, one of the principal authors of the French counterinsurgency doctrine admitted that such wars are fundamentally unwinnable and
that the best that could be hoped for would be to stem the spread of terrorist
cells and reduce violence to levels that the French public might eventually
come to accept (Paret 1964, 29–30). In so many ways, then, the French
colonial wars (and the war in Algeria in particular) were dominated by
ideological concerns; they were conflicts in which winning the hearts and
minds of the vast civilian populations of France and its colonies represented
the keys to victory. This fact made psychological warfare, the control and
manipulation of the media, the dissemination of propaganda, and the tactical
use of both terrorism and torture the means on which both sides relied to
wage what turned out to be protracted, bloody, and traumatic struggles. Of
course, in the end the French were forced to concede defeat; the contradictions underpinning the war effort in Algeria fractured both the military and
civil society in dangerous ways, and the emergence of the Organisation de
l'Armée Secrète made it clear that the conflict in Algeria was actually manufacturing terrorism within the ranks of the French military.

Interestingly, in 1966, in the wake of the French defeat in Algeria and in the
midst of a war the United States had inherited from the French and redefined
as the "frontline" in a global war against communism, the American anthropologist Marshall Sahlins warned against repeating France's tragedies. He
claimed that, in the end, "Advanced anti-communism trades places with the
enemy. It becomes opposite communism, and 'opposites' are things alike in
every respect save one" (Sahlins 2000, 249). Thus, he predicted that in its final
stages, "Vietnam will be marked by the imitation of the enemy's techniques"

(Sahlins 2000, 249). In Sahlins's estimation, the contradictions inherent in the U.S. war effort made it inevitable that, like the French, the Americans ultimately would become the very thing they were committed to destroying. "Winning" in Vietnam could and would only come at the cost of "losing" American hearts and minds.

To demonstrate this point, Sahlins drew attention to the activities of American advisers who moved from village to village in Vietnam to spread propaganda and organize and train anticommunist cells to resist Chinese domination—a task they learned to perform from studying Maoist revolutionary warfare doctrine. However, the Americans' imitation of their Chinese enemies only began there, for the work of these American advisers frequently went beyond the mere education or "motivation" of the civil defense forces to the "forced destruction of people's beliefs" (Sahlins 2000, 249). In the worst-case scenarios, the advisors' work involved "the tortuously exacted confession and conversion" of captured communist insurgents (Sahlins 2000, 249).

Here it is worth briefly quoting Paret's study of French counterinsurgency doctrine: "If the Algerian war was a conflict of ideologies . . . the *conversion* of the enemy constituted a mission of central importance. The winning of Moslem adherence could justify the French stand better than anything else, in their own eyes and in world opinion" (Paret 1964, 62; my emphasis). This being the case, the French, armed with the Marxist psychology of Chakhotin, firsthand knowledge of Chinese indoctrination methods used to revolutionize the Viet Minh, and the help of Catholic social psychologists such as Georges Sauge, developed a rigorous method for dealing with their most thoroughly indoctrinated enemies. "The first step in the process was to 'disintegrate the individual.' The internee was isolated, his fears and guilts were exploited by his monitor" (Paret 1964, 64). Then, once the internee's identity and convictions had been disrupted, they were exposed as fictions and replaced by new truths. In simple terms, once the ideological demons had been exorcised from the enemy's mind (a process the French called "*lavage de crane,*" or "brainwashing"), a secondary process of "brain filling (*bourrage de crâne*)" would commence with the goal of bringing about a true conversion (Paret 1964, 64).

Sahlins noted that the American advisers he met were particularly adept at facilitating this procedure and that their successes owed to the fact that they eschewed the use of physical force, relying instead on the methods the communist opposition had developed: they psychologically destroyed their prisoners and patients. In simple terms, after the Vietcong prisoner had been brutalized by his South Vietnamese captors, the Americans defied his expectations of further physical torture or execution by identifying with him, befriending him, and shielding him against both real and imaginary threats. Then, using time and confusion to their advantage, they issued an appeal to the prisoner to reciprocate and provide them with a bit of useful information to prevent the compassionate Americans from having to turn him back over to the real enemy—the South Vietnamese.

The principal goal of this procedure was simply to elicit a confession, which had the double benefit of yielding military intelligence and (by way of betrayal and guilt) severing the prisoner's bond with his comrades, thereby bringing him to what the interrogators described as "the lowest point in his life in terms of meaning and existence" (Sahlins 2000, 252). Finally, in what Sahlins claims was an "unintentional parody" of the Chinese techniques, the prisoner was then handed back to his South Vietnamese handlers and informed that his confession was not a sufficient guarantee of individual salvation. To be reborn as a full-fledged anticommunist, further rehabilitation and reeducation would be necessary. At that point, the prisoner's options were simple: voluntary conversion or a disgraced and solitary death.

Finally—and most important, perhaps—the interrogators Sahlins questioned admitted that they secretly respected and admired the Vietnamese prisoners they simply could not break, attesting to the emotional interdependence that developed between the Vietnamese enemy and the American adviser in the arena of interrogation. "The prisoner's successful resistance is the interrogator's greatest satisfaction: his strength proves their strength, his will their will, his conviction their conviction" (Sahlins 2000, 253). In other words, the Americans interrogators had to fail to "convert" Vietnamese prisoners to confirm the righteousness of their cause and preserve their own hearts and minds. They had fallen into the kind of "hopeless contradiction" that ultimately guaranteed the American defeat in Vietnam (Sahlins 2000, 253).

A Second Look at the Abu Ghraib Abuses

Transforming a chosen Iraqi detainee into an intelligence asset at Abu Ghraib certainly seems to have entailed "breaking" him or her—that is, it involved bringing the detainee to the "lowest point in his life in terms of meaning and existence" (Sahlins 2000, 252). We now know that in Vietnam this point was reached at the moment of confession, and it was followed by a "rehabilitative" process of some kind. However, it is not clear whether this held true in the Iraqi case. The Iraqi prisoners at Abu Ghraib were subjected to pro-tracted abuse that involved the violation of cultural and religious taboos, sexual humiliation, dog attacks, and compromising photographs,[24] but none of the investigations conducted in the wake of the abuses disclosed whether this nightly drama was part of a larger process that might have been followed by clever American interrogators promising to burn photos and release and protect prisoners in exchange for information. Instead, the official reports all present the abuse as examples of the kind of naked coercion that television would have people believe is familiar to American police detectives but is utterly alien to American soldiers.[25] We are thus confronted with important questions. Were the abuses at Abu Ghraib really linked to an attempt to implement a radically new American strategy for combating terror? Or did they actually demonstrate residual traces of the American counterinsur-gency strategy from Vietnam? Were they attempts at conversion or literal examples of naked coercion? Not surprisingly, perhaps, I think the answer to this question is "both."[26]

First, it is important to recognize that the bulk of the abuses at Abu Ghraib were committed by troops assigned to the 205th Military Intelligence Brigade (a conventional military-intelligence unit permanently stationed in Wiesbaden, Germany) and the 372d Military Police Company (a conven-tional U.S. Army Reserve unit from Cresaptown, Maryland), outfits that had not been deployed to Afghanistan and that had little specialized training regarding operations in the Middle East. In other words, the majority of the accused abusers at Abu Ghraib were ordinary enlisted soldiers assigned to support units—not CIA / Special Operations personnel or private contractors —and they were almost completely unfamiliar with post–9 / 11 changes to the protocol for the treatment of enemy combatants prior to their arrival in Iraq. In other words, they had been trained to conduct affairs in much the same way Sahlins described, and they became familiar with the new, post–9 / 11 guidelines and techniques for dealing with enemy combatants "on the job."

Next, it is important to recognize that even if selected prisoners were not actually being prepared by U.S. handlers to operate as "snitches" or infor-mants under the threat of blackmail in one or more U.S.-run detention facili-ties, the calculated use of sexual shame and humiliation that had formed the backbone of the Pentagon's covert "Copper Green" program had undoubt-edly made its way into Abu Ghraib via members of what the guards called the OGAS.[27] As the former CIA counterterrorism chief Cofer Black put it in testimony before Congress in September 2002, "After 9 / 11 the gloves came off," and it was decided that bringing terrorists to "justice" would require the adoption of extraordinary measures. Thus, several new counterterrorist task forces staffed by veteran CIA and Special Forces operatives were created and given the proverbial green light to do whatever had to be done to capture or kill suspected terrorists—including conducting secret interrogations at Abu Ghraib and other detention centers.[28] In fact, the Fay and Jones report clearly states that "the CIA's detention and interrogation practices contributed to a loss of accountability and abuse at Abu Ghraib. . . . Local CIA officers convinced military leaders that they should be allowed to operate outside established local rules and procedures" (Fay and Jones 2004, 43). In addition, a small army of privately contracted military and intelligence personnel was recruited to participate in America's global war on terror (at least four of whom were eventually alleged to have participated in the Abu Ghraib abuses), and little seems to be known about the interrogation practices or even identities of some of these personnel. However, it is obvious now that many of them were poorly trained; they were informed that the Geneva Convention protections did not apply to the Iraqi prisoners; and the interrogation techniques they used resulted in the deaths of a number of detainees, including Manadel al-Jamadi, whose iced corpse was featured in several of the infamous Abu Ghraib photos.

Again, however, I think it would be a mistake to think that experienced operatives *radically* broke with conventional, time-tested strategies for culling information from captured prisoners. In fact, Colonel Steve Kleinman, who was sent to Iraq in 2003 as part of a special delegation to advise on the interrogation of detainees, claimed that the problem was that the interrogators were trained on a Cold War model that was not applicable in Iraq (Mayer 2008, 247). As a result, they consistently asked the wrong kinds of questions, and when they received true responses they mistook them for lies, which led to a progressive ratcheting up of force (Mayer 2008, 247). Considering this, at least some of the OGA interrogators at Abu Ghraib actually may have been using methods very similar to those described by Sahlins. The key difference, of course, would have been that under existing circumstances, doing so would have required the U.S. Military Police personnel assigned to the prison to play the same role that the South Vietnamese torturers had played for American CIA and Special Forces interrogators during the Vietnam era. Thus, a structural formula for abuse may have been generated that involved American prison guards terrorizing Iraqi detainees via physical beatings, death threats, and the calculated manipulation of their cultural and religious taboos to help prepare them for their "conversion" experience.

All of this is, however, speculative. What is most important is the simple fact that in the overcrowded wards of the prison in the fall of 2003, when American morale was low, tensions were high, and the majority of the MPS on duty were reservists who had been forced to leave civilian life to serve in Iraq, the guards became increasingly sadistic. In fact, U.S. officials later called their behavior "illegal" and "aberrant," charging that the abuses they perpetrated went far beyond the already expanded list of acceptable interrogation practices. The big question is, "Why?" Was individual psychopathology the driving force behind the abuses? Did a few poorly supervised and trained bad apples simply take advantage of a set of confusing wartime circumstances to act out their sadistic fantasies? Or did the myriad contradictions inherent in the U.S. project in Iraq create a situation on the ground that somehow turned ordinary American soldiers into "criminals"? Just how over-determined were the abuses?

My own sense is that the sadism at Abu Ghraib became more intense during the period just mentioned *primarily* because, as had been the case in Vietnam, the enemy's refusal to be "broken" had become the only confirmation that America's "auxiliary" soldiers had to affirm the righteousness of America's wrongful presence in Iraq. If the detainees were not dangerous terrorists, there was no need for the prison or the guards, no need to have left families and jobs behind, no need to suffer and witness suffering daily in the dark recesses of a prison on the other side of the world, no need for the expected tour of duty to have been extended beyond September—no need for war. Thus, from the perspective of guards, the Arab prisoners had to offer up signs of their guilt, signs that would confirm that they held America and Americans in contempt, signs that might hint at their complicity in the ongoing campaign of attacks against U.S. targets or even in the capture and abuse of Private Jessica Lynch—signs that might allow the guards to indulge their fantasies of engaging the enemy in personal combat. Thus, a group of mostly innocent Iraqi detainees was subjected to increasingly severe beatings, insults, threats, degradations—acts of violence meant to produce anxiety, provoke resistance, and reveal hidden objects. When these special techniques generated "signs" of Iraqi resistance (in the forms of curses, prayers, refusals to comply, or psychotic behavior), the mandate to "break" them became refreshingly real for guards such as Charles Graner. I suspect that something similar held true for the more than one hundred other American soldiers who have been court-martialed for abusing detainees since the onset of hostilities in March 2003.

Diane Liang, a former member of the 327th Military Police Company stationed at Abu Ghraib during the time the abuses took place, supported this view in part when she answered the question of why the abuses occurred by saying, "I think it was just out of curiosity and boredom and anger." She continued,

> You're there 12 hours a day, every day, and you're pissed off at every-thing going on around you. We were told we were going home in September. You want to take out your anger against other people in the unit, but you can't do that. So some people took it out on the pris-oners. What [the MPS] did was wrong, but not everyone realizes that everyone in there attacked the Coalition forces and tried to kill us.[29]

Of course, we now know that not all the Iraqis sent to tier 1A were dangerous "terrorists." But Specialist Liang's testimony makes it clear that, for the guards, this notion operated as a convenient rationalization for the wrongful mistreatment of prisoners. Moreover, this rationalization was rein-forced by virtue of the regressive identification the MPS developed with the unconventional-warfare specialists who applauded their efforts and provided them with a sense of being part of something bigger and more important than perpetual guard duty.

Conclusion

In 1965, Sahlins went on a fact-finding mission to Vietnam, where he inter-viewed Special Forces and CIA personnel charged with culling information from captured Vietcong insurgents. His findings were published in 1966 in the article "The Destruction of Conscience in Vietnam," which claimed that American advisers were actually losing their hearts and minds rather than winning those of the Vietnamese people in a conflict hopelessly contami-nated by lies and contradictions. At bottom, Sahlins argued that the Ameri-cans were victimizing innocent Vietnamese to advertise U.S. military power (and the willingness to use it) to the expansionist government in China, and that in the course of doing so they were committing the very crimes they sought to prevent the Chinese from propagating—a fact that American ad-visers could not afford to accept, and one that they could deny only by finding and destroying Vietnamese communists, even where they did not exist. In Sahlins's words, "It is Vietnam's tragedy to have been chosen the battleground for America's stand against the forces of evil. . . . All the compromises and the self-deceptions of the Americans, and all the brutalization, originate in this contradiction" (Sahlins 2000, 233, 238).

Forty years later, Sahlins's analysis seems eerily applicable to the ongoing war in Iraq, a conflict whose real purpose seems to have been to advertise U.S. power to the "Axis of Evil" and to "shock and awe" those audacious enough to explore its limits. Indeed, it does not seem unreasonable to say that it has been Iraq's tragedy to have been chosen as the "frontline" in another war of transcendent purpose that key policymakers believe is America's historical destiny to fight and win. Moreover, the notorious abuses at the Abu Ghraib prison facility and the string of murders and massacres that have come to light in their wake make it clear that the contradictions underpinning the war have created a schizophrenic situation on the ground that is daily destroying Arab lives and American hearts and minds. They are calling into question how American anti-terrorists differ from the "evildoers" they are attempting to destroy—a question that neither American advisers nor policymakers can afford to entertain.

In this chapter I have attempted to show how some of these large-order contradictions have manifested themselves on the ground in Iraq. In doing so I have suggested that one of the central problems at Abu Ghraib was that the lower-enlisted soldiers convicted of abusing prisoners began to operate with a sense of impunity and self-righteousness that actually rivaled that displayed by their superiors. Here I am referring to the same sense of impunity and entitlement that inspired U.S. commanders to occupy Saddam Hussein's former palaces and prison chambers in the first place—a move that openly mocked the dissipated power of the former Iraqi regime and that flaunted America's ability to remake Iraq in its own image, inadvertently helping to catalyze an anti-imperialist insurgency in the country.

Interestingly, virtually every official investigation of the Abu Ghraib abuses agrees that the guilty guards operated with an almost pathological sense of impunity, and they all claim that this occurred because they were inadequately supervised; the abusers' aberrant behavior would have been held in check if the chain of command had not been fragmented. However, the fragmentation of the chain of command at Abu Ghraib seems to have been caused by a surplus rather than deficit of governmental authority, and in the case of Abu Ghraib, the military mantra "lead by example" seems to have worked too well rather than not well enough. Moreover, it seems to me that arguing that the problems at Abu Ghraib derived from a lack of adequate supervision is akin to admitting that, left to their own devices,

American troops would and will continue to denigrate and abuse the Arab-qua-"terrorist" enemies they encounter in Iraq and elsewhere. In short, this popular diagnosis, which will inevitable lead to a new emphasis on monitoring the ethical conduct of the *individual* soldier's actions, is largely self-deceptive and will not put an end to future abuses.

Unfortunately, Pentagon officials seem incapable of recognizing—or, at least, acknowledging—that the American soldiers fighting in Iraq and elsewhere today have been placed in a position where they must "lose" their hearts and minds to win on the battlefield. By this I mean that American combatants must provoke anti-American sentiments and create hatred and disorder in Iraq to justify being there (and everywhere else) to "win the peace." Poor policy decisions have thus trapped these soldiers in a perpetual double bind, and if the impulse to abuse innocents exists within the American ranks, I believe its existence is linked much more closely to a set of institutional pathologies than it is to individual psychopathologies.

Going further, insofar as these dedicated soldiers are acting as instruments of U.S. foreign policy in a series of new wars, they are inevitably exporting a (sub)culture that equates masculinity with violence, power, and control—that is, they are exporting a set of values that has been imprinted in the course of their military training and that is expressed, to greater and lesser degrees, in the forms of digital entertainment (music, games, pornography) soldiers consume in their downtime. Moreover, they are exporting these cultural forms in the context of a larger effort to "influence" local ways of life and transform an entire region. Every military commander is aware of this, and I would like to believe that they are all also aware of the inevitable risks that occupying such a position entails. As the abuses at Abu Ghraib (to use one example) have shown, culture is an integral dimension of the ongoing American war on terror, and until a greater emphasis is placed on understanding and influencing the American military (sub)culture, American military neocolonialism is bound to generate more unintended, but not necessarily unpredictable, tragedies.

Notes

The bulk of this chapter was written in December 2004 and circulated as an unpublished manuscript titled, "The Destruction of Conscience Revisited." Another copy was circulated at the Global Counterinsurgency Conference, University of Chicago, 2008. I thank everyone who read the paper and provided me with feedback and encouragement.

Thanks also to Seungsook Moon and Maria Höhn for their support and for the comments they contributed to the present version of the essay. Without their encouragement, it would not exist.

1. Seymour M. Hersh, "Torture at Abu Ghraib," *New Yorker*, 14 March 2010. For a complete list of government documents related to detainee abuse since 2003, see http://www.aclu.org/accountability/released.html.

2. See Amnesty International, "Beyond Abu Ghraib: Detention and Torture in Iraq," 6 March 2006, available online at http://www.amnesty.org/en/library/info/MDE 14/001/2006 (accessed 14 March 2010); American Civil Liberties Union, "ACLU Torture FOIA [Freedom of Information Act] Search," available online at http://www.aclu.org/torturefoiasearch (accessed 14 March 2010); Seymour Hersh, "The Gray Zone: How a Secret Pentagon Program came to Abu Ghraib." *New Yorker*, 24 May 2004.

3. American Civil Liberties Union, "Army Documents Show Senior Official Reportedly Pushed Limits on Detainees," 2 May 2006, available online at http://www.aclu.org/safefree/torture/25406prs20060502.html (accessed 14 March 2010).

4. James Schlesinger and colleagues (2004) note that plans were made approximately one year before the invasion of Iraq to house as many as 100,000 enemy prisoners of war once hostilities commenced. The same report claims that since November 2001, a cumulative total of approximately 50,000 detainees have been in the custody of U.S. forces worldwide.

5. Hersh, "The Gray Zone," 4.

6. Ibid.

7. Ibid.

8. The American military actually has a great deal of experience combating insurgency. However, until recently this form of warfare was the almost exclusive province of the U.S. Army Special Forces, which deployed its advisers overseas to work with indigenous police and military units on "Foreign Internal Defense" missions. In Iraq, however, the invasion and subsequent occupation resulted in the dissolution of indigenous police and military forces, and it turned the occupying army into an incumbent power forced to defend itself against what were, at least initially, treated as "terrorist" attacks (despite the fact that the U.S. State Department had defined "terrorism" as violence directed against "non-combatant" targets).

9. Steven Stefanowicz was an employee of CACI International. In his official report, Lieutenant-General Antonio M. Taguba (2004, 48) claimed that he suspected that Stefanowitcz and several other civilian contractors "were either directly or indirectly responsible for the abuse at Abu Ghraib," and he recommended that they be disciplined by their civilian employer: Hersh, "Torture at Abu Ghraib." According to executives at CACI, relations between the company and U.S. Department of Defense remain strong: CACI International, "CACI Responds to Allegations in the Media about Its Employees in Iraq and to Financial Community Interests," press release, 5 May 2004, available online at http://www.caci.com/about/news/news2004/05_05_04_NR.html (accessed 14 March 2010).

10. Interestingly, this notion is complimented in important ways in appendix G of Schlesinger et al. 2004, which is aptly titled "Psychological Stresses," and it refers to the Sanford Prison Experiment and a range of material related to the social psychology of aggression to suggest that the prison environment itself played a role in distorting the disposition to power and moral vision of the Abu Ghraib abusers.

11. These techniques included, but were not limited to, placing detainees in stress positions, stripping them and depriving them of sleep and warmth, keeping them hooded for long periods of time, and intimidating them with dogs. Alfred W. McCoy (2006) has documented the CIA's development of these and other unconventional interrogation techniques since the Cold War, making it clear that they were not invented by lower-enlisted soldiers.

12. The fact that photos taken with digital cameras were such an important part of the Abu Ghraib drama ought not to be overlooked. In my opinion, a strong argument could potentially be made that the incriminating photos the abusers took were symptomatic of the degree to which the enlisted ranks of the American military value storytelling, war trophies, cell phones, and pornography—all of which were condensed in the Abu Ghraib case. In fact, the commander of the 870th MP company at Abu Ghraib was court-martialed for taking nude photos of the female soldiers in his command and storing them on a government computer. However, I have chosen to say little about the photos in this essay because I think they deserve an essay in their own right. I hope that others take the time to analyze them in depth.

13. It is important to note that the claims I make in this portion of the essay derive from my own experiences as a U.S. Army infantryman and Special Operations soldier (January 1986–July 1992) and from conversations with both active-duty and former members of the military since. Therefore, although I believe that my claims are generally valid, I must also acknowledge that in many units they may be the exception rather than the rule.

14. It would not be difficult for me to offer an array of personal anecdotes to illustrate these points. However, in his recent, self-published book, Stan Goff, a retired master sergeant and former Delta Force operative, provides a plethora of such examples and does so with greater honesty and erudition than I am capable of here or elsewhere. Therefore, interested readers should consult Goff 2006.

15. For more on rape and war, see Brownmiller 1993; Stiglmayer (1994); Barstow (2001).

16. Quoted in Josh White, "MPS Blamed for Abu Ghraib Abuse," *Washington Post*, 4 August 2004, A1.

17. Quoted in Jacob Laksin, "Lynndie and the Left," 31 August 2004, available online at http://frontpagemag.com//Articles/ReadArticle.asp?ID=14883 (accessed 14 March 2010).

18. Interestingly, Xavier Amador, a psychologist called on by the defense in Private First Class Lynndie England's criminal trial, later testified that her " 'overly compliant' personality made her incapable of making an independent judgment about participating in the mistreatment and photographing of Iraqi prisoners at the Abu Ghraib prison in Baghdad": *New York Times*, 24 September 2004, *Testimony on Abu Ghraib*.

Likewise, Specialist Sabrina Harman was described by a prosecution witness at her court-martial as "a great person, always willing to help anybody." She was also described as being kindly, caring, and good to the Iraqis living in al-Hillah: T. A. Badger, "Female Soldier convicted in Abu Ghraib scandal apologizes for abusing Iraqi prisoners," Associated Press, 17 May 2005. Her aberrant behavior inside the Abu Ghraib prison was thus chalked up to a combination of poor judgment, a lack of knowledge regarding rules pertaining to the treatment of prisoners, and Charles Graner's malignant influence. Both of the women directly involved in the scandal were thus portrayed at their court-martials as passive (female) rather than active (male) participants in the abuse, again reproducing the notion that power, agency, and physical violence are masculine characteristics.

19. Quoted in David Finkel and Christian Davenport, "Records Paint Dark Portrait of Guard," *Washington Post*, 5 June 2004.

20. I conducted several unstructured interviews with former female soldiers who had become involved with the Veterans Administration or with the Veterans of Foreign Wars when they returned from Iraq. All of the soldiers were former enlisted personnel who had served in support units. The views expressed in these interviews may *not* reflect wider realities in the U.S. military very accurately; however, I think they do point to gender tensions that have emerged in the context of the conflict in Iraq that are worthy of further investigation.

21. It became clear in the course of our discussion that these sexual relations took many forms, ranging from voluntary consensual sex to sex for money or privileges.

22. This female noncommissioned officer also invoked the classic "dyke" versus "whore" distinction to explain how difficult it had been for her, as a heterosexual woman in a committed relationship, to deal with male soldiers—especially in Iraq, where more than ever soldiers seem to view refusing sex as a form of perversion: see Hampf 2004.

23. Another female soldier told me that two female soldiers in her unit had been raped in Iraq, but she added, "They should have known better than to be alone with the guys. . . . Male soldiers only think about three things: drinking, sports, and sex—and in Iraq, where you work twelve hours a day and you need outside contacts to get booze, [the lower-enlisted male soldiers] are sex crazed. . . . They act like they'll die if they have to go one day without it." It is also worth noting that reported cases of sexual assault within the U.S. military have skyrocketed since the invasion of Iraq in 2003. In 2002, the U.S. Army reported 783 cases of sexual assault. By 2004, the figure had risen to 1,700, and in 2005, it rose an additional 40 percent to 2,374 cases.

24. In the Arab world, dogs are generally considered "unclean" and polluting animals. The tactical use of dogs to break prisoners was therefore part of a larger, well-developed interrogation strategy predicated on a basic knowledge of Arab culture and psychology.

25. Not surprisingly, a large number of the personnel assigned to interrogate and guard the prisoners at Abu Ghraib were army reservists and privately contracted operatives who had been employed as police or prison guards in the United States before they arrived in Iraq. This is significant because in the U.S. penal system, criminals are

frequently detained, threatened with compromising information, and then released on the condition that they work as informants, or "snitches," to help authorities penetrate larger criminal networks. Given this, I think it is plausible to suggest that the abuse of prisoners that occurred at the Abu Ghraib facility represented the importation of a commonplace method of dealing with American *criminals* into an uncommon place—namely, an active war zone. However, this move is quite consistent with the Bush administration's *criminalization of the enemy* in the global war on terror.

26. The coexistence of competing theories and practices within the present-day U.S. military is symptomatic of the ongoing failure to establish a coherent policy regarding the way the military should be transformed to deal with post–Cold War challenges— that is, it is a consequence of unresolved debates regarding "force transformation."

27. Based on the photographic evidence, it seems highly unlikely that the Iraqi victims of the notorious "night shift" at Abu Ghraib had been targeted and supervised as part of this alleged program. Very few of the photos demonstrate a concern with linking culturally shameful acts to faces or other marks that would enable the photo to function as positive photographic evidence in a blackmail scenario. For this reason, I argue that the *paradigm* rather than the program of photographed sexual humiliation was adopted by the night shift as part of the softening-up procedure the accused abusers claimed intelligence personnel had encouraged them to carry out.

28. As Arno Mayer (2000) has pointed out, acts of vengeance nearly always precipitate cycles of violence and terror that can be circumvented only by the forceful intervention of a neutral third party whose sovereignty is unanimously recognized. This is crucial because America's status as the world's lone superpower, combined with the almost complete disregard the Bush administration has demonstrated for the authority and legitimacy of the United Nations in the wake of the 9/11 attacks, has created a situation in which the administration of "justice" in the so-called global war on terror is impossible. By positioning itself as both the wounded victim of terrorism and the self-righteous settler of scores worldwide, the United States has conflated vengeance with justice, criminalizing its enemies and announcing to the world that in the twenty-first century, might does make right. However, as Mayer reminds us, retribution is an ongoing, two-sided affair. Therefore, we should expect both the United States and its declared enemies to engage in increasingly violent cycles of what the U.S. State Department has defined as, "premeditated, politically motivated violence perpetrated against non-combatant targets" in the future (Office of the Coordinator for Counterterrorism, *Patterns of Global Terrorism 2002*, U.S. Department of State Publication 11038, April 2003, 13: online at: http://www.state.gov/documents/organization/20177.pdf [accessed 14 March 2010]. The retributive beheadings of captured Americans in the immediate aftermath of the release of the photos documenting the abuses at Abu Ghraib merely represent one example of this cyclical phenomenon.

29. Quoted in Trent T. Gegax, "Behind the Walls of Abu Ghraib," *Newsweek*, 25 May 2004.

EMPIRE AT THE CROSSROADS?

☆

MARIA HÖHN AND SEUNGSOOK MOON

For the past sixty years, the United States has presided over history's largest military empire. Despite the long and bloody war in Iraq and President Barack Obama's promise to draw down the troops stationed there, for this military empire there is no end in sight. As the past sixty years have shown, once bases are built, U.S. military commanders and military strategic planners are loath to give them up.[1] While some critics have exposed in recent years the degree to which the vast network of U.S. military bases project power across the globe, their existence has barely filtered into the national consciousness. Media sources in the U.S. rarely mention the bases when discussing America's footprint in the world. Consequently, most Americans would be stunned to hear that the United States maintains military bases in more than 150 countries.[2] The emphasis in national media coverage on America's sprawling military reach is generally on the troops (or their loved ones at home)—their heroism and willingness to sacrifice and how the troops represent that which is best about America (and all too often lacking in civilian life).[3]

Ann Laura Stoler's observation that "the United States is not a phantom empire just because it is a flexible one" (Stoler 2006c, 19) reveals how even this prominent scholar of empire ignores the physical manifestation of America's footprint in the world. None of the host countries, and especially the local women and men living in and around U.S. military bases worldwide, would ever consider the

United States a phantom empire. The bases are all too real even as their stance toward neighboring communities has become more defensive. Because of the ongoing war on terror, military bases, family housing, and associated facilities have been surrounded by tall fences and an unprecedented corridor of security barriers, checkpoints, and heavily armed guards (often provided by military personnel from the host nation). Indeed, bases that once hovered powerfully and often arrogantly over local communities no longer emanate that same confidence. To many of the locals now, the "indispensable" world power, as Madeleine Albright called the United States during the Clinton years, looks like an empire under siege.[4]

While the focus of our exploration has been on the military-base structure that ensured American power vis-à-vis the Soviets during the Cold War and in its aftermath, we argue that these military bases, and the interactions that take place there, need to be incorporated much more fully into the larger narrative of U.S. history. Claims of American exceptionalism and denial of empire for too long have obscured the fact that military bases have been constitutive of American empire building going back to the nineteenth century. What changed beginning with the Second World War was merely the fact that the United States "inherited" a substantial number of military bases from the British empire and took over bases from other imperial powers, such as Japan and Nazi Germany, as spoils of war. Yet the United States did not just "stumble" into this unprecedented empire (as the British liked to describe their own acquisition of empire). Beginning with its entry into the Second World War, the United States was determined to maintain its global presence, ensured by a web of military bases. The Cold War merely shaped the contours of the empire, much as America's War on Terror shapes it today.

With this collection, we hope to generate a more nuanced and empirically grounded exploration of the impact of U.S. military bases, both "Over There" and at home in the United States. Much more research is necessary to reveal the full scope of this unprecedented empire. The Philippines, where the United States maintained bases for almost one hundred years, and Panama and other countries in the Caribbean and Latin America have been seriously neglected. Even more important, despite the growing U.S. military involvement in the Middle East, almost nothing is known about U.S. military bases in Bahrain and Turkey, where the United States has maintained a substantial military presence for almost sixty years. In the past few years, scholars have taken on this critical task of making the empire more visible, and exposing the social and political effects of such an empire (Calder 2007; Cooley 2008; Gillem 2007; Go 2007 and 2008; Johnson 2004; Lutz 2009; Vine 2009). It is noteworthy, however, that these scholars for the most part come from fields outside American History and American Studies; most of them come from fields such as Anthropology, Geography, Political Science, the emerging sub-field of Global or Transnational Sociology, or are interested in the bases because of their interest in Peace and Conflict Studies. This neglect of the overseas bases by scholars of American History and American Studies reveals the extent to which the U.S. military empire is marginal to America's sense of its own history and identity.[5]

Significantly, because these military bases occupy the extraterritorial spaces guaranteed by Status of Forces Agreement (SOFAS) and function in the marginal contact zones or hybrid spaces where U.S. military and local civilians interact, scholars in host countries generally also do not claim them as part of "their" history.[6] In response to this gap in scholarship, both in the United States and "Over There," we have concentrated on South Korea, Japan and Okinawa, and Germany as a first effort to analyze the conditions central to the differentiated workings of the military empire on the ground: the type of host government, the composition of U.S. troops stationed, the location of military bases in relation to civilian populations, and racialized cultural differences between the United States and the host countries. Through our comparative approach we have learned that local conditions on the ground, as well as U.S. strategic considerations, shape how the empire exercises its power and man-ages the social costs of its global military presence. By studying these coun-tries, we have also discovered three very different models of power relations between the U.S. military and host societies: West Germany, with the most egalitarian arrangement; South Korea, with the most unequal one; and Japan and Okinawa roughly in the middle of this continuum.

It would be a mistake, however, to assume that the relationships between the United States and host societies remain static over time. While all three countries have been integral parts of the global system of U.S. power projec-tion, they should not be seen merely as passive pawns in America's imperial politics. As the contributors to this book have shown, improvements in economic conditions within the host societies significantly altered the degree of asymmetrical power relationship that defined how the U.S. military inter-acted with the host nation. This change would take longer in South Korea (the late 1980s) and Okinawa (the 1970s) than in West Germany (the 1960s), but the trajectory is unmistakable. Political democratization in the host societies also facilitated improvement in the relationships through the re-negotiation of established SOFAS and mitigating some of the most egregious limitations on national sovereignty. This shift has particular (albeit still limited) resonance for South Korea, where the United States had imposed a much less favorable alliance and a much higher social burden on the local population than it did in West Germany after 1955 and in Okinawa after 1972.

By bringing a worm's eye view to the interactions between the American military and host societies, we have uncovered not only the uneven social cost imposed by the United States, often in collaboration with local elites, but also how the daily interactions between American soldiers (and sometimes their families) and local men and women enabled locals to challenge hierarchical relations of gender, race, and class in their own societies and to subvert the power relations imposed on them by the empire. At the same time, the chapters reveal how America's imperial politics abroad has implications for gender roles in the United States; therefore, scholars of women's history and gender studies as well as global and transnational sociology need to pay more attention to what happens "Over There." The worldwide web of military bases also had significant implications for racial relations in the U.S. military and in American society at large. As scholars have shown in the past few years, much of the civil rights struggle was fueled by the fact that the United States took on the mantle of being the leader of the "Free World," and sent African American soldiers abroad where they experienced for the first time societies without Jim Crow race laws. Thus, for a more comprehensive understanding of race in America after 1945, scholars need to pay more attention to the peripheries of the empire and rethink the African American diaspora beyond the existing focus on the continental United States and the Caribbean.[7]

In light of the ongoing wars in the Middle East and shifting U.S. strategic interests in the region, we want to reflect briefly on the implications of America's post–Cold War posture. The collapse of the Soviet Union dramatically altered America's geopolitical interests, because the policy of "containment" that had encircled the Soviet Union with ground, sea, and air power no longer made strategic sense. While the anticipated "peace dividend" never came about, the United States did implement a massive contraction of bases in the continental United States and a significant drawdown of troops overseas. Most affected was Germany, where huge bases were converted and troops were substantially reduced, from more than 250,000 to some 70,000 soldiers.[8] In Japan, bases were consolidated in mainland Japan, the number of troops was reduced to some 50,000, and more of the base structure was moved to Okinawa. Furthermore, by 2012, some 8,000 Marines are scheduled to move from Okinawa to Guam. Comparable adjustment took place in Korea, where troop strength was reduced from roughly 37,000 to 30,000 and where bases are scheduled to move from the demilitarized zone to south of Seoul (mostly P'yŏngt'aek City). Although the U.S. military today occupies and controls a much smaller physical space in these countries, its global stance is hardly diminished. Indeed, the ongoing revolution in warfare technology has made its power even more effective and lethal.

Indeed, the realignments of the recent years do not indicate a retreat from empire, but merely reflect altering objectives as Islamic terrorism, the ever-pressing pursuit of foreign oil (in the Middle East and Africa), and the rise of China as a new superpower have been preoccupying military strategists. In place of the cumbersome and stationary Cold War bases, they envision strategic forward sites, or "lily pads," to ensure a more agile and efficient projection of U.S. power. This new type of base is intended to transform the U.S. military into a "lean" and "mobile" global fighting machine, unencumbered by military families and long-term involvement in host societies.[9] The recent negotiation and signing of a SOFA between Iraq and the United States in preparation for a long-term U.S. military presence suggests that the new focus on strategic forward sites does not mean that they will completely replace traditional bases.[10] Rather, the emphasis on the new type of base reveals the empire's strategic concern with maximizing its military efficiency and minimizing unpredictable human factors and political cost.

In the aftermath of 9/11, American military strategists introduced the term "arc of instability" to identify an extensive area encompassing North Africa through the Middle East, Pakistan, and the former Soviet republics in Central Asia to China as their new focus of asserting U.S. control. As a result of this dramatic geopolitical shift from Western Europe and Northeast Asia to this part of the world, a growing number of U.S. military bases are now located in developing countries. During the Cold War, less than 6 percent of all U.S. military bases were located in such countries (Calder 2007, 51). Those countries are not only poor but also politically unstable. In light of the findings in this collection, it is therefore likely that these new locations will produce patterns of asymmetrical power relations and deplorable social conditions similar to those that have been identified for South Korea and Okinawa. Racialized cultural assumptions toward the new host societies and the appalling lack of historical and cultural knowledge about them will only exacerbate this line of development.

The new global posture of the United States also means that a third of U.S. military bases overseas are now located in Islamic countries, where the U.S. presence has provoked tremendous opposition and violent backlash. During the Cold War, less than 1 percent of bases were located there (Calder, 51). The management of soldiers' sexuality in the new Islamic "host" nations espe-cially presents the military with unprecedented challenges. To deploy its troops during the Persian Gulf War (1991), the U.S. military had to assure the Saudi regime that U.S. soldiers would refrain from any sort of relationship with local women and that the military would not tolerate any arrangement of prostitution around U.S. bases. To live up to this commitment, the military organized rest-and-relaxation (R&R) trips for its troops to neighboring Bah-rain, where the United States has a huge naval port and where women from the Philippines and Russia work in a thriving sex industry (Baker 2004, 160; Enloe 1991, 103). In Iraq, the military faces a similar dilemma: to ensure a smooth occupation, soldiers are prohibited not only from drinking and pros-elytizing but also from initiating consensual romantic or sexual relationships with Iraqi civilians. According to a soldier with a twenty-year record of military service, "fraternization" lectures in Iraq were a world apart from those he had received in Germany twenty years before, when the motto had been "sleep NATO," meaning that in their sexual pursuits soldiers were safe with the women of America's allies in Europe. In Iraq, the lecture lasted a mere five minutes: "If any of you is stupid enough to wander outside the wire and become involved with a local woman, there ain't a damn thing we can do. Uncle Achmed [sic] is going to chop you into pieces—and your sweetie too. Enough said?"[11] This strict policy on soldiers' conduct might explain why a bordello in Baghdad's international Green Zone has been set up for the use of military and private contractors (Chandrasekaran 2006, 57).[12] Sig-nificantly, while the R&R trips to Bahrain since the invasion of Iraq in 2003 relied on an existing global sex industry, the bordello in the Green Zone implies that the U.S. military, just like in South Korea, Okinawa, and postwar Germany, was involved to some degree in regulating prostitution. Although the R&R facilities in Qatar, which are used by soldiers stationed in Iraq, keep a tight leash on GIs sent there, Qatar, like Bahrain, is a thriving center of sex trafficking in the Middle East. These lines of complex development suggest that America's strategic shift to the Middle East and Central Asia means that the U.S. military will have to rely to a larger degree on the global sex industry, which has exploded since the collapse of the Soviet Union.[13]

The ongoing strategic shift to more mobile forward sites and the deploy-ment of troops unencumbered by families also has far-reaching implications for military personnel. As agents of the empire, these soldiers, who dispro-portionately come from economically disadvantaged backgrounds or are members of racial minorities, have borne an asymmetrical burden of im-perial politics. Since 9 / 11, military personnel in the United States have been deployed away from home on average about 135 days a year; in the U.S. Navy, sailors have been away some 170 days; and in the U.S. Air Force, personnel have been away about 176 days. In the Army, soldiers now average a deployment abroad once every fourteen weeks.[14] Beginning with the war in Iraq, the U.S. military has been also tapping ever more extensively into the National Guard and Reserves, who resent the multiple deployments abroad.[15] To make up for manpower shortages, the military has also begun using "individual augmentees," experts with a particular and desirable skill, who are not integrated into a military unit. These soldiers experience especially serious stress due to the isolated nature of their deployment.[16]

Sending overly stressed and discontent soldiers who are separated from their families and deployed for short-term and multiple rotations abroad does not bode well for civilian-military relations. Such conditions are conducive to excessive drinking, prostitution, and violence against the local population. The short-term deployments mean that, even if they wanted to, the mostly male soldiers cannot get comfortable with their host societies or, perhaps, even establish consensual relationships with local women. To keep the soldiers content, it is very likely that the military will rely on local or migrant (often transnational) women to provide forms of emotional and sexual labor.

The strategic realignment of the U.S. military empire also has tremendous implications for female soldiers, given the military's misogynistic and homophobic subculture, especially at the level of daily interactions among soldiers (Britton and Williams 1995; Hampf 2004; Hillman 2005; chapter 12 in this book). Although Internet pornography has been banned by the military, its use has exploded among U.S. soldiers who are separated from their families, often on multiple and extended deployments. In Muslim countries, where sexual fraternization with the local population poses a serious threat to America's strategic goals, heterosexual relationships between soldiers have increased significantly, and this context increases the potential for sexual harassment of and violence against female soldiers. One soldier in Iraq told a female comrade that the "military sends women over to give the guys eye candy to keep them sane." In Vietnam, he continued, soldiers "had prostitutes to keep them from going crazy, but they don't have those in Iraq. So they have women soldiers instead."[17] Female soldiers have reported increased violence committed by male soldiers, and the fact that the military has been granting ever more "moral waivers" to recruits with criminal records only increases the chance for violence. According to investigation by the Department of Defense, almost one-third of a nationwide sample of female veterans seeking health care through the Veterans Administration reported that they were raped or exposed to attempted rape during their service; 37 percent of that group also replied that they experienced multiple rapes; and 14 percent said that they were gang-raped.[18]

Further, the doctrine of a leaner and more mobile military has increased the U.S. military's reliance on outsourcing to private contractors such as Halliburton and Blackwater (renamed Xe), which have been taking on tasks traditionally performed by soldiers. They train soldiers and assist in frontline combat, gather intelligence, provide force protection, cook meals for the soldiers, and provide a host of other services (Scahill 2007; Singer 2003).[19] Since the invasion of Iraq in the spring of 2003, the United States has spent more than $100 billion (or a fifth of war expenses) on private military contractors. The reported 180,000 private contractors in Iraq outnumber the approximately 140,000 U.S. soldiers deployed in the country in 2008.[20] The unprecedented growth of this industry is the result of the post–Cold War realignment of the military championed by former Secretary of Defense, Donald Rumsfeld, and the military's overextension in the aftermath of 9/11.

Like the military itself and the defense industry, the world of the privatized military industry is dominated by men and informed by a hyper-masculine warrior ethos. Many of its personnel are recruited from the ranks of military and Special Forces veterans. Unlike the U.S. military, however, these contractors are primarily responsible to their stockholders, because they are for-profit business corporations. Similar to U.S. military bases overseas and the defense industry in the United States, the privatized military industry is a hybrid entity that blurs the boundary between the military and civilian society. Due to their ambiguous status, privatized military companies also pose the problem of legal accountability when deployed on foreign soil because the U.S. military cannot charge them under the Uniform Code of Military Justice, and after private contractors have committed crimes, they are often spirited out of the country.[21]

As some publicized incidences of the killing of Iraqi civilians by American contractors indicate, these contractors basically enjoy the same extraterritorial privileges that SOFAS grant to GIS but they are not subject to the military justice system.[22] It is revealing that there was not a single case of prosecution against American contractors in Iraq during the first three years of the war, when more than 100,000 such contractors worked there.[23] While this situation was mitigated with the Iraqi government's ratification of an agreement in November 2008 that strips American contractors of their extraterritorial privilege,[24] the large presence of highly paid, single, male military contractors who are separated from their families has far-reaching implications for civilian–military relations. The situation around military bases in Kosovo, which hosts Camp Bondsteel, the biggest U.S. military base in the Balkans, is suggestive of the entanglement between privatized military operations and the global sex industry. As Kellogg Brown and Root, another private contractor increasingly used by the military, built and maintained Camp Bondsteel in the town of Urosevac, there were an average of nine brothels in each of thirty municipalities of Kosovo to cater to the Americans. Women in these brothels were often deceived or lured into the transnational network of procurement for the sex industry. In Bosnia, U.S. military contractors were involved in sex trafficking; several DynCorp employees purchased underage girls, some of them as young as twelve years old, to sell them into forced prostitution in the Balkans.[25]

The long and bloody war in Iraq and Afghanistan has triggered a serious rethinking among policymakers and military strategists. The continued reliance on "boots on the ground" as the war and occupation drag on in both of these countries suggests that Donald Rumsfeld's dream of lean and mobile "lily pad" bases needs to be shelved, at least partially, for now. Bases that had been slated for shutdown in Germany were given new life as military strategists recognized the usefulness of old allies and of an established and reliable infrastructure. Noteworthy changes are also occurring in South Korea, where Secretary of Defense Robert Gates has finally approved three-year tours of duty accompanied by families.[26] While this step was approved at last to improve the standard of living for soldiers, it will have significant implications for gender relations with the host communities. It remains to be seen, however, whether these most recent developments present a reversal of the lily-pad strategy or a return to the old model of base structure that supported American power in the past.

While this book presents an in-depth scholarly analysis of the changing scope of the U.S. military empire and the social costs entailed by such an empire, we are cognizant of the acutely political nature of our subject matter and its implications for local—and increasingly transnational—migrant men and women. The varying, yet immense, social costs they have borne for decades, and the growing resistance in many of the host countries, suggest an urgent need to transform the "empire at the crossroads." Their experiences with the U.S. military also highlight the deeply contradictory rhetoric of democracy that the United States has been using in its international relations. Neither of us is naïve enough to assume that the empire will retreat any time in the near future, but if the United States is serious about living up to its ideal of democracy, it needs to engage with host countries on a more level playing field. More equitable and transparent SOFAS, greater historical and cultural knowledge about host societies, and respect for those societies are just a first step toward a more egalitarian global power structure. Equally crucial to this more level playing field is a greater democratization of the host countries. The agency of local men and women in subverting existing hierarchical relations of gender, race, and class in their own societies that we have highlighted, suggests a possibility of democratization of civilian–military relations that might mitigate the worst aspects of overseas deployments for both locals and American soldiers. We hope that our book can facilitate the growth of public awareness of these difficult issues and will foster greater scholarly interest in America's place in the world.

Notes

1. Over the decades, the worldwide U.S. military-base structure has adjusted to changing strategic needs. Buoyed by Richard Nixon's rapprochement with China in the early 1970s, military planners at the Pentagon no longer anticipated having to fight a two-and-a-half front war (one front in Europe, one in Asia, and half in Africa). This shift led to a significant contraction of the American military in Asia, because a war with China was no longer expected. Beginning in 1970, for example, the number of U.S. troops in South Korea shrank from some 70,000 to 35,000–40,000. Occasionally bases were closed because host nations asserted themselves against U.S. tutelage. Prominent examples include President Charles de Gaulle's decision in the mid-1960s to ask the Americans to leave France and the refusal of the Philippine government to renew treaties for the Subic Bay Naval Base and Clark Air Force Base in the early 1990s.

2. See Catherine A. Lutz, "Bases, Empire, and Global Responses," *Fellowship*, Winter 2007, available online at http://www.forusa.org/fellowship/winter07/catherinelutz.html (accessed 29 March 2010).

3. See McAlister 2001 on the militarization of American society as a side effect of this global posture, and Bacevich 2003 for a critique of American militarism from a conservative perspective.

4. The same sort of phenomenon can be observed in U.S. embassies and consulates. They are closed off by heightened security measures and guarded by extensive surveillance. Often, whole streets surrounding U.S. institutions are closed off, imposing on the convenience of people who live in the vicinity.

5. Donna Alva, who is a scholar of American history, is the sole exception in this collection.

6. As a result, historians in the major host societies tend to overlook U.S. bases in their scholarly research, as well. In general, books on the bases are written by activists (and scholars as activists) as part of fact-finding reports and records of their activism rather

than for scholarly analyses. An exception is the work of Maria Höhn, but she is a scholar of German history in the United States; she could not have written the dissertation (on which her book GIs and Fräuleins is based) at a German university. This attitude toward the place of the bases in German history is changing in Germany, albeit slowly. It is noteworthy that both of the co-editors of this book are scholars who lead transnational lives.

7. Melanie McAlister is one of the few scholars who has singled out how the glorification of the military as the "cultural rainbow" that often eludes Americans at home affects gender relations: McAlister 2001, 8. For the impact on U.S. race relations and civil rights, see for example Höhn (2002, 2005, 2008, 2010) and Höhn and Klimke 2010. The German Historical Institute, Vassar College, and the Heidelberg Center for American Studies at Heidelberg University are supporting a research project that explores this connection, focusing for now on Germany as a case study. For first results, see aacvr-germany.org.

8. For a detailed description of base conversion, see Cunningham and Klemmer 2005.

9. See National Defense Strategy of the United States of America, cited in Michael T. Klare, "Imperial Reach," Nation, 25 April 2005, 13–18.

10. On 26 November 2007, President George W. Bush and Iraqi Prime Minister Nuri Kamal al-Maliki signed the "Declaration of Principles" in preparation for long-term security as well as economic and political relations between the two countries. Despite its name, this agreement resembles the SOFA that the United States signed with other countries hosting its troops: see Thom Shanker and Cara Buckley, "U.S. and Iraq to negotiate Pact on Long-Term Relations," New York Times, 27 November 2007. Throughout 2008, the two countries were involved in delicate negotiations over the SOFA: Alissa J. Rubin and Katherine Zoepf, "Iraqi Cabinet Wants Proposed Security Agreement Altered," New York Times, 22 October 2008.

11. The soldiers' blog (accessed July 2008) is no longer available online (http://www .communati.com / pzmiller / then-vietnam-war-and-now-iraq-war-fraternization-opposite-s-x).

12. Staff of the Coalition Provisional Authority told Chandrasekaran that the brothel was a "military thing" and that only the soldiers knew the location (2006, 57). For General Order 1, see "For One Night GIs Get a Taste of Home," Washington Post, 9 January 2009.

13. It is crucial to recognize that this distinction between military-regulated prostitution and the commercial sex industry is ethically ambiguous, at best. While the use of the civilian sex industry allows the military to avoid legal responsibility, the reality of impoverished countries in the former Eastern Bloc (the new republics in Central Asia and Eastern Europe) suggests that the sex industry there is generally entangled with the trafficking of women: "U.S. Stalls on Human Trafficking, Pentagon Has Yet to Ban Contractors from Using Forced Labor," Chicago Tribune, 27 December 2005.

14. Los Angeles Times, 6 January 2002.

15. Many of these veterans came from California and Texas and filled vacancies in National Guard and Army Reserve units to be sent to Iraq and Afghanistan in 2004 and 2005: Reuters, 30 June 2004.

16. "For Military Solo Sailors, Few Valves to Relieve Stress," *New York Times*, 2 November 2008.

17. Helen Benedict, "The Private War of Women Soldiers," 7 March 2007, available online at http://www.salon.com/news/feature/2007/03/07/women_in_military (accessed 12 April 2010). See also chapter 12 in this book. Intra-military sexual relations have also grown in South Korea since U.S. military authorities implemented the zero-tolerance policy on prostitution and trafficking in 2002. This information is based on Seungsook Moon's conversation with Tong-nyŏng Kim, a photographer and staff member at My Sister's Place, Tongduch'ŏn City, March 2007.

18. A recent report shows that the numbers of rapes in combat zones rose 44 percent from 2007 to 2008: Steven Myers, "Another Peril in War Zones: Sexual Abuse by Fellow GI's," *New York Times*, 28 December 2009.

19. For an insider's account of the private military industry, see Schumacher 2006.

20. See Steven Lee Myers and Sabroma Tavernise, "Citing Stability in Iraq, Bush Sees Troop Cuts," *New York Times*, 1 August 2008; James Risen, "Use of Contractors in Iraq Costs Billions, Report Says," *New York Times*, 12 August 2008.

21. Daniel McGrory, "Bosnia Sex Trade Whistler Blower Wins Suit Against Dyncorp," *The Times-London*, available online at http://www.rense.com/genera128/dyn.htm (accessed on 7 April 2010).

22. On 16 September 2007, Blackwater guards under contract to the U.S. Department of State shot unarmed Iraqi civilians, leaving seventeen of them dead: Alissa J. Rubin and Paul von Zielbauer, "The Judgment Gap," *New York Times*, 11 October 2007. There have been publicized incidences of U.S. soldiers' killing civilians, including the killing of twenty-four Iraqi civilians by a group of Marines in Haditha in 2006. But criminal charges against American soldiers were commonly dropped for "lack of evidence": Paul von Zielbauer, "The Erosion of a Murder Case against Marines in the Killing of 24 Iraqi Civilians," *New York Times*, 6 October 2007.

23. This immunity was introduced under the Transitional Administrative Law approved by Paul Bremer III, head of the U.S. Occupation Authority, in 2004. This order was intended as a substitute for a SOFA: Alissa J. Rubin and Paul von Zielbauer, "The Judgment Gap," *New York Times*, 11 October 2007.

24. James Risen, "End of Immunity Worries U.S. Contractors in Iraq," *New York Times*, 1 December 2008.

25. "U.S. Stalls on Human Trafficking, Pentagon Has Yet to Ban Contractors from Using Forced Labor," *Chicago Tribune*, 27 December 2005.

26. Eric Schmitt, "Gates Approves of 3-Year Tours for U.S. Troops in South Korea," *New York Times*, 4 June 2008.

REFERENCES

☆

Archives

AAA   Archiv des Auswärtigen Amt, Berlin

ASR   Archiv für Soldatenrecht, e.V., Berlin

AMHI   U.S. Army Military History Institute, Carlisle, Pa.

BK   Bundesarchiv, Koblenz, Germany

HH   Hessisches Hauptstaatsarchiv, Wiesbaden, Germany

HIS   Hamburger Institut für Sozialforschung, Hamburg, Germany

HQYB   Headquarters of U.S. Forces, Yokota Base, Tokyo

IANAS   Interdisziplinärer Arbeitskreis für Nordamerikastudien, Johannes Gutenberg Universität, Mainz, Germany

LK   Landeshauptarchiv, Koblenz, Germany

LOC   Library of Congress, Washington, D.C.

MMAL   General Douglas MacArthur Memorial Archives and Library, Norfolk, Va.

NAACP   Papers of the National Association for the Advancement of Colored People, Schomburg Center for Research in Black Culture, New York Public Library

NARA   National Archives and Records Administration, College Park, Md.

SF   Stadtarchiv Frankfurt, Frankfurt on Main, Germany

SK   Stadtarchiv Kaiserslautern, Kaiserslauten, Germany

UMAA / SCAP   SCAP Files of Commander Alfred R. Hussey, University of Michigan, Ann Arbor

Film and Media

Chermayeff, Maro, dir. 2008. *Carrier*. Documentary, PBS Home Video.

Cho, Keung-Ha, dir. 1964. *Yukch'eŭi kobaik* [Body confessions]. Film, Dong Seong Films, Seoul.

Chung, Y. David, and Matt Dibble, dirs. 2007. *Koryo Saram: The Unreliable People*. Documentary, Tangunfilms, Ann Arbor, Mich.

Fassbinder, Rainer Werner, dir. 1979. *Die Ehe der Maria Braun* [The marriage of Maria Braun]. Film, Albatros Filmproduktion, Munich.

Goodwin, Beth, and Donna Musil, prod. 2006. *Brats: Our Journey Home*. Documentary, Brats without Borders, Eatonton, Ga.

Kim, Il Rhan, dir. 2005. *Mamasang: Remember Me This Way*. Documentary, Pale Pink Skirt, Seoul.

Munhwa Broadcasting Corporation. 2003. *Ijenŭn malhalsu itda: sex tongmaeng kijich'on chŏnghwaundong* [Now we can talk about it: Sex alliance and the camptown cleansing campaign]. Seoul: Munhwa Broadcasting Corporation.

Nakae Yuji, dir. 1999. *Nabbie no Koi*. Office Shirous, Japan.

———. 2002. *Hoteru Haibisukasu*. Cine Qua Non Films, Japan.

Shin, Sang-ok, dir. 1958. *Chiokhwa* [Hell flower]. Film, Seoul Films.

Takagi, J. T., and Hye Jung Park, dirs. 1995. *The Women Outside: Korean Women and the U.S. Military*. Documentary, Third World Newsreel, New York.

Wilder, Billy, dir. 1948. *A Foreign Affair*. Film, Paramount Pictures, Hollywood, Calif.

Zeiger, David, dir. 2005. *Sir! No Sir!*. Film, Displaced Films, Los Angeles.

Newspapers and Magazines

Abendzeitung

Asahi Shinbun

Asia Times

BBC Monitoring Europe–Political

BBC Monitoring International Reports

Chicago Tribune

Chosun Daily

Christian Century

Chungang Daily

Congressional Record

Daily Yomiuri

Dong-A Daily

Ebony

Frankfurter Allgemeine Zeitung

Frankfurter Rundschau

Die Freiheit

General Anzeiger

Han'guk Daily

Hangyŏre
Hangyŏre 21
International Herald Tribune
Korea Herald
Korea Times
Kyŏnghyang
Life
Los Angeles Times
Mannheimer Morgen
Naeil
Nation
Neckarzeitung
Neue Presse
Newsweek
New York Times
Pacific Stars and Stripes
Pacific Sunday News
Pittsburgh Courier
Saarbrücker Zeitung
St. Petersburg Times
Sisajŏnŏl
Der Spiegel
Stars and Stripes
Der Stern
Time
Travel Magazine
U.S. News and World Report
Washington Post
Washington Times
Watertown Daily Times
Yonhap News
Yorkshire Evening Post
Die Zeit

Secondary Sources

Ahagon, Shoko. 1989. *The Island Where People Live*, trans. C. H. Rickard. Hong Kong: Christian Conference of Asia.

Albano, Sondra. 1994. "Military Recognition of Family Concerns: Revolutionary War to 1993." *Armed Forces and Society* 20 (Winter): 283–302.

Allen, Matthew. 2002. *Identity and Resistance in Okinawa*. New York: Rowman and Littlefield.

Alvah, Donna. 2007. *Unofficial Ambassadors: American Military Families Overseas and the Cold War, 1946–1965*. New York: New York University Press.

Angst, Linda. 2003. "The Rape of a Schoolgirl: Discourses of Power and Women's Lives in Okinawa." In *Islands of Discontent: Okinawan Responses to Japanese and American Power*, ed. Laura Hein and Mark Selden, 135–58. Lanham, Md.: Rowman and Littlefield.

Anonymous. 1959. *Eine Frau in Berlin* [A woman in Berlin]. Frankfurt on Main: Eichborn AG.

Appadurai, Arjun. 1996. *Modernity at Large: Cultural Dimensions of Globalization*. Minneapolis: University of Minnesota Press.

Arasaki, Moriteru, ed. 2000. *Profile of Okinawa*. Tokyo: Techno.

Aron, Raymond. 1974. *The Imperial Republic: The United States and the World, 1945–1973*. Cambridge: Winthrop.

Aussaresses, Paul. 2006. *The Battle of the Casbah: Terrorism and Counter-Terrorism in Algeria, 1955–1957*. New York: Enigma Books.

Bacevich, Andrew J. 2002. *American Empire: The Realities and Consequences of U.S. Diplomacy*. Cambridge: Harvard University Press.

Bach, Julian, Jr. 1946. *America's Germany: An Account of the Occupation*. New York: Random House.

Bailey, Beth, and David Farber. 1994. *The First Strange Place: The Alchemy of Sex and Race in Hawaii*. New York: Free Press.

Baker, Anni P. 2004. *American Soldiers Overseas: The Global Military Presence*. New York: Praeger.

Bald, Detlef. 1994. *Militär und Gesellschaft 1945–90. Die Bundeswehr der Bonner Republik* [Military and Society 1945–90. The Bundeswehr of the Bonn Republik]. Baden-Baden, Germany: Nomos Verlagsgesellschaft.

Barber, Benjamin R. 2001. *Jihad vs. McWorld: How Globalism and Tribalism Are Reshaping the World*. New York: Ballantine Books.

Barden, Judy. 1950. "Candy Bar Romance—Women in Germany." In *This Is Germany*, ed. Arthur Settel, 161–76. New York: Books for Libraries Press.

Bascara, Victor. 2006. *Model-Minority Imperialism*. Minneapolis: University of Minnesota Press.

Barstow, Anne Llewellyn. 2001. *War's Dirty Secret: Rape, Prostitution, and Other Crimes against Women*. Cleveland: Pilgrim's Press.

Bautista, Aubery A. 2005. "Filipino Women in Sex Industry." In *Filipino Women in Sex Industry and International Marriage*, ed. My Sister's Place, 101–43. Ŭijŏngbu City: My Sister's Place.

Beloff, Max. 1986. "The End of the British Empire and the Assumption of Worldwide Commitments by the United States." In *The 'Special Relationship': Anglo-American Relations since 1945*, ed. William Roger Louis and Hedley Bull. Oxford: Clarendon Press.

Bender, Peter. 2003. "America: The New Roman Empire?" *Orbis* 47, no. 1 (Winter): 145–59.

Bhabha, Homi K. 1994. *The Location of Culture*. London: Routledge.

——. 1995. "Signs Taken for Wonders: Questions of Ambivalence and Authority under a Tree Outside Delhi, May 1817." In *The Post-Colonial Studies Reader*, ed. Bill Ashcroft, Gareth Griffiths, and Helen Tiffin, 29–35. London: Routledge.

Biddiscombe, Alexander P. 2001. "Dangerous Liaisons: The Anti-Fraternization Movement in the U.S. Occupation Zones of Germany and Austria, 1945–1948." *Journal of Social History* vol. 34, no. 3 (Spring): 2001, 611–47.

Blaker, James. 1990. *United States Overseas Basing: An Anatomy of the Dilemma.* New York: Praeger.

Boggs, Carl, ed. 2003. *Masters of War: Militarism and Blowback in the Era of American Empire.* New York: Routledge.

Boose, Lynda E. 1993. "'Techno-Muscularity and the 'Boy Eternal': From the Quagmire to the Gulf." In *Gendering War Talk,* ed. Miriam Cooke and Angela Woollacott, 67–106. Princeton: Princeton University Press.

Botting, Douglas. 1985. *From the Ruins of the Reich.* New York: A. Allen & Unwin.

Bourdieu, Pierre. 1980. *The Logic of Practice.* Stanford, Calif.: Stanford University Press.

Boyle, Kay. 1963. *Smoking Mountain: Stories of Germany during the Occupation.* New York: Alfred A. Knopf.

Brandt, Allan. 1985. *No Magic Bullet: A Social History of Venereal Disease in the United States since 1880.* New York: Oxford University Press.

Britton, Dana M., and Christine L. Williams. 1995. "'Don't Ask, Don't Tell, Don't Pursue': Military Policy and the Construction of Homosexual Masculinity." *Journal of Homosexuality* 30, no. 1: 1–22.

Bromberg, Sara. 1999. "Feminist Issues in Prostitution." In *Prostitution: On Whores, Hustlers, and Johns,* ed. James E. Elias, Vern L. Bullough, and Gwen Brewer. New York: Prometheus Books.

Brown, Elizabeth I. 2005. "Bye, Bye Miss American Pie: Wives of American Servicemen in Southeast Asia 1961–1975." Ph.D. diss., University of Colorado, Boulder.

Brownmiller, Susan. 1993. *Against Our Will: Men, Women, and Rape.* New York: Fawcett Columbine.

Brünn, Dieter, ed. 1986. *Widerstand in der US-Armee. GI-Bewegung in den siebziger Jahren* [Resistance in the U.S. Army. The GI movement in the 1970s]. Berlin: Harald Kater.

Busch, Noel F. 1948. *Fallen Sun: A Report on Japan.* New York: D. Appleton–Century.

Butler, Judith. 1997. *The Psychic Life of Power: Theories in Subjection.* Stanford, Calif.: Stanford University Press.

Calder, Kent. 2007. *Embattled Garrison: Comparative Base Politics and American Globalism.* Princeton: Princeton University Press.

Campbell, Kurt M., and Celeste Johnson Ward. 2003. "New Battle Stations? The Pentagon Is Planning the Greatest Change in the U.S. Overseas Military Posture in Fifty Years." *Foreign Affairs* 82, no. 5 (September–October): 95–103.

Carlson, Allan. 1993. "Your Honey or Your Life: The Case for the Bachelor Army." *Policy Review* 66 (Fall 1993): 45–52.

Center for Strategic and International Studies. 2002. *Path to an Agreement: The U.S.–Republic of Korea Status of Forces Agreement Revision Process.* Washington, D.C.: Center for Strategic and International Studies.

Chai, Alice. 1993. "Asian-Pacific Feminist Coalition Politics: The Chongshindae / Jugunianfu ('Comfort Women') Movement." *Korean Studies* 17: 67–91.

Chakrabarty, Dipesh. 2000. *Provincializing Europe: Postcolonial Thought and Historical Difference.* Princeton: Princeton University Press.

Chandrasekaran, Rajiv. 2006. *Imperial Life in the Emerald City: Inside Iraq's Green Zone*. New York: Alfred A. Knopf.

Chang, Yun-sŏn. 2000. "P'aju yongjugol yullak yŏsŏngdŭl [Prostitutes in Yongju Village, P'aju]." *Sindonga* (July): 354–65.

Chatterjee, Partha. 1989. "Colonialism, Nationalism, and Colonized Women: The Contest in India." *American Ethnologist* 16, no. 4 (November): 622–33.

Chaudhuri, Nupur, and Margaret Strobel, eds. 1992. *Western Women and Imperialism: Complicity and Resistance*. Bloomington: Indiana University Press.

Cho, Hae-il. 1974a. "America." In *Cho Hae-il sosŏljip America* [Cho Hae-il's novel collection America], 269–366. Seoul: Minŭmsa.

———. 1974b. "Tae'nat [Midday]." In *Cho Hae-il sosŏljip America* [Cho Hae-il's novel collection America], 253–66. Seoul: Minŭmsa.

Cho, Hyŏng, and P'il-hwa Chang. 1990. "Kunghoesokkiroge nat'anan yŏsŏngjŏngch'aek sigak: Maemaech'une taehayŏ [The perspective in women's policy written in the stenographic records of the National Assembly meetings: Regarding prostitution]." *Yŏsŏnghaknonjip* 7: 83–100.

Choi, Chungmoo. 1998. "Nationalism and Construction of Gender in Korea." In *Dangerous Women: Gender and Korean Nationalism*, ed. Elaine H. Kim and Chungmoo Choi, 9–31. New York: Routledge.

Chŏn, Kyŏng-il. 1991. "Kijich'onŭi ch'inmijojik hanmich'insŏnhoe [Camptowns' pro–American organizations Korean American Friendship Society). *Mal* 65: 170–73.

Chŏn, Kyŏng-ok, Sung-nan Yu, Ŭn-sil Kim, and Hŭi-sŏn Sin, eds. 2005. *Han'gukyŏsŏng, chŏngch'isa hoesa* 2 (1945–1980) (A history of Korean women in politics and society, vol. 2). Seoul: Sookmyo ng Women's University Press.

Chŏng, Chae-hun. 1988. "Maech'une kwanhan chŏngbujŏngch'aegŭi pyŏnch'ŏnkwa kŭ ponjil [The shift in the government policy on prostitution and its substance]." *Nogji* 22 (December): 157–65

Chŏng, Chin-sŏng. 1997. "Ilbongun wianso chŏngch'aegŭi suripkwa chŏngae [The establishment and development of Japanese military comfort station policy]." In *Ilbongun wianbumunjeŭi chinsang* [Truthful state of Japanese military comfort women], ed. Council for Resolving the Problem of the Military Comfort Women, 101–18. Seoul: Yŏksabip'yŏngsa.

Chŏng, Sŏng-gŭn. 1967. "Wurinara yullakyŏsŏngŭi hyŏnghwangkwa kŭ taech'aek [The state of prostitutes in our nation and its countermeasures]." *Pŏphaknonch'ong* 8: 65–87.

Christy, Alan. 1993. "The Making of Imperial Subjects in Okinawa." *Positions* 1, no. 3: 607–39.

Cline, Lydia Sloan. 2003. *Today's Military Wife: Meeting the Challenge of Service Life*, 5th ed. Mechanicsburg, Penn: Stackpole Books.

Cobin, Alain. 1990. *Women for Hire: Prostitution and Sexuality in France after 1850*, trans. Alan Sheridan. Cambridge, Mass.: Harvard University Press.

Cohen, Eliot A. 2004. "History and the Hyperpower." *Foreign Affairs* 83, no. 4 (July–August): 49–63.

Cohn, Carol. 1988. "A Feminist Spy in the House of Death: Unraveling the Language of Strategic Analysis." In *Women and the Military System*, ed. E. Isaksson, 288–317. New York: St. Martin's Press.

———. 1993. "Wars, Wimps, and Women: Talking Gender and Thinking War." In *Gendering War Talk*, ed. Miriam Cooke and Angela Woollacott, 227–46. Princeton: Princeton University Press.

———. 1994. "Sex and Death in the Rational World of Defense Intellectuals." In *The Woman Question*, ed. Mary Evans, 118–37. London: Sage.

Cooley, Alexander. 2008. *Base Politics. Democratic Change and the U.S. Military Overseas.* Ithaca: Cornell University Press.

Coomaraswamy, Radhika. 1995. *The U.N. Special Rapporteur on Violence against Women,* Article 205. Geneva: United Nations.

Cortright, David. 1975. *Soldiers in Revolt. The American Military Today.* New York: Anchor Press.

Cosamas, Graham, and Albert Cowdrey. 1992. *Medical Services in the European Theater of Operations.* Washington, D.C.: Center of Military History, U.S. Army.

Critchlow, Robert D. 2005. *U.S. Military Overseas Basing: New Developments and Oversight Issues for Congress.* CRS Report for Congress RL 33148. Washington, D.C.: Congressional Research Service.

Cunningham, Keith, and Andrea Klemmer. 2005. *Restructuring the U.S. Military Bases in Germany: Scope, Impacts, and Opportunities.* BICC Report no. 4. Bonn: Bonn International Center for Conversion.

Dakyuinp'o. 2004. *Puggŭrŏun migunmunhwa tabsagi* [A record of exploring the shameful culture of the American military in South Korea]. Seoul: Pug'ijŭ.

D'Amico, Francine, and Laurie Weinstein, eds. 2000. *Gender Camouflage: Women and the U.S. Military.* New York: New York University Press.

Davis, David Brion. 2000. "The Americanized Mannheim of 1945–46." In *American Places: Encounters with History—A Celebration of Sheldon Meyer*, ed. William E. Leuchtenburg, 79–81. New York: Oxford University Press.

Davis, Franklin M., Jr. 1967. *Come as a Conqueror: The United States Army's Occupation of Germany 1945–1949.* New York: Macmillan.

DeGrazia, Victoria. 2005. *Irresistible Empire: America's Advance through Twentieth-Century Europe.* Cambridge, Mass.: Harvard University Press.

DeGroot, Gerard J., and Corinna Peniston-Bird, eds. 2000. *A Soldier and a Woman: Sexual Integration in the Military.* Essex: Longman.

Doezama, Jo. 1998. "Forced to Choose: Beyond the Voluntary versus Forced Prostitution Dichotomy." In *Global Sex Workers: Rights, Resistance, and Redefinition*, ed. Kamala Kempadoo and Jo Doezema, 34–50. New York: Routledge.

Domentat, Tamara. 1998. *Hallo Fräulein. Deutsche Frauen und amerikanische Soldaten* [Hello, Miss: German women and American soldiers]. Berlin: Aufbau Verlag.

Domestic Economy. 1947. Frankfurt on Main: Office of the Chief Historian, European Command.

Douglas, Mary. 1984 (1966). *Purity and Danger: An Analysis of Concepts of Pollution and Taboo,* ARK edition. New York: Routledge.

Dower, John W. 1986. *War without Mercy: Race and Power in the Pacific War.* New York: Pantheon.

———. 1999. *Embracing Defeat: Japan in the Wake of World War II.* New York: W. W. Norton.

Doyle, Michael W. 1986. *Empires*. Ithaca: Cornell University Press.

Duke, Simon. 1989. *United States Military Forces Installations in Europe*. Oxford: Oxford University Press.

Duus, Masayo. 1995 (1979). *Haisha no Okurimono* [A Gift from the Defeated], paperback ed. Tokyo: Kōdansha.

Eisenhower, John, ed. 1978. *Letters to Mamie*. Garden City, N.Y.: Doubleday.

Eisenstein, Zillah. 2007. *Sexual Decoys: Gender, Race, and War in Imperial Democracy*. London: Zed Books.

Eland, Ivan. 2004. *The Empire Has No Clothes: U.S. Foreign Policy Exposed*. Oakland, Calif.: Independent Institute.

Elshtain, Jean B., and Sheila Tobias, eds. 1990. *Women, Militarism, and War: Essays in History, Politics, and Social Theory*. Savage, Md.: Rowman and Littlefield.

Ender, Morten. 1996. "Growing Up in the Military." In *Strangers at Home: Essays on the Effects of Living Overseas and Coming "Home" to a Strange Land*, ed. Carolyn D. Smith, 95–106. New York: Aletheia Publications.

Enloe, Cynthia. 1983. *Does Khaki Become You? The Militarization of Women's Lives*. Boston: South End Press.

——. 1989. *Bananas, Beaches, and Bases: Making Feminist Sense of International Politics*. London: Pandora.

——. 1991. "A Feminist Perspective on Foreign Military Bases." In *The Sun Never Sets: Confronting the Network of Foreign U.S. Military Bases*, ed. Joseph Gerson and Bruce Birchard, 95–106. Boston: South End Press.

——. 1993. *The Morning After: Sexual Politics at the End of the Cold War*. Berkeley: University of California Press.

——. 2000. *Maneuvers: The International Politics of Militarizing Women's Lives*. Berkeley: University of California Press.

Enriquez, Jean. 1999. "Filipinas Prostituted around U.S. Military Bases: A Nightmare Recurring, This Time, in Korea." In *Sŏngsanŏbŭro yuipdoen oegugin yŏsŏnge kwanhan hyŏnjang silt'ae chosa pogosŏ* [A fieldwork report on foreign women trafficked into the sex industry], 91–100. Seoul: Korea Church Women United Counseling Center for Migrant Women Workers.

Evans, Jennifer. 2001. "Reconstruction Sites: Sexuality, Citizenship, and the Limits of National Belonging in Divided Berlin, 1944–58." Ph.D. diss., State University of New York, Binghamton.

Fay, George R., and Anthony R. Jones. 2004. "AR 15–6 Investigation of the Abu Ghraib Detention Facility and the 205th Military Intelligence Brigade." Reprinted in *Torture and Truth: America, Abu Ghraib, and the War on Terror*, ed. Mark Danner, 403–579. New York: New York Review of Books.

Fehrenbach, Heide. 1995. *Cinema in Democratizing Germany: The Reconstruction of a National Identity in the West, 1945–62*. Chapel Hill: University of North Carolina Press.

——. 2005. *Race after Hitler: Black Occupation Children in Postwar Germany and America*. Princeton: Princeton University Press.

Ferguson, Niall. 2002. *Empire: The Rise and Demise of the British World Order and the Lessons for Global Power*. New York: Basic Books.

———. 2005. *Colossus: The Rise and Fall of the American Empire*. New York: Penguin Books.

Field, Norma. 1993. *In the Realm of a Dying Emperor: Japan at Century's End*. New York: Vintage.

Figal, Gerald. 2001. "Waging Peace in Okinawa." *Critical Asian Studies* 33 (March): 37–69.

Firestone, Juanita M., and Richard J. Harris. 2003. "Perceptions of Effectiveness of Responses to Sexual Harassment in the U.S. Military, 1988 and 1995." *Gender, Work and Organization* 10, no. 1: 42–64.

Fleckenstein, Bernhard. 1987. *Die Beziehungen zwischen allierten Truppen und deutscher Bevölkerung im Spiegel empirischer Ergebnisse. Vorträge und Beiträge der Politischen Akademie der Konrad Adenauer Stiftung* [The relationship between allied troops and the German population based on empirical studies. Papers and contributions of the Political Academy of the Konrad Adenauer Foundation]. Munich: Sozialwissenschaftliches Institut der Bundeswehr.

Forgash, Rebecca. 2004. "Military Transnational Marriage in Okinawa: Intimacy across Boundaries of Nation, Race and Class." Ph.D. diss., University of Arizona, Tucson.

Foucault, Michel. 1980. *History of Sexuality, Volume I*. Trans. Robert Hurley. New York: Vintage.

Frankenstein, Luise. 1954. *Soldatenkinder. Die unehelichen Kinder ausländischer Soldaten mit besonderer Berücksichtigung der Mischlinge* [Children of soldiers. The illegitimate children of foreign soldiers with special consideration for those of mixed race]. Munich: Internationale Vereinigung für Jugendhilfe.

Frederiksen, Oliver J. 1953. *The American Military Occupation of Germany 1945–1953*. Darmstadt, Germany: Historical Division, U.S. Army in Europe.

Freedman, Dan, and Jacqueline Rhoads, eds. 1989. *Nurses in Vietnam: The Forgotten Veterans*. Austin: Texas Monthly Press.

Freud, Sigmund. 1959. *Group Psychology and the Analysis of the Ego*. New York: W. W. Norton.

Frevert, Ute. 2004. *A Nation in Barracks: Modern Germany, Military Conscription and Civil Society*. New York: Berg.

From Nogŭŭnri to Maehyangri Publication Committee. 2001. *Chuhanmigunmunjehaegyŏlundongsa: Nogŭnriesŏ Maehyangriggaji* [A history of the Korean people's movement to solve problems of the U.S. Forces in Korea: From Nogŭnri to Maehyangri]. Seoul: Kip'ŭnjayu.

Fujime, Yuki. 1991. "Akasen Jūgyōin Kumiai to Baishun Bōshihō [Redline District Union and the Prostitution Prevention Law]." *Joseishigaku* [*The Research Society for Women's History*] 1:16–36.

———. 1998. *Sei no Rekishigaku* [*Historical Study of Sexuality*]. Tokyo: Fuji Shuppan.

———. 1999. "Reisen Taisei Keiseiki no Beigun to Seibōryoku [The U.S. Military and Sexual Violence during the formation of Cold War System]." *Josei, Senso, Jinken* [*Women, War, Rights*] 2 (May): 116–38.

———. 2006. "Japanese Feminism and Commercialized Sex: The Union of Militarism and Prohibitionism." *Social Science Japan Journal Advance Access* 9, no. 1: 33–50.

Fulbright, J. William. 1967. *The Arrogance of Power*. New York: Random House.

Gardner, Lloyd C., and Marilyn Blatt Young, eds. 2005. *The New American Empire: A Twenty-First Century Teach-In on U.S. Foreign Policy*. New York: New Press.

Gassert, Philipp. 2001. "Mit Amerika gegen Amerika. Antiamerikanismus in Westdeutschland [With America, against America. Anti-Americanism in West Germany]." In *Die USA und Deutschland im Kalten Krieg. Ein Handbuch* [*The United States and Germany in the Era of the Cold War, 1945–1990: A Handbook*], ed. Detlef Junker, Vol. 2: 750–60. Stuttgart and Munich: DVA.

Gayn, Mark. 1948. *Japan Diary*. New York: William Sloane Associates.

Geis, Margaret. 1952a. "Morale and Discipline in the European Command 1945–49." Historical Division, European Command. Karlsruhe, Germany.

——. 1952b. "Negro Personnel in the European Command, 1 January 1946–30 June 1950." Historical Division, European Command. Karlsruhe, Germany.

Geis, Margaret, and George J. Gray. 1951. *The Relations of Occupation Personnel with the Civilian Population, 1946–1948*. Occupation Forces in Europe Series. Historical Division. European Command. Karlsruhe, Germany.

Gerson, Joseph, and Bruce Birchard, eds. 1991. *The Sun Never Sets: Confronting the Network of U.S. Foreign Military Bases*. Boston: South End Press.

Geyer, Michael. 2001. "Cold War Angst: The Case of West German Opposition to Rearmament und Nuclear Weapons." In Hanna Schissler, *The Miracle Years: A Cultural History of West Germany, 1949–1968*, 376–408. Princeton: Princeton University Press.

Gher, Jaime M. 2002. "Status of Forces Agreements: Tools to Further Effective Foreign Policy and Lessons to Be Learned from the United States-Japan Agreement." *University of San Francisco Law Review* 37 (Fall): 227–56.

Gill, Lesley. 2004. *The School of the Americas: Military Training and Political Violence in the Americas*. Durham: Duke University Press.

Gillem, Mark L. 2007. *America Town: Building the Outposts of Empire*. Minneapolis: University of Minnesota Press.

Go, Julian. 2007. "The Provinciality of American Empire: 'Liberal Exceptionalism' and U.S. Colonial Rule, 1898–1912." *Comparative Studies in Society and History* 49, no. 1: 74–108.

——. 2008. *American Empire and the Politics of Meaning: Elite Political Cultures in the Philippines and Puerto Rico during U.S. Colonialism*. Durham: Duke University Press.

Go, Julian, and Anne L. Foster, eds. 2003. *The American Colonial State in the Philippines: Global Perspectives*. Durham: Duke University Press.

Goedde, Petra. 2003. *GIs and Germans: Culture, Gender and Foreign Relations*. New Haven: Yale University Press.

Goff, Stan. 2006. *Sex and War*. Self-published by Lulu.com.

Govern, James. 1957. *Fräulein*. London: Calder.

Grant, Will. 2002. "Here, There, Everywhere: The N[ew] S[tatesman] Guide to United States Military Bases." *New Statesman* 131 (January 28): 32–33.

Green United and the Coalition of Movements to Reclaim U.S. Military Bases. 2004. *2004 nyŏn chuhanmigungji hyŏnwhangbogosŏ* [A 2004 field report on the U.S. military bases). Seoul: Green United and the Coalition of Movements to Reclaim U.S. Military Bases.

Grossmann, Atina. 1995. "A Question of Silence: The Rape of German Women by Occupation Soldiers." *October* 72 (Spring): 42–63.

Gusterson, Hugh. 1996. *Nuclear Rites: A Weapons Laboratory at the End of the Cold War*. Berkeley: University of California Press.

Gutmann, Stephanie. 2001. *The Kinder, Gentler Military: Can America's Gender-Neutral Fighting Force Still Win Wars?* New York: Scribner.

Habe, Hans. 1949. *Walk in Darkness*. London: George G. Harrap.

———. 1957. *Off Limits*, trans. Ewald Osers. New York: Fell.

Hampf, M. Michaela. 2004. "'Dykes' or 'Whores': Sexuality and the Women's Army Corps in the United States during World War II." *Women's Studies International Forum* 27: 13–30.

Hardt, Michael, and Antonio Negri. 2000. *Empire*. Cambridge, Mass: Harvard University Press.

Harris, Richard J. 1999. "Changes in Patterns of Sexual Harassment in the U.S. Military: A Comparison of the 1988 and 1995 DOD Surveys." *Armed Forces and Society* 25, no. 4: 613–32.

Harvey, David. 2003. *The New Imperialism*. Oxford: Oxford University Press.

Hassner, Pierre. 2002. "The United States: The Empire of Force or the Force of Empire?" Chaillot Paper no. 54. Paris: European Union Institute for Security Studies. September.

Hauser, William. 1973. *America's Army in Crisis: A Study in Civil–Military Relations*. Baltimore: Johns Hopkins University Press.

Hawkins, John Palmer. 2001. *Army of Hope, Army of Alienation: Culture and Contradiction in the American Army Communities of Cold War Germany*. Westport, Conn.: Praeger.

Hayashi, Hirofumi. 2005. "Amerika gun no Seitaisaku no Rekishi—1950 nen dai made [History of U.S. Military Sexual Measures—To the 1950s]." *Josei, Senso Jinken* [Women, War, Rights] 7 (March): 94–118.

Headquarters of the Movement to Root Out American Soldiers' Crime, ed. 2002. *Migunbŏmjoiwa han-mi SOFA* [American soldiers' crime and the Korea–U.S. SOFA]. Seoul: Turimidia.

Hein, Laura, and Mark Selden, eds. 2003. *Islands of Discontent: Okinawan Responses to Japanese and American Power*. Lanham, Md.: Rowman and Littlefield.

Heineman, Elizabeth. 1996. "The Hour of the Woman: Memories of Germany's Crisis Years and West German National Identity." *American Historical Review* 101, no. 2: 359–95.

———. 1999. *What Difference Does a Husband Make? Women and Marital Status in Nazi and Postwar Germany*. Berkeley: University of California Press.

Heinrichs, Christine Willard. 2007. "Women Fill Technical and Leadership Roles in Today's Defense Industries." *Diversity/Careers in Engineering and Information Technology*. Www.diversitycareers.com. Accessed 10 April 2010.

Henke, Klaus-Dietmar. 1995. *Die amerikanische Besetzung Deutschlands* [The American Occupation of Germany]. Munich: R. Oldenbourg Verlag.

Herbert, Melissa. 1998. *Camouflage Isn't Only for Combat: Gender, Sexuality, and Women in the Military*. New York: New York University Press.

Hersh, Seymour. 2004a. "Torture at Abu Ghraib: American Soldiers Brutalized Iraqis." *New Yorker*, 10 May.

———. 2004b. "The Gray Zone: How a Secret Pentagon Program came to Abu Ghraib." *New Yorker*. 24 May.

Higashi Mineo. 1992. *Child of Okinawa*. In *Okinawa: Two Postwar Novellas by Oshiro Tatsu-*

hiro and Higashi Mineo, ed. and trans. Steve Rabson, 79–118. Japan Research Monograph 10. Berkeley: Institute of East Asian Studies, University of California.

Hillman, Elizabeth Lutes. 2005. *Defending America: Military Culture and the Cold War Court-Martial*. Princeton: Princeton University Press.

Hirano, Kyoko. 1992. *Mr. Smith Goes to Japan: Japanese Cinema under the American Occupation, 1945–1952*. Washington, D.C.: Smithsonian Institution Press.

Hodge, Carl Cavanagh. 2005. "America's Empire by Default." *Orbis* 49, no. 1 (Winter): 61–73.

Höhn, Maria. 2002. GIs *and Fräuleins: The German–American Encounter in 1950s West Germany*. Chapel Hill: University of North Carolina Press.

———. 2005. " 'Ein Atemzug der Freiheit': Afro-amerikanische GIs, deutsche Frauen, und die Grenzen der Demokratie (1945–1968) [A Breath of Freedom. African American GIs, German Women, and the Limits of Democracy]." In *Demokratiewunder. Transatlantische Mittler und die kulturelle Öffnung Westdeutschlands, 1945–1970* [The Miracle of Democracy. Transatlantic Mediators and the Cultural Opening of West Germany, 1945–1970], ed. Arnd Bauerkämpfer, Konrad H. Jarausch, and Marcus Payk, 104–28. Göttingen: Vandenhoeck and Ruprecht.

———. 2008a. "The Black Panther Solidarity Committees and the *Voice of the Lumpen*." *German Studies Review* 31, no. 1 (February): 133–54.

———. 2008b. " 'We Will Never Go Back to the Old Way Again': Germany in the African American Debate on Civil Rights." *Central European History* 41, no. 4 (December): 605–37.

———. 2010. "The Black Panther Solidarity Committee and the Trial of the Ramstein 2," in *Changing the World, Changing The Self: Political Protest and Collective Identities in 1960 / 70s West Germany and the United States*, ed. Belinda Davis, Martin Klimke, Carla McDougall, and Wilfried Mausbach. New York: Berghahn Books, 2010, 215–39.

———. 2011. "Love Across the Color-Line: The Limits of German and American Democracy, 1945–68," in Larry Greene and Anke Ortlepp, eds., *Germans and African Americans: Two Centuries of Contact*. Jackson: University of Mississippi Press.

Höhn, Maria and Martin Klimke. 2010. *A Breath of Freedom. The Civil Rights Struggle, African American* GIs*, and Germany*. New York: Palgrave.

Hough, Patricia. 1979. "The Socio-Cultural Integration of German Women Married to American Military Personnel." Ph.D. diss., Free University, Berlin.

Houppert, Karen. 2005. *Home Fires Burning: Married to the Military—for Better or Worse*. New York: Ballantine Books.

Howes, Ruth H., and Michael R. Stevenson, eds. 1993. *Women and the Use of Military Force*. Boulder: Lynne Rienner Publishers.

Hutton, Bud, and Andy Rooney. 1947. *Conqueror's Peace: A Report to the American Stockholder*. New York: Doubleday.

Ignatieff, Michael. 2003. *Empire Lite: Nation Building in Bosnia, Kosovo, and Afghanistan*. Toronto: Penguin Books.

Iha Masakazu. 1998. "Kandō o Hada de Shiru [Knowing Passion through Experience]." In *Eisā 360°: Rekishi to Genzai 1998* [Eisā in the Round: History and the Present (1998)].

Inoue, Kiyoshi. 1962. *Gendai Nihon Joseishi* [Modern / Contemporary Japanese Women's History]. Tokyo: San'ichi Shōbo.

Inoue, Setsuko. 1995. *Senryogun Ianjo* [Comfort Stations for the Occupation Forces]. Tokyo: Shinhyoron.

James, John C., and Terunobu Tamamori. 1996. *A Minute Guide to Okinawa: Society and Economy*. Naha City, Japan: Bank of the Ryūkyūs International Foundation.

Janeway, Eliot. 1945. "America's Moral Crisis." *Asia and the Americas* 45 (October): 466–69.

Jeffords, Suzan. 1994. "Terminal Masculinity: Men in the Early 1990s." In *Hard Bodies: Hollywood Masculinity in the Reagan Era*. New Brunswick, N.J.: Rutgers University Press.

Johnson, Chalmers A. 2000. *Blowback: The Costs and Consequences of American Empire*. New York: Holt.

——. 2004a. *The Sorrows of Empire: Militarism, Secrecy, and the End of the Republic*. New York: Metropolitan Books.

——. 2004b. Three Rapes: The Status of Forces Agreement and Okinawa. Japan Policy Research Institute Working Paper No. 97. January.

Johnson, Sheila. 1975. *American Attitudes toward Japan, 1941–1975*. Washington, D.C.: American Enterprise Institute for Public Research.

Juchler, Ingo. 1996. *Die Studentenbewegung in den Vereinigten Staaten und der Bundesrepublik Deutschland der sechziger Jahre* [The student movement of the United States and Federal Republic of Germany in the 1960s]. Berlin: Dunker und Humblot, GmbH.

Kagan, Frederick W. 2006. "The U.S. Military's Manpower Crisis." *Foreign Affairs* 85, no. 4 (July–August): 97–110.

Kane, Tim. 2006. "Global U.S. Troop Deployment, 1950–2004." The Heritage Foundation, Center for Data Analysis. Www.heritage.org / Research / Reports / 2006 / 05 / Global-US-Troop-Deployment-1950–2004. Accessed 12 April 2010.

Kang, Ok-kyŏng, Hyon-sŏn Kim, and Su-kyŏng Chŏn. 2001. *Kyŏnggidojiyŏk sŏngmaemae silt'aejosa mit chŏngch'aekdaean yŏngu* [A study of prostitution in the Kyŏnggi Province area and policy alternatives]. Tongduch'ŏn City, South Korea: Saewumt'ŏ.

Kang, Yŏng-su. 1989. "Hyangnaksanŏbŭi kihyŏngjŏk sŏngjangkwa ie taehan olbarŭn insigjŏngnibŭl wihayŏ [Toward an understanding of the monstrous growth of the entertainment industry]." *Kaech'ŏkcha* 26 (October) [Pioneers]: 121–40.

Kanzaki, Kiyoshi. 1953a. "Kanpan ni agatta Panpan." *Kaizo* ["PanPan(s) On Board."] 34, no. 6: 196–203.

——. 1953b. *Yoru no Kichi* [The Nights of Bases]. Tokyo: Kawade Shōbo.

Kaplan, Amy. 2002. *The Anarchy of Empire in the Making of U.S. Culture*. Cambridge, Mass.: Harvard University Press.

——. 2004. "Violent Belongings and the Question of Empire Today: Presidential Address to the American Studies Association, October 17, 2003." *American Quarterly* 56 (March): 1–18.

Kaplan, Amy, and Donald E. Pease, eds. 1993. *Cultures of United States Imperialism*. Durham: Duke University Press.

Kawahira Choshin. 1970. *Ryūkyū Ocho-shi: Okinawa no Tami to O* [A History of Ryūkyūan Dynasties: Okinawan Royalty and its Subjects]. Naha City, Japan: Gekkan Okinawa-sha.

Kawasaki, Hiroshi. 1988. *Saipan to Yobareta Otoko* [A Man Called "Saipan"]. Tokyo: Shinchōsha.

Kelsky, Karen. 2001. *Women on the Verge: Japanese Women, Western Dreams*. Durham: Duke University Press.

Kempadoo, Kamala. 1998. "Introduction: Globalizing Sex Workers' Rights." In *Global Sex Workers: Rights, Resistance, and Redefinition*, ed. Kamala Kempadoo and Jo Doezama, 1–27. New York: Routledge.

Kennedy, Paul. 1989. *The Rise and Fall of the Great Powers: Economic Change and Military Conflict from 1500–2000*. New York: Random House.

Kim, Chae-jun. 1970. "Kungmin, kukhoe, anbo [Nationals, the National Assembly, security]. *Sindonga* 73 (September): 140–47.

Kim, Chae-su. 1980. "Kijich'one kwanhan sahoejirihakjŏk yŏngu: Dongduch'ŏnŭl chungsimŭro [A social geographical study of military camptowns: Focus on Dongduch'ŏn]." *Chirihakyŏngu* 5: 274–94.

Kim, Ellim. 1990. "Yullakhaengwidŭng pangjibŏp kaejŏngŭl wihan yŏngu [A study to revise the Prostitution Prevention Law]." *Yŏsŏngyŏngu* 26: 85–118.

Kim, Hyŏn-sŏn. 2001. "Kijich'onmaemaech'unkwa yŏsŏnginkwŏn [Camptown prostitution and women's human rights]." Lecture presented at the Women's Peace Academy, Seoul.

Kim, In-suk. 1989. "Yullakyŏsŏnge taehan sahoebogji chŏngch'aekpunsŏk" [An analysis of social-welfare policy on prostitutes]." *Sahoebogji* 101 (Summer): 127–59.

Kim, Jinwung. 2004. "Ambivalent Allies: Recent South Korean Perceptions of the United States Forces Korea (usfk)." *Asian Affairs* 30, no. 4: 268–85.

Kim, Sŭng-t'ae. 1997. "Ilbongun 'wianbu' chŏngch'aek hyŏngsŏngŭi ilbonch'ŭk yŏksajŏk paegyŏng [The Japanese historical background of the making of the Japanese military 'comfort women' policy]." In *Ilbongun wianbumunjeŭi chinsang* [Truthful state of Japanese military comfort women), ed. Council for Resolving the Problem of the Military Comfort Women, 37–68. Seoul: Yŏksabip'yŏngsa.

Kim, Tong-nyŏng. 2007. "Han'guk, nanŭn han'gugi choa [Korea, I like Korea]." In *Turebangesŏ kirŭl mutta: Turebang 20junyŏn ginyŏmmunjip* [We ask a way at My Sister's Place: Twentieth anniversary writing collection], ed. My Sister's Place, 54–77. Ŭijŏngbu City: My Sister's Place.

Kim, Tong-sim, Sa-jin Kwak, Il-lan Kim, Yŏng-hŭi Han, Kyŏng-t'ae Pak, and Tu-yŏn Kim. 2003. *Kijich'on honhyŏrin inkwŏnsilt'aejosa* [A research report on the status of mixed-blood people in camp towns]. Seoul: State Human Rights Commission.

Kim, Yŏn-ja. 2005. *Americataun wangŏnni, chuggi obunjŏnkkaji agŭlssŭda: Kim, Yŏn-ja chajŏn esei* [A big sister in the America Town screams until five minutes before her death: Kim Yŏn-ja's autobiographical essay]. Seoul: Simin.

Kirk, Gwyn. 2007. "Yŏsŏngŭi chinjŏnghan anjŏn [Women's genuine security]. In *Turebangesŏ kirŭl mutta: Turebang 20junyŏn ginyŏmmunjip* [We ask a way at My Sister's Place: Twentieth anniversary writing collection], ed. My Sister's Place, 131–53. Ŭijŏngbu City: My Sister's Place.

Kissinger, Henry. 2001. *Does America Need a Foreign Policy? Toward a Diplomacy for the Twenty-First Century*. New York: Simon and Schuster.

Kleinschmidt, Johannes. 1997. *"Do Not Fraternize": Die schwierigen Anfänge deutsch-amerikanischer Freundschaft 1944–1949* ["Do Not Fraternize": The difficult beginning of the German–American friendship, 1944–1949]. Trier, Germany: Wissenschaftlicher Verlag.

Kligman, Gail, 2005. "Trafficking Women after Socialism: From, to, and through Eastern Europe." Paper presented at the Center for European and Eurasian Studies, University of California, Los Angeles. 11 March.

Klimke, Martin. 2010. *The Other Alliance: Student Protest in West Germany and the United States in the Global Sixties*. Princeton: Princeton University Press.

Knauft, Bruce M. 2007. "Provincializing America: Imperialism, Capitalism, and Counterhegemony in the Twenty-first Century." *Current Anthropology* 48, no. 6: 781–805.

Knauer, Sebastian. 1987. *Lieben wir die USA? Was die Deutschen über die Amerikaner denken* [Do we love the USA? What the Germans think of the Americans]. Hamburg: Gruner und Jahr.

Ko, Hyŏn-wung, Chae-wŏn Kim, Ra-mi So, Da-he Chang-Im, Tong-sim Kim, and Tong-nyŏng Kim. 2006. *Oegugin yŏnyein toip silt'aejosa mit chŏngch'aekbikyoyŏngu* [A study of the importation of foreign entertainers into South Korea and policy comparison]. Seoul: Ministry of Culture and Tourism and International Organization for Migration.

Ko, Yu-kyŏng. 2007. "Chuhanmigun chaebaech'iwa p'yŏnghwajŏk saengjonkwŏn [Relocation of the U.S Forces in Korea and the right to peaceful life]." In *Turebangesŏ kirŭlmutta* [We ask the way at My Sister's Place], ed. My Sister's Place, 234–61. Ŭijŏngbu City: My Sister's Place.

Kobayashi, Daijiro, and Murase Akira. 1992 (1961). *Minna ha Shiranai Kokka Baishun Meirei* [The State Prostitution Order that No One Knows]. Tokyo: Yūhikaku Shuppan.

Kobayashi, Yoshinori. 2005. *Okinawa-ron* [Treatise on Okinawa]. Tokyo: Shogakukan.

Koikari, Mire. 1999. "Re-Thinking Gender and Power in the U.S. Occupation of Japan, 1945–1952." *Gender and History* 11, no. 2: 313–35.

Korea Church Women United. 1999. *Sŏngsanŏbŭro yuipdoen oegugin yŏsŏnge kwanhan hyŏnjang silt'ae chosa pogosŏ* [A fieldwork report on foreign women trafficked into the sex industry]. Seoul: Korea Church Women United Counseling Center for Migrant Women Workers.

———. 2002. *Sŏngsanŏbŭro yuipdoen oegugin yŏsŏnge kwanhan Che 2ch'a hyŏnjang silt'ae chosa pogosŏ* [The second fieldwork report on foreign women trafficked into the sex industry]. Seoul: Korea Church Women United Counseling Center for Migrant Women Workers.

Korean Military Support Corps for the U.S. Eighth Army. 1993. *Katusaŭi ŏjewa onŭl* [The KATUSAS' yesterday and today]. Seoul: Mi p'algun han'gukkun chiwondan.

Korea Travel Newspaper Special Report Team. 1999. *Han'guk kwankwang 50 nyŏn pisa* [A 50-year hidden history of tourism in Korea]. Seoul: Travel Newspaper.

Kramer, Paul. 2002. "Empires, Exceptions, and Anglo-Saxons: Race and Rule between the British and U.S. Empires, 1880–1910." *Journal of American History* 88 (March): 1315–53.

———. 2006a. *The Blood of Government: Race, Empire, the United States, and the Philippines*. Chapel Hill: University of North Carolina Press.

———. 2006b. "The Darkness That Enters the Home: The Politics of Prostitution during the Philippine–American War." In *Haunted by Empire: Geographies of Intimacies in North American History*, ed. Ann Laura Stoler, 366–404. Durham: Duke University Press.

Kroes, Rob. 1996. *If You've Seen One, You've Seen the Mall*. Chicago: University of Illinois Press.

Kuisel, Richard. 1993. *Seducing the French: The Dilemma of Americanization*. Berkeley: University of California Press.

LaCapra, Dominick. 1999. "Trauma, Absence, and Loss." *Critical Inquiry* 25, no. 4: 696–727.

Lee, Clark. 1947. *One Last Look Around*. New York: Duell, Sloan, and Pearce.

Lee, Ulysses Grant. 1966. *The Employment of Negro Troops: Special Studies, United States Army in World War II*. Washington, D.C.: Office of the Chief of Military History.

Leuerer, Thomas. 1997. *Die Stationierung amerikanischer Streitkräfte in Deutschland. Militärgemeinden in Deutschland als ziviles Element der Stationierungspolitik der Vereinigten Staaten* [The stationing of American troops in Germany. Military communities in Germany as a civil aspect of the United States' stationing policies]. Würzburg: Ergon Verlag.

Levine, Philippa. 2003. *Prostitution, Race, and Politics: Policing Venereal Disease in the British Empire*. New York: Routledge.

Lilly, J. Robert. 1995. "Dirty Details: Executing U.S. Soldiers during World War II." *Crime and Delinquency* 42, no. 4: 491–516.

Lilly, J. Robert, and J. Michael Thomson. 1997. "Executing U.S. Soldiers in England, World War II: The Power of Command Influence and Sexual Racism." *British Journal of Criminology* 37: 262–88.

Lincoln, Brett. 2006. "Fiscal Year 2007 Federal Budget Proposal: Combined Mandatory and Discretionary Spending." *Defense Monitor* 35, no. 2 (March–April): 4.

Lindsay-Poland, John. 1996. "The U.S. Military Bases: Will They Stay or Go?" *NACLA Report on the Americas* 29, no. 5 (March–April): 6–9.

———. 1999. "Military Bases Close in Panama, New Bases Open in Ecuador and Dutch Antilles." *NACLA Report on the Americas* 33, no. 1 (July–August): 52–53.

Ling, L. H. M. 1999. "Sex Machine: Global Hypermasculinity and Images of the Asian Woman in Modernity." *Positions: East Asia Cultures Critique* 7, no. 2 (Fall): 277–306.

Lundestad, Geir. 1998. *The United States and Western Europe since 1945: From Empire by Invitation to Transatlantic Drift*. Oxford: Oxford University Press.

Lutz, Catherine A. 2001. *Home Front: A Military City and the American Twentieth Century*. Boston: Beacon Press.

Lutz, Catherine A., ed. 2009. *The Bases of Empire: The Global Struggle against U.S. Military Posts*. New York: New York University Press.

Lutz, Catherine A., and Jane L. Collins. 1993. *Reading National Geographic*. Chicago: University of Chicago Press.

Maase, Kaspar. 1992. *Bravo Amerika: Erkundigungen zur Jugendkultur der Bundesrepublik in den fünfziger Jahren* [Bravo Amerika. Explorations of West German Youth Culture during the 1950s]. Hamburg: Junius Verlag.

Maier, Charles S. 2006. *Among Empires: American Ascendancy and Its Predecessors*. Cambridge, Mass.: Harvard University Press.

Mann, Michael. 1984. *State, War and Capitalism: Studies in Political Sociology*. Oxford: Blackwell.

———. 2003. *Incoherent Empire*. London: Verso.

Markusen, Ann. 1999. *Arming the Future: A Defense Industry for the Twenty-First Century.* Washington, D.C.: Council on Foreign Relations Press.

Mason, R. Chuck. 2008. "Status of Forces Agreement (SOFA): What Is It, and How Might One be Utilized in Iraq?" CRS Report for Congress RL 34531. Washington, D.C.: Congressional Research Service.

May, Elaine Tyler. 1999 (1988). *Homeward Bound: American Families in the Cold War Era,* revised and updated edition. New York: Basic Books.

Mayer, Arno. 2000. *The Furies: Violence and Terror in the French and Russian Revolutions.* Princeton: Princeton University Press.

Mayer, Jane. 2008. *The Dark Side.* New York: Doubleday.

McAlister, Melanie. 2001. *Epic Encounters, Culture, Media and U.S. Interests in the Middle East, 1945–2000.* Berkeley: University of California Press.

McClintock, Anne. 1995. *Imperial Leather: Race, Gender, and Sexuality in the Colonial Context.* New York: Routledge.

McCoy, Alfred. 2006. *A Question of Torture: CIA Interrogation, from the Cold War to the War on Terror.* New York: Metropolitan Books.

McNinch, Joseph H. 1954. "Venereal Disease Problems, U.S. Army Forces, Far East 1950–53." Presented to the Course on Recent Advances in Medicine and Surgery, Army Medical Service Graduate School, Walter Reed Army Medical Center, Washington, D.C. 27 April. http://history.amedd.army.mil/booksdocs/korea/recad2/ch4-2.htm (accessed on 17 March 2006).

Meade, E. Grant. 1951. *American Military Government in Korea.* New York: King's Crown Press.

Mehta, Uday Signh. 1999. *Liberalism and Empire: A Study in Nineteenth-Century British Liberal Thought.* Chicago: University of Chicago Press.

Memmi, Albert. 2006. *Decolonization and the Decolonized,* trans. Robert Bononno. Minneapolis: University of Minnesota Press.

Merritt, Anna, and Richard Merritt. 1980. *Public Opinion in Semi-Sovereign Germany: The HICOG Surveys, 1949–1955.* Chicago: University of Illinois Press.

Meyer, Sybille, and Eva Schulz. 1985. *Von Liebe sprach damals keiner. Familienalltag in der Nachkriegszeit* [Nobody talked of love then. Family life in the postwar years]. Munich: Beck.

Miller, Laura. 1998. "Feminism and the Exclusion of Army Women from Combat." *Gender Issues* 16, no. 3: 33–64.

Mills, Karen. 1993. *Americans Overseas in U.S. Censuses.* Technical Paper 62. Economics and Statistics Administration, Bureau of the Census, U.S. Department of Commerce, Washington, D.C. November.

Ministry of Health and Social Affairs, Republic of Korea. 1958. *Sŏngbyŏngnyŏnbo 1957* [Venereal disease yearbook 1957]. Seoul: Ministry of Health and Social Affairs.

———. 1969. *Pogŏnsahoet'onggyeyŏnbo* [Yearbook of public health and social statistics]. Seoul: Ministry of Health and Social Affairs.

———. 1987. *Punyŏhaeng ŏng 40nyŏnsa* [A forty-year history of women's administration]. Seoul: Ministry of Health and Social Affairs.

Minton, William L. 1948. "Report of Essential Technical Medical Data." Prepared at

Rehabilitation Center, Office of the Surgeon, APO 6, Unit 4, U.S. Army Forces in Korea. NARA, RG 554, box P47.

Misra, Maria. 2003. "Lessons of Empire: Britain and India." *SAIS Review* 23, no. 2: 133–53.

Mitchell, Brian. 1989. *Weak Link: The Feminization of the American Military*. Washington, D.C.: Regnery Gateway.

———. 1998. *Women in the Military: Flirting with Disaster*. Washington, D.C.: Regnery Publishing.

Mitsui, Hideko. 2006. "The Resignification of the 'Comfort Women' through NGO Trials." In *Rethinking Historical Injustice and Reconciliation in Northeast Asia: The Korean Experience*, ed. Gi-wook Shin, Soon-won Park, and Daqing Yang, 36–54. London: Routledge.

Molasky, Michael S. 1999. *The American Occupation of Japan and Okinawa: Literature and Memory*. London: Routledge.

———. "Medoruma Shu: The Writer as Public Intellectual in Okinawa Today." In *Islands of Discontent: Okinawan Responses to Japanese and American Power*, ed. Laura Hein and Mark Selden. Lanham, Md.: Rowman and Littlefield, 161–91.

Moon, Chŏng-ju. 2005. "Kijuch'on yŏsŏngŭi samkwa kŏngang [Camptown women's lives and health]. In *Turebang yiyagi: Turebang 15nyŏn kinyŏmjaryojip* [Stories from My Sister's Place: Fifteenth anniversary resources collection], 326–35. Ŭijŏngbu City: My Sister's Place.

Moon, Katharine H. S. 1997. *Sex among Allies: Military Prostitution in U.S.–Korea Relations*. New York: Columbia University Press.

———. 2007. "Resurrecting Prostitutes and Overturning Treaties: Gender Politics in the 'Anti-American' Movement in South Korea." *Journal of Asian Studies* 66, no. 1: 129–57.

Moon, Seungsook. 1998. "Begetting the Nation: The Androcentric Discourse of National History and Tradition in South Korea." In *Dangerous Women: Gender and Korean Nationalism*, ed. Elaine H. Kim and Chungmoo Choi, 33–66. New York: Routledge.

———. 2001. "The Production and Subversion of Hegemonic Masculinity: Reconfiguring Gender Hierarchy in Contemporary South Korea." In *Under Construction: The Gendering of Modernity, Class, and Consumption in the Republic of Korea*, ed. Laurel Kendall, 79–113. Honolulu: University of Hawaii Press.

———. 2002a. "Beyond Equality versus Difference: Professional Women Soldiers in the South Korean Army." *Social Politics* 9, no. 2 (Summer): 212–47.

———. 2002b. "Imagining a Nation through Difference: Reading the Controversy concerning the Military Service Extra Points System in South Korea," *The Review of Korean Studies* 5, no. 2 (December): 73–109.

———. 2005a. *Militarized Modernity and Gendered Citizenship in South Korea*. Durham: Duke University Press.

———. 2005b. "Trouble with Conscription, Entertaining Soldiers: Popular Culture and the Politics of Militarized Masculinity in South Korea." *Men and Masculinities* 8, no. 1 (July): 64–92.

Moskos, Charles. 1970. *The American Enlisted Man: The Rank and File in Today's Military*. New York: Russell Sage Foundation.

Mosse, George L. 1985. *Nationalism and Sexuality: Respectability and Abnormal Sexuality in Modern Europe*. New York: Howard Fertig.

Müller, Emil-Peter. 1986. *Antiamerikanismus in Deutschland. Zwischen Care-Paket und Cruise Missile* [Anti-Americanism in Germany. Caught between Care Packages and cruise missiles]. Cologne: Deutscher Instituts-Verlag.

Münkler, Herfried. 2007. *Empires: The Logic of World Domination from Ancient Rome to the United States*, trans. B. Patrick Camiller. Cambridge: Polity Press.

Muppidi, Himadeep. 2004. *The Politics of the Global*. Minneapolis: University of Minnesota Press.

My Sister's Place, ed. 2003. *Kyŏnggibugbu kijich'onjiyŏk sŏngmaemaegŭnjŏrŭl wihan p'ihaeyŏsŏng chiwŏnsaŏp pogohoe jaryojip* [A report on projects to eliminate camptown prostitution and support women victimized by the prostitution in northern Kyŏnggi Province). Ŭijŏngbu City: My Sister's Place.

——, ed. 2005a. *Turebang yiyagi: Turebang 15nyŏn kinyŏmjaryojip* [Stories from My Sister's Place: Fifteenth anniversary resources collection]. Ŭijŏngbu City: My Sister's Place.

——, ed. 2005b. *Kijich'onjiyŏk sŏngmaemae pihaeyŏsŏng sangdamjiwŏn saryejip* [A collection of counseling support cases for women victimized by camptown prostitution]. Ŭijŏngbu City: My Sister's Place.

——, ed. 2005c. "Philippines–Korea Internship Program for the Prevention of International Trafficking and the Protection of the Rights of Filipina Migrants: Filipino Women in the Sex Industry and International Marriage." Report sponsored by the Asia Foundation, My Sister's Place, Ŭijŏngbu City.

——, ed. 2005d. *Sŏngmaemae mogjŏgŭi insinmaemae kŭnjŏrŭl wihan konggaet'oronhoe charyojip: sŏngmaemaet'ŭkpyŏlbŏpkwa kijich'on yŏsŏng* [Collection from a public discussion meeting to eliminate trafficking of women for prostitution: Prostitution Special Law and camptown women]." Ŭijŏngbu City: My Sister's Place.

——, ed. 2007. *Turebangesŏ kirŭl mutta: Turebang 20junyŏn ginyŏmmunjip* [We ask a way at My Sister's Place: Twentieth anniversary writing collection]. Ŭijŏngbu City: My Sister's Place.

Naimark, Norman M. 1995. *The Russians in Germany: A History of the Soviet Zone of Occupation 1945–49*. Cambridge, Mass.: Harvard University Press.

Nalty, Bernard C, and Morris McGregor, eds. 1981. *Blacks in the Military: Essential Documents*. Wilmington, Del.: Scholarly Resources.

National Association for the Advancement of Colored People. 1971. *The Search for Military Justice: Report of an NAACP Inquiry into the Problems of the Negro Servicemen in West Germany*. New York: National Association for the Advancement of Colored People.

National Campaign to Eliminate Crimes Committed by U.S. Forces in Korea. 1999. *Kkŭnnaji anŭn ap'ŭmŭi yŏksa: Migunbŏmjoe* [A history of pain that has not yet ended: Crimes committed by U.S. Forces in Korea]. Seoul: Kaemasŏwŏn.

——. 2002. *Migunbŏmjoewa hanmi SOFA* [Crime committed by American soldiers and Korea-US SOFA]. Seoul: Turimidiŏ

National Economic Board. 1947. *South Korea Interim Government Activities*, No. 27 (December). Seoul: United States Army Military Government in Korea.

——. 1948. *South Korean Interim Government Activities*, No. 29 (February). Seoul: United States Army Military Government in Korea.

National Military Family Association. 2005. "Fact Sheet: A Brief History and Introduction to the National Military Family Association." Alexandria, Va. June.

——. 2006. "Position Paper: Communities: Preparing for Transformation, Global Rebasing, and B[ase] R[ealignment] a[nd] C[losure]." March.

Nelson, Christopher. 2009. *Dancing with the Dead: Memory, Performance, and Everyday Life in Postwar Okinawa.* Durham: Duke University Press.

Nelson, Daniel. 1987. *Defenders or Intruders? The Dilemma of U.S. Forces in Germany.* Boulder: Westview Press.

Nishida, Minoru. 1953. *Kichi no Onna* [Women of the Base]. Tokyo: Kawade Shobo.

Noble, Harold J. 1975. *Embassy at War.* Seattle: University of Washington Press.

Nolan, Mary. 1994. *Visions of Modernity: American Business and the Modernization of Germany.* New York: Oxford University Press.

Nomura, Kōya. 2005. *Muishiki no Shokuminchishugi: Nihonjin no Beigun Kichi to Okinawajin* [Unconscious Colonialism: The Japanese People's American Bases and the Okinawan People]. Tokyo: Ochanomizu Shobō.

Norman, Elizabeth M. 1990. *Women at War: The Story of Fifty Military Nurses Who Served in Vietnam.* Philadelphia: University of Pennsylvania Press.

Nye, Joseph S. 2002. *The Paradox of American Power: Why the World's Only Superpower Can't Go It Alone.* New York: Oxford University Press.

——. 2004. *Soft Power: The Means to Success in World Politics.* New York: Public Affairs.

O'Donnell, Ian. 2004. "Prison Rape in Context." *British Journal of Criminology,* 44, no. 2 (March): 241–55.

Oh, Kyon-ch'i, Yŏng-gu Cha, and Tong-jun Hwang. 1990. *H'anmigunsahyŏmyŏk kwangyeŭi paljŏnkwa chŏnmang* [The development of Korea–U.S. military cooperation and its prospect]. Seoul: Segyŏngsa.

Oh, Yŏn-ho. 1990. *Tŏisang urirŭl sŭlp'ŭge hajimala* [Do not make us sad anymore]. Seoul: Paeksansŏdang.

Okazawa-Rey, Margo. 2005. "Margo Report on the Problem of Bi-Racial Children in Korea." In *Turebang yiyagi: Turebang 15nyŏn kinyŏmjaryojip* [Stories from My Sister's Place: Fifteenth anniversary resources collection), ed. My Sister's Place, 188–201. Ŭijŏngbu City: My Sister's Place.

Okuno Hikorokuro. 1978. *Okinawa Koninshi* [The History of Marriage in Okinawa]. Tokyo: Kokushō Kankōkai.

Oldfield, Sybil. 1989. *Women against the Iron Fist: Alternatives to Militarism, 1900–1989.* Oxford: Basil Blackwell.

Onna Tachi no Ima wo Tou Kai [Association to Discuss Today's Woman Question], ed. 1986. "Raundo Teburu: Chōsen Sensō Gyaku Kōsu no Naka no Onna Tachi [Round Table: Women in Korean War and the Reverse Course]." In *Jyūgoshi Nōto Sengo Hen* [A Note on History of Home-front, Postwar Volume]. Tokyo: Impakuto.

Ōshima, Yukio. 1975. "Kokusaku Baishun no Tenmatsu [The Whole Story of National Prostitution Project]." In *Nihon Josei no Rekishi,* Volume 13: *Senchu Sengo no Josei* [*Japanese Women's History: Women in Wartime and Postwar*], ed. Itsuo Tsubota. Tokyo: Akatsuki Kyōiku Tosho.

Ōta, Masahide. 2000. *Essays on Okinawa Problems.* Tokyo: Yui Shuppan.

Padover, Saul. 1946. *Experiment in Germany: The Story of an American Intelligence Officer.* New York: Duell, Sloan and Pearce.

Pae, Yong-gi. 1989. "Yŏsŏngŭi koyonggujowa yullakyŏsŏng [The structure of women's employment and prostitutes]." *Kwangjang* 188 (April): 59–69.

Pak, Annie. 1965. *Naebyŏrŭn ŏnŭhanŭre: paeginhonhyŏl yangkongjuŭi sugi* [In which sky is my star? An autobiography of a white, mixed-blood Western princess]. Seoul: Wangja Publications.

Pak, Chŏng-ch'ŏl, and Oh Sŭng-hwan. 2003. *Nŏhŭigk katusarŭl anŭnya: Ibangin sogŭi Ibangin, katusagk parabon chuhanmigun iyagi* [Do you know KATUSA? A story of the U.S. Military in South Korea told by KATUSA, foreigners among foreigners], revised edition. Seoul: Risu.

Pak, Chong-sŏng. 1994. *Han'gukŭi maech'un* [Prostitution in Korea]. Seoul: In'gansarang.

Pak, Pong-hyŏn. 2002. *Nŭhŭidŭri miguninjul ara?* [Do you think you're GIS?], vols. 1–2. Seoul: Ch'aengmandŭnŭn kongjang.

Pak, Wan-sŏ. 1998. "A Pasque Flower on That Bleak Day." In *The Rainy Spell and Other Korean Stories*, trans. Ji-moon Suh, 204–12. New York: M. E. Sharpe.

Paret, Peter. 1964. *French Revolutionary Warfare from Indochina to Algeria: The Analysis of Political and Military Doctrine*. Princeton Studies in World Politics no. 6. New York: Frederick A. Praeger.

Parker, Roy. 1952. "Sex and the Soldier." *Cornet* 32 (June): 103–6.

Peters, C., ed. 1992. *Collateral Damage: The New World Order at Home and Abroad*. Boston: South End Press.

Peukert, Detlev. 1992. *The Weimar Republic: Crisis of Classical Modernity*, trans. Richard Deveson. New York: Hill and Wang.

Pilger, John. 2004. "John Pilger Cheers the Islanders Fighting Dirty Tricks." *New Statesman* 133 (18 October): 22–23.

Pŏbjech'ŏ. 1952. *Migunjŏngbŏmnyŏngjip* [The collection of laws during USAMG rule]. Seoul: Pŏbjech'ŏ.

Poiger, Uta. 1999. *Jazz, Rock, and Rebels: Cold War Politics and American Culture in a Divided Germany*. Berkeley: University of California Press.

Pok, Kŏ-il. 1994. *Kaempŭ senekaŭi kijich'on* [Camp Seneca's camptown]. Seoul: Munhakkwajisŏngsa.

Powell, Colin L., with Joseph E. Persico. 1995. *My American Journey*. New York: Random House.

President's Committee on Equal Opportunity in the Armed Forces. 1963. *Equality of Treatment and Opportunity for Negro Personnel Stationed within the United States*. Washington, D.C.: U.S. Government Printing Office.

———. 1964. *Final Report: Military Personnel Stationed Overseas*. Washington, D.C.: U.S. Government Printing Office.

Quester, Aline O. 2002. "Women and Minorities in America's Volunteer Military." *Contemporary Economic Policy* 20, no. 2 (April): 111–21.

Ranciere, Jacques, and Peter Hallward. 2003. "Politics and Aesthetics: An Interview." *Angelaki* 8, no. 2: 191–211.

Renda, Mary. 2001. *Taking Haiti: Military Occupation and the Culture of U.S. Imperialism, 1915–1940*. Chapel Hill: University of North Carolina Press.

Render, Frank W., II. 1970. "U.S. Military Race Relations in Europe—September 1970." Memorandum to Secretary of Defense Melvin Laird, Washington, D.C. 2 November.

Rhee, Taek Hyong. 1986. *U.S.–ROK [Republic of Korea] Combined Operations: A Korean Perspective*. Washington, D.C.: National Defense University Press.

Richie, Donald. 1968 (1956). *This Scorching Earth*. 3d ed. Tokyo: Charles E. Tuttle.

Ricoeur, Paul. 2004. *Memory, History, Forgetting*. Chicago: University of Chicago Press.

Riley, Robin L. 2006. "Valiant, Vicious, or Virtuous? Representation and the Problem of Women Warriors." In *Interrogating Imperialism: Conversation on Gender, Race, and War*, ed. Robin Riley and Naeem Inayatullah, 183–206. New York: Palgrave Macmillan.

Ritzer, George. 2000. *The McDonaldization of Society*. Thousand Oaks, Calif.: Pine Forge Press.

Rose, Sonya. 1997. "Girls and GIS: Race, Sex, and Diplomacy in World War II Britain." *International History Review* 19 (February): 146–60.

Rosenberg, Emily. 1982. *Spreading the American Dream: American Economic and Cultural Expansion, 1890–1945*. New York: Hill and Wang.

Rosenthal, Debra. 1990. *At the Heart of the Bomb: The Dangerous Allure of Weapons Work*. Washington, D.C.: Addison-Wesley.

Ruhl, Klaus Jörg. 1980. *Die Besatzer und die Deutschen, Amerikanische Zone 1945–48* [Occupiers and Germans, American zone 1945–48]. Düsseldorf: Schwann.

———. 1985. *Deutschland 1945, Alltag zwischen Krieg und Frieden in Berichten, Dokumenten und Bildern* [Germany 1945. Daily Life between war and peace in reports, documents and pictures]. Neuwied, Germany: Hermann Luchterhand Verlag.

Sahlins, Marshall. 2000. *Culture in Practice: Selected Essays*. Chicago: University of Chicago Press.

Said, Edward. 1978. *Orientalism*. New York: Vintage Books.

Sams, Crawford F. 1986. *DDT Kakumei* [DDT Revolution], trans. Eiji Takemae. Tokyo: Iwanami Shoten.

Sandars, C. T. 2000. *America's Overseas Garrisons: The Leasehold Empire*. Oxford: Oxford University Press.

Sands, Phillipe. 2008. *Torture Team*. New York: Palgrave Macmillan.

Sassen, Saskia. 1998. "Service Employment Regimes and the New Inequality." In *Globalization and Its Discontents: Essays on the New Mobility of People and Money*, ed. Saskia Sassen, 137–51. New York: New Press.

Sato, Ikuya. 1991. *Kamikaze Biker: Parody and Anomy in Affluent Japan*. Chicago: University of Chicago Press.

Scahill, Jeremy. 2007. *Blackwater: The Rise of the World's Most Powerful Mercenary Army*. New York: Nation Book.

Schlesinger, James R., Harold Brown, Tillie K. Fowler, and Charles A. Horner. 2004. *Final Report of the Independent Panel to Review Department of Defense Detention Operations*. Report no. A347824. Washington, D.C.: Office of the Secretary of Defense.

Schnabel, James F. 1972. *Policy and Direction: The First Year*. Washington, D.C.: U.S. Government Printing Office.

Schraut, Hans Jürgen. 1993. "U.S. Forces in Germany, 1945–1955." In *U.S. Military Forces in Europe: The Early Years, 1945–1970*, ed. Simon Duke and Wolfgang Krieger, 153–80. Boulder: Westview Press.

Schroer, Timothy. 2007. *Recasting Race after World War II: Germans and African Americans in American Occupied Germany*. Boulder: University Press of Colorado.

Schultz, Elizabeth. 2000. *Those Days in Muramatsu: Diary by Mrs. Yumi Goto*. Publications of the Center for East Asian Studies, Electronic Series, no. 2. Lawrence: University of Kansas.

Schumacher, Gerald. 2006. *A Bloody Business: America's War Zone Contractors and the Occupation of Iraq*. St. Paul: Zenith Press.

Schwartz, Thomas Alan. 1991. *America's Germany: John J. McCloy and the Federal Republic of Germany*. Cambridge, Mass.: Harvard University Press.

Schwarz, Hans-Peter. 1981. *Die Ära Adenauer: Gründerjahre der Republik* [The Adenauer Era. Founding years of the republic]. Stuttgart: Deutsche Verlagsanstalt.

Scibetta, Barbara, and Elfrieda Shukert. 1988. *War Brides of World War II*. Novato, Calif.: Presidio Press.

Scott, Wilbur J., and Sandra Carson Stanley. 1994. *Gays and Lesbians in the Military: Issues, Concerns, and Contrasts*. New York: Aldine de Gruyter.

Segal, David R., and Mady Wechsler Segal. 2004. "America's Military Population." *Population Bulletin* 59, no. 4 (December): 1–40.

Seiler, Signe. 1985. *Die GIS—Amerikanische Soldaten in Deutschland* [The GIS. American Soldiers in Germany]. Hamburg: Rowohlt.

Shaw, Martin. 1991. *Post-Military Society: Militarism, Demilitarization and War at the End of the Twentieth Century*. Philadelphia: Temple University Press.

Shawver, Lois. 1995. *And the Flag Was Still There: Straight People, Gay People, and Sexuality in the U.S. Military*. New York: Haworth Press.

Sherry, Michael S. 1995. *In the Shadow of War: The United States since the 1930s*. New Haven, Conn.: Yale University Press.

Shimizu, Ikutarō, Seiichi Miyahara, and Shozaburō Ueda. *Kichi no Ko* [Children of the Bases]. Tokyo: Kōbunsha.

Shin, Eui-Hang. 1987. "Interracially Married Korean Women in the United States: An Analysis Based on Hypergamy–Exchange Theory." In *Korean Women in Transition: At Home and Abroad*, ed. Yu Eui-Young and Earl H. Phillips, 249–74. Los Angeles: Center for Korean American and Korea Studies, University of California, Los Angeles.

Shinseki, Eric K. 2003. *The Army Family: A White Paper*. CMH Publication no. 70–94–1, U.S. Army Center of Military History. Washington, D.C.: U.S. Army Chief of Staff.

Sievers, Sharon. 1983. *Flowers in Salt: The Beginnings of Feminist Consciousness in Modern Japan*. Stanford, Calif.: Stanford University Press.

Sin, O-sŏng. 1989. "Han'guk chŏnjaengjŏnhuŭi pogŏnŭiryo kwanhan yŏngu 1945–1959: Han'guk chŏnjaenggirŭl chungsimŭro [A study of health and medicine in the postwar period, 1945–1959: A focus on the Korean War period]. M.A. thesis, Graduate School of Health, Seoul National University.

Sin, Tong-ho. 1970. "Migungamch'ukkwa kijich'on kyŏngje [The reduction of U.S. Troops and the camptown economy]. *Wŏlgansawŏl* 4, no. 8: 30–31.

Singer, Peter. 2003. *The Rise of the Privatized Military Industry*. Ithaca: Cornell University Press.

Smith, Charles R. 1997. *Securing the Surrender: Marines in the Occupation of Japan*. Marines in World War II Commemorative Series. Washington, D.C.: U.S. Government Printing Office.

Smith, Howard. 1950. "Report on the Public Health Problem of South Korea." Washington, D.C.: U.S. Public Health Service.

Smith, Jean Edward. 1990. *Lucius Clay: An American Life.* New York: Henry Holt.

Smith, William Gardner. 1948. *The Last of the Conquerors.* New York: Chatham Booksellers.

Sōkagakkai Fujin Heiwa Iinkai, ed. 1982. *Heiwa he no Negai wo Komete.* Vol. 6: *Kichi no Machi (Kanagawa) Hen: Sayonara Bēsu (Base) no Machi* [Wishing For Peace: Base Town, Kanawaga Volume: Goodbye to the Base Town]. Tokyo: Daisan Bunmei Sha.

Sŏl, Tong-hun, Hyŏn-mi Kim, Kŏn-su Han, Hyŏn-wung Ko, and Sallie Yea. 2003a. *Oegugin yŏsŏng entŏt'einŏüi ilkwa sam* [Foreign women entertainers' work and life]. Seoul: Korean Sociological Association.

——. 2003b. *Oegungyŏsŏng sŏngmaemae silt'aejosa* [A study of the situation of foreign women in prostitution]. Seoul: Ministry of Gender Equality.

Son, Chŏng-mok. 1988. Iljehaüi maech'unŏp: kongch'angkwa sach'ang [Prostitution during the Japanese colonial rule: public prostitution and private prostitution]. *Tosihaengjŏngyŏngu* 3 (December): 285–360.

Song, Pyŏng-su. 1995 (1957). "Ssyori Kim." In *Ssyori Kim / Ch'ŏllo oe: Song, Pyŏng-su / Kwak, Hak-song* [Ssyori Kim / Railroad and other writings by Pyŏng-su Song and Hak-song Kwak], *Han'guksosŏlmunhakdaekye* [Korean novels collections]. Vol. 38, 11–30. Seoul: Dong'a Publishing.

Song, Yong-p'il. 1989. "Yullaksanŏbüi silt'aewa kŭ taech'aek [The actual conditions of the sex industry and its countermeasures]. *Kwangjang* (April): 70–78.

Sŏng, Yŏng-so, and Pong-yul Chang. 1970. *T'ŭkjip: Chuhanmigungamch'ukkwa Han'gugüi anbo* [Special: The reduction of U.S. troops and Korean security]. *Sindonga* 73 (September): 128–39.

Song, Yung-ok. 1997. "Origin and Development of the Military Sexual Slavery Problem in Imperial Japan." *Positions: East Asia Cultures Critique* 5, no. 1: 171–217.

Spickard, Paul R. 1989. *Mixed Blood: Intermarriage and Ethnic Identity in Twentieth-Century America.* Madison: University of Wisconsin Press.

Standifer, Leon. 1997. *Binding up the Wounds: An American Soldier in Occupied Germany 1945–1946.* Baton Rouge: Louisiana State University Press.

Stanton, Shelby L. 1989. *America's Tenth Legion.* Novato, Calif.: Presidio.

Starr, Joseph. 1947. *Fraternization with the Germans in World War II.* Occupation Forces in Europe Series. Frankfurt on Main: Office of the Chief Historian, European Command.

Stiglmayer, Alexandra, ed. 1994. *Mass Rape: The War against Women in Bosnia-Herzogovina.* Lincoln: University of Nebraska Press.

Stoler, Ann Laura. 1991. "Carnal Knowledge and Imperial Power: Gender, Race, and Morality in Colonial Asia." In *Gender at the Crossroads of Knowledge: Feminist Anthropology in the Postmodern Era*, ed. Michaela di Leonardo, 51–101. Berkeley: University of California Press.

——. 1992. "Rethinking Colonial Categories: European Communities and the Boundaries of Rule." In *Colonialism and Culture*, ed. Nicholas B. Dirks, 319–52. Ann Arbor: University of Michigan Press.

———. 2002. *Carnal Knowledge and Imperial Power: Race and the Intimate in Colonial Rule.* Berkeley: University of California Press.

———. 2006a. *Haunted by Empire: Geographies of Intimacies in North American History.* Durham: Duke University Press.

———. 2006b. "Imperial Formations and the Opacities of Rule." In *Lessons of Empire: Imperial Histories and American Power,* ed. Craig Calhoun, Frederick Cooper, and Kevin W. Moore, 48–60. New York: New Press.

———. 2006c. "Tense and Tender Ties: The Politics of Comparison in North American History and (Post) Colonial Studies." In *Haunted by Empire: Geographies of Intimacy in North American History,* ed. Ann Laura Stoler, 23–67. Durham: Duke University Press.

Stone, Vernon. 1949. "German Baby Crop Left by Negro GIS." *Survey* 85:579–83.

Sturdevant, Saundra P., and Brenda Stoltzfus. 1993. *Let the Good Times Roll: Prostitution and the U.S. Military in Asia.* New York: New Press.

Taguba, Antonio M. 2004. "*Article 15-6 Investigation of the 800th Military Police Brigade.*" Reprinted in *Torture and Truth: America, Abu Ghraib, and the War on Terror,* ed. Mark Danner, 279–328. New York: New York Review of Books.

Takara, Kurayoshi. 1997. "*Okinawa*" *Hihan Josetsu* [A Critical Introduction to Okinawa]. Naha City, Japan: Okinawa Bunko.

Takazato, Suzuyo. 1996. "I Refuse." *Bulletin of Atomic Scientists* (July–August): 26.

Takemae, Eiji. 2002 (1983). *Inside GHQ: The Allied Occupation of Japan and Its Legacy.* New York: Continuum.

Tanaka, Yuki. 2002. *Japan's Comfort Women: Sexual Slavery and Prostitution during World War II and the U.S. Occupation.* London: Routledge.

Teruya, Yoshiko. 2001. "Ryukyu and Its Role in Western Thought: Euro-American Peace Movements in the Early Nineteenth Century." In *Ryukyu in World History,* ed. Josef Kreiner. Bonn: Bier'sche Verlagsanstalt.

Timm, Annette. 1998. "The Legacy of *Bevölkerungspolitik*: Venereal Disease Control and Marriage Counseling in Post–W W II Berlin." *Canadian Journal of History* 33, no. 2 (August 1998): 173–214.

Titunik, Regina F. 2008. "The Myth of the Macho Military." *Polity* 40, no. 2 (April): 137–63.

Tobey, James A. 1948. "The Army and Venereal Disease." *American Mercury* 61 (October): 479–83.

Tomiyama, Ichirō. 1995. *Senjō no Kioku* [Memories of the Battlefield]. Tokyo: Nihon Keizai Hyōronsha.

———. 1998. "Okuni Wa? [Where are You From?]" In *Oto No Chikara: Okinawa—Koza Futtōhen* [The Power of Music—Okinawa: Koza Boiling], ed. DeMusik Inter, 7–20. Tokyo: Inpakuto Shuppankai.

Tompkins, Tom. 1981. *Yokosuka: Base of an Empire.* Novato, Calif.: Presidio Press.

Turner, Terence. 2007. "The Social Skin." In *Beyond the Body Proper: Reading the Anthropology of Material Life,* ed. Margaret Lock and Judith Farquhar, 83–106. Durham: Duke University Press.

Tylee, Claire M. 1990. *The Great War and Women's Consciousness: Images of Militarism and Feminism in Women's Writings, 1914–64.* Iowa City: University of Iowa Press.

Uezato, Kazumi. 2000. *Amerajian: Mō Hitotsu no Okinawa* [Amerasians: Another Okinawa]. Kyoto City: Kamogawa Press.

U.S. Air Forces in Europe. 1953. *Problems of USAFE Dependents, 1946–1951*. Wiesbaden: Historical Division, U.S. Air Forces in Europe.

U.S. Bureau of the Census. 1964. *U.S. Census of Population: 1960, Selected Area Reports, Americans Overseas*. Washington, D.C.: U.S. Government Printing Office.

———. 1973. *1970 Census of Population: Subject Reports: Americans Living Abroad*. Washington, D.C.: U.S. Government Printing Office.

U.S. Department of Defense. 1972. *Report of the Task Force on the Administration of Military Justice in the Armed Forces*, vols. 1–4. Washington, D.C.: U.S. Government Printing Office.

———. 1981. *Selected Manpower Statistics, Fiscal Year 1980*. Washington, D.C.: U.S. Government Printing Office.

———. 1990. *Cost of Dependents Overseas: Report to Congress*. Washington, D.C.

———. 2004a. *FY 2004 Baseline Data*. Washington, D.C.

———. 2004b. *Strengthening U.S. Global Defense Posture: Report to Congress*. September.

———. 2005a. *Worldwide Manpower Distribution by Geographical Area*. Defense Manpower Data Center, Statistical Information Analysis Division. 30 September.

———. 2005b. *The National Defense Strategy of the United States of America*. March.

———. 2006. *Quadrennial Defense Review Report*. 6 February.

———. 2007. *Base Structure Report. Fiscal Year 2007 Baseline*. Http://www.defense.gov/pubs/bsr_2007_baseline.pdf.

———. 2009. *Base Structure Report: Fiscal Year 2009 Baseline*. Http://www.defense.gov/pubs/pdfs/2009Baseline.pdf.

U.S. Department of State. 1976. "Muccio Telegram to the Secretary of State, Taegu, August 9, 1950." In *Foreign Relations of the United States, 1950*. Volume 7: *Korea*. Washington, D.C.: U.S. Government Printing Office.

Vazansky, Alexander. 2008. "Army in Crisis: The United States Army, Europe, 1968–1975." Ph.D. diss., Heidelberg University.

Vidal, Gore. 2002. *The Last Empire, Essays 1992–2000*. New York: Vintage International.

Vine, David. 2009. *Island of Shame: The Secret History of the U.S. Military Base on Diego Garcia*. Princeton: Princeton University Press.

Wagnleitner, Reinhold. 1991. *Coca-Colanization und Kalter Krieg: Die Kulturmission der USA in Österreich nach dem zweiten Weltkrieg*. Vienna: Verlag für Gesellschaftskritik.

———. 1994. *Coca-Colonization and the Cold War: The Cultural Mission of the United States in Austria after the Second World War*, trans. Diana Wolf. Chapel Hill: University of North Carolina Press.

Wainwright, Hillary. 1983. "The Women Who Wire up the Weapons." In *Over Our Dead Bodies*, ed. Dorothy Thompson, 136–45. London: Verago.

Wallace, Terry. 1970. "Bringing the War Home." *Black Soldier* 2, no. 3: 2–18.

Walker, Paul. 1991. "U.S. Military Projection Abroad." In *The Sun Never Sets: Confronting the Network of U.S. Foreign Military Bases*, ed. Joseph Gerson and Bruce Birchard, 35–46. Boston: South End Press.

Waltzer, Michael. 2003. "Is There an American Empire?" *Dissent* (Fall): 27–31.

Watson, James L., ed. 2007. *Golden Arches East: McDonald's in East Asia.* 2d ed. Stanford, Calif.: Stanford University Press.

Weigley, Russell F. 1984. *History of the United States Army.* Bloomington: Indiana University Press.

White, Osmar. 1996. *Conqueror's Road: An Eyewitness Report of Germany.* Cambridge: Cambridge University Press.

White, W. L. 1947. *Report on the Germans.* New York: Harcourt Brace.

Wildenthal, Laura. 2001. *German Women for Empire, 1844–1945.* Durham: Duke University Press.

Williams, Patrick, and Laura Chrisman, eds. 1994. *Colonial Discourse and Post-Colonial Theory: A Reader.* New York: Columbia University Press.

Williams, William Appleman. 1972. *From Colony to Empire: Essays in the History of American Foreign Relations.* New York: John Wiley & Sons.

——. 1980. *Empire as a Way of Life: An Essay on the Causes and Character of America's Present Predicament, along with a Few Thoughts about an Alternative.* New York: Oxford University Press.

Willoughby, John. 2001. *Remaking the Conquering Heroes: The Postwar American Occupation of Germany.* New York: Palgrave.

Wilson, George C., and Haynes Johnson. 1971. *Army in Anguish: Washington Post National Report.* New York: Pocket Books.

Wolinsky, Marc, and Kenneth Sherrill, eds. 1993. *Gays and the Military: Joseph Steffan versus the United States.* Princeton: Princeton University Press.

Wünschel, Hans Jürgen, ed. 1985. *Quellen zum Neubeginn der Verwaltung im rheinisch pfälzischen Raum unter der Kontrolle des amerikanischen Militärregierung April bis Juli 1945* [Primary sources regarding the reestablishment of the administrational structure in the Rhineland and Palatinate region under control of the American military government, April to July 1945]. Mainz: v. Hase and Koehler.

Yamada, Meiko. 1995. *Senryōgun Ianfu* [Comfort Women for the Occupation Forces]. Tokyo: Kōdansha.

Yea, Sallie. 2004. "Sex Trafficking of Foreign Women to United States Military Camp Towns in South Korea." Research report, International Development Program, Royal Melbourne Institute of Technology.

Yee, James. 2005. *For God and Country: Faith and Patriotism under Fire.* New York: Public Affairs.

Yi, Chae-ik. 2001. *Noran chamsuham* [Yellow submarine], vols. 1–2. Seoul: Samjingihoek.

Yi, Chŏng-hŭi. 2004. "SOFA kaejŏng: Chukwŏn hoebogŭi kkum [SOFA revision: A dream to recover sovereignty]." In *Puggŭrŏun migunmunhwa tabsagi* [A record of exploring the shameful culture of the American military in South Korea], ed. Dakyuinp'o, 448–61. Seoul: Pug'ijŭ.

Yi, Im-ha. 2004a. "Han'gukchŏjaengkwa yŏsŏngsŏngŭi tongwŏn [The Korean War and the mobilization of women]." *Yŏksayŏngu* 14 (December): 107–48.

——. 2004b. "Migunŭi tongasia chudunkwa seshuŏlt'i: Migunjŏngggiŭi maemaech'un munjerŭl chungsimŭro [The U.S. military occupation in East Asia and sexuality: The problem of prostitution during the U.S. Army Military Government rule]." In *Tonga-siawa kŭndae yŏsŏngŭi palgyŏn* [East Asia and the discovery of modern women), ed. East Asia Confucian Cultures Teaching and Research Group, Sŏngkyunkwan University, 259–99. Seoul: Ch'ŏngŏram midiŏ.

Yi, Man-yŏl. 1997. "Ilbongun 'wianbu' chŏngch'aek hyŏngsŏngŭi chosŏnch'ŭk yŏksajŏk paekyŏng [The historical context of Korea behind the making of the Japanese military 'comfort women' policy]." In *Ilbongun wianbumunjeŭi chinsang* [Truthful state of Japanese military comfort women], ed. Council for Resolving the Problem of the Military Comfort Women, 69–97. Seoul: Yŏksabip'yŏngsa.

Yi, Pae-yong. 1996. "Migunjŏnggi yŏsŏngsaengwhalŭi pyŏnmowa yŏsŏngŭisik, 1945–48 [Change in women's lives and consciousness during the U.S. military rule, 1945–48]." *Yŏksahakhoe, Yŏksahakbo* 150: 159–209.

Yi, Pŏm-sŏn. 1995 (1959). "Obalt'an [A stray bullet]." In *Amsajido / Obalt'an oe: Sŏ, Ki-wŏn / Yi, Pŏm-sŏn*, [Amsa map / A Stray Bullet and writings by Sŏ Ki-wŏn and Yi Pŏm-sŏn], *Han'guksosŏlmunhakdaekye* [Korean novels collections]. Vol. 35, 470–505. Seoul: Dong-a Publishing.

Yi, So-hŭi. 2001. "Migun pŏmjoi, kŭrigo chŏhangŭi yŏksa [GI crime, and a history of resistance]." In *Chuhanmigunmunjehaegyŏlundongsa: Nogŭnrieső Maehyangniggaji* [A history of the Korean People's Movement to solve problems of U.S. Forces in Korea: From Nogŭnri to Maehyangni], ed. From Nogŭnri to Maehyangni Publication Committee, 272–91. Seoul: Kip'ŭnjayu.

Yokosuka Keisatsushoshi Hakko Iinkai. 1977. *Yokosuka Keisatsushoshi* [Yokosuka City Police History]. Yokohama: Funatsu Insatsu.

Yoneda, Sakoyo. 1972. *Kindai Nihon Joseishi: Vol. Ge* [Modern Japanese Women's History].Tokyo: Shinnihon Shuppansha.

Yonetani, Julia. 2003. "Contested Memories: Struggles over War and Peace in Contemporary Okinawa." In *Structure and Subjectivity: Japan and Okinawa*, ed. Glenn D. Hook and Richard Siddle, 188–207. London: Routledge Curzon.

Young, Iris Marion. 2003a. "Feminist Reactions to the Contemporary Security Regime." *Hypatia* 18, no. 1(Winter): 223–29.

——. 2003b. "The Logic of Masculinist Protection: Reflections on the Current Security State." *Signs* 29, no. 1: 1–25.

Young, Robert. 1995. *Colonial Desire: Hybridity in Theory, Culture and Race*. London: Routledge.

Yun, Chŏm-gyun. 2005. Kijich'on yŏsŏng, Yun, Chŏm-gyun. In *Han'gukyŏsŏnginmulsa 2 (1945–1980)* [A history of Korean women characters, vol. 2, 1945–1980], ed. Kyŏng-ok Chŏn, Sŏn-ae Pak, and Ki-ŭn Chŏng, 130–87. Seoul: Sungmyŏng Women's University Press.

Yun, Il-wung. 1987. *Maech'un: Chŏnguk sach'anggawa ch'angnyŏ silt'ae* [Prostitution: The actual conditions of private brothels and prostitutes in the country]. Seoul: Tongkwang.

Yun, Yo-wang. 2001. "Wŏnju: Migungijirŭl Wŏnju siminŭi p'umŭro" [Wŏnju: American military bases encircled by Wŏnju citizens]." In *Chuhanmigunmunje haegyŏlundongsa:*

Nogŭnriesŏ Maehyangniggaji [A history of the Korean People's Movement to solve problems of U.S. Forces in Korea: From Nogŭnri to Maehyangni], ed. From Nogŭnri to Maehyangni Publication Committee, 161–69. Seoul: Kip'ŭnjayu.

Zeeland, Steven. 1996. *The Masculine Marine: Homoeroticism in the U.S. Marine Corps*. New York: Harrington Park Press.

Zeiger, Susan. 1999. *In Uncle Sam's Service: Female Workers with the American Expeditionary Force*. Ithaca: Cornell University Press.

Ziemke, Earl. 1975. *The U.S. Army in the Occupation of Germany 1944–1946*. Army Historical Series. Washington, D.C.: Center for Military History.

CONTRIBUTORS

☆

DONNA ALVAH is associate professor and Margaret Vilas Chair of U.S. History at St. Lawrence University. She is the author of *Unofficial Ambassadors: American Military Families Overseas and the Cold War, 1946–1965* (2007). She recently completed an essay on wives of U.S. military men in the Philippines between the Spanish-American War and the start of the Second World War and is working on a project on sexual assaults committed by U.S. servicemen in Okinawa after 1945.

CHRIS AMES is associate professor in the school of undergraduate studies at the University of Maryland University College. He has published widely on Japanese film and Okinawan history and culture.

JEFF BENNETT is assistant professor of anthropology and religious studies at the University of Missouri, Kansas City. His research on Abu Ghraib is informed by his experience as a former member of the U.S. Army Special Forces.

MARIA HÖHN is professor of German history at Vassar College. She is the author of *GIs and Fräuleins: The German-American Encounter in 1950s West Germany* (2002), which was published in German as *Amis, Cadillacs,"Negerliebchen"* in 2008. She is the co-author with Martin Klimke of *A Breath of Freedom: The Civil Rights Struggle, African American GIs, and Germany* (Palgrave 2010). A German version of that book is being published with Verlag Berlin-Brandenburg. She is also the co-director of "The Civil Rights Struggle, African America GIs, and Germany" at http://www.aacvr-Germany.org, a digital archive and oral-history collection that was honored by the NAACP in 2009 with the Julius E. Williams Distinguished Community Service Award.

SEUNGSOOK MOON is professor of sociology at Vassar College. She is the author of *Militarized Modernity and Gendered Citizenship in South Korea* (Duke, 2005) and its Korean edition, *Kunsajuŭie kach'in kŭndae: Kungminmandŭlgi, simindoegi, kŭrigo sŏngŭi chŏngch'i* (2007), elected one of ten books worth reading by the Korean Publication Ethics Commission in March 2007. She has also published numerous articles on gender and the military, nationalism, civil society and social movements, globalization, and cultural politics of collective memory and food in contemporary Korea. She is the Korea Book Review editor of the *Journal of Asian Studies* and chaired the Committee on Korean Studies, representing scholars of Korea in the Association for Asian Studies. She has also served on the editorial boards of *Gender and Society* and *Asian Women*.

CHRISTOPHER NELSON is associate professor of anthropology at the University of North Carolina, Chapel Hill. His work focuses on memory, critical theory, and intellectual history. He is the author of *Dancing with the Dead: Memory, Performance, and Everyday Life in Postwar Okinawa* (Duke, 2008).

ROBIN RILEY is an assistant professor in the Women's and Gender Studies Department at Syracuse University. She is co-editor with Naeem Inayatullah of *Interrogating Imperialism: Conversations on Gender, Race, and War* (2006) and co-editor with Chandra Talpade Mohanty and Minnie Bruce Pratt of *Feminism and War: Confronting U.S. Imperialism* (2008). Her research on gender, militarism, and war includes her current project on how Iraqi and Afghan women are depicted in the U.S. media.

MICHIKO TAKEUCHI is an assistant professor of history at California State University, Long Beach. She specializes in modern Japan, women, and oral and ethnographic history. She is working on a book manuscript tentatively entitled, "Pan-Pan Girls and GIS: The Japan–U.S. Military Prostitution System in Occupied Japan (1945–52)."

INDEX

☆

Page numbers in italics indicate illustrations or captions.

Korea Special Tourism Association (KSTA), 63, 341
Korea-U.S. Mutual Defense Treaty, 54
Kosovo, military prostitution in, 405
Koza Riot, 287–88
Kramer, Paul, 139n8
Ku Klux Klan, 314
Kŭm-i Yun, 355
Kunsan Air Base (Wolfpack), 337
Kyŏng-su Kim, 343, 344

LaCapra, Dominick, 306n2
language of masculine domination, 376–79
Latin America, U.S. military interventions in, 14
Law for the Prevention of Venereal Disease (1927), 120
Lee, Clark, 84
Lend-Lease, 7
Liang, Diane, 389
liberal imperialism, 13–15, 32n24, 34n34
Lilly, Robert, 132
Loving v. Virginia, 135–36
Luce, Henry, 33n27
Lynch, Jessica, 388

MacArthur, Douglas, 78, 87, 94, 236, 238
Mann, Michael, 165, 238
Mansfield, Mike, 322
Marines, U.S., 18, 34n39
marriage of GIs, 94, 100, 115, 134–37, 179–80; deceptive practices of, 352–53; to German women, 114, 117, 124–25, 127, 131; immigration regulations and, 65; military policy on, 22, 65, 124; to Okinawan women, 23–24, 181, 194–98; to South Korean women, 40, 43, 56, 65, 66, 76n92
Marshall Plan, 14
masculinity, militarized, 27, 29, 41, 68, 89–90, 350, 356–58
mass media, 4–5
May Laws, 110–11
McCarran-Walter Act, 180

McClintock, Anne, 79
McCrary, John W., 242
McDonaldization, 4–5
McNarney, Joseph T., 263
Medoruma Shun, 181, 189
Middle East, military bases in, 3, 8, 381, 401–2, 403
militarism, U.S., 204–5
militarization, gendered. *See* women in defense industry
military, U.S., 22; all-volunteer, 2, 137, 167, 200n14; feminine qualities and, 150–51; gender conservatism in, 94; recruitment quotas of, 152–53, 168–69, 313, 358, 403; sexual assault cases in, 394n23. *See also* racial discrimination, military
military, U.S., statistics, 358: on African American GIs, 35n44, 320, 325–26; on children and relatives of soldiers abroad, 149; on moral waivers for new recruits, 358; on Okinawa, 178; on percentage of unmarried soldiers, 171; on private contractor costs, 404; on racial distribution, 269–70, 325–26; on territory controlled, 108n71
military, U.S., statistics on deployments, 137; in Japan, 108n71; of married soldiers, 113, 124, 126, 167, 192; in Okinawa, 34n39; in post–Cold War era, 6, 400; by region before 1960, 8, 9–12; in South Korea, 254n9, 324, 331; in West Germany, 125
military, U.S., women in, 379–81; Abu Ghraib prisoner abuse and, 30, 393n18; consequences of new global posture on, 166; deployment statistics of, 137; KATUSA discourse and, 233, 246, 249, 251, 253; Second World War and, 123; sexual violence against, 394n23, 403–4; in West Germany, 270
military-base system, 5–12, 233, 234, 397, 400–401; in Cold War era, 8; compensation politics in maintenance of, 181–82; consequences of new global posture on,

Nixon, Richard M., 136, 268

Nixon Doctrine, 67, 68, 329

non-command sponsored (NCS) families abroad, 169

North Atlantic Treaty Organization (NATO), 10, 79

Nuremburg Race Laws, 130

Obama, Barack, 397

Obon (festival of the dead), 26, 288–89, 298–99

occupation prostitution, 126–28. *See also* military prostitution

O'Donnell, Ian, 378

O-jang Kwŏn, 345

Okinawa, 177–78; anti-American sentiment on, 187; colonial relationship of, with Japan, 17, 19, 26; compensation politics and, 181–82; economy of, 179, 180; gendered nationalist movements on, 182–83; identity politics and, 188–90; consequences of new global posture on, 170, 171; politics of remembrance on, 26, 288–89, 298–99; racial discrimination on, 192; U.S. occupation of, 178–80, 183–85. *See also* Japan

Okinawa, post-occupation military presence on, 17–19, 178, 181; crime rates and, 201n18; deployment statistics on, 34n39; economics of, 289; in film, 283–88; GI violence toward women, 171, 180, 190–91; in history, 199n5; military prostitution and, 104, 185; protests against, 26, 180–83, 186–90, 287–88; spatial element of, 286; troop drawdowns and, 400

Okinawa-Japan relations, 183, 185–86, 187, 188–89

Okinawan past: *eisā* for remembering, 288–305; in film, 283–88; gender and class representations, 307n20; present-day images of, 281–82

Okinawan women: as *eisā* dancers, 291, 307n20; GI violence against, 171, 180, 190–91, 199n5; hunger prostitution of,

178; suicide and infanticide and, 183, 189, 281. *See also* Japanese women

Okinawan women and GIS, 23–24, 177–78, 180–81, 194–98; balance of power between, 178–79, 193–94; differential criminal treatment of, 190–91; family positions on, 191–92; legends and, 185–86; marginalization of, 23–24, 176, 187–88; objectification of GIS by women, 192–93; otherization of, 187; treatment of, 184–85, 186–87, 189

Okinawan youth, 292–93

Oriental lady fetish, 192

Osan Air Base, Songt'an, 346, 349, 361n14

Ōta Masahide, 181, 187–88, 190

Other, the, 20, 98, 114, 144n64, 181, 187, 194. *See also* us–them binary

Padover, Saul, 115

Pak, Pong-hyŏn, 249

Pak Ok-sun (Annie Pak), 39–40, 51

pan-pan girls, Japan, 80, 91–93, 104; definition of, 78; economics of, 89; GI sexual conquest of, 98–100; MP supervision of, 85; statistics on, 87; VD inspections of, 88; victimization of, 102–3

Paret, Peter, 382–83, 384

Park Chung Hee regime, 325; camptown prostitution development and, 41, 56–57, 58, 61, 64, 68; junta of, 66; U.S. support for, 16

Patai, Raphael, 370–71

Pearl Harbor attack, 7

Perry, Matthew, 199n5

Pershing missile crisis, 259, 270

Philippines, 139n8

Polk, James, 320

Potsdam Conference, 7

Potsdam Declaration, 78

Powell, Colin L., 255n14, 256n32, 256n34

Presley, Elvis, 26, 273, *274*

prisoners of war, 140n15, 248, 384–85. *See also* Abu Ghraib prisoner abuse

prison system, American, 378

propaganda, wartime, 182–83, 185, 190, 261, 384

prostitutes, prostitution, 42; boundaries between romantic love and, 115, 117; British military and, 138n1; definitions of, 69n2, 80; legalization of, 55–56; South Korean policy on, 41, 44–46, 50–53; state licensed systems of, 85–86; zero-tolerance policy on, 338, 340, 349, 350. *See also* camptown prostitution; camptown sex workers; military prostitution; sex workers; trafficking of women for prostitution

Prostitution Prevention Law, 61, 63, 104

Psychological Operations Division (PsyOps), U.S., 329–30

Public Act (PA) 7 (1947), 44, 49

Public Health and Welfare Section (PHW) (SCAP / GHQ), 45, 85

Public Prostitution Elimination Law (1947), 61

Puerto Rico, 234–35

racial crisis of 1970–71, 27, *288*, 312–32

racial discrimination: Japan's cult of racial supremacy and, 22, 36n50, 82, 97; off-base, in West Germany, 314, 317, 319–20, 322–23; in Okinawa, 183–85, 192; by sex workers, 1, 64, 87, 90–91, 111, 327–29

racial discrimination, military, 22, 27–28, 130, 131–36, 249–51, 331, 333n11, 334n25; affirmative action programs, 321; exportation of, 116, 183–84, 242, 319–23, 325; German knowledge of, 318 Gessell report (1963–64) on, 335n34; institutionalization of, 111, 320, 329; interracial marriage policy and, 65, 94, 100, 115, 124, 179–80; against KATUSAS, 25, 235, 240–43, 256nn24–25; against Korean civilians, 43, 49; racial crisis of 1970–71 and, 312–23; special comfort facilities and, 87; in Vietnam War era, 314

racial purity, 36n50, 82, 87

racial superiority, military culture of, 2, 93–94, 240–45, 252–53, 325–26, 331

racism, white, 249–52

Ranciere, Jacques, 300, 304

Recreation and Amusement Association (RAA), 81, 85

Regulations Concerning the Acquisition of Prostitutes (1916), 42

Rehabilitation Training Center, 47, 48

religious women, aggression of GIS against, 117

Render Commission, 319–21, 331

rest-and-recreation leaves, 53

Revolution in Military Affairs (RMA) enthusiasts, 165, 174n19

Richie, Don, 90

Ricoeur, Paul, 296, 297

Rooney, Andy, 124

Roosevelt, Franklin D., 7

Rumsfeld, Donald, 155, 164, 171, 172, 367, 405

Russian camptown workers, 342, 352

Russo-Japanese War (1905), 42

Ryūkyū Archipelago, 177

Sahlins, Marshall, 366, 383–85, 389–90

Saka, Shinya, 81

Sams, Crawford, 85–86

Sanchez, Ricardo, 367

San Francisco System, 14

Sauge, Georges, 384

Schlesinger, James R., 366–67, 369

Schmidt, Helmut, 322

September 11, 2001, attacks, 2, 271, 277, 401, 402–3. *See also* War on Terror, U.S.

Seventh Army. *See* Germany, West, Seventh Army in

sexual labor to control male aggression, 42–46, 51–53, 81, 82, 403

sex workers, 57–58, 83; cost of services rendered by, 108n73; definition of, 69n2; as freelancers in South Korea, 55, 64; military prosecution of, 62, 89, 121, 122, 128, 133; patriotism as method of controlling, 23, 330, 344; in Philippines, 336n41; public treatment of, 46; trafficking and labor

MARIA HÖHN is a professor of history at Vassar College.
She is the author of *GIs and Fräuleins: The German American
Encounter in 1950s West Germany* (2002) and co-author, with
Martin Klimke, of *A Breath of Freedom: The Civil Rights
Struggle, African American GIs, and Germany* (2010).

SEUNGSOOK MOON is a professor of sociology at Vassar
College. She is the author of *Militarized Modernity and
Gendered Citizenship in South Korea* (Duke, 2005)
and *Kunsajuŭie kach'in kŭndae: kungminmandŭlgi,
simindoegi, kŭrigo sŏngŭi chŏngch'I* (2007).

Library of Congress Cataloging-in-Publication Data
Over there : living with the U.S. military empire from
World War Two to the present / edited by Maria Höhn
and Seungsook Moon.
p. cm.
Includes bibliographical references and index.
ISBN 978-0-8223-4818-4 (cloth : alk. paper)
ISBN 978-0-8223-4827-6 (pbk. : alk. paper)
1. Military bases, American—Foreign countries—History—
20th century. 2. Military bases, American—Social aspects.
I. Höhn, Maria II. Moon, Seungsook
UA26.A2094 2010
355.7—dc22   2010025721